the Way

to achieve success

Stephen Box

The Way
to achieve success

Stephen Box

Twitter @thestephenbox
www.thestephenbox.com
www.amazon.com/author/stephenbox

© 2017 Stephen Box. All rights reserved.

No part of this book may be reproduced, stored in a retrieval system, or transmitted by any means without the expressed written permission of the author.

Published

ISBN: 978-1-7396765-8-2 Hardback
ISBN: 978-1-7396765-2-0 Paperback
ISBN: 978-1-7396765-3-7 eBook

If— Rudyard Kipling - 1865-1936

If you can keep your head when all about you
   Are losing theirs and blaming it on you;
If you can trust yourself when all men doubt you,
   But make allowance for their doubting too;
If you can wait and not be tired by waiting,
   Or, being lied about, don't deal in lies,
Or, being hated, don't give way to hating,
   And yet don't look too good, nor talk too wise;
If you can dream—and not make dreams your master;
   If you can think—and not make thoughts your aim;
If you can meet with triumph and disaster
   And treat those two impostors just the same;
If you can bear to hear the truth you've spoken
   Twisted by knaves to make a trap for fools,
Or watch the things you gave your life to broken,
   And stoop and build 'em up with wornout tools;
If you can make one heap of all your winnings
   And risk it on one turn of pitch-and-toss,
And lose, and start again at your beginnings
   And never breathe a word about your loss;
If you can force your heart and nerve and sinew
   To serve your turn long after they are gone,
And so hold on when there is nothing in you
   Except the Will which says to them: "Hold on";
If you can talk with crowds and keep your virtue,
   Or walk with kings—nor lose the common touch;
If neither foes nor loving friends can hurt you;
   If all men count with you, but none too much;
If you can fill the unforgiving minute
With sixty seconds' worth of distance run—
   Yours is the Earth and everything that's in it,
And—which is more—you'll be a Man, my son!

the Way

Content

	Page
Forward by Prof Stefano Gatti, Bocconi Business School	i
Preface	iii
Acknowledgements	viii
Prologue – The journey begins	1
Week 1 – Rules of Engagement; this game called Business; Business philosophy; Morality and Integrity; Stress	45
Week 2 – Personal Integrity, Comfortable in own skin, Wardrobe Malfunctions	87
Week 3 – Working with, and understanding people; Persuasion; Benefits of written & verbal Rhetoric	109
Week 4 - The Art of War – Estimates, Waging War, Offensive Strategy, Dispositions	143
Week 5 – The Art of War – Strategic Power, Weaknesses & Strengths, Manoeuvring, Nine Variables	173
Week 6 – The Art of War – Deploying Troops, Terrain, Ninefold Earth, Incendiary Devices	205
Week 7 – The Art of War – Spies; Presence; Overcoming Anxiety	241
Week 8 – Capture your market without destroying it; Strike where they least expect it; Maximise the power of information; Move swiftly to overcome competitors; Employ strategy to master competition; Effective leadership; Look the part	257

Week 9 – Art of verbal & written presentation;   291
Don't get Personal; structure & preparation of Business
Development Proposal – Who, What, Why, When, How, How
Much; Importance of practical Impact & Risk Assessment

Week 10 – Finalise Business Development Proposal   327
including Risk; rose-tinted spectacles, managing distress,
structure of healthy & flexible companies, managing need over
want

Week 11 – Make your Strategy invisible;   349
Market dynamics; Business value drivers overview; people
versus technology; optimal organisational structure; managing
human resources; managing human frailty and insecurity;
Coaching performance – overcoming constraint; leadership skills

Week 12 – Managing change; managing IT projects;   389
managing people; the Value of Community; The value of a
family culture both domestic & International; Establishing
yourself as a leader

Week 13 – Executive behaviour – Humanity, Integrity,   425
Courage, Discipline; Use of Interpreters; impacts of culture;
International travel rules; dealing with family bereavement

Week 14 – Time out for refresh; Quickly move on   457

Week 15 – Managing impacts of Recession & Inflation;   465
Car Accident; If not broken keep moving; righteous self-pity
vs commitment; purging the past; atonement and moving on;
Retaining human touch

Week 16 – Executive role & remuneration;   491
managing maternity; Respecting gender equality; Social and
Welfare considerations; managing project failure; the value of
family in whatever form; the importance of Reciprocity

Week 17 – New Business Implementation Plan;   521
Negotiating skills

Week 18 – The role of business in the community;   555
Sexual harassment & intimidation

Week 19 – Christmas Break and study understanding   567
Balance Sheet & Income Statement

Week 20 – New Year; the need to recharge and refresh   575

Week 21 – Corporate Business Plan; Grooming spies;   579
nurturing alliances; delegation; dangers of intercompany
personal relationships

Week 22 – First executive decision; reality check;   611
Overcoming the fear of failure

Week 23 – Boardroom Protocols & Procedure; Changing   621
the guard under distress; the show must go on; managing
multiple hats; the need for fun

Week 24 – Dealing with grief; impacts of transition;   657
managing pain, rising to the challenge; the loneliness of
leadership

Week 25 – Time to take the baton; staying focussed;   676
exerting leadership

Week 26 – First Board Meeting; Implement Business Plan;   699
managing merger; the reality of hindsight – use of deception;
prepare for listing; the battle over, consolidation of victory
begins

Foreword

Professor Stefano Gatti – Antin IP Professor of Infrastructure Finance Bocconi University, Milan (Italy)

What makes a CEO a competent corporate leader?

This is probably one of the most controversial questions that a person like me, teaching in higher education institutions and business schools, faces every day of their professional life.

Is a CEO the best in class in terms of technical skills? Or are they a person able to build a team spirit so that their success is built on each team member's success? Is a successful CEO a problem solver? Or are they able to skilfully anticipate problems?

I have been teaching finance and investment banking for many years and it is exactly for this reason that I first met Stephen Box many years ago.

I was writing the first edition of my book "Handbook of Project Finance" and Stephen at the time was one of the partners of UNIVEST, a boutique of senior bankers devising hybrid solutions for complex International structured and project finance deals. Stephen was so kind to contribute a full chapter to that book, explaining the intricacies of insurance-based event risk solutions for infrastructure project finance.

If you look back at the long career of the Author, you will immediately see how eclectic his life and career have been. A former nuclear physics scientist, he moved easily to the City of London holding several high-level positions in international banking at some of the most reputed financial institutions. He then turned to hybrid and novel structured finance solutions, mainly for developing economies. Only his health prevented him from even higher achievements.

All in all, Stephen's career path well explains the comprehensive structure and content of this book.

The "Art of War" by Sun Tzu, is one clear source of inspiration to him. However, the reader will find much more in this novel. Yes, I use the word novel because, although this book could easily be used at any top business school worldwide as MBA course reading for a strategy or leadership course, it is in all senses a novel enjoyable by any aspiring executive.

The book is set in 1990 as the UK approaches a deep recession. A young lady, Melanie, is given the opportunity to prove herself capable of an important executive position at the construction fabrication company of choice. By luck, she meets Sebastian, an Executive Investment Banker who has recently retired. Sebastian becomes her mentor and teaches her the mental attitude, skills, and attributes that make for a successful corporate leader.

The table of contents illustrates the real-life journey Melanie encounters under the direction of Sebastian and, simply looking at the Content's titles, you can understand how pervasive Stephen Box's view of the executive role. Not only do you find – as expected – the technical aspects of the profession, but also the "soft skills" requirements, an attention to leadership and team building, topics like gender diversity/sexual harassment and much more.

The most direct comparison to the structure of this book is James Joyce's Ulysses. In that book, the novel was in all senses a journey. For Joyce, in a normal middle-class day; for Stephen Box probably a journey that lasted his entire life.

Preface

I was initially asked to record my management style as a case study by KPMG after the rescue of the securities division of a City bank. When asked to engage in this rescue, with the full endorsement of the Bank of England, the conventional wisdom, as proffered by the largest business consulting houses, was at least 2 years to rebuild. It took just 25 weeks to fully stabilise the situation, and a further 16 weeks to transform it into one of the best. A bemused executive would not accept that such a transformation was possible, including tripling trading turnover with 50% of the original headcount, so asked for a full audit. I did reserve the right to have the final say who conducted such an audit. After much searching, I finally accepted a senior partner from the Chicago head-office of the then Arthur Anderson to conduct this audit.

At the end of the process she came to sit with me to discuss her findings. She was so impressed with everything she found she wanted to know how I was able to assemble and mobilise such skills and enthusiasm so embedded throughout the division. She openly expressed that she could not recall another bank that could claim such competence and integrity in every aspect of trading operations. The conclusions of this audit report were very embarrassing for the executive fully endorsing every part of my Business Plan, and execution using my own management style including the first use of AI in a trading room to control credit and risk.

The great storm throughout the night of 15-16th October 1987 which brought London to a standstill proved beyond any doubt that the integrated nature of my organisational structure could withstand such shocks. We had a securities issue on the 16th October for Hanson Trust. Only some 25% of my overall staff made it to the office. Conventional wisdom would withdraw the issue for reschedule to a later date. The fact that any of my staff could turn their hand to any aspect of the business meant, after discussion with the underwriters, we could successfully launch to much acclaim. Although the concept of my *family* style of management as described herein matured whilst I built Chase Investment Bank, London in preparation for 'Big Bang' in 1986 it proved it could withstand the most demanding of challenges.

I was approached by a partner of KPMG to commission a Case Study of the rescue including my philosophy and management style. However, "The Art of War" by Sun Tzu is my bible of executive leadership and guided me well throughout my career. The selection and deployment of my *family* of resources is guided by the teachings of Sun Tzu. This book includes my gender-neutral interpretation of the 'Art of War'.

A few years later I was asked to mentor a woman who wanted to enter the world of City banking having completed her MBA with honours. I found her a position in a smaller bank hoping to give her some real-world experience before moving into the large banks. She heeded little advice and lasted but 4 months. At the sharp end of banking you win, or you fail. Such a stark differential creates clarity within the most competitive and combative corporate cesspit. A woman entering this cesspit needs to know the game, and the rules of the game. And I would suggest needs to fully understand the Art of War if she is to survive, let alone prosper. I was climbing the banking exec ladder in the late 1970's when women were first attempting to break into the upper echelons of banking. Having helped to create an informal club of rising execs of both genders, essentially to take care of the needs of a rising star without any of the potential baggage, I became very familiar with why most failed.

I have subsequently been asked by various organisations and institutions to mentor students, mostly female. The tradition of mentoring is that a mentor finds their protégé, not the reverse. My attitude has been very much to advise how to prepare to be mentored as there are rules of engagement. Whereas a number have subsequently found their calling, none proved worthy of mentoring, nor will rise the corporate executive ladder. However, I benefitted from the process as I could identify how the current world, including social media, impacts behaviour.

I recalled what one of my great mentors, Bernie Kramer, instilled into me. When I once asked him why he put so much on the line for me giving me the space to develop my novel ideas he told me that when I found someone worthy of such help I have a duty to do the same for them. He made the ultimate sacrifice for me, giving me the space to finish what is now called the internet. This book is dedicated to him and, within, I cameo his contribution to my success in his honour.

There is much debate today about women entering the alpha-male Boardroom. In my experience there is no mature, successful corporate Boardroom that fits such description. And this debate now includes proposals to force corporates to include women by decree. This idea is absurd. The global competitive environment requires that Executive Boards consist of the very best resources based on merit, not gender, colour, or ethnicity. Women need to understand that a Boardroom has codes of conduct which, although devised by men, are completely gender neutral as is the case in the higher Courts where women are accepted as equals enshrined in a code of dignity, respect, and conduct applicable to all who participate. This book discussed this issue in terms of think clan, not man.

Having not found a suitable woman to mentor in a corporate environment, and time is marching on, I decided to write down my ideas. Initially I considered a textbook to supplement the narrative taught at Business Schools using my version of Sun Tzu's teaching plus other techniques such as valuable corporate coaching. But Sun Tzu does not consider the influential peripheral issues such as family and emotional challenges, especially for a woman, and which can only reasonably be incorporated into a novel which does explore many of the challenges faced by potential executives, male or female, but wrapped in the additional challenges of life. I remembered a book called 'The Goal' by Eliyahu M. Goldratt and Jeff Cox that describes process dynamics but written as a novel to incorporate the human impact of sterile algorithms in real life. Four years later, and goodness knows how many hours at my desk, I have documented a series of lectures wrapped inside a story of the real-life issues that people must face whilst climbing the corporate ladder. Whereas much of what I've written applies to either gender, I have overlaid it with the additional issues faced by a woman. None of these lectures contradict or compete with the more academic textbook narrative of business schools. Indeed, it would be reasonable to state that these lectures teach what you do not confront at business school, but I would suggest that without this knowledge the business school narrative is of limited use.

Having set myself the challenge to write this book in 2014 I needed to find a platform that will appeal to anyone with the desire to succeed in any walk of life, thus have not used a banking background. My philosophy and techniques will work in any competitive environment. I also set it immediately prior to the explosion of social media as I've yet to see these new social media technologies benefit corporate leadership. Just as the Art of War is timeless, I hope the reader will find that the concept of *family* is likewise.

The year is 1990. The City of London is settling into its post Big Bang era but facing a deep recession. Technology requirements are dominating the corporate construction industry, but the recession will likely change the landscape from debt finance to cash rich developers.

Melanie is a 32-year-old account manager in the London office of one of leading construction fabrication companies in the UK. Even though she is fast becoming a significant business generator she has been overlooked twice in the space of 2 years for promotion in favour of lesser qualified male candidates in this totally male dominated sector.

A critical Director is declared terminally ill. The Chairman offers her the opportunity to fill his boots, but she must move to head office in Derbyshire to learn the business. She lodges with Sebastian, a formidable senior executive of the most influential bank in the world who has taken early retirement and retreated to Derbyshire to consider his future. He sees her executive potential so agrees to mentor her as far as she can reach. But is she strong enough for the ordeals she must face, the tough choices she must make, and the additional challenges she will face as a woman in a man's world to be accepted as an equal in a male dominated industry? She has just six months to prove herself.

Acknowledgements

When I decided to write this book, having retired from executive banking, it was as a tribute to the most valuable contribution to my success – **mentors**. From the age of 12 to my early 30's I was rarely without at least one wonderful mentor prepared to commit their valuable time, knowledge, and experience to channel my enthusiasm and help me on my way. I would like to pay tribute to some of my most important mentors. Without exception these were people I did not seek out; they found me – the true mentor profile.

My first mentor was Frank Saunders, the Deputy Head of the High School in Atherstone, Warwickshire as well as my mathematics teacher. He took me by the ear one day to tell me I belonged at the adjacent Grammar School so what was I prepared to do about it. Until his intervention I had never been encouraged to study although I had an inquisitive mind. He gave his own time to both encourage a thirst for knowledge and teach me after school so that I could sit the 13+ examinations and transfer to Grammar School. Frank was the hero who encouraged me to dream, believe, and succeed.

During my Grammar School years my primary mentor was Patrick (Pat) Burley, founder, and owner of Burley Metals in Birmingham. He originally undertook to coach me in rifle shooting; a sport for which I had a flair. However, after one disastrous behaviour day at Kingsbury Rifle Range he took me by the ear and suggested I needed to take matters seriously if he was to continue expending his valuable time with me. He taught me the ditty that I live by to this day.

If you have a job to do,

Be it big, be it small,

Do it well, or not at all.

My father would not support my education past the age of 16 despite the intervention of my Grammar School and the County Education Officer. His view was that if I wanted to study further, join the military. This was a parting of the ways that was never reconciled albeit I found out he dined out on my various successes. I would be the first person in our entire family history to go to university.

Where I grew up in the Midlands, engineering was the primary industry. Not really understanding where my future lay in the mid-1960's I joined Doulton Insulators near Tamworth as a Management Trainee and who sponsored me through day release and night school to secure Ordinary National Certificates in Mechanical Engineering, Electrical Engineering, and Electronic Engineering. I did them all at the same time because I had no reference to direct me, nor did I feel any of them as my calling. Come to my rescue one Ken Ridgeway, Head of Technical Design for Doulton Insulators. He told me I did not belong there and encouraged me to apply for an advertised position as Assistant Scientific Officer at the Atomic Energy Research Establishment (AERE), Harwell. We are now in 1968, amid the liberation of youth in the UK. Everything was changing, and my move to Harwell radically and rapidly changed my life.

My primary mentor at Harwell was Sir Basil Rose, Head of Nuclear Physics. Having spent 4 months in the Harwell Training School where, after undertaking aptitude tests, I was assigned to the Nuclear Physics Division in the Industrial Physic Group. This group was initially located at the Wantage site but moved to Harwell and located in Hanger 7. Basil Rose had a PA, Jill Lincoln, who knew of my family situation so encourage Basil to take me under his wing. This was a major blessing. He ensured that I went to university, was recognised for my work including the design and development of the x-ray tube that made the CT scanner possible, and encouraged me to take advantage of my age and lack of family responsibilities to go seek my fortune elsewhere when the retirement of Sir Solly Zuckerman, chief scientific adviser to the British Government, triggered the Civil Service takeover of science, tearing the very heart out of scientific research in the UK. Many great talents moved to the USA. I did a Dick Whittington routine (minus cat) and moved to London treading the streets looking for work as an out of work nuclear physicist, but with extensive knowledge of computers which were at the beginning of their introduction into commercial activities.

Throughout my life, generally through the lack of direction, I have set myself goals. At school I was labelled a dreamer if I inadvertently disclosed such goals. At eighteen years of age, then at Harwell, I set myself a goal that by my 30th birthday to have travelled the World and be paid to do it, and to be self-sufficient. By my 30th birthday I had travelled the World, including using most Concorde routes, stayed in the best hotels, and enjoyed the best restaurants. For my 30th birthday I bought myself a new Porsche 928 for cash, the most expensive Porsche roadcar at that time.

In early 1976 (the USA bicentennial year) I was recruited to the then Marine Midland Bank at their headquarters in Buffalo, New York State. They had an enormous IBM computer installation processing their global business. They suspected this system was being fraudulently manipulated. Whereas I knew how to talk to this computer, what questions should I ask? In steps the SVP, Operations (whose name escapes me after all these years) who sent me to school for 3 months to study international finance and economics. I found my resting place for the remainder of my career. In December 1976 having solved their problem, culprits identified, I was on my way back to London, in demand.

At the beginning of 1977 I was recruited into Chase Manhattan Bank, in the City of London. They were developing systems and where I drove the international transactions processing. I had more than one senior person take an interest in me. I devised an automated capability to facilitate interest rate arbitrage under Bill Bigalow, Head of Money Markets, and developed the concept of the rolling money book where trading positions moved around the world at the close of business each day thus preventing exposure to turbulence in the markets whilst any time zone was closed, and which was fully implemented by all major international banks during the early 1980's. My reward was sponsorship through Business School.

I was then head-hunted by the then Citicorp International Bank, the largest bank in the World, to devise and implement a global systems strategy for all Merchant Banking activities. The first week there I was sent to New York to meet the then President and CEO of the Bank, Walter Wriston; probably the most influential banker of the 20th century. A real street fighter, he introduced me to Sun Tzu, and became my most important mentor educating me how this World really works. What he taught me, and exposed me to, was infinitely more valuable than any university degree, and the basis of this book. I understood the real drivers of the global economy; every conceivable banking transaction; use; characteristics; risk; and processing. It was a 10-minute conversation with him, a long week of work with the brilliant Peter Savage who devised the X25 communication protocol and 128bit encryption protocol, and some USD600 million which led to the global technology base in October 1979 that is now called the internet. Tim Berners-Lee brought the World-Wide Web to the attention of the World in 1984 but using the first Global Intranet which was fully operational in 1979.

There is reference in *the Way* to an environment described as the worst cesspit of sharks and crocodiles. This is the environment in which I cut my teeth as a junior exec. I encountered the good, bad, and downright ugly in executive leadership and senior political leadership. This is where, under the guidance and belief of great mentors, I both learnt and developed most of the skills described in this book.

This brings me to one incredible mentor in Citicorp in the form of Bernie Kramer, COO in London. This man picked me up, dusted me off, and sent me back to work more times than I can remember. He was like a father to me and why he has a cameo role in this book. The latitude he gave to me to explore seemingly impossible ventures and solutions, and the defences he put up to shield me from any fallout, will never be forgotten. To this day I hold myself responsible for his untimely death on the day we finally succeeded with the global intranet as he had a heart attack a few days before defending me against a vicious reproach from a vile CEO.

Another great influence on me, John Botts, Head of Global Securities, and the most powerful player in the international securities market, picked up the reins after the death of Bernie including shielded me from the envious backlash of Citibank because of what we had achieved with a miniscule fraction of the resources available to Citibank. Success has its downside.

And with great reverence I must include Jack Mudge, senior member of the Civil Aviation Accident Investigation Authority, but more importantly my valued neighbour in West London. Such a calming influence when my corporate blood boiled. His mantra was to keep faith in yourself, never surrender your goal, and never despair.

In the early 1980s my mentored days were over. Indeed, I was now mentoring the next generation. But one achievement is worthy of mention as it resulted directly from the latitude afforded me by my great mentors and attracted significant attention. In late 1983 I was asked by Willard 'Bill' Butcher, the then Chairman and CEO of Chase Manhattan Bank, to devise and implement a plan for the creation of Chase Investment Bank in London ready for 'Big-Bang' in 1986. This mandate gave me the opportunity to apply all of the valuable knowledge and experience gained to both create my *family* style of management (described in this book) and to devise technology that revolutionised the way the international financial markets worked. Initially this involved combining the power of a hitherto ignored IBM computer, the System 38, and fibre optics to provide novel online trading and decision support systems. This attracted the attention of IBM who invited me to define the processing requirements of a completely new type of computer resulting in the AS400 and help to define and build the graphical interfaces in the then Presentation Manager (now MS Windows) to facilitate global trading and risk management – the first trading system using Artificial Intelligence was born.

In 1988 Sir Robert "Robin" Leigh-Pemberton KG PC, Governor of the Bank of England and Peter Morgan, former Director of IBM and then Director General of the Institute of Directors, nominated my entry into DeBretts - *Distinguished People of Today*.

If you have the will, you will find the Way

Prologue

Chapter 1

Melanie sat at her desk glum and despondent. Despite the late August sunshine, all she could think about was the latest company announcement staring her in the face. Again, she has been overlooked for promotion. They have hired Maurice Fulmer, five years her junior, to head the commercial client account department.

'It's time for you to look elsewhere girl' she heard herself mutter under her breath, *'I've been here for nearly ten years. I know this business inside out, but I'm a woman, and women should get married and have babies – not pursue a career.'*

Some 150 miles away in Matlock, Derbyshire, Charles Aldridge sat at his desk overlooking the factory reading the release about the hiring of Maurice Fulmer. He wasn't happy about this hiring and had made his feelings known to the Business Development Director, Michael Chimes. Michael argued that Maurice was the son of the CEO of one of the largest commercial construction companies in the South-East and was a tactical move to ensure Aldridge Fabrications Ltd was the supplier of choice. He further argued Melanie was planning her wedding and would likely have babies soon thereafter as she was already 32 years of age, and her biological clock is ticking. Thus, her priorities would likely change in the coming months.

He couldn't argue against this logic without using his superiority, but he knew Mel – she had been with the company since leaving university, and from the opening of the London office. She'd worked hard on her career, and he didn't see her as someone who would jettison her ambitions unless she felt unappreciated, as she surely will after this latest setback.

As Chairman, CEO, and owner, he could override decisions. But Michael was the head of business development and should select his own team. Charles needed another solution before he loses his very capable Mel.

He picked up the notice and strolled down to the office of Jim Spalding, his long-standing friend, fabrication engineer, and Production Director of the company. He put the notice on his desk.

'Have you read this?' pointing to the notice.

'Yes, I have. Mel must be well pissed-off.'

'I agree. This is the second time in the past two years Michael has overlooked her capabilities. He has a misogynous streak. He does not accept women in positions of seniority. How's your health situation? Have you received the results of your latest tests?'

Jim, now approaching his sixty-third birthday, suffered from various health issues, and had already discussed early retirement with Charles, not least because the environment surrounding a fabrication factory was not helping his respiratory problems.

'I need to give you six-months-notice of retirement hoping I can manage that long. We cannot delay the fateful day when I cannot function anymore. You need to seriously think about and find a replacement for me as there are no obvious candidates within the company.'

'Jim, I have an idea. Bear with me for a minute. I like Mel, and I think if she wasn't a woman, she would already have a senior position here, maybe even executive. She has a complete understanding of the business, and fantastic relationships with most of the top commercial architects in London. Is it not true you have complete confidence in her ability to collect the technical data you need from architects and reliably convey it to you?'

'Why, yes. She has my complete confidence. Why?'

'I would like to bring her up here to Matlock on secondment for six months to shadow you so we can see what she's really

Prologue

made of when treated properly. If I'm right about her, I see her as a formidable director of this company for the future. What do you think?'

'Look Charles, we both have a high regard for her. But what will possess her to give up the high life of London to live up here? She's planning her marriage, and he works in London. Why would she just up and move here for six months?'

'Instinct, my dear Jim, instinct. I sense she is looking for success in her career. Part of that path will be to delay her marriage if appropriate. They already live together so what difference to being married. I'm going to London on Thursday to attend a meeting with her and her new architect client to discuss a new project. Let me sound her out.'

'Okay, if she's seriously up for it then I'm happy to have such a pretty, young lady as my shadow. Beats the hell out the shadow cast by my bag of bones, and she's very bright and capable. Will be good fun for me.'

'Let's keep this to ourselves. I'll let you know how she reacts when I'm back on Friday.'

He returned to his office with more of a spring in his step knowing Michael cannot argue against this move – if Mel agrees, and it will take her from under his control.

Chapter 2 - Thursday

The architect meeting with Mel was arranged for 2pm. The days of getting up at the crack of dawn to get a commuter train from Derby to King's Cross station in London for a morning meeting had long gone. The 10:01am train would get him into King's Cross around 11:30am – just in time for lunch. The meeting with the architect was in Holburn so he arranged to meet Mel for lunch and briefing at the Renaissance Hotel in Holburn at noon. She thought nothing irregular about this plan as this architect was a potential new client needing the corporate connection, and she liked Charles.

He was already at their table in the hotel restaurant when she arrived. She immediately spotted him as it was near empty at this early time. Their eyes met, and with a big smile on her face, she approached the table as he stood to greet her.

After ordering lunch, he asked for a profile of this new client, who he noted was female. He listened intently as she profiled the architect, her practice, and their upcoming project requiring some new fabrication ideas. After he felt satisfied with the brief, and they had exchanged pleasantries during the main course he decided the time was right to spring his plan.

'Mel, I owe you an apology, and I'm embarrassed about it.'

She looked at him startled and confused 'You owe me an apology – for what?'

'For not informing you of our plans for you before Michael announced the hiring of that Maurice Fulmer guy. You must have been very disappointed, and for that you have my sincere apology.'

'What plans are you talking about?'

'I have a proposition for you, young lady. It may sound a little strange to you initially but hear me out as this is a proposal that recognises your talent, contribution, and loyalty to this company, and I think you're ready for a challenge.'

'Okay. A little confused but thank you for thinking of me. What do you have in mind?'

'Mel, you've been with us for nearly ten years. In fact, you were one of the first four people to start the office in London when we decided we needed a presence in the highest growth area in the UK. You've demonstrated your intellect and skills in understanding how to translate architectural concepts into fabrication solutions. Your degree in maths have served you well. You show initiative and capability in your dealings both with clients and within the company. You're not only liked, but also respected.'

Prologue

He paused for a sip of water to see how his flattery was being received. He was satisfied the door was open to his proposal, so continued.

'What is more remarkable is you're a woman in what is essentially a man's world which must have its obstacles and frustrations. You could reasonably suggest you've twice been overlooked for promotion in the past two years because you're not a man. I'm guilty on the first occasion as I could not fully appreciate why a woman would want a career in this predominately male construction industry. Times are changing, and I've been a little slow to come to terms with women in important positions throughout industry.'

He paused again to let this declaration sink in.

'Something happened earlier this year which made me realise the significant role my wife, Edna, played in the development of this company. I met Edna just after the war when I demobbed from the Royal Engineers Regiment. This country required much rebuilding, and I wanted to be part of it. Edna and I quickly married as we lived in a 'live for today' environment. We had nothing other than my demob money, but I saw a need, and developed prefabricated houses which were both fast and cheap to build.'

With a reflective smile on his face 'They were intended only as a short-term solution, but some 40% of them are still occupied today – 40 years later.' He paused 'My generation adopted the view that a woman's role was to have and nurture children, and to keep house. This attitude was promoted by the Government well into the 1960's as, the 'baby boom', was necessary to replenish the people lost in the war. Although equality for women started in the mid-60's progress with acceptance on the ground has been slow, and I'm as guilty as the next man.'

'Earlier this year it dawned on me just how much I owe to Edna in the development of my business. In the early years she was my confidante, advisor, loyal supporter, and backbone – to name but a few of her valuable contributions. She played as much a part, if not more, than my management team. It was both a humbling and enlightening experience. It opened my eyes to the contribution a capable woman can make, and which turned my attention to how little I had appreciated the value you bring to my company.'

'Mel, I've stopped looking at you as a woman, beautiful as that picture is in my mind, and now look at you as a valuable resource – potentially executive material. I'm not getting any younger, so I need to nurture the next generation of management, not least to pay for my retirement.'

He took another sip of water. She took the opportunity to speak.

'What do you have in mind for me?'

'You probably realise Jim is not in good health. He has been advised by his medics to tender 6-months-notice of retirement. After much consideration both Jim and I believe, much against conventional wisdom, you are the best candidate to fill his boots.'

'What I'm proposing to you is to come to Matlock on secondment for six months to shadow Jim whilst maintaining only your architect client contacts. If you prove successful, you can decide if you want to fulfil your duties from Matlock, London, or both locations. If you prove you can cut it, then you could also have Jim's place on the Board. This is what I wanted to tell you before the Fulmer announcement. I hope you can forgive me for my tardiness.'

With her head in her hand and elbows on the table 'I don't know what to say. I'm extremely flattered by your proposal but left in a state of shock. You're the first person in my career to date to acknowledge my value. Thank you.'

'If I can repeat what I think you have suggested, it would be helpful to me. You want me to come to Matlock to work with Jim as a transition to merging his role with my existing role with the possibility of a Board position. You're testing me to see if I have what it takes to become an executive of this company.'

Prologue

'Close, but one small, but important factor. Both Jim and I already think you are right for this role. But you must convince yourself and others you can deliver. What you will undertake is probably the most important function in the company. Jim has been with me from the beginning. He and I were Royal Engineers together during the war, and I trust him with my life. Can you fill his boots is a question only you can answer.'

'Wow. Stating it like that makes me feel nervous and inadequate. Jim is a legend in this company. Everyone out there knows him, or of him. My father was an engineer during the war, so I understand the mentality and the discipline. If you want to give me the chance, I'll grab it with both hands as I yearn for the opportunity to find out if I'm good enough for high office, and to prove myself.'

'I understand you're planning marriage which is, and should be an important part of your life, as it was with Edna and myself. Will this influence your decision to accept this opportunity?'

'The wedding is eight months away so no problem. I probably must spend most weekends back here, not least to see my mother who is still devastated by the loss of my father earlier this year. But I don't see this as a problem either, if you don't, as I can plan necessary visits with architects accordingly.'

'I hope your mother will forgive me for dragging her daughter to Matlock, especially if she's still grieving the loss of your father. So not at all a problem. And we would cover your travel expenses. Jim has to keep to regular hours so no late nights or weekend working.'

'I'm really stunned with your offer and really appreciate your faith in me. How do you suggest we move forward? Does Michael know of this?'

'Michael knows nothing of this proposal as I wanted your reaction before informing him of my decision. What I propose is you come to Matlock on Monday next week for the week on the premise you are briefing Jim on new projects including our meeting this afternoon. You will have the time to work with Jim and myself, so you fully understand the role we expect you to fulfil. Before you leave Matlock, I would like you to either commit to the requirement, or decline. Either is acceptable so long as you are honest and committed. Do we have a deal?'

'Yes. We have a deal. Thank you so much for the opportunity. I hope I live up to your expectations.'

'You're a talented lady; overlooked by this company for too long. It's my pleasure to offer you this opportunity. I believe you will deliver, but it's for you to believe you can do it. It will be hard work as it's time limited, and you'll face hurdles not faced by a man. We'll be there for you as Matlock is not as advanced in equality as London in our industry. But if you can cut it with our hard-faced workforce in Matlock, London will be a breeze.'

'I'll speak with Michael as necessary to inform him what I've agreed with you but will not tell him of the secondment until we have agreed this between us. Please clear your desk of any important issues before travelling to Matlock or bring them with you. I'll get Mary to make your travel and accommodation arrangements.'

She was still a little dazed at this discussion, so he arranged for the bill. 'Time to get back to work lady. Are you ready for our meeting?'

'Yes, sir. I just need to visit the bathroom.'

Chapter 3 - Friday

'Mary, can you please arrange travel and accommodation for Mel next week? She will arrive Monday afternoon and leave Friday after lunch. We want to make her feel good about moving here for a while so no awful hotels or B&B's.'

'You want to impress her? Can I suggest an unusual place about three miles away and is used by Aarden Industries for their head office executives? I've a good relationship with my

Prologue

counterpart there who tells me this place only accepts executives. Do you know Merton Hall on Sydnope Hill? Sebastian Ryder is the owner – a former senior banker. It's highly recommended by my friend.'

'Mel is not an executive. And would this place be suitable for a single woman? I've met Sebastian at various functions. He's respectable but lives alone.'

'My friend claims one of the executive female directors from the parent company in Germany prefers to stay there and describes him as one of the most interesting people she's met. Absolutely no reservation about his behaviour. It's expensive at £160 B&B. He also provides dinner for a further £40 so long as confirmed by 6:30pm and served at 7:30. The lady executive claims the food is excellent, and you would pay at least this amount for the wines he serves. Apparently, the accommodation is spectacular.'

'Sounds great, but how will you get Mel there with the executive requirement?'

'You tell me to organise it and I'll do the rest.'

He smiled in resignation. She had been with him for many years, and he knew she had her ways. 'Okay, contact Sebastian and see if he'll accommodate Mel for four nights next week, and on your head be it. I'll pick her up in Chesterfield and take her there to inspect this spectacle for myself.'

'He'll want to meet her, so you can inspect each other.'

Whilst she made the arrangements, he went to tell Jim Mel was receptive to their plan, and she would arrive Monday afternoon. Jim was happy with this news. He felt suddenly much better and started the process of re-arranging his spacious office to accommodate a desk for her.

Charles went home for the weekend very pleased with himself. He had reversed his attitude towards career women, outmanoeuvred the misogynistic Michael, and had a good feeling about nurturing the first female executive of the company after 40 years of male domination. And the architect they met was proposing a fabrication technique that is very new. He knew the inventor and was looking for an opportunity to lead the sector with this material. *'Next week will be interesting.'*

Chapter 4 – Monday

Charles was at Chesterfield station at 3:30 to meet her. He drove her straight to Merton Hall; about a 45-minute drive. During the journey she updated him on events in the London office, especially regarding Maurice. He was not impressed with this appointment as it may improve their chances of business with one player, but likewise it could discourage others. Mel had proven that relationships with the major architects, an initiative she had promoted, was far more productive.

They arrived at Merton Hall. Charles had not been here since Sebastian purchased it some five years ago in a dilapidated state, and then spent some two years, whilst still a banker in the City, completely renovated both the buildings and the grounds approaching twenty-six acres. After the description by Mary, it intrigued him to meet Sebastian and see why his accommodation had such acclaim.

The gates opened as though expectant of their arrival, and he drove to the front door. Mel could only marvel at what she was viewing. Everything about this place filled her with delightful surprise. She expected a hotel. What she saw was a beautiful mansion with manicured gardens. *'Charles is certainly pulling out all the stops for me'* she thought.

They were greeted by a tall, handsome man in his late 50's, maybe early 60's, but with the physique of someone twenty years younger. He was dressed in a T-shirt and shorts, but his stature was self-assured and imposing.

Prologue

'Charles, we've briefly met before at various functions. Welcome to my home. And this must be Melanie, your protégé,' reaching for her hand.

'Please come in. I've prepared afternoon tea so we have time to clear any issues you may have.'

'So that's how Mary did it' he thought as they were guided to the lounge *'my protégé. But she's right. This place is spectacular. He must have spent millions renovating this home.'*

After tea Seb took both of his visitors to view the accommodation for Mel. Her comment was 'wow'. His was an audible 'better than a 5-star hotel'. Both were more than satisfied, and Charles had no reservation about the response he would get from her finding such a place.

As it was now past 5pm, they decided there was no point her visiting the factory today. She should settle in, and he would collect her at 8:30am in the morning.

'We really should have dinner one evening as we have, to date, not had the opportunity to know each other at the community functions which I'm very pleased to note your support. I'm somewhat embarrassed you have already lived here for some two years, and I've not invited you before. And this house is stunning. My wife would be in raptures inspecting what you have achieved here. Why don't we get through this week, and I'll call you?'

'That would be delightful. If your wife would like to look around, why don't I invite you to dinner here. You would be most welcome.'

'Thank you. We can discuss where when I call.'

Charles left, leaving her with her travel case. Seb helped her to her suite and, after checking for any dietary issues, encouraged her to unpack, relax, and come down to the kitchen when ready. 'Comfortable house clothes are the appropriate dress code, and dinner will be ready at 7:30.'

After unpacking, changing into her house clothes, and conditioning herself to the overwhelming feeling she was in some exotic palace – far better than anything she could dream of owning, she strolled downstairs to the kitchen.

Seb was organising dinner.

'Do you mind if I have a nosey around this magnificent house of yours?'

'Please do. I'll give you a guided tour after dinner in any event.'

'In that case would you mind if I hang around and chat with you?'

'It would be my pleasure. If you have the compelling need to feel useful, you can help me with dinner. Alternatively, I'll open a bottle of wine and you can relax while I prepare dinner.'

'I would love a glass of wine; and would be happy to help if I can.'

He organised wine and then continued to prepare dinner.

'We'll start with smoked salmon and soft goat's cheese, followed by my take on ragú, after which you can have fresh fruit and/or a selection of cheese with coffee. Essentially, you are joining me for dinner. In case you are not fully informed you can join me for dinner any evening so long as you let me know by 6pm and join me at 7:30. I do try to play tennis on Tuesday evenings in which case I would leave you dinner, unless you can join me at 6:30.'

Having absorbed this information, she sat for a while observing this unusual host. He appeared very ordered, but in a very calm and relaxing way. She found herself comfortable with where she was. The surroundings are sumptuous; he had lovely relaxing music in the background, and she felt a warmth which totally nullified any anxiety about being alone in this house with a stranger.

She had encountered B&Bs of various standards, some friendly family environments, and some were just in it for the money. But she had never encountered what she classified as a 5-star+ B&B. *'This is better than a quality hotel'* she thought, *'but why does he need to do this? Can't be the money. Must ask him over dinner.'*

Her thoughts were all over the place trying to absorb this whole and sudden change in her life. The confession by Charles had moved her. Finding this place to house her in comfort to make her feel welcome, further moved her. She felt wanted and is Charles now to fill the role of her father who had passed away from a sudden heart attack during the last Christmas holiday? She was an only child, and her father was the stalwart of her strength dealing in a male-dominated industry.

By the time she had returned to the present he was ready to serve.

'Are you comfortable to eat here, or would you prefer the dining room?'

'I'm not dressed for dinner, so here will do nicely, thank you.'

He dressed the table with the appropriate accoutrements before delivering the starter for both. He sat opposite her.

'You've been lost in your thoughts for some time. I hope you are not uncomfortable with the unconventional nature of this situation.'

'Not at all. I was reflecting on the massive shift in my life over the past few days. I knew nothing of this before last Thursday. I find this whole situation a little bewildering.'

'If it's of any comfort Aldridge must think a lot of you because the lady who phoned me on Friday knew of my criteria for guests but was most persuasive you are worthy of such exacting criteria even though you are not yet there. She even asked if I'm prepared to take a six-month contract to accommodate you during the working week. Aldridge has never used me before, and there are decent hotels in Matlock.'

'Mary, the lady who called you, has been with Charles for many years. She can be very assertive. Sometimes I think she runs the company. It sounds like Charles and Jim, the Production Director, are sticking their necks out for me for reasons I don't yet understand. I only hope I can meet their expectations. I have this week to decide if I want to accept their challenge, and whether I feel confident to deliver.'

'I would suggest Charles is canny enough to know you can achieve what you want. The question for you to answer is what do you want? Are you committed to a successful career and is this the route to your goal?'

'I guess I have this week to consider these questions, especially as it will require major changes in my private life.'

He noted a change in her mood. He needed to bring her back to the present as she would need much more time and information before reflecting on what lifestyle changes are involved.

'As you are my guest for this week, and potentially for the next six months, I'm interested to know Melanie as a person. Are you prepared to tell me a little about yourself?'

'My friends and colleagues call me Mel. I'm 32 years old and have worked for Aldridge since leaving university. I live with my fiancée in West London, close to the office, and we are planning our wedding in early spring next year. My job is to create the linkage, both personally and technically, between the architects, their concepts, and the fabrication realities.'

'Impressive role. What did you study at university?'

'Applied Maths and Philosophy. My dad was an engineer. He guided me in his image although greasy hands was a step too far.'

They both laughed. *'She has a good sense of humour'* he thought as he served the ragú.

'So, you've been with Aldridge for about ten years.'

'Yes. I joined them just as they opened the London office. There were four of us. Now there are 28 staff covering the South-East, mainly London. Other than PA's I'm the only female.'

'Aldridge has done well as a business and is still 100% owned by Charles. This suggests he's a shrewd businessman. You could learn much from him.'

'This ragú is delicious. Is your recipe a secret?'

Prologue

'I rarely work with recipes, just ideas and techniques. Rarely do repeats taste the same as much depends on what ingredients I have available. But thank you for the compliment. I try my best to please my clients.'

'Why do you think you're here?'

'It stunned me last Thursday when he put this proposal to me, especially as, last Monday, I was overlooked for the second time for a key role in the London office. And now, housed here in this fabulous mansion, I'm being asked to consider a key role in the head office. I guess the real story will unfold over the coming days.'

'On the basis information is the key to good decisions could I show you around my humble abode, so you know what is available to you, and where it is. We can have dessert while you ask any questions you have about your stay here.'

He guided her through the expansive hallway to the extension at the back of the house. He switched on the lights to reveal a swimming pool, changing room, gym, and sauna.

'Gosh. What a lovely pool. How long is it?'

'20m, and the depth is adjustable between 1.4m and 2.5m.'

'How does it work?'

'The pool has a false bottom with hydraulic controls to move it up and down. If I want to use the pool for aqua exercise, I will set the depth to 1.4m. If I want to dive, then 2.5m. 1.8m is enough for swimming. The controls are over here. You set the required depth, and the hydraulics will respond. If you go from extreme to extreme, it takes about ten minutes to adjust.'

'You are welcome to use any of these facilities as much as you wish. I use the pool from 6am to 6:30am but you're welcome to join me.'

'Thank you. Mary told me to bring my gym and swimming kit. Now I can see why. It's lovely.'

He extinguished the lights and steered her towards the main body of the house, and then right, into a dark room. He switched on the lights to reveal a small cinema, but with comfortable sofas and armchairs.

'You can choose from over one thousand movies and documentaries. If you want to use this room, I'll show you how to select what you want to watch. Everything is streamed and menu driven, so there are no physical discs involved.'

'Very nice. But I don't think I'd watch a movie in here on my own.'

He continued around the house showing her the spacious conservatory, lounge and dining room eventually arriving back in the kitchen. She found the whole house impressive, beautiful, and daunting at the same time. She had never been inside such a magnificent home.

They were back at the table where she settled for fresh fruit whilst he indulged in his preferred cheese and coffee.

'Do you have any questions about the facilities here?'

'Not at this moment. Can I ask you a personal question?'

'Of course, you can.'

'You're obviously wealthy so why allow total strangers to use this lovely house? It cannot be the money no matter what you charge.'

'Good question. I'm very discerning about who stays here. I prefer corporate executives, or equivalent senior public servants. And if they're from abroad then even better. There are several companies in this area owned by, or engage with, foreign entities. Although I've left the glamour of the big stage in the City I still like to discuss geo-economics and politics with people who really know what is happening out there, rather than rely on mostly ignorant pundits who fill our screens and ears with their own ill-informed views. Thus, I like to have such people as my dinner guests to engage in conversation and debate in a relaxed atmosphere.'

'I don't fit any of your criteria, so why allow me as your guest?'

Prologue

'I am intrigued to know what Charles sees in you, and what he has planned for you. Mary referred to you as his protégé. He and I have only met briefly on occasions when we are supporting local worthy causes. But he's well known here and has a good reputation. His business must be worth tens of millions, he employs over 100 people here, and he has built this business himself. For him to nurture a woman in such a male-dominated industry makes you interesting. He can see something in you he considers worthy of attention. I was still being mentored at your age, so I know the process. So, for now, if you're interesting enough for him to commit serious resources to your career progress, you're okay with me. I look forward to seeing how you progress in the coming days and, although we're strangers, should you feel the need to voice any thoughts or concerns you have outside of the Aldridge environs then please consider me as a safe ear.'

It was now approaching 10pm. She was tired and needed some quiet time to absorb the events of today.

'Would you mind if I go to my room as it's been a long day, and I need to be fresh tomorrow.'

'Certainly. I would suggest breakfast at 7:45 if Charles is collecting you at 8:30. What would you like?'

'What do you have?'

'Usually omelette, juice with toast or fresh bread.'

'Fresh bread sounds nice. I'll have the same as you. Good night.'

She went to her room.

As he prepared the dough for fresh bread for the morning he reflected on the revelations during the evening.

Chapter 5 - Tuesday

Charles arrived on the dot of 8:30. She was in good spirit and ready for work having enjoyed her breakfast.

'Good morning Charles. Thank you for collecting me.'

'My pleasure my dear. Does the accommodation meet with your approval as we've never used this facility before?'

'Absolutely wonderful, thank you. You should see the facilities here – magnificent.'

'And what about Sebastian?'

'Lovely man, and what a cook. The food here is better than many good restaurants I know. This is an unusual place but thank you for finding it for me. I feel very appreciated.'

'You can thank Mary for finding this place. Apparently one of our neighbour German subsidiaries uses it exclusively for their visiting execs.' He thought to himself *'We got this bit right. Now to convince her to accept our challenge.'*

'We're only a few minutes from the factory so soon there.'

He pulled into the factory entrance, through the gates, and parked in his designated parking space. They were quickly in his office.

'Why don't you go say hello to Mary and discuss any needs you have. I'll be with you in about ten minutes.'

She had been to the factory frequently before to meet with Jim, so she knew her way around.

'Good morning Mary. Thank you for all your help to get me here.'

'Hello, my dear and welcome. Tell me everything about Merton Hall, and the famous Mr Sebastian Ryder. I've found his bibliography, or whatever you call it. Very impressive career. What's he like in person? My friend at Aarden tells me one of the female directors from head office in Germany always insists on staying there.'

Prologue

'It's lovely, really lovely. And he's very nice, and a great cook. I'll take you to see the place if you like to satisfy your intrepid curiosity.'

'I'm so pleased my dear. I usually try to check out new places before we use them, but your visit was all of a rush. Jim is looking forward to have you work with him. He's already installed a desk for you in his office.'

She took breath 'Is there anything you need, my dear?'

'Not that I can think of at present, thank you.'

'Well, you just let me know if you need anything. It will be so nice to have another woman around here on this floor.'

Viewing her diary 'You're out to lunch with Charles and Jim today, and I'll take you back to Merton this evening.'

'You can come in and meet the famous Sebastian, and I'll give you a quick tour, but be prepared to gasp.'

'Wonderful. Can't wait. I can hear Charles coming so it looks like you're off to work. See you later.'

Charles took her to Jim's office where indeed there was a desk awaiting her. There was a company computer, so she had everything she needed to function.

'Mel. How lovely to see you and welcome to your new home for a while. We'll discuss your assignment, should you choose to accept it, over lunch. But for now, why don't you give me your version of the requirement discussed last week with your new architect client. Charles told me how impressed he was with the concept and the architect, a woman no less. Let's try to put together a competent proposal and win this order.'

'Hello, Sebastian? This is Mel. I want to tell you I'm having lunch with Charles and Jim, so no need for dinner. Maybe just a snack. It's your tennis evening, but I should be there before 6:30.'

'That's fine. My tennis partner has called off tonight, so I'll be here. You can have as much, or as little as you like at dinner.'

'Mary is bringing me back today. She would like to do her usual nose around if okay with you.'

'No problem. Does she want to stay for dinner?'

'Let me ask her.'

'Mary, would you like dinner at Merton this evening?'

'I would love to my dear, but my husband might object. Maybe another time. But thanks for the offer.'

'Sebastian, she needs to get home tonight, but maybe another time.'

'Okay. See you this evening.'

Mary and Mel arrived at Merton just before 6pm. Mary got the tour and was on her way before she changed into her house clothes. She went downstairs to find Seb in the kitchen preparing a variety of cold dishes with fresh bread.

'So how was the first day of your new adventure?'

'Good. I now have a clearer idea of what they require of me, and why they want me to succeed. The task is daunting in just six months, but I appreciate their belief in me, and would like to give it my best shot.'

'Could I suggest your future is about what you want to achieve rather than pleasing others. Where do you see yourself in 10 years from now? Do you want children? I would also advise the higher you rise, the lonelier it gets. Are you comfortable in your own space?'

'Mary tells me you're a famous banker, with an impressive career. You've trodden the career boards. How did you start, and what did it take for you to succeed where others failed?'

'Mary has been researching me. I hope she'll be kind enough to keep her knowledge to herself. I came here to get away from such nonsense. It's in the past, and I would like to keep it that way.'

'I'll ask her not to alert the gossip media. She's a real gossip. But you know what I face so do you have knowledge that will help me in my choices?'

'Mel. I don't have first-hand knowledge of the female choices that will confront you. I was on the career ladder when women first entered banking looking for a professional career. It was a bear pit for them compared with my route. Just being taken seriously was miraculous. Many fell away, not because they lacked the knowledge or capability, but because of the bigotry of a majority alpha male chauvinist order who thought women should contain their career goals to breeding children. It's not so bad today, but how many women make it to the top – so few they are practically celebrities or own the business? It will take what the Greeks call thárros, grit, for you to succeed in a man's world. You mentioned yesterday about being overlooked twice before for male alternatives who were probably not as good as you, so you know how it feels. Remember these feelings because they are the start for you if you rise through the ranks. You must manage your emotions, disappointments, misogyny, sexism, and character assassination so you'll need a thick skin. There are but a few top spots compared with many vying to take them. The rules of engagement become more savage and ruthless the higher you reach.'

'Wow. You make it sound awful. But was there one asset you can identify that gave you the edge?'

'Good mentors. People who can pick you up, dust you off, and put you back on the track. You appear to have a mentor in Charles. Good start as he has successfully survived many battles in his time. I doubt he has the knowledge to add the female edge, but a good start.'

'So, you had good mentors to help you.'

'From being a teenager, all the way through to senior executive.'

'How did you find these mentors?'

'You don't find them, they find you, as with Charles.'

'And what makes a good mentor?'

'Mostly they have been there, seen it, and done it. They see something in you that you cannot see yourself, or you're still too rough around the edges to succeed. They know, with guidance, you have what it takes to be successful. A bit like a good sports coach who shows you how to win, but they can't do it for you. Most importantly, they believe in you.'

'Are you such a mentor?'

'I owe it to my mentors to pass on my knowledge and experience to the next generation. I have mentored – especially towards the twilight of my career.'

'Do you have any pointers for me in my quest?'

'I don't know you well enough, yet. I'll have a better idea when you've decided your future later this week. I can only suggest you need to believe in yourself and your destiny and show the courage to reach for it before others will believe in you. You need to be committed. You'll have to make tough choices requiring sacrifice on your part. Let's see how you fair this week. Charles sees something in you which I hope is more than sympathy for your cause as a woman. For now, I watch with interest.'

Chapter 6 – Friday

It was Friday morning. Mel was packing, thinking through what her choice will be. She had spent every evening having dinner and chatting until bedtime realising Seb was the most experienced person in life she had ever met. She learnt so much from him she felt a different person already. He had no airs and graces and never spoke down to her. He had never tried to tell her what to do, just expressed ideas for her to think about. But she still did not feel ready to provide Charles with a decision today, not least because she wanted to discuss how this might work in relation to her fiancée.

It was time for breakfast.

'Good morning Seb. I have a problem. I'm not ready to make my decision before I speak with my fiancée. Marriage is supposed to be a partnership, so I want his support.'

'Do you need his consent to accept this challenge?'

'No. But I would like his support.'
'And what if he doesn't support you?'
'Then I have one of your nasty choices to make.'
'Are you ready to make such choices?'
'Can I answer with a question?'
'Sure, fire away.'

'I know this is not your affair, and I'm just an inexperienced young woman in your eyes, but I've really enjoyed our chats this week. You've opened my eyes to so much I need to understand and learn. I also trust you more than anyone else to be honest with me; brutally, if necessary. My father was my rock until he passed away. I need that rock for this decision. So, my question is, should I feel the need for guidance over this weekend, can I phone you?'

He looked at her for a moment as he thought *'she's serious about the choices she needs to make. Why not?'*

'Sure, you can. Tomorrow I may be out in the morning. Sunday is fine.'

'Thank you so much. But what do I say to Charles? He expects my decision today.'

'How about the following approach? Tell him you are very grateful for this opportunity. You now have a grasp of the challenge, and the choices involved. You would like to see if you have the support of your fiancée and determine the changes you will need to make to your own lifestyle to commit to the challenge. You also have your mother to consider having recently lost your father which leaves her alone. Tell him you fully understand your obligation to him by accepting this challenge and, therefore owe it to him to be fully committed from the start. Therefore, you'll call him as soon as you're ready to make a total commitment to this opportunity. He'll respect the fact you're serious about your obligations to him, and the commitment to be successful.'

'Thank you. If I knew you better, I would give you a big kiss just like I did with my dad. I feel stronger already.'

the Way

'I think you'll be fine. It looks like Mary has arrived. Are you ready?'

'My case is in the hall.'

'If you take this challenge would you want to stay here, or get your own place?'

'You can inform your German director lady she needs to look elsewhere for at least 6 months.'

'And how long before you start?'

'I'll need a week to clear my desk in London and organise myself.'

'You'll need a car here to get around. No convenient public transport here. And you can use this address for mail.'

'I have a car, and too much luggage to bring on the train. Would you mind if I brought a few things to remind me of home?'

'Your room is your space whilst you're here. I'll never enter your room unless you need me to. The only rule is you don't wreck it.'

She smiled 'I would never consider wrecking anything in your beautiful home.'

'Off you go, and good luck if I don't hear from you again. It has been a pleasure meeting you.'

'Thank you so much for everything, and the beautiful accommodation and food.' She hesitated, then gave him a kiss on his cheek, and was on her way.

As she was travelling back to London after lunch, she spent the morning with Jim going through the various contracts requiring some interaction with the client in the coming week. She could usefully visit with these clients and thus a productive way to finish the week.

Having finished this task Jim asked her for her thoughts about what she wanted to do.

'The task is a very attractive opportunity, and I feel privileged you're offering it to me. I owe it to you to be totally committed if I accept. I need a couple of days to quietly reflect on this requirement to be sure I'm ready to make this commitment, as failure is not an option I want to consider.'

'That's very reasonable and, may I say, a mature response. You've grown this week already. For my part I'm fully supportive of your preparation to take over from me. For what it's worth I agree with Charles you have what it takes for this job, and it will be fun to grow you into it.'

'You're very kind to me. I also enjoy working with you and would enjoy the experience gained from your vast knowledge. I'm only sorry you find yourself in this position.'

'Thank you. But I hope to leave my role in good hands. Charles is waiting to speak with you so be on your way, and I hope to see you back here soon.'

'She popped in to see Mary to be sure Charles was not busy.

'He's on the telephone, so give him a few minutes. How have you left things with Mr Ryder?'

'His name is Seb, and I've left it you'll call him if we need his services again.'

She laughed 'So you just said goodbye and left. Please Mel, you have spent more time with him than anyone else. Do you want to spend your 6 months with him?'

'He gave me much to think about. Really useful advice. Much to consider. So yes.'

'He's off the phone. Off you go.'

The meeting was very relaxed, and she used the approach proposed by Seb regarding the way forward. He was happy with her sincerity and took her to lunch on the way back to Chesterfield to catch her train. She also had his agreement to a telephone call over the weekend if she had any further questions, or indeed, a decision.

Chapter 7 – Friday evening

Having fought her way through the throng of Friday commuters, people going somewhere for the weekend, and visitors dragging suitcases at King's Cross St Pancras International station onto the overcrowded underground, she finally arrived back at her West London apartment around 6:30. Phillip, her fiancée, would not be home before 7pm so she needed to think about dinner. Eat in or eat out was the choice. She would prefer to eat in, but inspection of the contents of the fridge suggested otherwise, unless a quick shopping trip is undertaken.

'A hot bath I think before dinner' she thought. A glass of wine and a hot bath was her preferred retreat.

She pondered on her thoughts during the train journey home which had resulted in as many questions as answers. *'Forget the job, what about my lifestyle?'* She liked London with all it offered. *This is where the action is. What is there for me in Matlock?* She knew her secondment would not end at 6 months and then operate from London. Now she understood the nature of the job it was unrealistic to think she could run the production side of the business remotely. She would have to be in Matlock for at least half of her time.

She heard the apartment door open. 'Hi sweetheart, I'm home. Where are you?'

'In the bath. Pour yourself a glass of wine and join me.'

'Okay, on my way.'

They kissed, and he sat on a stool beside her.

'How was Matlock? I hear the Peak District is one of the most beautiful parts of England.'

'Didn't see much of the countryside; too busy. But it was a shock coming back into King's Cross during the rush hour wading through all those people. No point in trying to hurry anywhere.'

'Did you miss me?'

He kissed her again 'I'll show you later.'

They both giggled.

'Thought you might have arranged for dinner at home tonight.'

'I didn't know when you would be back, so I arranged for it to be delivered at 7:30.'

'Fantastic. I have a lot to tell you. Better here than shouting in a restaurant.'

'I'll go organise the table while you find something sexy to wear, or not. We have much catching up to do after dinner.'

'Naughty boy. I'll be ready in 10 minutes.'

Their food arrived. Her favourite Italian food. *'Perhaps tonight is not the time to talk shop'* she thought.

Their night was typical of lovers who had spent time apart.

Chapter 8 - Saturday

When they finally awoke on Saturday morning, she wanted to get his agreement to discuss her career plans. It would be football today with his mates as Chelsea were at home, and he was a season ticket holder.

'Phil, much happened this week presenting a serious opportunity for me to progress my career to executive level. For the first time I feel appreciated by the company, but we need to talk about what they expect of me. I need to give them an answer this weekend so when can we talk?'

'Need to leave here at 11 o'clock to meet the lads before the game. Probably late when I get home. Tomorrow morning is the earliest, but what's so important we need to make time this weekend? You've been away for a week so why can't it wait a few days?'

'My career. A real opportunity for me to advance to executive level.'

the Way

'Are you serious? Just last week they shit all over you for the second time, and you're now telling me they think your executive material. Where're they coming from?'

'Last week was a mistake. The Chairman has stepped in to make it right. My visit to Matlock was to lay the foundation for my progress to Board level. But it means me going on secondment to head office for 6 months. This is what we need to discuss.'

'What is there to discuss. You don't have time to spend 6-months away on secondment. We're getting married in 8 months and you have much to arrange.'

She felt shattered. *'Is he as misogynistic as the men she dealt with in business?'*

'Did you hear what I said? They want to prepare me for a Board position – a real career opportunity that will open many doors for me. Why aren't you pleased for me? Why won't you support me in this challenge?'

'Sweetheart, why Matlock? London is where the action is. What can you learn in Matlock you can't learn here?'

'Because Matlock is where the key Board members live. They need 6 months to prepare me to take over the most important executive role in the company. The head office is in Matlock. London is just a regional branch office. So, the real action is in Matlock and thus where I need to be. But I want your support.'

'I need to go meet the lads ready for the match. We can talk tomorrow but don't expect me to be enthusiastic about you being away for 6 months.'

She could not believe how negative he was without even talking it through. *'What did Seb say about information being the key to good decisions. He's not interested in the information, or my career, just what is convenient for him. Let's go see what my mother thinks.'*

She arrived at her mother's just in time for lunch.
'Hi mum, how are you?'
'I'm all right my dear. How was your trip?'

Prologue

'Full of surprises. I'll tell you over lunch.'

'Will you set the table while I serve up?'

Once seated, she began her story starting with her meeting with Charles in London, then the opportunity on offer, lodging with Seb, and then the shocking reaction of Phil this morning.

'It all sounds wonderful my dear, but what about Phillip? His reaction is typical of a man. Wants you to focus on children, not your career. Sounds like you have to make some hard choices.'

'What would dad have said?'

'He would tell you to follow your heart and your instincts. Marriage requires compromise, but not the surrender of your soul. If you really feel in your heart this opportunity is right for you then you must convince Phillip it is good for both of you.'

'Easy to say. Not so easy to do.'

'My darling, you are a very talented woman. You have your father's passion for achievement. He was so proud of you. If you believe in yourself follow your dreams. People who really love you will support you.'

'Thanks mum. You've told me what I need to hear. You're confirming what Seb told me. As I see it, I have three seasoned mentors encouraging me to accept this challenge. Do you mind if I have a chat with Seb? I need him to advise me on something.'

'Go ahead. You do what you need to do. This Seb has clearly influenced your thinking in a good way. Maybe he can show you what you need to do.'

She lifted the phone and dialled his number. He answered on the third ring.

'Seb, it's Mel. I would like your input on how to square this away with Phillip. He's against me being away for six months.'

She related their discussion this morning. 'Your advice regarding my conversation with Charles worked perfectly. How do I convince Phillip this opportunity is good for both of us?'

'Have you decided where your destiny lies?'

'If you mean am I accepting the challenge, then yes I am.'

'Good. For what it's worth you have made a bold, but good choice. Do you need a mentor?'

She smiled 'If you are speaking of a wise sage by the name of Sebastian then I would think myself very lucky, and humbly grateful.'

'Then listen up lady because life is about to get much tougher, and you'll need to be mentally fitter, smarter, and more astute. From what you've told me today I don't see a rosy future for you and Phillip, but so long as you wish to persevere with this relationship, I'll help you keep it on track.'

He then explained a strategy to get Phillip onside.

'Have you got all of that, or do you need a recap?'

'No, I have it, and thanks once again. I think I'll be thanking you many times in the coming months.'

'If you tire of using those words, the silent version you used with your father will suffice. But unconditional commitment from you is what I'll expect.'

'I'll remember that.'

Her mother had listened to their exchanges and indicated she would like a word with him.

'My mother would like a word if you don't mind.'

'No problem. Put her on.'

'Hello Mr Ryder. My lovely daughter has spoken highly of you, and I thank you for encouraging her in her career. She had a strong father and misses his wisdom. I applaud her decision to reach for higher things, but she will need help and guidance. She clearly believes you will be there for her, and I'm very grateful to you. Can I please ask you to take care of my little girl as she's all I have left in this life?'

'Dear Mrs Southgate, please call me Seb, or Sebastian if more acceptable. Thank you for your kind words, and I hear your concerns. Mel will face many trials in her quest over the coming months and years, especially as a woman. I cannot fight her fights for her, but I'll endeavour to be there with guidance, and a first-aid kit when required.'

Prologue

'As you're playing such an important role in her future, you may call me Vera. If I can ever be of help to you in your guidance, please call me as I would like to play my part in her success if I have anything to offer.'

'Vera, you are her cherished mother, and only remaining family. She loves you dearly. Just be there for her with your love and support as her journey can be very de-humanising albeit I'll endeavour to avoid such an outcome.'

'Thank you, Sebastian. I hope to meet you one day as I think I'll hear much about you over the coming months. I'll say goodbye and hand you back to Mel.'

'Thank you yet again, I'll drive up next Sunday afternoon if this is good for you.'

'No problem. I'm sure Mary will contact me to prepare for your stay. You concentrate on putting your life in order as you'll need a clean slate for your journey. Have you informed Charles of your decision?'

'Not yet. He's my next call now I have my head straight, and my wonderful mentor onside.'

'Please don't forget Charles, and probably Jim will play significant mentor roles during your journey.'

'I fully appreciate that, but they don't have your worldly experience with career women. I see how men in my industry treat significant female architects, so I need you to make me strong.'

'Bring your boxing gloves as I didn't see you do any exercise during your stay. This must change as you need to keep physically fit as well as mentally. Do you play tennis?'

'Not for some years, but I played in my teens, and at university.'

'Good. Then part of your reciprocity will be to develop your game such that you are a capable doubles partner to me. A more interesting way to keep fit. And you should regularly use my pool.'

She laughed 'Deal, my master.'

the Way

'You can retain your cheek. It works for you. Now go get this show on the road. If you need me for anything, just pick up your phone.'

'Thank you, my master. I'll see you next Sunday if you don't hear from me earlier.'

'Bye lady, and good luck tomorrow.'

'Bye Seb, and thanks.'

'Okay young lady, I can see that you interact well with this man, and he'll be there for you. Go make your father proud. He was always confident that you would do well in life.'

'Thanks mum.'

She sat consumed in her decision, and its implications for her.

'Mum, can I ask you a question I've not asked before, but it's very relevant now?'

'What is it?'

'Are you disappointed I've not produced any grandchildren for you?'

'My dear I already have a child who has given me so much joy over the years. Whether or not you bear children is your business. After having you it didn't concern either of us if we had another. You brought all the light to our lives we needed and still do. It's for you to decide if your career can include children, and when. Don't have children on my account as it's a major commitment, but also ensure you'll not have regrets. Only you should make your choices. Your biological clock may be ticking, but you can also adopt so don't allow such things to hold you back from your dreams. Your father would tell you to dream, believe, and achieve. You must follow your own path.'

She was in tears. She had never heard her mum speak in this way before. It was now clear she was the quiet strength behind her father. It reminded her of the revelations by Charles about his wife, Edna. She hugged her mother to prevent the escape of this moment.

'Thank you. I never knew you felt this way. You've lifted a burden from my shoulders. Thank you so much. I love you so dearly.'

'Your father was a good man who never had much time for social fads, or what others thought. He was strong and focussed as you now need to be. I only want for you what you want from life. I have you. It's enough.'

Chapter 9 - Sunday

It was mid-morning Sunday. She was already up preparing her "To Do" list. He didn't arrive home until after midnight, worse for wear from the after-match trip to the pub with his mates. He was still snoring away.

Her night had been agonising. She still had not made the call to Charles. She wanted to keep her upcoming marriage on track but was not happy her intended partner for life was not taking her quest seriously. *What to do?*

She reflected on her conversation with the only man she instinctively knew she could trust and be there for her – after just one week. She has told him she will return, and he will mentor her. She picked up the phone and dialled the number for Charles.

'Good morning, Charles. I hope this is not an inconvenient time for you.'

'Not at all. I've kept my time free to help you through your thought process.'

Her eyes welled with tears as she realised how many people were rooting for her.

'Charles, I've made my decision. I want to accept your kind offer and will dedicate the next six months to prove myself worthy of your support.'

the Way

'Fantastic news. Thank you, Mel. You have my full support throughout what will probably be a hard journey for you. But I know you'll make me proud of you. I'll inform Jim, and I'll contact Michael to inform him of my decision regarding your future with us. He'll know of your plans by the time you arrive at the office tomorrow. Will you stay with Sebastian?'

'Yes please. He was instrumental in my decision.'

'We noticed the rapid change in you last week and guessed he was in the loop. I'll ask Mary to ensure you have your chosen accommodation for the next six months. If you can give me his number, I'll phone him myself. It's about time he and I get to know each other as he'll no doubt play a significant role in your progress. To have someone with his worldly experience in the loop makes the cost irrelevant.'

She gave him the telephone number she had for Seb.

'Good. I'll let him know whatever you need will be covered.'

'Thank you. You're all very kind to me.'

'Thank you for believing in us. I'm delighted with your decision. We'll make this work for both of us.'

'I'll try my best. I intend to travel up to Matlock next Sunday so I can start on Monday. I'll be bringing my car, so I won't need to be collected.'

'That's fine. I'll speak with you during the week, but we look forward to you joining us next week. Thank you, Mel. Goodbye for now.'

She heaved a sigh of relief. It was done. Now back to her list in earnest as he emerged, bleary-eyed, and brandishing a hangover.

'Hi sweetheart. Who were you talking to?'

'My Chairman, Charles Aldridge.'

'What do you need to talk to him about on a Sunday?'

'I needed to inform him I'm accepting the position at head office on the basis I can return to London at weekends. He agreed.'

'I thought we would talk about this today?'

Prologue

'We said Sunday morning. It's nearly noon. If you cannot take our future seriously, then I must make decisions I feel are important for us.'

'Sorry sweetheart. Last night was a little heavy. You should have woken me up.'

'I don't see this job as an issue now I'm here at weekends. You travel with your job, so what's the difference?'

'So, what you are saying is you'll be in Matlock during the week, but back here at weekends.'

'Yes, although if this weekend is anything to go by, I have to question whether or not I should bother on weekends involving football.'

'My plan is to come home Friday evening and return on Sunday afternoon unless your plans make such a journey irrelevant.'

'When do you intend to start this secondment?'

'It'll take me next week to clear my desk, so I'll drive up to Matlock next Sunday. I need a car there but can use the train at weekends. The person I'm to replace is very ill so I must complete this task within six months as his medics insist he cannot continue beyond this if he lasts six months. So, I must do what is necessary to ensure continuity.'

'Wow. If you put it this way then, at least, I understand why you need to be there. I don't like it but let's see how it goes. At least we'll get weekends together.'

'We could occasionally have more time as I still have a responsibility for my architect clients. When I need to visit with them, I'll either travel down Thursday evening, or travel back on Monday evening.'

'So, in six months you'll replace this guy, and be an executive, with an executive salary. Sounds good. They'll have to pay you full salary when you get pregnant. We need to celebrate. Let me shower and clean up. Time for brunch to celebrate and toast your success.'

He made his way to the bathroom.

the Way

She looked up to the ceiling *'Thanks Seb. You're a genius. I'll remember the philosophy you deployed. Easier to ask for forgiveness than to ask permission, wrapped in a little confuse and destroy. Great. Your strategy worked perfectly. Another big kiss for you.'*

'Sebastian? This is Charles. Good news. Mel has accepted our offer and will return next Sunday. Whatever she needs will be covered. Do you need a contract?'

'Good afternoon, Charles. Good news indeed. No contract required. Your word is good for me.'

'It did not escape our attention she made significant strides forward as a person last week, so I assume you're a very welcome contributor to the development of this young lady. Could we meet for lunch, say Tuesday at the golf club at 12:30 to get to know each other better. We share an interesting project, and I would welcome any thoughts you have to achieve the best possible outcome.'

'Tuesday is fine with me. Do I need to observe any dress code for the restaurant as my suits are essentially moth-balled?'

'Jacket, but no compulsion for a tie.'

'Good. I'll see you there on Tuesday.'

'Should Mary contact you politely indicate we've already agreed the way forward. I should be able to intercept her, but I'm not in the office tomorrow morning.'

'No problem. Bye.'

Chapter 10 - Monday

Within minutes of arrival at her office on Monday morning Michael Chimes entered.

'I had a call from Charles yesterday. It transpires last week was more than a review of current projects. So, you're moving to Matlock for six months to assume the responsibilities of Jim. Why he thinks you can do that job, get married, and probably quickly have children is beyond me. Can you ensure you hand over your construction clients to Maurice before you depart? We need to ensure continuity. Good luck.'

He left.

Normally she would feel hurt by such abrupt and sexist comments, but she felt elated. She was out from underneath this male chauvinist pig, and would hopefully return at least his equal in seniority, if not above. The very thought made her tingle with delight. This week would be a chore but would pass quickly. She was smiling with joy and looking forward to the future for the first time in months.

Chapter 11 - Sunday

She was ready before noon to start her drive to Matlock. The decision about what to take with her was far too onerous so practically emptied her wardrobe and drawers. As she intended to travel by train at the weekends, she did not want to carry more than a weekend bag, nor carry anything larger returning. Her car was full. She also had a box of memorabilia on the passenger seat including photographs of her mum and dad. These would be her home-from-home items. She knew she had enough space at Merton for far more than she could ever need, so no embarrassment with the amount of luggage. She was prepared for anything.

It was the last full week of August, and a very pleasant summer's day. The drive to Matlock would take about three hours. She wanted to arrive in plenty of time to unpack, and to avoid the late afternoon traffic. She said her goodbyes to Phil who, again was recovering from a football hangover, and started her journey to a new beginning.

She felt a sense of adventure, a new chapter in her life. Secretly she couldn't wait to get back to Merton Hall.

the Way

She finally arrived at the gates after an uneventful trip. She pressed the buzzer. The gates glided open as if bowing to greet her. As she pulled into the parking bay he had allocated for her, he came out to meet her in his standard attire of T-shirt and shorts.

'*He looks great*' she thought as she switched off the engine and got out of the car. They greeted each other as would a friend with a hug and a kiss on each cheek. She then gave him two further kisses on each cheek 'I owe you those for last weekend.'

'Thank you, and welcome to your new home.' He saw the luggage in her car 'Are you staying long?'

She laughed 'I couldn't decide what to bring, so brought everything.'

'Would you like any refreshment before we call the baggage boys to unload your car?'

He was teasing her. 'I need the bathroom, and if you could arrange a cold drink, this would be splendid, my man.'

'I think madam knows the location of facilities at this establishment, so I'll see you in the kitchen bar in a few minutes.' They both laughed as they made their way to the house.

When she returned to the kitchen, he had prepared two glasses of Prosecco. He handed one glass to her and offered a toast.

'Let us toast your new life here. I sincerely hope you enjoy your stay, and I look forward to observing you grow in stature over the coming months. I hope you achieve your dreams.'

They clinked their glasses and drank. Her smile ran from ear-to-ear.

'He picked up a key and electronic fob and handed them to her. This is your key to the house, and your fob to open the gates. It works from about 20m away, so you can activate it as you approach them, and they will open for you to glide straight inside. They close by themselves.'

Prologue

'Wow, my own keys to Merton Hall. Now I know I've arrived.'

'Seb, before we start this adventure I'm very grateful to you for this opportunity, and I put myself totally in your hands. If I step out of line, I consent to correction. If I offend you, shoot me down. From now on you're not my host, you're my master and I'll endeavour to live up to your expectations of me.'

'Quite a speech lady, but very much appreciated. If you want to achieve the very best possible outcome in the allotted timeframe, you'll need to work hard, both here and at Aldridge. There will be bad times when you will hate me and/or them. But there will also be good times, and even fun times. If I come down hard on you it's for your benefit, not mine, but I'll also likely feel your pain. I'll not enjoy seeing you cry in despair, but sometimes you will only understand the gain after you experience the pain. Does this bother you?'

'The one thing I know about you is I can trust you to take care of me, and I hope this trust comes to my mind in any bad times.'

'Good enough. I have a little surprise for you later. Why don't we get your luggage to your room, change into something more comfortable, and we can chill on the sundeck.'

'What's the surprise?'

'Wouldn't be a surprise if I told you.'

It took three trips to unload her car as some items, such as coats, were loose. She only unpacked enough to find a top and shorts before re-joining him on the sundeck where he had the Prosecco on ice. She immediately noticed the BBQ had been primed, ready to light.

'We're having a BBQ. Is this the surprise?'

'No, but it's a lovely day, so a BBQ is an obvious choice.'

'Great idea' still trying to see if she could identify the surprise.

She sat absorbing the view. She had not been up here before, nor had she seen the grounds.

'What a fabulous view. You can see for miles. How much of this land is yours?'

the Way

'All the way to the golf course below – about 400m.'

'You're completely secluded up here. What a great place to sunbathe.'

He left her to relax and absorb the warm, scented air as she panned the raw, but beautiful Peak District horizon. He fired the BBQ with South African kameeldoring wood as the aromatic burn added extra flavour to the food but took some time to render down to charcoal.

After a while they heard the gate buzzer.

'You expecting visitors?'

'Yes. They come to celebrate your arrival.'

'She looked puzzled.'

'Come with me to welcome our guests.'

He opened the gates and two cars entered. She immediately recognised the Range Rover owned by Charles, but the other SUV was unfamiliar until she saw the driver. It was Jim, and they both had their wives with them.

She rushed to greet them both with hugs, and introduced to their respective wives, Edna and Margaret. 'What a lovely surprise and thank you for coming to see me.'

Charles introduced Seb to the ladies.

'Welcome to my home. Please come inside and tell me what you would like in the way of refreshment. I have Prosecco on ice for those interested.'

They all took Prosecco and toasted Mel. Charles led with 'To your future with us. May you enjoy the journey, and we look forward to our first lady executive.'

'Mel, I know these ladies are keen to survey our abode so could you please show them around while I attend to the BBQ.'

'Sure. How much can I show?'

'Whatever is available to you.'

Jim piped in 'Do you mind if I tag along? I've heard so much about this place from Charles and Mel I would like to see it for myself.'

With Prosecco in hand, they followed her for their tour.

Prologue

Charles turned to Seb 'This is a great idea of yours. My wife was starting to wonder what I was up to with Mel. Now everyone in this venture can meet, and we can start this process on the right footing. She looks happy enough so here's to a successful venture and thank you so much for your help.' They toasted success.

'I need to move food up to the deck. Could you help me?'

'Of course. What would you like me to take, and where is the sundeck?'

'If you could take these dishes, and return for the rest, and follow me.'

Once on the sundeck Charles could only marvel at the architecture, and the vista. 'You really have made a wonderful home. I'm only sorry not to see any of our fabrications. But if you have plans to build further, please let me know first as I would love to contribute to such a stunning property.'

'Thank you. I have further plans I could discuss with you, but not until we have concluded our current project.'

The others appeared in a state of shock as they entered the deck. Edna spoke first 'Charles told me your home is special. Always the one for understatement.'

They all laughed.

Edna continued 'You really have done a magnificent job restoring this property. It was dilapidated when I last saw it.' Turning to Mel 'And I understand that you, young lady, are also quite special, and these two fuddy duddies and Sebastian are attempting a "My Fair Lady" routine on you. If at any time you need female interaction you are free to call me. I accept their intentions are honourable, but since when have men understood women?'

Everyone laughed loudly, including Mel. 'Thank you, Edna. I'll certainly call you if necessary.'

Everyone settled down as Seb prepared the BBQ. Both wives were keen to chat with Mel as they had heard good things from their husbands. The afternoon went well.

the Way

The guests left around 7:30 leaving Seb and Mel to clear up in the kitchen.

'That was your idea, wasn't it?' No response. 'You're a real clever clogs, and I loved the "My Fair Lady" analogy. You must be Professor Higgins, Charles probably Colonel Pickering, and Edna as Higgin's mother.' Trying an East End accent 'Will I have to speak proper as part of the process?' she teased.

'No, my dear. Your spoken English is already worthy. But we have to ensure the words you utter are appropriate.'

She poked him in the ribs 'I's only a poor flower girl, my master.'

Later that evening, as they relaxed in the lounge chatting, he decided she must start her daily exercise routine tomorrow.

'I need to revise your daily routine, starting tomorrow. What time do you intend to get to your office?'

'I've agreed 8:30.'

'So you need to leave here at 8:15 which means breakfast at 7:45. Therefore, you need to be out of bed no later than 7 o'clock, straight down to the pool. You do two lengths in glide mode to warm you up, and then ten laps in race mode. Then you shower, get ready for work, and be in the kitchen ready for breakfast at 7:45. Any questions?'

'No, my master.'

'Is this master thing something you're serious about, or are you teasing me?'

'No, my master. It's my way of differentiating between what I'll do without question, and what I may challenge.'

'Okay, I accept the use of this token. Interesting idea.'

'Next. When you arrive home tomorrow evening, I want you in your gym kit ready to train for 30 minutes. I'll show you what program I want you to follow tomorrow. I do not intend these exercises to generate a muscular body. They are core and toning exercises.'

'What is the measure of success you seek, my master?'

Prologue

'When you can catch me, or even beat me, swimming ten lengths of the pool you will be at a level that only requires maintenance. Remember, I'm about twice your age so beating me is no big deal.'

'And the purpose, my master?'

'Sitting in an office all day is not good for you. A healthy mind needs a healthy body. We need to keep toxins under control to maintain alertness. You'll feel much better in yourself after a week. Then it will be self-evident to continue an exercise regime.'

'There is one other thing that will conflict with your current thinking, but for me to develop you into quality executive material I need more time than just evenings. Aldridge can advance you to what they need for their business, but I would like to push you to see if you are capable of any executive role in any company. To do this I need a few weekends, at least, where you stay here to give me the time I need to develop specific techniques with you. How do you feel about this requirement?'

'If you need me here, then so be it. Can we try to select weekends when Chelsea are at home or involved in a London derby as I would probably stay here for those weekends in any event. Phil and his mates disappear for the whole day so no loss other than popping down to see my mum on a Saturday. I would also like to see Matlock and the surrounding area when we have time.'

'Great. I'm sure this will work as I have no specific curriculum, just much to teach you.'

'I've agreed with Charles not to take any annual leave during these six months. If necessary, I can use my leave to tack on an extra couple of weeks with you full-time if we need it. I'm still in awe of how much time and effort you are prepared to give to me, and without reward. You asked for my commitment to success. You have it.'

the Way

He looked at her somewhat astonished thinking *'I don't know what happened this past week, but she is now clear in her objectives. Impressive.'*

'Why don't you unpack and get yourself settled. We'll start our adventure in earnest tomorrow.'

'Good night and thank you for your belief in me. You don't know how strong it makes me feel.'

'Good night. See you bright and early tomorrow.'

Week 1

Chapter 12 – Monday

She was in the pool at 7am following her instructions to the letter. The water felt good against her body, and there was no hint of chlorine. *'I wonder what he uses to keep this water so clean and fresh?'* she thought. *'Must ask him.'*

She dutifully arrived at breakfast at 7:45, said her good morning with a kiss on his cheek. She chatted with him expressing how nice the water was. He told her he uses an ionised copper sulphate solution. Healthier for the skin. She was both interested and satisfied with his answer, as unusual as everything about this man, finished her breakfast, and left for the office in good spirit.

When she arrived at her desk, there was a lovely bunch of flowers, and three "Good Luck" cards. *'These people are so lovely to me'* she thought, *I can't possibly let them down.'* Mary arrived with a mug of tea for her and welcomed her back.

'As you're now here, permanently' making quote marks with her fingers around the word "permanently", 'I need to run through some boring, but necessary Code of Practice for the factory. Pop along when you have some time.'

She spent the morning with Jim explaining to her how he approaches a project, the procedures he had developed over the years to ensure there were no cracks in the process and quality control, and what was required by the technical drafting department for them to plan the production process. Aldridge prided itself on custom design, and thus why they could work with architects on new concepts in design and fabrication technique.

After lunch he invited her to take a walk with him around the site. During WWII this had been a military air base. Although plots were sold off over the years for other industrial development to fund expansion of fabrication facilities, the retained site was still substantially larger than required for current production. The airfield had been used primarily for bombers so had a wide concrete apron and runway. They had widened this to about three times its original width so the total concrete slab for the site was some 300m x 100m. They walked to the building at the far end.

This building was a former aircraft hangar. There were a series of hoppers at the far end. 'This is where we fabricate concrete structures, and hence why this building is at the end of the site. I'm not allowed in this building any longer because of the dust. But I'll get Tom to find you some overalls, a hard hat, and show you what's inside.' Pointing to the hoppers 'We used to make our own concrete, but the standards today are so rigid we only make concrete for prototypes. For smaller work that can be transported we buy in ready-mix from a local certified supplier. Otherwise, we build the steel superstructure around which we pour the concrete on the client's project site.'

They walked back the 100m or so to the next factory, just behind the office block. Again, a large building, same width but longer than the previous one. 'You already know this building is where we produce extruded fabrication products, and there is also a section engaging in wood fabrication, mostly for churches and restoration work although still used in modern domestic architecture. Again, I can no longer enter this building, but this is not the reason for this tour.'

He turned towards the space between the two factories and pointed to it. 'This is the space I want to show you. For some time now we have been watching the development of polymer materials for use in the construction industry. We know the inventor at the forefront of this technology in the UK, and who lives not far from here at Chester-le-Street. Charles has become very friendly with him and, indeed, helped him to achieve the independent certification of some of his ideas at Cardiff

Week 1

University. They are meeting tomorrow because your new project provides the opportunity to use this polymer technology. I took the liberty of speaking with Teresa Yardley, the architect, last week and she is agreeable for a proposal based on this technology. We have for some time now quietly planned for a factory to produce polymer fabrication in this space. If we compare these materials with concrete, they are half the weight, eight times the strength, dramatically improved thermal and sound insulation, and far easier and cleaner to mould. As a polymer, the thermal expansion characteristics can be a challenge, but the architect does not envisage this as a problem compared with the benefits. Importantly, the fabrication process is materially cheaper than a concrete equivalent.'

'The size of the order for your project would fully justify the construction, and the timeline works as well. So, my dear, you may have brought us the next big advance in this company to use these products, and you will be the first Production Director to deliver such products. You're not merely taking over from me, you are forging the next generation in material technology. Your order; your project. This could be your legacy. I want your involvement in every conversation regarding this new development. I would also like you to keep this to yourself for a while until we can secure the licenses we need, but I thought it useful to show you you're overseeing the next generation of this business.'

'Wow. I realised Teresa had something special on her screen when I saw the outline design, and now you tell me we can help her to do something special with it. Sounds exciting. Can I mention it to Seb just in case he needs to factor something into his program for me?'

'Okay. As he has become an important part of your development, but please, no-one else.'

When she arrived home, she quickly changed into her gym kit and presented herself for instruction. He went through a series of exercises for core strength, toning, and cardiovascular. He had already made a chart of the exercises, and the number of repeats.

Having completed her program, she readied herself for dinner before relaxing in the kitchen watching his preparation.

During dinner she told him about her day at Aldridge, and the plans they had to introduce polymer fabrication. He quizzed her about this new polymer material, and then it was time for work.

'My master, can you give me some idea of the scope of our activities over the coming months?'

'Before I do can I tell you my ideas regarding the best use of our time. I think we should designate the time you're ready for dinner, and throughout dinner, for you to tell me what happened during the day, and any issues relating to material already covered. After dinner we'll deal with new material. How does this sound to you?'

'Sounds like a plan.'

'As week's progress we should develop a two-way feedback mechanism where I determine what, and how you are integrating your new knowledge into your work, anything not covered but expected of you, and thus tailoring the process.'

'The subject matter is multi-faceted but can be broken down into general headings such as your attitude, your behaviour under stress, several philosophical tools, physical and mental well-being, managing stress, understanding the rules of the game called business, psychology of business relationships, and if we have time, the financial structure of business. Please take this list as preliminary as I'll probably think of others. I haven't defined a specific curriculum as I prefer to respond to need, capability, and desire. During the initial weeks I intend to concentrate on the characteristics you must possess to have any chance of survival in the corporate jungle. As your personal skills develop, we'll move on to the skills needed to do your job. Your role, as an exec, is essentially strategic, driving the business forward. We will study the elements of strategy and risk, and how to apply them. You can always study the financial tools you need to know yourself as there are many textbooks on this subject.'

'But before we engage in these subjects, I would like to instil a few ground rules. When I ask you to do something you're not obliged to comply. If you want to learn, I'm prepared to help. You cannot cherry pick important aspects of your knowledge needs. You can walk away at any time. If I think I'm wasting my time I can ask you to leave. I have no contractual commitment to your endeavours; everything is by mutual consent.'

'The most important aspect of this relationship is trust. I expect you to trust my direction and decisions as they will always be in the best interest of your desire to become serious executive material. Is this understood?'

'Yes, my master.'

'If we start with the premise you desire to arm yourself with the knowledge and capability to survive as a corporate executive, what do we mean? I could arm you with everything you need to be an executive at Aldridge very quickly. However, the skills needed for Aldridge are only a microcosm of what you'll need for a major corporate. My experience is at the very top of the largest cesspit of sharks and alligators, whereas I would consider Aldridge a den of pussycats. I would like to train you to the full extent of your potential. Many people question why top executives earn such large remuneration packages. These people do not understand the demands of such a role. Only the fittest and best equipped survive. Are you prepared to reach for your full potential?'

'Yes, my master. Is there any significance to the sharks and alligators?'

'They're fierce predators with few if any natural predators. Both have survived for thousands of years. Alligators are relentless pursuers who will work in groups and devour anything in their sights. If they lose a limb, it will grow back, i.e.

they can recover from major setbacks. Sharks will even attack each other for food or supremacy. Very fitting at the very top.'

'Let's define the profile of a corporate executive. First, and foremost they understand business is a game. You walk onto the pitch when you arrive at the office in the morning, you fight to win throughout the day, and then you leave the pitch when the game is over, and you go home. When you go home, you relax and become a normal human being again and attend to family affairs, keep fit, and develop your skills.'

'Think of a soccer team. They develop the skills and fitness to play the game. When they enter the pitch two teams go head-to-head with the aim of winning the game. They fight for possession of the game using skill and ploy trying to outmanoeuvre and outplay each other. Think of the law and regulators as the referee to keep the game legal, albeit you will see infringements not detected by the referee. At the end of the game the players who have been knocking seven bells out of each other, shake hands and walk off the pitch as friends. Does this picture resonate with you?'

'Now I think about it I can understand the sport analogy, but are you seriously telling me you switch off when you leave the office?'

'If you want to retain your sanity, recharge your batteries, and have a family life you must learn to do this. Those who take business too seriously and personally soon burn out.'

'I've met executives who think the company depends on them, thinking the whole business will collapse if they don't appear for some reason. These people are fools, and I've happily fired such people because they're a liability. Do they seriously believe the corporation will fold if they're killed or otherwise suddenly die? I think it was Margot Fonteyn, the great ballerina, who remarked one should always take one's work seriously, but one should never take oneself seriously.'

She thought about her own behaviour for a moment 'I've always taken my job seriously, even had sleepless nights worrying about a decision made, or whether I've done enough to secure an order. Now you tell me this is the last thing I should do.'

'The second skill you most certainly need, especially a woman, is theatre. The business world is a stage, and you're an actor. Your acting ability plays a major part in your ability to succeed in debate, argument, and maintaining discipline. A good actor can convince you they are happy, in pain, your best friend, angry, sad, in love, sincere – whatever the role needs, but when the clapperboard signifies the end of the scene, the actor immediately returns to their natural self.'

'We'll engage in much simulated role play, especially negotiation skills. There will also be times in the coming months when I'll let rip at you. I'll let you into a secret. If you take my pulse rate, it will not increase one beat. You cannot concentrate if you're emotionally involved. I can tell you this knowing you'll forget this fact when I let rip because it will be so convincing to you.'

'Before I forget I'll mention something drummed into me at the start of my exec career by the Chairman of the bank who became a fantastic mentor. He made it clear when I walk through the office door, onto the field of play, I must leave my politics, nationality, religion and any other ideology or dogma at the door. My job was to adopt the philosophy of the bank and engage equally with people throughout the world whatever their background. The bank would decide who was a suitable client and I must accept and respect that view. There is no room for personal prejudice in the corporate environment.'

'As a woman in a generally male dominated world, you need additional skills. You need to be very confident in your abilities, and comfortable in your own skin. You will face intimidation, sexism, and personal attack, both mentally and physically. You must be able to stand your ground without flinching under any circumstances. I'll flush out your mental weaknesses and

the Way

attempt to correct them. I'll also teach you how to defend yourself against physical abuse.'

'You'll hear people speak of winning or losing arguments. Neither is a productive outcome. In argument, the skilful negotiator knows a win-win is the most desirable outcome. Therefore, each will try to convince the other of their position, but in a non-confrontational manner allowing either to move their position without appearing to concede. Both sides will freely adjust their positions towards an optimum outcome both parties can endorse. This is by far the supreme outcome.'

'To be a successful negotiator, you need to read people. Why are they motivated towards a specific outcome? Is there a hidden agenda? Why are they so accommodating? Do they have a personal motive? The list is long. You must be aware of being lulled into accepting things at face value. You must hone your instincts and listen to them.'

'Ultimately you are the architect of your own destiny. You only need the tools and the knowhow.'

'How are we doing?'

'You've just turned my whole philosophy and behaviour on its head. Boy, how wrong I've been. I studied philosophy, but nothing like this.'

'When you speak with an architect expounding the qualities of Aldridge against your competitors do you call upon Aristotle to formulate your rhetoric and then deliver it with conviction?'

'Not consciously. But I think you are about to prove I do.'

'Not now. I don't want to get into detail. My aim tonight is to start to develop the framework of your new mentality, give you an idea about the skills you need, and to give you just enough to start you thinking, which will open your mind to what is to come. I need you to buy into the game and theatre ideas as this mentality is imperative to your success.'

She paused while she thought about what she was hearing. 'Seb, you're describing a whole new world to me. Can you really teach me all of this in just six months?'

Week 1

'You're a bright lady, and willing to learn. Listen up, open your mind to new ideas, accept I'll not lead you astray, and you'll accomplish much in the time available. Probably not to the level of a corporate exec, but all the tools you need to further develop and hone your skills.'

'I'll give you a taster. If I tell you to toughen up, I'm asking you to remove emotional content from your argument and decision process, and never take things personally. Be an observer, and respond to what you see from a calm, remote perspective. From my experience, this is the tough part for a woman.'

'And you'll teach me how to fight, like martial arts?'

'I could, but no. I'll teach you how to respond to and neutralise gropers and molesters in the workplace. This will be a Sunday activity. We can advance to muggers and beyond if you spend enough weekends here.'

'I've already decided to spend this weekend here to get myself properly installed, and to find my way around. So, I'm available for whatever activities you think useful.'

'Good. I'll plan accordingly. By the way, I haven't explained the house rules. I have a housekeeper, Georgina, who works Monday through Friday, but excluding Bank Holidays. She will clean your room, bathroom, and take care of towels and bed linen. She can also take care of your personal laundry unless you prefer to do it yourself. Her husband, Peter, takes care of the gardens and routine maintenance. You have the run of the house and grounds except for my study area. Any questions?'

'No. Although I would normally take care of my own laundry, I think you will keep me very focussed and busy whilst here. Therefore, I would appreciate Georgina taking care of it if you don't mind.'

'No problem. Use the laundry basket in your bathroom. It's late lady. Enough for today. You have much to think about before dinner tomorrow when I'll go through the golden rules of becoming a successful executive.

the Way

'Have you mentored a woman before?'

'No. Didn't find one who either needed my support or attracted my attention. I suppose we all helped each other when I was climbing the exec ladder, and this provided a good insight into the differences in the process for women. I was also asked to help a woman refine her MBA dissertation, probably because I might employ her after graduation.'

'What happened?'

'She pulled herself up from an administrative position through an MBA program, seeing herself eventually as businesswoman of the year. She graduated top in class. She wanted to see how the banking world worked so I found her a position in a lower bank. Within six weeks the shock to her system was taking its toll. Throughout her MBA program she had become used to working on problems in groups and having time to pontificate solutions. A senior banker spends much of their time making serious decisions on their own, on the fly – the markets won't wait. Harvard Business School regard a corporate executive successful if 85% of their decisions by value are correct. In banking at least 95% with no thinking time. She didn't last three months, and I heard nothing of her afterwards. It's a tough game, and you need to be up for it. So off you go and sleep tight. No thinking or dreaming about work.'

'Good night, my master.'

Chapter 13 – Tuesday

By the time she arrived home she had considered the game and theatre ideas and had also discussed these ideas with Jim who found it interesting, conceding they were probably right. Over dinner she confirmed her acceptance of this framework and was ready to move on.

Week 1

'Tonight, I will outline some golden rules you must understand and apply. I will briefly discuss the importance of each rule, and then we can expand on any you feel you need a deeper understanding. This is vital information, so listen up.'

'I'll start by stating the rule and then explain.'

'Go to work each day willing to be fired.'

'If you don't have confidence in yourself, why should anyone else? Be true to yourself. If you find you can't do the job, or don't enjoy it, either quickly shape-up, or resign and move on. Being fired is not good for your CV, your self-esteem, or job prospects. It's so important your career is on your terms.'

'Circumvent any orders aimed at stopping your dream.'

'You will encounter times when you are being directed to suppress your own intuition and judgement without good reason. Do not do this. Think of the playing field. A defender will attempt to convince you psychologically you cannot get passed them. If you buy into this, you will never get passed them.'

'People will try to put you down – imposed supremacy.'

'When a peer or senior sees you as a threat to their position the typical response will be to suppress you. They could use the tactic of our previous defender who psychologically convinces you that you cannot get past them, they can restrict your ability to perform, strategically speak badly about you to your peers and/or seniors, steel your thunder, or try to get your demoted, or even fired.'

'This can be more than one person, especially if butting against the corporate immune system. Use these rules to work underground until you can defeat this obstacle. Never let go of your dream.'

'Do any job needed to make your project work, regardless of your job description.'

'Job descriptions are for low-level employees who cannot think for themselves. Executives need to do whatever it takes to achieve the goal in an ever-changing world. If your people are struggling to meet your deadlines do not stand there getting hot under the collar – help them. Was your expectation and deadline realistic? If not, adjust it, and learn for the future. Sometimes just being there maintaining the tea and coffee supply, rather than stalking the floor, can make the difference.'

'Find people to help you.'

'The more people you can recruit to help you the easier the task. Heroes rest in graves. Smart people find collaborators.'

'Follow your intuition about the people you choose; and work only with the best.'

'Very important to hone your instincts and listen to them. Do not tolerate or carry anyone. The better the people around you the better the result. A few good people will always be better than an army of mediocre people. We'll discuss this much more when we study "The Art of War" written some 2,500 years ago.'

'Work underground for as long as you can - publicity triggers the corporate immune system.'

'The corporate immune system is one of the most divisive beasts you will encounter. This is the status quo, conventional thinkers who do not want their cosy existence disturbed by new ideas or, indeed, you to outshine them. We will discuss the corporate immune system many times as this presents itself more times than you can imagine. "We have always done it this way" is classic corporate immune system.'

'Never bet on a race unless you are running in it.'

'We can interpret this several ways. Probably the most important is not to accept a task for which you will be accountable if someone else is telling you how to do it. If you're being offered the task, then the assumption is you're capable of delivery. If you're accountable for the outcome, then you **must** be in control of the delivery mechanism.'

'If you think you cannot deliver, be very careful about accepting it on the basis the originator will guide you through. Ask yourself why they're asking you to deliver if they claim they can do it themselves. If in doubt, back out. Do not be accountable for anything over which you have no control.'

'Remember it is easier to ask for forgiveness than for permission.'

'My favourite line in My Fair Lady, the film, is when Eliza leaves Higgins in the middle of the night she encounters Freddie who then serenades her with his love for her. Her response is good advice - don't tell me, show me. Sometimes explaining to people what you want to do is beyond their belief or understanding. Therefore, their response will be to prevent you from attempting delivery. If you feel this response is likely then don't ask; just quietly do it, i.e. show them. Results speak for themselves. If it goes wrong, it's easier for them to forgive you knowing the fallout.'

'Be true to your goals but be realistic about the ways to achieve them.'

'If you try to impose your way to success, you will probably be frustrated, and face animosity. You need to take people with you and move at a speed which keeps people with you. And never use your seniority or sexuality to exert your aims – this always fails.'

'Honour your sponsors.'

'Remember who pays your salary every month. You have an obligation of loyalty, and to deliver your best. Never take them for granted. Your sponsors include shareholders.'

'I would like to share one important caveat to this rule. Winston Churchill succinctly described it when, in later life and having fallen out of favour, was concerned about history being kind to him, so he wrote it himself. As a corporate executive you're obligated to comply with a majority vote unless illegal. If, however, you truly have good reason to believe the proposed course of action erroneous or will not achieve the desired outcome then you must record your thoughts. The best way is to log your reservations in the minutes of the meeting. For example, should the majority vote be to expand business in an anticipated buoyant market, but you have reliable information to suggest the market is far from resilient and likely to tank, and you have adequately expressed your views, then declare you will support the outcome of the vote, but you would like to formally record your opposite view of market expectations in the minutes. Ensure the minutes reflect your view before they're sealed. If the corporate strategy goes very wrong leading to heads rolling, the minutes will record you were right and thus history will be kind to you.'

She looked up from her notes. 'Wow. It must take a lot of courage to oppose in such a way. Has this happened to you?'

'More than a few times, especially in recent years. Indeed, next year will prove my parting shot correct and which will cost the bank tens of millions, and vulnerable to takeover. Courage has nothing to do with it. If you are at peace with your convictions, then you have a responsibility to express them.'

'Can you tell me about your parting shot, and what will prove your stance?'

'Not this evening. We have much to cover. Let's move on.'

'Some 85% of a solution is understanding the problem.'

'Smart people never accept a problem from the perspective of anyone else. Just because someone else looks at something as a problem does not mean they're right. Analyse the best data and evidence available and reach your own view. Unless a life or death situation don't get involved in the urgency of someone else. Stand back and take a calm look at the issue and it will probably reveal a different perspective. Someone else's problem is not yours.'

'Assume nothing. Assumption is the mother of failure and poor judgement.'

'Mark Twain captured the essence of this rule when he commented "It's not what we don't know that gets us into trouble; it's what we know for sure that just ain't so."'

'Do not make major decisions based on the word of someone else.'

'Major decisions, especially those against which you will be judged, require a full evaluation by yourself. Take advice if required but you don't know how thoroughly someone else will have reviewed the situation or options available. You also need to guard against any mischievous or malicious content intended to do you harm.'

'Never commit to paper what you don't want to bite you in the future.'

'If you receive or hear of something that hits you emotionally, do not respond until you have sat back, calmed down, and rationalised the motive of the originator. Many people have suffered career setbacks being judged by a response in the heat of the moment.'

'Do not get into battles before you understand the war.'

'It is very easy to get involved in taking sides without understanding the background. If it's not your battle stay away from it. Wars can get personal. Don't mediate or take sides lest you find yourself the sacrificial lamb.'

'Anticipate the worst, reach for the best.'

'If you always anticipate the worst that can happen, you can never be disappointed, and it shows you fully understood the issue. And I don't mean become a pessimist. You need a positive attitude at all times to reach for the best outcome but be alive to what can go wrong.'

'Any self-respecting banker will always analyse the downside risks of any project before analysing the upside potential. If you don't analyse in this order, the upside can blur the downside. There must be an assumption someone thinks the project worthwhile or else why would you look at it. But it takes a skilful, disciplined mind to see the inherent downside risks, and thus fully appreciate the overall project risk/reward potential.'

'Life is simple; only people make it difficult.'

'Don't assume a solution on paper can be translated into the desired outcome. Human factors such as know-how, culture, language, commitment, conviction need to be considered. This is where understanding the people you are depending upon to deliver is so important.'

'I remember my first encounter with this issue. We were implementing a new financial product into our portfolio. As the young exec delegated this task, I developed the processes to both transact and manage this product in London. As we intended to promote this product globally, I sent all this data to the various offices where it was needed. After a week or so the Hong Kong office claimed the process did not work even though we successfully implemented it in London and New York. I spent hours on the phone with the Hong Kong office, working myself into a state of despair. One of my wise mentors told me to get on a plane and visit with these people. It took less than half a day to realise there was a cultural issue needing a different approach. Within a day I understood the issue and agreed a suitable way to solve it. For any problem there is a solution, but there can be many ways to get to that solution. A valuable lesson that helped me on many occasions, especially in negotiations.'

'Do not ask others to do what you are not prepared to do yourself.'

'Obvious and important.'

'You don't have to like other players. You don't have to take them home.'

'Far too many people choose colleagues based on whether they like them. I've worked with some exceptional people who disliked me intensely but enjoyed the challenges I presented to them. The results were generally ground-breaking and substantially enhanced my career. Exceptionally bright people can be very difficult to work with and manage. Harness their confidence and enjoy the results they develop.'

'You have no friends on the field of play, only colleagues.'

Week 1

'Do not trust anyone on the field of play. Even though you play in a team, remember every team member has their own self-interest in their mind and will use and abuse anyone to exert their own prominence. Human nature.'

'Avoid working with people who are inconsistent or moody.'

'Far too many execs bring their moods into the workplace, and I don't mean theatre. If they have an argument with their wife before leaving for the office, they bring it into the office. This affects their consistency in approach to both their work and to their staff. You've probably met these people. I'll do whatever is necessary to rid myself of such people. They're a menace.'

'I've seen this situation arise where someone who is extremely good at one level is promoted to the next level and finding themselves in unknown territory. We refer this to this as the Peter Principle. For example, I've seen an accomplished accountant promoted to CEO. This move from an essentially objective role to a more subjective role impacts their personal security and they become out of their depth with these new demands. They try to rationalise everything back to the comfort of their objective approach. Frustration results in unpredictable behaviour.'

'Ironically some of the worst offenders are women. How often have you heard someone say a female exec is a bitch to work for? These women suffer insecurities which are expressed ruthlessly against subordinates. They have not mastered the skills to survive the jungle. We will endeavour to ensure your skills are honed to prevent such insecurities.'

'This is very different to people who work for you. Very talented people can be emotionally unstable. You need to learn how to manage these people as rule books and conventional practise will not work. You need to win their confidence that you care for them and will look out for them. Some need a special environment to perform, but don't pamper them. They need to understand the reference points between bending and breaking the rules. They are intelligent; they will comply once they understand you have reached out as far as you can.'

'Understand the games people play.'

'People play psychological games, both in private and business. There is a book I'll give you called "The Games People Play" by Eric Berne which classifies behaviour into three psychological states, and how people interact with each other across these states. When you understand how the games are played you will know how to both observe how others use this behaviour, and how to use it yourself to avoid or resolve conflict.'

'Silence is golden.'

'One of the most valuable characteristics of a good negotiator is knowing when to sit back and stay quiet. It's the "he who blinks first" syndrome. The drama in a piece of music is not created by the black notes on the manuscript, but by the space between them. Think of "Jaws" the movie. Just two notes and then silence tells us all we need to know. Far too many people in business, especially sales, feel they need to fill empty spaces in a conversation because the quietness makes them nervous. When you have said what you need to say, be quiet. Wait calmly and patiently to see what happens.'

'Keep it Simple.'

'During your stay here, you will encounter the KIS principle many times. Always look for the easiest route of least resistance to an end. If people cannot explain something to you in terms you can understand, then it's reasonable to conclude they don't understand the subject. When explaining something try to find everyday analogies to illustrate what you want to convey. I've met many people who think being very technical or using obscure words makes them look intelligent and superior. They have forgotten the first principle of language: to communicate.'

'Pillow Talk'

'This involves using sexual encounter with your opponent to engage in off-guard conversation. We'll discuss this at length as a separate subject because women cannot play the same rules as men.'

'Don't be afraid to stand alone if conviction is there.'

'If you're convinced you're right, and feel able to demonstrate this given the opportunity, stay with your conviction, even if you're alone. Find someone who believes you and then spread the word underground until you have enough momentum to go back to the non-believers.'

'Learn how to seed new ideas, as opposed to sounding out.'

'Seeding is incidental. A casual "By the way have you heard anything about [something of interest]" is seeding. Sounding out is a deliberate conversation.'

'Seeding is a great way to foster support for a new idea you want to exploit. Even if the person you have seeded does not pursue the subject, they'll remember they have heard about it somewhere, and thus their mind will be open to persuasion.'

'There is no right or wrong, black or white.'

You will hear people, especially politicians, constantly use the words right or wrong. This is pure rhetoric as right and wrong vary with time and culture. At any one time the extremes are better defined as acceptable and unacceptable. Same with black and white which are inevitabilities regarding life and death, night and day, but otherwise are shades of grey. For example, is abortion right or wrong? The answer is neither as it's a function of culture, religious belief, etc. Is a solution black or white? No, as even $2 + 2 = 4$ can be demonstrated to be 5 if the mathematical framework is changed. Is killing your fellow man right of wrong? Neither as we send armies to war intending to kill the enemy. So here we have shades of grey determined by sanction. Not only is it inadvisable to use these terms, other than convenient rhetoric, you should not think in these terms either as it closes your mind to alternate ideas.

'Rhetoric'

'As a student of philosophy, you should already be fluent in the component parts of rhetoric and how to use it to sell an idea and win support. I would add a valuable component to this. Do not used 100 words if 10 will deliver your message. By the time you get to the 100th word most will have forgotten where you started.'

'Maybe I'm being a little slow today, but I don't quite understand what you're telling me. Is it possible for you to find a way to demonstrate your ideas? What am I saying?'

'I think we are back to My Fair Lady. Don't tell me, show me.'

'Good. We'll undertake several sessions on presentation and delivery as it's not so much what you say, but how you express yourself that gets attention. Theatre.'

'We have covered much this evening, but these rules need to be part of your philosophy. They will define your behaviour within the corporate environment. Do I need to recap any of these rules for you? We'll certainly assume them in this process.'

Her head was spinning with all this information, but it made sense to her. 'I would like to write down the rules, probably while you prepare dinner tomorrow. I see the logic but would like to have something I can refer to until fully embedded in my mind.'

'Good enough. You've had a busy day so let's close for this evening. What we must avoid is burnout. We'll find a pace that does not tire you after a busy day at the office.'

They said their goodnights as she was made her way to bed, exhausted.

Chapter 14 - Wednesday

It was mid-morning on Wednesday. The telephone rang.
'Hello.'
'Sebastian, my darling. They tell me I have been forsaken for another woman. Please tell me this is not true.'

Week 1

'Guten Morgen, Carmen, wie geht es dir?'

'I was good until I was informed of your new woman, and for six months, I hear. How can you do this to me, my darling? I need to come to England next week to see you.'

'What to do?' he thought. *'Might be good to have interaction between Mel and an existing successful female executive.'*

'Carmen, I do have a lady staying here for a special project. It would not be appropriate to have other guests here during this project. However, just for you, no-one else, no substitutes, and you don't mind using my guest room, I could make an exception.'

'Does your guest room have a comfortable bed, and a bathroom?'

'Of course.'

'Then my darling what else do I need? I will be there next Monday afternoon around 2pm as the factory is closed. Would you like your usual Schnapps?'

'As always, vielen Dank.'

'Thank you, my darling. I knew you would not let Carmen down.' She threw a kiss down the phone and was gone.

'That's one problem solved,' he thought.

He found Georgina to tell her of the arrival of Carmen and to ensure the guest room be ready before she leaves on Friday, as next Monday is a Bank Holiday.

During dinner he told her about the imminent visit by Carmen. This would change the program whilst she was there, but as a successful female executive, they could have some useful exchanges from a female perspective, and maybe even some useful role play, where she can hone her techniques against Carmen. Three nights will allow real testing of progress in a closed environment.

The table was cleared. Time to work. 'Tonight, we'll look at some interesting philosophies that are useful tools for manoeuvring yourself in the jungle of corporate rivalry. I hope your degree subjects of philosophy and applied mathematics will allow a swift comprehension of some of these topics. For example, if I give you a list of philosophical issues fundamental to your decision skills could you tell me which ones you think you already understand.'

This time she had her notebook, already used to write down the rules from yesterday as he prepared dinner, handy and ready.

'Cause and Effect'

'The first skill you need is to quickly determine if you are observing the cause, or merely an effect. The subsequent skill is to analyse an effect to determine the cause. Sometimes the effects are very secondary to the cause. It takes skilful analysis to strip back to the real cause. Much deception can be applied for mischievous or malicious reasons. Is a decision or behaviour of someone being influenced by something happening in their private life? If you cannot determine the true cause, you cannot determine a suitable solution.'

'Inevitability and Consequence'

'Being able to determine inevitable outcomes is a valuable skill. Most people focus on consequence as a driver to inevitability. This is nonsense. Consequence is a variable which will determines the timeline impacts of the inevitable. For example, in your business it can be inevitable a building will be built, but when can be subject to the outcomes of available finance, planning consent, objections, etc.'

'Information and fact'

'We are constantly swamped with information when making decisions. Understanding the use and abuse of data to skew decisions one way or another is invaluable. Sifting information, or ranking as it is more frequently known, into fact, speculation, supposition, and misleading is a vital skill for making good decisions. When someone provides you with data as part of a decision process you need to ask yourself if they have any vested interest in the outcome. If so, then you need to put a low rank of the quality of this data. Ranking the quality of information is important in good decision making.'

'Permission and Forgiveness'

'We have already mentioned it is easier to ask for forgiveness than to ask for permission. You have seen the application of this on Phillip, but it has far more serious application. You will encounter situations where you know you can deliver a radical outcome, but there is much opposition from the status quo. This could be for several reasons such as fear of the unknown, not invented here, and jealousy of the standing you will earn if successful. If you truly believe you can deliver, and the benefits outweigh the risks then it is easier to just do it. If it goes wrong, then you can plead your case for forgiveness which is easier to secure knowing the outcome.'

'Confuse and Destroy'

'This is a manoeuvring technique to break down a formidable objection, but without a singular argument. We also know this as smoke-screening. A good example of this can be demonstrated using a group of people who all firmly believe the same thing. Take each member of the group and tell them the same story about what they believe, but each time change a critical piece of information. For example, if you have a good guy and a bad guy in your story juxta position the names of the good and bad characters. Now get them all together to discuss the essence of the story. They all have different versions – which one is right? Thus, you confuse, and destroy the belief.'

'Plausible deniability and responsibility'

'Used extensively by secret service agencies this is a way of structuring events such that if they go wrong, the party involved will either accept responsibility, or they will have engineered a smokescreen to show plausible responsibility lies elsewhere.'

'Any problem with any of these?'

'Not tonight, but I may come back for more clarification as I digest and apply them.'

the Way

'Look out for any of these being played out in your workplace.'

'Before we finish, let us deal with stress in the workplace as every successful exec can readily manage stressful situations, even when everyone else is frantic. Stress is usually self-inflicted. It can express insecurity, not being able to manage your workload, imposed by some third-party unreasonable demand or failure, fear of being found wanting, or any combination of the above.'

'All sources of stress break down into three components, being your own lack of confidence, someone else's lack of confidence in you, or your inability to manage the game. All ultimately are your failings. If you are out of your depth, quickly learn to swim, or step back into shallow waters. Stay with the rules, respond calmly to your environment, and do not take any stress home.'

'In the first two or three weeks of your training I'll be watching for any stress and help you understand how to manage it. Thereafter I'll come down hard on you if I see you allowing stress into your game.'

'But I see stress in the workplace all the time. It would be unusual to not see Michael in some mode of stress. And then he stresses everyone else.'

'It's clear to me Michael is out of his depth, and thus the stress. You must stay above such inadequacy by being good at what you do, and comfortable in your own performance. Stress is a total waste of time and emotional energy.'

'It's getting late, so if no questions, let's call it a day.'

Chapter 15 – Thursday

'Tonight, I want to concentrate on morality, integrity, and any which way you can.'

'If we look at the human tribe known as corporate executives, we'll see, as with any tribe, you have degrees of good and bad. At the extreme of the good end of our curve we find executives who have endured this process without loss of moral fibre, dignity, and integrity – few, but noted. If you think of the standard behaviour of our executive tribe as a Gaussian Distribution, then they are at the 15% extreme. At the other end of the curve we have animals who have no morality at all, and concepts of dignity and integrity do not exist in their lexicon. They only care about themselves and money. Many will use far too much alcohol and probably drugs such as cocaine both socially, and to keep themselves up. They are also shrewd, ruthless, can be very charming when they want something, and can appear to have an appealing, exciting lifestyle. Think of Satan in Milton's *Paradise Lost*; the oratory, rhetoric and manipulation they use to trick their way to influence. Avoid these people at all costs, especially a woman.

'Then there is the mass of people between these extremes who have a mixture of talent and cunning, and varying standards of behaviour.'

'I'll give you an example of the bad people. We got wind of a deal being proposed to a major oil company we wanted as a primary client. We knew we could put a better offering to the client but the account executive at our competitor bank had a superior reputation. I sat in a meeting discussing the options available to us. One exec suggested we get his two young sons, both at private school, hooked on drugs to distract him from his work – and he was serious.'

'These people are divisive and have no interest in collateral damage so long as they get their deal. I have no qualms about the ruthless nature on the field, but I will not involve innocent by-standers.'

'A good example of behaviour extremes is most of these people will engage in pillow talk if the need and opportunity exist. It's a valuable tool for covert intelligence gathering which can provide valuable information not obtainable elsewhere. No-one should get hurt, and it can result in a just and fair outcome, or more usually to gain a market advantage.'

'As recruitment policy exists today, the target is a secretary or PA who invariably is a woman. She could be directly connected to a competitor exec, or better still to the CEO. The latter is usually more informed, with less likelihood of detection.'

'The methodology is very simple; give her something she cannot get for herself. A special night out is best. Non-consumable gifts should be avoided as these could give her away and provide valuable evidence in an investigation. If she is single, then anything is fair game. It's far more difficult and complicated if she's married. However, a married woman is still game as she is likely to keep such liaisons covert. Smart CEOs employ middle-aged married women as their PAs to deter such situations. But ego driven execs want a young, attractive PA, making her a certain target.'

'You, as a relatively young, single, attractive woman exec make a special target as you have much to lose, if caught. You may think you are not the target but, ultimately, a man treats you as a trophy. The worst you can do is cause him problems within his own relationship. He can destroy you. I have seen a few women use it in a double agent role where the man thinks he is engaging in valuable pillow talk, but is being fed dangerous, misleading information intended to skew his thinking. Once this misinformation has been deployed the man needs to know he has been used in order to protect the reputation of the woman.'

'My advice to you is never use it for your own end, and never allow yourself to be abused, no matter how clever a charmer he is. Remember, everyone has a price. If you accept the price, make sure you can live on it for the rest of your life. Live by the rule that no relationship survives involving two career execs, and you'll be safe.'

'My advice to young female execs is to find a trusted male lieutenant to act as a spy, using, and funding pillow talk if appropriate.'

'I have experienced young female execs try to use their sexuality to gain an advantage in their rise to fame. They're used for a while, sometimes passed around, and then dumped, career finished.'

'Casual affairs are okay between consenting, rising execs, but not where there is any possible conflict of interest. You will note that if relationships occur within a corporation, they will have you decide who will leave, or be told.'

'When I was a budding exec, women were just starting to rise through the ranks. The sharks and alligators swooped at every opportunity, and they devoured many of these women. I knew one of the rising stars quite well as we shared a passion for the opera. She invited me if she needed a partner for corporate purposes to avoid any potential advances, and vice versa. Occasionally we would spend the night together as she knew I wasn't looking for a relationship, and neither was she, but we both had sexual needs. We were chatting about this issue and realised we could assemble a club of like-minded people to enable young execs to perform their business, and satisfy their natural needs, in a controlled environment. She assembled the women, and I found the guys. It worked brilliantly. Everyone shared their interests and sports such that if you needed a partner for some activity, you could select the most appropriate club member.'

'When I think back it worked better than normal relationships because, with the best will in the world, the chances of a couple having the same interests and sports is low. One night I would go to the opera with a woman who loved opera, and the following night partner another woman in a tennis match. Weekends away, or other occasions could be accommodated when the woman did not want to go alone. Everyone got what they needed in the safety that everyone was in the same boat, so don't rock it. One positive consequence for the guys was the reduction in honey-trap cases where woman wanting a fast-track to the executive lifestyle, stalked up-and-coming execs and allowing themselves to become pregnant contrary to their protestations they were on the pill.'

'Have you used pillow talk in your career?'

'It has proven useful both internally and externally occasionally.'

'Why internally?'

'As a young exec it is sometimes useful to find out how you are viewed at the top, or to extract skeleton-in-the-cupboard information to cause problems for an exec causing you problems.'

'Can you give an example?'

Thinking for a few seconds 'I can think of one that could have been disastrous for my career had I failed. When I was a young exec, we had a local CEO who was from an old establishment family in the USA – essentially untouchable, and an arrogant bully. We also had a Director of Operations, Bernie, who guided me like a father, kept me out of trouble, and looked out for me if I got into trouble.'

'Bernie was aging, sitting out his time to retirement. I found myself with a technical issue which meant a delay in delivery of the first global intranet some five years before the internet became public; considered by the CEO as an opportunity to impose himself on the project and me. Until then I had a free rein to oversee this important project. But once it would likely work and give us significant competitive advantage with global corporates, he wanted and was looking forward to the kudos when the bank President arrived a few days later. Bernie tried to defend me but took such an arrogant verbal beating by the CEO he suffered a heart attack. He died three days later. As it happened the delay in delivery was only a few days and didn't matter.'

'It outraged me. I wanted to chop this bastard down to size. But how? His PA, who was a little older than me but still single, had already imposed herself upon me when she brought papers for signature and my new flight tickets for my next trip to my house in West London. I had flown into Heathrow from New York that morning and was due to leave for Hong Kong the following morning, so stayed at home taking care of my mail and other chores. It was a lovely summer's day, and I had a sundeck not overlooked from anywhere. She took sun whilst I read the papers – in only her panties. I called her in to ask something about the content of these papers. She strolled in as she was and sat with me. One thing led to another.'

'Thus, I decided to find out what skeletons were in the CEO's cupboard as I knew she was discreet, but did not like him, especially after the Bernie incident. This provided rich pickings over the space of probably half a dozen pillow talk sessions, but what to do with this damming information. There was an influential weekly journal read by most senior bankers. I knew the female editor quite well having met her at various functions. I approached her with my file. It cost me a very wild night, and a mild bout of Venereal Disease to get her to publish. He was gone 24 hours after publication, never to be heard of again. It was worth the effort.'

She thought about the image he created *'My name is Ryder, Sebastian Ryder, licenced to kill.'*

'Did anyone realise it was you who brought him down?' she asked.

'Two execs mentioned if it was me, suggesting they knew, then well done. The CEO had few friends. But no direct questions. Why would they want to know in such a politically fuelled situation?'

'Normal inquisitiveness, and a real feather in the cap for you.'

'Neither is appropriate. The outcome is enough. Not knowing the events behind the result means you never have to lie to protect anyone. And never fall into the trap of suggesting a name if anyone asks. If enough people suggest the same name during a witch-hunt, then that name is assumed guilty. All you say is the deposed had many enemies. It's not your war so stay out of it. His PA knew, but we ensured there was no evidence of any untoward connection between us, and she had an equally strong affection for Bernie, and loathing for the CEO. She was not challenged to my knowledge – far too distressing for her having already lost Bernie.'

'You've had an interesting life. Us underlings watch this stuff on TV or cinema not realising it really exists. Amazing.'

Chapter 16 – Friday

She looked tired when she arrived home from the office. He was pleased she went to the gym, as usual, additionally followed by a swim. He was appreciating her commitment. He noted it must have been a tough week for her, but she wasn't looking for sympathy.

When she arrived in the kitchen ready for dinner, he had a glass of prosecco waiting for her. 'Thank you. Are we celebrating something?'

'Your commitment, and survival of your first week.' He toasted her.

'How do you feel having been bombarded by both camps this week?'

'The combination of Jim's calm, gentle approach to the technical aspects of fabrication, and your significantly more brutal revelations about my naivety have proven challenging, but I find myself wanting more. It's like having a peek into another world. I feel myself morphing into a person I've never met before.'

'Is this new person where you want to be, or a strange alien?'

'I feel like a chrysalis bursting out of its dark existence into a butterfly, exposed to the light, but now needs to learn how to fly. I guess I feel exposed, but strangely alive.'

'Progress indeed. Tonight, we'll only deal with any issues you have, and then relax. You've done well, but in need of a little fun. We can also go to our local pub if you like.'

'Thanks, but I'd prefer to take a glass of wine, and have a soak. Early night is needed.'

Chapter 17 – Saturday

She was enjoying a casual breakfast 'What do you have in mind for me today?'

'Back to civilisation for you, I think. You've worked hard this past week, so I think you deserve a little free time. I need to do the weekly shop in Matlock. You're welcome to join me in which case I'll also show you around both the town, and locale. Perhaps we could have a nice lunch somewhere. What do you think?'

'Lovely idea. I've been to the factory a few times but never had time to see what the fascination is with this part of the world.'

'Get yourself together, and I'll show you.'

He used his Range Rover car, so they were high enough to see over most edges. Although Matlock is not within the Peak District National Park, it is still a beautiful mix of craggy hill and dale with the river Derwent flowing through the dales.

'Do you have your tennis kit with you?'

'No, I don't have anything anymore.'

the Way

'Okay. Sports shop first. We start to play tomorrow so we need to get you organised.'

'Is this part of my training, or because you need a partner?'

'I don't **need** a partner, although if you're good enough then it would be nice to play together. I think it part of your training. Many deals are done, or at least moved along, playing sport. The two predominant games are golf and tennis because they keep people together for a reasonable length of time, and in isolation from interruption. If you can play either sport at a reasonable level, you'll find yourself in demand and, therefore in play.'

He let her digest this idea. 'Does this make sense to you?'

'As with so many things this week I've never thought of it, but it makes sense.'

'There is also another reason for wanting to see how you play. Tomorrow morning I'll start to train you in self-defence. Most of the exercise regime I've mapped for you is to develop core strength, balance, and mobility. Tomorrow afternoon we go to my tennis club where I want to see how you generate the power you need to play a tennis shot. It will help me to refine your training. Self-defence is not about physical strength; it's about generating power.'

'I see. So, in six months I'll fight like Bruce Lee, and play tennis like Steffi Graf. Have you ever played at Wimbledon?'

'I play my tennis at Queen's Club when in London, and I'll certainly teach you to respect martial arts tomorrow.'

'*Ooops*' she thought '*flippancy not appreciated by my master.*'

It took some time to find the 'right' racket for her, and she took her own time selecting shoes and clothing. All done he decided to take her around Matlock showing her the historic buildings, and where to find more practical needs such as the Post Office. Lunch on some craggy peak went by the wayside because of the time in the sports shop so they found a nice pub in town.

She found it interesting to shop in a supermarket with a man, and especially where the man is the lead. With her and Phil he never went with her to shop for food. She noted how carefully he selected fresh produce and knew exactly what he wanted. *'Impressive. A man who has been at the pinnacle of the business world is happy to do his own grocery shopping'* she thought *'can I teach Phil how to shop for us – not likely'*.

Chapter 18 – Sunday

It was after 8am when he heard her making for the pool, and another 45 minutes before she appeared for breakfast. He was sitting reading the newspaper.

'Am I too late for breakfast?'

'What would you like?'

'Have you already eaten?'

'No. I decided to wait and have breakfast with you.'

'Sorry if I kept you waiting. My eyes took a long time to open.'

'I'm not surprised. Your system must be in shock after the week you've endured.'

She smiled 'Batteries did need an extra charge. What are the options?'

'I'm opting for a full English this morning, with just a snack before we go play tennis.'

'Sounds good. But can I have a small full English?'

'One full, and one-half full English coming up. Fresh juice with it?'

'Hmm, sounds good.'

'As it's a nice day, I thought of showing you around the grounds before our self-defence. Walk off breakfast. I might even show you my tractors.'

'You have tractors? Big boy's toys' laughing 'and what do you use them for?'

There is a lot of maintenance required to keep nature from turning the land into a jungle. Woodland to thin, grassland to keep down, fences to fix to name but a few of my country chores.'

'This I have to see. Do I need green wellies to stomp the land?'

'Sometimes they come in useful.'

After breakfast she helped him with the dishes and then found a pair of suitable walking shoes.

Because the property was 'L'-shaped she had only seen the land from the sundeck which was at the back of the extension forming the base of the 'L'. There was a path leading around the extension giving access to the rear of the main building where there was a beautifully laid southwest facing garden protected by outbuildings and a walled garden to the east. To the west she could see an orchard, and two modern barns. From there the pastureland flowed down towards the golf course with woodland on the right-hand side. She already knew the view across the landscape but being on the ground made it seem more real.

'What a lovely garden. If I'm getting this picture right, the garden is very formal at the house, and slowly gets less formal until it becomes a field thus blending the garden into the natural landscape. How clever is that?'

'Well spotted. I wanted to encourage wildlife and insects, but not too close to the house. And blending is better than a truncating fence. Shall we start over by the walled garden which still has an orangery although I use it for grape vines.'

Week 1

He opened the solid gates into the walled garden to show her the produce cultivated there, and the grapevines which were heaving with grapes. 'Much of the vegetables and fruit we eat are cultivated here, so you know it's fresh.'

He closed the door to keep out unwanted animals and walked down towards the golf course.

They chatted as they strolled along the gradients and observing the wildlife about their business. She found this very relaxing, picking wildflowers and generally enjoying the clean, fresh air. The area around the factory was industrial resulting in poor air quality so here, just three miles away, was a pleasant surprise. And, of course fresh air in London is a pipe dream.

As she walked through the woodland, she realised she hadn't done this in years. How lovely it was to smell the scent from the trees and plants; to see various varieties of mushrooms growing in the shade of the trees, or on long ago fallen trunks, to hear the wind rustle the leaves, and to hear the birds sing their various melodies.

When they reached the barn containing his agricultural equipment, he tapped in the code to open the roller door. She could see he was not kidding about three tractors of different sizes plus an array of equipment from trailer, backhoe, front bucket, snow plough to hedge cutter.

'Wow, so many boy's toys. Can I drive one of your tractors?'

'Have you ever driven one before?'

'No, but how hard can it be?'

'If I decide to give you lessons, you'll find out. They design a tractor to overcome adversity thus when it's moving it's not easily stopped if the driver doesn't know how. I would have to put a large flashing 'L' sign over the cab to warn the neighbours of the potential danger of a runaway tractor.'

'That's not fair, and even sexist. I drive a manual shift car with no problems.' Quickly realising he might be testing her emotional reaction 'Anyway would be one way to meet the neighbours.'

Having returned to the house they sat in the kitchen to have a drink.

'Are you ready to fight with me?'

'Do I have to go gently with you, or can I let rip?'

'The more real it is the better. In martial arts it's all about feel, awareness, and power generation. I want you to feel the contact so you know what it's really like when you need to use it. Perhaps I should warn you you could get hurt, but the hospital's not far away.'

'You're kidding, right?'

'Have I kidded you to date? Help me clear the living room floor and then we'll bring in two mats from the gym.'

Once he had the room as he needed, he asked her to walk towards him and collide with him shoulder to shoulder – and mean it. She walked forcefully towards him. As she reached him, she felt herself lifted off her feet, flying through the air, and landing on the couch. 'Ouch. How did you do that? I didn't see you even brace yourself.'

'What just happened I've witnessed a few times. You have a woman walking along a corridor carrying papers and coffee. Mr machoman walks towards her pretending not to see her, splats her against the wall; papers and coffee flying everywhere. He's very apologetic as he helps her to her feet, but he has transmitted his message he's superior man, and don't forget it. To combat this, you need awareness, and balance.'

'Are you okay to try the next move?'
'Will it hurt?'
'Depends how well you fall.'
'I want you to come up behind me and grope my butt with you left hand. You need your right hand for tennis this afternoon. If this has happened to you in the past, you know how it feels. So, go for it.'

As she grabbed his right buttock all she saw was a flash before her eyes just before she felt her wrist being locked turning her through ninety-degrees face down on the floor, her hand very painfully locked back against her arm. She couldn't move.

'Now try to break free.'

As she tried to turn the lock tightened, and the pain increased. 'Please, you're hurting me.'

He let go. She just lay there trying to hold back tears. He left her for a few seconds to compose herself.

'Are you angry with me?'
'You really hurt me.'
'Then you can express anger against me in the third, and final attack for today. On your feet.'

She got herself onto her feet, visibly distressed.

'This time I'm going to attack you. I'm trying you grab you by the scruff of your neck. When my hands make contact, you will clasp your hands lightly at waist level, and bend your knees. Then with all your power drive your arms up between my arms moving your arms outwards using your forearms against my elbows. Using that same power, you're going to rise onto your toes on one foot and drive your other knee hard into my groin. Are you angry enough to do this? No holds barred remember. You need to feel the power. Ready?'

Without giving her chance to think he reached for her. She did as he had instructed. She couldn't throw his arms away from her, but her knee made good contact with his groin. He fell to the floor in pain. She dropped down beside him 'Are you okay?'

'Give me a minute.'

'You really meant it about the pain. This is tough.'

He eventually sat up, and she sat beside him. 'How did that feel? Did the emotional anger help you react?'

'I just did what you told me. You didn't give me time to think.'

'What would you say if I told you that maybe in three months, I can teach you to be so effective at all three moves today you will stop most men in their tracks? No-one will be able to splatter you against a wall, grope, or molest you.'

'Do I assume it will be a painful three months as my shoulder and wrist are not very happy.'

He smiled at her 'Give me your wrist.' He started to gentle feel to ensure nothing was out of place, and then massaged the carpal area. After a few minutes he rubbed his hands together violently to generate as much heat as possible and then cuffed her wrist. She could feel the soothing. 'How does that feel?'

'Good, thank you.'

'How about your shoulder?'

'It hurts at the joint with my arm.'

'Pull your T-shirt over your shoulder so I can get at the joint.' Again, he checked the joint; and with one hand on her shoulder and the other on her elbow gently rotated her arm. Then he applied heat to the joint. 'How's that?'

'Much better, thank you. How's your groin?'

'Still groaning. I'll need padding when I teach you how to at least triple the power you applied.'

'Why did you let me do that to you?'

'I wanted to see if you had the nerve to do it. I did help you by making you angry with me, albeit in a good cause. It's no good playacting this stuff because when you need it you must do it by instinct and mean it. You don't have time to consciously think, your subconscious must react naturally. You now know how painful the wrist lock can be, and how much more pain you feel if you try to break free. When I teach you how to apply the lock, you know you're safe and can increase the pain at will if they try to break free. Thus, you have the confidence you're safe. So how was the lesson?'

'Painful. But if you can teach me to defend myself like this, I'll forgive you. All too often men think they can touch me, especially on the London Underground. It will be good to react - painfully.'

'We need to add a belly slap and toe-grind to your arsenal to deal with people in confined spaces. I will add these to the program.'

What is a belly slap and toe-grind?'

'The belly slap is a simple but very effective way of winding someone in close proximity, and a toe-grind is where you accidentally on purpose slam your heel down on the toes of one foot of your groper and turn towards him with you heel still in place on his toes. Very painful.'

'Go take a gentle swim to ease your shoulder. Then we should have a snack. We leave for tennis in one hour.'

'You look good in your new kit. Are you happy with it?'

the Way

'Yes, it feels good. Let's see if I can remember how to play.'

Although it was club mixed doubles afternoon, he took a separate court so she could concentrate on her game rather than risk embarrassment.

'I'm going to feed you some balls which I want you to hit back to me.' He watched closely to see how she approach the ball, positioned herself, and then struck the ball. He was not surprised to see she had not been taught how to generate power into her shots. He spent the remainder of the session next to her with a basket of balls showing her how to prepare for a forehand strike and deliver power to the ball.

As it was a lovely evening, they took dinner up to the sundeck.

'How do you feel about this past week now you have some idea what is in store for you?'

'A little embarrassed to tell you the truth. You have opened my eyes to so much I feel I should already know. For instance, I studied philosophy at university for three years, and promptly stopped when I got my degree. I listen to you and see I should have continued to apply what I'd learnt and extend it into the workplace. After a week in the pool and gym I feel much better in myself. I guess I've had a wake-up call, but I'm enjoying the experience. And this school is such a lovely place to be.'

'What do you think after having to look after this naïve woman? Do you think I have a chance of making your hard work worthwhile?'

'I agree with Charles. You have potential. But it will get harder for you in the coming weeks as we call upon you to make tough decisions and choices your current emotional content will either resist or call wrong. You'll need much courage to break down these emotional barriers. My prognosis is if you sincerely believe in the desired outcome, we'll get you there. A good actor will "kill" someone in a fight with the ferocity demanded by the script, but then go home and not even think about it. They did what was expected of them. Job done. You must adopt the same attitude.'

'But the actor doesn't really kill their adversary, it just acting.'

'You will not actually kill any of your adversaries, but you may end their career. It cannot be personal.'

'From what you've told me about Carmen it will be interesting to see what she has to deal with in real life, and how she approaches her adversaries.'

'I think you'll like her. You'll find her overwhelming initially, but she is accomplished at being a woman in a man's world.'

the Way

Week 2

Chapter 19 – Monday (Bank Holiday)

They were sitting having breakfast. 'Seb, can I ask you some questions about you?'

'Sure. What do you want to know?'

'I can now see the attractiveness of this area, but I sense you could live anywhere you want to. Places like Monte Carlo, Monaco, Cote d'Azur, anywhere. Why here?'

'I spent a long career travelling all over the world, meeting many influential movers and shakers, staying in the best hotels, dining in the best restaurants, enjoying the very best in opera, sport, and everything else. Many would consider this lifestyle privileged, but the rat race is a dog-eat-dog environment. And you're wed to the social networking involved. As someone with no family responsibilities, I additionally found myself elected to fulfilling social engagements at the weekends. My life was engulfed in both work and social responsibilities. What you come to understand is how superficial it all is. You're expected to appear at many functions, most of which required you to play your part in the game of one-upmanship. Here I'm unknown, living in beautiful, raw countryside with no requirement for posturing or pretence, realising how wonderful this planet, if you're prepared to standstill long enough to feel it. I no longer have to dress in suits every day, nor have to socialise with people I'd prefer not to.'

'That explains your rebellious dress code, but why here?'

'I wanted my freedom. Living in a city, especially the social communities you've mentioned, you're expected to join the social set. I wanted my own space to wander at liberty with no expectation of interaction with anyone. Living in the Highlands of Scotland did cross my mind, but my desire to feel warm sunshine for at least a few months each year brought me here. Having honed my shooting skills near to here, I was familiar with this area, so it was an informed choice. With easy access to Manchester and London, and thus international airports, it's easy to travel if I feel the need. You've only had the minutest of taste for this area to date. When we have a free day, I'll show you places around here so beautiful they'll take your breath away.'

'Can't wait to see it, especially through your eyes. Living in London can be both a buzz and superficial. I suppose at my age the buzz still overrides the bad bits. As you must wait for Carmen to arrive, I'll go explore myself today. Can you point me in the right direction?'

'I'll give you maps and point out where you may like to visit.'

'Thanks. I want to get back around 5'ish to do my gym workout before dinner.'

'Another subject. What do you do during the day when I'm at work? I don't see you as someone who wastes a single minute.'

'Looking after you is exhausting. At my age I need to rest during the day.'

'Sure. You can cut the crap about your age. Time wise you may be aging but looking at you it would be easy to cut twenty years off. Seriously, what is a normal day for you?'

'I rise at 6am and go straight to the pool for my morning swim. Around 6:30 I go to my study to see what's happening out there, with keen interest in the financial markets. I may place some trading instructions if I see something of interest. Then I prepare breakfast for whoever is here. Depending on the weather I may return to my study to write or, if the weather is nice, go help Peter. I also visit London for a few days each month, but on hold for a while.'

'Can I see your study?'

'Sure. Follow me.' He led her up the stairs but instead of turning left towards the bedrooms, he turned right along a corridor which included his bedroom suite. He opened the door to his study and let her in. On one wall were two shelves with three screens on each overlooking a large desk. On the desk was a PC and three keyboards. To the left of the desk, and behind the door, she could see banks of electronics. All the screens were showing numeric data or graphics. Next to them was a TV switched on to a news channel, but no sound, with ticker data running along the bottom. Between the desk and the outer wall was a floor to ceiling bookcase crammed with books and piles of magazines.

To the right of the door there was a seating area with a couch and two wing chairs.

'This looks like something out of NASA. What are all these screens telling you?'

'Market data from around the world, and a direct feed into my broker in London.'

'So, you're still active in the financial sector.'

'I like to dabble to keep myself current.'

'Interesting. I'd like you to show me what you do here, if it's not intrusive. I've always wondered what goes on behind the walls of the buildings in the City.'

'Maybe, but not today as you need to get going if you want to go sightseeing.'

Carmen drove through the gates a little after 2:30. They greeted in the typical German three cheek kisses, and he helped her with her luggage to his guest room. He had a snack ready for her.

'Now darling, tell me about this special project that has interfered with my favourite hotel in the whole world.'

'One of the local, very successful, fabrication companies,' she interrupted him 'You mean Aldridge Fabrications my darling,' just to let him know her intelligence network knows the story.

'*Mary, the gossip,*' he thought. 'Okay. Aldridge has a key director who has serious health issues and must retire within six months if he survives that long. There is no obvious replacement within the company. Although there are no females on the management team, the Chairman has identified a woman in the London office who has worked with this director for some years, and he thinks executive material. He wants to mentor her into the role while she shadows the sick director. I had her here for a week, and I agree she has potential, but needs to learn how to survive in the corporate jungle – as you have done. So, I've agreed to help in the process during the evenings.'

'She could not ask for a better teacher, my darling. Your good judgement, especially here in England, has saved my arse frequently. Where is she? It is Bank Holiday here, no? What is she like?'

'She's out surveying the local countryside. She'll be back around 5 o'clock as she has a routine she must observe every day.'

'Bad boy taskmaster, eh?'

'Her name is Mel,' another abrupt interruption 'Mel is short for Melanie, no?'

'Mel is short for Melanie.'

'What a quaint English name. Go on.'

'She's 32 years old, very attractive, good sense of humour, but still naïve in life. She's committed to this opportunity, and I think she has what it takes to make it.'

'Praise indeed, my darling. I have a new project here in England, so I need to come here for 3 days every month during the first week of each month. I would like to book this with you. I will watch development of Mel with interest. I might learn something myself from this master teacher.'

'Would you like to help me in areas more in need of a female touch? I would value your experience as a woman who has fought her way to the top.'

'If this means I have my booking then why not, my darling? Might be fun.'

'She operates in a male-dominated industry, especially here at the factory. I need her to get comfortable in her own skin so men cannot intimidate her.'

Week 2

'You mean like in her own naked skin, as we would in Germany.'

'Exactly. I can teach her how to stand her ground generally, but not when she's physically compromised.'

'So, you want me to get her into the pool with me, and maybe the sauna.'

'This would be a great start if you can do it. When she returns, she has a routine of 30 minutes in the gym. If you could go with her, and then into the pool, it would be a good start.'

'Would you like me to get her into the pool with us in the morning for our morning swim?'

'If you can manage that during your stay you will significantly advance by cause.'

'Leave it to me, my darling. I know why this must be done and understand why this could be difficult for you. The conservative English roses here are so embarrassed about their bodies. Why is this? We all have one. What we must do with her is normal in my country. Will you join me on the sundeck? Shame to waste this lovely sunshine.'

'Why not? Prosecco?'

'Would be lovely, my darling. See you there in 5 minutes. I need to change.'

Once settled on the sundeck, both naked, they continued to talk. She told him about her new project in Matlock to expand UK production of air conditioners specifically for the domestic market, including the construction of a new production line.

They heard the gates open. 'This must be her. Let me introduce you.'

'My darling, will we have time for the gym, pool and sauna before the lovely dinner you will prepare for us. Say 8 o'clock tonight, so I do not need to rush her.'

'Do you think you can achieve all of this in one go?'

'It is a natural progression, my darling.'

'Do you have any special request for dinner?'

'One of your wonderful pasta dishes would be my choice.'

the Way

'Pasta it is. And thank you for your help.'

As they slipped back into clothes 'My darling you are my favourite person in the whole world after my family, and I like what you are trying to do for this woman. Think nothing of it. One of your wonderful bottles of Pinotage would help to celebrate my success, no?'

He never tired of her way of getting what she wants without appearing to ask. But one of his better wines would be small reward for achieving this vital task.

They were already in the kitchen as she entered. 'Hi Seb, and you must be Carmen. Very nice to meet you. Seb has told me good things about you. Do you mind if I call you Carmen?'

'Hello, my dear, Carmen is fine. My darling Sebastian has told me all about your adventure into my world. Come sit with me and let us become acquainted.'

He excused himself whilst Carmen started her play 'I have to think about dinner so will leave you ladies to it.'

'Carmen has taken total control and authority and thus in control. No escape for Mel against such a strong woman,' he thought as he went to his pantry.

They chatted, or more accurately Carmen interrogated her for some minutes. Mel finally found space in the conversation to inform Carmen of her need to go to the gym.

'Would you mind if I join you? I've done nothing today except sit on a plane, in a car, and now here. My body could do with some exercise.'

'See you there in 5 minutes.'

As Carmen approached the gym, she flicked the switch for the sauna. She then allowed Mel to show her prescribed routine. She took great interest and participated fully.

After they completed the program, they were both sweaty.

'Invigorating, my dear. Shall we swim to cool off?'

'I don't have my swimsuit down here.'

Week 2

She stared at Mel for some seconds for maximum effect. 'Why do you need a swimsuit here in this wonderful pool? We are alone. Come, you don't need such things.'

With some theatre 'Ah, English prunes are embarrassed about their bodies.'

Mel was laughing. 'What is the matter dear, have I said something wrong?'

'I think you mean prudes. You eat prunes.'

'Ah yes. My English. Prude, yes English prude. Come, my dear' as she led her to the changing room and quickly removed her gym kit 'you cannot survive as an English prude in the executive jungle.'

Mel could not help but notice her completely tanned body, and no reservation showing it. She swirled her body 'see my dear, complete tan'.

She surrendered and removed her gym kit, following Carmen to the pool.

'Are you a swimmer, my dear? Can I race you as I do with my darling Sebastian every morning?'

'You swim naked with Seb in the morning?'

'Without fail. He is good to race with and maybe one day I will beat him. It is exhilarating to swim naked. Come. Try it.'

They dived in and were soon racing. Mel soon forgot her nakedness and felt exhilarated as the water stroked her body. After ten lengths they stopped, panting from the exertion, and hung on the edge of the pool together.

'Was not good, my dear? You are a good swimmer. I will enjoy racing with you.'

'It felt great. Thank you.'

'Let's to the sauna for 20 minutes to complete our program. We can chat some more.'

There was no point in protesting as Carmen collected two towels and led her to the sauna which, after charging the hot stones with water, was ready. Mel noticed Carmen chatted as though this situation was the most natural thing in the world.

She was still very aware of her nakedness, although Carmen was very matter of fact about it. Carmen sensed her unease.

'My dear, you are concerned about something, no?'

'I'm not used to being naked like this.'

'In my country, and most of Europe, this is normal, even in public facilities. At home my family, I have two teenage boys, all swim together in our pool without clothes, and in the sauna. It is also not unusual to walk around our home without clothes. We are all the same. We don't understand the British. We always find it funny when they come to sauna with swimwear. Why such inhibition? When you are in a man's world you cannot show any embarrassment about your femininity.'

'I've heard about this, especially Scandinavia. I don't know why we cover up here, but it's part of our way I guess.'

'My dear if you want to succeed you must be comfortable in your own skin. There will always be times when you are compromised in public, usually with men. You must be confident enough to stay calm, and in control. If you maintain your poise you move the game in your favour.'

'Are you suggesting it's okay to be naked around Seb?'

'I would say it is a good place to start. He is a lovely man to be with.' Moving closer as though someone was listening 'If not happily married he would be my ideal man.'

'Isn't he a little old for you?'

'My dear. How old you think I am?'

'Around mid-forties.'

'Thank you, my dear, but my darling Sebastian needs to work on your observation skills. I am a career executive with two teenage children. I did not have these children before I had secured my career. Therefore, I am 54 years old.'

'Wow. I'm so sorry. You look fabulous. You must tell me your secret to looking so fantastic.'

'You stay fit, allowing you to manage the stresses of corporate life. Be confident in your own skin and think positive. You will tone over the coming weeks, although you have a beautiful body already. You must maintain it, not with chemicals, but with exercise, good sleep, and a strong mental attitude. Does this make sense to you, my dear?'

'You echo what Seb tells me.'

'His incredible career makes him ideal to teach you. He has the experience, and the scars, so is better than so-called career development courses where none of the presenters have played the game, and certainly not at his level.'

'My dear, he has never made any inappropriate advances to me. We can be playful, no more. I never feel uncomfortable in his presence, even when naked. If I am in a rush in the morning, and I need to iron my shirt, I will be in the laundry room in my underwear. I rarely wear underwear – never a bra – for dinner. I sometimes walk from my room to the pool naked. I don't even think about it. This place is like my second home.'

'What about if you are having a period, I mean menstruating.'

'We are speaking in general terms. For such times, you will wear panties, but only because of hygiene. There is nothing embarrassing about menstruation. It is normal for a woman.'

'We have been in here long enough, my dear. Why don't we go shower off and return to our rooms as we are?'

They left the sauna, showered, dried off, collected their gym kit, and strolled back to their rooms. He could hear the giggles in the hallway and noticed two naked bottoms climbing the stairs. *'Well done, Carmen. You're one hell of a lady.'*

Both women reappeared some fifteen minutes later for dinner, still chatting and laughing. He noticed Mel was not wearing a bra.

'Welcome ladies. Your dinner is ready to be served. Please take your seats.' He put a towel over his arm for effect and poured wine for Carmen. 'Would madam check the wine is to her taste?'

She played her part, swirling the wine around the glass and taking a sip 'Very nice. Thank you, waiter.'

the Way

He poured more into her glass, and then for Mel and himself.

He had prepared wild boar carpaccio for a starter knowing this would please Carmen, and she gasped with delight at his pasta main course. 'My darling, this restaurant is definitely my favourite. The food, wine and company are always delicious.' She raised her glass 'to my new friend Melanie, my darling Sebastian, and the best food on the planet.'

After the toast 'my darling, do you think I could send my husband here for cooking lessons?' Much laughter.

By the time they finished dinner it was after 9:30 (10:30 in Germany). 'My darling, and my dear new friend, I must to bed. Very busy day tomorrow whipping these English chauvinists into shape. As always, it has been a pleasure to dine with my fabulous hosts. I can't wait to join you tomorrow evening.'

She turned to Mel 'We have a date in the gym at 6 o'clock tomorrow evening, no? Much nicer to exercise with good company.'

Mel read this as an instruction more than an invitation. Carmen departed to her bed.

'You appear to have gelled well with Carmen. How was your time in the gym as you were both there much longer than expected?'

'I got the impression my master orchestrated our session. But I understand why this was both necessary and valuable. She is an experienced executive who knows what it takes to climb the ladder and survive. I cannot argue with her experience or advice. I'm not yet ready to join you in the pool in the morning, but I realise I need to overcome my resistance. Please give me time.'

'Do you understand why you need to overcome any anxiety about yourself and be confident in your own skin?'

'She suggested if I can stay poised in compromising situations, the game changes in my favour. I'm not sure I understand what she means.'

'Let me try to explain. You are in a meeting where you are the only woman. You have a wardrobe malfunction where the top buttons on your low-cut blouse pop revealing a little too much of your lacy bra. How would you react?'

'I'd make my excuses and get the hell out of there as quickly as possible.'

'And where does that leave you in their eyes, especially when you return looking flushed and self-conscious?'

'So what should I do?'

'What do you think Carmen would do?'

'She's clearly a formidable woman, but what would she do?'

'Try this for size. She would look them in the eye and say something to the effect: Oops. Do you know how much I paid for this blouse? Gentlemen, should this wardrobe malfunction prove a distraction I'm happy to take an adjournment to find another top?'

'And, of course, as with every consummate executive, you have a spare top in your office for such events. I always had a spare shirt in my office because you could be sure that on the day you needed to look your best, you'll have a coffee spill ten minutes before the meeting.'

'It would take one confident lady to keep her cool in such circumstances. Is this where we're going with me and Carmen?'

'If I told you Carmen would probably turn the whole situation to her favour with any embarrassment being with the men, could you handle that?'

'So, my master will teach me how to keep my cool and bury my natural self-consciousness.'

'Yes, but we start by making you comfortable in your own skin. Ever since Adam and Eve noticed their nakedness in the Old Testament book of Genesis, people have been anxious about being exposed in public. You hear of prisoners being stripped of their clothes in the clear attempt to humiliate them to break their spirit. Imagine being at some event that gets a little exuberant or even out of hand and someone unclips your clothing such that

the Way

they expose you. Are you going to fold and become the butt of this joke, or can you turn the situation, so you're in control of the joke, thus retaining your dignity? Let me tell you about a real experience where the capability to stay calm and poised probably saved her life.'

'We had an account manager, Kimberley, an American in her late 20's. Part of her patch was North Africa – strange territory for a woman, but she was tough and confident, even at her tender years. She knew all the tricks of a rising star – minimal makeup, clothes that did not smack of female, nor stood out in a gathering of men. She was not a glamourous stunner, but very attractive.'

'She was in Algeria when war broke out with Morocco. The Americans were backing Morocco so there was acute anti-American sentiment. We had to get her out, but she would not be safe trying you use the airport. To be an American was good enough for summary execution. To be an American banker meant a slow, humiliating death. To be a female American banker meant the unimaginable – probably extensively gang-raped and beaten or stoned to death.'

'There was no point sending in another American, and she could not get to the Embassy because it was surrounded. The Algerians had no quarrel with the British and, as a Brit, I could move around freely. I would need to collect her from her hiding place under the cover of darkness and drive her across the desert to Tunisia hoping not to get caught. We could not get word of our plan to her – no internet, or the new-fangled mobile phones in those days.'

'I had difficulty quietly finding a suitable vehicle for hire that would stand the rugged landscape of the desert route I needed to take, which was an old track used by smugglers. By the time I'd secured a Land Rover, and fuelled up, it was late. When I got to her, she was already asleep. There was no time to get dressed as I sensed I was being followed – they knew she was in the country. She just grabbed her bag so as not to lose her passport, sneaked out the back way and we were on our way. All she was wearing was a night top and shorts.'

'We drove along the highway until about 10km from the border where I got off the road and headed for the track provided to me by the Tunisians who would meet us at the border. About 2km from the border dawn was breaking. We ran into an Algerian patrol. I put my foot to the floor, navigating around obstacles as bullets spit through the air around us. Thankfully, this patrol was typical of Arab conscripts who had no idea how to aim, just pointing in the general direction and pulling the trigger.'

'As we approached the Tunisian border, the Tunisian army returned fire, albeit over their head to avoid a political incident, and we safely crossed the border. Our papers were checked to ensure we were the people expected, and an officer gave her a jacket before we drove to Tunis – the first place I could get clothes for her.'

'Not once, throughout the whole recovery mission, did she show any signs of discomfort or embarrassment, even though her breasts were barely concealed by her top. If you know how Arabs react to such a state of undress of a woman in public, you'll know she attracted much noisy attention at the border crossing, and at the entrance to the department store where I bought her new clothes. She did not bat an eyelid at her exposure and made little attempt to cover herself. She was a gutsy lady who knew keeping her poise meant she was in control, and onlookers kept a discrete distance.'

'We remained good friends until she moved back to the States to take a senior position with Bank of America. I have no doubt she made the grade as a senior executive.'

'Could you keep cool under such circumstances?'

'I don't think so unless I was numb with fright.'

'She was calm and responded to every instruction without hesitation. She knew I had enough to think about already without her causing me problems. When I asked her, some months later, how she felt during that trip, she told me I was lucky she remembered I used to rally drive, or else she would have taken the wheel. One tough cookie.'

'You cannot prepare yourself for every conceivable eventuality, but you can prepare yourself to be resilient and resourceful. Only then can your brain function clearly. This is what I aim to achieve with you.'

'Then, my master, I will achieve it. I'm sure Carmen will drag me kicking and screaming across the resistance boundary if I don't do it myself. That would be embarrassing.'

She remembered something Carmen had said 'Seb, can I ask you a personal question?'

'You can ask me anything you want, though you might not always get an answer.'

'A comment Carmen made in the sauna reminded me of a question I wanted to ask last week. Were you ever married?'

'What did Carmen say?'

'Her comment was if she weren't already happily married, you would be her ideal man.'

'Interesting. There's no room in a marriage for two strong executives. They would likely kill each other. In fact, I would like you to study Carmen over the next couple of days and tell me what you detect about her as a person.'

'Okay, but you haven't answered my question.'

'Yes, I was briefly married, a long time ago. I was in my mid-20s and establishing my senior executive career.'

'Talk about getting blood out of a stone. What happened?'

'She died three years later in tragic circumstances.'

'I'm so sorry. Can you tell me about it?'

'I've answered your question if you don't mind. All I will add is it was the darkest and most painful period of my life. After I focussed on my career. Reliving that time gives me great pain.'

He recovered his composure 'It's late lady. You need your sleep.'

'I would like to know of your past, and how you made it to the top. Carmen is clearly in awe of your achievements.'

'Let's first focus on your career. Off to bed with you. You have an early start in the morning.'

'Yes, my master. Good night' as she kissed him on the cheek. She had hit a raw nerve which revealed a tender vulnerability. She wanted to understand his past; but all in good time.

Chapter 20 – Tuesday

She arrived for breakfast just as Carmen was driving out of the gates. 'She must get there before anyone else.'

'Her body clock is on European time, and she likes to catch up with things in Germany before she starts here. But she will be back here by 6pm so her day is not that long.'

'It was a good idea to let her stay. She adds a dimension you would find difficult to convey. I like her.'

'Just a twist of fate, and opportunity taken.'

Both women were back before 6pm and made their way to the gym. Then a swim, finishing in the sauna.

They chatted for some time as Carmen reinforced the game and theatre philosophy.

'Seb explained to me about keeping cool during a wardrobe malfunction. Has it happened to you, and if so, how did you deal with it?'

'In my experience wardrobe malfunction is a way of life for both men and woman. For a woman they can be simple like a broken heel, a laddered stocking, broken zip, and many others. These are just silly and should not be a problem to anyone; only inconvenient. Then we have more embarrassing problems such as buttons failing on a low-cut blouse, a zip, or any other issue which would be considered a distraction. If you are the only woman amongst men, you need to know how to handle the men as they have stopped thinking of you as colleague executive, and now see you as a woman with an exposure problem. You need to reverse this change in attitude quickly.'

'So, if you popped your blouse buttons enough to reveal underwear during a meeting what would you do?'

'Have some fun with it. You expose your bra. You sit on a beach with far less of a bra, or even no bra, with many people. I quickly assess how I might use this malfunction to my advantage. I may pretend I do not know, even though I can see all eyes on my bra. If there is someone there who is not being co-operative during the meeting, I may ask him if there is a problem. He knows where he is looking, so I cause him a little discomfort. Destabilise him. Either he will tell me about my buttons, or I will look down and see for myself. I will then make a joke about it, and ask the men if we can continue, or would they find my exposure too distracting. At no time do I try to excuse myself or show any discomfort or embarrassment. Carmen now has control of the meeting. If it is not going my way, then I can suggest an adjournment which allows me to change and regroup my thoughts. If things are going my way, then I continue knowing my malfunction will distract at least one man thus improving my chances of leaving the meeting with what I want.'

'You can seriously manipulate in this way?'

'My dear, I tell you a secret. Sometimes I engineer a malfunction, so Carmen gets what she wants.'

Mel was laughing, 'You're some lady. I can see why you're successful.'

'I think Sebastian already tells you to always look for positives in a negative, no?'

'Yes, always see the positives.'

'This is the attitude you need in any compromising situation. Turn it to your advantage. Then you win. Is good?'

'Yes, very much so. Thank you.'

Carmen thought for a moment. 'My dear, careless female executives can regularly cause themselves wardrobe problems. For one week in every four weeks a woman will menstruate. Her body will change. Her breasts will fill out. Her tummy will bloat. For these occasions, a smart executive will be prepared.'

'How do you cope with such problems?'

'For me I have in my wardrobe clothes one size more for such weeks some the same as my normal clothes. In this way, it is not obvious because I am comfortable. This works for me, but every woman is different, so you must find what works for you.'

'I've never thought about it in this way before. Thank you. I'll adjust my wardrobe accordingly. We should go. Seb does not like us to be late for dinner.'

Chapter 21 – Wednesday

They were back in the sauna to complete their evening routine.

'What are your views on pillow talk?'

'My darling Sebastian teaches you well. What did he say to you?'

'He told me to avoid it. Use a male lieutenant. Only get involved if I want to plant false information that will win the day.'

'Mel, my dear, using it to plant false information is a very dangerous strategy, and you really need to know what you are doing. Many years of experience before you even think of such a thing. Better you let a lieutenant, you call him, do it for you. This way you do not expose yourself, and you can deny any knowledge of the activities of your lieutenant.'

'I would never betray my husband or my family for the sake of business. My husband is not a jealous man, but we share a loyalty to each other I will not compromise for this game called business. There is always another job, but only one family.'

'What about your relationship with Seb? If you could sleep with him, would you?'

'Very personal question, my dear, but I will answer you as this is part of the learning process. There is a big difference between sleeping with a man, and an affair. Sex is just gratification, whereas love is an emotional desire. I travel many weeks each year. If I am away for more than a few days, my husband would not deny me gratification so long as I do not take it home in any form, and he never hears of it. Certainly I think of Sebastian as a possible source of gratification knowing it will never be known. But only if he and I are here alone. I took hold of his penis one day in the pool when we were having a little argument. Carmen knows how to win the day. And we fool around in the shower in the changing room. But nothing more in the past. I also think because I now come here every month sex with Sebastian steps over the line of casual gratification. So, Sebastian and Carmen can have fun, but not sex.'

'Interesting philosophy. Never thought of sex as just being gratification, but if you are away from your partner, and it's discrete, then it fulfils a need.'

'Do you masturbate, my dear, or use sex toys?'

'Yes, occasionally, why?'

'Is this not sexual gratification? All you do is replace your toys with a man. You do not need to care for the man, just what he can do for you.'

'As I'm quickly learning, our chats in this sauna are very illuminating. Thank you for speaking with me so frankly.'

'You have much to learn and understand about life. If Sebastian thinks you are worthy of this knowledge, I am ready to help. We need more women executives in this world.'

After Carmen had retired for the night, they sat talking in the kitchen.

'Any interesting revelations in the sauna this evening?'

Yes. Interesting. Do you know she creates wardrobe malfunctions to help her win argument?'

'Would not surprise me. She's one resourceful woman.'

'And she absolutely agrees with you about pillow talk. In fact, she suggests I should never get involved in the planting of false information. I should use a lieutenant so I can deny any knowledge. Must sit under your heading of plausible deniability.'

'Good point. Hadn't thought of that.'

'She told me you have fun sometimes in the changing room shower, and she grabbed you by the penis during an argument. But you cannot be her sex toy because she comes here too often.'

'Never argue with the likes of Carmen with your pants down. I know she has considered sex, but she knows the rules. No repeats; don't take it home.'

'So this isn't just her rule?'

'No. It's the rule book for those who spend much of their time away from home.'

'And what about the one who stays at home?'

'They draw the short straw unless they also go away. Never on your own doorstep. Too visible.'

'You have a rule book about sexual activity for travelling executives. Wow, a whole new world for me. What else is in this rule book?'

'It's a rule book about travelling where sex is just one section. We'll get to it at some point in your education.'

'Can't wait.'

Chapter 22 – Thursday

Carmen had left before Mel appeared for breakfast. 'I didn't say goodbye.'

the Way

'She'll be back in a few weeks. She's looking forward to see how far you have grown by then.'

That evening, over dinner, Seb asked for her thoughts about Carmen.

'Very interesting lady. Clearly successful, and very comfortable in her own skin. But constantly using her own name suggests an element of insecurity. I'm not sure why this is but will think about it. She uses a lot of face to hide her insecurity and seems to get away with it. Maybe the men around her find her amusing in a funny sense.'

'You don't think using her name has anything to do with the familiar and formal nature of the German language, or the use of the word "I" in English?'

'No. I don't think it's that. I think she needs to let her listener know who she is. Possibly something to do with being a lone woman on an Executive Board of men. I'll think on it and we can discuss it again.'

'We should get back to your studies. As it's Thursday, and you leave for London in the morning, why don't we recap what you have learnt to date, and possibly expand on issues of immediate interest?'

'That works for me. Would you mind if I drive this discussion? I have some thoughts that will be best addressed in a particular order.'

'Please do. The faster we get to a two-way dialogue, the better.'

They spent the remainder of the evening recapping rules and philosophies, elaborating where appropriate, but without expanding the general narrative.

Chapter 23 – Friday

When she appeared for breakfast, she had her weekend bag with her as she would go straight to Chesterfield station to reach London in time to meet with one of her architect clients.

She kissed him on the way out, telling him she would be back for dinner on Sunday.

Chapter 24 – Sunday

She entered the gates a little after 6pm. She appeared subdued as she strolled to the house. He was in the kitchen preparing for a BBQ. The sun was still hot, so why be inside?

'Hi Seb', as she kissed him.

'How was your weekend?'

'Nice to be back.'

'That bad. What was the problem?'

'When I got home on Friday evening, the place was a tip. He's done nothing to keep the place tidy. He even had his washing piled up waiting for me to do it. Other than the time I spent with my mum, I spent most of the weekend clearing up. What is it with men? They expect their mothers to clear up after them until they get married and then expect their wife to do the same. We both work so why don't we share the chores?'

'I hope you don't include me in your generalisation.'

'That's a good point. You, a very successful banker, take care of this place, and me, although you have Georgina.'

'Big house. But I do all the cooking.'

'I'll concede on those points. What did you do?'

'Mainly shopping on Saturday. Went out for dinner on Saturday evening with friends, and tennis this afternoon.'

'That's another thing, you do the food shopping. Can't even get Phil to come with me, let alone do it himself. Ordering a take-away is his limit.'

the Way

'Come lady. Get yourself into your house clothes, grab a bottle of something, and join me on the sundeck for a BBQ.'

'Be there in five minutes.'

Week 3

Chapter 25 – Monday

'This week we'll prepare you for the main thrust of your studies over the coming weeks including your mindset for the rigours of the Art of War – probably the most important philosophy required by a successful executive.'

'Tonight, we will study how to analyse and understand the behaviour of people in the workplace. Carmen tells me you need to improve your observation skills, so we'll deal with this before we discuss the games people play.'

'How many times in your life have you met someone, formed your first impressions of them, only to find later you were completely wrong about them?'

'Too often to count.'

'What was your primary source of information about them?'

'I guess it was visual.'

'Exactly. Our eyes are the most prejudicial sense we have and, if not disciplined, is the most dangerous. Our interpretation of visual information is our next most dangerous sense as the way we interpret data from our eyes can be heavily skewed by our perceptions, expectations, and failure to fully understand a picture. Your own prejudicial constraints can evoke your brain to refuse to accept what you actually see because it goes against your belief and so you recreate the picture in your mind to something more akin to your belief system.'

'Then we have pure ignorance, or lack of knowledge of how to interpret what you see. Carmen told me you miscalculated her age by some margin even though she had already given you information to help your eyes to be accurate. I need to teach you to absorb and believe what your eyes observe without constraint or prejudice and then interpret this picture with knowledge and information from other senses, so you have reliable data to analyse. If you cannot see a true picture of a potential enemy, how can you expect to know, and defeat them?'

'If you use your eyes objectively, and your senses are tuned, you can discern much about someone else with the slightest movement of their eyes.'

'If you remember back to last week, I told you about the need to leave your nationality, politics, religion and any other ideology and prejudice at the door on entering your workplace. This is to ensure your mind is open to whatever you encounter and thus can deal with the reality of whatever confronts you. It's fundamentally important you deal with what is, not what should be, or could be. When we study the Art of War in the coming weeks, you'll see how important it is to accurately assess a situation and person if you are to respond in the most effective way. I will dig out some pictures where some content is misplaced or out of context. We'll train your brain how to capture and analyse the information provided by each picture without prejudice so you can apply it to your powers of observation.'

'When you next undertake client visits, besides a complete recollection of what was discussed including the actual words and tone used by your client to express a relevant view or opinion, I'll expect you to recall what your client was wearing, what make of computer they use, if they had a bookcase what books were on the shelves, and were they well ordered, or just lying on the shelves. What type of jewellery did they wear, especially their type of watch? Was their dress code appropriate? If not, were they nervous, or relaxed? I need you to observe an environment, capture any useful information, and then process it to see what it tells you about your client, or their business. In fact, I would like you to keep a notebook of such meetings capturing all the data I've mentioned, and any impressions and thoughts you drew from the meeting. You should write this visit report as soon after the meeting as possible, and certainly before

Week 3

engaging in another meeting. We'll then analyse each meeting to see how well you extracted everything possible from it.'

'Wow. My dad used to play a game with me where he would hold a tray containing several unrelated objects for a minute or two, cover it, and ask me to recall all the objects. If I appeared cocky, he would expect me to tell him where on the tray each object is located. You're now saying I need to deploy an adult version of this game as part of my training.'

'What's the model of your car, and its registration number?'

'It's a Ford Escort. Registration starts with a "D" and has the letters "AFC" – Arsenal football Club. Can't remember the numbers.'

'Your car is a Mk IV Cabriolet 1.6l, and the registration is D437AFC. Interesting you use word association to remember the letters as we will develop this technique. Do you know the year it was first registered as in the first "D"?'

'It was three years old when I bought it, so makes it 1986.'

'Good. Using association again rather than backtracking from the current letter. This is what we need to enhance.'

'Do you have any questions as this is an important topic? You will have many situations where your observation of just some small detail will make the difference.'

'No. I accept the need as Carmen has already told me, and I will attempt to keep my eyes open from now on.'

'It's more than keeping your eyes open, it's keeping your mind in the present. Far too many people think of anything other than the immediate situation.'

'Okay. Let's move on to people.'

'If I were to say to you the nicer the person, the more you need to be cautiously aware of them, what would you think?'

'Are you suggesting the nicer the person the more I need to be on my guard with them? Bit counterintuitive for me.'

'There you go. You allow prejudice and emotional content to cloud your judgement. Let us contain our argument to the workplace. It's counterintuitive to believe any capable executive can also be a genuinely very nice person. Charming, courteous, pleasant company, considerate, can put you at your ease, is perfectly okay, but any more is deception theatre. If you think back to our analogy of a football team, can you really believe, when in play, the players are very nice to each other, even their own team players. We are talking about very competitive people who will use all their charm and guile to achieve their aim, ultimately for their gain, at your expense, if necessary. Rule of thumb is the more successful, the more ruthless.'

'As it ever occurred to you that far too many great comedians are usually very lonely and reclusive people in real life? Look how many have tortured lives and die alone, or even commit suicide, yet you remember them as being hilarious and likeable. Think Peter Setters, Tony Hancock, Spike Milligan, and Kenneth Williams as good examples.'

'This also applies to the life and soul of the party person. Generally insecure or lonely.'

'If an executive, even on your side, is being overtly nice to you, do not be flattered. Ask yourself what they want from you. If you're lucky enough to have a good mentor whose only interest is your success, you can lower your guard. But, as you may have noticed, mentors are not very nice to their students.'

'That's not fair. I think my mentor is very nice to me.'

'Bear this in mind as we progress.'

'But are you saying I need to question everyone's motive for being nice to me? Sounds paranoid.'

'Not at all. You just need to be aware of the context of the situation in which you find yourself and tune your senses accordingly. Pleasant is okay, but overtly nice should ring alarm bells rather than relax your defences – think pillow talk. We'll study all of this at some length over the coming weeks so for now please accept the principle.'

'I sense Carmen analysing me all the time, even over dinner, so as my master wishes.'

'We can encapsulate the essence of what you must learn into a short motto:'

Be Aware, Be Prepared

'Let's move on to another topic – power. In a competitive environment the players are invariably intent on exerting power over everyone else. Think of male animals gathering their harem during the mating season. The males will fight each other, to the death in some cases, to exert their supremacy. In the executive world there are many ways to exert power. You need to be aware of such challenge and not be intimidated. If they're more powerful than you feign retreat, but not submission. If they're of similar power to you, let them know they do not intimidate you so go play elsewhere. If they're subordinate to your power base, quietly put them in their place. I tend to engage in the typical Clint Eastwood stare. Says far more than words.'

'I've seen that stare. Sends shudders down my spine.'

'The next subject will appear a contradiction, but there is a logic to it. The subject is urgency. We touched on this before but let me expand a little. If the building is on fire, or you're bleeding to death, it can be argued the situation is urgent. Most other situations are subjective. Yet people will come to you, possibly in distress, insisting you must act urgently. Think before you respond. Is this situation really urgent, or is it panic by the messenger? Does the situation appear worse than it really is? Is it a ploy to get you to respond without thinking? Remember urgency is subject to interpretation.'

'Another form of this is when you're asked to provide an answer by a certain time. Is this timeframe real, or arbitrary? If real, then you can only respond based on the data available, and there will be times when you must do this. If arbitrary then you should not feel the need to respond in the allotted time if you have a reasonable argument to support your delay.'

the Way

'Remember when Charles wanted your decision on the Friday before you left, but you weren't ready. You explained why you needed a little more time, and he respected your need. This is normal so don't feel threatened or intimidated by artificial deadlines.'

'Can I end tonight's session on a philosophical note? Life should be simple, but people make it difficult. For example, people tend to resist change as it can interrupt their comfortable routine and calm. But this attitude is unreasonable as life is a progression of change. I would not attempt to count the number of times I can see a solution to a problem requiring change only to find those who need to adopt such change become the real challenge. Thus, in general, life is difficult. Embrace this and you change your mindset from negative burden to positive challenge.'

Chapter 26 – Tuesday

'Tonight, we'll study the games people play. The book I gave to you was essentially written around social intercourse. But you engage with people in the workplace at both a formal and social level, so I think it relevant as a useful tool especially when dealing with people who are more emotionally driven.'

'I'll give you the building blocks around the games people play and show you how they fit together. Then we'll examine each of the building blocks until you understand how they work, and more importantly, how to use them. You will find you can use them in your personnel life, as well as your business life. For example, the best, sure way to win an argument with someone in Child mode is to side-wind them.'

'What do you mean by side-wind?'

'Generally, it is a distraction that will not be ignored but I'll explain more in a moment.'

'You'll learn there are three stances you can take in a debate or argument: Parent, Adult, and Child. These are symbolic names which can be defined in psychology as ego states, but they describe the stance you take. All of us unconsciously use all three states in our daily lives. If you know consciously how to use them, switching from state to state as the need dictates, you can almost always win, or at least diffuse the argument. For example, the Child in us demands certainty. The Child in us wants to know day will follow night, mother will always be there, and the bad guy will always get it in the end. The Adult in us accepts there is no certainty to anything. The Parent uses more judgemental rationale or uses emotion to change the position of an argument.'

'When the Parent or Child in us dominates, the outcome is predictable. When the Adult dominates, the outcome is not predictable. In arguments you should generally avoid adopting the Adult stance. The person starting the argument will likely adopt the Adult stance from the beginning. You must arm yourself with the answers to their possible arguments, and present them in the Parent stance, using the Child stance where necessary to bring them down into the Parent stance. When they are in the Parent stance, it will be easy for you to diffuse their argument, and possibly sell your alternate argument and the outcome will be a predictable success.'

'A side-wind is a Parent stance to offset a Child stance, where the child is too young to understand the Parent and Adult stance albeit they will adopt them in their argument. If you directly argue with a child, they will adopt the Adult stance and you will do the same and you'll get nowhere, just frustration. A typical Adult stance for a child would be to answer every one of your arguments with "Why?". This is a face-to-face direct confrontation. You need to think of a way to distract the child with something more interesting to them. If you can do this, they will soon forget the argument and be on their way. So rather than argue directly, you feed a different stimulus in from the side, hence sidewinder. As adults, we can use a significant distraction or a diversion to break a logjam in an adult argument.'

She looks at him. 'Now you're a psychologist.'

'No, but I'm a trained negotiator so I know all the various ploys people utilise to get their way. As a negotiator, I need to move the argument where I need it to be without the other side feeling beaten or manipulated. The best result from any negotiation is a win-win, and I'll teach you this.'

'So, you just play games with people to get what you want.'

'Life is a game. What you need is to understand the rules of the game and be clear in your arguments. Knowledge is king.'

'So how long will it take me to understand all of this?'

'Once you have mastered the principles, we'll regularly use them, until they transfer to your subconscious mind and thus part of your way of life.'

'You don't know how you currently use your Adult, Parent and Child states, but you use them. When you fully understand these things, you can use them with great effect. My role is to give you a fast-track introduction, and the books you should read to continue your education.'

'For example, where did you get this fish? Adult response – the local fishmonger; Parent response: why is there something wrong with it? The Adult response is informative. The Parent response is defensive.'

'Let me try to give you an example in the workplace. Emotional content is the scourge of executive life, but it happens. We're all human. All types of stress can lead to emotional response. A good executive will have a release valve allowing this emotional content to dissipate without undue impact. But there are those who release it on some subordinate; possibly even in public, and which I consider as unforgiveable. Others let it get to them.'

'An exec arrives at your office in a frenzy about some disagreement you may have and rants at you, most certainly in

Adult mode. How do you deal with this? There is no point in you joining this argument in Adult mode. You have two choices which will require your honed skills in reading the situation. If you sense you can calm the situation in either Parent mode, or even Child mode, then you apply these. The Parent mode would be something to the effect of inviting them to sit and discuss this over coffee. The interruption created by the delay in securing the coffee allows them to calm a little – a distraction where you show concern by moving away from your desk to somewhere comfortable to sit.'

'If you feel the need to drop into Child mode to encourage them into Parent mode, you need a more tuned read of the situation as you cannot imply resignation to the argument. Your adopted stance is one of hurt. Why are you speaking to me this way? What have I done to deserve this tirade of abuse? If they do not quickly switch into Parent mode and essentially apologise for their outburst, you must quickly switch to Adult mode to end this encounter, but not before you have seeded your view of the world. Your response would be along the lines of I do not agree with you as I think this, but I don't have time for this right now so let's defer it until later. This is where the fewer words needed to express your case is very important. They then have an opportunity to calm and consider your response before another encounter. You could even use your spy network to find out about the underlying emotional issue, so you are better prepared next time.'

'Does this make sense to you?'

'I sometimes think I'm the release valve for Michael Chimes. Whenever he's in a mood, I get the sharp end of it.'

'Okay. Let's analyse this situation as this is real to you. Has he ever made a pass at you, invited you out for drinks after work, or anything similar?'

'When he first started with Aldridge, he invited me for drinks after work, but I declined unless part of a group. He used to look at me in a predator man way, but now more in a pain-in-the-arse way.'

'What about his personal life? Is he married? Does he have children? Does he appear happily married, or does he spend most evenings after work out socialising?'

'He's married and has two children. Don't know about the state of his marriage other than he appears most mornings in a mood, but I don't know if this is a family issue or a hangover. He spends most evenings during the week purportedly entertaining clients.'

'What do you think he thinks about you?'

'By the way he treats me, I would say I'm a thorn in his side. I'm a woman he cannot have. He can't fire me, not least because I deliver a good job, and have the support of both Jim and Charles. He once told me to stop wasting my time with architects, but I already had approval from Jim to explore this opportunity, and he knew it. I'm not one of the lads, and he can't use me as his floozie when entertaining his client mates. The only way he thinks he can exert power over me is ensuring I don't get promoted.'

'Interesting. Let's deal with the simple parts first. You are an attractive, and single woman. You're fair game for any man.'

'But I'm engaged to be married!'

'Irrelevant. You're not married, and all that matters to a man.'

'Your lack of information regarding his personal life would indicate you do not have a good relationship with his PA. We'll discuss the need for spies as part of your career; and PA's are an excellent source of valuable information. Then we have your relative longevity with Aldridge, and especially with Jim. This makes him feel impotent. He has a member of his team who can appeal above him for support when necessary. Thus, you have not convinced him you're on his team, and what you're doing is valuable to the team. Thus, why you don't get promotion. From what I've seen of the Aldridge management there is Charles, to a lesser extent, Jim, and the remainder is the required ego boost on business cards.'

'Does this mean you don't think Michael has misogynistic tendencies?'

'If we look at the information we have, and rank it for reliability, we conclude any misogynistic component is purely speculative. As you do not have the intel regarding his private life, we cannot derive any reliable information regarding his predatory instinct towards you. What we know is Michael has every reason to consider you as not a part of his team, and able to usurp him, which is confirmed by your presence here.'

Gulp. 'I've never looked at the situation this way. I still think Michael has a misogynistic streak, but I accept your analysis.'

'It's not your fault. You've never worked for an ordered corporate environment so don't understand the need for loyalty to your responsible executive. This problem has been caused by the unwitting way in which Charles runs the company. I'll teach you how good organisations are structured to ensure such problems cannot occur. You'll also learn the importance of being aware of what is happening around you, and the absolute need for good intel within your own organisation to assist your awareness.'

'Are we back to pillow talk?'

'Any which way you can for valuable information, as you will see in the Art of War.'

Chapter 27 – Wednesday

'Tonight, we will expand on your existing knowledge of rhetoric as applied in the workplace. As already stated in the rules of engagement, persuasion is very important. More often than not, it's the way you pitch an argument that wins the day.

the Way

It's of little use if you have a great idea, product, or strategy if you cannot sell it to needed collaborators.'

'Aristotle, as you well know, was a great philosopher, and a great politician. As you also know political debate is usually in the form of spoken debate. Thus, the art of persuasion is fundamental to a politician hoping to win the argument. Aristotle studied this art and developed rhetoric as a means of persuasive dialogue. He came up with the three accepted components required in any speech to effectively deliver your message in a way that optimises your chance of success. As you should be aware, these components are logos, ethos, and pathos.'

'Aristotle's original work has been tinkered with through the ages to what we have today. My version, and what I want to teach you, uses the following definitions.'

'"Logos" is the essential logic of what is wrong, and what needs to be done about it, for example, "this is the problem, and we need to do something about it". Please note the use of "we" not "I".'

'"Ethos" is the credibility and/or integrity of the speaker to address this problem and propose a solution. For example, "I have studied this problem in some detail, and because of this, I think we should do this". This is the only part where the word "I" is used.'

'"Pathos" is the emotional content to energise people into believing you are doing this for the greater good and thus they should support you.'

'So, you see it's not rocket science. Are you with me so far?'

'Yes', she said attentively. 'Fairly easy really. This is the problem that needs fixing, I know how to fix it, but I need your support.'

'Not quite, but not bad. You haven't stated the consequence of not fixing the problem. A few examples will hone you into the specifics.'

'But before we start, we use rhetoric in the form of speech, so you must get a specific commitment from your audience to hear

Week 3

you out before they contribute. Please note we are not speaking of oratory as per Cicero as this would require years of practice. It's very important your audience agree to give you the floor until you've finished. If you allow yourself to be interrupted, your chances of success significantly reduce.'

'Furthermore, time and place are important. You cannot allow distractions such as telephones, another engagement, etc. Your audience has to be relaxed and prepared to give you the floor and their undivided attention for whatever time you need.'

'The reciprocity of this is you must know their attention span and keep your argument within their timeframe.'

'So, creating your environment is very important.'

'In business, we extend rhetoric being voiced because it's not always possible to get all the collaborators you need into one space, especially in an international organisation. Thus, we have a written version of rhetoric which is different to the language of a conventional report. If you think of the great oratory speeches by Churchill, he spent much time preparing these speeches choosing and weighting every word on paper. Then he added delivery, which is theatre. He was a master at both written and spoken argument, albeit I understand he studied Cicero with some zeal to perfect his oratory skills. Nice if you have the time but unnecessary for our purpose.'

'If you think of a conventional report, it should be factual, considered, and reasoned. This makes it a hard, if not a boring read for a busy executive, and thus will not be top of their reading list unless it motivates them to engage. So how can you ensure they read your report? Let's consider why you buy a new product you have never considered, or even needed before. Someone thinks of a clever way to attract your attention and keeps you engaged for the short time needed to stimulate you with the essential need you have for the product.'

'I guess you mean advertising.'

'Correct. If you remember when we discussed business philosophy, I stressed the need to not use more words than necessary to express your point. If you want collaborators to support your report, you need to stimulate them to read it. You need a catchy piece of written rhetoric which can be read and digested within a few minutes, and which stimulates the interest to read more – your report. And I don't mean the executive summary at the front of a report. This is the second step, a convenient short recap. Your supplemental page of rhetoric is read once, and then, job done, is discarded. The number of reports and proposals landing on my desk in a week made it impossible to read all. So, what was my filter mechanism? First, select required reading, being information valuable to me. Thereafter bin anything that does not capture my imagination in the first two minutes. Therefore, a page of cleverly written rhetoric can prove invaluable, if only to amuse the reader; whatever it takes to get your report to the top of the stack. I took the view if the writer has no respect for my time, then I have none for theirs.'

'At all times you must write for your reader. You must consider how to phase your argument to make it easy for them to read and digest.'

'All of this also applies to presentations. It never ceased to amaze me that people think they can treat a presentation as a major event for which time has no importance. They forget you have other items on your own agenda, so they must treat delivery as a presentation of a summary to see if of interest.'

'I have been part of what we term business rounds in various countries. Part of this process allows pre-selected companies or organisation to discuss a particular investment requirement with the delegates. These people would be allocated thirty minutes, sometimes only fifteen minutes, to make their pitch. My role would be to advise them on the viability of their requirement regarding external investment. They would bring bulky project reports more appropriate to a sales pitch than an investment forum. Then you would find the presenter would have to keep referring to paperwork for key factors in the project, things they should know by heart if they know their project.'

'If a client could not articulate the essential components of their requirement to me in six minutes without referral to notes, certainly no more than 10 minutes, then I took the view they did not understand their requirement and binned their proposal.'

'You must have been a tough person to deal with, even brutal. Why only six minutes?'

'I once presented a very complex US$6 billion project to investors involving both capital investment and public offering for a developing economy. It took me a few seconds short of six minutes to sell this project to the investors including identifying specific country risks. No-one ever presented anything as remotely complex to me.'

She looked up from her notes 'So, you measure others by your own capabilities.'

'Hmm. Not exactly. I measure others by their respect for my time and input.'

Chapter 28 – Thursday

'To wrap up your studies for this week I want to talk about time management, and the discipline you will need to ensure you hit your objectives every day.'

'The characteristics of a successful executive are they are self-starters, highly motivated, and disciplined in how they manage themselves. Without these fundamental characteristics the world would quickly close in on them and swallow them up. If you need someone to manage you or guide you in your workload, then forget being an executive. Having said this, my definition of a great PA is one who can manage her boss without them realising it. At the end of the day it's the PA who ensures you are in the right place, at the right time, with the relevant material.'

She stopped writing 'I can identify with the PA bit. Mary most certainly manages Charles, although he's very aware of it, but grateful most of the time. I've also encountered executives who are invariably late for meetings with no apparent regard for the inconvenience to others.'

'I said they're disciplined in how they manage themselves. They'll achieve what they want. The executive type you mentioned is so selfish in their own objectives and self-importance they have little concern about how this might impact others. I have also met many such people. My view is you are honour-bound to be punctual, thus showing respect for those with whom you engage. This is part of your integrity. Those who ignore this will find themselves unable to arrange meetings or frowned upon. Too important to be refused is ego driven; a means to exert superiority but can also cause them problems when they really need help. I would readily find reasons to avoid such people. If the need to meet was important I would set the meeting on my terms where it was clear I only had a short window of time between other "important" appointments for which I could not be late. Managing peers is an important part of your success.'

'Then there are those who always claim they need to meet with you urgently. Quickly establish this is the case, remembering what I've already expressed about urgency. Then apply the boy who cried wolf to your response to these people.'

'As an executive the demands on your time can be onerous. You and your PA must be ruthless in managing such demands. You start your day with a written To-Do List; not one of these new electronic time managers; but something in your face throughout the day. Rank the tasks based on urgency with special regard to time critical. There will be tasks more compelling than others. There will be tasks you would prefer to shuffle to the bottom of the stack. It's easier to start the day with one of these more unsavoury tasks for no better reason it's one less to do, and the day can only get better. Be realistic when making your list as your discipline should dictate on normal days, you complete all tasks.'

'Try to picture your transition to executive as moving away from the pack to be the pack leader. No-one is telling you what to do. The pack looks to you to instruct them. You must develop the discipline to manage your own time, set your own tasks, think for everyone else in the pack, and take care of them. It's a lonely position so the temptation will be to mix with them. You cannot. Your authority vests in the gap between you and them.'

'The plague that creates the most havoc to an executive's schedule is meetings. Lower-level people love meetings. It is a plausible way to consume much time with little effort, but rarely produces outcomes worthy of the resources consumed in such endless discussions.'

'Over the years I found the optimum result was no more than two meetings per day lasting no longer than one hour. Only crisis meetings could circumvent this rule. Note, this included meetings with the President and CEO of the bank. Although they found this frustrating at the beginning, they grew to understand how important it was in an environment where markets can swing in minutes.'

'My most important mentor, and President of the bank, worked with the philosophy it takes no more than two people to make great decisions, up to five people can valuably discuss options, up to ten people comprise a think-tank where ideas are kicked around and developed, and any more is a conference where no decisions are made. He rightly claimed the more people involved in a decision, the more mediocre the outcome. He cited so-called democratic governments as the clear proof of this.'

'Let me illustrate an experiment you can try for yourself in the workplace. Find a problem that impacts across several processes. Ask for a meeting with representation from each of the

the Way

processing areas. Define the problem, and then ask for a 5 – 10 minutes adjournment for each to consider their response. Then move around the table asking each for their thoughts regarding a solution. After everyone has responded with their thoughts, request each person to re-articulate the problem from their process perspective. You will likely find your original problem has been reshaped to suit their own perspectives. The more people present, the more likelihood of diversity. Listen carefully. This is important information about any implementation issues. Detect people who are receptive to the problem and the need for a solution rather than those who prefer to distance themselves. This will help you to shape an implementation plan most likely to succeed.'

Always remember there are two components to a solution, the logical/rational solution, and the ability of your resource base to implement a solution. Who makes the decision?'

She was not sure where this was going having never consciously encountered this scenario. 'I suppose you try to find consensus.'

'Could take a while, and likely to be more being all things to all people, thus likely to be mediocre. But there are two scenarios to consider. The first is you already know what needs to happen so your meeting is about the best way to sell your solution. The second, less impressive, is you are seeking guidance thus in think-tank mode.

In the first scenario you make the decision having considered the human delivery issues articulated by the people at the meeting. A skilful executive will propose the solution in such a way each person feels they have contributed. They are sold, and will deliver, but only one person made the decision.'

'If your solution is far from what can easily be sold then you need to switch into impose mode. This is where you appreciate life is simple, only people make it difficult. But your approach will be something akin to *having listened to and considered all the ideas and positions expressed my preferred solution is ……., so can we*

Week 3

discuss how we can implement this solution. You now need to keep the meeting focussed on your solution but try to end the meeting on an inclusive note.'

In the second scenario you can either derive a solution from the information gathered during the meeting and thus sell it back as above or accept more time is needed for reflection but set a time on probably the next day to reconvene to establish a solution inferring a solution has to be found, and quickly. Thus, you have participated in a think-tank or even conference mode where no decision is made.'

She was confused. 'But why have company executive Boards if this philosophy works?'

'Not the same unless the CEO is a one-man show with a Board of compliant executives. A Board meeting of a corporate which functions under collective responsibility comprises a strategist, the CEO, and a team of tacticians, the executives, who bring the skill sets together that collectively drive the business. These executives are also strategists in their chosen skill set. A good example would be the military example of a Commander-in-Chief, the Air Commodore of the Air Force, the Admiral of the Naval Fleet, and the Field Marshal of the Army. They all play a part on the battlefield, but the Commander-in-Chief decides the nature of the encounter and manages the overall battlefield. If it is a land-based encounter then the principal decision to engage will be between the Commander-in-Chief and the Field Marshal, with the navy and air force providing required support on demand. All four sit together at the table so there is commitment to deliver on all aspects of the plan.'

'But how do you differentiate between a strategist and a tactician in the Boardroom?'

'A strategist will define the goal. A tactician will devise the best means to achieve the goal.'

'But we digress. Back to time management. When you were at university what was the typical duration of a lecture?'

'Fifty minutes. Why?'

the Way

'Do you know the significance of this duration?'

'Something to do with attention span, or ability to absorb information.'

'Correct. Research suggests people tend not to stay focussed for over fifty minutes without a break. Thus, as a rule, I would suggest you do not allow meetings to last more than one hour. Unless a Board or crisis meeting, be very reluctant to attend open-ended meetings. They feed the lazy but waste your time. There are some novel ideas today to stop these endless sessions. One involves not having chairs in the meeting room, so everyone stands. Apparently meeting times dramatically shortened.'

'If you agree to a meeting, ensure the aim of the meeting is clear from the outset. As soon as it meets the aim, leave the meeting.'

'If a meeting comprises over five people, including yourself, question if this meeting is worth attending. Send a deputy, or just refuse to attend until the aim is more defined.'

'As an executive, your role in the day-to-day is ensuring existing plans are working as they should, and to be available if something extraordinary occurs. Otherwise, your role is to devise the strategy going forward. You will have much information to absorb and must have the time for your own research. In the final analysis decisions are yours, and for which you will be accountable. So, ensure your instincts are well nourished with the data you need to make great decisions. You are only deemed as good as your last major decision.'

'Make time to walk your floor twice every day you're there. The purpose of this is to let your people know you exist and approachable; to harvest valuable feedback from the people at the coalface, both internally and externally; and to sense issues you can address before they become toxic. A good plan on paper is not the same as real life. The problem with plans on paper is no matter how much consideration you give to the human element in devising the plan, humans are infinitely variable resources. Plans implemented will need to be adjusted to the available resource base to maximise value. The only way you hone this skill is by walking the floor.'

'Be close to your critical people. Let them know you're there. Let them know you have time for them when needed. A good example of this occurred a few years ago when I joined an old English bank as Director responsible for all Global debt instruments. They expected me to take residence, as was traditional, on the sedate nineteenth floor with the other executives from other divisions of the bank. It caused quite a stir when I insisted my office be in the thick of the operations on the first floor. The CEO responsible for all securities visited with me typically twice a day, having explained to him the reason for my decision was to feel and sense what was happening in the markets throughout the day. Far too many executives use meetings, memos, and reports to determine their strategy. I honed my senses on the floor of the trading room. This allowed me to differentiate between trends which would fizzle out, and trends to which we needed to quickly adapt. After a while he could feel the atmosphere and understood the relevance to strategic planning. He moved his office to the first floor.'

'Another aspect of time management can seriously impact the business. There are those who are so incapable of disciplined management of their time, or so consumed in their own importance, they cause chaos and discontent. I speak of those who regularly cancel appointments or meetings at short notice, where short notice is a function of the inconvenience to the other participants. There will always be times when cancellation or deferment cannot be avoided, but this should be exceptional, and is different to abuse of the time management of others. Within an organisation such behaviour will lead to discontent amongst the abused. If this happens with customers, expect these customers to find an alternative supplier and spread word in the market about such abuse. It becomes irrelevant you are the best supplier if the customer cannot benefit through such abuse. There is always another competitor ready to deliver if you fail. A capable executive should not, on a regular basis, need to quickly respond to extraordinary events at the expense of scheduled activity. And always remember a bird in the hand is worth two in the bush. Do not risk losing existing customers in anticipation of maybe securing a new customer.'

'In summary, it is very important you do not allow others to manage your time for their convenience, nor do you abuse the time of others. Apply integrity and even-handedness to your time management and you will gain respect. Some will not like this approach, but they will learn, and come to appreciate your fair and reasonable management of your time. A simple rule is you should always have the time for those who depend on you, and to those to whom you are accountable.'

'Any issues with any of this?'

'No. It all makes perfect sense but, as with everything this week, requires a complete revamp of how I work and schedule my time. I need to work on these requirements now so when I take over from Jim, I have a more disciplined approach to how I work. Really interesting about peer management, but this is back to team players on the field of play. I get it. Enthusiasm can be abused. Can we stop now as I'm tired?'

'Sure. Off you go and sleep well. Tiredness makes people ineffective.'

Chapter 29 – Friday

She arrived home visibly exhausted. He thought she was feeling the strain of working during the day, and again in the evening.

'Someone looks like they need a drink.'

'My master observes well. But I would like a swim first. I'll skip gym tonight if you don't mind as I want to recap some material this week, and I want an early night.'

'Sounds like an acceptable plan. Go have your swim. I'll speed up dinner and have a nice drink ready when you're ready.'

He thought for a moment. *'Dinner here will feel like our normal classroom routine. Lovely evening. Dinner on the deck should change her mood.'*

When she returned, he was not there; just a glass of prosecco on the table, and a note telling her dinner is on the deck. *'What a great idea'* she thought with a smile.

On the sun deck he had a pizza oven which was fired, and almost ready. He had prepared pizza dough and had a variety of toppings ready for selection.

'Thank you. This is a nice idea.'

'Take a lounger and chill for a while. The oven is nearly ready.'

He took a lounger next to her. 'Am I pushing you too hard? Do I need to recalibrate the workload?'

She put her hand on his arm. 'No. You've given me so much to think about that's not just knowledge, it makes me re-evaluate my whole way of thinking. It's not the load making me feel tired, it's a sense of inadequacy. I've spent the past ten years strolling around in blissful ignorance. Now I meet the most wonderful teacher who, quite unintentionally, makes me feel an idiot in need of a brain transplant. And, more importantly, I can see how much I don't know. But why don't I know this? Okay, some of the corporate stuff would reasonably be new to me. But the stuff about character, attitude, observation, self-discipline, and well-being – what have I been doing these past years? It's depressing.

'He saw the tears rolling down her cheeks, so sat up to face her and hold her hand. 'You're being too hard on yourself. They've left you to your own devices these past years. I can't imagine you've had any management training courses, or any other formal training. But I did not agree to this process lightly. You are a very bright lady who only needs direction to grow in stature. For what it's worth you have a gold star for one simple, but powerful statement. You can see how much you don't know. You've opened a receptive door into your mind. The knowledge will now pour in, and you'll find it exciting and fulfilling. Maybe a little overwhelming at the beginning.'

She turned her tearful face to meet his 'Thank you. Overwhelming, clearly. But it means a lot to me you consider me worthy of your time and incredible knowledge. Boy, do I need to wake up and get in the groove!'

'Why don't we relax this evening unless you have a burgeoning desire to offload your questions. We have all weekend to talk through whatever is on your mind. Come, tell me what toppings you would like on your pizza while I prepare the base.'

'See. You can even make your own pizza, which is yet more of what I can't do.'

'Have you ever tried?'

'No.'

'Then your first lesson in making a pizza. You take this piece of dough and copy my actions to make the base.'

He had her spinning the dough to extend it out to form a base. She was soon laughing as she aborted and restarted the process until she managed what would pass for a base. She then applied the passata and cheese base before selecting toppings. Soon they had their pizzas.

'You see, nothing to it. Next time I'll show you how to make the dough and you can be on pizza duty.'

She felt much better as they ate and chatted about everything and anything while they enjoyed the remainder of the sunshine, their pizza, and prosecco.

A little after 9pm she asked for a glass of red wine, and announced she would take a long bath, and an early night.

Week 3

Chapter 30 – Saturday

She appeared for breakfast a little after 8am although he knew she had used the pool.

'How do you feel this morning?'

'Much better, thank you. And thanks for a lovely evening. Just what the doctor ordered. Sorry about the tears.'

'You're very welcome. And please don't concern yourself about the tears. There will be more as we progress unless I turn you into an unfeeling, hard-nosed robot which is not my intention. You are safe to shed your tears here. I'll be here for you. What would you like for breakfast?'

'Have you eaten?'

'No. I decided to wait for you.'

'Then whatever you're having on a smaller scale, will do nicely.'

Once breakfast was on the table, he felt he needed to bring her back from her thoughts.

'Do you feel like getting back to civilisation today? I have shopping to do if you would like to come with me. Or you could wander off on your own to explore. It will be a lovely day.'

'Do you mind if I hang out with you? I do want to talk, but in small chunks, if possible.'

'No problem. Why don't we do what I intended the first weekend you were here and take you somewhere into the countryside for lunch? We'll do the shopping first and bring it back. Perhaps you can select your favourite ingredients, and I'll try to put them into a nice meal during the week.'

'Sounds great.'

'Okay, I need fifteen minutes to clear up, and then five to change.'

'I'll help you clear up and then be ready in ten minutes.'

Shopping done and stored away they set off for the notorious Snake Pass, the A57 road that winds its way through the Peak District between Sheffield and Manchester, and now replaced by the far less onerous trans-Pennine M62 motorway. When they reached the Ladybower Reservoir, he parked in a lay-by opposite. As she got out of the car and scanned the reservoir to the south of the road, she gasped at the sheer beauty of the vista with the reservoir bending away to the east surrounded by forested hills.

'Seb, this is beautiful, stunningly beautiful. Can we sit a while and absorb this wonderful landscape?'

'Of course, we can. Let's cross the road, over the fence and sit on the bank for a while.'

He helped her across the fence avoiding the nettles and brambles and wandered some twenty yards toward the water's edge. She sat quietly for some minutes scanning all she could see.

'This place is so peaceful. Now I understand your fascination with this part of the world. It's so lovely.'

After a while they continued their drive towards Glossop but stopped at the Snake Pass Inn at High Peak for lunch. They sat outside looking south over the Peak District where to the west the hills were baron, stripped of their forest and foliage by the acid rain from the factories of Manchester during the Industrial Revolution, although there were signs Mother Nature had healed her scars and plants and trees were growing again, albeit in scattered clusters. To the south and east the land had escaped the polluting smoke so was lush with vegetation. The contrast was stark, and Seb explained how, in the winter, Snake Pass is generally impassable, and the damaged landscape is forbidding.

They took their time with lunch finishing more than an hour after they arrived, but she was in no hurry to leave.

'Are you ready to discuss your first chunk of recap?'

'Absolutely not. Not here. This is a real recharge for me. Thank you for bringing me here. I love it. Can we go walking through the hills one day?'

'There is one of the most beautiful walks in the Peak District near to Matlock. And there is also a cable car which rides across

Week 3

the same dale, so you can view it at ground level and from above. We could walk to the far end of the cable car, and ride high above it coming back.'

'Sounds great. When can we do it?'

'Tomorrow soon enough?'

'Do we have the time?'

'It's what you need, so it's part of our time. Your absorption level will significantly improve after a refreshing return to nature. The walk is about two hours, the cable car ten minutes, so we can do it in half a day.'

'Where are we going from here?'

'We carry on through these baron hills to Glossop and then head south to Buxton which is a spa town some 600m above sea level. Quick look around there as parts of it are delightful. Then it's downhill all the way back to Matlock, but through very lush countryside.'

When they finally returned to Merton, it was late afternoon. 'Can I phone my mum to see how she is and have a chat?'

'You can phone your mother anytime you wish. You don't need to ask.'

She reappeared over one hour later. 'Mum sends her regards, and thanks you for taking care of me. I'm going to the deck to read for a while.'

'Okay. I'll bring supper up when it's ready.'

When he arrived with supper, she was chilling on a lounger. He noticed the book by her side was 'Games People Play'.

'How are you getting on with the book?' bringing her out of her thoughts.

She got up to help him unload the tray and set the table. 'Really interesting. I think I now have a good grasp of the ego states and how they work in various scenarios. Interesting section on relationships. Must try out some of these techniques on Phil next weekend. You speak of the more mundane, but necessary, items on a To-Do list. Getting such items onto our combined list is a real chore, and to even get his attention to do or discuss them usually requires sexual favour. This must change. He needs to share responsibility for all the tasks we have to deal with.'

'And how is your mum?'

'She's okay. Missed me today, but she's very keen for me to progress. I told her about this past week and the impact it had on me. She was her usual sympathetic mum and then side-winded me with,' as she paraphrased her mum 'does he beat you? Does he abuse you? Do you accept what he tells you, and can you question him? Well then, medicine is rarely nice to swallow, but it's what you need to get better. I could hear my dad in her voice.'

'How do you feel now?'

'Far less fragile. Today was lovely, and it helped a lot.'

'Do you want to talk about it?'

'This past week I feel like I've been shredded. Even concepts in the third person hit raw nerves. And when you used me as the example, I felt gutted. I came here thinking I'm very capable at what I do, and able to handle myself. This week has shattered these illusions. I feel stripped naked, incisively dissected, lying there bleeding to death. I lost my belief in myself. I ask myself what you see in me because I feel so devoid of reality.'

'Then, young lady, I would say this past week was very successful. Think back to your first week here, considering this opportunity. Every evening we spoke at length. What you did not realise was those discussions were an intensive interview. You don't yet have the tools to realise what was happening so your guard was down. I would hit you with a concept to see how you would react. It was my evaluation to see if I could work with you. Last week I demolished views you had which would constrain your mind to what is coming. Painful as it was for you, your mind is now open.'

'Let me attempt to introduce some perspective into your concerns. The knowledge I'm presenting to you was gained from two years at Business School, some three to four years finding my way with the help of some very good mentors, and then some thirty years of experience. Let's forget the experience as you cannot teach this. Therefore, it took me some six years to gain the knowledge you're invited to grasp in as many months. You are playing catch-up, but if successful, you will be close to where I was at your age for a company the size of Aldridge.'

'You have the disadvantage you have not experienced a typical corporate environment. Charles and Jim built Aldridge from scratch, neither of them having worked for anyone else in their lives. Their only managerial skills will have been gleaned from their military service. But you cannot argue with their success. I've examined the filed accounts for Aldridge. For such a small company with no formal corporate infrastructure, the turnover is phenomenal, they have substantial land-bank in their fixed assets, no debt, and their profits are consistently good. They also have a very loyal customer base. If Aldridge came to me as a banker for corporate lending my only concern would be the lack of a succession plan. Charles and Jim are fundamental to their success, everyone else is replaceable. This is not good for lending purposes. But they don't need it, so who would ask them to reflect upon these shortcomings as a risk? My guess is Charles totally relies on his auditors for corporate compliance as the Financial Director is only a young guy not long qualified.'

'What I found interesting is the London office is an indulgence in terms of revenues. Charles could close the London office, keep just the existing and significant corporate retail business, resulting in improved cash flow and profit. I would be interested to speak with him to understand his thinking unless it's the usual qualification argument; if we're good enough for the big players, the small player is safe to engage.'

'I have to be careful to stay away from too much corporate structure with you for now as the last thing you need is to go to the office and realise policy and procedure do not comply with what I teach you. Worse still, I don't want you telling Charles what changes are needed because of what you learn from me.

Therefore, I'm concentrating in these initial weeks on your personal development. Thankfully, you are only finding it emotionally tough. Intellectually you appear to be coping well, which means I can move on to the serious philosophy in the coming weeks, starting on Monday. I alerted you from the beginning tears were likely, so don't be embarrassed. I would prefer you to shed tears when you feel the need so we can refresh you and move on. I don't want you to build stress or be brave for the wrong reasons. Does this resonate with you?'

'Put that way, yes, but my huge question is why are you doing this for me? Every time I feel stressed in this process, I rebuke myself for not appreciating your wonderful guidance and care. But why? What's in it for you?'

He thought for a moment. 'Let's say I owe it to someone who gave far more for me. Will this suffice for now?'

She could sense the pain in his words. This was not some frivolous reason. It was real. It was enough for her not to probe further. 'That was heartfelt. I hope one day to deliver for you.'

'If you can do that, I'll be very grateful.'

Chapter 31 – Sunday

Breakfast was a late affair for them, not least because they could not start their walk before 10am.

'We have two choices. We can scale the slopes of Masson Hill to the Heights of Abraham, and return by cable car, or take the cable car up to the top and walk down. Which is your preference?'

'I find it easier to climb than to walk downhill, so my choice is to climb.'

'Okay. We'll leave the car at the base station of the cable car and make our way up. It's a steep climb over stony paths that zig-zag their way up, so be prepared. However, the rewards at the top make the effort worthwhile.'

'Can't wait. Let's go.'

They parked the car, crossed the river Derwent over a footbridge and commenced their climb. After a while they reached the Great Rutland Cavern, a remnant of the lead mining of this area purportedly dating back to Roman times, reaching its heyday in the 17th Century. The colours in the rock face were stunning when lit by a flashlight.

After exploring the cavern, they pressed on up to the summit where they encountered the Victoria Prospect Tower, built by the then out of work lead miners to celebrate the reign of Queen Victoria. The climb had taken over two hours as they reached the base of the tower. They scaled the tower to the top. She moved around the tower marvelling at the spectacular vistas of the Derwent Valley below and the splendour of the surrounding Peak District. She could see two castles.

'Seb, which castles are they?'

He pointed to the Riber Castle, and then to the Willersley Castle.

'Wow, Seb. I'll never question why you chose to live here again. England's green and pleasant land at its best. And smell the air. So clean and fresh. Thank you for showing me this wonderful place. Can we just savour this vision for a while?'

'There's no hurry to get back.'

He watched her as she breathed in the air, filling her lungs again, and again. She was using all her senses to capture every aspect of this captivating place. The tired woman of Friday was now revived and refreshed, knowing her usual respite in London was far away, but she didn't care. This is where she needed to be right now.

Eventually she turned to him with an ear-to-ear smile. 'This is great. Thanks.'

'Are you ready to try the cable car? First alpine cable car in England.'

the Way

She sat in the cable car as it slowly descended across the valley, not knowing where to look. Every angle had a different picture, but which one to prefer?

As they got out of the cable car, she put her arm through his. 'Can I invite my wonderful master to lunch somewhere? It's such a lovely day, so if my master knows of a suitable place where we can eat outside, this would be my preference.'

Having experienced her stress from the past week, he retreated from any further discussion on her progress unless prompted by her. However, he felt he needed to add some perspective to managing stress to ensure she did not descend into despair again. She was now primed for what he knew would be a taxing four weeks of study, and which he wanted her to enjoy. He saw his opportunity whilst enjoying a simple supper.

'Now you're refreshed can I finish this week with some thoughts about managing yourself to know when you need a break, and how to ensure you listen to this requirement. Your reaction on Friday to the stresses of the week suggests you've been testing your resolve to the point of despair. This is not healthy or needed. You were successful in determining you have much to learn, and your mind is now open. But your reaction was depressive negativity rather than positive enthusiasm. You have also experienced taking a break allows you to recharge, albeit imposed by me. Allow me to give you some pointers that will help to apply discipline to your need to take time out to recharge when needed.'

'I'm sorry if I've been a pain. I let everything get to me last week. I guess you would say I'm unrealistic about my current knowledgebase, so I beat up on myself. But thanks for a wonderful weekend. Glad I didn't go back to London. What does my master suggest?'

'You have not been a pain. This weekend has been enjoyable, and I appreciate the opportunity to help you through this distress, not least because we start to study your new business

Week 3

philosophy next week and I need you fresh for this challenge. But I need positive enthusiasm, and you must call time when a break is needed.'

'First, a little philosophy. For others to believe in you, you must believe in yourself. You must differentiate between what you know, and understand what you don't know, but know where to find such knowledge. Thus, your mindset is quiet confidence in your ability, not ego or arrogance. True champions do not have words such as "can't", "impossible", "rules", "status quo", "mistakes", and "convention" in their vocabulary. For them, the impossible merely requires a little thought whereas miracles are within reach with a little application. And there is no room for error. This is the mindset I expect from you going forward.'

'Wow. Back to earth with a bang.' As she hit the table with her hand.

'As for knowing when you need a break, you need to remember what we have already discussed on this subject. When you leave your work each day you must switch off. The way I managed this is very much the same as a football player. They put on their kit to play and switch into play mode. After the game they remove their kit and switch back into normal life. When I put on my suit in the morning, I was ready to play. When I got home and removed my suit, I switched from business to pleasure. You need to find this mindset in a way works for you. One reason I send you to the gym when you arrive home is to give you that switch.'

'You must always remember you have a life. You work to live but must never live to work as you will quickly burn out.'

'The other situation you most certainly need to find your own way to manage is when you feel stressed with your workload. You cannot possibly rely on decisions made when you are physically and/or mentally exhausted. You must discipline yourself to defer any such decisions until you have refreshed and recharged. You may feel pressured by superiors or peers to make decisions under such pressure, but you must defer. I should add what I refer to as stress is severe exhaustion. I'll teach you to manage day-to-day stresses that would otherwise crumble most people.'

'How did you manage such stress?'

'The primary stresses I faced occurred when travelling from office to office across the globe and time zones with little sleep. If I felt I could not function effectively, I located the nearest ClubMed resort and booked myself in for a few days. It was easy to drop off the radar in those days.'

'Did your bank not object to you disappearing without notice?'

'My PA would reschedule my remaining visits. As for my peers and superiors, they knew I would deliver and committed to delivery, so they accepted my behaviour knowing I needed a time-out. With the financial implications of my typical decisions, they respected I would only make them in the best interest of the bank.'

'Phew. On that note I better go to my bed and get myself ready for a tough week. Goodnight. And thanks again for this weekend. I really appreciate how you take care of me.'

Week 4

Chapter 32 – Monday

She arrived for dinner. There was a book next to her place settings on the table. 'The Art of War' by Sun Tzu. 'Sounds a little desperate for the corporate world.' She looked inside the cover. He had written an inscription:
"My Dear Mel.
 If you follow the teachings of Sun Tzu,
and keep this book by you in times of volatility and conflict,
you will find the guidance you need.
Best wishes,
Sebastian.
10th September 1990."
'Powerful words, my master. Who is Sun Tzu?'
'I'm surprised you didn't study him in your philosophy lessons. That book was written as a series of essays around 500 BC and is as relevant today as it was then. Most Western military academies use it as a standard reference book. Major business schools look upon it as a bible for business leaders. We'll study much of his teaching over the coming weeks so you can understand the philosophy and learn how to translate his thinking into everyday business practice.'

'But let's have dinner first so you can tell me about your day.'

She explained the polymer fabrication techniques were gaining momentum, and she would meet with the principal inventor tomorrow to discuss the practical issues of commercial fabrication techniques with these materials.

Dinner finished it was time for study.

'Sun Tzu's essential philosophy is the supreme art of war is to subdue the enemy without conflict. If you think about it this is the ultimate win-win scenario. No costly time and effort, no-one gets hurt, no battle-scarred landscapes to repair, no bitterness to overcome; everyone is happy. We've already discussed the negotiator's win-win scenario where both parties converge to a common acceptance.'

'The great Generals are not those who win lots of battles, but the ones who can prevent carnage by bringing both sides together in peaceful settlement. Great business leaders avoid expensive hostility; they achieve results by consent or superior tactics.'

'Wait a minute. To date, you've been talking about cesspits, sharks, alligators, no morality, conflict and being fitter than your competitor. Now we speak about peaceful settlement. I don't get it.'

'You must be capable of all the strategic and tactical aspects of conflict resolution because you'll not always be able to resolve issues peacefully, but it must be your priority. Don't go looking for a fight if you can avoid it. There will be those who know of your formidable fighting skills and this knowledge will encourage them to submit, desist, or be amenable to a peaceful settlement if you can formulate an acceptable solution. General George Patton told his soldiers on the eve of a significant battle during WWII that the point of war is not to sacrifice your life for your country but rather to force the other dumb bastard to sacrifice their lives for their country. Whereas there is logic to this statement, the choice to engage in battle has to be Plan B.'

'I should probably add a counterbalance to the impression I've given to you. If business is to function effectively and prosperously for society, then ethical morality must be at its core. In theory, the imperialist days of the likes of the East India Company and the American railway barons is over, at least in the Western world. However, this is not my experience, especially in Third World economies with natural resource wealth, corrupt leadership, and cheap labour. Ruthless companies exploit the law, engage in corruption, and anything else which furthers their greed regardless of any moral or social consequences. If you're prepared for the lowest common denominator, if only to ensure you can thwart such behaviour, then you can survive.'

'You will find a multitude of translations specifically targeted towards the corporate executives and managers. I studied the original General Samuel Griffith's 1963 translation which is a qualified academic English interpretation of the original essays, and I prefer to revert to this text when I need to. However, I'll provide you with a simplified interpretation for your studies, especially where the original text contains ambiguities requiring complex interpretation. Like with any language you don't really understand the culture behind the language until you can think in that language; something we will consider when we address the needs of a global executive. For now, we only need to accept that when these essays were written much was described in imagery and allegory coupled with the idealism of Confucius. This combination provokes thought beyond defined conventional thinking. Thus, the text provides hints and suggestions of how to apply his skills to present-day situations.'

'Personally, I find many of the executive translations lose some of this original philosophy as they are audience targeted, but you can purchase the executive version if you want an overview of modern text as applied to the corporate world. In the time available I'll contain our primary study to what you need to understand for small to medium capital companies. We can look at extension to global corporations, time permitting.'

'Executive translations tend to summarise these essays to ten principles for competitive success; typically described as:
- Learn to fight
- Do it right
- Expect the worst
- Burn the bridges
- Pull together
- Show the way
- Know the facts

the Way

- Timing is everything
- Do it better
- Keep them guessing.'

'I don't like the tone of this list. It sounds like a war chant. Typical American approach where they think themselves as the greatest and most powerful nation on earth. Think about the Vietnam War where the Americans adopted the strategy they could outgun and outlast the Vietnamese. Look how that ended. During my career, I've witnessed many head-to-head corporate battles in the USA using this same macho attitude of overestimate your own resilience and underestimating the enemy; most of which ended in tears. The corporate landscape, notably in the USA, is littered with examples of how not to fight wars. Therefore, my own preferred corporate principles are:
- Capture your market without destroying it
- Strike where its least expected
- Invest in the best market information
- Move swiftly to overcome competition
- Employ smart strategies to achieve your goal; and
- Effective leadership is essential to success.'

'We will study each of my preferred principles until you understand what they mean, and how to deploy them.'

'However, we'll study the thirteen essays as presented in the ancient text, probably one each day, so you can understand the underlying philosophy of these principles. Unfortunately, the original text was in an ancient dialect, so we need to examine the essence of what he's saying to attribute the nearest words in our language. The thirteen essays are:
- Estimates
- Waging War
- Offensive Strategy
- Strategic Dispositions
- Strategic Power

Week 4

- Weaknesses and Strengths
- Manoeuvring the Army
- The Nine Variables
- Deploying Troops
- Terrain
- The Ninefold Earth
- Incendiary Attacks
- Using Spies.'

'As you can see these headings relate to military conflicts, but they equally apply to any form of conflict or competitive environment. In the ancient past the Sovereign State secured the resources it needed to prosper and protecting the people. Therefore, Sovereign States had armies to secure wealth, materials, and food from wherever they could find them. Today, the State provides security in the form of armies and intelligence to protect the integrity of the nation, and corporations are the means of securing resources and applying them to the needs of the people and State. But the same rules and philosophy applies, especially where demand exceeds supply or, indeed, supply exceeds demand. Here in the UK we refer to the State as UK plc whereby the management; the Executive of the Government, provides security, healthcare, infrastructure, schooling, laws and other society-based services. They collect the funding they need using taxation. The people are both the stakeholders and the customer. Corporations organise the resources they need to provide the food, goods, and services needed for people to live their lives. They employ people; their army, and they are owned by investors which, if a listed company, includes the people whether directly or through their pension funds.'

'I have translated these essays in relation to corporate activity, but we can apply this philosophy to any activity requiring human resources to co-operate towards a common goal, including individuals. Even organisations such as NGO's and charities need to compete for donations if they are to survive. An

the Way

informal social group seeking new members to achieve a critical mass need to consider how to make membership attractive, and then how to market themselves.'

He handed her printed notes titled *"Estimates (Planning)"*. 'There is no particular order to these essays, and you'll note because of the integrated nature of this philosophy, he repeats some issues across essays, albeit they may be in a different context. Should you try to equate my presentation back to the Samuel Griffith book I have taken liberties to reflect in Sun Tzu's time he speaks of physical armies meeting on a battlefield adopting specific strategies and tactics. In today's world the armies reside in offices and unlikely to confront each other so many strategies and tactics can be deployed simultaneously. I have merged individual verses that deal with specific battlefield tactics to simplify translation. I have also taken liberties to change the wording of some clauses to make them less clumsy to read, and I've omitted his summaries unless I feel the need to recap more complex philosophies. With these exceptions versus should corelate. My intent is to introduce this valuable philosophy and show you how to approach translation.

'Let's start with *"Estimates"* which translates to *"Planning"*; the essential first step to any competitive campaign. I will also attempt to make my interpretations gender neutral for association.'

Sun Tzu says: *War is a matter of vital influence to the State; the province of life or death; the road to survival or ruin. It is mandatory that it be thoroughly studied.*

Translated – A corporate (the State) survives by being competitive. The executive is the instrument of competitiveness. Competition determines who will grow in stature, and who will fade, who succeeds and who fails, who profits and who loses, which companies live, and which die. Therefore, your ability to be competitive determines your power, influence and prosperity, and thus corporate activities need to be carefully planned, and properly executed.

Week 4

Sun Tzu says: *We estimate using five principles to calculate our strategy. These five principles are first is **moral influence**, second is **climate**, the third is **terrain**, the fourth is **leadership**, and the fifth is **doctrine**.*

*By **moral influence** I mean that which causes the people to be in harmony with their leaders, so that they will accompany them in life and unto death without fear of mortal peril.*

Translated - He is referring to the **moral influence** of the corporate. This determines how your employees, customers and investors feel about you, so corporate image is important. If your image is good, then employees will support you with excellence in product and service delivery, and people will purchase what you sell, and thus help you achieve your corporate goal.

'Think of the way corporates such as Apple, Coca Cola, and McDonalds present themselves and their products to the World.'

By **climate** I mean the interaction of natural forces; the effect of winter's cold and summer's heat and the conduct of military operations in accordance with the seasons.

'***Climate*** translates to the political and economic climate that influence your ability to be competitive. If you don't understand and adapt to the current climate, you will not survive. We can split this into primary and secondary influences. Primary influences directly impact your market. Secondary influences are external factors that likely impact your market albeit you need to be aware rather than directly factor into your planning.'

'Your business sector is London and the South-East. Primary influences will be the state of the construction industry in London. Is the market optimistic with the demand for new commercial buildings and can they be delivered at an attractive price relating to market rental income levels? Secondary influences could be the attractiveness of London as a place to be by foreign companies looking to open offices in the UK. How competitive is London regarding rental prices, taxes, communications, transport infrastructure, etc compared with comparable, alternative cities?'

the Way

By **terrain** I mean distances, whether the ground is traversed with ease or difficulty, whether it is open or constricted, and the chances of life or death.

Terrain refers to how well the corporation is organised and managed. Structure and flexibility determine the capability of an organisation to enter and dominate a market.

By **leadership** I mean the General's qualities of wisdom, sincerity, humanity, courage, and strictness.

Leadership translates to the quality of leadership of the organisation. It follows that if you have established quality leadership, then the organisation and management will be lean and fit enough to recognise changing circumstances and to act expediently. The essential qualities of leadership are wisdom, sincerity, humanity, courage, and discipline.

'If you think back to your studies of Confucian Idealism, you'll remember that although society was authoritarian, there was no conscription. A man would not participate in a cause he did not believe to be reasonable or just. To assemble an army the Sovereign and General needed to create belief in the cause before men would be truly committed. Good Generals needed to be great leaders. Likewise, the armies of today, the corporate workers chose who they wish to work for.'

By **doctrine** I mean organisation, control, assignment of appropriate ranks to officers, regulation of supply routes, and the provision of principal items used by the army.

'The doctrine that such a leader will impose is organisation, control, assignment of tasks to the most capable, think the unthinkable; achieve the impossible, i.e. core beliefs. This includes the professional ability of securing facts – the reality of the conditions and circumstances in a competitive situation. Without factual data, you cannot plan properly. Quality information is so important in the decision process even spies are an essential component of the fact gathering methodology. Does this make sense to you?'

Week 4

'Much of it ties back to your rules and philosophies, but on a generic scale rather than individual. Smart cookie this Sun Tzu. I can understand his thinking, and your learned translation. How did he come to light as my understanding is much ancient Chinese philosophy was suppressed by Chairman Mao, especially from around the time of Confucius which is about the same time as Sun Tzu?'

'You're right in that Sun Tzu was a contemporary of Confucius, but I'm sure you studied in Chinese philosophy leadership is about character. The *Art of War* is a spiritual philosophy, not a technical rule manual. His philosophy is based on strength of character, knowledge, wisdom, and insight so thus applies to life as much as to military conflict. Would it surprise you to learn Chairman Mao used this philosophy to unite China? He quoted Sun Tzu frequently. Let's move on.'

Sun Tzu says: *Having paid heed to the advantages of my plans, the General must create situations which will contribute to their accomplishment. By "situations" I mean that he should act expediently in accordance with what is advantageous and so control the balance.*

Translated – Having laid a plan, effective and controlled execution are vital to success. A skilful executive builds the strongest possible team from the resources available. The actions and reactions of the competition reveal how to be smarter. Surprise your opponent with your willingness to quickly adapt to changing circumstances, demonstration of your innovative use of quality information and resources.

Earlier Sun Tzu spoke of five principles that must be included in the planning stage. He then refers to seven elements that can only be applied once the campaign is in progress: essentially thinking on your feet. The following verse refers to these elements, but the principle is what matters.

Sun Tzu says: *All warfare is based on deception. Therefore, when capable, feign incapacity; when active, inactivity. When near, make it appear that you are far away; when far away, that you are near. Offer the enemy a bait to lure him; feign disorder and strike him. When he concentrates, prepare against him; where he is strong, avoid him. Anger his General and confuse him. Pretend inferiority and encourage his arrogance. Keep him under strain and wear him down. When he is united, divide him. Attack where he is unprepared; sally out when he does not expect you.*

Translated – A wise executive knows the art of deception. Never let your opponents know you. Keep them off-balance. Keep your plans disguised and under the radar. Ensure the information they require about you is either not available or is purposely but convincingly erroneous. Disrupt your opponents, indirectly if possible. Divide and conquer where possible. Do what they least expect.

'One of the most effective, and least expensive tactics deployed today is to create discontent, disharmony, confusion, in-fighting and betrayal amongst your competitor's executives. If you can distract them in any of these ways their position will weaken thus victory is yours if exploited effectively.'

Sun Tzu says: *Now if the estimates made in the temple before hostilities indicate victory it is because calculations show one's strength to be superior to that of the enemy; if they indicate defeat, it is because calculations show that one is inferior. With many calculations, one can win; with few one cannot. How much less chance of victory has one who makes none at all! By this means I examine the situation and the outcome will be clearly apparent. When we look at it from this point of view it is obvious who will win the war.*

Translated - The chief executive who plans carefully before engaging with a competitor understands how to leverage their own skills, the strengths of the people around them (executives), and those of the organisation. Every possible response of the opponent must be fully considered ensuring all bases are covered. With careful planning it can be predicted which actions offer the most valuable opportunities. With superior execution of the executive plan valuable opportunities created translate into ultimate success.

'It might be helpful if I recap the essentials. The ability to win a campaign requires leadership with vision who can define and instil quality core beliefs and mission. They must also have reliable information about the marketplace of interest and understand the external influences such as economic and political climate.'

'Before launching a campaign, the leadership must establish the following:

- who is better managed and established on the field of play
- who has the most capable resource base
- who is better positioned to take advantage of the current conditions
- who is better organised and disciplined
- who is stronger both in resources and position
- who is better prepared
- who is more motivated towards success
- what is the likely cost in time and resources.'

'Finally, what strategic advantages exist? Think the unthinkable; think beyond current boundaries. Search for strategic advantages and conditions. Be creative; apply the unexpected. Replace any weakness with strength; training. Examine the situation continuously, analysing the strengths and weaknesses of your competition.'

She was frowning 'I'm beginning to see why you express the need for his teachings to become a way of life for me if I'm to be successful. I still can't understand why we didn't study this philosophy at university. Especially as you call it a bible, and you say this book is a fundamental part of Business School learning. Would you mind if we call it a day so I can quietly read the Forward and the background to these teachings?'

'Good idea. We've finished this essay. Over dinner tomorrow we can deal with any thoughts you have before we move on to the next essay.'

Chapter 33 – Tuesday

Charles had set the meeting for 10am. They all convened in the Boardroom where Charles introduced Dennis Potter, the creator of the polymer materials they were proposing to use in construction fabrication. Mel sat there in such resources under the radar would ensure Aldridge could secure required quantities at attractive prices before the emergence of any competitive demand. And using waste organic materials and the waste ash from power station cooling stacks as core ingredients made it more impressive, not least because of how cheap it all would be. Much was being discussed in the World about recycling waste product. She was now involved in such a process, potentially on a grand scale. Fabrication was becoming exciting for her.

After lunch she couldn't wait to get back to the office with Jim and discuss the opportunities. At the end of this discussion Jim had a satisfied grin. She was hooked. Fabrication was no longer just a job to her. The potential enthused her. She would now learn quickly.

She couldn't wait to tell all to Seb who was fascinated to see her rapid change in attitude to her work. This was both good, but a potential distraction to her other studies. He would need a little careful management to bring her back to the task in hand.

'Now dinner is out of the way how did you get on with your reading last night?'

'Great. It's not the easiest text to read but the background content was fascinating. I'm ready to progress.'

He handed her his translation notes. 'Tonight, we'll study the essay on *Waging War*. As the title suggests this essay is about how to engage in a conflict. However, he focusses more on the consequences of conflict, what not to do, and when not to engage. This follows the doctrine of the ultimate art of war is to win with no expensive conflict.'

'Sun Tzu used a variety of terms for key players. I have adjusted these, so there is a consistency to aid your understanding. A Sovereign will mean the owners of a corporate, such as the shareholders. The General is the corporate CEO. Commanders are the executives, and which can include the CEO. A State is a corporate entity. An army comprises the exceptional resources, as opposed to normal daily corporate activity, specifically assembled to engage in a proposed campaign.'

Sun Tzu says: In order to establish an army, the General needs thousands of chariots, tens of thousands of wagons and carts, and hundreds of thousands of soldiers. Supplies must be transported over thousands of Li. There will be expenses for officers and staff, expense for soldiers, chariots, leather armour, arrows, spears and swords, stipends for the entertainment of advisers and visitors, and expenses for many different things. Thousands of pieces of gold will be expended each day to establish the army.

Translated - In essence, he is saying that to wage any sort of campaign will require resources in both manpower and organisational resources. This applies to any campaign whether a major structural change within your own organisation, the opening of a new office in a foreign country, launching a new product, fighting a hostile action by a competitor, fighting for competitive advantage, and many more events requiring specific resources including takeover bids against a competitor. The greater the scope of the campaign the greater the expenditure of resources. Such resources must be available before launching any such campaign. Thus, step one is to budget the cost of a campaign to determine whether the means justifies the intended aim. If not, the campaign will be difficult to justify.

This puzzled her 'Surely we cannot classify internal issues as a conflict.'

'Human nature is generally averse to change. Major change internally can require the same tactical approach as to external

the Way

conflicts if you want to avoid unnecessary and costly upheaval. The corporate immune system can be a powerful enemy.'

Sun Tzu says: Victory is the main object of war. If this is long delayed, weapons are blunted, and morale depressed. When troops attach cities, their strength will be exhausted.

Translated – Victory is the essence of any conflict. But prolonged conflicts are not only expensive, they will demoralise resulting in exhausted and depleted resources.

She needed clarification 'Do you have any views on what constitutes a prolonged campaign. Are we talking months or years?'

'I generally found you should contain any campaign to no longer than three months, even if you expect it could take longer. I can motivate a resource base of people for three months, but horizons further out in time soon become lost in the haze of daily life. You may know it will take longer but try to break it down into logical units of activity within a three-month horizon. The situation can change in a three-month horizon and thus can influence subsequent activity in any event. Even pregnancy is discussed in terms of three trimesters even though it's known to last nine months.'

'We will return to campaign or project horizons as we progress, especially in relation to technology and IT projects.'

Sun Tzu say: When the army engages in protracted campaigns the resources of the State will not suffice.

Translated - We continue to look at the cost of protracted campaigns. There is no point engaging in a protracted campaign if it completely depletes your own resources.

Sun Tzu says: When your weapons are blunted, and ardour damped, your strength exhausted and treasury spent, neighbouring rulers will take advantage of your distress to act. And even though you have wise counsellors, none will be able to lay good plans for the future.

Translated - He is saying if a campaign weakens you to a point where you become a target from a competitor, no matter how good your plans for the future, you will not be around to see them through.

Sun Tzu says: *Thus, while we have heard of blundering swiftness in war, we have not yet seen a clever operation that was prolonged. For there has never been a protracted war from which a country has benefited.*

Translated - Whilst we know hastily executed campaigns can be troublesome, we have never seen successful campaigns that are protracted. A successful campaign should not be complicated. To win, do simple things well, and quickly. Strategies that are complex, or waste time and exhaust resources have no value.

'Think of both World Wars, and the Vietnam War. What was the cost in resources, and what benefits they achieved? Today there are many protracted civil conflicts throughout the World created from ideology or vested interests of the few but destroying the lives of many innocent people and valuable infrastructure. When they finally end through capitulation or exhaustion who can afford to rebuild the country?'

'You will find many corporate campaigns such as the merger of Agfa and Gevaert around 1964 are classic Business School case studies of ill-considered and protracted campaigns. Both Agfa and Gevaert lost out to Kodak who took full advantage of the situation.'

Sun Tzu says: *Thus, those unable to understand the dangers inherent in employing troops are equally unable to understand the advantageous ways of doing so.*

Translated – Executives who do not understand how to balance risk versus reward dynamics cannot succeed in today's business environment. Planning, speed of execution and innovation are the keys to success. Only those who can manage the uncertainties and ambiguities of rapid execution, i.e. thinking on your feet, can profitably manage delivery of innovative products and services. Only those who understand the

the Way

knowledge gained from over-zealous failure can achieve lasting success.

Sun Tzu says: *Those adept in waging war do not require a second levy of conscripts nor more than one provisioning. They carry equipment from the homeland; they rely on provisions on the enemy. Thus, the army is plentifully provided with food.*

Translated – A skilful executive does not hesitate to fully utilise the resources at their command. Appropriate resources are utilised to engage the competition immediately. They extract precious information from direct contact with valuable contributors. They do not waste time talking to corporate staff or people who are further removed from the competitive situation. Being one step ahead of the competition is worth more than anything else. A wise executive does not need to revise plans because of poor execution.

Sun Tzu says: *When a country is impoverished by military operations it is due to distant transportation; carriage of supplies for great distances renders the people destitute.*

Translation – When an executive fails in competitive operations, it is because of overdependence on poor knowledge and rumour being that body of unchallenged assumptions which everyone thinks of as true. Assumption and rumour exist in every organisation. The value of information offered by people who do not know the market and competition is practically zero, particularly in times of rapid change. Decisions made on such information impoverish the executive and the organisation.

Sun Tzu says: *Where the army is, prices are high; when prices rise the wealth of the people is exhausted. When wealth is exhausted the peasantry will be afflicted with urgent exactions.*

Translated – Prolonged campaigns are expensive. Expect your competitors to wait until they expend your resources before seeking to take advantage. Fortune is won by outstanding performance when the competitor is exhausted.

Week 4

Sun Tzu says: *With strength thus depleted and wealth consumed the households in the central plains will be utterly impoverished and seven-tenths of their wealth dissipated.*

Translated – In a prolonged campaign requiring huge commitment from human resources, moral and enthusiasm will wane significantly reducing their commitment and enthusiasm.

'I can't stress enough the importance of keeping staff motivated. I have witnessed so many campaigns that are ill-conceived, far too ambitious, or totally ignore the impact on the daily lives of their staff. Pushing people for long hours over a protracted period shows complete ignorance of resource management. In my early days as a banker, I had many opportunities to observe this poor leadership in action, especially IT projects. Much of what I'll teach you is derived from the guidance of Sun Tzu and my practical experience learning how to effectively manage resources to maintain commitment and enthusiasm.'

Sun Tzu says: *As to government expenditures, those due to broken-down chariots, worn-out horses, armour and helmets, arrows and crossbows, lances, hand and body shields, draft animals and supply wagons will amount to sixty percent of the total.*

Translated – The most expensive information is that which is out-of-date or erroneous. Sixty percent of the value of information is gained from timeliness and accuracy. Resources spent gathering misinformation are wasted. Relying on misinformation will consume large amounts of funds and manpower.

Sun Tzu says: *Hence the wise general sees to it that his troops feed on the enemy, for one bushel of the enemy's provisions is equivalent to twenty of his; one hundredweight of enemy fodder to twenty hundredweight of his.*

Translated – The wise executive harvests timely information from valuable sources and competitors. One new product idea generated from discussion with real customers is worth any number of ideas generated by consultants or headquarters staff.

the Way

Sun Tzu says: *The reason troops slay the enemy is because they are enraged.*

Translated – In order to dominate competition, resources – from top to bottom – must be passionate about the services they provide and the products they represent.

Sun Tzu says: *They take booty from the enemy because they desire wealth.*

Translated – To capture the spirit of employees, we must offer them defined and valuable rewards. Reward a group for gaining customer share. People should also be able to receive rewards based on individual merit.

Sun Tzu says: *Therefore, when in chariot fighting more than ten chariots are captured, reward those who take the first. Replace the enemy's flags and banner with your own, mix the captured chariots with yours, and mount them.*

Translated – When someone provides outstanding service, reward them openly. Make this service an example for others to follow by providing sure and meaningful rewards for excellence.

Sun Tzu says: *Treat the captives well, and care for them.*

Translated – Treat valuable people who migrate from your competitor well; train them thoroughly. We build the success of the organisation using the combined success of all its members.

Sun Tzu says: *This is called "winning a battle and becoming stronger".*

Translated – This is how you dominate one situation and create the resources to seize the next opportunity.

Sun Tzu says: *Hence what is essential in war is victory, not prolonged operations. And, therefore the General who understands war is the Minister of the people's fate and arbiter of the nation's destiny.*

Translated – The important requirement in competitive operations is quick results, not prolonged activity. The executive who understands how to energise people and dominate a marketplace will become the essence of the company's success.

'To quickly recap on the significant points, the aim of any campaign is swift victory; not wasting time, and certainly not prolonged campaigns. Leaders who completely understand their business and deploy smart strategies control the campaign achieving victory with the minimum of resources and a minimum of damage. Such leaders do not need to regroup, re-plan, or require additional resources to execute their plans.'

'Leaders who do not understand their business or the perils of conflict do not know how to assemble and advantageously deploy appropriate resources.'

'Il-considered prolonged campaigns deplete resources, depress morale, and can bankrupt you, or at least deplete you to the point you become an easy target for another competitor.'

'A successful campaign is measured by its net gains. It's wasteful to capture market advantage but ignore the awe of the simplicity of the process. Her teachings under Seb made her realise planning to secure opportunity to secure the physical and human resources of your competitor needed to support such gain. Gaining competitors and making good use of their resources within your organisation allows you to become stronger and more dominant. Treat such captives well and train them in your ways so they become part of you.'

'So, what do you think we can learn about waging war?'

'If I use your list of corporate principles, I think move swiftly with well-trained resources and smart strategies that can be adapted to changing situations.'

'Well done. Impressive. Your summary fully captures the essence of waging war.'

'My wise master's translation makes it easy for me to understand. I could not derive your translation from the original text. I'm starting to see how you translate, but not there yet. The relevance is clear, even to a junior like me. I'll say goodnight, thank you, and go read this essay again.'

the Way

Chapter 34 – Wednesday

He handed her his translation notes. 'The subject tonight is *Offensive Strategy*. As the title suggests he focusses on winning strategies.'

Sun Tzu says: In general, the best policy is to conquer an entire country intact: to destroy the country is inferior. To capture the enemy's army is better than to destroy it; to take intact a battalion, a company or a five-man squad is better than to destroy them. For to win one hundred victories in one hundred battles is not the acme of skill. To subdue the enemy without fighting is the acme of skill.

Translated – It is better to dominate a market with superior innovation, products, and service than to splinter it with destructive tactics. To destroy a competitor is inferior to gaining their resources intact through takeover. To capture a competitor's market is better than to destroy its reputation; to recruit a competitor's productive employees is better than to put them out of work; to capture a competitor's distribution channels is better than tarnishing their company's image. To win one hundred head-to-head battles with a competitor does not require great skill but is costly. To win the approval of an entire market without competitive battles, i.e. become a sole source provider, is the superior goal. Those who reach this goal do so with a strategy of unrelenting attention to delivery and service. Instead of fighting expensive head-to-head battles, they innovate to create superior products and service.

'Ancient warriors knew how to use their military to defeat the enemy's army, but not in battle. They overpowered the enemy's country, but not by force. The goal was to take things whole. In this way soldiers were not killed, and the sovereign gained the largest booty. Therefore, a general who wins his battles by destroying other armies is not the ultimate warrior. The ultimate warrior is one who wins the war by forcing the enemy to surrender without fighting any battles.'

Week 4

Sun Tzu says: *'The best military strategy, then, is to use superior positioning to attack the enemy's strategy. After that use diplomacy. After that use military force as a threat. Only after all else has failed do you attack your enemy.*

Translated - In essence he is saying that bull at a barn door is no approach to a campaign. It is far better to achieve your aim by consent than by imposition. The ideal strategy is to make a competitor's products or services obsolete through innovation. The next best way is to market yourself more effectively. The next best strategy is to create better ways of providing products and services. Only if these options fail, do you consider confrontation with your competitor.

Sun Tzu says: *The worst policy is to attack cities. Attack cities only when there is no alternative. To prepare the shielded wagons and make ready the necessary arms and equipment requires at least three months; to pile up earthen ramps against the walls an additional three months will be needed.*

Translated – The worst strategy is to attack a competitor's reputation or products directly. We can define this form of strategy as desperation. To engage in destructive competition is ultimately self-defeating. Your aim is to provide superior service which generates high levels of satisfaction in your interest markets. Ruining a competitor's reputation, which takes time and resources, and perhaps destroying your own in the process, is not a productive policy.

Sun Tzu says: *If the General is unable to control his impatience and orders his troops to swarm up the wall like ants, one-third of them will be killed without taking the city. Such is the calamity of these attacks.*

Translated – If an executive cannot control their own impatience and seeks to destroy their competitors by direct attacks, they will waste significant resources accomplishing nothing. The impact of such a strategy is disaster.

Sun Tzu says: *Thus, those skilled in war subdue the enemy's army without battle. They capture his cities without assaulting them and*

the Way

overthrow his state without protracted operations. Your aim must be to take All-under-Heaven intact. Thus, your troops are not worn out and your gain will be complete. This is the art of offensive strategy.

Translated - The skilful executive conquers with knowledge and creative imagination. They create better products; explore and expose unmet needs; unerringly seeks to provide greater satisfaction. They outwit competitors without resorting to head-to-head battles or lengthy campaigns. The aim is to secure interesting markets intact by appearing superior in all respects. Thus, resource requirements will be proportionate, and gains maximised. This is the art of effective competitive strategy.

Sun Tzu says: *Consequently, the art of using troops is this: when ten to the enemy's one, surround him; when five times his strength, attack him; if double his strength, divide him; if equally matched you may engage him; if weaker numerically, be capable of withdrawing; and if in all respects unequal, be capable of eluding him, for a small force is but booty for one more powerful.*

Translation – The philosophy of competitive strategy is this:

If your customer base is already significantly larger than your competitors' press the competition hard through aggressive service. Dominate the situation with your presence. Spend your resources on research and innovation.

If you have twice as many customers, make sure you understand why they are choosing your product and why they might choose your competitors'. Talk with your marketplace. Talk with your competitors' marketplace. Refine and differentiate yourself. How are you different? How are you superior? If you share power and influence equally with your competitors, seek to divide the market into smaller, more profitable niches which you can dominate. Further, seek new markets for existing services. What additional services can you provide? Can you meet needs outside your currently defined marketplace? Look at yourself through fresh eyes.

If you are weaker than your competition in any given market, hold your position if you can, but be prepared to leave in favour of a more profitable market you can dominate. Remember, many advantages flow from dominance. Greater profit is one; better morale is another.

If an existing market is draining your resources, find or create another as fast as you can. A slow death is death nonetheless. And if your products are, in all respects, inferior to your competitors', abandon those markets. Even desire and intense effort cannot overcome fatal flaws. Invest your resources in a more promising situation.

Sun Tzu says: *Now the General is the protector of the State. If this protection is all-embracing the State will surely be strong; if defective, the State will certainly be weak.*

Translated – Executives are leaders charged with the survival and growth of themselves and their organisation. If a leader is smart and courageous, they and their organisation will surely prosper and grow. If a leader is passive and weak, they and their organisation will surely die. Success or failure depends upon leadership.

Sun Tzu says: *Now there are three ways in which a Ruler can bring misfortune upon his army: when ignorant that the army should advance, to order an advance or ignorant that it should not retire, to order a retirement. This is described as "hobbling the army"; when ignorant of military affairs, to participate in their administration. This causes the officers to be perplexed; when ignorant of command problems to share in the exercise of responsibilities. This engenders doubts in the minds of the officers.*

Translation – Here we are considering the influence of a superior (Ruler) who is not directly involved in the conflict. A high-ranking executive, owner, or shareholder can cause trouble for themselves and their organisation in three ways, namely:

First, they can cause serious problems by acting out of ignorance. For instance, not understanding when to avoid competitive actions they cannot win. Or, when winning in ongoing competitive actions, they fail to see opportunity. High-

the Way

ranking executives who issue orders without first-hand knowledge hobble themselves.

Second, they can cause problems by focusing on rules rather than customers. When procedure-minded executives attempt to govern company actions with cumbersome rules, employees are confused, and customer service suffers. Organisations whose purpose is to provide service for their own sake rather than for the sake of the customer (e.g. Governments) can afford burdensome rules since customer service is not a priority. Aggressiveness, flexibility, and creativity, however, govern innovation and growth. An effective executive must thrive on uncertainty and ambiguity.

Third, they can cause problems by promoting those lacking skill and courage. When an executive is appointed to a position of authority based on factors unrelated to ability, employees become sceptical and suspicious. This inevitably lowers employee morale. Good leadership is everything. Authority must reside in the hands of those who can lead.

Sun Tzu says: *If the army is confused and suspicious, neighbouring Rulers will cause trouble. This is what is meant by the saying 'a confused army leads to another's victory'.*

Translated – If employees are confused and demotivated by the actions of a high-ranking executive, competitors will steal their markets. Internal weakness gives strength to competitors.

Sun Tzu says: *Now there are five circumstances in which victory may be predicted. He who knows when he can fight and when he cannot, will be victorious. He who understands how to use both large and small forces will be victorious. He whose ranks are united in purpose will be victorious. He who is prudent and lies in wait for an enemy who is not, will be victorious. He whose Generals are able and not interfered with by the Sovereign will be victorious. It is these five matters that the way to victory is known.*

Translated – Five indicators predict who will dominate:

A leader who knows when to fight, and when to wait, will win.

Week 4

A leader who uses resources appropriate to the challenge will win.

A leader who is enthusiastic and innovative will win.

A leader who uses accurate, timely information to make decisions will win.

A leader not burdened by onerous rules or troublesome staff will win.

Sun Tzu says: *Therefore, I say know the enemy and know thyself; in a hundred battles, you will never be in peril. When you are ignorant of the enemy but know yourself, your chances of winning or losing are equal. If ignorant both of your enemy and of yourself, you are certain in every battle to be in peril.*

Translated – If you know your markets, your competitors, and yourself, your strategies will not fail, even if you're challenged a hundred times. If you know yourself only, but are ignorant of your markets or your competitors, you can expect to fail as often as you succeed. If you are ignorant of yourself, in addition to your markets and competitors, you will fail every time.

'To recap the essential message is the most valuable victories are those achieved by consent, not conflict. Your first aim is to convert competition into allies. If this is not possible, then your first step is to attack their strategy. Then disrupt their alliances. Only if these steps fail do you consider conflict, but never against strength.'

'Always pitch strength against weakness. Know yourself and your strengths; compare these with your competition. If you are weaker either strengthen your resource base; or defer. Know when you can be on the offensive; and when you need to be defensive. Be prepared.'

'And finally, campaigns should only be managed by those with extensive knowledge and experience. External interference from above should be avoided; or ignored. Ensure your mandate to campaign is robust.'

'That's it. Any thoughts?'

the Way

'Much of this relates back to your initial teaching. Know yourself; know your enemies; and know your market. Then apply self-discipline and cunning to wait for opportunity. Define your strategy, believe in yourself, and surround yourself with the best resources available before engaging. All makes good sense.'

'Not bad. Can you see how to apply his wisdom to your work?'

'I will ensure that I adopt this philosophy as I realise that I will encounter situations where I will need such discipline, even at a non-executive level.'

Chapter 35 – Thursday

They were sitting having dinner. 'I would like to stay here this weekend, although I'll pop down to visit mum on Saturday. As we're studying a whole essay per evening, I need some time to digest this new world for me.'

'No problem. We'll not start a new essay tomorrow in any event. I agree that there is much to absorb so we can use tomorrow evening for any recaps you may need, or just relax. You can also use your train journeys as quiet reading time. You're welcome to join me with some tennis club members for dinner on Saturday evening should you have need of a little respite.'

'Thanks. It will be nice to socialise with real people.'

'Our discussion tonight is *Strategic Dispositions* or *Positioning* which concerns itself with the need for flexibility to sense opportunity.'

Sun Tzu says: Ancient great warriors first made themselves invincible. Then they awaited the enemy's moment of vulnerability. Not to be conquered depends on oneself; to conquer depends on the action of the enemy. Thus, those skilled in war can always remain unvanquished, but the enemy may not be vulnerable. Therefore, one who cannot conquer, defends. But one who can conquer, attacks.

Translated – Effective executives position themselves and their products and services in situations where they will survive attack. Then they wait for an opportunity to act on a vulnerability within a competitor. Survival depends upon careful defence; the opportunity to beat competition depends on the action of others. Therefore, while an effective executive can always manage to survive, they may not necessarily be able to engage a competitor. Only attack a competitor when you are capable of victory.

Sun Tzu says: Ancient warriors were not victorious through infinite wisdom or through boundless courage. Rather, ancient warriors made no mistakes. Every strategy foretold victory. Thus, those who defended well hid in the deepest recesses of the ninefold earth. Those who attacked well struck from the highest reaches of heaven. By waiting for the enemy's vulnerability, they surely triumphed.

Translated – Successful executives do not necessarily have extraordinary wisdom, or reckless courage. They are competent at positioning themselves and their organisation where they cannot be attacked, miss no chance to exploit opportunities presented by their opponents, and do not make mistakes.

Sun Tzu says: To foresee a victory which the ordinary man can foresee is not the acme of skill. To triumph in battle and be universally acclaimed "expert" is not the acme of skill, for to lift an autumn down requires no great strength; to distinguish between the sun and moon is no test of vision; to hear the thunderclap is no indication of acute hearing. Anciently those called skilled in war conquered an enemy easily conquered. And, therefore the victories won by a master of war gain him neither reputation for wisdom nor merit for valour for he wins his victories of an enemy already defeated. Therefore, the skilful commander takes up a position in which he cannot be defeated and misses no opportunity to master his enemy. Thus, a victorious army wins its victories before seeking battle; an army destined to defeat fights in the hope of winning.'

the Way

Translated – To foresee victory considered a foregone conclusion does not indicate superior capability. To achieve victory through embarrassing confrontation or emotional exploitation takes no great skill. Effective executives win victories that appear easy but only because of skilful foresight, planning, and execution rendering competition already defeated.

Sun Tzu says: *Those skilled in war cultivate moral influence, preserve the laws and are therefore able to formulate victorious policies.*

Translated – Competent executives take the moral high ground and formulates strategies within the law that may be challenged but not broken.

Sun Tzu says: *Now the elements of the art of war are first, measurement of space; second, estimation of quantities; third, calculations; fourth, comparisons; and fifth, chance of victory. Measurements of space are derived from the ground. Quantities derive from measurement, figures from quantities, comparisons from figures, and victory from comparisons. Thus, a victorious army is as a hundredweight balanced against a grain; a defeated army as a grain balance against a hundredweight. It is because of disposition that a victorious General is able to make his people fight with the effect of pent-up waters which, suddenly released, plunge into a bottomless abyss.*

Translated – Successful executives understand the art of war, position themselves and their organisations to withstand attack, positions themselves to dominate their market, identify and exploits opportunities provided by the competition, and ensures their people and resources are committed, innovative, and well trained and motivated to meet any challenge.

'Any questions?'

She considered for a moment. 'All very clear and informative. As always, the translation by my master makes the complexity of the original text readily understandable. I could not envisage being remotely capable of such translation. Possibly why it is not so well known; it needs considerable knowledge to interpret. Is that it for today as I would like to quietly consider the teachings of this week? New world for me. I need to let it sink in.'

'We've finished; and thank you for your attention this week. It can't be easy for you to take this punishment after absorbing the needs of your new role at Aldridge during the working day.'

She looked shattered. 'It is a little overwhelming, but as Sun Tzu says I must take advantage of every opportunity to position myself to be a successful executive.'

They both laughed as she gathered her notes and departed for her room. 'Good night'.

Chapter 36 – Friday

Mel arrived home tired but satisfied she had made real progress both at work and in her studies. She found the Sun Tzu teachings a little overwhelming at the beginning but now had a good grasp of the philosophy. Describing this philosophy to Jim over lunch each day helped her confidence in her grasp of the fundamentals. And she was now hooked on fabrication. Progress indeed.

Having completed her gym session, she arrived for dinner to find a glass of wine ready for her. Life was good. A lovely dinner, and a long soak in her bath with a glass of wine would provide a fitting respite to the revelations of Sun Tzu. Her confidence in her journey was growing. It was not a labour. It was stimulating.

Chapter 37 – Weekend

Mel left early for London to see her mum. She drove to Derby station to catch her train to London as she wanted to shop in the Derby centre shopping mall on her way back.

She arrived back at Merton happy with her day, took a swim, and readied herself for dinner with Seb and his tennis friends; the first socialising in Matlock since commencing her development program. She wanted to wear a dress but settled for slacks and a top to stay with Seb's casual approach.

Breakfast was late on Sunday morning as it was nearly midnight when they returned from dinner. It was such a lovely day Mel took a walk in the grounds taking her notes with her before succumbing to her weekly painful combat training followed by tennis in the afternoon. At least she now knew other tennis club members and thus not an outsider anymore.

Week 5

Chapter 38 – Monday

Charles popped in to see her. He saw a book on her desk.
'*The Art of War*. Can I take a peek?'
She looked up at him, 'Sure.'
He read the inscription by Seb. 'Wow, some recommendation. Is this what you're studying?'
'Yes, three, maybe four weeks on just this philosophy. But it's really interesting, especially when translated into the corporate world by Seb. Can't believe it was written around 2,500 years ago, but still as relevant today as it was then. This guy, Sun Tzu, knew his business.'
'How do you study it?'
'There are thirteen essays, so we study one each evening with the proviso if I haven't completely understood the significant aspects, then we stay with that essay the following evening. He gives me a handout,' pointing to the pile underneath the book 'which has the original text followed by Seb's translation of the essence of the Sun Tzu text to show me how to translate the original text.'
'He obviously thinks this book is significant. Do you think I should study it?'
'To him this book is a bible of corporate game play. I'm starting to appreciate why. Apparently, it's required study at most major Business Schools. Why don't you come along one evening and sit in? I think you'd enjoy his approach to translating the original text into corporate strategy and tactics.'
'Do you think Sebastian will mind my intrusion?'
'Of course not. Would you like me to set it up? Come to dinner, after which we study for about two hours.'

the Way

'I would like to see how he teaches you. Could we say tomorrow evening as I need to get an evening pass from Edna?'

She smiled at this thought 'I'll let him know this evening. Might be fun to see how a canny businessman like you reacts to the text.'

'Can I borrow the book? I'll send Mary out to get a copy.'

'No problem. Seb has more copies if you can't find one. There are books that already translate the original text into modern day corporate language if that would work better for you. Seb prefers to work with the original text, but you need to know how to translate it.'

'I'll get her to get both. Thanks. Never too old to learn.'

'I can also get another copy of Seb's translation notes if you like.'

'Let me start with the books and we can go from there. Thanks.'

'Did you want something?'

'Ah, yes. Can you give me specs of some of the fabrication requirements for Teresa Yardley? I want Denis Potter to study them to see if they will work in polymer material, and how we could make them.'

'No problem. Have them on your desk this afternoon.'

'Thanks Mel. Jim will be in around lunchtime. He had a bad night.'

'Sorry to hear that. I'll treat him gently this afternoon.'

....

When she arrived home, she informed Seb about the request from Charles to sit in on tomorrow's lesson and has sent Mary out to buy the book. He would join them for dinner at 7:30.

The thought of teaching a canny businessman like Charles amused Seb. 'Should be interesting to see how he reacts to such teachings. Shall we progress? Tonight, we'll study the essay called *Energy* or as I prefer to call it, *Strategic Power* which explains how to organise your company to appear far stronger than your competitor. We see this in the animal kingdom where a male will have features that make them look bigger and stronger than the competition. It's better if the show of strength is real, but deception can be just as effective.'

'When we discuss organisation management, I'll illustrate why multi-layered organisations find it difficult to respond quickly to change or competition. The flatter the organisation the easier to manage, and faster to respond to changing requirements.'

Sun Tzu says: *Generally, management of many is the same as management of few. It is a matter of organisation. And to control many is the same as to control few. This is a matter of formation and signals.*

Translated – A clearly defined organisational structure with good management ensures no matter what size the organisation it will operate effectively. The larger the organisation, the more important the need for effective chains of command and internal communications.

'I would add the flatter the structure, the better. The more layers the longer communication takes and the more likely communication will be distorted. Think of the circle of people where you inform one in the loop of a piece of information with the instruction to convey this information to the person next to them. The more times it's repeated, the more likely it will change its form.'

Sun Tzu says: *That the army is certain to sustain the enemy's attack without suffering defeat is due to operations of the extraordinary and the normal forces.*

Translated – To sustain a competitor attack a competent executive will activate both orthodox and unorthodox responses which are intended to create a deterrent even if a false perception of the ability to respond.

Sun Tzu says: *Troops thrown against the enemy as a grindstone against eggs is an example of a solid acting upon a void.*

Translated - When capable executives dominate a situation, it is because they create opportunity and understand timing. They know how to demonstrate strength and apparent weakness, reality and illusion. Competitors are confused as to where or what to defend.

Sun Tzu says: *Generally, in battle, use the normal force to engage; use the extraordinary to win.*

Translated – In competitive situations, conventional tactics are normally used to confront the opponent. But it is the opportunity created by unexpected tactics, i.e. innovative use of people and information, that makes victory certain.

'Perhaps it would be useful to differentiate between extraordinary and normal forces. Let me create a picture in your mind using a military example. In the UK we have the regular army supported by elite forces such as the SAS and Royal Marine Commandos. They use the elite forces in small groups in fast covert strikes to disrupt the enemy by cutting supply routes such as bridges and railways, mislead the enemy where to attack, or even to take out the command centre. Spies can also plant false information to the enemy. This disruption reduces the effectiveness of the enemy and thus allows the regular army to be successful with fewer losses. When we progress to real corporate examples using my six headings remind me to discuss Sir Gordon White's hostile takeover of Smith-Corona in 1986 because it was a classic application of this Sun Tzu philosophy.'

'One other point whilst I think of it. When using elite forces to destroy or disrupt supply chains, the wise General will avoid destroying the capability of the enemy to retreat. Sun Tzu is very clear the enemy must always be allowed to retreat honourably. During the Dunkirk evacuation of allied forces in 1940 Hitler made the mistake of continuing to attack the allied forces and the boats effecting the evacuation rather than surround the beach but allow the beaten allied forces to retreat honourable. Many considered Dunkirk a humiliation, but I've spoken with a soldier who survived the evacuation in June that year. This disgraceful attempted annihilation of allied forces by Hitler had the opposite effect; it put fire into the bellies of the allied forces to strike back, which successfully occurred exactly four years later in 1944. In

Week 5

the corporate world once victory is yours allow your competitor a graceful retreat as this could well lead to a friendly takeover leading to a much-enlarged market share.'

Sun Tzu says: *Now the resources of those skilled in using extraordinary forces are as infinite as the heaven and earth; as inexhaustible as the flow of the great rivers. For they end and recommence; cyclical, as are the movements of the sun and moon. They die away and are reborn; recurrent, as are the passing seasons. The musical notes are only five in number, but their melodies are so numerous that one cannot hear them all. The primary colours are only five in number, but their combinations are so infinite that one cannot visualise them all. The flavours are only five in number, but their blends are so various that one cannot taste them all.*

Translated – This paragraph is a very clear example of how Sun Tzu uses both imagery and allegory to ensure his meaning is clear. He uses music, painting, and cooking to depict the senses of hearing, sight, taste, and smell. He is saying if you freely use all your know-how, instincts and senses you have an infinite variety of options available to you. Rid yourself of status quo, ideology, conventional wisdom, and dogma. Let your mind absorb information from wherever it is found and think the unthinkable to develop unexpected tactics. The executive who is skilful at using creative and innovative tactics has infinite resources with which to confound competition.'

Sun Tzu says: *In battle, there are only the normal and extraordinary forces, but their combinations are limitless, none can comprehend them all. For these forces are mutually reproductive; their interaction as endless as that of interlocking rings. Who can determine where one ends, and the other begins?*

Translated – Competition between organisations and the marketplace gives rise to opportunities for both conventional and exceptional tactics. The possibilities provided by the innovative use of people and information is limitless. Conventional and exceptional tactics create one another in the ebb and flow of conflict, like a circle which has no start or

the Way

endpoint. Your opponents cannot tell where one tactic ends, and another begins.

Sun Tzu says: *When torrential water tosses boulders, it is because of momentum. When the strike of the hawk breaks the body of its prey, it is because of timing. Thus, the momentum of one skilled in war is overwhelming, and his attack precisely regulated. His potential is that of a fully drawn crossbow; his timing, the release of the trigger.*

Translated – When your resource base is honed into a powerful force, it is capable of overwhelming an opponent. For the skilled executive, opportunity is like a missile launchpad; timing is the trigger that will shoot a missile with deadly accuracy. Competition is put under intense pressure before unleashing overwhelming power with unfailing results.

Sun Tzu says: *In the tumult and uproar the battle seems chaotic, but there is no disorder; the troops appear to be milling about in circles but cannot be defeated. Apparent confusion is a product of good order; apparent cowardice, of courage; apparent weakness, of strength. Order or disorder depends on organisation; courage or cowardice on circumstances; strength or weakness on dispositions.*

Translated – In the chaos of organisational conflict or a competitive marketplace, the skilled executive recognises patterns in the activities of rivals, while apparently using their own resources randomly, appearing to move in disorganised circles, but cannot be defeated. Apparent disorder comes from expert organisation. Creating an illusion of fear comes from great courage. Seeming strength and weakness comes from confidence.

Sun Tzu says: *Thus, those skilled at making the enemy move do so by creating a situation to which he must conform; they entice him with something he is certain to take, and with lures of ostensible profit they await him in strength. Therefore, a skilled commander seeks victory from the situation and does not demand it of his subordinates. He selects his men and they exploit the situation.*

Translated – An effective executive, skilful at manoeuvring competitors in competitive situations, creates favourable

Week 5

opportunities by luring his competitors into vulnerable positions with the promise of easy gains. There he waits with overwhelming power derived from combining the conventional with the extraordinary; the obvious with the innovative. In this way the wise executive creates victory through their own initiative. They do not depend on others for success. They select the most appropriate resources to execute their purpose at the critical moment.

Sun Tzu says: *He who relies on the situation uses his men in fighting as one rolls logs or stones. Now the nature of logs and stones is that on stable ground they are static; on unstable ground, they move. If square, they stop; if round, they roll. Thus, the potential of troops skilfully commanded in battle may be compared to that of round boulders which roll down from mountain heights.*

Translated – If your people are not well organised and motivated, they cannot readily react to situations. Resources must be organised and honed for action at all times. Thus, a skilful executive creates a powerful resource base capable, at the right moment, to hurl at his competitor with overwhelming force.

'Any problems before I recap?'

'I'll tell you after your recap.'

'His first verses refer to building a sound organisational structure. Regardless of size use the same fundamental principles of structure and management. The control of any corporate is a function of effectiveness of organisation and internal communications.'

'Then he discusses the application of overwhelming power against competition – whether real or deception. He talks about conventional, or direct force to confront an opponent. The force used to strike at the weaknesses of an opponent he refers to as extraordinary, or indirect force. Keeping your opponent confused about your plan of attack is the key to success. Know when you can apply strength against weakness. If you confront

the Way

with direct force, and engage weakness using deceptive indirect force, your opponent will not know where to defend.'

'Finally, he speaks of coordinating momentum and timing. Essentially your actions must have the energy of momentum delivered at the most advantageous time. Effective organisation will maintain order amidst apparent confusion. Good planning will create favourable circumstances; and maintain high morale. Your strength or weakness is a function of such planning. Quality leadership will unite the people and resources creating the energy and momentum for victory.'

'Powerful stuff, my master. Build your resource base into a bulldozer, catch your opponent off-guard, and bulldoze them away.'

'Sounds like you've got it. Enough for this evening unless you want more.'

'Time to reflect. Goodnight.'

Chapter 39 – Tuesday

Charles had joined them for dinner. 'This food is delicious. No wonder your German executive lady speaks so highly of this place. Before we start Mel's study what is it about this Sun Tzu that make you regard the *Art of War* as a bible for executives? I've read the introduction, and a piece from an exec translation so I get the context, but who was this guy, and why so revered?'

'The story goes that, having read the thirteen essays, Ho Lu, the King of Wu, wanted to know if his ideas could be applied universally. With Sun Tzu's assurance they could, the King asked if this included women. Again, he received assurance from Sun Tzu this was possible. The King ordered the 180 women who lived in the palace to be brought outside where it was agreed Sun Tzu would train them in military drill.'

'Sun Tzu split them into two companies, each one headed by a favourite concubine of the King. The women did not take the exercise seriously and were soon in fits of laughter at the drill they were asked to perform. Sun Tzu tried more orders, but to no avail. He took the view, as his orders were clear, there was no discipline in the ranks. He announced something to the effect that if the commands are not clear, then it is the fault of the General. But if the orders are clear and the soldiers disobey, then it is the fault of the officers. He ordered the two lead concubines beheaded. The King protested, but Sun Tzu reminded the King he was the General, and the discipline of the army was his responsibility. He then appointed the next two women in line as platoon commanders and restarted the drill process. This time the fearful women performed the drill perfectly without a sound. Sun Tzu informed the King his women's army was ready to serve. The awestruck King appointed Sun Tzu as his General, and he went on to win many great victories for his Sovereign.'

'His man management may have been brutal, but he demonstrated a clear and strong line of command can create a loyal and motivated force capable of anything. Although I was never allowed to behead anyone, I did not tolerate any breaches of discipline, give favour, or carry anyone, yet I had very happy, loyal, and capable staff. I had a simple objective; if they take care of me, I'll take care of them.'

'But why compare business to war? I've done both and I know which I prefer.'

'The *Art of War* is essentially a paradox because the objective is to win without conflict. But sometimes it requires the threat of a conflict to focus people. Let me paraphrase some lines I heard in a movie. *A war demands clarity. It brings people together with a common purpose where everyone knows their part.* General George Paton told his troops on the eve of battle in WWII that the point of war was not to sacrifice your life for your country, but rather to force the other dumb bastards to sacrifice their lives for their country. If you are forced into conflict this would be very Sun Tzu.'

'If we think about why something declared as a classic deserves such accolade, we need to consider why it continues to resonate with people throughout the ages. When I first encountered the *Art of War* in the 1970s the world was a different place compared to today. We did not have the global village or the technology we have today. The world was still a place of distant lands and disharmonious cultures. Today markets and cultures are far more aligned and integrated. My translation today is somewhat different to that in the 1970s albeit the underlying philosophy is still as relevant. Thus, my preference to refer to the 1963 text as it's not clouded by reinterpretation – it maintains its original purity. If we think about contemporary interpretations of the plays of Shakespeare, we see they're presented in the context of the modern world, but they do not change any of the words of the play as they're as relevant today as they were when written. Does this make any sense to you?'

Charles thought for a moment 'I get the Shakespeare bit as I've attended a few contemporary performances. I guess what you're saying is we analyse the text in context to the current environment and it will make good sense. Amazing.'

Seb gave him a moment and then continued 'In business you fight for survival irrespective of whether you are the protagonist or the victim. Indeed, you can be both at the same time. Leadership and focus are essential, just as with an army, if you are to survive. Surely you have faced battles during your business career?'

'I suppose that's true. After the war it was possible for anyone with an enterprising spirit to build a business, especially in the construction sector, because there was so much to do to rebuild the country. By the mid-1950s the workload reduced, so we did fight for our share of the business available. Many failed. By the 1970s it became cut-throat. Many businesses either merged, sold to the big construction companies, or died. Although we had some lean years, we survived by building good relationships, produced a quality product at the right price, and could survive the recession storms because we had no shareholders breathing down our necks.'

'Perhaps it would help if I give you a summary of the thirteen essays, and the approach to interpretation. Each essay contains a thorough analysis of the political, psychological, and material factors involved in conflict but, in Taoist terms, we can achieve success as much by not doing, as doing – Yin and Yang. So you could say the Art of War, as per Sun Tzu, is as much about knowing what not to do and when not to do it as it is knowing what to do and when to do it in order to achieve success in your objectives.'

'The first essay, Estimates, describes the importance of strategy, planning, and budgeting – the processes any executive undertakes to determine the pros and cons of any proposed strategy.'

'The second essay, Waging War, stresses the consequences of conflict. He emphasises speed over protracted campaigns and stresses the importance of conservation of energy and material resources. Consuming vast quantities of resource in conflict is not a winning way.'

'The third essay, Offensive Strategy, concentrates on planning a campaign. Again, the emphasis is to avoid conflict. Neutralise your competition by foiling their plans and rendering them helpless. Make yourself invincible. Preserve as many resources as possible on both sides. No point conquering if you have destroyed the value.'

'The fourth essay, Strategic Dispositions, defines the need for adaptability and inscrutability. Be formless. See vulnerability and act quickly to seize the opportunity.'

'The fifth essay, Strategic Power, describes the use of momentum to overpower. Use the unity of purpose and coherence of the organisation to appear invincible. Utilise both orthodox and guerrilla warfare with infinite variations of tactics to confuse and destroy your enemy. This includes psychological warfare.'

'The sixth essay, Weaknesses and Strengths, and the one we will study this evening, describes the need to drain the strength of your opponent whilst conserving your own. Test your opponent to gauge their resources and capabilities whilst not revealing your own. Make them chase shadows. Divide and conquer.'

'The seventh essay, Manoeuvring the Army, deals with attacking weakness; not strength. How to avoid exposing yourself. When to strike, and when to walk away.'

'The eighth essay, The Nine Variables, is mostly about leadership, and the qualities of a capable leader. This permeates down to the quality and discipline of the resources available to a leader.'

'The ninth essay, Deploying Troops, concerns itself with how to approach conflicts. He speaks of favoured terrain and conditions. Containing your own resource base to hold the line irrespective of the action of the opponent. Await your moment. How to use psychology to overcome a stronger opponent. Much again about leadership.'

'The tenth essay, Terrain, continues to consider tactical manoeuvring and adaptability, but in respect of the environment in which you find yourself; the need for discipline and good intelligence being fundamental to how to conduct yourself in various situations. This is very much about know yourself and know your enemy.'

'The eleventh essay, The Ninefold Earth, speaks of various encounters, from a brief skirmish to large encounter and defines the way to resource and manage each situation. Human nature plays a major part in managing each encounter.'

'The twelfth essay, Incendiary Attacks, is more about the need for compassion when using destructive fire power. He warns against using excessive and destructive force unnecessarily, citing a nation destroyed cannot be restored, nor the dead restored to life. Conflicts should not be born from anger or provoked from wrath.'

'The thirteenth and final essay, Using Spies, describes the fundamental need for spies, and the various types of spies that can be utilised. He also describes how such spies should be managed and rewarded.'

'The reason these essays have survived and are so revered is they are a comprehensive political, psychological, and practical approach to conflict, and how to avoid it.'

'Why don't we use tonight's session to demonstrate this? It's the essay regarding weaknesses and strengths.' He passed a copy of his handout for this session to both Charles and Mel. 'In this handout you will find a copy of the original text followed by my translation of the essence of the text as applied to the corporate world. I'll read out loud the original text and my translation. We can then explore each paragraph as you require.'

Sun Tzu says: *Generally, he who occupies the field of battle first and awaits his enemy is at ease; he who comes later to the scene and rushes into the fight is weary. And, therefore those skilled in war bring the enemy to the field of battle and are not brought by him.*

Translated – Those who thoroughly prepared for conflict from wherever it comes are at ease with their state of readiness. Those who are unprepared can be rushed and exhausted. A skilful executive anticipates conflict ready to respond, never allowing competition the advantage of surprise.

Sun Tzu says: *One able to make the enemy come of his own accord does so by offering him some advantage. And one able to prevent him from coming does so by hurting him.*

Translated – A skilful executive lures their competition to advance by offering them apparent advantage; but prevents his competition from attacking by revealing apparent disadvantage. Hence, competition advances only when a skilful executive is prepared.

Sun Tzu says: *When the enemy is at ease, be able to weary him; when well fed, to starve him; when at rest, make him move. Appear at*

the Way

places to which he must hasten; move swiftly where he does not expect you.

Translated – A capable executive keeps his rivals on the move, and in the dark as to why. If a competitor is comfortable; create difficulties. If a competitor is satisfied, stimulates dissatisfaction. If a competitor is calm; create agitation. The skilled executive acts where the competition must rush to defend; and penetrates where his competitors least expects.

Sun Tzu says: *That you may march a thousand li without wearying yourself is because you travel where there is no enemy.*

Translated – A skilful executive positions his resources with ease because he occupies territory not contested by others.

Sun Tzu says: *To be certain to take what you attack is to attack a place the enemy does not protect. To be certain to hold what you defend is to defend a place the enemy does not attack. Therefore, against those skilled in attack, an enemy does not know where to defend; against the expert in defence, the enemy does not know where to attack.*

Translated – An effective executive's offensive attacks positions competitors cannot defend; thus successful. An effective executive's defensive positions never fail because they are, or projected to be too strong to be attacked. Against such a skilled attacker, the competition does not know which positions to defend; against such a skilled defender, the competition does not know which positions to attack.

Sun Tzu says: *Subtle and insubstantial, the expert leaves no trace; divinely mysterious, he is inaudible. Thus, he is master of his enemy's fate.'*

Translated - The best strategies are subtle. They have no discernible form. The best strategies are kept secret so they cannot be discovered. Formless and invisible; one can control a competitor's destiny.

Sun Tzu says: *He whose advance is irresistible plunges into his enemy's weak positions; he who in withdrawal cannot be pursued moves so swiftly that he cannot be overtaken.*

Week 5

Translated – When a skilled executive applies pressure to his competition, he focusses on weak positions. If in withdrawal; leaves no discernible weak positions.

Sun Tzu says: *When I wish to give battle, my enemy, even though protected by high walls and deep moats, cannot help but engage me, for I attack a position he must succour.*

Translated – If all considerations indicate it is time to attack a competitor, even when this competitor hides behind a large reputation or a closed door, the competitor is forced to respond if an important issue or a critical market is threatened.

Sun Tzu says: *When I wish to avoid battle I may defend myself simply by drawing a line on the ground; the enemy will be unable to attack me because I divert him from going where he wishes.*

Translated - If it's not the right time for an encounter, even if a competitor postures and threatens, a competitor can do no harm if no obvious target is available to aim at.

Sun Tzu says: *If I am able to determine the enemy's disposition while at the same time I conceal my own then I can concentrate, and he must divide. And if I concentrate while he divides, I can use my entire strength to attack a fraction of his. There, I will be numerically superior. Then if I am able to use many to strike few at the selected point, those I deal with will be in dire straits.*

Translated – Effective executives stress the competition whilst retaining their own freedom. They divide and disrupt the competition while keeping themselves intact. They distract the competition while remaining focussed. Hence, they are able to use many resources to pressure positions which are supported with fewer resources. They create overwhelming leverage. They concentrate strength against weakness.

Sun Tzu says: *The enemy must not know where I intend to give battle. For if he does not know where I intend to give battle he must prepare in a great many places. And when he prepares in a great many places, those I have to fight in any one place will be few. For if he prepares to the front his rear will be weak, and if to the rear, his front will be fragile. If he prepares to the left, his right will be vulnerable, and*

the Way

if to the right, there will be few on his left. And when he prepares everywhere he will be weak everywhere.

Translated – The less a competitor knows about where you intend to focus your attention, the stronger you are. If a competitor is forced to spread resources to meet your challenge, each position will be weaker. If a competitor strengthens one position, they likely weaken another. If they strengthen the support for one product, they likely weaken another. If they concentrate on one position, they likely undermine others. If they try to strengthen all positions, they will likely weaken every position – essentially divide and conquer.

Sun Tzu says: *One who has few must prepare against the enemy; one who has many makes the enemy prepare against him.*

Translated – You are strong if you cause the competition to react to you; you are weak if you must react to the competition.

Sun Tzu says: *If one knows where and when a battle will be fought his troops can march a thousand li and meet on the field. But if one knows neither the battleground nor the day of battle, the left will be unable to aid the right, or the right, the left; the van to support the rear, or the rear, the van. How much more is this so when separated by several tens of li, or, indeed, by even a few!*

Translated – If an executive controls the time and place of an encounter, they can make careful, detailed preparations without risking failure. If they do not control the time and place of an encounter, no matter how many resources are throw into the conflict, preparations will be inadequate, and failure likely.

Sun Tzu says: *Although I estimate the troops of Yüeh as many, of what benefit is this superiority in respect to the outcome? Thus, I say victory can be created. For even if the enemy is numerous, I can prevent him from engaging.'*

Translated – If you control the situation, how can the competitor's resources help them, even if they are greatly superior? With control, those with skill can craft victory. Even if a competitor's resources are substantial, with control you can make them lose their will to engage.

Week 5

Sun Tzu says: *Therefore, determine the enemy's plans and you will know which strategy will be successful and which will not; agitate him and ascertain the pattern of his movement. Determine his dispositions and so ascertain the field of battle. Probe him and learn where his strength is abundant and where deficient.'*

Translated – Probe competition carefully to determine which strategies can win and which will lose. Spar with competition to determine what positions they will defend, and where they intend to attack you. Probe various positions to determine where they are strong and where they are weak. Compare your resources with their resources to determine relative sufficiency and insufficiency.

Sun Tzu says: *The ultimate in disposing one's troops is to be without ascertainable shape. Then the most penetrating spies cannot pry in nor can the wise lay plans against you. It is according to the shapes that I lay the plans for victory, but the multitude does not comprehend this. Although everyone can see the outward aspects, none understands the way in which I have created victory. Therefore, when I have won a victory, I do not repeat my tactics but respond to circumstances in an infinite variety of ways.*

Translated – Strategy should be formless and invisible to your competitor. The best spy cannot discover a formless strategy; the sharpest advisors cannot determine an invisible strategy. Defeat the competition by controlling the situation, but don't allow competitors to discover how you control it. Even though all can see victory was accomplished, none can understand how. Results are obvious, but methods remain hidden. Successful strategies should never be repeated. Every conflict represents a new and unique situation.

Sun Tzu says: *Now an army may be likened to water, for just as flowing water avoids the heights and hastens to the lowlands, so an army avoids strength and strikes weakness. And as water shapes its flow in accordance with the ground, so an army manages its victory in accordance with the situation of the enemy. And as water has no constant form, there are in war no constant conditions. Thus, one able*

the Way

to gain the victory by modifying his tactics in accordance with the enemy situation may be said to be divine.

Translated – Successful strategies are shaped by the circumstances of the conflict. Successful strategies avoid complex methods and find easy ones. Just as the flow of water is shaped by the contour of the land, the flow of victory is shaped by the actions of the opponent. As water has no constant form, the tactics of victory have no constant form.

Sun Tzu says: *Of the five elements, none is always predominant; of the four seasons, none lasts forever; of the days, some are long and some short, and the moon waxes and wanes.*

Translated – In nature, no single element is superior to all others in every situation. Each of the four seasons comes and goes. Some days are longer, and some days are shorter. The moon waxes and wanes. Thus, the executive who crafts victories by successfully adapting plans and resources to the strengths and weaknesses of opponents and their surrounding environment is called a genius.

'Perhaps I should recap the salient messages from this essay. The first message is to grasp the initiative. If you are ready for confrontation, then you are at ease so you can attack at will, especially if your opponent is not ready. Skilful practitioners control the battlefield. You either offer some luring advantage to encourage your opponent to engage; or stifle your opponent's ability to engage.'

'We can summarise the next message as confuse and destroy. He speaks of the element of surprise, and how to harass your opponent. When your opponent is at ease; force them to chase shadows to weary them. When they appear well-fed; starve them. When they are at rest; make them move. Move swiftly where least expected forcing your opponent to react in haste.'

'Then he speaks of different tactical positions depending upon whether you are the aggressor or defending. If you are the aggressor, attack the unprotected will ensure victory. If you are skilled in attack, your opponent will not know where or what to defend. Apply your strength against their weakness. If you are defending, then hold what you defend by making it hard to attack. An expert in defence will ensure the opponent does not know where to attack. And should you decide to withdraw do it swiftly so your opponent cannot catch you.'

'We then move on to relative superiority. If you can determine your opponent's position whilst concealing your own, you can concentrate your attack to force your opponent to divide; use strength to attack these divided positions; ensure your opponent cannot determine where you will attack next, thus forcing your opponent to spread resources defending different positions and thus you can pick off what you want using many against the few. The few can only defend.'

'The value of intelligence information is a major contributor throughout these essays. Those who know where and when a battle will be fought can marshal their resources to best advantage. Even if your opponent's resource exceeds your own victory is still possible if intelligence is skilfully managed to discourage your opponent to engage. Knowing your opponent's plans also allows you to determine if your plan will work. We can also use valuable intelligence to stir your opponent in order to reveal patterns of response, and to probe for strengths and weaknesses.'

'Again, throughout these essays, he constantly refers to flexibility in approach and the fluid nature of tactics. Strategies to a degree, and most certainly tactics, adapt to the changing environment. As rushing water has no constant form as it weaves its course according to the obstacles it encounters, tactics must remain fluid as the battlefield unfolds. Learn to shape your opponent in your favour with tactical obstacles without revealing your own shape. Find and exploit any weakness.'

'There we have it.' Looking at Charles 'Did any of this essay strike a chord with you?'

'Fascinating. As Mel told me yesterday the power of his words is in the translation to the ways of the corporate world today. Your considerable experience enables your translations to be relevant and invaluable. I guess much of it I have learnt through trial and error over the years. But I'm glad I decided to join you this evening. Very illuminating. Can't wait to see how Mel uses these teachings in her quest. And I would appreciate a copy of your translations for all thirteen essays. Never too old to learn.'

'I'll send copies with Mel.'

'I'll leave you to your studies as it's getting late. Thank you so much for dinner, it was delicious. And thank you again for such a generous contribution to Mel's quest. I really appreciate it.'

'Mel is an attentive student. I have great hopes for her.'

Charles turns to Mel. 'Dear Mel. Thank you for the invitation this evening. Gives me a much clearer understanding of both your effort and commitment to your quest. We all have great hopes for your future with us.'

'Thank you, Charles. Let me show you out.'

Charles left and Mel returned to her place at the table.

He wanted to know her thoughts about this evening. 'What do you think about Charles's presence this evening?'

'Not really sure other than impressed with your translation. I'll know more in the morning after he's slept on it.'

She gathered her paper. 'If we've finished, I'd like to go to bed now. I never know if Jim will appear, so I have to prepare myself for the pressure of his job during the day.'

'We've finished for today. If you have a particularly hard day that warrants deferring your study, please tell me. No point grinding you into the ground.'

'Thanks. Good night.'

Week 5

Chapter 40 – Wednesday

Having dropped her bag at her desk she took the essay translations to Charles.

'Good morning, Mel. Thank you for the invitation last night. Most illuminating. I'm in awe of the effort you put into your day job and then go home to such intense study. Need to be careful we don't burn you out.'

She smiled, 'If my evenings were a chore you're probably right. But studying with Seb is so interesting. He's very alive to burnout, especially if I'm coping during the day without Jim. If I need a break, he's very understanding. But I always want more. I didn't work this hard when at uni, but I'm having fun. How did you find it?'

'Shall we just say I will be devoting some time to these translations and certainly look forward to seeing how you apply these teachings in your work.'

'I can't wait to have the opportunity to apply my newfound knowledge. Still some way to go with Sun Tzu and then we'll study real case studies showing how this knowledge was deployed in the corporate world.'

'Don't you think Aldridge a little small for jungle warfare?'

'Never too small. You've survived many changes in the business landscape over the past forty years, and now fabricator of choice. Aldridge must be in someone's sights as a target. Need to be alert and ready.'

'You'd better keep your eyes open. But I'm serious. This journey is not about burning you out. That degree of resilience is not required here.'

'Please don't worry, Charles. I only study new material with Seb four nights each week. If I go home at weekends, I leave Friday evening although I use the train journey to recap my week. If I stay here at weekends, we recap the week on a Friday evening if necessary, and we never work on Saturday. And Carmen, the German exec lady, is here three nights per month.

the Way

We don't engage in formal study while she's here, but we have some fascinating discussions including how she survives in the corporate jungle as a woman. She's the only woman on their Board so she knows a few tricks.'

'Margaret tells me she's a tough lady. Hope to meet her sometime. But until then it's time for work, so on your way. I have calls to make.'

Over dinner she related her conversation with Charles.

'I like Charles. A bit old school, but most certainly a tough, shrewd businessman. Succeeding him will need a good person. Let's see if we can make you eligible.'

'Tonight, we study the seventh essay which describes the art of manoeuvre. This essay can be considered a conundrum when compared with his view on maintaining the moral high ground as it speaks much of deception as an important art of war. But what he's addressing is the need for misleading tactical activities which distract your opponent. Today we refer to such activities as smoke and mirrors. Let's begin.'

Sun Tzu says: *Normally, when the army is employed, the General first receives his orders from the Sovereign. He assembles the troops and mobilises the people. He blends the army into a harmonious entity and encamps it.*

Translated – Once an executive understands the need to engage competition, they gather appropriate resources, carefully organises them, and assembles them under their control.

Sun Tzu says: *Nothing is more difficult than the art of manoeuvre. What is difficult about manoeuvre is to make the devious route the most direct and to turn misfortune to advantage. Thus, march by an indirect route and divert the enemy by enticing him with a bait. So doing, you may set out after he does and arrive before him. One able to do this understands the strategy of the direct and the indirect.*

Translated – The most difficult aspect of competition is how to out-manoeuvre your competitor. Winning depends upon using information effectively. In planning an attack, or indeed a defence, gather quality information about your competitor and their markets. Determine where the real advantages and disadvantages lie for both. Determine what is real and what is illusion. Controlling the information available to your competitor enables you to misdirect your competitor and lead them astray. You can make them adopt a less effective strategy by creating false perceptions. Thus, even if you start your preparation later than your competitor, you can be ready before them by misleading them. Only those who understand the subtleties of controlling information flows can achieve this.

Sun Tzu says: *Now both advantage and danger are inherent in manoeuvre. One who sets the entire army in motion to chase an advantage will not attain it. If he abandons the camp to contend for advantage the stores will be lost.*

Translated – Manoeuvres can gain advantage or can avoid loss. If you seek to gain advantage, timing and resource allocation is critical. Do not mobilise resources before you are ready to advance as this will slow you down allowing your competitor to escape and whatever opportunity you had will be lost.

Sun Tzu says: *It follows that when one rolls up the armour and sets out speedily, stopping neither day or night and marching at double time for a hundred li, the three commanders will be captured. For the vigorous troops will arrive first and the feeble straggle along behind, so that if this method is used only one-tenth of the army will arrive.*

Translated – If you skip necessary preparation and move too hastily into a difficult conflict situation, even if you toil day and night, you will have little chance of success. Your efforts will be scattered. Your resources wasted. Your motivation destroyed.

Sun Tzu says: *In a forced march of fifty li the commander of the van will fall, and using this method but half of the army will arrive. In a forced march of thirty li, but two-thirds will arrive. It follows that an army which lacks heavy equipment, fodder, food and stores will be lost.*

Translated – Adequate preparation having determined what mix of resources to apply at what time is essential to successful

the Way

manoeuvre. It is unwise to risk anything less. It follows that if you lack effective training, proper equipment, adequate financial backing and timely information you will be defeated.

Sun Tzu says: *Those who do not know the conditions of mountains and forests, hazardous defiles, marshes, and swamps, cannot the march of an army. Those who do not use local guides are unable to obtain the advantage of the ground.*

Translated – An executive who does not know the minds of the competition, and the political and market environment, cannot prepare and focus appropriate resources. An executive who does not know his competitor's objectives, resources, and allies cannot know with whom to form alliances. If an executive does not deploy inside informants and spies to discover his opponent's strengths and weaknesses, he cannot make successful plans.

Sun Tzu says: *Now war is based on deception. Move when it is advantageous and create changes in the situation by dispersal and concentration of forces.*

Translated – Success against a competitor depends on deception. If your competitor knows your strategy, no matter how good you are, you can be defeated. Focus on your objectives and keep your strategy secret. By constantly changing your visible activity you keep your competition off-balance.

'Sun Tzu says: *When campaigning, be swift as the wind; in leisurely march, majestic as the forest; in raiding and plundering, like fire; in standing, firm as the mountains. As unfathomable as the clouds move like a thunderbolt.'*

Translated – Keep your methods hidden. You can move swiftly or slowly; you can attack fiercely; you can stand firm like a mountain; you can strike like lightning from the darkness, powerful and unpredictable. Keep your competition guessing.

Sun Tzu says: *When you plunder the countryside, divide your forces. When you conquer territory, divide the profits.*

Translated – Divide your competition's resources and you can plunder his positions. Cause them to lose focus and you will conquer. Share the spoils.

Sun Tzu says: *He who knows the art of the direct and the indirect approach will be victorious. Such is the art of manoeuvring.*

Translated – If you move without restriction, whilst hampering the movements of your competitors, you will win. The secret of winning is knowing how to manipulate perceptions. Make distant threats seem near, and nearby threats seem distant. Make unworkable strategies seem productive and workable strategies seem unproductive. Deception is the art of manoeuvre.

Sun Tzu says: *The Book of Military Administration says: 'As the voice cannot be heard in battle, drums and bells are used. As troops cannot see each other clearly in battle, flags and banners are used. Now gongs and drums, banners and flags are used to focus the attention of the troops. When the troops can be thus united, the brave cannot advance alone, nor can the cowardly withdraw. This is the art of employing a host. In night fighting use many torches and drums, in day fighting many banners and flags in order to influence the sight and hearing of our troops.*

Translated – Conflict can generate confusion potentially hindering wise reasoning. Clear communication among members of your resource group can be more difficult. Develop specific communication methods which can refocus attention on your objectives. If your resources are unified by clear communication, those who are aggressive will not attempt unwise initiatives, and those who are overly cautious will not ignore opportunities for gain. This is the way we manage people during conflict.

Sun Tzu says: *Now an army may be robbed of its spirit and its commander deprived of his courage. During the early morning spirits are keen, during the day they flag, and in the evening thoughts turn towards home. And, therefore those skilled in war avoid the enemy when his spirit is keen and attack him when it is sluggish and his*

the Way

soldiers homesick. This is control of the moral factor. In good order, they await a disorderly enemy; in serenity, a clamorous one. This is control of the mental factor.

Translated – A competitor's manpower can be demotivated; a hostile executive can be distracted from his purpose. If you watch a competitor closely, you will observe their spirit is high in the early stages. Later their spirit will diminish. As matters drag on, they will be eager for a resolution. Use this to your advantage.

Avoid your competitor when their spirit is high. Apply pressure when your competitor is lazy or tired. Time your actions according to the spirit of your competitor. This is psychological warfare.

Sun Tzu says: *Close to the field of battle, they await an enemy coming from afar; at rest, an exhausted enemy; with well-fed troops, hungry ones. This is control of the physical factor.*

Translated – Await a chaotic competitor with discipline. Await a disordered competitor with calm. In this way you control your position. Wait for your competitor to come to you. Gather critical information. Analyse it in depth. In this way, you and your resource group will be thoroughly prepared.

Sun Tzu says: *They do not engage an enemy advancing with well-ordered banners nor one whose formations are in impressive array. This is control of the factor of changing circumstances.*

Translated – Do not engage with a well-prepared competitor. Do not challenge a well-managed group. Wait for the situation to change. Manage conflict in this way.

Sun Tzu says: *Therefore, the art of deploying troops is when the enemy occupies high ground, do not confront him; with his back resting on hills, do not oppose him. When he pretends to flee, do not pursue. Do not attack his elite troops. Do not gobble preferred baits. Do not thwart an enemy returning homewards. To surround an enemy, you must leave a way to escape. Do not press an enemy at bay. This is the method of deploying troops.*

Translated – Do not confront or oppose strength.

Do not pursue a competitor when they appear to move away from a strong position. This may be a false retreat to lure you away.

Do not attack a competitor's sharpest people.

Do not attempt to grab an apparent advantage without investigation. It may be bait in a competitor's trap.

If your competitor is withdrawing from their position, do not pursue. They are already defeated.

When a competitor has exhausted his resources, give them a way out. Let them retain their ability to earn a living. Do not destroy them as this may prove to be a costly way to win.

There is no need to press a desperate competitor. Desperation itself will bring defeat.

This is the essence of winning in direct attack.

'There we have it. Much of the translation of this essay is self-explanatory so I'll only recap the main points for reinforcement purposes.'

'The art of manoeuvre is to gain advantage. There are many forms of manoeuvre, and he identifies some key ones such as deception, turning misfortune to advantage, apparent changes intended to confuse your opponent, and devious activity.'

'He speaks of critical mass of resources before engaging, but counsels caution when using alliances without fully understanding their interest. And ensure all involved profit from spoils.

Using deception is to allow you to rally support and deployment before your opponent can deploy. This diffuses the ability to do you harm.'

'Established processes is an area of weakness, especially communications amongst leaders and resources. In a conflict situation your opponent can intercept and deploy such established processes. So, stay away from standard processes of communication during conflict – create an ever-changing structure that maintains clear communication within your own

the Way

resource base but does not allow penetration to the advantage of your opponent.'

'Finally, he speaks of gaining the mental advantage. Do not fight battles you cannot win unless an intentionally distracting skirmish. Preserve your best resources for the main plan. Be flexible; adapt quickly to changes in circumstances. Do not allow your opponent to manoeuvre you, and do not press a desperate opponent so hard that they have nothing to lose.

Chapter 41 – Thursday

This evening we will address the Nine Variables, or the factors that determine when and where to fight.

'Sun Tzu said: *Only a general who is flexible and knows how to adapt his strategy to changing circumstances can command victorious troops. Therefore, do not garrison troops in abandoned lands. Unite with allies where roads intersect. Do not linger in desperate ground. Make contingency plans in surrounded land. Fight if attacked in dead lands. Do not assume the enemy will not come. Prepare for his coming. Do not assume the enemy will not attack. Rely instead on strong defence.'*

Translated – Once an executive has entered competition for position, they should observe the following rules:

Do not create a situation that is isolated or far from required resources.

Do not create a situation that has many weak positions that cannot be defended.

Communicate with allies and arrange for mutual support.

Make contingency plans in case the competition moves quickly to challenge your position.

If pressed into action, be ready to delay an encounter until you are ready.

Week 5

In making strategic choices some methods should not be used; some people should not be attacked; some issues should not be argued; and some markets should not be contested.

During competition, sometimes communications from distant resource members should not be acknowledged.

Therefore, only an executive who is flexible and can adapt strategy to changes in circumstances can effectively manage his resources in competition.

An executive who is not flexible enough to adapt strategy to changes in circumstances, even with wide knowledge of people and methods, will not take advantage of this knowledge. Even if they recognise advantageous situations, they will not assign the right resources to do the right thing at the right time.

A smart executive considers both gains and losses in his strategic calculations. By considering gains, plans can be geared to yield the maximum profit; by considering losses, problems can be foreseen, and plans modified to overcome them. A smart executive creates losses for the competition to constrain him from movement; minor irritations to keep him occupied; and uses perceived benefits to move him about and keep him busy.

So, to be effective in competition do not assume your competitor will not attack; instead rely on preparation to assure your victory and on strong defences to defeat him.

'Sun Tzu said: There are five flaws in character which are dangerous for a General. If he is reckless, his men can be killed. If he is cowardly, his army can be captured. If he is quick-tempered, he will react in anger. If he is self-important, he can be deceived. If he is attached to his men, he will hesitate at a critical moment. These five flaws are serious faults in a General, and in military operations are calamitous. The ruin of the army and the death of the General are inevitable results of these shortcomings. Consider them well.'

Translated – There are five flaws in character that can be exploited to defeat an executive engaged in competition:

If reckless, can be encouraged to waste resources;

the Way

If timid, resources can be usurped;
If short-tempered, can be provoked to be rash;
If self-important, can be deceived with flattery;
If overly concerned about popularity with his resources, will hesitate before making unpopular decisions at critical moments.

These five flaws greatly restrict an executive's potential success. They cause tremendous loss in competitive situations. These five flaws cause executives to fail and companies to die. Eliminate them in yourself.

'Do you see any of these flaws in yourself?'

'None my master will permit me to retain by the end of this journey.'

They both laughed.

'Let me quickly recap the important point before we close this essay.'

'Do not allow any ideology or rules to constrain your consideration of tactical options, albeit within the law. Understand your mission, gather the best available resources, and concentrate on your plan. Do not dwell where advantage cannot be gained. Carefully foster alliances where necessary. When your options are limited, revert to strategy. And only fight when there is no alternative.'

'Always be alert to business opportunities not worth the costs; competitors you should not attack; counterparties you should not engage with, positions you cannot win, and intelligence you should treat with caution.'

'Advantage alone is not enough to engage. What would you do if in your opponent's position? What would your opponent do to gain a perceived advantage? Can you use third parties to dissuade your opponent from seeking such advantage?'

'Always be prepared for attack from competition ensuring adequate defences to critical aspects of your business at all times.'

'Much corporate failure can be attributed to faulty leadership. Heroes and egotistical bravery lead to recklessness and destruction. On the other hand, being overly cautious leads to cowardice and defeat. Uncontrolled anger leads to vulnerability to insults. Delicate honour leads to sensitivity, insecurity, and unhelpful reactions. Worry leads to over-solicitude and subjective blunders.'

'Do you still worry about the decisions you are asked to make?'

'Don't have time to worry anymore. And my master would be on my case if I did. So time for bed. Much to study and think about. Good night.'

Chapter 42 – Friday
Mel home for w/e

Chapter 43 – Sunday
When he arrived home from tennis a little after 5pm he noticed Mel was already back. He finds her reading on the sun deck.

'You're back early. Is there a reason for your enthusiasm for your venture, or has something happened?'

'Phil has run out of business shirts, and I refused to launder them for him. He left around 11 o'clock to have his mother do them for him so I made my way back. He wasn't at all pleased when he left, so I can't imagine him being good company when he returns. He needs to get used to looking out for each other before we get married. I'm not his slave, nor do I accept I always do the cleaning and laundry. He'll learn.'

the Way

Week 6

Chapter 44 – Monday

This evening we'll study the essay on Deploying Troops. In this essay, as in others, he uses water allegorically. If the water is calm, then he refers to stability. If the water is turbulent, this refers to a state of change or transition. If the water is raging, then he refers to great instability or disruption. If he refers to water finding its own way, he is describing the path of least resistance.

He handed her his prepared notes.

Sun Tzu says: *Generally, when taking up a position and confronting the enemy, having crossed the mountains, stay close to valleys. Encamp on high ground facing the sunny side. Fight downhill; do not ascend to attack. So much for taking positions in mountains.*

Translated – Generally, when confronting competition use the following rules. Avoid unnecessary obstacles and difficulties. Assemble the most knowledgeable people, organise them appropriately, train them effectively, and equip them well. Do not engage in complex conflicts with inadequate resources.

Sun Tzu says: *After crossing a river you must move some distance away from it. When an advancing army crosses water do not meet him at the water's edge. It is advantageous to allow half his force to cross and then strike. If you wish to give battle, do not confront your enemy close to the water. Take position on high ground facing the sunlight. Do not take position downstream. This relates to taking up positions near a river.*

Translated – If you need to reorganise your company before an encounter complete it quickly and let it stabilise. A stable organisation is best placed for conflict. When the competition is reorganising do not challenge them when they start because they will revert to their former structure to position themselves

the Way

against you. It is better to wait until their reorganisation is some halfway complete.

Sun Tzu says: *Cross salt marshes speedily. Do not linger in them. If you encounter the enemy in the middle of a salt marsh, you must take position close to grass and water with trees to your rear.*

Translated – If you are engaged in conflict do not institute large-scale organisational change yourself. Stick with accepted and easily understood methods and procedures. Maintain a stable organisation. Keep administrative matters simple and clear. Do not waste time with unnecessary activity.

Sun Tzu says: *In level ground occupy a position which facilitates your action. With heights to your rear and right, the field of battle is to the front and the rear is safe.*

Translated – You can manage conflict more readily when your emotions, your organisation, and your markets are stable. Different competitive situations may require different tactics for success. But as far as possible maintain stability during conflict situations. Do things the easy, well-understood way. Operate from positions which can be defended.

Sun Tzu says: *An army prefers high ground to low; esteems sunlight and dislikes shade. Thus, while nourishing its health, the army occupies a firm position. An army that does not suffer from countless diseases is said to be certain of victory.*

Most organisations like stability. People work better with methods, procedures, and equipment they understand. They are more comfortable if they know what is going on. They dislike being in the dark. People who are comfortable and stable have healthier emotions and sharper minds as are necessary for competitive success.

Sun Tzu says: *When near mounds, foothills, dykes or embankments, you must take position on the sunny side and rest your right and rear on them.*

Translated – When you face a challenge or obstacle focus on the benefits of success. Create motivation and innovation through enthusiasm. In this way your people draw strength from your example.

Sun Tzu says: *When there are raging waters in deep mountains, a place surrounded by heights with low-lying ground in the centre, terrain resembling a covered cage, places where troops can be entrapped and cut off, land is sunken, and where mountain gorges are narrow and where the road is sunken, you must march speedily away from them. Do not approach them. I keep a distance from these and draw the enemy toward them. I face them and cause him to put his back to them.*

Translated – When there is excessive change or uncertainty it will affect your ability to compete. If you must work within a rapidly changing or highly uncertain environment, wait until the flood of change or uncertainty has subsided. There are also dangers inherent in every competitive situation because of commonly held assumptions or assertions of undocumented information such as rumour and gossip. Always challenge the validity of any such information and encourage your people to ignore it. If your competitor bases their movements on such information, encourage them as most of it is baseless so it weakens an opponent who bases their defence on it.

Sun Tzu says: *When on the flanks of the army there are dangerous defiles or ponds covered with aquatic grasses where reeds and rushes grow, or forested mountains with dense tangled undergrowth you must carefully search them out, for these are places where ambushes are laid, and spies are hidden.*

Translated – When you must compete in an environment that provides only incomplete understanding of the movements or tactics of the competition, be astute and vigilant in the search for traps and ambushes. Challenge anything which appears unusual.

Sun Tzu says: *When the enemy is nearby but lying low he is depending on a favourable position. When he challenges to battle from afar he wishes to lure you to advance, for when he is in easy ground he is in an advantageous position.*

the Way

Translated – If your competitor is ready to challenge but remains calm it is likely they rely on some critical advantage. If your competitor seems unprepared for conflict but challenges you from afar, they are tempting you to leave your defensive positions and advance. They probably occupy a position which gives them an advantage. Investigate it thoroughly before moving.

Sun Tzu says: *When the trees are seen to move the enemy is advancing.*

Translated – If there is unexplained activity in the market or agitation among members of your markets, your competition may be positioning behind the scenes.

Sun Tzu says: *When many obstacles have been placed in the undergrowth, it is for the purpose of deception.*

Translated – When your competitor sets hidden traps and obstacles, they are trying to confuse you. If your ordinarily supportive markets suddenly distance themselves from you, your competitor is preparing to make a sudden and prepared attack.

Sun Tzu says: *Birds rising in flight is a sign that the enemy is lying in ambush; when the wild animals are startled and flee he is trying to take you unaware. Dust spurting upward in high straight columns indicates the approach of chariots. When it hangs low and is widespread infantry is approaching. When dust rises in scattered area the enemy is bringing in firewood; when there are numerous small patches which seem to come and go he is encamping the army.*

Translated - Be alert to any unusual signs from your competitor. If there is a great deal of erratic activity they may be preparing to move quickly. If the activity level is steady and organised, they are preparing to move cautiously. Look for patterns of activity that show where they are gathering information about your activities.

Sun Tzu says: *When the enemy's envoys speak in humble terms, but continues preparations, he will advance. When their language is deceptive, but the enemy pretentiously advances, he will retreat. When*

Week 6

the envoys speak in apologetic terms, he wishes a respite. When with no previous understanding the enemy asks for a truce, they are plotting.

Translated - If your competitor's communications sound self-effacing but they otherwise appear confident they are preparing to advance against you. If your competitor's communications are evasive but aggressive in tone, they are preparing to withdraw. If your competitor comes to you with a generous offer to consider, they may need time to regroup. If your competitor suddenly wants to begin peace negotiations without any apparent reason, they are plotting against you.

Sun Tzu says: *When light chariots first go out and take position on the flanks the enemy is forming for battle. When his troops march speedily and he parades his battle chariots he is expecting to rendezvous with reinforcements. When half his forces advance, and half withdraws he is attempting to decoy you. When his troops lean on their weapons, they are famished. When drawers of water drink before carrying it to camp, his troops are suffering from thirst. When the enemy sees an advantage, but does not advance to seize it, he is fatigued. When birds gather above his camp sites, they are empty. When at night the enemy's camp is clamorous, he is fearful.*

Translated – If your competitor deploys their resources aggressively, they are expecting an encounter. If your competitor partially advances and then partially retreats, they are trying to lure you out of your defensive position. If your competitor resorts to trickery or subterfuge to sustain their position, they are facing some difficulty. If your competitor sees an obvious advantage but does not advance, they are weary or distracted. If your competitor wanders aimlessly in discussion, they are uncertain how to proceed. If your competitor speaks loudly, they are reticent to proceed.

Sun Tzu says: *When his troops are disorderly, the General has no prestige. When his flags and banners move about constantly he is in disarray. If the officers are short-tempered they are exhausted. When the enemy feeds grain to the horses and his men meat and when his troops neither hang up their cooking pots nor return to their shelter, the*

the Way

enemy is desperate. When the troops continually gather in small groups and whisper together the General has lost the confidence of the army. Too frequently rewards indicate that the General is at the end of his resources; too frequent punishments that he is in acute distress. If the officers at first treat the men violently and later are fearful of them, the limit of indiscipline has been reached.

Translated – If your competitor is in turmoil their leadership is not effective. If your competitor's communications are in disarray, their thinking is chaotic. If your competitor's representatives are short-tempered, they are under emotional stress. If your competitor uses their last available resources to challenge you, they are desperate. When your competitor's people whisper among themselves in clandestine groups, your competitor is losing their loyalty. When your competitor hands out too many rewards they have lost the ability to motivate their people. When your competitor hands out too much retribution they have lost control of their people. When your competitor publicly criticises their community, they have lost the plot.

Sun Tzu says: *When the enemy troops are high in spirits, and although facing you, do not join battle for a long time, nor leave, you must thoroughly investigate the situation. In war, numbers alone confer no advantage. Do not advance relying on sheer military power.*

Translated – When a competitor confronts you as if prepared for an encounter, but neither advances nor retreats, you must study the situation carefully. Search for important factors you may have overlooked. In conflict it is unnecessary to have the most resources to win, but It is important not to challenge recklessly using force alone.

Sun Tzu says: *It is sufficient to estimate the enemy situation correctly and to concentrate your strength to capture them. There is no more to it than this. He who lacks foresight and underestimates his enemy will surely be captured by him.*

If you concentrate your resources in determining a competitor's strength, and carefully study their movements, you will win. If you underestimate a competitor's strength and do not consider the meaning of their movements, you will lose.

Sun Tzu says: *If troops are punished before their loyalty is secured they will be disobedient. If not obedient, it is difficult to employ them. If troops are loyal, but punishments are not enforced, you cannot employ them. Thus, command them with civility and imbue them uniformly with martial ardour and it may be said that victory is certain. If orders which are consistently effective are used in instructing the troops, they will be obedient. If orders which are not consistently effective are used in instructing them, they will be disobedient. When orders are consistently trustworthy and observed, the relationship of a commander with his troops is satisfactory.*

Translated – When managing people if you castigate an individual before they feel loyalty to you, they will not obey your orders in the future. Furthermore, once a person feels loyalty, but general discipline is not enforced, they will not follow orders either. Without complete loyalty it is hard to use people effectively.

Therefore, if you manage your employees through an appropriate organisational structure and maintain control through appropriate discipline, your people will be loyal and competent.

If you train and organise your employees with clear expectations, they will perform in a competitive situation. If you train and organise your group with vague expectations, they are ill-equipped to perform.

When expectations are clear and organisational structure is appropriate for the task, people will trust their leaders.

She looked up from her reading 'This last section is about how to manage troops. In today's corporate environment what do you think makes a good leader?'

'First and foremost, such a person must clearly know their business. What I mean by **clearly** is it must be clear to all staff by continued demonstration of organisational skills and decisions by the leader. Then a good leader will have a flair for the human aspects of leadership. This means they know it's people who deliver outcomes, not rules and procedures – these merely provide a framework discipline to the pathway of delivery. As I have said before, a leader does not have to be liked, but they should not be disliked. Occasionally hard decisions must be made, and these must be fair and impartial to command acceptance and respect. A good leader will treat staff equally as family with no favouritism using the principal if staff take care of their leader, then the leader will nurture and care for them. And of course no worthy leader will be remote from their staff; leadership is a two-way conversation.'

'Can I recap this essay and then we can discuss any thoughts you have? The first verses concern how to position yourself, so you maximise your strength. Keep your key resources close to you as they represent your strength. Position yourself to the disadvantage of your opponent, i.e. make it difficult for your opponent to attack you. Also prevent your opponent from taking advantage of any available strength that may threaten you.'

'Then he speaks of seeking the high ground. What he means is you should always know the health and well-being of the resource pool to ensure maximum strength. Never occupy imperilled positions; let your opponent occupy them.'

We then address the need to be ever vigilant. Watch for signs your opponent is on the move. Study the actions and mood of your opponent's resources. For example, if your opponent is providing lavish incentives the resource base is depleting. Treat every potential opponent as a threat; being careful not to underestimate them.'

'Then we address leadership again. Treat you people with respect and humanity. It is then easy to instil a sense of discipline and loyalty. Trust and confidence must be mutual; otherwise it has no value.'

'What is your experience with leadership in the corporate world?'

'I've met far too few exceptional leaders whether corporate or political. I've met some good leaders, but I would say a significant number of business leaders are mediocre or plain bad. Exceptional leadership appears effortless, albeit you know this needs continuous excellence. I would classify good leaders as people who know their business but have scant regard for the resources they marshal. What I will add is if you meet someone who thinks they have a divine right to lead, especially through birth right, they cannot lead. Easy prey in a competitive situation. Leaders lead because people will follow them. I guess I should exclude people such as cult leaders who use psychology to enlist frailty, disillusionment, dislocation, etcetera. A sign of a good General is one who will ensure their troops are properly fed and watered before they feed themselves. Far too many so-called corporate leaders today will ensure their own fat-cat compensation before considering the people who make it possible for them.'

'Wow. Are good leaders that difficult to find?'

'We are studying an exceptional General – 2,500 years after he lived. How many great leaders can you name in the past 100 years?'

'Well Winston Churchill must be up there. I guess Field-marshal's Rommel and Mountbatten are candidates. Political leaders could be Mahatma Gandhi, Mustafa Kemal Atatürk, John F. Kennedy, Martin Luther King – how am I doing?'

'Impressive, but what about business leaders?'

'More difficult. What about Warren Buffett, Bill Gates, Steve Jobs, Onassis, Rockefeller, and your mentor bank President?'

'Again, not bad. I assume you mean my mentor, Walter Wriston. But that we can name them, suggests they are not plentiful. And that's my point. Of course, there are many unsung heroes who successfully ran divisions or subsidiaries, and there are also entrepreneurs like Richard Branson. And I'm surprised you didn't mention any great soccer managers as they manage significant corporate assets and enter onto the field of conflict every week.'

'Didn't think of that. Need to open my field of view.

'It's worth noting that great leaders are able to master complexity. Problems in business are multidimensional requiring multidimensional minds to formulate multidimensional solutions. The complexity of a requirement must be understood as part of a solution. Therefore, leaders must excel in a diverse range of knowledge in seemingly unrelated fields. They can seek detail from others but must understand the principles themselves to know from where to seek appropriate information.'

'But how many have such diverse backgrounds?'

'Anyone with a truly inquisitive mind who is prepared to follow ideas and thoughts wherever it takes them. A thirst for knowledge is a prerequisite. Think of Sun Tzu. How would he know what size of army he would need, and the skills needed by this army and how to deploy these skills if he did not understand every aspect of warfare? Great leaders have a complete understanding of their art.'

'Don't see myself as a great leader. Judging by my life to date my eyes are closed most of the time.'

'But you can learn to open them and explore what you observe.'

'A work in progress, I think. Are we done this evening as it's late?'

'Sure. You're good to go. Any questions can be dealt with over dinner tomorrow. Good night.'

Chapter 45 – Tuesday

'We are progressing well with Sun Tzu. We now study essay 10 which is titled **Terrain**. In this essay we look at the tactical manoeuvring and adaptability to the environment in which you find yourself. This essay is very much about knowing yourself and knowing your enemy. If you remember your ancient Greek, Apollo's 1st Commandment to all mortals is Gnosti Seautum – Know thyself. All great leaders know their strengths and their weaknesses. They know what they know; and know where to secure what they don't know. They surround themselves with loyal resources to supplement their skills. Knowing yourself gives you the confidence and self-assurance to be successful. Knowing your competitor allows you to win. Let's get started.'

Sun Tzu says: *Ground may be classified according to its nature as accessible, entrapping, indecisive, constricted, precipitous, and distant.*

Translated – We can describe the six competitive situations as accessible, ensnaring, indecisive, restricted, difficult, and speculative. Note: the change of descriptors.

Sun Tzu says: *Ground which both we and the enemy can traverse with equal ease is called accessible. In such ground, he who first takes high sunny positions convenient to his supply routes can fight advantageously.*

If all competitors can penetrate a given market easily, then the situation is accessible. When the situation is accessible, try to be first to establish a strong position. This gives you an advantageous position to set the access criteria.

Sun Tzu says: *Ground easy to get out of but difficult to return to is entrapping. The nature of this ground is such that if the enemy is unprepared and you sally out you may defeat him. If the enemy is prepared and you go out and engage, but do not win, it is difficult to return. This is unprofitable.*

Translated – If it is easy for either side to engage in a competitive situation, but once involved, difficult to withdraw, then the situation is ensnaring. When your competitor is unprepared, you can challenge them. However, remember that once you are involved, if your investment in funds or manpower is high, you may not be able to withdraw. Therefore, it is unwise to challenge your competitor if they are prepared.

the Way

Sun Tzu says: *Ground equally disadvantageous for both the enemy and ourselves to enter is indecisive. The nature of this ground is such that although the enemy holds out a bait I do not go forth but entice him by marching off. When I have drawn out half his forces, I can strike him advantageously.*

Translated – If both sides have difficulty entering and leaving a competitive situation then neither side may be able to win. Do not challenge a competitor when you are not confident of winning, even if they are weak. It is a waste of resources. Instead, if you can, make your competitor waste their resources. Wait for a better time for an encounter.

Sun Tzu says: *If I first occupy constricted ground, I must block the passes and await the enemy. If the enemy first occupies such ground and blocks the defiles, I should not follow him; if he does not block them completely I may do so.*

Translated – Restricted markets are difficult to access. Stringent technology requirements, professional knowledge, regulation, or financial demands may present significant challenges. If you can access the market first, build stronger barriers in your favour. From this position you have the advantage, and you can afford to wait for your competitor's advance knowing what they will encounter. If your competitor has already established themselves strongly in this market, they have the advantage. Do not attack unless they have unwittingly left you an opening.

Sun Tzu says: *In precipitous ground, I must take position on the sunny heights and await the enemy. If he first occupies such ground, I lure him by marching off; I do not follow him.*

Where both sides have difficulty accessing a market if you arrive first, establish a strong position, and wait for your competitor to advance. If your competitor already has a strong defensive position, stimulate them to waste time and funds defending their territory. But, do not move too quickly if they retreat. This may be a trap.

Week 6

Sun Tzu says: *When at distance from an enemy of equal strength it is difficult to provoke battle and unprofitable to engage him in his chosen position.*

Translated – Speculative competitive situations involve important or profitable constituents who may be unknown or remote. These situations are equally risky for both sides because they may involve taking actions whose costs and consequences are largely unclear. In a speculative situation it is usually difficult to create circumstances in which you can win. Therefore, it is generally not advantageous to advance.

Sun Tzu says: *These are the principles relating to six different types of ground. It is the highest responsibility of the General to inquire into them with utmost care.*

Translated – We are back to the importance of careful planning.

'Okay so far?'

'As usual I'll study more carefully, but no problems.'

'Good. Let's move on to the leadership.'

Sun Tzu says: *When troops flee, are insubordinate, distressed, collapse in disorder or are routed, it is the fault of the General. None of these disasters can be attributed to natural causes.*

Translated – During competitive operations failure can spring from six different conditions. These conditions are not created by fate but are caused by executive mistakes. These conditions are lack of resources, lack of direction, lack of performance, lack of discipline, lack of order, and lack of competence.

Sun Tzu says: *Other conditions being equal, if a force attacks one ten times its size, the result is flight.*

Translated – If, all other things being equal, an executive instructs a poorly equipped, supplied, trained, organised, or funded group to challenge another group adequately resourced in these areas, the cause of the ensuing failure is lack of suitable resources.

Sun Tzu says: *When troops are strong and officers weak the army is insubordinate.*

the Way

Translated – If the people in a group are committed, but their managers are weak, the cause of failure is lack of direction.

Sun Tzu says: *When the officers are valiant and the troops ineffective, the army is in distress.*

Translated – If a group's leader is committed, but the people are poorly trained or demotivated, the cause of failure is lack of performance.

Sun Tzu says: *When senior officers are angry and insubordinate, and on encountering the enemy rush into battle with no understanding of the feasibility of engaging and without awaiting orders from the commander, the army is in a state of collapse.*

Translated – When operating executives are angry or defiant or when they become emotional and challenge competitors without receiving orders to do so, the cause of failure is lack of discipline.

Sun Tzu says: *When the General is morally weak and his discipline not strict, when his instructions and guidance are not enlightened, when there are no consistent rules to guide the officers and men and when the formations are slovenly the army is in disorder.*

Translated – When the chief executive is weak, lacks personal authority, cannot motivate people, and training is poor, or when people's tasks are unclear and organisation structure is vague, the cause of failure is lack of order.

Sun Tzu says: *When a commander unable to estimate his enemy uses a small force to engage a large one, or weak troops to strike the strong, or when he fails to select shock troops for the van, the result is rout.*

Translated – When the chief executive cannot develop effective operating plans, when they misunderstand competitors' actions, or when they underestimate the resources needed to complete tasks, the cause of failure is lack of competence.

Sun Tzu says: *When any of these six conditions prevails, the army is on the road to defeat. It is the highest responsibility of the General to examine them carefully.*

Week 6

Translated – The above six conditions lead to failure. Every executive needs to investigate them carefully and rectify any deficiencies.

Sun Tzu says: *Conformation of the ground is of the greatest assistance in battle. Therefore, to estimate the enemy situation and to calculate distances and the degree of difficulty of the terrain so as to control victory are virtues of the superior General. He who fights with full knowledge of these factors is certain to win; he who does not will surely be defeated.*

Translated – A thorough understanding of any competitive situation is fundamental in conflict. An effective executive understands their markets, opponents, themselves, and the realities all parties face, and thereby controls victory. They correctly estimate the difficulties of alternate strategies and calculates the resources required. They know the strengths, weaknesses, and capacity of the people involved in the situation – both their own and those loyal to the opponent. An effective executive wins because they take the time to know all these things and applies knowledge to take advantage of the opportunities they uncover.

Sun Tzu says: *If the situation is one of victory but the Sovereign has issued orders not to engage, the General may decide to fight. If the situation is such that he cannot win, but the Sovereign has issued orders to engage, he need not do so. Therefore, the General who in advancing does not seek personal fame, and in withdrawing is not concerned with avoiding punishment, but whose only purpose is to protect the people and promote the best interests of his Sovereign, is the precious jewel of the State.*

Translated – If the chief executive calculates success is probable, they should go ahead even if their advisers think differently. If they calculate failure, they should stop even if advisors propose to advance. An executive who competes but does not seek to gain personal glory; who acts but does not seek to avoid responsibility; whose only goal is to benefit their

the Way

markets and organisation is the organisation's most precious asset.

Sun Tzu says: *Because such a General regards his men as infants they will march with him into the deepest valleys. He treats them as his own beloved sons and they will die with him.*

Translated – If you treat your people like family, they will repay you with loyalty and will work for you through thick and thin.

Sun Tzu says: *If a General indulges his troops but is unable to employ them; if he loves them but cannot enforce his commands; if the troops are disorderly and he is unable to control them, they may be compared to spoilt children, and are useless.*

Translated – But, if you are so generous with your people you cannot manage them; so kind, you cannot maintain order; or so disorderly, you cannot direct them, it is like spoiling your child. Once spoiled, they are no longer effective.

'Good commanders are both loved and feared.'

Sun Tzu says: *If I know that my troops are capable of striking the enemy, but do not know that he is invulnerable to attack, my chance of victory is but half. If I know that the enemy is vulnerable to attack, but do not know that my troops are incapable of striking him, my chance of victory is but half. If I know that the enemy can be attacked and that my troops are capable of attacking him, but do not realise that because of the conformation of the ground I should not attack, my chances of victory is but half. Therefore, when those experienced in war move they make no mistakes; when they act, their resources are limitless. And therefore, I say: "Know the enemy, know yourself; your victory will never be endangered. Know the ground, know the weather; your victory will then be total.*

Translated – In timing actions, if you know your group has the resources to succeed, but do not know whether your competitor is vulnerable, your chance of victory is 50:50.

If you know your competitor is vulnerable, but do not know if your group has the resources to succeed, your chance of victory is 50:50.

If you know your competitor is vulnerable, and know your group has the resources to succeed, but do not know if the competitive situation allows you to win, your chance of victory is also 50:50.

Hence those executives who experience success advance only when they have full knowledge. As a result, they need not consider retreat.

Know your opponent, know yourself, you will not lose. Know the competitive situation, and the markets involved, then victory will be assured.

'Any questions before I recap the main points?'

'I think much of this essay is about the qualities of a leader.'

'Well observed. Let me recap. The first verses require you to understand your battlefield in a conflict situation, or markets in a competitive situation. Be first to secure the best positions but, in questionable markets, let the competition enter first to determine if valuable opportunity exits. Try to develop your strength in niche markets and vigorously defend profitable and unique markets. Pursue only weakly defended markets, but distant markets can be difficult to serve or defend.'

'He then again refers to leadership. If you attack strength, you will likely lose. If your instructions are clear, all will act with confidence, if unclear disorganisation will ensue. When you cannot accurately assess the overall situation, the probable result will be disaster. Know how to evaluate the strength of your opponent. Be shrewd in evaluating dangers and difficulties. It's not enough to know what you should do; you must also know how to put it into practice with consideration to your available resource base. Do not act in your own self-interest. Your job is to act in the best interest of your organisation and its people. And never be afraid to retreat from a bad position. Save your resources to fight another day.'

'And, finally, to leaders. Knowing yourself is not enough; you must also know your opponent, especially the leader. Your

the Way

chances of victory are greatly enhanced when you attack weakness and avoid strength.'

Chapter 46 – Wednesday

'The eleventh essay we will discuss is the **Ninefold Earth**, or nine battlefield terrains and how to approach each in terms of allocating and managing your own resources. We have already discussed that in Sun Tzu's time the State was all-encompassing, so we need to update this scenario to the modern world in which we find ourselves. In the corporate world of today terrain could be a marketplace, a product, or service and I will collectively refer to these as territory. In the first Sun Tzu verse I will use his nine classifications but will then rename some of them for the same reason, including in his verses.'

Sun Tzu says: *In respect to the employment of troops, ground may be classified as dispersive, frontier, key, communicating, focal, serious, difficult, encircled, and death.*

- *When a feudal lord fights in his own territory, he is in **dispersive** ground.*
- *When he makes but a shallow penetration into enemy territory, he is in **frontier** ground.*
- *Ground equally advantageous for the enemy or me to occupy is **key** ground.*
- *Ground equally accessible to both the enemy and me is **communicating ground**.*
- *When a State is enclosed by three other States, its territory is **focal**. He who first gets control of it will gain the support of All-in-Heaven.*
- *When the army has penetrated deep into hostile territory, leaving far behind many enemy cities and towns, it is in **serious** ground.*

Week 6

- *When an army traverses' mountains, forests, precipitous country, or marshes through defiles, marshlands, or swamps, or any place where the going is hard, it is in **difficult** ground.*
- *Ground to which access is constricted, where the way out is tortuous, and where a small enemy force can strike my larger one is **encircled** ground.*
- *Ground in which the army survives only if it fights with the courage of desperation is called **death**.*

Translated - In respect of deploying resources territory may be classified as dispersive, frontier, key, accessible, focal, serious, difficult, encircled, and speculative.

- If a competitor attempts to challenge your territory before you can concentrate and focus your resistance, you are in a **dispersive** situation because your resources feel at ease in your territory and thus complacency is the enemy within. Caught napping, in short.
- If you are attempting to probe a competitors' territory to test for reaction, this is **frontier** territory where you have no predetermined base.
- If you are attempting to capture territory equally advantageous to your competitors, this is **key** territory.
- We call interesting territory equally accessible to both yourself and your competitors **accessible** territory.
- Rich, fertile territory which is also the focus of competitors is **focal** territory with rich pickings for the winner.
- When you have or need to work hard to penetrate a territory, this is termed **serious** territory.
- When you have encountered much resistance, not from competitors, but from the territory itself such as political rebuff, this is **difficult** territory.
- Territory where access is difficult, and once in can be very costly to withdraw is called **encircled** territory.
- When you are entering a hostile market in unfamiliar territory where outsiders are not welcome, and you must fight every step of the way then you are in **speculative** territory.

the Way

Sun Tzu says: *Therefore,*
- *do not fight in dispersive ground;*
- *do not stop in the frontier borderlands;*
- *do not attack an enemy who occupies key ground;*
- *in communicating ground do not allow your formations to become separated;*
- *In focal ground, ally with neighbouring States;*
- *in deep ground, plunder;*
- *In difficult ground, press on;*
- *in encircled ground, devise stratagems;*
- *in death ground, fight.*

Translated – Therefore,
- Do not engage in conflict in your own dispersive territory, you will only destroy your own precious infrastructure. Fortify your territory to rebuff your competitor's attempts.
- When probing frontier territory do not stay there. Regroup back in your own territory.
- If your competitor beats you to key territory, do not engage in conflict as they will be ready to defend their positions.
- In accessible territory keep your resources tight and focussed.
- In focal territory find allies who can help you to act swiftly.
- In difficult territory, be prepared to do what must be done to remove resistance and win; or withdraw.
- In encircled territory something as simple as a single opposing politician can block your way. To win in such circumstance requires innovative resources who can neutralise or remove any such blockage.
- In speculative territory you require extraordinary resources who know and understand failure is not an option.

Sun Tzu says:
- *In dispersive ground, I would unify the determination of the army.*

Week 6

- *In frontier ground I would keep my forces closely linked.*
- *In key ground, I would hasten up my rear elements.*
- *In communicating (accessible) ground, I would pay strict attention to my defences.*
- *In focal ground, I would strengthen my alliances.*
- *In serious ground, I would ensure a continuous flow of provisions.*
- *In difficult ground, I would press on over the roads.*
- *In encircled ground, I would block the points of access and egress.*
- *In death ground, I could make it evident that there is no chance of survival. For it is the nature of soldiers to resist when surrounded; to fight to the death when there is no alternative, and when desperate to follow commands implicitly.*

Translated –

- In dispersive territory the executive needs to re-energise and focus resources to protect their territory against interlopers and investigate why they were caught napping.
- Probing frontier territory can be for several reasons such as testing the resolve of your competitor to protect their territory, or a distraction whilst attempting to outmanoeuvre a competitor and such probes will be elite resources on various skirmishes. It is fundamental these resources are kept close and informed.
- When pursuing key territory, the executive needs to be alive to changing resource requirements to quickly overcome obstacles and ensure these resources remain committed and focused on the task.
- When pursuing accessible territory, prepare to be attacked by competitors.
- When pursuing focal territory be prepared to seek alliances from other interested entities.
- When in serious territory, ensure you have the right resources and backup.
- When pursuing difficult ground be prepared to withdraw.

the Way

- In speculative territory, having decided to pursue it, you must be prepared for anything, and be resilient in pursuit. 'We will look at this subject in detail using General Electric's pursuits to win a major stake in the Chinese market.'

She looked up from her notes 'I'm having some difficulty understanding the essence of these nine situations.'

'This whole essay is about human nature. If we look at the dispersive territory situation. Here the people are at home with their friends and families. Someone spots a competitor is exploiting a weakness in their defences. Do they stay in the office and bolster this defence, or do they give priority to the school play they are expected to attend by their children? It's clear both are important. An executive always shoulders the burden of protecting their territory whilst keeping costs as low as possible. Therefore, managing their resource base is invariably a myriad of conflicts. But it is essential they have built-in mechanisms to capture both the weakness in their defences and the recognition a key resource has a reasonable priority to specific family matters. Then both can be accommodated by deploying a different resource.'

'At the other end of the spectrum there is no point allocating human resources to a speculative situation if they have young families. Resources sent into speculative situations can be deployed far away from home for long periods of time. These resources are fighting for the right of the company to penetrate a forbidding environment, and they must be fully committed – not dealing remotely with distracting family matters or longing to see their families. What Sun Tzu is articulating here is the need to understand how humans will react and perform in given situations and thus what can and cannot be achieved with any given human resources. We will speak about managing human nature and people at length in future sessions.'

'Having dealt with the nine territory situations let us explore how he deals with the human characteristics of leadership.'

Week 6

Sun Tzu says: *The tactical variations appropriate to the nine types of ground, the advantages of close or extended deployment, and the principles of human nature are matters the General must examine with the greatest care. Anciently, those described as skilled in war made it impossible for the enemy to unite his van and his rear; for his elements both large and small to mutually co-operate; for the good troops to succour the poor and for superiors and subordinates to support each other. When the enemy's forces were dispersed they prevented him from assembling them; when concentrated, they threw him into confusion. They concentrated and moved when it was advantageous to do so; when not advantageous, they halted.*

Translated – In managing competitive actions effective executives make it difficult for competitors to defend all aspects of their positions, understand and coordinate use of their resources, support weaknesses in their organisations, and communicate effectively with their territory. When a competitor's resources are spread around effective executives prevent their concentration. When resources are concentrated, effective executives prevent their coordination. Effective executives advance their position when it is advantageous, and stop when not.

Sun Tzu says: *Should one ask, "How do I cope with a well-ordered enemy host about to attack me?" I reply: "Seize something he cherishes and he will conform to your desires."*

Translated – In the days of Sun Tzu when faced with a well-ordered army of overwhelming odds the favoured response was to capture an object or kidnap someone so dear to the opposing ruler he would not sacrifice for victory. Today civilised society would condemn such violation. But a smart executive faced with such odds would seek something that could be used as a bargaining chip. This could be identifying a lesser territory that could be sacrificed to appease your aggressor or purchase a company that would appeal to your aggressor, or even threaten to disclose some inflammatory information that would damage the company. It may also be possible to form an alliance with

the Way

another competitor who would thwart such an attack. The recent emergence of formidable asset-stripping predators is a constant reminder to executives they must maintain themselves at maximum strength ensuring they have the resources to thwart any attack. As Sun Tzu says on many occasions in these essays, the possibilities are only limited by our ability to think.

Sun Tzu says: *Speed is the essence of war. Take advantage of the enemy's unpreparedness; travel by unexpected routes and strike him where he has taken no precautions.*

Translated – A capable executive will readily identify failures in his competitors such as unprepared for challenge, lack of foresight, or lack of caution. Our executive will quickly exploit such failings. Any delay in response will lose the advantage.

She looked up again 'Does this mean our capable executive is on the field of play 24/7.'

He smiled 'No. Opportunities are not on a production line, they are periodic. Larger corporates tend to have an elite core unit specifically tasked with continually analysing competitors and takeover targets looking for opportunities worth exploiting. And asset-strippers have small armies tasked with scrutinising markets for valuable opportunities and can pounce with no warning on unsuspecting companies who have failed to optimise value for their shareholders.'

Sun Tzu says: *The general principles applicable to an invading force are when you have penetrated deeply into hostile territory, your army is united, such that any defender cannot overcome you. Plunder fertile country to supply the army with plentiful provisions. Pay heed to nourishing the troops; do not unnecessarily fatigue them. Unite them in spirit; conserve their strength. Make unfathomable plans for the movement of the army.*

Translated – In general, competitive actions will succeed only if people are wholly committed to them. When people are committed, they have a unified purpose. When they are unified no attacker can overcome them. The nature of people, when committed, is to strive to reach their goal. Put an organisation into a situation where they have no choice but to commit to your goals and they will exceed your expectations. When you move into a market, study your competitor's methods. Use their experiences to avoid mistakes. Keep your people healthy. Conserve their energy. Cherish their morale. Do not unnecessarily burden them. Carefully plan how to best use your resources. In this way you will be prepared to take advantage of unexpected opportunities.

Sun Tzu says: *Throw the troops into a position from which there is no escape and even when faced with death they will not flee. For if prepared to die, what can they not achieve? Then officers and men together put forth their utmost efforts. In a desperate situation they fear nothing; when there is no way out they stand firm. Deep in a hostile land they are bound together, and there, where there is no alternative, they will engage the enemy in hand to hand combat. Thus, such troops need no encouragement to be vigilant. Without extorting their support, the General obtains it; without inviting their affection, he gains it; without demanding their trust, he wins it.*

Translated – Lead your organisation to its goals. Give your people no alternative – either they attain your goals, or they fail. If the alternative is failure (potential loss of job), what worthwhile person will not do their best to avoid it? When worthy people are committed, they do not fear failure. When they are focussed on a common goal, they are calm. When they are deeply involved in their work, they desire to succeed. Under these circumstances worthy people stay alert. They follow instructions and procedures without supervision. They work diligently without unnecessary promises or guarantees.

Sun Tzu says: *My officers have no surplus of wealth but not because they disdain worldly goods; they have no expectation of long life but not because they dislike longevity. But throw them into a situation where there is no escape and they will display immortal courage.*

Translated – On the day a major project is started every worthy person may complain because they know how much

the Way

work needs to be done. But when they find their backs against the wall, they will exceed expectations because they are engaged and committed.

Sun Tzu says: *The troops of those adept in war are used like a simultaneously responding snake. When struck on the head its tail attacks; when struck on the tail, its head attacks; when struck in the centre both head and tail attack. Should one ask: "Can troops be made capable of such instantaneous co-ordination?" I reply: "They can." For although the men of Wu and Yueh mutually hate one another, if together in a boat tossed by the wind they would co-operate as the right hand does with the left. It is thus not sufficient to place one's reliance on hobbled horses or buried chariot wheels. To cultivate a uniform level of valour is the object of military administration. And it is by proper use of the ground that both shock and flexible forces are used to the best advantage.'*

Translated – A group of resources skilled in conflict, can counter from any angle. One may ask: "Can people in my organisation become committed and cooperative?" The answer is: "Yes they can." It is normal for people within the same organisation to disagree. But throw them together into a lifeboat battered by a storm and they will help each other survive in the same way the right hand helps the left. Once you are in command of competitive actions, you cannot depend on a large organisation or abundant funding for your success. The goal of leadership is to encourage people to work together to achieve desired goals. A thorough understanding of the competitive situation will reveal how to manage both the weaker and stronger parts of your organisation so all can cooperate to achieve the goal.

Sun Tzu says: *It is the business of a General to be serene and inscrutable, impartial and self-controlled. He should be capable of keeping his officers and men in ignorance of his plans. He prohibits superstitious practices and so rid the army of doubts. Then until the moment of death there can be no troubles. He changes his methods and alters his plans so that people have no knowledge of what he is doing.*

He alters his campsites and marches by devious routes, and thus makes it impossible for others to anticipate his purpose.

Translated – An effective executive creates a situation of cohesion through their own skill, discipline and commitment, planning strategy in secret and managing its execution with clear and direct commands, not allowing everyone to know all details of the plan. In this way competitors cannot be forewarned. Cooperation between resources is essential to success. Speculation is denounced and rumours killed among constituents. In this way the morale of people remains focussed. They can change direction and alters methods at will. No competitor can anticipate direction or destination. Competitors do not understand the nature of the challenge until it is too late to counter.

Sun Tzu says: *To assemble the army and throw it into a desperate position is the business of the General. He leads the army deep into hostile territory and there releases the trigger. He burns his boats and smashes his cooking pots; he urges the army on as if driving a flock of sheep, now in one direction, now in another, and none knows where he is going. He fixes a date for rendezvous and after the troops have met, cuts off their return route just as if he were removing a ladder from beneath them.'*

Translated – The business of an executive in command is to bring his resources together and put them into a situation where they must commit to the goal. They configure resources to facilitate the highest level of performance necessary to succeed. They create a situation where complete success or total failure are the only options. They push resources forward and then burn the bridges behind them. There is no escape from commitment. They lead resources up the ladder of high expectations and then, when the time is right, kicks away the ladder. In this way, although resources do not know details of the plans, when the executive asks them to perform, they obey as the sheep obey the shepherd.

the Way

Sun Tzu says: *One ignorant of the plans of neighbouring States cannot prepare alliances in good time; if ignorant of the conditions of mountains, forests, dangerous defiles, swamps and marshes he cannot conduct the march of an army; if he fails to make use of native guides he cannot gain the advantages of the ground. A General ignorant of even one of these three matters is unfit to command the armies of a Hegemonic King.*

Translated – Do not ally with those unwilling to meet the challenge of competitive actions. Those unaware of the opportunities and obstacles are not competent to command an organisation. Those who do not employ local specialists and consultants cannot take advantage of their competitor's weaknesses nor react to unexpected circumstances. Those who are ignorant of how to manoeuvre in different competitive situations cannot be successful.

Sun Tzu says: *When a Hegemonic King attacks a powerful State, he makes it impossible for the enemy to concentrate. He overawes the enemy and prevents his allies from joining him. It follows that he does not contend against powerful combinations nor does he foster the power of other States. He relies for the attainment of his aims on his ability to overawe his opponents. And so he can take the enemies cities and overthrow the enemy's State.'*

Translated – When a capable executive moves into a competitor's territory, they do not allow their competitor to combine forces with allies. They impose their will on their competitor. They do not allow their competitor to rely on others for strength.

Sun Tzu says: *Bestow rewards without respect to customary practice; publish orders without respect to precedent. Thus, you may employ the entire army as you would one man.*

Translated – A worthy executive disdains arbitrary reward systems preferring to reward on merit and delivery. They will also not constrain themselves or their resources complying with irrelevant bureaucratic systems or tradition. In this way all people are treated equally.

Week 6

Sun Tzu says: *Set the troops to their tasks without imparting your designs; use them to gain advantage without revealing the dangers involved. Throw them into a perilous situation and they survive; put them in death ground and they will live. For when the army is placed in such a situation it can snatch victory from defeat.*

Translated – Lead by example, not with words. Motivate people with the expectation of profit. Do not tell them about the risks involved. Put them into situations where they can choose either commitment or failure, nothing else. When worthy people face this choice, they will find the strength to win.

Sun Tzu says: *Now the crux of military operations lies in the pretence of accommodating one's self to the designs of the enemy. Concentrate your forces against the enemy and from a distance of a thousand li you can kill his General. This is described as the ability to attain one's aim in an artful and ingenious manner.*

Translated – To create circumstances favourable to you first feign going along with your competitor's program. Make your competitor believe you are going in the direction he has determined for you. Lull him to sleep. In this way when you execute your carefully developed plan you can overcome your competition.

Sun Tzu says: *On the day the policy to attack is put into effect, close the passes, rescind the passports, have no further intercourse with the enemy's envoys and exhort the temple council to execute the plans.*

Translated – From the moment competitive operations begin, maintain strict secrecy. Instruct commanders to execute the plan.

Sun Tzu says: *When the enemy presents an opportunity, speedily take advantage of it. Anticipate him in seizing something he values and move in accordance with a date secretly fixed.*

Translated – When your competitor shows weakness move rapidly to take advantage. Seize what the competitor values most. Make your competitor react in accordance with your wishes.

Sun Tzu says: *The doctrine of war is to follow the enemy situation in order to decide on battle. Therefore, at first be shy as a maiden. When*

the Way

the enemy gives you an opening, be swift as a hare and he will be unable to withstand you.

Translated – Adapt your strategy according to the movements of your competitor. Put yourself into a position to gain decisive shares of the market. Begin your action quietly and secretly. When your competitor exposes their weakness, move quickly. In this way your competitor will not be able to respond.

'That's it. So, to recap, his initial verses speak of choosing your battleground or market that is your most likely to win and defend. For each opportunity you must carefully consider the potential obstacles. There is no point attacking, or even defending, where you have no advantage. Where you cannot advance or retreat concentrate on protecting yourself. If progress is difficult, stay on the offensive. When facing significant odds resort to strategy, fighting courageously to overcome.'

'We then consider how to shape your opponent's strategy to your advantage. Do anything within the law to disrupt your opponent. Examples are infiltrate and disrupt their internal communications, deplete their morale, fracture their cohesion, and dis-harmonise their alliances. Only advance your plan when you can gain advantage; otherwise hold your position. Seize any initiative that will put your opponent on the defensive. And finally, do not dwell. Speed is essential. Move rapidly when appropriate, missing no opportunity for advantage.'

'Now we look at the morale of your own resources, instilling the ethos that victory is the only option. The more successful you are the greater the morale of your resources making future success certain. Devise winning plans and solicit optimal resources. Ensure the consequences of failure are understood. If fighting for survival, unity of purpose develops its own strength. Be ready to absorb attack in one place; and strike back in another.'

'Then he looks at motivation. Foster structures and relationships that encourage internal cooperation. Strength alone does not win. Victory results from a tenacious resource base

Week 6

united in purpose. Set and encourage high standards of performance. Fully utilise any advantage or strength within your battlefield environment.'

'The next verses relate to managing the situation. Manage calmly, even in the heat of battle, and keep your people united. You need to be just; but maintain order. Be careful what you say lest it's used against you. Ensure everyone is motivated to succeed. This will keep your opponent guessing.'

'Such leadership fosters winning ways. Such leaders are knowledgeable in the ways of both allies and opponents. They understand the field of conflict and the people who can win. This enables such leaders to shape strategy to the situation.'

Chapter 47 – Thursday

'We are close to the end of our study of Sun Tzu. Just two more essays. As you are going back to London for the weekend, and Carmen will be here next week, we'll have to leave the final essay until this time next week. But tonight, we'll deal with Incendiary Attacks, or Destroying Reputation. This essay is as much about restraint as it is attacking competitors as this type of attack can quickly backfire. For this reason, I would like to add a cautionary note to that provided by Sun Tzu more relevant to today. In today's world of fast communications, in skilful hands perception versus truth can be deployed as a powerful weapon. Targeting the reputation of people can be a double-edged sword. One silly mistake can swiftly turn your sword against you. It's well understood if you face an army led by a great General, your best chance of victory is to eliminate the General – but note, this means killing the General, a definitive solution. In the corporate world this would be deemed murder which is a criminal offence and thus an option not legally available to you. Therefore, if you wish to deploy incendiary attack against people, you must be sure of success which requires considerably more research and strategy than attacking the reputation of an organisation. If it becomes personal, then we are into vendetta where the prescribed rule is to dig two graves.'

She interrupted 'But you told me you successfully destroyed the reputation of your CEO when your mentor, Bernie, died. Wasn't that revenge?'

'The emotional relationship was with Bernie. He was my catalyst to remove an incompetent Commander from the field of play. It took considerable effort and research before I was prepared to move against him because I knew just one small error in detail could be swiftly utilised to discredit my attack. He had considerable resources available to him to create a smokescreen of perception. Before such smokescreen had dispersed to reveal the truth, my career would be over. Thank goodness for the wisdom of Sun Tzu, and which guided me throughout.' He paused to reflect.

'I have a good recent example of catastrophic backfire in my summary of the Art of War when Alan Bond, an Australian businessman tried to dethrone 'Tiny' Rowland, the CEO of Lonhro plc. But for now, let's begin.'

Sun Tzu says: *There are five methods of attacking with fire. The first is to burn personnel; the second, to burn stores; the third, to burn equipment; the fourth, to burn arsenals; and the fifth, to use incendiary missiles. To use fire, some medium must be relied upon. Equipment for setting fires must always be at hand.*

Translated – Destroying a competitor's reputation is the least desirable and most dangerous competitive operation. However, it can be extremely effective if deployed with great skill. There are five areas which can be a focus for attacks on reputation: personnel or personal relationships; organisational products or individual performance; customers or employees; suppliers or supporters; and capital resources of financial backing. Your competitor must have a credible, serious weakness that can be exploited or exposed before you can destroy his reputation.

Week 6

Further, the facts and resources necessary to carry out this task must already be at your disposal.

Sun Tzu says: *There are suitable times and appropriate days on which to raise fires. Suitable times means when the weather is hot and dry. Suitable days means when the moon is in Sagittarius, Alpharatz, I, or Chen constellations, for these are days of rising winds.*

Translated – Destroying reputation depends on the legal, political, and economic environment. The political and economic currents must carry bad news effectively for the damage to spread. The appropriate time for starting a campaign to destroy a competitor's reputation is when there are other difficulties present on the political or economic scene. This is particularly true when there are problems within the organisation for which they have not yet found a convenient scapegoat.

Sun Tzu says: *In fire-attacks one must respond to the changing situation. When fire breaks out in the enemy's camp immediately co-ordinate your action from without. But if his troops remain calm bide your time and do not attack. When the fire reaches its height, follow up if you can. If you cannot do so, wait. If you can raise fires outside the enemy camp, it is not necessary to wait until they are started inside. Set fires at suitable times. When fires are raised up-wind do not attack from down-wind. When the wind blows during the day it will die down at night.*

Translated – To destroy a competitor's reputation effectively, you must focus your attention on one of these five objectives and adapt your attack to meet the requirements of that objective.

First try to cause a credible crisis within your competitor's most loyal constituents because this is the most effective method. If a crisis rapidly erupts, follow up quickly with pressure from outside. But if you cannot stir a crisis right away and your competitor remains calm, press your outside attack with caution. Let the campaign do as much damage as possible. As soon as a weakness or opportunity appears, then attack, otherwise delay.

If you determine you need to destroy a competitor's reputation and the timing is right, start the campaign even if you

the Way

must start outside of their constituency. It is not always possible to get close enough to your competitor, particularly if they are clever.

Attempting to destroy a competitor's reputation is a dangerous business. After you have started a destructive campaign, make sure you are not caught in the backlash.

As political and economic currents change direction, be prepared to modify your tactics, or abandon the campaign if the time and currents turn against you.

Sun Tzu says: *The army must know the five different fire-attack situations and be constantly vigilant. Those who use fire to assist their attacks are intelligent; those who use inundations are powerful. Water can isolate an enemy but cannot destroy his supplies or equipment.*

Translated – To destroy a competitor's reputation effectively, you must focus your attention on one of these five objectives and adapt your attack to meet the requirements of that objective. Executives must be capable of defending themselves and attack others under the strategic situation. Destroying reputation is a method of permanently defeating your competitor. Other methods of competition require great expenditure in resourcing, and even if successful results may not be permanent. A destroyed reputation may cost you nothing more than a few well-placed words. More importantly once destroyed a reputation is hard to restore.

Sun Tzu says: *To win battles and take your objectives, but to fail to exploit these achievements is ominous and may be described as wasteful delay. Therefore, it is said that enlightened rulers deliberate upon the plans, and good Generals execute them. If not in the interest of the State, do not act. If you cannot succeed, do not use troops. If you are not in danger, do not fight.*

Translated – To defeat a competitor and take control of the situation without being able to benefit from victory is a misfortune. Competing for the sake of competition is a waste of time and resources besides being an unwanted risk. Therefore, a smart executive first weighs the benefits to be gained from mounting any challenge. Once determined it is appropriate, engage to win. Do not attack your competitor's reputation unless you can profit from it. Do not consume resources unless there is a corresponding gain. Do not act aggressively unless you are in danger.

Sun Tzu says: *A Sovereign cannot raise an army because he is enraged nor can a General fight because he is resentful. For while an angered man may again be happy, and a resentful man again be pleased, a State that has perished cannot be restored, nor can the dead be brought back to life. Therefore, the enlightened ruler is prudent, and the good General is warned against rash action. Thus, the State is kept secure and the army preserved.*

Translated – An executive should not compete out of emotion or attack out of anger. Move when it is profitable; stop when it is not. While it is true emotion can return to reason, and anger to pleasure, it is also true a destroyed reputation cannot be restored, and a dead organisation cannot be returned to life. Therefore, a smart executive moves wisely and cautiously to ensure their own weaknesses are minimised, reputation preserved, and their own organisation remains intact.

'To recap, this essay is about matching optimal resources to a conflict to win without expending more resource than is necessary. He speaks of using the optimal resources including disrupting the opponent, forcing depletion of their resources. Creativity in deployment is superior to frontal attack.'

'Then he speaks of consolidating gains and exploiting any opportunities that arise. He encourages and rewards the spirit of enterprise, but carefully lays plans for the next attack to avoid losing advantage. Restraint in the heat of success is important. Attack only when you see material advantage; do not expend energy and resources in self-gratification or anger as losses cannot be recovered. Be prudent, avoiding rash actions in the heat of the moment.'

the Way

'There are many recorded battles in history where one side has forced another to retreat leaving adrenaline fuelled troops and their commanders baying for blood. A poor leader who has not planned the next move has allowed troops to pursue in disarray, eventually confronting an opponent who has regrouped or who find themselves fighting for their lives. This reckless pursuit turns the initial victor into the vanquished. We even see instances where this is a planned strategy referred to as entrapment.'

'On that note, unless you have any questions, we'll call it a day. You're away this weekend so we'll re-commence on Monday.'

'Good night, and thanks for this week. Really interesting.'

Week 7

Chapter 48 – Monday

Carmen arrived just minutes after Mel who was still in the kitchen with Seb. 'My darling Sebastian. So nice to be back. And Mel, lovely to see you. We go to the gym and sauna together?'

'Hi Carmen. Yes. See you in the gym in about 10 minutes.'

After the gym they sat in the sauna together. 'So how has it been since I was last here?'

'Life changing. I've learnt so much. Can I ask you some questions as I would like to understand certain things from a woman's perspective?'

'My dear, you can ask Carmen anything. But have you overcome your English prude yet? Do you swim with Seb?'

'No, not yet. I think it would help me if you were here the first time.'

'No problem. You join us tomorrow morning. It will be good for you. You will see. Now what do you want to ask me?'

'What are your thoughts on makeup in the workplace? I notice you use makeup, but not much.'

'My dear, you present yourself to the situation. This includes both clothes and makeup. Think how you want to be seen by your colleagues. Do you want to be seen primarily as a beautiful woman, or capable colleague? I dress for the occasion. As you may have noted my clothes for the office are nice but do not scream female. Conservative I think the English word. My makeup is minimal, and no strong perfume. These people must see me as a strong and serious executive with defined expectations from them. They must never think me just a woman who can be circumvented by reference to other executives in Germany. Does this answer your question?'

'Great. Thank you.'

the Way

She leaned over to Mel as though sharing a secret. 'Sometimes I play game with executives who think they can play with Carmen. If we have dinner away from the office Carmen will dress as woman forcing them to observe the courtesy afforded a woman of stature whilst I play them off against each other. I call it my Cleopatra role. Can be very amusing for Carmen. But takes skill to make it work for you.'

'I would love to be a fly on the wall for such an occasion.'

'Being woman in this male dominated world can be much fun when you understand the game. A woman can always beguile a man. Maybe as my project here develops there may be an opportunity to show you.'

'I look forward to see Carmen in action.'

'What has my darling Sebastian been teaching you?'

'The most painful part is the self-defence.'

'He teaches you to fight!'

'It's not really fighting. He teaches me how to deal with a groper or molester. How to neutralise them with enough pain to discourage them from trying again. So far, I have three defences for open space, and two when you're in a tight space like on the underground and someone is too close, or even touching you.'

'You can show Carmen these things?'

'Sure. Which do you want me to show you?'

'I have a manager here who is always too close to me when we walk. He is so close he touches me. I can feel his breath on my neck. I do not like.'

'Stand up' as she stood herself shoulder to shoulder. Mel issued a belly slap. Carmen crumpled back to the bench gasping for air.

When she caught her breath 'Mein Got, that hurt, but I did not see you do anything.'

'Powerful isn't it. Would you like me to show you how to do it?'

'Please, yes. Can you show me now in here?'

She demonstrated the movement to her and let her try it on her. She soon had it.

'I try on Sebastian before dinner. If I can stop him, then I try on this nasty manager tomorrow. Thank you, my dear. This school is very good for Carmen also.'

When Carmen entered the kitchen for dinner, she strolled up to Seb and administered a belly slap. He immediately folded gasping for breath. She helped him to a chair. 'Sorry my darling, but I learn this from your student, but I needed practice before I use it tomorrow. Are you all right, my darling?'

He looked at her 'You don't need any more weapons. You're Carmen.'

'There is a manager at the factory who is always too close to Carmen. Tomorrow I change this thanks to Mel.'

Mel came into the kitchen and saw him still folded on the chair. She could not help herself laughing. 'It worked then.'

'Please do not laugh, my dear. Can't you see my darling Sebastian is in pain?' they both laughed.

Chapter 49 – Tuesday

She could hear Carmen and Seb in the pool as she approached. *Am I ready for this?* She quietly edged her way along the walkway to the pool, past the gym and dressing room, but out of sight. Peaking around the corner, she caught the eye of Carmen. 'Mel, you come to join us. The water is lovely.'

It was too late to retreat. She walked to the edge of the pool, dropped her robe, and jumped into the water. It did feel good, but she kept her shoulders below the water. 'Morning'.

Carmen was first to get to her. 'Do your warmup laps my dear, and then we race.'

the Way

She needed no more encouragement to be on her way. When she got back both Carmen and Seb were standing at the pool edge. 'Sebastian, my darling, you are the starter. Are you ready? Ten laps.'

They both stood ready. They heard him say 'on your marks, go.'

Once she was halfway through the first lap, the water streaming against her body felt good. She quickly forgot her nakedness as she concentrated on her race. She could hear Carmen by her side, but she could not allow Carmen to beat her; not with Seb watching. By the fourth lap she was in her stride with a good rhythm knowing she still had more if needed. As she turned her head towards Carmen, she could see she was staying with her. On the eighth length, they were neck and neck. *'Time to turn up the pace'* she thought. As she turned for the ninth lap, she got a good kick off the wall and increased her pace. When she turned for the final length Carmen was about a metre behind her. She swam the last twenty metres with every ounce of strength she could muster, arriving at the pool edge some two metres ahead of Carmen. She was panting for breath, but elated, forgetting all about her nakedness. Carmen reached over to congratulate her. They hugged.

'You are a good swimmer, my dear. Perhaps one day I see you beat Sebastian.'

Seb got out of the pool and stood at the edge to lift both out. It was the first time she had seen him naked. *'Great body, good muscle tone'* she thought as she reached up for him to grab her hand. They stood at the poolside together as they dried off.

'See you ladies at breakfast in thirty minutes,' as he put on his shorts and T-shirt.

She went back to her room elated. She'd done it, and it wasn't the ordeal she expected. It was more exciting than she had imagined, especially when she noticed him looking at her. She wasn't quite in Carmen's exhibitionist mode, but she was not uncomfortable.

Week 7

When she arrived for breakfast Carmen was already at the table. 'Well my dear, you broke through the prude barrier. Congratulations. You swim with us each morning I am here to get used to your new freedom. We make you strong, comfortable in your own skin. I will see you this evening for our usual routine.'

After Carmen had left, he sat with her. 'Are you okay about this morning?'

'Surprisingly good. I've been fretting about it these past weeks, wondering if I could do it. I think over the next few days it will become a big tick on my to do list and shouldn't be a problem after Carmen has left. The more I do it, the more natural it will become. I might even invite you to take a sauna with me to see how I react to a more static situation.'

'Okay. Just let me know when. Try not to plan it. If you come home and have something we need to discuss, then suggest we use the sauna. Then you have the distraction you need to take your mind off your nakedness.'

'Good idea. We could do the routine I do with Carmen so we would swim together before the sauna.'

'But never feel compelled to do it. You now know why you need to be comfortable in your own skin, but you don't need to do anything you would prefer not.'

'Relax, Seb. If Carmen tells me I need to do this, then I'm good with it. As she said I'm safe here to roam around naked so what better place to get used to the idea. I hear you and she sunbathe naked on the sundeck. How can I join you unless I do the same?'

'Okay. As you have some time before you leave, and it's such a lovely morning, why don't you have a stroll around the garden to set you up for the day?'

'Great idea. See you before I leave.'

Mel was in the kitchen with Seb when Carmen arrived. She almost danced across the driveway into the house, went straight to the kitchen, kissed him, and then hugged her with a big kiss.

'Carmen has triumphed. No-one comes near Carmen again. Thank you, my dear Mel. You are good teacher. You must show me more of this self-defence. I will go change first.'

'What have you done? Now I must teach both of you! You better go get changed.'

He made space in the living room and laid two mats. They both came down the stairs together, and into the living room. 'What do you want to practise with Carmen?'

'Groper, I think.'

He extended his arm 'show me the moves to secure the wrist lock before you turn your attacker.'

'She grabbed his wrist and arm as he had taught her.'

He turned to Carmen, 'We don't play at this. It's full on so you know what it feels like for real. Do you understand? If you don't want pain now is the time to back away.'

'Mel already shows me how you practice, and she is still breathing. I'm ready.'

He turned to Mel 'Turn your back to Carmen. Now Carmen come up behind her and grope her.'

As soon as Carmen touched her buttock, she reached back to grab her wrist, spun around and completed the move spinning Carmen to the floor and holding her in a wristlock.

She was elated. 'Carmen, try to break free.'

Carmen was not about to be submissive as she tried to turn and spin her legs towards Mel to upend her. Mel was alert to her moves. She increased the pressure on her wrist, moving her legs out of range.

'Mel, Mel, Mel, you hurt Carmen. Please let me go.'

She held her grip for a few more seconds for effect and then threw her arm away from her. Carmen turned on her back and soothed her wrist. Mel had a big smile on her face. She had done it for real, not knowing which side Carmen would attack her, and it felt so good. She was feeling a power rush.

She reached out to Carmen to help her to her feet. 'Are you okay?'

Week 7

'And this is how he teaches you?'

'Yes. Full on pain.'

'Very impressive, my dear. And Carmen can learn this?'

'Only takes a few lessons to get the grip right. You don't need much strength once you have the grip, just balance. Your attacker will follow your moves because of the pain in their wrist. This is the first time I've done it for real. It feels great.'

'I know this feeling this afternoon when I slapped that man. Wow, what a rush. So, we learn this. What does Carmen need to do?'

'Okay ladies. I'll leave you to it. I need to prepare dinner. Mel, only go through the moves to secure the wrist. No more throwing tonight. I suggest you both have a gentle swim and sauna before dinner to sooth any pain. Dinner in one hour.'

Mel worked with Carmen for some twenty minutes going through the order of moves necessary to secure the lock on the wrist before turning your adversary. They practiced to where a further twist would surely force the adversary to the floor. Then they skipped the gym, had a gentle swim, and made for the sauna.

Carmen was still buzzing from her success this afternoon. 'You must tell me more about what you learn here. My darling Sebastian takes your education seriously in all respects. There must be much Carmen can learn.'

'We've spent the past weeks studying the *Art of War*.'

'Aah, this Sun Tzu man he speaks of so highly. I have not found this book in German but if you spend weeks on it, then Carmen must also study.'

'We still have one essay left. I think Seb is waiting until you leave before we finish it.'

'Would you mind if Carmen sits in with this study so I can see how to study this *Art of War*?'

'Not at all. I think we'll be too late to start this evening, but we could do it tomorrow evening. Will mean we have no sauna, just gym, and a swim.'

the Way

'Good. We do it. Let us go prepare for our lovely dinner.'

Over dinner they agreed with Seb to study the final essay of the *Art of War* together, and Carmen insisted they added fighting to their routine during her next visit.

Chapter 50 – Wednesday

They both returned earlier than usual, and completed their gym, swim, and dinner by 8pm. Seb handed a copy of the *Art of War* to Carmen suitably inscribed and then handed a copy of his teaching notes with a more readable version of the sayings of Sun Tzu to both.

'Okay ladies, I'll read the sayings of Sun Tzu, my brief translation into the corporate world, and then we'll discuss what he means, and how this knowledge can be used in the corporate environment. As you see, the essay we are studying relates to the use of spies.'

'Sun Tzu says: *When an army of one hundred thousand is raised and dispatched on a distant campaign the expenses borne by the people together with the disbursements of the treasury will amount to a thousand pieces of gold each day. There will be continuous commotion both at home and abroad, people will be exhausted by the requirements of transport, and the affairs of seven hundred thousand households will be disrupted. One who confronts his enemy for many years in order to struggle for victory in a decisive battle yet who, because he begrudges rank, honours and a few hundred pieces of gold, remains ignorant of his enemy's situation, is completely devoid of humanity. Such a man is no General; no support to his Sovereign; no master of victory.*'

Translated – Investing resources for a specific competitive situation removes these resources from alternative uses. Money and manpower already committed to conflict cannot be used for more productive purposes.

Week 7

Competitive intent can continue for many years while competitors attempt to position themselves for a decisive encounter. As time passes costs mount putting a strain on resources. The reason smart executives win victories, achieve outstanding successes, and surpass others is they know their competitor's objectives, resources, abilities, and activities. They know the mindset of the targeted markets. Furthermore, they win because they confuse their competitors about their own intentions and circumstances.

'What do you think he is suggesting with these words?'

Mel felt Carmen probably needed a little guidance regarding how Sun Tzu used indicative expressions, so she knew not to read it literally. 'Seb, I think you need to explain to Carmen which expressions are not to be taken literally.'

'You're right. I'm sorry.'

He explained to Carmen how Sun Tzu expressed environment, size, time, cost, and distance.

Carmen was quick to understand. 'I think he says before you start an expensive fight with anyone, be sure you have quality information about your enemy. And for this you need spies. Is this correct?'

'Not bad. Can I add you need to understand the importance of using spies, and you must not begrudge their cost, which is nothing in comparison to the costs of staging a war.'

'Let's move on.'

'Sun Tzu says: *Now the reason the enlightened Sovereign and the wise General conquer the enemy whenever they move, and their achievements surpass those of ordinary men, is foreknowledge. Foreknowledge cannot be elicited from the spirits, nor from gods, nor by analogy with past events, nor from calculations. It must be obtained from men who know the enemy situation.*'

Translated – This critical information, or intelligence, is not provided by wishful thinking or speculation. It's not provided by examining past events or activities. It's not provided by gathering, measuring, or analysing marketplace or corporate data. Valuable intelligence comes from people who have first-hand knowledge and personal experience about their competitors and their markets.

Carmen was reading as Seb was speaking, and then laughed. 'You say this man writes this over two thousand years ago. He should sit in meetings with Carmen. How many times does Carmen hear I think, I feel,' and then animated 'and maybe they see it in a dream? They expect Carmen to commit budget and resources to such nonsense. Carmen has many spies, so Carmen is well informed and knows the right path.'

Mel thought Carmen had taken over the session, but what she had to say, and that she could relate Sun Tzu to her daily work, could be interesting so decided not to compete. She may learn something and could always repeat this essay after she leaves.

'Sun Tzu says: *Now there are five sorts of secret agents to be employed. These are native, inside, double, expendable, and living. When these five types of agents are all working simultaneously and none knows their method of operation, they are called "The Divine Skein" and are the treasure of a Sovereign. Native agents are those of the enemy's country whom we employ. Inside agents are enemy officials whom we employ. Double agents are enemy spies whom we employ. Expendable spies are those of our own spies deliberately given fabricated information. Living agents are those who return with valuable information.*'

Translated – There are two goals for intelligence activities. The first is to obtain accurate, timely information about the objectives, resources, and activities of competitors and their markets. The second is to provide the competition with appropriately misleading information about your own objectives, resources, and activities. There are four sources that can be used to receive and transmit intelligence: general sources, internal intelligence, counterintelligence, and moles.

By combining these four sources of intelligence no-one can know how your information is obtained or provided. A powerful, but mysterious network is created. This network is the most precious asset of a chief executive.

Local sources of intelligence are those easily accessed in the majority of corporates. Local sources of intelligence include, for instance, people at conventions, low-level employees of the competition, trade publications, national publications and journals, manufacturers' representatives, and advertising. Local sources are good channels for disseminating misleading information targeted to confuse the competition. But beware of gossip and rumour.

Internal sources of information are people working for, or with the competition, their customers, and service providers who have access to important data. These sources are primarily executives and technical staff, but also include clerical people at lower levels who have access to critical information, particularly in companies with an unrestricted flow of information.

Counterintelligence agents are competition agents or moles within your company who have been converted to your use. They are the most valuable agents. But remember counterintelligence can be used by your competition as well. Some of your informants are likely counteragents. When you discover a counteragent, use them. Provide the competition with misleading information. The counteragent will be believed, at least, for a while.

Moles are agents on your payroll who have regular jobs with the customers or service providers of your competitors.

Carmen interceded again. 'This is good. Carmen did not know of these five types of spy. But it makes good sense. Tomorrow, when I fly home, I will list my spies according to this and see where I need more.'

She turned to Mel 'You see, do not use pillow talk yourself to plant fabricated information. Makes you expendable.'

Seb was amused at how Carmen interpreted Sun Tzu, but she obviously knows the essence of what is being said.

the Way

'Sun Tzu says: *Of all those in the army close to the commander none is more intimate than the secret agent; of all rewards, none more liberal than those given to secret agents; of all matters, none is more confidential than those relating to secret operations.*'

Translated – No activity is more closely tied to success than effectively gathering and disseminating intelligence. No reward should be greater than that given to those who provide essential intelligence. No operations should be more secret than those related to intelligence activities.

'Sun Tzu says: *He who is not sage and wise, humane and just, cannot use secret agents. And he who is not delicate and subtle cannot get the truth out of them. Delicate indeed! Truly delicate! There is no place where espionage is not used.*'

Translated – Only a supremely wise and subtle executive can make effective use of intelligence. The impact of intelligence is so pervasive, so encompassing and so universal there is no activity where it cannot be put to good use.

'Sun Tzu says: *If plans relating to secret operations are prematurely divulged the agent and all those to whom he spoke of them shall be put to death.*'

Translated – Intelligence must be kept secret. If plans for gathering and dissemination of intelligence are known, all involved are doomed to failure.

Carmen was really animated 'Is it true today we can execute all those who ruin our plans with loose talk? This would be so nice. Too many times men have tried to cause Carmen problems by divulging my plans to the enemy. I would love to kill these men, of course after cutting off their balls with nail clippers.'

Mel was animated with laughter as she visualised the delight of Carmen reeking her revenge in this way.

'Sun Tzu says: *Generally, in the case of armies you wish to strike, cities you wish to attack, and people you wish to assassinate, you must know the names of the garrison commander, the staff officers, the ushers, gatekeepers, and the bodyguards. You must instruct your agents to inquire into these matters in minute detail.*'

Week 7

Translated – It does not matter what type of competitive actions are planned, or whose reputation is to be attacked; it is necessary to know the names of the executives involved, their assistants, advisers, and any close service provider including drivers; even their spouse and other close family. Informants and agents must provide this data.

'Sun Tzu says: *It is essential to seek out enemy agents who have come to conduct espionage against you and to bribe them to serve you. Give them instructions and care for them. Thus, double agents are recruited and used. It is by means of the double agent that native and inside agents can be recruited and employed. And it is by this means that the expendable agent, armed with false information, can be sent to convey it to the enemy. It is by this means also that living agents can be used at appropriate times.*'

Translated – Converting your competitor's own agents achieves a critical advantage. Therefore, they should be lured with profit, guide them, and protect them. In this way they become part of your counterintelligence network.

'Sun Tzu says: *The Sovereign must have full knowledge of the activities of the five sorts of agents. This knowledge must come from the double agents, and therefore it is mandatory that they be treated with the utmost liberality.*'

Translated – A quality leader will know all aspects relating to intelligence activities. They must understand counterintelligence is the most crucial element to success in competitive operations. And they must understand the reward for counterintelligence work should be generously proportionate to the risks involved by such spies.

'Sun Tzu says: *And, therefore only the enlightened Sovereign and the worthy General who can use the most intelligent people as agents are certain to achieve great things. Secret operations are essential in war; upon them the army relies to make its every move.*'

Translated – Great leaders rely upon quality intelligence to plan their strategies. Spies are the essential component of such intelligence.

the Way

'That's it, ladies. I don't think I need to recap this essay – the shortest, but possibly the most important for corporate leadership. Any questions?'

'Sebastian, my darling, I am so grateful to Mel for allowing me to sit with you both this evening. In previous visits you have always spoken so highly of this ancient sage, but Carmen has not listened. Tonight, I see Carmen can profit from such teachings. Mel has told Carmen you have translations for these essays. Would you allow Carmen copies of these so Carmen can study this wisdom?'

'Of course. I'll have a set for you at breakfast.'

Chapter 51 – Thursday

'Now Carmen has become more involved in your development have you changed any of your views about her?'

'Last night was very interesting. The way she could totally relate to Sun Tzu was revealing. I think I've changed my mind about her using her name as a form of insecurity. I think she uses it as a ploy. It's part of her act. She wants her adversaries to see her as a woman, part of her manoeuvring process. She lets the men think she's not really in their league, and then she cuts their feet from under them. I think she's a smart lady, and I'll bet during the next few days she'll devour the other essays seeking out more, or better ways to be victorious, as Sun Tzu would say. She's some lady.'

'I applaud your observations. What about the physical side? How did you leave it with her?'

'She's up for it. She was really buzzing with her belly slap success. I think the more she can hone her powers over men, the more powerful she'll feel. My guess is during the next visit she will master the basics, and then I think she'll possibly find a reason to stay over a weekend. I told her we practice on a

Sunday so it's in her head that if she wants to become proficient in these skills, she'll need to spend at least a day with you. Alternatively, she could stay on a Friday and hone her skills with you. We'll see. But she wants these skills.'

'Do you want to go over anything from last night as Carmen did steal your show.'

'No. We all know about spies. Sun Tzu expanded upon common perception, especially with the distinct types of spy. I understand the importance of them, and how to utilise them. In fact, I can identify my existing spies albeit I had not thought of them as spies until last night. Yet again my master has opened my eyes, and the revelations are very illuminating.'

'That's it for this week unless you have any questions.'

'As I'm going to London tomorrow for the weekend, I'll study Sun Tzu on both train journeys, and more, time permitting. I know I must commit to this philosophy and can see why.'

the Way

Week 8

Chapter 52 - Monday

'Now you've had time to study Sun Tzu let me return to my consolidating six principles for the corporate environment:
- Capture your market without destroying it
- Strike where it's least expected
- Invest in the best market intelligence
- Move swiftly to overcome competition
- Employ smart strategies to achieve your goal
- Effective leadership is essential to success.'

'This will be more like a prepared lecture with accompanying notes unless you have questions as we progress. I've used real examples and Business School case studies to illustrate my point, but always remembering the Art of War is multidimensional in concept with infinite variables. You need to think generically and apply the philosophy according to the situation you face. Unfortunately, I don't have examples relative to the size of Aldridge. My sphere of influence was global corporates, and these provide a more dramatic illustration of the use and abuse of the Art of War philosophies. But I've chosen corporate examples that have recently played out or are still playing out.'

'Let's start with what we should have learnt during this 20th century to date using the original essays as written.'

By far the biggest lesson is that ill-considered warfare results in costly devastation and destruction. The two World Wars cost millions of dead all over the world, devastated much of Europe and Asia, and left even the victors weaker and poorer than when war began – think UK.

Subsequently, during four decades of the Cold War, America spent substantial resources to prevent communism spreading across the world. In the process billions of dollars have been expended on armaments all over the world, including countries that could ill afford them. Finally, we have witnessed the demise of communism with its planned market economy revealed as fantasy. The Cold War has ended, and the military tensions between the superpowers will hopefully subside, albeit I do not anticipate any decline in the perceived need for more warfare resources. Vietnam was yet another senseless war where no-one won anything, but many suffered on both sides.

Not that major conflicts have been eradicated. Hovering underneath the East-West conflict regarding communism is another referred to in higher circles as the North-South conflict, more commonly known as the Islam versus Christianity problem. Unfortunately, we do not have the same clarity as we had with capitalism and communism. Islam is a fractured ideology, especially between Sunni and Shi'ite Muslims. The conservative fundamentalists have divergent toxic views. It's very difficult to determine which would be a better, integrating faction. In our need to understand the meaning of life, and death, humans created the unique construct that their striving to make a difference gives meaning to their lives thus human ambition has been the force creating culture and ideology, myths and legends. But the "vaulting ambition" Shakespeare attributed to Macbeth has been behind history's most spectacular follies and tragedies; religion being at the forefront.

In contrast to decreasing military competition, the end of the Cold War facilitated economic competition between countries and global corporates to a new and higher pitch. Global competition has become ferocious, and leaders of nations and leaders of corporations both understand business "is a matter of vital importance to the State . . . the road to survival or ruin."

As in Sun Tzu's age of the Warring States, today's business world is one of continual competition between companies as they strive for survival and success across the world. Faced with scarce and expensive resources and an ever-changing economic environment, competitors seek even the slightest advantage.

Meanwhile, executives attempt to cope with the overwhelming volume of information coming at them from market research and the mass media. Add to this a variety of consultants clamouring for service contracts, trying to sell strategic insight or the latest management fad. The result is often not clarity, but perplexing confusion; not composed, but seemingly chaotic. It becomes ever more difficult to build a coherent, cohesive strategy unless you're smart enough to disseminate data to identify between fact and fiction.

To overcome this problem, it is essential to gain understanding of a philosophy geared toward competition, survival, and success. One that is both integrated and holistic—one that has stood the test of time. The Art of War's principles of strategy is that philosophy. This session discusses the first two principles of Sun Tzu's philosophy followed by two more tomorrow, and the final two on Wednesday, showing how they are all interrelated.

The Goal of Strategy: Capture your market without destroying it

Many city-states, countries, and empires have been built by leveraging their specific history, geography, know-how, and resources to control their environment. Thus, they were able to survive, achieve stability, expand, either dominate or build alliances with their neighbours, and ultimately prosper for hundreds of years.

The Roman Empire grew from a small area surrounding Rome to extend from Britain to the Black Sea to Egypt to Gibraltar. The structure of the Roman Empire could be deemed a peaceful coexistence of strategic alliances mostly forged by military might and controlled from Rome. It lasted over 500 years. The Mongol Empire began with a single nomadic tribe in central Asia but grew to rule lands from China to India to Europe. And, of course, the sun never set on the British Empire for several centuries.

the Way

Businesses, like countries, have a specific history, culture, and asset base in terms of products, facilities, and services. But how do we judge whether a business is successful? The Western view is a business exists to generate income primarily to provide a return on investment to stakeholders. In contrast, the typical Asian view is a business exists primarily to provide jobs for its employees. Although both views differ, there is one constant between them; to meet either goal a business must survive and prosper. Therefore, successful businesses, like successful countries, are those that may have started small but grew on their successes; surviving and prospering over many years.

If the goal of business is to survive and prosper its strategy must be "to take All-Under-Heaven intact"- that is to capture its marketplace. It must identify the markets it wants to capture and commit the resources to achieving market dominance in those markets whether by overwhelming force or strategic alliance. This will ensure its survival and prosperity. There are many examples of companies that have achieved this, especially in technology such as computers, telecommunications, and cars. They began in their local markets but used creative strategy to bring value to the global marketplace, grew quickly, and continue doing business successfully for many years. They had to establish themselves in their industry or niche, enabling them to protect themselves in their home markets, and then shape the global forces in their industry in their favour. Their success is defined by the relative market dominance they achieved.

Market dominance can appear in many forms; technology leadership, brand recognition, or cost and cash flow management are some signs of it. We can also think of market dominance in terms of market share. Companies with dominant market share in an industry segment or an entire industry are more able to influence industry and markets, direct its evolution, and establish an excellent competitive position. Their powerful position allows them to set the industry's standards and thus define the field of play. Firms that have achieved dominant market share most likely also enjoy the advantages of higher customer loyalty, larger sales volumes, better economies of scale, and strong distribution capabilities. In addition, substantial data and research have shown that market share and profitability are indivisible in a range of industry environments. These same advantages tend to increase revenues and lower unit costs, thus increasing profitability. If a company can achieve relative market dominance, prosperity will be their reward.

In the 1970s and 1980s, Japanese companies, with their long-term view on strategy, emphasis on competition and survival, and belief that business is warfare, supported this thinking. Japanese companies have been very successful at capturing market share and achieving a dominant position in many industries, making significant inroads in both the European and U.S. markets. This has provided them with the ability to influence their respective industries, even after the U.S. and European markets started to successfully challenge their dominance. However, it should be noted in the car manufacture sector, both US and Japanese manufacturers chose peaceful cooperation and coexistence using strategic alliance over competitive warfare. We have yet to see if the resource commitment by the Japanese to such long-term strategies is sustainable as over-investment in the long-term can significantly exceed the shelf-life of its products and thus become a burden in the future.

If you hope to win all without fighting, you must utilise strategy and tactics that enable you to capture market share prosperously without destroying your industry or your market. Remember market dominance is the means; survival and prosperity are the end game. Thus, the essence of good business is to win without conflict as with the car manufacturers. Conflict requires expensive resources which are not endless, and if depleted leave you defenceless. Outright price confrontation, as witnessed in the airline and tobacco industries, should be avoided.

Avoiding Strength

Unfortunately, pitting strength against strength is all too often the preferred method of competition among many Western countries. Although the entrepreneurial culture of the USA has yielded some of the largest and most successful global corporations, the domestic USA's corporate landscape is littered with examples of such failed campaigns. This is because the direct approach is embedded in Western culture. It appears in our legends, our sports and, at times, in our military adventures. It's two titans in armed combat – victor takes all. It's the frontal attack philosophy; impatient, unsubtle, and heads down testosterone driven Rambo.

Because strength-on-strength attacks are so direct, they can often become personal. As executive wills and egos flair, usually fuelled by the media, these debilitating battles last much longer than they should, with emotional content replacing cool focus.

This tendency towards direct, head-to-head competition results not only from our culture but also comes from a line of reasoning that is misguided, yet dangerously appealing. The thought process starts along the line if a competitor has been successful by being the lowest-cost provider, or by increased spending on R&D, marketing, and distribution then we can do the same. This imitation philosophy leads to executives attacking strong competition at its strongest point. This strategy becomes a campaign of attrition; invariably ending in failure. The Vietnam War is a good example.

Attack Weakness

Attacking weakness is the skill of master strategists. They don't use pretentious ego to prove themselves. Even the mighty lioness does not need to chase the fastest antelope in the herd; she runs down the slowest which significantly increases the chance of satiating the appetite of her young.

In business, there are several ways you can apply Sun Tzu to create a situation where your company's strengths can be pitted against your competitor's weakness. You might attack weakness in their value chain. If they are strong in manufacturing, but distribution is weak, you can reinforce your distribution channels to court their customers. Better still secure their distributors and make them your ally or resource. Japanese companies applied this strategy where they leveraged their strength in consistent quality manufacturing to secure favour with distributors throughout Europe and the USA.

If your company is a major player in a market with a few large companies and many small ones, then secure your increase in market share by absorbing or eliminating the small players one at a time, thus surrounding the other major players and securing market-share without confronting them.

'You could also go into "emptiness, strike voids, and bypass what he defends" by creating new products, attacking niches in the market, or entering new geographic markets.'

CNN, ESPN and MTV are good examples of strategies utilising new technologies to create products targeted at specific niche markets. Whilst conventional TV networks fought to gain each other's market share by ever more sitcoms and bad guy versus good guy law enforcement series, these new competitors avoided the strengths of these major players by targeting what they did not provide. With CNN it's 24/7 world news, ESPN provides 24/7 sport, and MTV 24/7 music video. They all leveraged the new delivery system of cable TV. They avoided their larger competitors, penetrating their market where they least expected.

'Sound familiar?'

She smiled 'Sun Tzu – Manoeuvring.'

'Well done. Interestingly MTV provides the established music industry with a new means of promoting its products, and the musical film industry revived by delivering the block-buster songs through MTV as a promotional vehicle for their new musical films. Rather than the established industries trying to subdue this interloper, they embraced the benefits provided to themselves.'

'Creative bands such as Queen exploited MTV with heralded music videos, probably the most famous of which is *Bohemian Rhapsody* which is claimed to have established MTV as the channel of choice for music aficionados.'

It will be interesting to see how CNN develops over the years as it does not attract subscription-based delivery. Its survival depends on sponsorship, advertising, and quality, unbiased reporting. Will this need for sponsorship to support advertising revenue cause CNN to bend to the particular doctrine of a major sponsor wishing to deploy CNN to their own ends? It's expensive to have anchors in every country. This is a potential conflict which could challenge the independence of CNN.

General Electric, the US giant conglomerate, chose a similar approach by investing heavily in emerging markets. The end of the Cold War and the shift to capitalism around the world opened new market opportunities for adventurous companies in need of new markets. General Electric made it a priority to deploy resources to China, India and Mexico. The CEO, John Welch, wants General Electric established in these countries before the competition follow their lead. The same is happening in banking as known and reliable banking in these emerging economies is very much needed by such conglomerates.

Then we have the successful pre-emptive move into primary, secondary, and undergraduate classrooms around the world by Apple Computers before any other personal computer vendor creating a very loyal customer base.

Another US company, Hewlett-Packard, having established its dominance in the word processing, business calculator and printer market, engaged in a philosophy of making its products quickly obsolete by a continual development of new features and technology thus stimulating a regular churn rate by its loyal customers. This philosophy may be challenged in the coming years by concerns for the unnecessary wastage of functional resources as people become more environmentally conscious and recycling becomes a prominent consideration.

I assume you know of Tiny Rowland, chairman of the UK Lonrho conglomerate – much in the press with the Harrods takeover debacle. Most of Tiny Rowland's corporate battles are vicious. He's a very hard man, an enemy no one wants to have. He finds weaknesses in his adversaries and ruthlessly exploits them. He is renowned for courting allies no matter of repute, exploit them, and then drop them once their usefulness expires. Very much the enemy of my enemy could be a useful ally.

His most merciless recent victory was over the Australian tycoon Alan Bond, whom he at first befriended as a potential "white knight" when Lonrho was being stalked by another predator, Asher Edelman. Bond bought out Edelman's stake, boasting of himself as Rowland's natural successor and continued buying up shares. Rowland's response was to turn on him with savage intensity, publishing a 93-page document claiming Bond, sustained by a fragile pyramid of borrowings, was technically insolvent. Bond's bankers demanded their money back, and he faced bankruptcy and jail.

'The story is still running regarding his vicious dispute with Mohamed Al-Fayed over Harrods.'

Attacking Weaknesses at Boundary Points

Boundary areas, unclear lines of demarcation, disharmony between business units, or even dependency on a key resource, are all examples of weakness. These boundaries are typically found where there is a fundamental difference in thinking such as between R&D and manufacturing, manufacturing and distribution, marketing and development, sales region, geographic culture, or even between a competitor and its business partners, and can be exploited to good effect. I was even the subject of such an attack. We were in dispute with a larger investment bank. I was the lead for my bank, and we were outmanoeuvring our larger competitor whose intransigence was complicating the situation involving senior resources and

the Way

expensive lawyers. I received a call from a head-hunter offering me a far superior package to join our competitor bank. I accepted on the understanding I would not participate further in the dispute other than suggest an equitable settlement which was accepted by both banks saving face and restoring valuable resources back to their day jobs.

Attacking Psychological Weaknesses

Attacking your competitor can be psychological, directed at, and focussed on the mindset of your competitor. We can exemplify this in high-tech industries such as computers. Customers of computer companies have large investments in installed systems. The rapid change in technology development means computer companies need to regularly churn their products. They will court their customers informing them of the upgrade benefits of the next model well before release to allow for planning, and confirmation of staying relevant in the coming years. Armed with this valuable information competitors can then use rumour and cast doubts on the efficacy of the proposed updates through the likes of industry journals, press releases, and trade shows. The trade press then become more involved, as do competitor software providers. The disquiet can cause a breakdown in customer loyalty, or deferment of upgrade causing your competitor to spend resources trying to reassure customers, and deferred cash flow. This is the least resource-intensive means of attacking a competitor – *'the supreme excellence in war is to attack an enemy's plans.'*

I have experienced companies so focussed on seeking the weaknesses of their competitors they forget to use the same tactical skills to look at themselves for their own weaknesses. Looking within is as important as looking out. If key resources to your success are not honed, or even procured, this situation needs to be rectified as a priority. Therefore, you must test your own weaknesses, as your competitors surely will.

What I must avoid with you is the status quo approach. Far too many execs get locked into safe strategies using the same strategies as others in their field; usually imitation. Some years ago, it was a well-known adage you would not get fired for buying IBM. Great for IBM, but rarely good for your business. As Sun Tzu says complex problems, such as competitive strategy, require specific solutions that are not always the most obvious option. To be successful, you must not follow strategies your competitor is pursuing. If you copy someone else, at best, you can only be second best. You must find your own specific strategy to secure victory.

Chapter 53 – Tuesday

Invest in the best market intelligence

The best market intelligence can be described as foreknowledge so let us start by defining what we mean by foreknowledge. Foreknowledge is knowledge of something before it exists or happens but not projecting the future based on the past; it is not trend analysis. Foreknowledge is first-hand insight and a thorough understanding of your competitor, their strengths, weaknesses, plans, and people. Wherever such information is gleaned, it must be accurate, reliable, and preferably confirmed through unconnected sources. When you hear the expression *information is king*, what we mean is valuable information.

Unfortunately, much of what passes as competitive analysis can be very shallow, even with the computing capabilities of today. Can't beat an old-fashioned spy. There are major corporates who use the larger investment banks as a source of strategic advice because they amass significant data of both the market and the players to service their investment clients. These banks are more adept at dissecting a corporate to find opportunities for M&A, funding, or listing. Fee-based revenue is the bread-and-butter of investment banks so they pro-actively search for opportunity.

You must completely understand the capabilities of your competition, and their plans. To know this, you must delve into the minds of your competitor's executives. You must know their CV's in depth so you can anticipate their preferred approach. You must know the culture within your competitor. Is your competitor very structured and thus unlikely to respond quickly, or are they fleet afoot? Do they have a strong, collective responsibility Board, or are they essentially CEO driven?

Some types of companies are better at understanding their competitor's capabilities and mindsets. Companies in the takeover business, hostile or otherwise, must be able to analyse their target on an informed and continuing basis because their business depends on such thoroughness. When you see a merger or acquisition go sour, in most cases it's because the lead company failed in its analysis thus misjudging the situation.

For example, Hanson plc, a British-based company, currently one of the ten largest companies in the UK, is a conglomerate that grows primarily through acquisition. It has an excellent track-record of successful takeovers and profitability. One of their key skills is to target companies, parts of which can be sold off to reduce debt; sometimes covering the cost of the original acquisition. For example, in 1986 they executed a hostile takeover of Smith-Corona in the USA for $930 million. They quickly sold off its real estate and other divisions for $964 million keeping the typewriter and chemical divisions, essentially for free. Critical to Hanson's success is a thorough understanding of their executive opponents. They have an excellent, dedicated staff for in-depth research of targets, and key contacts with the major investment banks who can provide them with their insight into both the target company and its management. This combination of rigorous analysis and reliable intelligence is competitive research at its best.

Know Yourself

Foreknowledge does not stop at knowing your competition. You must also know your own strengths and weaknesses. Some of this will be from your own company data. But this is only part of the story. How are you perceived by the marketplace? Who are your customers and are they loyal? Who are your key personnel, and what would be the impact to you if they were no longer available to you? Can you identify potentially disloyal personnel who could be recruited as spies by competitors? What weaknesses can you exploit within your company if you were with the competition? All of this and more is first-hand analysis obtained by knowing your own company intimately. When not travelling I made it a point to "walk the floor" of all areas of the bank pertinent to my responsibilities twice each day talking to people. These relationships are important. If you are a stranger to these people, they will not open their minds to you about their real thoughts and concerns.

I presume you have already realised the Production Director role must be conducted at the coal face. I also hope you walk the floor regularly to feel the environment. This is also the place where you can quickly detect problems. Was there a problem with a delivery? Was it addressed positively and quickly? It's better that a subordinate employee reports to his leadership that there was a small problem which was quickly fixed, rather than you have a problem. Avoiding mole hills becoming mountains induces customer loyalty. Makes you dependable, even if a little more expensive.

Deploying Information Technology

Computer technology is now entrenched in most aspects of corporate activity from transaction processing, management information, design systems, and even computerised manufacturing machinery. There is a common view that computers will eventually control the world as we see processors capable of artificial intelligence infiltrate the corporate world. We can see this technology as a blessing; and a curse. It concentrates

the Way

valuable information for yourself, and for your competitor if not adequately protected. For example, when computers first entered banking for transaction processing purposes systems were designed to display the whole transaction irrespective of the level of input required as a transaction progressed through processing stages to ultimate settlement. This is highly sensitive information. My settlements team would speak with counterparts in other banks gaining valuable information which would allow us to significantly profit from this lax approach.

We introduced a concept in computer systems known as *views*. What any member of staff saw on their screen depended on their login information. Very much minimum need to know approach in order complete their task. Only key managers could view the whole transaction.

We will discuss the use and abuse of computer technology in business later in this process.

Know your market

It's an imperative you know the "terrain" on which you are competing; and the business environment in which you wish to operate. A regular flow of in-depth market research and analysis generated both internally and externally from reliable sources to understand your market, how your market is evolving and any constraints to growth you need to consider is fundamental knowledge.

Are you a market leader, or follower? If a market leader, how do you stay ahead of your competition? If a follower is there anything you can do to influence leaders to your advantage?

Identifying architects as the future of the influence of Aldridge in fabrication, together with Charles identifying the potential role of polymer products is a bold initiative which, if proven correct, will allow you to take a dominant position in the future.

Whoever has the best customer information has competitive advantage. Such information can be utilised to create close ties with customers. The resulting informed information facilitates rapid response to customer needs.

Deception

One of the critical ways to thwart attacks by your competitors is to ensure they cannot fully understand you, or your plans. This is achieved by deception. By leaving the trojan horse seemingly abandoned outside the walls of Troy, and supposedly sailing away, the Greeks deceived the Trojans into taking the horse within the city in celebration. After night fell, the Greek soldiers emerged from the horse, opened the city gates, and sacked Troy.

To beat your competitors, you must first deceive its intelligence gathering mechanism about the true nature of your business plans – a confuse and destroy philosophy. This will cause your competitor to waste resources in the wrong direction and possibly create weaknesses in them for you to exploit.

If your architect plan proves good, the fact you're leading this charge rather than Michael is an unintended deception as your competitors will watch where Michael is focusing his efforts.

If we go back to the Hanson takeover of Smith-Corona Sir Gordon White, the CEO of Hanson in the USA, and who led this charge, first moved to acquire Smith-Corona with a formal tender offer of $60 per share. The management of Smith-Corona was also interested to buy the company themselves and made an offer to the shareholders of $70 per share. In response Hanson increased its bid to $72 per share. In an attempt to thwart Hanson, the Smith-Corona management contracted with Merrill Lynch an option to buy two of its best performing divisions at a substantial discount if Hanson succeeded in its bid. Hanson promptly withdrew its tender offer which, on Wall Street, indicates withdrawal. Smith-Corona management thought the battle over so let down their guard in pursuit of their management buyout. Hanson quietly purchased a 25% stake in Smith-Corona on the open market, increasing Hanson's stake to 27%. The Smith-Corona management was furious and launched a lawsuit. Hanson launched a countersuit and won on appeal. Hanson then purchased even more stock until Hanson held over one-third of the stock. This thwarted the management buyout which required approval by two-thirds of shareholders. Hanson then thwarted the Merrill Lynch option and finally completed the takeover of Smith-Corona making a handsome profit. The key to Hanson's success was deceiving the Smith-Corona executive into thinking they had withdrawn. The poor management of Smith-Corona underestimated the skills of Hanson, and their own ineptitude.

Lawful deception comes in many guises and colours. You can use the media to misguide your competitors by withholding or disguising key information about a new product. If a competitor uses the media to test if you are about to launch a new product, or enter a new market, you can legitimately be canny in your response even if you have no such intention. Leave them guessing for as long as possible. As part of an attack strategy against a competitor, it's an accepted ploy to allow your competitor to think you're not strong enough. Encourage them to underestimate your potential giving you the element of surprise when you launch your offensive.

However, such tactics require discipline within your company. To mislead requires control to ensure your deception is convincing. If you are a public company, you must have the confidence of your shareholders lest they misread your intentions and dump your stock. Regulators expect filings to represent a true and fair picture of the company. If your filings are quarterly, you only have a ninety-day window to deploy a deception and make your move. People within your company must maintain secrecy, and information regarding real intent should not be collated where it can be read by unauthorised people. A private company like Aldridge can be very playful because Charles is the only shareholder, and Aldridge has no requirement to file quarterly information.

Week 8

Move Swiftly to Overcome competitors

It's now well established in modern warfare a small elite force such as the English SAS or American Navy Seals applied swiftly with good intelligence can overcome substantial odds with good results.

Events at the start of the second World War illustrate a more bruising account of the cost of not being able to respond. Germany was advancing on France. The large, well-equipped French army was spread out and entrenched behind the Maginot Line in expectation of trench warfare. But the Germans introduced a new element of speed in the form of fast-moving tanks supported by infantry moved around in trains and trucks; a new paradigm in warfare known as blitzkrieg. Even though the French had more and better tanks, the French strategy meant they spread them around in small numbers and could only move as fast as the infantry who were foot-soldiers. Using divisions of Panzer tanks with overwhelming firepower, the Germans could quickly break through enemy defences moving on into vulnerable areas to create chaos and confusion. Once behind the lines they kept moving, ignoring pockets of French army resistance which were swept away later. Thus, a smaller, lesser equipped German army using a strategy of speed, shock, and concentrated firepower caused France to surrender after only a few weeks even though on paper the French army was much larger and better equipped.

This inability by the French military elite to strategize and respond to attack revealed itself a few weeks later when asked by Winston Churchill to surrender the French navy fleet to British control, and which was anchored in a safe port in North Africa. Again, the French procrastinated. But Churchill was familiar with warfare. He wanted these ships as the UK was not suitable prepared for war. But he saw how swiftly Germany could attack and could not risk these naval ships falling into the hands of the Germans, so ordered the French fleet be sunk. This

the Way

compounded the embarrassment of the French military who again showed their lack of understanding of the art of warfare.

The irony of Blitzkrieg is it was Winston Churchill who, in 1916, saw the need for tanks to allow manoeuvre in warfare, and it was called a tank as a deception it was carrying water to the front-line.

Therefore, size and resource base are not important if you have the speed to overcome these impediments allowing you to exploit your opportunity before your lumbering competitor can respond.

In the Hanson takeover one factor contributing to its success was the ability to assess the counter-situation and respond quickly. From concept of strategy to victory took about one hundred business days, including the Court battles. Sir Gordon White did not allow his enemy any time to rest or regroup in this relentless battle.

I would say speed is critical to success because it allows resources to sustain and exploit the resulting market momentum once your strategy is victorious. German military philosophy was to launch simultaneous attacks and determine which one was stalling, and which succeeding. Instead of sending reinforcements to the one stalling, they increased resourcing to the successful attack. This allowed them to push deeper into enemy territory, cut off areas of resistance from their supply routes, and continue the tempo and momentum of attack. Later, after securing their position, they could readily defeat any remaining enemy strongholds. Classic Sun Tzu.

This same strategy applies to business. If you have two new products in the marketplace with one doing well and the other poorly, which do you choose to add additional resourcing?

Management often respond to the product not performing. Their logic is the one performing well already has momentum. This results in the performing product being starved of resources just as it is gaining market acceptance. When you have a breakthrough, you must exploit it. Therefore, Sun Tzu would say reinforce success, and starve failure. When you have exploited a weakness in your competitor's product line with a winning product of your own pour resources into your product to consolidate your position.

You encounter this problem time and time again. A company launches a new car but not sure how the market will respond so not prepared for a major success. They launch the car. The market loves it. The company cannot deliver market demand. The momentum has gone, and customers buy elsewhere. We see companies release a range of sizes for a new product but read the market incorrectly. The company expects primary demand for one size and heavily resource this size, whilst the market demand is for another. We saw this recently with the launch of the IBM AS400 range of computers. Despite market data suggesting the larger machines would be the primary choice of customers, IBM stockpiled the smaller units, leaving customers with at least a six month wait, if they could wait.

Another element of speed is your own capability to deliver. Can you reduce your business cycle-time in terms of development, materials supply, manufacture, distribution, and sales? But other factors should be addressed as importantly, if not more importantly. These are the decision processes within the company, and the speed at which you can generate customer awareness and product take-up.

Timely executive decisions are fundamental to seizing opportunity. The essential ingredient is fast and reliable data. But how fast does information from the field filter up to the right level? How long does it take for feedback and recommendations from subordinates to filter up to the right level? How long does it take to rank and compile data into a plan? As mentioned earlier companies that depend upon mergers and acquisition to build their products and sustainability have skilled and dedicated resources to this task. But for most companies it is part of an executive's busy schedule. For these companies, there must be the discipline and the will built into the culture to ensure

the Way

decisions are timely. Much of this is down to leadership which we will discuss tomorrow.

Chapter 54 – Wednesday

Employ smart strategies to achieve your goal

To defeat competition, you must first make them conform to your strategy, your rules, your will. You must seize the advantage and make your competitor meet you at the time and place of your choosing. To master your competition in this manner is what Sun Tzu meant by "shaping".

Smart strategies "shape" your competition. Such strategies not only attack the resources of competition, but more importantly, the minds, thinking, and morale of its executive team throwing them off balance, and thus ready for defeat.

Direct impacts are gaining and holding strategic positions in the marketplace, using technology to gain advantage, securing key buyers and distribution channels to deny competitors access to key markets.

Indirect impacts send signals to the market that bait competition into committing strategic mistakes such as leading them into unprofitable markets and directing them away from markets you desire.

Then we must consider alliances which further our cause at the expense of the competition; even stealing your competitor's alliances.

Effective leadership is paramount to success

During my career I have witnessed good leaders, mediocre leaders, and bad leaders. Occasionally I have witnessed great leaders. I would say the basic difference is the ability to analyse a situation, make a decision, and quickly action such decision effectively.

Vision is a description you will often associate with a great leader. I have witnessed such vision and was taught the skills to disseminate the important global political and economic drivers that determine inevitability, with consequences of global events defining the timeline of such inevitability. As an executive I was expected to define 5-year projections where the first 3-years were expected to be accurate with the fourth year being within reasonable margins of error (consequences) and the fifth year a logical projection. For each subsequent year this 5-year plan would be advanced one year having tested the accuracy of the original projection.

The discipline of this skill is beyond the scope of your initial training with me as it requires an acute understanding of global economics but, time permitting, we may look at how you would project the UK economy over five years – a skill you will need.

This is certainly one task where leadership with vision cannot be replaced with analysis from the likes of economists who work with models that do not account for the human implications. Knowing and understanding key political leaders is fundamental to clear corporate leadership. Knowing the political church of political leaders who can significantly influence events, and their personal objectives whilst in power, can dramatically influence economic activity.

This may sound daunting. However, there is one component in this equation that significantly aids corporate thinking – political leaders usually have a four to five-year term in office thus, despite what they might say, they will most certainly impose their impacts in the short-term, especially if seeking re-election. Thus, predicting likely events is not so difficult.

In addition to knowing your markets, economic, and political environment, a good leader will know their resource base in detail including an intimate relationship with key resources. Leadership requires connection with resources. Such connection is not imposed; its earnt. We have already stated the qualities required for leadership; such qualities being evident rather than assumed.

Chapter 55 – Thursday

Charles asked to speak with her. He had a request from Michael that she hands over her architect clients as she could not possibly service them properly from Matlock. As he was the Business Development Director, all business leads should go through him. As Mel no longer reported to him, she should no longer be involved in business generation.

'But Charles, it was my initiative that brought us these clients. I nurtured them when Michael was telling me I was wasting my time, and now we have the possibility to engage directly with a project using the polymer material. I know these architects; the relationship is with me. In any event, my view is we've lost our way in this new world of computer technology, and we need to get back in the race, but with architects and developers, not main contractors.'

'Good argument, Mel. I have invited Michael to meet us here next Wednesday to put all arguments on the table. Should give you time to put something together that supports your view. For what it's worth I agree with you, but he is the Business Development Director for major corporates. I would suggest you need a good case to keep your clients, but you have until Wednesday to put it together.'

'I think it's time to deploy Sun Tzu as I can think of at least one tactical strategy that would suggest we should not announce our deployment of architects to our competitors in this way, just as you have kept the polymer opportunity under wraps.'

'That's a good start, my dear. Can't wait to see Sun Tzu in action.'

Week 8

When she got home, she poked her head into the kitchen 'We need to talk, we have a real challenge I need to prepare before next Wednesday. See you in the gym in five minutes. I'll switch on the sauna before I get ready.' She was gone.

It required a quick adjustment to dinner to eliminate need for supervision.

When he got to the gym, she was already there and had started her routine. He saw no reason to exercise with her so sat on a bench. 'What's this challenge?'

'Michael Chimes has proposed to Charles he takes control of my architect clients. He's struggling to get new business, and I have three lucrative contracts in process. His most recent bids all failed, so he wants to steal my contracts.'

'Isn't he the Business Development Director and thus responsible for new business?'

'Yes, but these clients are my initiative, and I've nurtured these clients myself. He has taken no interest in any of them and has met none of them. When I've needed executive support, it has always been Charles.'

'What does Charles think about this proposal?'

'He's not keen, but it's up to me to make the case to keep them under my control. I'm being tested, and this is a test I must pass. I need your help.'

'Okay. You better give me a full brief of where you are. What was your reason to pursue these clients? Why do you think they'll work better with you? Let's get as much data as possible and then structure an argument.'

'No problem. Time for a quick swim, and then we can talk in the sauna.'

They went to the changing room where she was out of her kit quickly and on her way to the pool. He stripped, collected two towels, and joined her. After her ten lengths, she was ready. They quickly towelled down and entered the sauna.

Before she had time to settle, he asked her to give him the history from the inception of her initiative, including why she started with architects, and which took her some fifteen minutes to deliver. As he expected, she had the instinct to see things were changing in the commercial office sector, but still did not have the skills to articulate the business argument.

'Okay, lady, let's out of here and go do some work. When you're ready can you go to my study. As you walk through the door, turn immediately right. You'll see a cupboard where I keep stationery supplies. Pick up two pads and pens and bring them to the kitchen. I'll go finish preparing dinner.'

He noticed she had completely forgotten about her state of dress, or lack of it as she towelled down, picked up her gym kit and was on her way to her room.

After dinner they cleared the table leaving only their pads and pens.

'Let's start by looking at the headings we need to cover. Can you tell me what you think we need to both defend your position and demolish your opponent?'

'Using my teachings of Sun Tzu, I need to set out my battlefield. Therefore, I need to state why I thought to approach architects, the relationships developed, and why this strategy should be kept under the radar for as long as possible.'

'You have overlooked one essential ingredient. This is not about you. It's not personal. It's about the game called business.'

'But these are my clients I've developed over the past two years.'

'They are clients of Aldridge developed by you in the name of, and on behalf of Aldridge. They're not your clients. Do we really need to return to your first week here? Let me suggest headings which I would like you to flesh out without any personal content. Let's start with a heading to reflect why you thought this initiative necessary. Start writing.'

Background to the Initiative – what changes did you see in the market that stirred you to develop these relationships?

Evidence to Support this Continuing Initiative – what are the economics to support this continuing initiative.

Changes in the Market that Support this Initiative – changes in the way the market is evolving, why architects are leading the charge, and why relationships with them will be more productive for Aldridge than current clients. To this you can add the relevance of new fabrication materials.

Changes needed within Aldridge to respond to Market Changes – changes in philosophy, marketing process, architect support, design support, and anything else that needs to change within Aldridge to capitalise on this opportunity.

And finally, **Why this Initiative should remain concealed from Competitors** – this is where you can certainly use Sun Tzu in support of your arguments.

'Do these headings make sense to you?'

Somewhat sheepishly, 'Yes my master. I apologise for my personal content.'

'You have one hour to flesh out these headings noting what you don't know and thus need to research.'

Feeling somewhat deflated, she quickly started to consider her task.

It was after 9:30 by the time she considered her task as complete as possible. 'I'm ready to progress to the next stage.'

'What information do you need to structure your argument?'

'I need to formalise information gleaned from my architect clients, why the new breed of financier/developers are changing the landscape, ditto for computer technology, and economic data for where I think the market is heading. I know what needs to change within Aldridge to meet these new opportunities.'

'Okay. It's getting late. Write a list of questions for your architects. This will be a survey so you will contact each architect and put your questions to them recording their answers looking for both correlation and inconsistency. I will look at your questions while you breakfast, and you can use time tomorrow to contact as many architect clients as possible to secure their response. We can then examine the strength of your data over the weekend. I'll seek the economic data you require.'

Chapter 56 – Friday

After she had left for the factory, he reached for the telephone.

'Good morning Charles.'

'Hello Sebastian. What can I do for you this fine morning?'

'Mel has informed me of her task for next Wednesday. It gives me an opportunity to apply much of what she has learnt. I've asked her to poll her architect contacts today with a set of questions so we can get a clear picture of the current trends. Do you have any paperwork on the polymer technology you could share with me regarding its commercial viability?'

'Sure. I'm very optimistic this technology will provide good opportunities for us. I'll send it with Mel this evening.'

'I will also chat with old banker friends who specialise in the commercial sector. Banks are always five years ahead of the curve in technology so where they are today is where the general commercial sector is heading. Are you prepared to let her lead the debate with her arguments?'

'Most certainly. It's her patch. She needs to defend it. I want to see what she can do.'

'Good. She'll be fully prepared. I'll also go with her to London on Saturday to get her properly rigged out. No good being good if you don't look the part. It will put her into a different mindset if she is suitably dressed for the occasion.'

'How much do you think she must spend?'

'She's starting from a zero base so I guess between £1,000 and £1,500 should do it.'

'But Sebastian, I would be surprised if she has that budget.'

'Not a problem.'

'No, no, Sebastian. You already contribute far too much to this project. There will be some additional papers in the package this evening you should keep from Mel. Open it privately.'

'You really don't need to do this. I consider it an investment on my part.'

'That's very kind of you, but we need to share the costs of this project. I now have the feeling Wednesday will go as I believe it should, so the cost is immaterial. I look forward to what she delivers. I'll also ask Jim to speak with Teresa Yardley about the market trends as they have a working relationship. Will be good backup if Mel stumbles. Michael is likely fighting to justify his existence, so he'll be prepared.'

'As you wish. I hope you won't be disappointed.'

'I somehow think if she can deliver at the level you teach her, she will teach us a thing or two about corporate wrangling.'

'Thanks for the call, but I have to go now. If you need anything else in support material, tell Mel.'

She waited until after lunch to hit the phone to her architect clients. Friday afternoon is wind down time, so people will chat. She already knew where Teresa Yardley was focussed, so only eight others to call. She had her list of questions on one pad, and another to record the responses. Also, a good opportunity to catch up with them as her time in Matlock had restricted her contact.

It took two hours to complete her task, but she was happy with the responses. Jim had been quietly listening throughout. He was impressed with her easy relationship with her contacts, even more impressed with the questions, and the casual way she presented them. Perfect to extract unguarded answers. He was looking forward to Wednesday as he had already lost faith in Michael to deliver. He saw Wednesday as a first nail-in-coffin day for him.

When she got home, she was content her day had been productive. She was now able to articulate the changes in the construction market in London that made her initiative valuable. Her confidence in this task was growing.

Over dinner she recounted her day with enthusiasm. Seb produced the economic data she needed which would certainly influence much of her argument.

the Way

'Thanks for this. I would not have known where to get such incisive data. This economic projection will change the way forward for Aldridge so I must grasp what you've written.'

'But not this evening young lady. I would suggest your preferred relaxation of wine and soak as this weekend will be busy.'

Chapter 57 – Saturday

They were both up early and on their way to Derby to catch the train to London. He decided not to waste their time on the train so tried to explain what he expected her to purchase in the way of clothing fit for a young exec.

'Boardrooms can be alpha male domains. Alpha males created them, and the culture is very much alpha male, and even cronyism. I know of older banks that do not have any female toilet facilities on the executive floor. They do not encourage women into this domain. The alpha males are not about to change their culture to accommodate any politically correct requirement for female executives. This culture cannot be changed from the outside, only from within. Until there is a critical mass of female executives within any one corporate, little will change.'

'We see much lobbying of Governments for equality, but now is not the time to impose females onto executive Boards even if possible. The changes to global capitalisation in 1986 made business more challenging. You will see many companies built on cronyism fail or be swallowed as competition gets fiercer. Only the smartest and fittest will survive. Therefore, Boards will become more merit orientated, but will women be in the mix? Time will tell.'

'As a woman you need to fit into your surroundings without directly imposing the fact you're a woman. Let me use an example in the High Court as you've probably seen this on TV. There are several accomplished female barristers who attend the High Court. If you notice how they present themselves, you'll see they mimic the robes and short bar wig uniform of the male barristers, but it's still obvious they are women. What the female barrister tries to achieve with her dress code is people look at her and see a barrister who is a woman, rather than a woman who is a barrister. This differential is very important regarding how seriously you're taken. And don't forget there are now highly respected female judges in both the High Court and the Court of Appeal without any changes to either protocol or procedure to my knowledge. This success by women can readily be translated into corporate Boardrooms with a little understanding of the protocols.'

'The dress code for men is very limited in that it's suit and tie albeit there is some relaxation to this in newer corporates. A woman who dresses in a manner that makes the men conscious of the freedom women have in their dress code against their own will cause resentment, jealousy, envy. Whatever their reaction, they see a woman acting as an exec – not good. You need to belong to the clan to be acknowledged as an exec who is a woman, so you dress accordingly. It doesn't mean you can't be stylish and look very nice. Some male execs will have bespoke suits that look stunning, whereas others will wear off-the-peg suits long overdue at the cleaners, but the uniform is the same. You can have a stylish skirt or trouser suits and fit into the clan very well.'

She sat there thinking, *'Exactly as Carmen advised. These two certainly sing off the same hymn sheet so what they say must be right.'*

As soon as they arrived in London, they took the underground to Moorgate Station. He knew the shops around Moorgate, Liverpool Street Station, and the Lloyds Building where female high-fliers did their business clothes shopping. They spent the £1,500 provided by Charles, and more in less than two hours. It never ceased to amaze him how much more expensive clothes for women exceeded comparable clothes for men which generally required more material. However, he was satisfied she was fully equipped to suitably adorn any boardroom.

They grabbed a quick lunch before making their way to Bank Tube Station to catch a train to Ealing to visit with her mother, arriving a little after 2pm.

'Hello mum. This is Sebastian.'

'So nice to meet you. Please come in and make yourself comfortable.'

He quickly assessed this house had been left to decay after losing her husband. She was obviously lonely and somewhat lost without him. There were photographs of him and their daughter scattered around the living room – living with her memories. He dutifully sat back and observed mother and daughter exchange their news, only joining in when invited, and quickly out again. This visit was about mother and daughter maintaining contact, something he had not done with his parents.

Mel needed the bathroom. Her mum invited him to come closer. 'Thank you for taking care of her. She looks so happy and full of life. Can I tell you something you can only disclose to Mel when I've gone?'

'Yes, of course. But she may have finished with me before then.'

'Sebastian, I'm very sick. My time is short. I don't want my daughter worrying about me now she has a real opportunity to better herself. But tell me honestly, is she going to achieve her dream? Will she make it to the top? I need to know this as I might not last long enough to see it for myself.'

'Vera, she's a dream student. Every time she's tested, she more than delivers. I have no doubt she'll do very well. Her first test in a real Boardroom will happen this coming Wednesday. I'll phone you to tell you how she performs.'

'My Goodness. So early in a Boardroom. Will she be ready?'

'Yes, she's ready to be tested. She's worked hard, and I have every confidence she'll do well.'

They could hear Mel returning. She mouthed 'Thank you' with tears in her eyes as they resumed their positions.

Mel could see her tears. 'What's the matter mum?'

'I was just telling Sebastian about you and your dad. I miss those days. Sorry, my dear, I'm just being silly.'

She put her arm around her mum 'Your happy memories are not silly. I know you miss dad, but you still have me.'

'And what a prize to have my dear. Such a wonderful daughter' as she gathered her composure so as not to embarrass her guest.

During the train journey back to Derby she spoke much about her mum, and her loneliness now she was on her own. Although she had good friends around her, they were not there when she switched off the light to go to sleep, or in the morning when she awoke. These times are the realisation your lifetime partner, friend, lover, and confidante is no longer with you.

He was listening intently to detect if she knew of her mum's revelation to him, but other than a general concern for her wellbeing he detected nothing. *'Another shock in store,'* he thought to himself.

They finally arrived home, having stopped to eat on the drive back from Derby to Matlock, very satisfied they had achieved their objectives.

Chapter 58 – Sunday

When she arrived at the pool he was striding along in the water.

'Morning Seb. What are you doing?'

'Aqua aerobics. Get in, I'll show you.'

the Way

She dropped her robe and dived in, finally realising she could easily stand at this depth. Her breasts floating on the water. 'You've changed the water depth.'

'1.4m is ideal for this purpose. Good core exercise without loading any joints.'

He returned to the pool edge next to her. 'Essentially the water will resist your attempts to stride along the pool, so you need more force and energy through your legs, thighs and hips. Good for your tennis, and your self-defence. Stand upright with your arms by your side facing along the pool. Starting with your right arm and right leg stride out. The end of the stride should have your hand above your foot just below the surface. Then stride with you left leg and arm in the same way. For each stride push as hard as you can without losing your footing. Ready? Let's go.'

As she was slightly behind him, she could copy his motion but found keeping up with him difficult. By the time she had reached the far end of the pool she was feeling it in her legs. *'This is hard.'*

'This next lap we go backwards with essentially the same motion in reverse. Ready? Go.'

She found this more difficult to stay on her feet, so adjusted her pace accordingly. They repeated this exercise four more times both forward and reverse.

'I can really feel it in my thighs. This is hard work.'

'Have you had enough, or can we try one more exercise?'

'I'll try.'

'Turn sideways. We'll walk sideways but bringing the lagging leg through to the lead position. You need to have your knees slightly bent. Ready? Go.'

She was facing him so watching how he did it. When they reached the far end of the pool, they reversed the process to return.

'These are exercises you can use as an alternative to swimming. When you can do ten lengths of the forward stride comfortably try it with your knees bent so the water is up to your shoulders.'

'Time for breakfast. Do you want a swim, or have you had enough?'

'I'll do a few lengths and join you in about twenty minutes.'

He was out of the pool, had a quick shower in the changing room, on with shorts and T-shirt ready to prepare breakfast.

Over breakfast Seb suggested they spend some time assembling her data under each of the headings, and then to arrange the data into a logical, coherent argument. Then, as it was a lovely day, they would take a walk around the grounds to develop her argument to determine if there were any gaps needing further consideration. This would also allow Seb to see how much of the data accumulated she could both remember; and understand its role in her argument.

Having completed this task, they had a light lunch before leaving for their afternoon tennis.

the Way

Week 9

Chapter 59 – Monday

'Tonight, we need to anticipate what Michael can throw at you to justify taking the architect clients. Why do you think he needs them in his portfolio?'

'He has recently lost three lucrative contracts. I don't think he has any significant alternatives. He has potential projects in the design stage, but construction work appears to be slowing down.'

'Why did he lose the three contracts? What value was involved? What discounts had been applied? What margins were envisaged?'

'I don't know exactly, but I do know the fabrication requirements were complex.'

'Tomorrow look at all three projects. Find out exactly why Aldridge lost them and validate these projects are going ahead with alternate fabricators. What services would have to be provided as part of your margin? Were the jobs initiated by developers, main contractor, or someone else? Had you applied your alternate process to any of these projects would you have been in a better position to secure them? You must find his weaknesses. Remember, do not attack strength, only weakness. Got all that?'

'Loud and clear. I should be able to establish all his existing closed business, and business in process because every project must come here for technical appraisal. This time tomorrow I'll know everything about his business portfolio including potential future business.'

the Way

'Good. Now let's examine why he's struggling to find new business. The economic data I gave you. How much of it do you understand?'

'The data you gave me about the influence of technology on new build projects confirms what the architects told me. The data on the recession and securitisation will require explanation for me to see how they fit in my arguments.'

'Let's deal with the impact of a recession. When we speak of a recession, we are indicating a decline in economic activity including construction. During such periods interest rates rise and bank lending reduces. Has your mortgage interest rate increased this year?'

'Yes. Twice.'

'You are suffering the early days of recession. You can expect more rate rises in the coming months. But why are we entering recession? America is already in recession. When America coughs, the world sneezes. Add to this the turbulence in Eastern Europe we are seeing a period of uncertainty regarding global trade and thus reduced economic activity. The impact on Aldridge will be a reduction in construction activity requiring bank lending as the banks tend to withdraw construction lending during recessions. Projects will be shelved unless the developer has the capital to proceed. For those construction companies lucky enough to ride a recession, margins will be squeezed. As your architect clients are backed by cash-rich investor/developers, their construction projects are likely to proceed. You have positioned Aldridge to take advantage of these projects, albeit margins will be squeezed by the developer.'

Okay. I've got that, but what is securitisation?'

'Securitisation refers to the capitalisation of a future stream of quality income. This type of financing allows investors to replace banks for lending purposes. The most common securitisation products relate to mortgages and credit card receivables where good quality mortgages or credit card receivables can be bundled into packages, typically £100 million, and sold to the investor community who receive an attractive interest rate for essentially parking these assets. In your case a developer will occupy a new office building with quality tenants with a good covenant to support their rental obligations. These future rental streams will be converted into a capital amount from investors which can be used for future development. The developer does not dispose of the building but will repay the capital to the investors at the end of the term of the securitisation issue – typically 6 – 7-years is favoured by investors currently. Thus, they can build a portfolio of property essentially using the same capital.'

Chapter 60 – Tuesday

As soon as Jim arrived at his desk Mel had her questions regarding the data she needed. Jim was happy to explain to her what had happened with the three deals lost, acknowledging had they been given the opportunity to work with the architect at the technical design stage Aldridge would likely have secured at least two of these projects. This was the ammunition she needed, and Jim was very aware of this; secretly looking forward to the confrontation with Michael.

When she arrived home that evening, she was quickly through her gym routine and ready for both dinner and the completion of her preparation for tomorrow.

'This is the data regarding corporate business generation by Michael. We could have; should have secured two of the lost projects. And, yes, they are all proceeding to be developed.'

'Looking at this data, I would suggest Michael has not registered the inevitable recession. A serious weakness on his part. You can attack this with assuredness without attacking him personally. This lack of foreknowledge will seriously impact

the Way

Aldridge far in excess of the three contracts lost. So, let us weave your defence to make this weakness your strength.'

'As this is a verbal argument to where do we look for help?'

'My old friend Aristotle.'

'Good. What headings can we attribute to Logos – We've Got A Problem?

- Technology is changing the market; office buildings need to be cheaper to build with shorter life expectancy
- Architects are looking for new materials/fabrication technology to reduce costs
- Since deregulation of the financial markets in 1986 London is the global city of choice
- There is a new breed of cash rich developer working directly with architects pushing Lead Contractors down the decision chain
- Asset-backed Securitisation of rental income has provided an alternative source of finance to developers allowing them to retain ultimate ownership of their properties
- Recession is looming with a possible 2-year deep recession raising interest rates and reducing the availability of conventional bank finance

'Good. Now apply Ethos – My Credibility and Support of the Problem.'

- Have spent 2-years speaking with architects about the challenges they face
- Architects, not Lead Contractors, have confirmed the need for new materials and fabrication technologies as seen with the three recent lost contracts
- The need to develop the former dockland area of London to meet demand
- New companies such as Land Securities are backed by cash investors are building portfolio working directly with major architect firms

- Investors like the quality of asset-backed securities thus removing control away from the banks regarding construction finance and facilitating building retention using the rollover capability of securitisation
- Reliable information from senior bankers confirming the USA is already in recession, instability regarding the recently liberated Eastern European states, will result in certain recession in Europe
- Banks withdraw from property finance during recessions. Bank interest rate is already 9%, inflation is at 13%; both are set to increase in the coming months

'Now construct your Pathos – What We Need To Do.'
- Need to be proactive with these new developer/architect alliances as a valuable contributor. Teresa Yardley has already agreed to second one of our senior fabrication designers to assist with a new project at market rates – usually part of our margin with Lead Contractors.
- Need to change the way we address these market changes, especially computer-based technical support

'Very good. Before you flesh out these headings, what battlefield structure do you think you need to defeat Michael?'
- Planning over the last 2-years suggests we are no longer speaking with the right people – we've lost our way
- The impending recession suggests we must *Manoeuvre* into alliances with these specific developer/architects applying valuable input to enable us to dominate this most lucrative Terrain
- We need to train and position our key technical design resources to engage in the business procurement process
- We must restructure our own army to meet the challenges of this new territory
- We must hide our strategy from our enemies until such time as we have captured this market.

the Way

'Has this loyal servant of Sun Tzu complied with his teachings?'

He was laughing at her direct application of the 'Art of War'. He could see the cheeky smile on her face. 'Great. You can't lose. Convert your Logos, Ethos, and Pathos into short sentences remembering to write sentences as you would speak them. This is a verbal narrative. You will more easily remember your argument if your notes reflect how you verbally present.'

Chapter 61 – Wednesday

She sat at breakfast unsure about what was about to happen. 'Are you sure I'm ready for this confrontation?'

All you need to remember is not to get sucked into an emotional battle. You must not get personal at all. He'll likely try to destabilise you, challenge your view, suggest you are out of touch with reality. He may belittle your experience against his years in the industry. At this point you've won the argument. Remember his attitude towards you. You need to show him you're more aware of the market and how you would respond to the changes that are imminent. Then sit back quietly and let him drown himself. Do not be tempted to hold his head under water. You're above such things. Just be an observer to his self-inflicted downfall.'

'All sounds good, but it's hard not to take his attacks personally.'

'You told me about his reaction when you'd decided to take the challenge. How did you feel then?'

'Elated I was out from under him.'

'Today you're on even terms knowing his strategy is wrong. He can't shout you down. Put your plan out there with quiet confidence.'

'So, you have faith in me?'

Week 9

'Absolutely, as do Charles and Jim or they would not put you in this position. Remember what Charles said to you. He's confident you can deliver, but are you? Use the power and energy of three people who believe in you and go deliver. Now away with you and do what you have to do.'

She gave him her customary kiss on the way out, 'as my master wishes.'

Charles popped in to see her. She looked great in her new business suit. 'Well, my dear, you certainly look the part. Are you feeling okay?'

'Before I delve into my view of the market, can you ask him where he thinks we are, and the prospects for the next few years?'

'That, my dear, is the first question before any discussion about assuming your architect clients. You've worked hard under your own initiative to win these clients. I'm not readily handing them to Michael without believing he can service them at least as well as you do.'

'Thank you.'

Michael arrived, and it was decided to get straight down to business. Jim made it clear to Michael he was only playing a support role in this discussion, and Mel was the lead speaker regarding the architect clients.

Charles started the meeting. 'Michael, before we discuss your request to assume the architect clients currently serviced by Mel could you appraise us of where you think the London corporate construction market is going, and how we secure our share of this business?'

Michael took a pile of folders from his briefcase and put them in front of him. 'The current situation in London is competition is increasing as lead contractors try to keep costs down to win business. Developers are trying to squeeze ever more out of the construction phase as lease rentals are becoming ever more challenging. There is a general move towards developers minimising construction costs and maximise rental streams, so they can make a quick exit of buildings, fully occupied, to the likes of pension funds. We've not been successful in the last three bids, essentially because the fabrication requirements need to be flexible to accommodate the new technology requirements in these buildings. I feel we need to work with the architects to simplify the fabrication needs so we can compete.

Charles interrupted, 'Is it reasonable to assume the buildings associated with the three lost bids are being built?'

'Yes. They found fabricators who are prepared to cut their margins to the bare bone to win the business.'

'Can we not influence the issues causing us problems? After all, we are generally the fabricator of choice.'

'This is why I think bringing the architects into our portfolio we can have a better influence with the lead contractors.'

'How is Maurice Fulmer working out?'

'He's slowly but surely building relationships that will work for us in the medium to long term.'

'Has he closed any business to date?'

'Not yet, but we have interesting prospects.'

Charles turned to Mel, 'What's your take on the current situation and our prospects.'

She took a deep breath and steadied herself 'Having spent a great deal of time with major architects over the past two years there is indeed a pressure on them to design buildings cheaper to construct. The reason for this is advances in technology, mainly computer technology in the workplace. A revolution in technology advances is expected, and thus challenges building design to accommodate it. These challenges are so dramatic that trying to redevelop buildings built as little as fifteen years ago is proving so expensive it's cheaper to demolish and rebuild. We are also seeing companies shying away from a traditional twenty-five-year lease down to ten – fifteen-year leases with break clauses to provide flexibility to the lessee, but also reducing the value of the building using conventional valuation methods. The other challenge they face is to minimise disruption to both pedestrians and transport during the construction phase. Councils are now charging for the degree and duration of disruption adding to the cost of the project. The challenge for architects is to move away from a building designed to last 80 – 100 years, to a building designed for just 30 – 50 years before refurbishment or even redevelopment. This challenges conventional build techniques. They need prefabricated structures that are cheap and fast to construct in the expectation that such buildings can be demolished and replaced in as little as 25 years, thus the cost has to reflect the likely income stream from occupation.'

Charles interrupted her 'And what would be your approach to positioning Aldridge to take advantage of this change in the landscape?'

Thank you, Charles' she thought as she continued 'Architects are looking for cheaper materials and fabrication techniques to keep costs and build times to a minimum. Jim and I looked at two of the three projects we lost recently. It was clear that had our technical expertise been involved with the architect during the design phase the required fabrications would have been simplified allowing us to gain the business without sacrificing margin.'

Michael tried to protest. Charles diffused his protest 'Please Michael, let Mel finish.'

She continued 'I think we need to be proactive with the architects informing them of new materials and fabrication techniques they can deploy to achieve their objective. We have started this process with Teresa Yardley. She has requested we second one of our technical designers to her team for a minimum of three months to help them with the technical design. In the past we have provided this service to the Main Contractor as part of our delivery, i.e. as part of our margin. Teresa Yardley is prepared to pay market rate for such secondment. It also puts us in the top spot to secure the order as, in her case, we are the only company offering the fabrication technique. Therefore, I think the future is working directly with architects from inception thus making us an integral part of the project.

'I can illustrate my concerns by reference to what I've observed here over these past weeks. During the past year our technical design team have switched from drawing boards to computer CAD systems. But the distance from their office to our office means when they want to show a design to Jim or me, they need to print a drawing or bring a disc. This building does not lend itself to basic technology, yet I see in the near future we not only need direct connections within the company, but we also need direct connections to the architects who can design ideas, send them to us for technical evaluation and budget, thus allow a more effective collaboration. And of course, we'll need to study CAD driven fabrication machinery in the workshops to use our technical drawings to fabricate the requirement. We're behind the curve. We need to adapt to secure our position as fabricator of choice.

She took a sip of water to let this information sink in.

'Whilst it's true pension funds are taking some of these buildings onto their own books, this is a traditional approach for such funds. There is a new breed of property company, owned by investor developers, who now retain their buildings. Deregulation of the financial markets in 1986 has made London the global city of choice. Much more development is needed with a fast build time. We saw the Barclay Brothers develop Canary Wharf. However, other developers see more opportunity within the confines of central London. New banking instruments allow them to securitise the income streams of new build with quality lets at costs below rental yields allowing them to readily finance more development. Therefore, they will build relationships with preferred architects as part of their business model.'

Week 9

'I also have it on good authority the rumours of an impending recession are indeed correct. More importantly, my source suggests for two years of this recession we should plan in terms of a deep recession. This means interest rates will rapidly increase making borrowing far more expensive. Banks will not only withdraw from commercial property lending but also call existing loans with riskier clients. This will fuel a decrease in commercial property values and stifle new build. That is except for this cash rich new breed of developer who will see the opportunity to scoop both redevelopment and new-build sites at a discount knowing once the recession is over, there will be a clamour for new office space. The new developers have some three years to develop this space at a discount as contractors will reduce their margin to stay in business.'

'I propose we restructure the London office to provide full technical support to architects during the design process and steer our marketing away from Main Contractors to developer/architect collaborations. We have a value-added service we can offer, and my view is we become part of the collaboration when the opportunity arises. Fixed sum Design and Build and lumped sum JCT contracts are becoming the norm for major projects thus moving the Main Contractor a further step away from the project development.'

Michael could not contain himself any longer. 'Charles, this is all hearsay. Our traditional approach has been to bid under the Main Contractor. This has been successful in the past, and I don't see it changing anytime soon.' He turned to Jim 'Surely you don't think the world is about to change according to Mel?'

Jim had been quietly listening, his chest expanding with pride as he listened to her argument. 'Not only do I believe it, but I've spoken directly with Teresa Yardley who confirmed what Mel has just outlined. It was I who suggested to her we get involved from inception. She jumped at the idea, and I'm currently briefing Simon Wardle from our technical design team to go work with her people using a new material Charles and myself have been tracking for some time. Technology is changing the world, and we need to position ourselves to be part of it. I fully support Mel's approach, and she should guide us how to develop our thinking as it was her initiative some two years ago to build relationships with major architects.'

Charles turned to Mel 'The serious piece of your proposal is the impending deep recession. Is your source who I think it is?'

'Yes, after research with his fellow bankers. The USA is already in recession, inflation here is approaching 9% pushing bank rates to close to 14%, and the disarray in Eastern Europe is creating many economic difficulties.'

'This is serious. I need to get out there and ensure as much of our bread-and-butter retail business as possible is closed by year-end.'

Charles turned to Michael 'Anything you want to add?'

'I need to go away and test what Mel has just suggested if you are confirming the quality of her sources.'

You do that and get back to me.'

Charles looked at Mel again, 'Anything you want to add.'

'Yes, I think I have one more pertinent contribution. We have spent some two years under the radar developing the architect relationships I've fostered. We're at the point where we can now convert this effort into valuable business, especially in light of the impending recession. I propose we keep this opportunity under the radar until we have consolidated our position with these architects without alerting our competitors. Therefore, we should not add these architects to our mainstream business flow – it will expose our strategy. I would propose, however, Michael could quietly start to nurture other architects fronting cash-rich developers, but only him as I'm sure if Maurice Fulmer's father got wind of what we're doing, we could lose the initiative. I would propose to continue, with Jim, to consolidate the architects we already have in play.'

Charles looked at Mel with a large grin on his face as he thought *'Sun Tzu.'* He remembered the Weaknesses and

Strengths session he attended. 'You do that. Mel, can you write up your thoughts about restructuring both here and the London office to accommodate your ideas? Let's reconvene when we have had time to digest her report. Michael, you quietly look for more architects that fit Mel's profile and ensure all our retail opportunities in your region are pushed to close before the year-end. When does Maurice Fulmer's probation expire?'

'I think five months makes it end of the year. Why?'

'Mel's right. We don't need a double agent spoiling our business. If he hasn't closed significant business he originated by December, let him go.'

'Right gentlemen (pause) sorry Mel, and lady, this conversation stays in this room. Mel, use Mary to type up your report. Distribution only to the people in this room, and to be kept under lock and key when not in use. No discussion with anyone outside of this room. Any questions?'

Michael collected his paper 'Better get back to London and start my research.'

After Michael had left for London, Charles called in both Jim and Mel. He had three glasses and a bottle of champagne on his desk. Congratulations Mel, you were magnificent. I hope that put to rest your poor treatment by him in the past. And I suppose I don't need to ask where you got all of that financial data.'

'The need for it came from the teachings of Sun Tzu, and the data came from my trusted collaborator.' They all laughed.

Charles shook his head in submission 'I really must study this pre-historic General some more.'

'We need to move forward quickly and reposition ourselves to meet these new challenges. Can you arrange to go visit with your architect clients to see how we can support them, especially with new materials and fabrication techniques. Both myself and Jim are available for support for such visits. The more support you have for your approach by year-end, the better.'

the Way

They each took a glass 'To our future, and to Mel who has shown us the way.'

Charles looked at Mel thoughtfully, 'I would assume Sebastian will help you to orchestrate your report.'

She looked at him nervously, 'Yes, unless you instruct otherwise.'

'No, no, my dear. Don't be alarmed. My concern is the amount of quality detail it will contain. Can't allow such detail out of this office. Michael will be feeling vulnerable, so we must not arm him with valuable information he could use as an entry to another position with a competitor. Let Jim and myself see your report when ready and we'll decide how much of it we give to Michael.'

Later Charles phoned Sebastian to congratulate him yet again for his contribution.

Upon entering the kitchen, she had a very satisfied grin on her face.

'How did it go?'

She said nothing, walked up to him and gave him a kiss on each cheek before taking a step back to curtsy 'My master was right, as always. Your humble student is most grateful.'

He smiled at her theatrics. 'You may rise my humble student. Your master only gave you the means, you delivered the result. You should be very proud of yourself. After your session in the gym, we will celebrate.'

'As my master wishes.'

Once dinner was served, he asked her how the meeting went.

Charles obliged me by asking him to lay out his argument first. Then I started by....' He interrupted.

No. I already know this from Charles. What I'm interest to know is how did it feel? What were your thoughts as the meeting progressed?'

'The first specific thought I had was the tactical advantage of getting Michael to put his arguments on the table first. It may sound silly, but Sun Tzu was laying out the battlefield in my head as he spoke. I could see what resources I needed to defeat him. It was weird, but my adrenalin was flowing, and my concentration absolute.'

'I knew I didn't need all the arguments we prepared, so I didn't use them. I merely attacked each of his views and, frankly, demolished him. I think Sun Tzu would have praised his student for minimising the resources deployed.'

'Did you keep yourself in check; remote from the attachment you have to these clients?'

'At no point did I see these relationships in jeopardy, so it didn't concern me. It was all over in ten minutes.'

'Do you think you can remember all the processes you have used in these past days to prepare yourself for battle, and then how you managed the battlefield?'

'I have it all written down, so yes.'

'That was not the question. These processes must be embedded in your memory so you can recall them at will.'

'Then I will embed them. But we haven't finished my master. Charles wants me to put my arguments and proposals into a report for further discussion. He is also being very canny about how much of your valuable contribution will be shown to Michael – thinks he'll sell it for a new job.'

'Ah, the shortcomings of small businesses. As I have said before, Michael may be a director, but Charles, and to a lesser extent Jim, make all the decisions. What we'll do is to generate a Business Development Proposal as would be required by a larger corporate so you have the experience of both qualitative and quantitative analysis. It will require much more effort, but the experience will be invaluable to you.'

Chapter 62 – Thursday

After she had departed for the office, he picked up the phone and dialled.

'Vera? It's Sebastian.'

'Hello, my dear, I've been waiting for your call.'

'I couldn't phone you last night. I spoke with the Chairman after the meeting. She did good – strong, confident, and frankly spectacular performance. I'm so proud of her.'

He could practically hear her tears down the phone, 'Thank you so much. When I pass on, I'll find her father and visit with the angel that put you together and thank them for their kindness to my lovely Melanie. Will you keep her safe for me as she so much believes in you?'

'I will be there for her whenever she needs me, I promise.'

'You're a good man. While she has you, she'll be strong.'

'Vera, do you need anything? I cannot stand by and see you in need. Can I organise any medical treatment for you, if only to ease your pain?'

'Thank you for thinking of me. You are already doing all you can do for me.'

'Bye, Sebastian, and thank you for calling.'

At the office Jim was in, but Charles was out visiting. She was anxious about what Seb had told her during her sessions with him about bringing big corporate into Aldridge. 'Jim, this report you want. How far can I go in discussing changes needed to Aldridge to meet the challenges I've outlined because I don't want to offend the opportunity you've given me?'

He could sense her concern. 'My dear, yesterday you gave us quite a shock with your presentation. I had gleaned some issues from Teresa, but nothing like the bombshell you dropped on us. But we cannot argue with what you said. I think the preoccupation with my health has resulted in us taking our eye off the ball. We've been caught napping and we need to wake up to the challenges ahead. Thank goodness your eye is most certainly on the ball, and with Sebastian in your camp you've been able to provide us with a needed reality check. Even now Charles is out there nurturing his sources to accumulate and close business to keep our order books full for at least a year. We have been caught in recessions before without prior warning, and suffered, especially having to let people go because we didn't have enough work on our books. But you also see we're a community business so lay-offs hurt us personally. Sebastian has prewarned us this time and we need to respond to protect our people. So, my dear, you can be as thorough and blunt as you feel is necessary. We'll take it on the chin, analyse your ideas in the spirit presented, and respond accordingly. It sounds like we need to make some tough decisions so help us to make good ones. Does this help with your anxiety?'

'Thank you, Jim. I still feel like an apprentice and don't want to tread on anyone's toes.'

'My dear Mel, your growth rate into this business is stunning. As of yesterday, you are not my apprentice, you're a very worthy colleague and valuable contributor to this business. I expect you to challenge whenever you feel the need. You won't always be right but never let that stop you from looking for improvement to our business model and expressing your view. If you need any input from me, just ask.'

She looked at him tenderly. *'What a lovely man'* she thought before getting her head back into play. 'Thank you for your confidence in me. It means so much to me. I do need some information from you, mostly about the cost implications and lead times for introducing new fabrication ideas into production.'

'Are you ready with your questions?'

the Way

'Yes.'
'Then let's go through them.'

She was sitting in the kitchen in preparation for dinner and their evening session. 'I intend to stay here this weekend but want time out to go see my mum on Saturday.'

'No problem. While I finish preparing dinner, why don't you start your report with probably the most important part – why should anyone read it. You have two minutes of reading to capture the attention of your reader and encourage them to read on. So, what skill set do you think we need as a template?'

She recalled this conversation in her first few weeks. With a cheeky smile on her face, 'Can I call on a friend? His name is Aristotle.'

'Do you have his number?' They both laughed. 'So, what information do we need?'

'I guess we need to define the issue, why it exists, and the impact on Aldridge if they don't respond. Then we need to show from my experience over the past two years how we can assert ourselves into this changing world and then argue what we need to do to be successful.'

'Okay, you have all of your notes we put together for your presentation. You have ten minutes to write your summary that can be read within two minutes. Off you go.'

Seb finished preparing dinner.

'Seb, I'm ready.'

'Read it to me.'

'Technology is changing the landscape of the corporate environment. The growth curve of technology is unpredictable, but it is fast. Office buildings need to be capable of accommodating the ever-increasing demand for new technologies requiring wiring and rewiring a multitude of networks, data and voice highways, and power distribution including a more secure uninterrupted power supply to critical technologies. Then we have the increasing demand for clean air

Week 9

and air-conditioning required to keep technology within its operating temperature range. This ever-changing landscape within corporates also tends towards large, open-plan office space which are far easier to adapt to new generations of technology but increasing demands on architects to build. The rapid and unpredictable growth in technology and thus the building design considerations mean corporate tenants do not want to commit to long leases on buildings that may not readily adapt to future technology. Developers are thus looking to architects to design flexible buildings, with faster build, using more cost-effective materials such that redundancy can be reduced to some 25 – 30 years. In addition, intelligence sources suggest that the impending recession will be deep for some two years.'

'Having built relationships with seven significant architects over the past two years all of which are directly involved in major projects in London we now have their confidence to the point where we are providing direct technical fabrication support to Teresa Yardley and expect this to be duplicated in other practices. I have engaged in detailed discussion with these architects and now understand the basis of their commissions being provided by cash-rich developer/owners.'

'The corporate marketplace for new buildings is changing. To survive, we must understand what is needed from Aldridge to achieve market share. We need to restructure our approach, familiarise ourselves with technologies that can help us to offer a premium service to this new breed of developer/owner. We have built the relationships giving us a clear lead over our competitors. Now we need to convert this knowledge both within Aldridge and with our client portfolio to capitalise on this opportunity. This Business Development Plan describes the changes in the marketplace, the changes we need in our business model to secure our position in it, and the changes within Aldridge to ensure we can perform and delivery as expected of the Aldridge brand.'

the Way

'That's it. How did I do?'

'Excellent. Let's have dinner and then map out the report content.'

Dinner finished, he felt a little background to the intended use of such a report would help to clarify what she needed to include, and how to package it concisely as possible.

'Let me outline what this type of business development proposal is intended to convey, especially if it requires a significant change in business practice. A change in business practice and/or a significant investment requires considered, and reasonable argument with supporting evidence. The best mechanism I ever encountered for such reporting was at a major American bank. They had a well-documented process called an MEP (Major Expenditure Proposal) which contained a proforma report structure for just about any corporate investment requirement anywhere in the World. Wish I still had it. But, having used it many times, I quickly appreciated any such proposal must present the relevant information as succinctly as possible. If you think in terms of Who, What, Why, When, How, and How Much you have a good template to ensure you include all the information required to facilitate a decision to proceed. Does this make sense to you?'

'Other than understanding what is included in each of your headings I'm okay so far.'

'I also want to distinguish between a Business Development Proposal and a Project Plan. It's unlikely you can fully quantify the changes needed in a Business Development Proposal. Indeed, it could well propose various options in which case you would provide an indication of magnitude of investment requirement both in terms of financial and resources for each option. Think planning as per Sun Tzu. Once a decision has been made, then the next process is a fully costed Project Plan which will have substantially more detail, and budgets against which implementation can be monitored. Still with me?'

'How do these two processes differ from a Business Plan?'

'A Business Development Proposal will typical propose modifying the working practice of one facet of your existing business or add a new facet to the existing business such as a new product or service. A Business Plan encapsulate the whole business including any Business Development Proposal once it becomes an approved Project Plan.'

'So, there is an escalation process culminating into a Business Plan.'

'Correct. For example, your Business Development Proposal will include changes needed both here and in London to satisfy your proposed change in the way you service corporate clients in London. There is little or no justification for consuming the time and effort required to fully cost these changes until there is agreement in principle to adopt your proposal. However, to show you have a full grasp of your proposed changes, you need to provide budgets and timelines against which the efficacy of your proposal can be evaluated, and which must be supported in terms of new business generation opportunity. Thus, your Business Development Proposal will be qualitative supported by reasonable quantitative justification. I should also add you will need a risk section at the end of your proposal. This risk section will define the business risks involved in adopting your proposal, and the business risks of not adopting your proposal. You will need to think through the specific risks to Aldridge as you have a much clearer picture of Aldridge than me. I can suggest possible risks, but you must determine the relevance to Aldridge.'

'In terms of integrity, the arguments in your proposal need to be balanced. There is no utopia or Armageddon, just hard business realities. No unqualified assumptions; no speculation. There must be no overt indication you are emotionally committed to your proposal – this will raise questions about your objectivity. How are we doing?'

the Way

She smiled at his last comment, knowing he was referring to her personal attachment to her architect client. 'Loud and clear, my master. But I still need to understand your headings.'

'Okay. I'll summarise each, and then you should start to complete as much under each heading as possible tonight, tomorrow, and tomorrow evening if you still have fuel in your tank. Alternatively, you have two train journeys on Saturday you could use productively. However, let me alert you to the folly of working on public transport in full view of others. You must always assume the person looking over your shoulder, or at your papers is a spy for the competition. I worked for one of the largest banks in the World who had a policy that you engaged in no business whatsoever in unguarded surrounding including discussion in a restaurant. Although I liked this policy as I could relax whilst flying, the impact of non-compliance only really hit me when I travelled to New York in my usual casual clothing sitting next to a corporate banker from another large bank working on a funding proposal for a major corporate I knew we were courting. I read the whole proposal memorising the proposed transaction details which I then relayed to the appropriate account officer in the bank. We stole this transaction by offering better terms. Hence why any breach of this policy meant instant dismissal no matter how senior. As you have witnessed, Charles is very cautious about who knows the information in your proposal. Respect his judgement.'

'My master, the teachings of Sun Tzu would require me to be beheaded for such folly so I will be careful.'

He was smiling as he started to define the headings suggested to her.

Who

Define all players involved, and their involvement. In your case external players include architects and their developer backers. Internally you include all players existing or proposed, impacted by your proposal.

What

What is the opportunity in your proposal? You will include both external and internal considerations. This includes changes in economic circumstances, market demand, etc.

Why

Why are you making this proposal? What has changed in the market you think needs your proposed response. You will need to support your views with credible evidence.

When

This is the timeline during which your proposal needs to be enacted to capture the opportunity.

How

This is the mechanisms needed, both externally and internally, to implement your proposal. In your case you will discuss the proposed nurturing and technical support for architects both directly and indirectly. And then the internal corporate changes to ensure quality delivery to your clients.

How Much

This is indicative, but realistic costs to implement your proposal against a timeline of expenditure. To this you will project the likely value of business generated even if it relies more on business not lost as with the three contracts lost recently.

Risk

This is two parts. The first part is the risks you are averting or avoiding by implementing your proposal. The second defines the exposure to your business of not implementing your proposal. Disruption to your business during implementation is also a potential risk to business continuity.

'Do you think this enough to get you started?'

'Yes. I would like to try to flesh out each heading, reverting to you if I have questions.'

'Good enough. Let's see what you can do. One other piece of advice which may help you is to use concise bullet points under each heading. Once you're happy you've captured all issues under each heading then, in many cases you top and tail each bullet point and you have your proposal. Helps to keep your verbiage to a minimum. Respect the time of your reader.'

Chapter 63 – Friday

She hadn't sat at her desk for more than a few minutes before she received a call from Michael. 'Good morning, Mel. I don't want to make too much noise on the street so I thought I would liaise with you to determine which architects you haven't already approached are linked to these finance rich developers?'

'He has no idea how to find them. What does he do all day?' Remembering not to take it personally, 'I do know two practices that operate specifically in the City. I can give you their names, but there are others operating in Central London.' With much pride she knows this business better than him, 'The large estate agents are a good source of such intelligence.'

'Thanks, Mel. Good thinking. Is this where you found your clients?'

'I found three architects this way but would readily pursue this source as they are so close to the developers.' She was buzzing inside. *'Not so chauvinistic now, you creep.'*

'Of course, they are. Should have thought of that. If you can give me the names of the two City practices, I'll get on it, and then go speak with the larger West End agents.'

She gave him the names and quickly ended the call.

Jim had listened with much amusement as he could tell what she was thinking by the tone of her voice. 'That must have been a satisfying call, my dear. Must feel good to be needed by him.'

'Certainly was. But mustn't gloat. Seb would have me beheaded.'

They both laughed.

Week 9

'It's okay. Your secret is safe with me. You deserve a little gloat after the way he treated you. How's your proposal developing?'

'I now have my instructions what to produce but I need some technical input from you.'

'Let's do it. The faster we have your report, the faster we can get ourselves back into the game.'

That evening she finished integrating the input from Jim into her proposal, but then found herself stumped on the Risks section. *'Do I ask Seb, or Jim? Seb has already stated he's not the right person. Wonder if I should call Charles for advice.'* She picked up the phone to Charles. 'Good evening Charles. Sorry to disturb you but I'm working on my proposal and find myself short on experience in one vital part. Would you be free over the weekend as I want to finish ASAP but don't want to disturb Jim?'

'I applaud your diligence in this task so, of course I'll find time to help you. Tomorrow is my golf day, but Sunday morning would be convenient.'

'Don't worry about tomorrow as I'd like to visit with my mum. But Sunday sounds good. What time, and where?'

'Come to my house. I'm sure Edna would like to see you again. Say 10 o'clock?'

'Great, and thanks.'

'Thank you, Mel. You're an inspiration. Can't wait to see your proposal. See you Sunday.'

She informed Seb of her call with Charles and retreated with a glass of wine to enjoy a good soak.

Chapter 64 – Saturday

As soon as breakfast was over, she was on her way to Derby to catch her train to London. On the way back she intended a little retail therapy in the large shopping mall close to Derby station so parked her car there rather than the station car park.

Arriving in London just before 11am she was soon on her way to Ealing to arrive around noon. As she walked in, she could see bunting as though it was her birthday. This bunting repeated the words "Congratulations Melanie".

'What is this, mum? Why the bunting?'

'My wonderful daughter succeeded in a corporate Boardroom. Your father would be so proud of you.' She had tears in her eyes as she hugged her daughter.

'I've also made your favourite cake to celebrate.'

She wanted to tell her mum she didn't have to go to so much trouble but seeing how happy she was, chose to let her have some cheer. 'It's so lovely mum. Thank you.'

'Over lunch you must tell me all about your first confrontation in a corporate Boardroom. Sebastian told me you were fantastic. Passed with flying colours. How wonderful.'

'I see. Spying on me now. Since when have you and Seb been on chatty terms?'

'When he was here last Saturday, he mentioned your trial, and I asked him to let me know how it went. He was kind enough to call me on Thursday.'

Over lunch she related how Seb prepared her, and then not only how she demolished Michael but also alerting both Charles and Jim to the impending recession. And now she was preparing a report about the changes needed in Aldridge to meet new challenges in the market. The smile on her mum's face radiated light into the otherwise gloomy room.

As an afterthought 'Mum, I'm no longer the apprentice, I'm part of the management team. I still have much to learn but I've proven I can perform at a senior management level.'

'I am so proud of you. I must remember to thank Sebastian. Look at you. What a confidant woman I have as my treasured daughter.' No mention of Philip throughout the conversation.

She had used the train journeys to flesh-out her notes, having secured seating on both journeys to prevent any possible oversight. Charles was not aware of her typing skills, but should he ask tomorrow to see what she had already written she would transcribe her report to her personal computer so she would have hard copy she could give him. By the time she arrived back at Derby her first draft was safely in her notebook. The extra-long stay with her mum meant it was late. Shopping trip aborted, she drove home.

Over dinner she related her day with her mum, and used the train journeys to type her report.

Seb could see she was emotionally drained. 'I applaud your commitment to your task, but please don't burn yourself out. We have another full week starting Monday. How long do you think you need with Charles? Will you be back for tennis?'

She thought about how the day might go with Charles. As he had suggested Edna would like to see her again, she erred on the side of a long visit. 'I think you should count me out of tennis tomorrow, if you don't mind, as I envisage lunch, and then a chat with Edna.'

'No problem. So long as you limit the work time, socialising with someone different will help you relax. A change is as good as a rest. I'll see you for supper tomorrow. And no more work tonight. You're obviously emotionally drained from you visit with your mum so let's chill this evening. Do you want to go out somewhere, or just chill here?'

'I want to type my notes into my computer and then I'll engage in my favourite chill if you don't mind. I saw a smile on my mum's face today I haven't seen since my dad died. Need to think about a way to keep her smiling.'

'A worthy cause. If I can help in any way, please feel free.'

the Way

'Thanks, Seb. I know you're there for me. Sorry if I've made your evening boring.'

'Not at all. I shall join my friends at the pub. Haven't seen them for a while.'

Chapter 65 – Sunday

When she arrived at the Aldridge family residence Edna greeted her. 'Melanie, my dear, so lovely to see you. I've heard good things about you but how is Higgins treating you?'

Mel smiled with her reference to Seb as Professor Higgins, 'he's so good to me. Hard, but fantastic education.'

Charles tells me you put a full day in at the factory, and then at least another two hours in the evening. And now weekends. My goodness, they'll burn you out. Do I need to stem this abuse or are you at peace with it?'

'Thank you, Edna, for your concern, but I'm enjoying this journey. Seb won't let me burn out. He was concerned about me working today but I want to understand something from Charles's perspective, but he doesn't have enough time without distraction during the week.'

'Okay, my dear. But if you need me, I'm here for you. Charles is in his study. I'll show you the way. I hope you can stay for lunch. I'm so looking forward to hear from you how you are progressing.'

'Thank you, Edna. I'd love to stay for lunch if not inconvenient for you.'

'No bother at all my dear. I've been waiting weeks to chat with you again. I hear so much about you, but I want to hear it from you. This is his study. Please just go in.'

Week 9

She entered whilst Edna lurked in the doorway.

'Mel, my dear. So nice to see you. What can I do for you?'

'In the template Seb has provided for my proposal I need to add a section on risk which has two parts; the first being the potential risks to Aldridge adopting my proposed changes in corporate structure, and the second being the business impact of not adjusting to this market change.'

'Sounds a little too corporate for Aldridge. I will assess the risks of your proposal myself and ensure we minimise the impact.'

'That's fine for you. But if I'm to play an active part in the future of Aldridge, I need to understand these risks. You are best placed to help me define and understand the relevant risks so I can formulate implementation understanding these risks.'

Edna was still standing in the doorway listening. 'Quite right my dear. Charles assumes either people can mind-read him, or him knowing these issues is enough. Charles, you asked Mel to embark on this journey to the benefit of Aldridge, and her revelations last week certainly show her commitment so you must share your knowledge with her.'

'Do you have your proposal with you so I can see what I need to consider?'

'This is only my first draft, but I think it contains a broad outline of my proposal.'

Once in his hand he asked what she would like to drink whilst he read. Edna took her to the kitchen telling Charles to come for her when ready.

It took Charles over 20-minutes before he came to join them in the living room. He was carrying her proposal. 'Mel, did these numbers come from Jim?'

'Yes. We compiled them on Friday.'

My dear, this is more than enough for me to work with. You need not spend more time on this for my benefit.'

'Thank you, but my master requires me to produce a Business Development Plan to his corporate standards. As he provided much valuable input, I consider it my duty to comply with his exacting standards.'

Ah, yes. He told me he intended to push you as far as you can reach. I'll respect that and look forward to seeing such a document. Has Jim seen this?'

'No. I only finished it yesterday.'

'My goodness Mel. You're allowed some playtime. Did you see your mother yesterday?'

'Yes. I spent around three hours with her. Thrilled and supportive of my progress.'

'You must not sacrifice seeing your mother in the name of exacting standards. I like Sebastian's contribution to your journey, but your mother needs you.'

'Fear not, Charles. I'm driving the completion of this proposal, and Seb has expressed your concerns already. But I'm having fun. I have three wonderful mentors willing to help me. I'm grateful for the opportunity and I'll do whatever it takes to succeed. But you're right; this journey must include maintaining a close relationship with my mum. Seb won't allow otherwise.'

Edna decided this conversation needed to change. 'As this proposal appears to require substantial changes to Aldridge, I would like to be part of this discussion, so I know what to expect. Can I suggest we defer this discussion until after lunch so we can use the dining table as I assume Melanie would like to take notes. I will start lunch now so to be ready by 12:30. This will give us plenty of time to cover everything that needs to be considered.'

Charles looked at her. 'I could do with some time to think through the risks. I assume Seb will scrutinise my input, so I need to ensure I comply with exacting corporate standards.' He looked at Mel. 'Does your ancient warrior have a section on risk?'

'Oh, yes. Much on risk assessment.'

'I really need to study him more.'

Week 9

Mel, sensing a difficult moment, 'Could I help you with lunch whilst Charles gathers his thoughts?'

'That would be lovely my dear. We can have a good chat as we toil.'

Lunch over they cleared the table and readied themselves for Charles to express his thoughts.

'The first, and major risk with this proposal is providing Michael with so much valuable information. You worked hard under your own initiative to understand the changes in the corporate construction market in London. Although you asked for my support for this initiative, I don't remember giving you any input. And the information you added from Sebastian is invaluable to support your proposal. There is no doubt in my mind we must restructure our approach to capture this opportunity, but how without risking this valuable data being used by Michael to enhance his own position, probably with a competitor. The problem I have is diluting this information without degrading your proposal.'

He was struggling with his thoughts, so they stayed silent.

'I spoke with Jim before lunch. He told me about your conversation with Michael on Friday. By all accounts, you educated him how to find the best architect firms to approach. The fact he couldn't work this out for himself tells me he's out of his comfort zone.' He paused to think. 'Young lady, should Michael ask you about your report, it's still a work in progress until I can work out what I can disclose to him.'

'Understood.' *'Wow. How right was Seb?'*

Edna spoke. 'Charles, can you explain to me what changes need to be made, and why your reservations.'

He recounted Mel's initiative to change the focus for contracts having identified changes in direction in the market. Both he and Jim became involved recently and now realise her initiative is valuable. And now she has argued her case including alerting him to the impending economic recession. 'My darling, our preoccupation with Jim's health has taken our eye off the ball, and Michael was not there to alert us to these material issues. Mel has proposed major changes to the way we market our services to big corporate activity including restructuring activities both here and in London to meet these challenges. This is radical, but also provides the opportunity to introduce Dennis Potter's new fabrication techniques. We must act with some urgency to capture this opportunity before our competitors get wind of what we're doing.'

Edna, now turning to Mel, 'Well my dear. It would appear my husband's instincts about you are well founded, and the investment in you is already yielding dividends. Congratulations. I'm here for you whenever you feel the need.'

'Thank you. Much appreciated. And thanks for allowing me to be part of this process. Watching Charles use his vast experience to rationalise these issues is valuable to me.'

Charles interrupted. 'Mel, my dear, you proved yourself worthy last Wednesday which makes you a valuable member of my management team. You must be fully involved in the strategic management of Aldridge from now on. Indeed, you must lead the charge on your proposal. I will support you in every way you need, especially visits to potential clients, as it's not reasonable to expect Jim to travel. He can pick up the delivery needs after we've captured the business opportunity. I've already started to capture as much of our mainstream business as is possible before the year's out, to ensure our order books are full for at least a year. We'll need £2.5million to create a fabrication facility for the Potter fabrications. We have this money, but we need to secure business against it to trigger such an investment.'

'Charles, can I ask you a more general question which will help my thinking?'

'Certainly. What is it?'

'Seb has analysed Aldridge. He concluded the London corporate market is not a full contributor to Aldridge profitability, and Aldridge can easily survive without this business. What I'm proposing will cost money, especially in technology and technical support to architects. Is this a consideration armed with the knowledge of an imminent deep recession?'

'Good question my dear. And interesting Seb is scrutinising our business, no doubt to keep his teachings relevant. I initially created the London office as a loss leader, albeit I would never allow it to run at a loss today. There is an accelerating shift to out-of-town shopping centres; some of them large shopping malls. I want to capture this business without our margin being squeezed. If we are actively engaged in major projects in London, we are already pre-qualified for these shopping mall projects thus eliminating most of our competition. We already have one such project on our books, and I'm close to securing a second. These two projects alone are half of our order book capacity for a year. And because we can deliver and install a lorry load of windows in one visit, our installation costs substantially decrease. Does this answer your question?'

'Essentially what Seb suggested. *Smart cookie.*'

'I should give Mary a bonus for getting you in with Sebastian. What a valuable resource for your development; and to our business.'

Edna decided they had drifted away from the purpose of Mel's visit. 'Charles, my dear, time is moving on and you've not dealt with Melanie's questions about risk.'

'Sorry Mel. I have some thoughts regarding risks. I'll deal with some now, and others in the office. I have what I need from you, but I accept the idea you should complete this task as deemed appropriate by Sebastian. If you need to make any changes or additions to the body text you already have, can you complete this task ASAP? Please give a copy to Jim and, if necessary, a fresh copy for me. We can add your section on risks in the coming days during which time your proposal is incomplete and thus you do not need to lie to Michael.'

the Way

'If you consider Michael as a major risk, how do you propose we develop this business?'

'We have enough architect clients to test and establish the best way to work with these clients. Thankfully, they are still under your control, and will stay this way until at least the year-end. You and I will pursue this business as "part of a learning curve" as far as Michael is concerned thus nothing passes through the London office. Jim and you will control the technical support from here. We need to test how to keep our new clients satisfied with our services. There is no need to populate the London office with technical support staff until we know the scope of support required. I will keep Michael busy on other opportunities.'

Before I speak to my list of risks, do you see any you wish to address?'

'A particular risk I've thought about is architects poaching our technical designers. The architect may engage a technical designer on secondment, like them, and try to poach them.'

'We can contract against poaching.'

'Can I suggest an alternative approach? I think we should not resist such poaching. We should agree a transfer fee with the architect commensurate with the hiring costs and training of a replacement. We will have one happy client and another happy former employee with good feelings about us. The architect spends no more than they would recruiting a technical designer themselves, and our happy former employee knows where to go for the best advice and product delivery.'

He gave her a wry smile, 'Do I detect you intrepid ancient General in this approach?'

'Friendly and grateful allies are more useful than enemies. And we potentially have a valuable spy.'

He laughed. 'I love it. More of this thinking please. I'm beginning to see the value of this risk section. Anything else?'

'Another consideration is convincing architects our internal security will keep their valuable designs confidential including not sharing design techniques with other clients. If we can convince them of the integrity of our support process, they will be more open and thus closer with us. And, no, I haven't found a solution for this as there is a technical computer related aspect, and potential employee leakage. I'm interested to know how law firms wrestle with this problem.'

'You've stumped me. I fully accept the valuable nature of the risk. I'll ask our law firm how they do it and get back to you.'

'Okay, lady. Enough for today. I've written down some risks I've considered. Take it with you and let's address them during the next few days. And, of course, any others you've considered as Sun Tzu is far better at this than me.'

When she arrived home Seb was still not back from tennis, so she worked off lunch in the gym, have a swim and then relax on the sun deck. Much to think about.

He caught her deep in thought. 'Chilling or thinking?'

'Hi Seb. A little of both, I think. Interesting day.'

'Did you get what you need?'

'Yes, and no. Much information about how Charles sees business. You were right about the reason for the London office, and his disregard for Michael as an executive of Aldridge. I think risk to him is instinctive. He's very happy with my proposal but doesn't want me to officially finish it until he can decide how to deal with Michael. Initially expected me to lie to Michael, but then used the incomplete risk section as a reason for its incompletion. I certainly keep my architect clients and he will help me develop them into business contracts. All-in-all an interesting day. Even Edna participated.'

'Okay. Enough for today. Did you have lunch?'

'Full Sunday roast.'

'Light supper and then chill. Busy week coming.'

the Way

Week 10

Chapter 66 – Monday

She was working at her desk when the phone rang. It was Phillip. He had learnt she had been seen in Ealing on Saturday and wanted an explanation. She explained she needed to work but had taken some time away on Saturday to visit her mum because she's not well. He announced he was on business in Derby on Wednesday, and they should meet up in the evening and spend the night together at his hotel. She agreed, but with mixed feelings. After putting down the phone, she felt uneasy but did not know why.

It took her some time to get back to the risk list provided by Charles. Jim could expand on some risks, but she would have to speak with Charles about others. He was in Manchester today, so they would have to wait. She concentrated on the body text, after which she gave a copy to Jim for comment. They consumed much of the afternoon analysing her proposal, what changes within Aldridge would need to be implemented, and how.

When she arrived home, her telephone conversation with Phillip was still on her mind.

'Seb, I got a call from Phillip this morning. The jungle drums told him I was in Ealing on Saturday, so why didn't I visit with him? He wants to meet me in Derby on Wednesday evening, probably for the night. What do you think?'

'What does this have to do with me? If you want to see him, then go.'

'I'm not sure I want to mix my life here with my life in London. I'm not at peace with the tone of his call. I feel like I'm being summoned.'

'He's your fiancé. Surely you have no secrets from each other. You worked hard on Friday, and you spent all day yesterday working with Charles. Not difficult to understand you have work to do with just a little respite for your mum on Saturday.'

'Not sure he'll see it that way.'

'Go to the gym, have a swim if it would help, and we can explore your anxiety over dinner.'

She arrived in the kitchen for dinner as usual but had changed her persona.

'Still want to discuss your anxiety about meeting with Phillip?'

'No. I've decided he has no place in my life here; is far removed from my role under your direction and should not be a topic of discussion between us. I've dwelt too long on this already this week. I will go meet with him to understand his attitude and see where we go from there. What I must do in the next two days is finish my proposal.'

'Okay. Let's enjoy dinner and then see where you are.'

Dinner over and table cleared, she gave him a copy of her latest draft explaining Charles was not available today so would address the remaining risks tomorrow. They went through each section noting any ambiguities or omissions. Within an hour she was satisfied the final draft tomorrow would comply with the standards set. All she needed was to complete the section on risk after her meeting with Charles. She went to bed satisfied her first ever business proposal fully articulated her ideas and met with support from her mentors. And what she had learnt about Aldridge in the process made the effort worthwhile.

Chapter 67 – Tuesday

She spent the morning huddled with Charles and Jim finalising her Business Development Proposal and then deciding how much can be released to Michael.

'The problem we face my dear Mel is the quality of this report is so good it's difficult to find any of it I want to disclose. Sebastian is teaching you at such a high level against what we need. The result is valuable information for which our competitors would pay richly to get a copy.'

'Why don't I construct a watered-down version containing only what I disclosed last Wednesday plus some outline information about the proposed restructure of our offices and associated risk issues?'

'That's still too much in writing, but you do that and let us both have copies.'

With this they adjourned back to work stripping as much sensitive detail out until all she had was a barebones version providing both Jim and Charles a copy. The day passed with no further thought of her impending visit with Phillip.

Tonight, we examine what constitutes a healthy, flexible company. As a banker, looking at a corporate seeking funding for some project or venture, the first test applied is its hierarchy and internal communications. For instance, if this corporate is steeped in hierarchical levels, we would consider this a negative. Such a company will be steeped in artificial rule and protocol structures that effecting change will be like trying to turn around a mighty oil taker; takes forever.

'Then we try to gauge if the people at the bottom of the hierarchy know more about the direction of the company than the executives. It would surprise you how often this is the case. This signifies poor leadership.'

'If you think about the dynamics of a company there are only three functions, namely strategy, tactics, and delivery. If we

the Way

translate this into Sun Tzu, we have a General who plans strategy, his commanders who deal with the tactical delivery, and the army who effect the delivery.'

'So why do people think companies require more layers? If we look at a conglomerate, then we have an added layer of strategy in the group Board which usually comprises the CEO and CFO of each of the Group subsidiaries.'

'You will also note many companies have a chairperson or president and a CEO. Traditionally the Chairperson/President role looks outward in an ambassadorial role, whereas the CEO looks after the performance of the company. Some companies combine this role, but this is not favoured by investors in listed companies – too big a role for one person. It's also usually the Chairman/President figure is more experienced than the CEO offering both wisdom and oversight when needed.'

'A company the size of Aldridge can get away with a dual role, not least because they are the owner and founder of the company. The risk is if something happens to Charles what happens to the company. Who will ensure continuity? Even customers with a long-term relationship, but expecting time critical components, will see this as a risk. Should Aldridge ever find itself large enough for a listing, investors would expect these roles to be split.'

'We would scrutinise each member of the executive and any key resource. How qualified are they? What have they achieved before? How well do they function together? Are there any weaknesses in the form of shortfall in necessary skills and capability? Banks lend to people, not projects. During my career I have seen projects that are viable so long as managed by the right people. I have encountered the same project presented by two different companies; one rejected for lack of quality of management but accepted by the second company.'

'Let's get back to our corporate pyramid and examine how well it complies with the Teachings of Sun Tzu. If you remember back to the *Use of Energy* essay, it states that management of the

Week 10

many is the same as management of few. It's a matter of organisation. And to control many is the same as to control few. This is a matter of formations and signals.'

'If we think about the structure of Sun Tzu's army, he organised his troops into tactical and support units. He would have a unit of chariots to disrupt an advancing enemy, respond to any attempt to outflank him, or use their speed to get behind the enemy and disrupt from the rear. There would be archers to soften advancing lines. And there would be the main body of soldiers with their hand weapons to engage the enemy. Each unit would have a commander converting the strategic objective into tactical delivery. In the absence of field telephones and memos each unit would have a flag that uniquely identifies each unit to enable the command centre to monitor the shape of the battlefield, and another set of flags to disperse instructions, i.e. communications.'

'In our corporate environment we have tactical and support units referred to as departments and divisions. Each such unit will have a commander or line manager to oversee delivery, and a General or executive defining the strategic objective as requested by his sovereign or CEO. Our tactical units are directly engaged in the production and delivery of our product or service, and the support units comprise element such as human resources, regulatory and compliance, and accounts.'

'Whichever way you look at it there is only a requirement for three levels of hierarchy. So why, in many corporates are there more. If you examine such structures they're inherited from the days of order and compliance attitudes, ego driven – whatever they are they're poor management. In today's world, corporates need to be dynamic and flexible to survive. Outmoded hierarchical structures do not facilitate fleet o' foot.'

She was confused. 'But surely armies have a hierarchy in the ranks such as corporals and sergeants. My dad was a sergeant. If what you say is true, why do armies need them?'

the Way

'Good question, and one I put to a senior military officer when I was formulating my views. Interestingly, he was very much a proponent of Sun Tzu so understood my request. He explained that there are two very specific reasons for non-commissioned officer ranks. First, a battlefield is very different to corporate conflict. People die on battlefields, and the soldiers do not go home at the end of the day to their families before resuming the battle the next day. Second, should the commander be killed, someone must step in immediately to assume command to hold the line until a replacement can be found. Thus, why soldiers are taught, as part of their basic training, they must obey orders from a higher rank. Such hierarchy is considered an essential contingent asset for the maintenance of order on the battlefield.'

'He was right. Our corporate armies are not being asked to risk their lives, and they go home at the end of each day. In the event they suffer the demise of a commander, or even a General, there is time to regroup. Corporates do not need overt contingent assets in the form of hierarchy.'

'However, you can create an advantageous perceived hierarchy without labels. If you have two people both doing the same task, but one is far more experienced than the other and thus contributing more, we can reward their efforts through remuneration. In this way the less experienced is incentivised to become better at the task to achieve the same level of reward.'

'One of the important reasons for avoiding hard hierarchy in the ranks is change management. I've managed environments where responding to market changes is a way of life, and these can occur every 3 – 4 months. And this change must occur within the existing resource base, as they will also be learning what adjustments are needed in processing to accommodate such change. My way of managing such change was to select the most appropriate project leader with a small team of selected skills from the existing operations people, whatever discipline. They would determine the required changes, formulate an

Week 10

implementation plan, and then oversee the change. Once completed, this project team would dissolve back into the operation.'

'Now consider how this would work if hard hierarchies existed. Let's presume the most appropriate project leader is a lower hierarchy to other members of the project team. Would this create a management problem because a lower hierarchy person was now acting as a temporary commander? Of course, it would. Human nature.'

'You have a vehement disregard for hierarchy. Is this derived from bad experiences?'

'I was asked to join a bank where I faced twenty-four pay-grade levels just for the operations people. And this bank wondered why their level of performance was well below market average, and morale was low.'

'What did you do?'

'I wiped this whole structure away from my division, including superfluous titles. I instructed each line manager to mark every person under them to market value, make any adjustments necessary to remuneration, and then move forward with no such demarcations. Everyone would then be rewarded on merit and contribution.'

'What did the bank say?'

'By then I had a reputation for delivery. If you wanted me, you had no choice but to accept my ways. Don't ask me to do a job and then tell me how to do it. Remember our rules? All, but one bank adopted my ways as soon as they realised the value.'

'Implanted in my brain. What happened to the bank that didn't?'

'It realised the error of its ways far too slowly and is about to fail.'

'Wow. You must have rattled some cages in your time.'

'Investment banking is a dynamic environment where only the most skilful survive. However, such skills need firm, competent management, not irrelevant constraint. Look at the recent collapse of Barings Bank. The writing was on the wall months before, but the internal culture constraints, and poor management from the top, meant no control within the bank. It only takes a small error of judgement to cost £millions, or even bring the bank down. If we could see it from the outside, why couldn't they?'

'You will see the same situation play out with corporates who build so much constraint into their structures they cannot possibly adapt to moving situations which makes them a target for takeover, or demise.'

'Anyway, enough for this evening. Remember, flat structures make for dynamic environments with good communications. The more layers you have, the less adaptable you are, and errors in communications are an exponential function of the number of layers it needs to traverse; and takes longer. Try drawing a schematic of the layers within Aldridge.'

Chapter 68 – Wednesday

When she arrived for breakfast, she was unsure whether to be excited she would meet Philip in Derby after work, or reticent about his intrusion into her life here. His attitude towards her visiting her mother last weekend, but not spending time with him, had disturbed her. He could sense her continued anxiety.

'How do you feel about this evening?'

'I'm not sure. I never envisaged him involved in my time here. I see no reason to mix my life here with my life in London.'

'Why don't you treat it as an opportunity to defend your decision to come here, and the serious nature of the opportunity. Your decision to spend last weekend here, other than a compassionate desire to spend a few hours with your mother on Saturday, was geared to your workload, and thus legitimate.'

'As usual, my master looks to the positive. I hope one day to have such clarity of thought.'

'Time to go. Wish me luck?'

'You don't need luck. You make your own. Off you go now and don't worry yourself. I'll see you when I see you.'

She engrossed herself in her work during the day but couldn't help feeling somewhat anxious as the day progressed. By the time she left for Derby she had decided not to seek forgiveness as she had done nothing wrong. She would explain the demands on her time and defend her decisions.

Chapter 69 – Wednesday evening

It was late. He was watching the Ten O'clock News on TV. The gate alert sounded – a mechanism that warns him his gates are opening without his intervention. He went to the kitchen to see headlights on the drive. She parked but did not leave her car. He waited, but no movement so went to her car. She was slumped over the steering wheel. He opened her door. She was sobbing. He bent down and put his arm across her shoulders. She looked at him. Her appearance in the outside lighting was dishevelled. He lifted her out of the car, kicked her door shut, and carried her into the house.

After sitting her on the sofa, he could see a welt on her left cheek. She saw his reaction, buried her head, and sobbed more. He brought a bowl of warm water and a towel to clean her face, tenderly working around the welt.

'You're home, and you're safe. Tell me where it hurts.'

'She pointed to her cheek.'

'Is there any pain anywhere else?' She nodded in the negative.

'Let me take you coat.'

She complied without resistance.

the Way

He poured a cognac. 'Take a sip of this' handing it to her.

Again, she complied, but screwed up her face as the cognac hit her tongue. She did not like cognac, but he knew this would get her attention.

He sat next to her and held her in his arms to comfort her. 'Can you tell me what happened?'

'He was so angry with me. Our marriage is off. My ring is in the gutter somewhere in Derby.' Her sobbing resumed.

'How do you feel about it?'

'Wretched.'

'Why?'

'Because it's my fault.' She was now burying her head into him, still sobbing.

He knew this was not the case, but she was in no state to listen to reason.

'Will you let me take care of you tonight?'

'She nodded in agreement.'

'I'll take you upstairs and put you to bed. We can talk in the morning.'

'I don't want to be alone.'

'You're coming with me. I'll comfort you tonight. You need to sleep.'

He carried her to his room, undressed her, not least to check for any other injury, and put her into his bed. He undressed and joined her, extinguished the lights, and wrapped his arms around her. He could feel the tears still flowing on his chest. He rocked her for a while to allow her to calm, and then gently stroked her back. She was soon fast asleep.

Chapter 68 – Thursday

When she opened her eyes, she was still wrapped in his arms. It took a few moments for her to collect herself and assess the situation. He was looking at her with a comforting smile.

'Good morning. How do you feel?'

'Have you held me in your arms all night?'

'I did what you needed. How do you feel?'

'Very stupid.'

'Will you allow me get to you through this?'

'You must think me such a fool,' as she bowed her head into his shoulder.

'Yesterday has gone. Let's concentrate on today. Do you need the bathroom?'

'Yes.'

'Then go, and then come with me.'

He took her to the pool. 'Morning swim young lady but keep your face in the water for as long as possible during the glide lengths.' He followed her to let her know he was with her.

'Now I'll give you a half-length start. You must make every effort to stop me catching you.'

'Please, master. I don't feel like this today.'

'I'm not asking; I'm telling, so go.'

She started her swim. When she was halfway, he alerted her he was coming as he started to chase her. By the third lap, she could hear him closing in on her. '*I will not let him pass.*' She was angry with her master. She stepped up her pace.

He purposely stayed a little behind her as he saw the increase in pace, but he wanted more effort. By the end of the tenth lap they finished together. She held onto the pool edge, gasping for breath.

'Can I see your face?'

She looked at him, still recovering.

'Good. The water has reduced the swelling on your cheek, and around your eyes. How do you feel?'

the Way

'Certainly awake.'

'Come, I'll get you ready for work.'

'I don't feel like going to the office like this if you don't mind.'

'But I do mind. You have a responsibility to do your job. Your pain is self-inflicted, so only you pay the price. Come with me.'

He hauled himself out of the water and lifted her out. He towelled both and took her grudgingly back to his room.

'I'm going to do something I haven't done in a long time, so please listen to what I say as this is important for you.'

She followed him, still annoyed he was sending her to the office. She was thinking of the embarrassment when they see her face. He started the shower and tested the water temperature. He encouraged her in and joined her.

'Before I start please listen to what I say. I'm about to cleanse your body of everything to do with last night. All I want you to do is imagine that my cleansing is shedding you of all the bad feelings you feel. Just lose yourself under the warm water. This is about drowning your sorrows and washing away your pain. Do you understand?'

She nodded in affirmation.

He put her under the showerhead and drenched her from head to foot. He wanted her to feel like she was drowning. Then he applied shampoo to her hair, gently massaging her head as he slowly spread the shampoo throughout her hair. He left the shampoo in her hair, which straddled around her face, while he gently cleansed her whole body down to the spaces between her toes, taking his time to ensure she responded to each movement. He then rinsed her off as though under a waterfall.

After stopping the water flow, he left the shower, collected a towel, and invited her out. The towelling process was as tender as the cleansing. His final act was to put a towel around her hair.

'How do you feel?'

'That was the most beautiful experience in my life. Very intimate, but lovely. We must do it more often.' She was smiling.

'No problem. Please go to your room and get yourself ready for work while I prepare breakfast. You should not require much makeup to obscure the bruising. The pool did a good job.'

She was still fragile, but did comply, appearing for breakfast some 20 minutes later.

'I really can't face the office today. Must I go? Whatever happened to compassionate leave?'

'Why, who died? If you seriously expect to be an executive, it's important you pull yourself together and do your job. And you must deliver a day's workload. You must learn when you get knocked down, you must immediately return to your feet. If you fall and crumple, you'll be trampled. You will not recover. You must stay on your feet, no matter how painful. Now off you go; you're already late.'

As soon as she was on her way, he called Charles. 'Good morning, Charles. You have a somewhat fragile lady on her way. Phillip assaulted her. Her marriage is off. Please ensure she gets no sympathy, especially from Mary. She must carry on with her work, but please keep her off the factory floor. You can cut her a little slack, but please don't allow her to fold. If you can keep her in check, I'll have her back to normal tomorrow.'

'You're a hard man, but the results to date are impressive. Against my fatherly instinct, I'll do as you ask. Ah, I see her driving through the gates. I must alert the others. I'll call if we have a problem.'

He alerted Jim, and then Mary making it clear to her that today she must avoid her normal habit of ignoring him, or she would have to deal with Sebastian. No point is saying she would have to deal with him.

Mary intercepted her to assess the situation. Her eyes were still a little swollen, but otherwise she looked all right.

'Let me get you some coffee dear. I'll bring it to you in a few minutes. What do you want me to do if Phillip phones?'

'Not available, ever again.'

the Way

Jim ignored her face and continued their work as usual. 'Good morning Mel, I have a new project for us to study when you're ready, and I've had some thoughts about your Business Development Proposal which may help your understanding of this business and how we implement your ideas.'

When she arrived home, she looked emotionally shattered. Any hope of compassion was soon thwarted as she was told they would talk after her exercise, which could, on this occasion, be a swim if she preferred.

When she finally arrived in the kitchen, she saw he had prepared her favourite dish. A glass of wine was already poured. She felt better already.

'Is my master angry with me?'

'On the contrary, my dear, you have completed a task of great importance to your progress.'

'And what task is that?'

'The painful consequences of rose-tinted spectacles.'

'I don't understand.'

'Please let us have dinner before we complete this valuable lesson. Enjoy.'

'You know this is my favourite, so I'll enjoy even though totally confused why you appear to celebrate the breakdown of my marriage plans.'

'We are indeed celebrating, but not for the reason you state.'

She looked at him with despair but decided he would reveal all in the fullness of time. For now, she only wanted to eat as her lunch break had been consumed speaking with her mother.

After dinner, they adjourned to the lounge.

'Do you want to talk about what happened last night?'

'We were having dinner and talking about my work here. Without thinking about it, I spoke of you and your role in my progress. Then he wanted to know more about you. When he realised I live here alone with you, he wouldn't move on. When we got back to his room, he demanded to know what was going on between us, convinced there was more. He was angry that I preferred to spend weekends with you rather than him. When I protested my innocence, and told him to grow up, completely forgetting my games people play, he hit me. That was it. I told him we were through and left. When I got to my car, I yanked off my engagement ring and threw it into the gutter.'

'Now my precious student, let us review events since you started this challenge. Please recap the reaction of Phillip when you informed him of your plans to engage with this process.'

'He was very negative.'

'This was a red light. Why did you ignore it?'

'What do you mean?'

'You have the choice in any situation to see things exactly as they are – reality – or as you would like to see them – delusion, or as is commonly referred to as through rose-tinted spectacles. Executives are faced with such situations almost daily and need to immediately determine the efficacy of the situation before them. They must not, under any circumstances, impose their own preferred reality to the picture. I would suggest you fell afoul of a regular female delusion regarding marriage. The planning of a marriage should be a joyful experience. The reality is it's stressful, especially for the woman, and a pathway, once started, appears irreversible. Too embarrassing to call it off after alerting everyone. Thus, the signs all's not well are ignored, even though "happy ever after" is clearly not in the cards.'

'The lesson you have just learnt is you must be alive to your senses and believe what they tell you; not what you prefer. You pain is self-inflicted and thus not worthy of compassion. You must accept your error of judgement, and thus fault for your situation, and not expect, or accept any sympathy. You must accept this error as a valuable lesson in life and put it behind you immediately. I expect you to work a normal day tomorrow. Any questions?'

the Way

'My master, I find it difficult to argue your accurate, but brutal analysis. I will comply with your instructions, but would ask one minor, but important concession to help me comply.'

'Tell me.'

'I'm still feeling fragile, although I completely accept your rebuke. It has been a hard lesson for which I seek just a little compassion. Will you hold me again tonight and cleanse me in the morning to get me through this? I need to sleep, and you're clearly proficient in this task.'

'Your request is granted, but you must deliver tomorrow. When quietly sitting at your desk, I want you to imagine you're wearing your rose-tinted spectacles. Go through the motion of tearing them off your face and throwing them into the waste bin. Rid yourself of these painful illusions.'

'It will be as my master requires.'

'She started to cry. 'What a fool I am. I have one conversation with you about Phil, and you immediately know the inevitable outcome. I'm so blind and stupid. You must think me an emotional basket-case. I wanted so much to believe in our marriage I became immune to the signs. I will double my efforts to not mask reality with emotional desire.' Her sobbing was intense.

He knew this was a valuable part of the cleansing process so just quietly held her.

She calmed a little. 'I spoke with my mum today about Phil. She told me it was probably for the best and then reminded me you had expressed concern during our conversation that weekend I was making my decision. You're so right about me being blind to the signs. Why do you have belief in me?' She burst into tears again.

Once she had calmed a little, he took her to bed. As she snuggled into him, 'why would you celebrate my pain? You were almost gloating.'

'I was not gloating. I was having great difficulty framing an event which would allow you to feel the pain of delusion. You gave it to me on a plate. A great lesson for you, and relief for me. Now to sleep with you, young lady. You must be exhausted.' He wrapped her in his arms and stroked her back. She was quickly asleep.

Chapter 69 – Friday

Mel arrived in the office as usual with no signs of emotional stress. Charles came to inform her Jim was with the medics today and might not appear at all. He could not help but notice her frame of mind. *'Sebastian certainly knows how to weave his magic with her'* he thought as he returned to his office.

She went through Jim's in-tray and dealt with everything needing attention. Then she cancelled her wedding arrangements. Mary informed her Phil had phoned three times since yesterday. She was not interested. She wrote him a letter to tell him she had cancelled their wedding, and he should look for alternative accommodation.

It was time to get her mind back on her quest, but now with more vigour and focus. She knew she had faltered. It was time to show commitment and resilience. Remembering her instructions, she imagined herself wearing rose-tinted spectacles, ripped them from her face, and launching them into the bin.

She spent the afternoon talking to her architect clients, sounding them out on a more cooperative relationship as per her Business Development Proposal. The response was encouraging. She would give them time to absorb the concept and then arrange to go meet with them.

By the time she arrived home, she was mentally exhausted, but feeling good about her refreshed commitment. She had satisfied herself she had unloaded constraining baggage from her life, freeing her to pursue her own dreams.

the Way

He saw the tiredness but could feel the change in attitude. She had survived distress and was quickly moving on. Nothing needed to be said.

After dinner he took her to his local pub to meet his friends. This took her mind off work, after which she shared his bed again.

Chapter 70 – Saturday

Over breakfast she appeared a little down. 'You have something on your mind. Anything I can help with?'

'Look at me, Seb, I'm 32 years old, my marriage plans have just fallen apart. I don't have my weekend respite. Surely work isn't the only thing left in life?'

He knew this story. He had this conversation with a young female exec many years ago which led to the City Club, which satisfied the frustration she was feeling. What to do. He was not prepared to fulfil her sexual needs himself but letting her go out to find it for herself in her state of mind could complicate matters even more.

He remembered a technique he used with a woman some years ago, which she called "the hand in the dark". *'Could this work, or would it be a step too far?'*

'Mel, come sit with me, I have an idea I want you to consider.'

'If you remember back to our discussion about pillow talk, I described a young exec's club to overcome the frustrations of execs trying to fulfil natural needs without the complications of relationships. I think this is where you are. You have sexual needs you cannot fulfil. Am I on the right track?'

'That, and some fun is about right. What do you have in mind?'

'I'm not getting involved with you sexually. But I have a technique, similar to the cleansing process, which could tie you over until you can return to the real world and find another solution to your needs. This technique is right on the red line, so we have to agree some rules.'

'I love the cleansing process, so tell me what you want to do.'

'I refer to it as a hand in the dark. The only contact between us will be my hand, which will explore and caress you all the way to orgasm. You cannot touch me for any reason until after I've finished, and you will not attempt to take it any further once I've finished. Is this something you would like to try?'

'You are some incredible teacher. You want to satisfy my needs with just your hand. And you think you can resist taking it further afterwards. The idea is totally off the wall, but if it's as good as cleansing, then why not? I want to be in your arms again tonight so how does this start?'

'You can either roll over, so you have your back to me, and I'll start on your back after which you roll onto your back in a submissive form and let my hand weave its magic. You can fantasise to your hearts' content. If you don't want the backstroking, then just roll onto you back with your hands in surrender mode.'

'If this is as good as cleansing, you'll have one happy woman. Not sure about not indulging in sex, or touching, but you always seem to know what works for me, so go for it.'

'Do you have any preference for night or morning?'

'How about I just roll over when I feel the need?'

She thought about this conversation for a while. 'I can't believe some of the conversations we have. You are one extraordinary dude. If you were a woman, I'd be thinking Mary Poppins.'

The very idea he could satisfy her needs with just one hand tickled her as she tried to imagine how this would work. But it put a spring in her step as they engaged in the weekly shop for food. She was in a better place and spent the afternoon on the sundeck absorbing some necessary vitamin D.

the Way

Later, when they were in bed, she curled up in his arms, deciding to see what he could do. She rolled onto her back, arms in surrender mode. 'Okay hand, let's see what you can do.'

'Just close your eyes and let yourself go.'

He started by stroking down the arm nearest to him to her armpit and then continued down the side of her body to her thighs. He stroked across her tummy and moved up to her breasts, which he caressed, squeezed, and stroked until both nipples were fully extended. The tension in her body had gone. He continued to stroke all the parts he knew served him well those years ago. Finally, he moved between her legs where he found the evidence her juices were in full flow. He stroked the lips of her vagina as she purred with delight. Finding that most sensitive of parts, he gently stroked behind the head, knowing a slow burn would produce the best result. It took some minutes before he could feel the build to orgasm. He kept to a slow build as he felt her reaching the point of no return. Then her hips jolted with the first wave of orgasm. The spasms became more violent and frequent until she exploded, clasping her legs together. He kept his hand firmly between her legs to encourage every spasm of orgasm. As she calmed, he removed his hand.

She just lay there, still purring.

'Whoever taught you how to do that deserves a gold medal. No man has ever achieved anything like that orgasm.'

She rolled to face him and put her arms around his neck. 'That was so good. Can I have it on demand?'

'Does it solve the problem in the short-term?'

'When have you not solved my problems? It was fantastic. Every night, please, and twice at weekends.'

'Let's stick to weekends and special occasions as you would not have more than that before. All I'm attempting to do is to understand the need and emulate what our City Club created, in part, to satisfy this need. It won't be good to have you in my bed during the week. We're not lovers.'

Chapter 71 – Sunday

She woke with a smile on her face. She still could not believe what happened last night, but she felt good. This type of care was so new to her.

She watched him open his eyes. She wanted to give him a big kiss on the lips but thought better of it as she knew this was out of bounds, so a kiss on the cheek and a big smile would have to do.

'Someone is bright and cheery today.'

'I had a dream that a magic hand touched me in the night and instilled joy into me. It was a lovely dream.'

'How do you know it was just a dream?'

'Are you telling me it was real?' She threw the duvet from them and lay on her back in a submissive position. If it was real, show me.'

'A bit brazen, you hussy.'

She turned her head towards him 'I feel like a brazen hussy this morning. Indulge me.'

As he had full access to her, and could see her, he leaned up on his elbow so he could reach all of her, this time starting with her face and neck.

After her orgasm she lay there, eyes still closed, with the biggest smile on her face. He didn't know where she was in her mind, but she was certainly satisfied with life.

When she finally turned her head towards him, her eyes were bright and her smile broad. 'Thank you. You have completely cleansed me of Phil. He could never do that to me, and it's better than sex with him. I can continue my work with no remorse from last week thanks to my brilliant master. The hand in the dark is a fantastic therapy. I don't need more than this in the coming weeks.'

'Are you ready for our swim?'

'Where you lead, your student will follow, my master.'

the Way

After their swim and shower, they sat over breakfast. 'Seb, I'm 32 years old, but compared with your worldly experience, I feel like a naïve little girl. You have so much to give, and I want to learn as much as I can from you. If I openly invite you to take me anywhere you want to go with me, is this okay with you? I don't mean the mentor role, but life in general. You know so many things, and you never cease to amaze me with how well you can read me. Last week I could never have imagined being bathed in a shower by you, sleeping in your bed naked, and certainly not the hand in the dark. Now I want to know what more you can give. I feel so comfortable with you, I'll go wherever you take me. You don't need to ask anymore. Just scoop me up and show me life.'

'My dear lady, I don't plan anything for you, I just respond to a need. First, thank your blessings you collided with Carmen or else stripping you off and drowning you in the shower could have been a disaster. And certainly, no hand in the dark. I can't predict anything. Your consent to go where I think you need to go removes a weight from my mind as I don't want this project to end badly or abruptly. Yes, you are inexperienced, but you have shown your willingness to explore, which makes life easier for me as the things I can show you are all part of the package you need out there. Other than a few bruises now and again, I'll not harm or abuse you, no matter what I ask of you.'

She got up, went to him, and kissed him on both cheeks. She held his face in her hands, 'I know you won't harm me. I have never felt so cared for. You've got me through a difficult time by quickly moving me on. Most people would only try to comfort me and supply me with Kleenex. I can go to the office tomorrow with a clear head and a smile on my face. This makes you special to me.'

Week 11

Chapter 72 – Monday

When she arrived at the office, it was apparent to Jim the events of last week were behind her. He could not but marvel at her resilience. *'Charles is right. This lady has what it takes. And the magic Sebastian brings is remarkable. Time to bring her truly into the fold.'*

'My dear, today we need to expose you to the greater workings of Aldridge. You are already familiar with the commercial aspects in London but, as you now see, it's but a microcosm of our total business. Are you ready?'

She parked her car as usual, but walked to the house, head down, shaking it in disbelief. She entered the kitchen and dumped her bag, still head down. He found this amusing but said nothing.

'Hi, Seb.'

'Hi. You paint an interesting picture this evening. What can't you believe?'

'I've worked for Aldridge for ten years and thought I knew how this company worked. Until today I knew very little, if anything. Charles and Jim keep everything about this company so close not even the technical design team knows how most orders originate. I'm stunned.'

'Do you want to tell me now, or keep me in suspense whilst you do your gym routine?'

'I'm still trying to get my head around what happened today so let me do my routine. Maybe then I'll be less confused.'

He smiled with amusement, 'Can't wait. See you later.'

the Way

She collected her bag and wandered off to her room, still shaking her head.

She wandered back at 7:30 and sank into her chair at the table. He had already poured her a glass of wine. 'Thanks. Need a drink tonight.'

He put her food in front of her, still amused at her bewilderment.

'Are we any clearer about today, or are you still in shock?'

'Sorry.' She took a deep breath. 'Yet again I feel somewhat naïve and stupid. Ten years I work for a company I know nothing about. And now I know, the only person I can tell is you.' She curled herself as though in a secret meeting 'I'm now part of the inner sanctum of a secret society, and you must keep what I tell you within these walls, under pain of death. Do you understand?'

He played along 'I've lived in the inner sanctum for many years, so your secrets are safe with me.'

She feigned checking to see if they were alone. 'Aldridge has secret agents all over the place. They collect information about new developments and redevelopments and feed it through minders who report only to Charles and Jim. Orders flow from this information, but only Charles and Jim know the origin of these orders and keep this knowledge secret. Even the payments to these secret agents are handled only by Jason Tyler, our Finance Director. I think Charles is a descendent of Sun Tzu.'

'I think you're telling me Aldridge sources its order book through indirect agents. This is not an unusual process. Think of insurance companies, and motor companies who use third party agents to sell their products.'

'You're right, my learned sage. But with those companies, everyone knows the agent works for the supplier. This is not the case with Aldridge. Only the inner sanctum know the agents are on the books of Aldridge.'

'I therefore assume Charles has sources of lead generation who are quietly rewarded for putting the business to Aldridge.

Again, not unusual. Questionable in some situations regarding impartiality, but not unusual.'

'So why all the secrecy within the company? Even the London office doesn't know half the story in the South-East, including Michael.'

'As I've told you before, your London office is a bit of an anomaly. Charles has developed a lead generation model which works for his mainstream business. I would think he expects the London office to survive or fall on a different model, more akin to larger commercial projects. He's too canny to let Michael hide behind an existing working model. You've developed a better opportunity than Michael for the larger commercial projects. I'm sure if a suitable model can be developed for London, this would be duplicated in Manchester, and Liverpool as two cities on the development curve.'

'He's secretly looking at Edinburgh as well.'

'Smart move. Devolution of Scotland won't go away. Edinburgh is the logical seat of a new Assembly. This will stimulate much development across the board. And not far away from here.'

'But I still don't understand the nature of the stunning revelations today. What has made your feel naïve and stupid, as you put it?'

'I've been with Aldridge on the origination side for ten years. I've been here ten weeks shadowing Jim, looking at all projects. I've never looked at or noticed anything about mainstream order generation. Only today do they sit me down and explain how they generate business. Why have I never been interested enough to find out? Have I been sleep-walking these past ten weeks? Where are my instinctive powers of curiosity and observation?'

'Ah, I see. You feel you should have at least observed how orders are generated before being told. Sounds like Charles is very adept at keeping his business strategy secret, even from someone under whose nose this is playing out. Very Sun Tzu. So, what did he tell you?'

'I thought we had a small army of salespeople covering Manchester and Liverpool. I find we have just three on the payroll, and more than forty more in the form of mostly architect practices, commercial estate agents, local council property departments, and commercial property insurance brokers. They feed into the three salespeople who then define the orders with the purchaser. We pay the indirect originators a commission for the referral. Same applies in each region of the country. We have a total of seventeen salespeople covering the entire country with more than two hundred indirect originators. Total annual mainstream sales around £60 million. The order book typically extends out about one year. Incredible.'

'I told you Charles had a solid order book from loyal sources. The fact he keeps it so secret means his competition cannot attack him. Their loyalty is probably founded on more than a commission. My guess is Aldridge offers a quality and reliable product at a reasonable price with no delivery issues.'

'That's right. And Aldridge also offers a backup service. If the window is broken, we guarantee a glass replacement in two business days. If the frame is damaged beyond repair, we offer a full replacement within five business days. And we've never failed to deliver.'

'Charles is a canny businessman. He's even recession proof with such a small sales force on the payroll. To offer such a backup service, he must also have preferential supply-side agreements. You should be honoured he now trusts you with such valuable information. Consider how valuable such information would be to his competitors.'

'Can I assume my master is not disappointed in me for not already knowing this structure before now?'

'Absolutely not. The lesson from today is how, as an executive, you must keep valuable strategy concealed from anyone not directly involved, and even then, on a need-to-know basis. I'm grateful Charles considers you committed and trustworthy enough to share such information with you. Let's me know he's happy with your progress. Do you now understand the significance of these revelations?'

'Now I understand the significance, and no rebuke from you, I feel much better. Thank you.'

'I must get a video camera. Your arrival home and subsequent theatrics in the kitchen earlier were priceless.'

'Now you're making fun of me. What's our topic of study this evening?'

'This evening we will discuss market dynamics in the form of supply & demand, and price elasticity.'

'Other than I may have heard of these expressions can I declare your last statement should be considered as gobble-de-gooks.'

He laughed. 'Don't worry. We're not about to delve deep into these subjects. You can study as required; and you have the mathematical skills to understand the various algorithms. What I want to achieve is merely to make you aware of these subjects and their relevance to business. You need to understand the principles, even in a company like Aldridge.'

'Let's start with supply & demand. It should be clear to you if a product or service is desirable, it inclines you to purchase if the price is right. There are two ends to this curve. The first is where a product has mass appeal. But where to set the price? This is where knowledge of your market is essential. If you can determine the volume of demand by the marketplace for any given price, you can set your price to optimise revenues. Too high a price and you'll restrict your volumes. Too low a price and you will forfeit valuable profit. This is completely different to the computations to minimise the cost of the product to you. If you can make a product for £15 and sell it for £100 you make a good profit. But if you can make the same product to the same quality for £10, typically in a third–world economy, you make even more profit. Even better if someone else produces the product for you so you have none of the tooling costs or need to be concerned how long the shelf-life of your product. In this latter case you supply only for as long as you have demand, take your profit, and move on to another product. Does this make sense to you?'

'Yes, if we're speaking in general terms.'

'Okay. Let's look at the other end of the curve. This is where exclusivity creates demand. These will be products deemed to be so exclusively limited in supply that demand will be much greater than supply, and thus a substantial premium can be commanded for these products. Typically, we include prime quality watches, cars, jewellery which command a premium far more than the cost to produce. By restricting supply to less than demand, we can control pricing.'

'But why would you not increase supply and take a lesser price?'

'Exclusivity. People will pay a premium if they know only the few can own such a product. The more people who can afford a product, the less the kudos of ownership. These products are a badge of wealth. And, of course, the quality of craftsmanship will be confined to a relatively few specialists in making such products. Can you think of the most exclusive of products?'

'I guess you speak of one-offs like a work of art.'

'Exactly. Think of the prices paid for art masters. There is only one such painting, sculpture or other artefact, and thus its price will be what the highest bidder is prepared to pay to exclusively own it.'

'If suppliers want to maximise their prices, but consumers want to minimise their costs, how do we set the price for a product or service? And how do you know how much product to make available?'

'To determine the price and quantity of goods available to the market, we need to find the price point where consumer demand equals the amount suppliers are willing to supply. This is called "market equilibrium". The central idea of a free market is that

Week 11

prices and quantities move naturally toward equilibrium, and this maintains market stability.'

'If we look at Aldridge, and specifically at their retail window production, we could plot a supply/demand curve to determine optimal sales volumes. But this curve has an external component that will significantly affect how we read this curve. We would need to know the limits of production capability for the current workshop. In addition, we need to understand the supply-side costs at various volumes of purchase in both extrusions and glass. There will no doubt be stepped prices to Aldridge based on volume commitments.'

'Then we have external influences from competitors. How much of the market at our price point is already provided at the price/quality level we aim to produce, i.e. what market share can we capture.

'When producing your own product with substantial capital investment, understanding your role and how to capture market share is critical to establishing a healthy business.'

'If we now consider price elasticity, we are referring to the impact of price increase on demand. When considering what price to set for a product or service, not all products behave in the same way. The extent to which the demand for a product is affected by the price you set is known as "price elasticity of demand".'

'Inelastic products are those people always need, but in a finite quantity. Electricity is an example of an inelastic product; if power companies lower the price of electricity, consumers probably won't use additional power in their homes, because they don't need more than they already consume. If electricity prices rise, demand is unlikely to fall significantly, because people still need power.'

The obvious inelastic products you will already be aware of is Government duty levels on goods such as alcohol and fuel. Governments choose such commodities because they can continue to increase taxes because they are inelastic. These are consumables most people think they cannot do without lest they restrict their lifestyle. After each Government budget, any rises in duty on these commodities will be met with anger from the public, but then they will grin and bear the rise as they continue to consume as before. Very few will be forced to change their consumption so prices can rise with little impact on demand. The only recourse from the consumer is at the ballot box assuming an alternative Government is prepared to pledge to reduce these duties.'

'Other goods, generally labelled as luxury items, suffer more badly from price increases as there is high price elasticity. These goods are nice to have; but not needed in daily life. If these good are priced too high, people will do without them. The supplier can easily price themselves out of the market. Interestingly, it's these good that can suffer when inelastic prices rise. When taxes and duties go up people need to tighten their belts on elastic products to afford their continued inelastic consumption. The typical victims are leisure spending such as restaurants and pubs.'

'Where do you think retail windows produced by Aldridge sit on the elasticity curve?'

'They're not inelastic because there are other suppliers ready to undercut prices. However, they're not overly elastic either. Aldridge and its nearest rival, Pardow, work together to keep newcomers in check on pricing. If they find a newcomer destabilising the market, they work together to rid themselves of this troublesome problem. Aldridge and Pardow will compete for business, but they won't break agreed rules between themselves on undercutting. But if anyone else tries to steal their business, they will work together to put them out of business, if they can. Self-preservation.'

'Well done. You have grasped this subject well.'

'With a little cheating. Jim covered this subject with me during our pricing session.'

'Why cheating? I'm happy you understand this subject and how it applies to Aldridge. I think enough for this evening.'

Chapter 73 – Tuesday

She was studying a quotation Jim had prepared. Towards the bottom of the quotation there was a row of abbreviations that were circled if a necessary component of the quotation; each representing either a fixed sum or a percentage of the product makeup cost and covered several fixed, variable, or risk contributions. She knew most of them, but on this one particular quotation there was a fresh one marked 'SA' £600. 'Jim, what's this additional cost on this quote?'

He looked at it. 'Ah, yes. This is a special window for a new home. The problem is that it is being built on a steep gradient and we'll need a special crane to lift this window off our lorry at the bottom of the slope and align it for installation. They want us to take responsibility to provide the crane and lift this window into position. This is an unusual request as major commercial jobs have their own cranes for such tasks. Thus 'SA' stands for Site Access and will cost £600. To this we add the risk components not covered by the crane hire.'

He thought for a moment. 'It occurs to me I've not fully explained all these codes, what they represent, and how we cost each. Our task this morning is to correct this oversight. Let's get started.'

When she emerged into the kitchen for dinner Seb was still busy preparing. 'Any fresh revelations today?'

'Oh, yes. More secrets. Today it was the secret codes for job costing. Our quotation paperwork has a series of codes printed towards the end. They keep the meaning of these codes secret from the design team and the sales and marketing people. Only someone in accounts knows how to convert these codes into a monetary value, but we do not detail it on the quotation. Even Michael does not understand how this system works.'

'Sounds like another mechanism to keep your competition guessing.'

'Certainly is. All we do is to circle the codes that apply to the quotation for accounts to make up the paperwork. All very hush-hush. We created an extra code today, albeit Jim put the amount next to the code as it's a special situation.'

'Charles and Jim don't need to fight off competition because no one can see how they engage. Can you see Sun Tzu in how they operate?'

'Every day. Charles may not know Sun Tzu, but he sure as hell knows the Art of War. Jason keeps most of these number current as he knows the associated cost structure. They even recover around twice the cost of their insurance policies.'

'Why twice?'

'They figure that if they have a major claim, their premiums will rocket. So, they build a sinking fund to offset any such increase.'

'And another thing. They have a mechanism to manage discount expectations, especially for retail business. They have a potential discount capability up to 10% built into the pricing. But if you want this discount, or more, you lose the right to choose your date for delivery, and the replacement guarantees. Most clients retract from seeking discount.'

'Brilliant. They attribute specific value to any discounts thus thwart such requests without loss of face of the client. And should another client learn of any discounts intending to achieve discounts for themselves, Charles merely has to state the value reduction in delivery. The more I see of the internal workings of Aldridge the more respect I have for Charles. And there're encouraging you to get closer and closer to their business. Signs are good. Let's eat.'

Week 11

This evening I want to discuss the essential value drivers of a business. We are not about to enter the business school function of analysing the effectiveness of companies and how they are valued. This is a topic for self-study, or maybe you will attend business school. All I want to do with you is to explain the nature of business value drivers, to enable you to understand what they are and how to manage them.

'The essential value drivers stem from your operations, investment, and financing. Operations value drivers include your rate of sales growth, operating profit margin, and corporate tax rates. The combination of these equates to your operating cash flow. As you can see each of these drivers has their own characteristics. Your growth of sales determines the volume of business you undertake, but the larger this becomes the greater the infrastructure to service this growth. Your operating profit margin determines what funds are available to service future growth so there is no point reducing margin to increase sales if this does not produce the profit you need to grow. Corporate tax rates determine how much of your income can be used for future growth; thus Governments tend to keep these taxes as low as possible in order companies can invest in growth because this creates jobs.'

'The investment value driver relates to the working capital requirement you need to service your production and any fixed asset acquisitions you may need for expansion. This can range from a significant new machine, a new building, or even a corporate acquisition, all of which involving depreciation of the investment over some years.'

'Then we need to finance our activity with a combination of fixed capital and retained working capital which can include term financing from a financial institution. Using a rate of return on fixed capital determined by a minimum dividend expectation of investors, or the yield that could be achieved by investing these funds elsewhere, commonly referred to as the opportunity cost, we can compute a cost of capital. If you do not have the appropriate level of capital to support your business activities, you are deemed to be insolvent as you cannot meet your obligations as they fall due.'

'I want to explore the interrelationships between these value drivers so you can understand the pricing exercise you and Jim have been exploring this week. Are we okay so far?'

'The term value driver is new to me, but I can see what you mean.'

'Okay. You are in business to make money by selling something such as services, products you make, or products you source and sell. If we look at Aldridge, they fabricate the products they sell, which means for example they purchase base materials such as extrusions and glass and assemble these as finished shop fronts.'

'During this process Aldridge needs to meet the costs of the base materials it purchases, it needs to provide the environment, the machinery needed to fabricate, and the manpower. We term these operating costs and define the costs to engage in the product process. Some people call these direct costs whilst I prefer the term - cost to do business. The time it takes from arrival of base components to the time the finished product is shipped to the customer will define the working capital required to support the order process. If we then permit the customer a further grace period before payment is received by Aldridge, it will require further working capital to service the carry cost.'

'Managing this process is fundamental to good cash flow management and which minimises the working capital requirement. I would imagine Charles negotiates a deposit that triggers the order process, a further payment when the goods are ready to ship, and then a final repayment of any retainer between 30 – 60 days after delivery.'

'He will also negotiate terms with his suppliers which optimise between a favourable price and minimising the gap between his payment to suppliers and his receipt from the customer. How he manages this determines how well he controls

Week 11

the working capital requirement of the company. Of course, he also must support the sales process and administration costs as well, which all adds to the working capital requirement. The careful management of this process is valuable in keeping the working capital requirement as low as possible and thus a value driver to the business.'

She interrupted. 'From my experience to date Aldridge pays its suppliers 10% upon order, 50% within 7 days of delivery to Aldridge, and then the remaining 40% some 30 days later which means the fabrications have been shipped and installed at least 2 weeks before the final payment. On the sales side it is 10% with order even if the delivery is months into the future, and this is non-returnable as it covers the design process. Then a further 30% to trigger the manufacture process, 50% within 2 days of installation, and the 10% retainer 30 - 45 days later.'

'If the timeline of outflows and inflows of payments is managed as well as you indicate, I would say Aldridge have all of their operating costs covered with minimal working capital. Do all of your customers pay on time once they have the product?'

'The larger customers can be slow, but not if they want good service in the future. One or two large contractors take the view they control the order flow on big projects so are at liberty to take as much time as they like to pay. We have a built-in element to our pricing to help to fund this plus a 3% over bank base rate for late payment, which doesn't appear to bother large contractors. I also think Charles has an agreement to do the same with our principal competitor so contractors cannot play us off against each other.'

'They are probably paying debt service in excess of this penalty level for their project, so Aldridge are essentially funding their project at a cheaper rate. So long as Aldridge does not need to use bank funding to cover this lateness of payment, then both probably win. Canny move to secure agreement with

the Way

your competitors to adopt the same structure – the power of alliances.'

'Let's move to sales growth. In a manufacturing environment, management of sales growth is complex and requires careful management. You will see representations of sales growth as a smooth curve, but in practice it would look like a series of steps. Your operating environment is geared to an optimal production volume. When that volume is reach it will require capital investment in space and production capability to facilitate further growth. Before this is agreed much effort is required to determine how your marketplace will grow, and what portion of this growth you're likely to capture. Only when you are convinced you can capture enough business to justify the investment do you expand production.'

Chapter 74 – Wednesday

Charles popped his head around the door. 'Dennis Potter will be here this morning. I think it's time for you to become fully involved with this new material. Jim will be here soon, so why don't we all convene in the Boardroom at 11 o'clock.'

I think tonight we should discuss business, and the way we, as humans, engage. As you have not, to date, encountered a typical corporate structure, I will start with an overview of the corporate world having worked for both American and British banks throughout the world. My preference, by far, is the American corporate culture primarily because it's founded on meritocracy and enterprise whereas there is still far too much class cronyism in the UK.'

'There is a general view that this new age of technology and globalisation will create a culture where know-how is the key requirement of success. This implies we'll have a select workforce of people with this know-how and unemployment will be high. I would prefer to believe the advancement of technology will be a period of self-realisation for the masses with the final destruction of class barriers, the restructuring of organisations to encourage performance, and the realisation of human resource potential. I think it will take people with know-how to achieve this but not necessarily technical or commercial know-how, more human resource performance and contribution know-how.'

'This reminds me of a conversation I had some years ago with Henry Kissinger. I sat next to him during a flight to New York. We were talking about business culture, during which he made two very astute observations about the difference between the American and British attitude to business. The first relates to the value of capable and experienced human resources to the economy. In the UK, when someone reaches 65 years old, the tendency is to give them a carriage clock and retire them. So, one day we have a valuable resource with a wealth of knowledge and experience, and the next day nothing. There is no such equivalent in the USA. People work until they want to retire or can no longer fulfil their duties. For key resources there will be a succession plan along the lines of the person will take retirement but on full pay whilst the company has a successor shadow until ready to take over. The economics are the retiree is on retirement pay plus whatever it costs to increment this to full pay, providing the company with the equivalent of the retirement pay to cover the costs of the shadow. No valuable resource knowledge and experience is lost in the process.'

'The second relates to venture capital. We have so-called venture capitalists in the UK who are supposed to stimulate innovation and facilitate the technology transfer to bring these ideas to market. I took a client to such a prominent company some years ago. Our client needed £500,000 to facilitate their business venture, which I thought was credible. I was appalled at the approach of the venture capital people. They wanted to achieve the offered participation for half the investment, have one of their people put on the payroll to oversee the investment, and required an onerous and expensive monthly reporting package. They also wanted a charge over the client's personal assets. This is one of the major problems with corporate management in this country – companies run by accountants. This approach stifles enterprise.'

'Contrast this with the same requirement in the USA where venture capital companies tend to be funded and run by entrepreneurs who have grown their own successful businesses. Such a proposal will be analysed, contingency funding set-aside if needed, creative input provided without charge, and no personal asset charge. This is an enterprise culture that encourages innovation and risk.'

'What happened to your client?'

'I was so disappointed with the attitude of the venture capital company. I discussed it with some banker and broker friends, resulting in five of us committing the funding, along with our knowledge and access to potential supply and technology transfer partners. It proved an outstanding success resulting in a major corporate purchasing the company, which we negotiated for him. He is now a multi-millionaire, and the research and development director for that company.

'Sounds like a great white knight story. Did you ever do this again?'

'Funnily enough I remember one summer's afternoon sitting with colleagues discussing what we did as bankers that brought value to the world. We had clients with projects they could show to their grandchildren. We had sources of investment which could tell their grandchildren they were part of the project. Although we provided much expertise in ensuring the project was viable, we played no more part than a marriage broker. Our conclusion that day was we were parasites feeding off our knowledge and capability to bring people together, but nothing tangible to show our grandchildren. We did not make or build anything. The upshot was we decided to engage in at least one project each year resulting in something we could show our grandchildren. The irony is I never succeeded on the grandchildren front.'

'Did you ever consider venture capital as a career move?'

'There's a huge difference between having some fun with a hobby and engaging full time. The contra to our success stories is the inventors who have no concept, and thus the contribution value, of the resources required to take something they invented and built in their garage through the technology transfer process to market. I engaged with one inventor who had solved a significant issue in computer technology, but only on paper. I found a global company who was prepared to commit more than $500 million to bring this concept to reality. It would have been a major leap forward in computer technology. They offered him a fabulous deal with a guaranteed minimum annual royalty of more money than he could reasonably spend. But he could not comprehend the significant risk commitment value and declared the deal far short of his expectations. We sat there dumbstruck. To date, some five years later, his invention has not seen the light of day. No, my preference was to deal with professionals. But we digress from our topic tonight, so let's save such stories for leisure time.'

'Any new venture requires planning. Where is the market, how do we capture it, who are our competitors, how do we produce the product, how do we penetrate the market, etc. From this we can define the resources we need both in human resources and technology. The balance between human resource and technology is complex. With technology you can switch it on when you need it, and off when you don't. It doesn't need sick leave or holidays, requiring only periodic maintenance. We can consider human resources an asset if they perform well. However, they can also be a necessary evil if they come with too much State oversight; they get sick, they need holiday leave, maternity leave, need much maintenance, and they can behave in ways that confound and frustrate.'

the Way

'Achieving this balance is extremely complex, not least because business is not a linear function. Life and business are not predictable and thus, as per your teachings, adaptability and fleet of foot are necessary to be successful. Whereas technology can replace human endeavour in linear processing, it cannot respond well to abstract aberrations that cannot be foreseen but may make the difference between success and failure. Until technology can think like humans, we need people to engage in business functions. Okay so far?'

'Sounds very Sun Tzu planning. But won't artificial intelligence replace human resources?'

'Interesting idea. We installed AI into our trading room. Traders tried to use it to find anomalies in the markets which they could profitably trade. It went okay in stable markets once we refined the associated rule tables. The first time it was let loose on a volatile market, it went berserk. We had trades coming out of our ears. Far too many to process, and settlement was a nightmare. And far too many with insignificant amounts of profitability after we applied transaction costs. We had to seriously limit capability. It was frightening what could happen if many trading shops had this capability. The markets would go into meltdown as these systems started to chase the impact of other such systems without any reference to reality. However, it allowed me to automatically manage trading and credit lines.'

'The best way to illustrate what we found is to consider a traffic jam where all vehicles have live feeds about traffic. If just one of these systems detected that by taking the next left turn you could be navigated away from the traffic, you have value. But what about if every system gave the same instruction? All we do is to move the traffic jam – no value. I think AI has a role, but we will still need humans to make seemingly irrational decisions which avoid anarchy by computers. We are told AI systems will learn from their mistakes. So, after it has crashed you and your car into the wall, and probably killed you, it will learn not to do it again. The coming years will be interesting as

Week 11

processing power increases, but I don't see computers ruling the world in my lifetime. But we digress.'

'Managing today's technology is relatively straightforward. Put it into a suitable environment, give it the care and attention it needs, supply it with appropriate inputs and it will diligently deliver the required outputs. Human resources require a completely different management approach.'

'When I first joined the corporate environment, human resources were compartmentalised into departments each engaged in a specific business process. There were hard boundaries between these departments including walls, doors, and culture which includes language. It could be argued this structure kept information on a need-to-know basis. But this isolation was the enemy within because the cost implications in terms of unnecessary duplication, interface errors, misunderstandings, and processing imperfections could be significant. If you look in the bookcase in my study, you will find a book titled *'The Goal'* by Eliyahu Goldratt. This book addresses how the best-laid process dynamics plan for multi-function production lines can be confounded by human resources, and the cost of not understanding and managing this impact. Interestingly, this book is written as a novel to emphasise sterile textbooks full of algorithms do not work in practice when human interaction is required in the process. Reading this book, and later the Ricardo Semler article I'll give you tomorrow, reinforced and further developed the progressive management techniques resulting in my major successes. This book has sold millions of copies, so struck a real chord. I commend this book to you as it will certainly open your eyes to the real management issues involved in multi-dimensional business processes.'

'If you don't mind the intrusion into your inner sanctum, I'll collect it on my way to bed.'

'No problem. Any questions on the topic this evening?'

Can you explain more about process dynamics?'

the Way

Process dynamics is usually associated with industrial production lines. However, the same ideas can be adapted to any type of operation requiring more than one type of discipline to achieve a desired output.

In any balanced system, whether industrial, manufacturing, or commerce, the resourcing must exactly equal the capacity to meet demand. If this is achieved, our performance will have been optimised as our throughput meets expectation and our inventory is minimised. It does not necessarily mean, however, our operating expense base is optimised; but more on this later. Let us first analyse the characteristics of our balanced system and the ordinary constraints which can radically unbalance our system.

Most systems have a variety of processes, some in series, some in parallel, and others providing peripheral intervention such as information technology. In a balanced system it's assumed each process has the same mean processing capacity, but we will show how yields can fluctuate widely from expectation through inherent constraints. Let us assume we have a simple two process system in which the first process is essential human effort with a mean output level of 25 units per hour and in one day is expected to generate 175 units. The second process is an automated process with a capacity of 25 units per hour. This automated process starts one hour later each day but must be shut down after seven hours each day for essential maintenance. On the face of it, this system should balance with optimum throughput maintained.

In the first hour of the first day some human resources are slow to meet their target, so only 19 units are produced in the first hour. These 19 units are moved to the automated process. In the second hour of the first process more productivity is achieved as the work becomes familiar and 22 units are produced which are then transferred to the second process. As the day progresses the hourly output of the first process are 24, 26, 28, 28, & 28 respectively meeting their target of 175 units; and feeling very pleased with themselves. However, the throughput for the day of the system was only 165 because our automated process can only handle 25 units per hour. In its first hour it was constrained by the first process in that only 19 units were presented, 22 units in the second hour and 24 units in the third hour. Therefore, in each of the first three hours the second process was constrained by the first process and, although the first process can make up the production by over performing, the second process cannot oblige. Therefore, as the automated process is shut down at the end of the first day, there are still 10 units that must be carried over to the next day. It does not take much imagination to comprehend the impact if erratic production from the first process continues over a few days. Unless the automated process can be continued in excess of 7 hours each day, then balanced capacity can never be restored.

This situation can equally apply if the second process is a dominantly human resource process as some tasks take a given time to complete and are not prone to a shorter time frame. If both processes are human resource driven, then friction can develop between the two processes because the first process is either unaware of the inherent constraints on the second process, or just being inconsiderate. To achieve the organisational throughput requirement of 175 units per day, the second process would have to utilise overtime procedures or increase capacity, either of which both increase costs and possibly impact morale.

'As you read *The Goal*, you'll see just how disruptive humans are to process throughput. Managing throughput in a multi-process environment is a skilful art-form, more to do with managing people than knowing algorithms. I developed my own techniques in the bank and which I will describe to you when we discuss managing people.'

'Interesting, especially as we have production lines. It's also reassuring that technology will not be replacing humans anytime soon. So, I guess you will teach me how to manage human resources.'

Chapter 75 – Thursday

They were sitting having dinner discussing her day at the office.

'By the way, how much reading newspapers and trade press do you fit into your week?'

'Probably not as much as I should, but my 6-month program consumes so much of my time. I constantly revisit Sun Tzu and the other material you give to me, and I engage in discussion with Jim when we have any free time. And my architect clients are an excellent source of current information. Why do you ask?'

'As you grow in stature information relevant to your business, and the economy in which you operate will be a key driver in your decision process. You need to stay current with any information that could affect your business plans. And before you say it, I'm aware that with vast amounts of information in circulation, how is it possible to read so much.'

'How did you cope in the bank as there must be much more for you to absorb than in the fabrication business?'

'Each morning I would watch the early morning news being the most current source and then scan the Financial Times on the way to the office. We had an information officer who would scan the financial press in whatever form looking for news or articles of interest, sorting the considered and informative from the speculative chaff, compile this onto a few sheets and distribute it. Each piece selected would include its source for further reading. The best I encountered was pro-active in that you could inform her of any subject matter of interest to you for selection. Instead of a pile of newspapers and periodicals, you had a few sheets to read over coffee. She was also useful in the event something unusual had come to your attention. As she had read much of the available material, you could ask her if she had encountered anything about the unusual event of interest, or you could ask her to find anything out there. Good system. Made for efficient knowledge gathering.'

'Was she capable of sifting relevant information?'

'I think she had a degree in political economics and statistics but wanted ultimately to be a press officer. She was certainly a very good communicator. It was an important job, and she was very capable.'

'Don't think Aldridge could stretch to such a person. But I understand what you mean, so I need to give it some thought. I've finished with dinner. What's our subject tonight?'

'You should read the article I gave you from the Harvard Business Review called "Managing Without Managers" by Ricardo Semler describing a refreshing view on how to facilitate and enable people to perform and contribute to the overall success of their business. Probably the strongest reason for his success in transforming a near bankrupt company into one of the most successful companies in Brazil is he realised he could get performance and contribution from his staff by treating them as adults. His underlying reasoning for this was that, outside of the office and factory environment, people elect governments, serve on local government and other associations with committed enthusiasm, lead community projects, raise and educate families, and make decisions every day about their future. Friends solicit their advice. Salespeople court them. Children and grandchildren look up to them for their wisdom and experience. But when they enter their working environment, the company transforms many of them into adolescents by over-zealous and inept control, rules, and procedure, as well as expecting them to follow instructions without question.'

'He quickly found by facilitating and enabling performance the employees responded by substantially increased contribution to the company. By allowing people to do at work what they naturally did outside of work paid substantial dividends. So why is it that many businesses continually underestimate the limits of human potential?'

the Way

'It's reasonably accepted, in general, groups of people work together more effectively in a crisis situation than in a normal, stable environment. An explanation for this could be the control, order, compliance system breaks down under crisis conditions and people assume a more focussed role appropriate to the task-in-hand rather than the role defined for them in their normal environment. Also, in the crisis scenario, people tend to work together and are prepared to turn their hand to whatever is required to achieve the overall objective.'

'In most crisis situations reflection reveals surprise at the performance, and especially the performance of people who ordinarily would not be credited with the ability to perform at such levels. How many heroes and superstars have emerged as a result of crisis?'

'What is it about crisis that allows such performance and achievement to flourish? Could it be there is no time to consider superfluous hierarchical protocol, or who should do what task, or deliberate levels of commitment, or be deterred by all the other areas of constraint we have discussed.'

'What is it about crisis that highlights qualities in us as human beings hitherto not detected. I heard an apt piece of dialogue in a movie about the benefits of an occasional war. It went something like "war provides a clarity of purpose where everyone understands the objective, and everyone knows their role".'

'If we go back to Sun Tzu, we quickly understand that in a dynamic marketplace in which you wish to compete, adaptability is required to meet new challenges.'

'As we already know, human nature is generally not comfortable with change – most humans like their comfort zones. Therefore, they tend to exercise constraint in its various forms to resist change. However, a valuable new idea today becomes tomorrow's convention wisdom (status quo) so we will explore different types of constraint to determine if they are relevant to our goal, and if so, how can we overcome such constraint in order to optimise delivery of our goal.'

'On the basis of my favourite line from 'My Fair Lady', she interrupted, 'Don't tell me, show me,' with a smile on her face.'

'Good. You were listening. We have progress.'

'Trying to explain something for which there is embedded constraint is generally a losing battle. Therefore, I devised a demonstration so my staff could see for themselves the impact of their constraint. The first part of this demonstration deals with Constraint versus Co-operation.'

'You'll need a volunteer from your audience. Never use outsiders in any of these demonstrations, as the objective is to get your staff involved. You'll need a chair, a bin, and up to three small bean bags, tennis balls, or similar as projectiles.'

'Sit your volunteer on the chair and place the bin 2 – 3m behind the chair so your volunteer cannot see it. Give the volunteer the 3 projectiles and explain that you have placed the bin 2 – 3m behind the chair, and you would like the volunteer to throw the projectiles behind one at a time to see if they can hit the bin. Gather your audience around the demonstration but ask them to keep quiet. Let your volunteer throw the 3 projectiles. In most cases none will hit the bin, but statistically it is possible, and if it happens see if the volunteer can repeat it at which time you refer to random chance.'

'Now ask for a second volunteer (preferably not from the same department as the first volunteer) to help the first volunteer (who must not look at the position of the bin). Without direction, ask the second volunteer to work with the first volunteer by indicating after each throw where the projectile lands in relation to the bin. Note if they discuss if they should switch task. Hopefully, after a few throws the thrower will hit the bin. Note how the volunteers interact to identify if the second volunteer is committed to the success of the task; or is an unconnected third party.'

the Way

'Now you need a third volunteer, again preferably from another department, and different gender if volunteers 1 and 2 are of the same gender. Now you give instruction on how they might approach this task. You tell them they must select, amongst themselves, the best thrower, the most appropriate person to stand in front of the thrower at a distance equivalent to the distance of the bin behind the thrower to direct the throw, and the best person to stand close to the bin to give feedback on the result of the throw. They can have three projectiles each as thrower to determine the best person for each of the tasks. Once they have decided their roles, sit the thrower, change the position of the bin, ask the other 2 volunteers to take their positions, and commence the task. The person standing in front of the thrower cannot pace the distance to the bin – they must judge the distance visually from no closer than the thrower. Placing the bin off-centre adds a new dimension to this task. What you are looking for and want to achieve (with encouragement if necessary) is a total commitment by all three volunteers to the success of the task. If they are not working well together, get the audience involved. If you succeed in getting everyone involved in the outcome you have vaulted a major hurdle in your culture change.'

'After any revelry and applause has subsided, ask the audience if they can identify the difference between the three scenarios. What you seek is an understanding that, in scenario 1, the task was random, demoralising, and unlikely to succeed. In scenario 2 there was neither order nor combined commitment to the task which increased the effort with uncertain outcome. In scenario 3 the volunteers worked together to optimise the resources against the various tasks and encouraged each other to succeed, thus they bought in to the outcome as a team. If the audience got involved, you also created a spirit of togetherness.'

'You also point out that these 3 volunteers came from different departments, but combined their skills, without constraint, to achieve the goal. Therefore, is it reasonable to

Week 11

allow departmental or skill boundaries to constrain the achievement of the overall goal?'

'The point of this exercise is, without feedback on our performance, it is very difficult to modify or correct our actions. However, if we are provided with good information we can translate into revised action, then our performance can improve.'

'This experiment also demonstrates the power of team effort where there is a single objective on which to focus by the whole team. The translation of observation into accurate feedback that is executable, i.e. in a form that can be reasonably actioned by the recipient, then a result can be achieved. I would stress the point that the information not only has to be accurate but also useable. For instance, if the thrower has no co-ordination in the way they lob the ball perhaps it is worth changing the thrower to a more appropriate member of the team, or to coach the existing thrower to lob in a more co-ordinated manner. The more expedient view would be to change the thrower, but this is not necessarily the best overall response if, indeed, a little coaching with the thrower would achieve the objective.'

'This balance between identifying the most appropriate resource in a team, and coaching team members to improve their performance is an important task for any manager. Poor decisions may stagnate performance of a team player and, thereby, reduce the effectiveness and hence overall contribution of the team.'

'The next step is to demonstrate the impact of Constraint versus Communication.'

'This is a continuation of session one, either immediately or a later occasion, and uses the same props. It's a mistake to attempt to combine sessions 1 & 2 as the objectives are very different. The power of these sessions rests in a single objective that will cause your audience to think about what they experienced and discuss their thoughts with their colleagues.'

'You start this session by referring back to the outcome of session one, and then pose the question 'what about if our 3 volunteers all speak different languages?' No matter how committed they are individually to the goal, they need to be able to communicate to achieve it. Although not critical, if you can find 3 volunteers in your audience who can speak different languages then you have an ideal scenario for this demonstration.'

'Let us first examine what this session is attempting to address.'

'In the 1960's the young became liberated, but conventional wisdom identified and compartmentalised skills into named disciplines such as accountant, clerk, etc. The most serious was the redefinition of scientist to physicist, mathematician, biologist, chemist, etc. Where such labels were considered good order, you only need to consider that the person who designed the neuron processor for computers actual conceived his design studying the behaviour of the ordered roles of individual ants in seemingly chaotic ant colonies. There are many examples of the ridiculous nature of this compartmentalising of skills. Did Isaac Newton consider himself a physicist, or what label did Leonardo da Vinci ascribe to himself?'

'Compartmentalisation may have provided some convenient rationalisation of skills into identifiable comfort zones but has little or no relevance to how the World really works. Indeed, these artificial compartmental barriers have created many uncertainties that have fundamentally constrained our ability to progress. The costs of such constraint can be measured – and with serious negative impact.'

'The elements of this compartmentalising we seek to address is the progression of such process to a point where groups within compartments created their own identity by inventing technical language, jargon, acronyms, and abbreviations that allowed them to converse amongst themselves in the knowledge outsiders will not understand them. The dim-witted thought this clever, the ambitious as a weapon of superiority. Even the youngest of these compartments, IT, is guilty of this attempt to

Week 11

identify and isolate their profession. How many acronyms, abbreviations, and jargon can you think of that mean different things to different groups of people?'

'Business managers used these compartmental conventions to structure departments and then try to get these departments to perform in harmony with a real World of no such boundaries. The first time I encountered the serious nature of this problem was in the mid-1970's when computers were first being introduced to automate operational activities such as accounting, securities settlements, stock control, payroll systems, etc. At this time, I was learning how all the various components of a bank functioned. Not only did I need to learn a whole series of different technical jargon for each department, but identical functions could have a completely different language across departments needing to interface with each other. It was like a picture of a battlefield, the army would have their view of it from the ground, and the air force from the air. Their descriptions would be different, although they are referring to the same battle. An onlooker would not be able to relate one description to the other. This lunacy was not only time consuming, it created a great deal of confusion for systems analysts and programmers as they tried to systems test with the relevant departments. It sometimes took a very smart systems analyst to see departments were describing different views of the same data, rather than 2 different databases. As an observer, it became evident these ardent artificial boundaries, which were self-serving, caused severe constraints, and cost the business much unnecessary time, effort, and cost.'

'A few years later, when I was given my first strategic operational management responsibility over what was euphemistically called back-office operations with a mandate to automate as much as possible, I was determined to break this departmental boundary culture as a priority and create a partnership of skills communicating in a common language, and flexible enough to meet the variable demands of business.

the Way

However, easier said than done. The staff had their departmental structures in which they felt comfortable, the managers had their important egos, and me, the new boy on the block, without an established track record.'

'My mandate was to develop automated systems in London that could be implemented throughout the World to integrate management and financial activities so central senior management could readily establish a picture of its global activities and exposures. I quickly, and painfully learnt that my problem was to be magnified across cultural boundaries as I started with the naïve view that if I could crack the problem in London, as the principal hub, then I could repeat it in all the other locations. Not only was this idea not true, I also found that the systems themselves could not be implemented in all other centres without modification to meet cultural difference in working patterns.'

'Having decided a formal approach would be defeated by protectionism, I contrived several short, informal talks portrayed as introducing myself, my team, and what we proposed to do. This section essentially emulates these sessions, albeit refined over the years, and which proved very effective, achieving amazing results.'

'This second session deals with the language barrier in a way the participants realise for themselves such barriers exist, and good communication across the whole operational platform is fundamental to success.'

'This language problem was further compounded by IT professionals. In those early days of computers (pre-PC's) IT people developed their own technical jargon which was totally baffling to anyone else, amplified by the fact that computers at the time were the new demon coming to take jobs away from operational staff. IT people, in general, were paid very well and so were eager to preserve their identity to maintain their status. Thus, it was equally important to get them to understand the limitations of their effectiveness by using such jargon. How

Week 11

many systems can you think of, even today, that have failed, are way over budget, and/or late delivery through a basic misunderstanding of the requirement. The two principal reasons for this are 1) IT people tend to approach systems from the perspective of using the most current technology (rather than what technology best addresses the business problem), and 2) users look to functionality which is second nature to them and thus taken for granted (not disclosed) during the design phase.'

'Communication is the bridge to achieve the goal, but how do we build this bridge in a way all parties are comfortable to cross it?'

'Our base assumption is our 3 volunteers cannot communicate verbally. Although an extreme example, it clearly illustrates the point as several the audience will have experienced this problem at the most basic level when travelling abroad, thus will have experienced the frustration of making themselves understood. This is a serious constraint to successfully completing the task.'

'Instruct your volunteers to engage in the task as described in session 1 without communicating verbally (unless you have volunteers who can speak 3 different languages in which case they can each use a distinct language). In this case we would hope to see the volunteers using words and sign language in an attempt to teach each other the relevant words such as 'throw', 'ball', 'left', 'right', 'too far', 'not enough', etc. They quickly realise the frustration of not being able to communicate, and they must find a way to do this to complete the task.'

'If you don't have volunteers with language skills then they must use sign language, and if they're clever, teach each other some sounds that represents the words they would like to use, i.e. create a language.'

'Your audience should find this process amusing. Ensure you stop the process before the amusement turns to boredom in order to stamp the point home.'

the Way

'I use a real example of my own experience to illustrate that, even if they all speak the same language it does not mean they can communicate – which is the object of this session. My example goes as follows:

I remember early in my career having a manager who prided himself on his vast vocabulary, and his eloquent delivery. He also prided himself on his commitment to learn a new word every day and use it whenever he could. He even suggested I should expand my vocabulary and take elocution lessons. What he was impervious to was for all his eloquence and vocabulary, he spoke, but did not communicate as very few people understood what he was trying to convey because of the unfamiliar words he chose to use. I was taught to write for your intended reader with the foremost objective of communicating what you intend. This applies equally to the spoken word where you have the benefit of immediate feedback so you can adjust accordingly.'

'The same applies if you use skill specific jargon, abbreviations, acronyms, etc. to people outside of your sphere of skills: you speak – but do not communicate. I make a point of stopping people in their tracks if they start to use such language. For example, if someone uses an abbreviation that has various meanings in different contexts, I'll stop them and ask them to define the abbreviation for the sake of clarity.'

'You conclude this session by asking your audience to note each time they have a conversation with another member of staff where jargon, abbreviation, acronyms, etc do not compute. Stop the person using such language and see if you can find, between you, another way to convey the intended meaning of the conversation. The same applies to any written internal correspondence. Tell the recipient to underline the technical language which is causing them difficulty and send it back to the sender for clarification.'

'If you've captured the imagination of your audience, you'll start to see a dramatic improvement in communication throughout the operation.'

'Thus, with a simple demonstration of a basic task you've clearly demonstrated the need for good communication.'

'Wow. I see so much Sun Tzu but applied within your own organisation.'

'Sun Tzu makes it clear that you must be well organised with good communications.'

'There is one more topic I would like to cover this evening. It relates to people taking responsibility. The scenario is you assume control of a group of people who are dysfunctional whether from poor management, low morale, no leadership, or whatever. You are the new kid on the block. They want to see what you can do.'

'Let's consider what a good manager attempting to rectify a bad situation might like to see from immediate subordinates as a process of restoration.'

Stage 1. You have a problem

'The worst situation you will face, short of the subordinate just not even mentioning problems unless prompted, is that you have a problem. In this case the subordinate has completely disenfranchised themselves from the problem or any responsibility for the solution. The attitude would be "I only work here. I'm not paid to solve problems. You're the manager". You need to start a process of enfranchisement.'

Stage 2. We have a problem

'We have a problem demonstrates a more reasonable attitude by the subordinate in that they have clearly enfranchised themselves with the problem, but they still accept no responsibility for the solution. They look to and expect the manager to determine the solution and to provide instruction for the solution. The attitude would be "We have a problem .... what do you want us to do about it?"'

Stage 3. We have a problem and I propose the following

the Way

'At this stage the manager has enabled, but not empowered, the subordinate to identify possible solutions on the basis of "don't just bring me the problem, bring me a proposed solution". This is clearly a major step forward in that the subordinate is accepting some responsibility for the solution to the problem. However, the manager is still required to be the arbiter of day-to-day problems that probable could, in most cases, be solved by the people concerned.'

Stage 4. We have a problem, and we are doing the following

'Our manager has now started to empower the subordinate, and the subordinate is starting to take responsibility for the solution although either the manager does not feel comfortable enough to allow solutions to be effected without their involvement, or the subordinate does not yet feel confident enough to effect the solution without sharing the responsibility with the manager.'

Stage 5. We had a problem

'Both the manager and the subordinate accept their respective responsibilities to the full. The subordinate has been vested with the power to take responsibility for their problems and fully supported in the execution of their own judgement as to the appropriate solution. The manager has developed a rapport with the subordinate that is truly a team attitude whereby the manager will only need to get involved with problems that cannot be solved by the subordinate alone. This means our manager has more time to manage the necessary evolution of the business rather than getting involved in the day-to-day issues which can be better solved by the subordinates responsible for the day-to-day activity.'

'In this process we have moved from the total disinvestment in problems by the subordinate to the complete acceptance of both the problem and the responsibility for the solution. You can achieve this with good leadership and coaching. Show them you can lead, and you will gain respect. Show them what you expect of them, and they will follow.'

'I've written a book called *'Coaching Corporate Performance'* which explains all of this in detail. I'll let you have a copy.'

'Thanks. Really interesting. I think I would enjoy working for you.'

'Any thoughts you wish to air before we close this session?'

'All crystal. Can't wait to read your book. Goodnight.'

Chapter 76 – Friday

'How do you feel about a normal session tonight? I appreciate it has been a hard week, and Friday is your normal chill night, but we lost a couple of days last week. We need to recover at least one, but Sunday would also be okay.'

'I'm okay. If you're prepared to make the time for me, I'm ready to engage. It was my fault we lost those days, so no complaints from me.'

'Yesterday we dealt with how to structure your troops of varying disciplines to understand the goal and their role in the delivery. Tonight, I want to cover human frailty and how you avoid allowing such frailty to impact performance and delivery.'

'The people involved are those prone to insecurity and anxiety. Even though they work within a group, they still can feel alone when it comes to making decisions which challenge them. Think of my use of the psychological states from The Games People Play. If I come to you and ask, *"did you write this?"*, you can adopt one of two of these states. If you are self-assured you might respond in the Adult state "yes, what do you think?". However, if you're insecure, anxiety will come to the fore and your response is likely to be a timid, "Why, what's wrong with it?".'

'I generally found such people were capable; but lacked belief in themselves. Such insecurity fosters a reluctance to seek help

the Way

from their fellow colleagues in fear of appearing inferior. This is where the strength of "family" is at its most powerful. In our private lives we look to family in times of distress. If you can create this same philosophy within your staff, as is most certainly the case in the military, these weaknesses can be dispelled by real support, or through coaching. You won't always win, especially in dynamic environments, because the frailty is so deep no amount of nurturing will suffice. They will need professional help, and probably a different environment.'

'Come to think of it I have a little game you can play anywhere which has helped many people to realise their anxiety is of their own making. If they can release their performance constraints, the anxiety disappears as their confidence builds. How good are you at catching a ball with one hand?'

'Not so good as with two hands. Why?'

'Why do you think this is, and are you better with your right hand than your left hand?'

'I guess it's hand/eye co-ordination, and I'm naturally righthanded.'

'Would you like to try a little experiment to investigate this constraint?'

'Sure. What do you want me to do?'

'Let's go to the passageway to the pool and I'll get a tennis ball.'

Once in the passageway he stood her at one end, and he stood about 5m away.

'Look at the ball, Mel. It has a clear band around it. I want you to concentrate hard on this ring. When I throw it to you, I want you to tell me which way I apply spin as it comes to you – your clockwise or anticlockwise. As soon as you see it shout it out. Ready?'

He lobbed the ball towards her such that it bounced before reaching her. She correctly identified the spin and caught the ball with both hands. He did this a few more times until she confidently determined the spin and caught the ball.

'This time I'm going to toss the ball to your right or left so you try to catch it with the appropriate hand. Ready, but remember you must tell me the spin direction before it bounces?'

He lobbed the ball to her righthand side. She correctly detected the spin and automatically caught it with just her right hand. He repeated this twice more before lobbing to the left hand where again she naturally caught it. Then he lobbed the ball to her left fast enough that it didn't bounce. She correctly determined the rotation at this speed and caught it with her left hand. He stood smiling at her astonishment.

'What do you think happened there?'

'I don't know. I'm stunned I could do that. How did I do it?'

'Constraint exists in your conscious mind. Your sub-conscious has no such constraint. However, constraint in your conscious can prevent your subconscious doing what comes naturally. I fully engaged your conscious mind determining the spin allowing your subconscious mind to catch the ball. We have tonight removed a constraint which should not occur again. You can use this game with anyone showing lack of confidence as I've never known it to fail if executed properly. Think of your increase in confidence now you have removed the constraint impeding your natural ability to catch the ball.'

'So, you're playing with my mind.'

'Not really. I'm merely demonstrating your uncertainty about catching a ball is misplaced as with other constraints we have already addressed or will address in the coming weeks. Come. Back to our studies. We've not yet finished for this evening.'

'The benefit of *family* nurture is the sum of the whole is greater than the sum of its parts. Everyone belongs, and everyone grows. Staff morale is high, even in times of challenging circumstances when the full force and effect of *family* overcomes; and staff turnover becomes incidental.'

'As in the *Art of War* Sun Tzu knew if he kept his troops nourished, well trained, and disciplined they would follow him

the Way

and deliver for him. It is rare to have bad troops; just bad leaders.'

'I have already explained my attitude to my staff; they delivery for me, and I'll deliver for them. But you must lead; and be respected for your leadership. They don't need to like you. I've worked with people who disliked me and/or I disliked them to the point of never considering interacting with them off the field of play. But you don't have to take them home at the end of play. So long as they are respectful of the goal, deliver, and do not create discourse on the field of play, I have no problem with such people as most will deliver beyond expectation just to spite you. I generally found that female leaders have a problem with this attitude.'

She interrupted. 'I think I would have a problem with someone in my team who felt badly towards me.'

'Why? How many friends do you have? And I mean real friends; people who will stand by you through thick and thin.'

'I'm looking at one. But not many. Less than a handful.'

'And that is the truth in life. You may know many people, but they are not your friends when your chips are down. I suggest to you that far more committed troops will follow a good leader through thick and thin than the leader will have friends who would do the same. This is the power of great leadership.

Let's discuss how a good leader interacts with their troops. The leader sets the goal, the rules, and the code of conduct. A good leader will ensure the troops know their leader cares about them but will not socialise with them off the field of play. A good leader will ensure troops are rewarded commensurate with their contribution whether by salary or bonus. This can be tricky as the corporate will have rules regarding compensation, and many times I've found corporations reward the leaders at the expense of the troops. Then they wonder why there is discontent amongst their troops and the media hound them about the unfairness.'

Week 11

'Sun Tzu was very much of the view that you share the spoils of success. Salaries tend to be determined by market forces in the form of supply and demand. Each individual member of staff defines their own field of speciality and thus defines their market value upon which their salary is based. However, when it comes to sharing the spoils far too many corporates use a percentage of salary for distribution purposes. Thus, a member of staff who can command a salary of twice another member will get twice the bonus for the same contribution. I have never seen this as fair, or a way to motivate staff. As soon as I was able to dictate how my staff were rewarded, I created a bonus pool from which every member of staff would receive an equal share regardless of salary. This motivated everyone to grow the bonus pool.'

A few years back I joined a bank to control its International Securities Division. They had a percentage of salary bonus structure, but not by market segment. So, the staff of a market segment that did very well would get the same bonus as a segment that did very poorly. The first year I had to stomach this ridiculous situation. But my people had worked hard to restructure themselves as determined by my resource plan, and we made exceptional profits for which I was offered a considerable bonus. I decided I would sacrifice half my bonus, and have it distributed equally amongst all my staff in addition to the bank's corporate bonus distribution. The following year I managed to get my operation removed from the corporate scheme and created a bonus pool structure which included myself and my line managers. That year my staff were fully rewarded for their exceptional contribution to the bank's profitability. We had people queuing to join our operation.'

'Very generous to sacrifice half of your bonus that way.'

'Not really. Whereas I laid down the business strategy, they delivered on it. Why should I receive all the spoils? In any event the tax rate on my bonus was around 80%. The maximum tax rate of my staff would have been around 40%. I lost very little disposable income, the taxman lost more than half of what I would have paid in tax, but I had a very happy and grateful staff willing to do whatever was required to maximise the bonus pool the following year. I easily recovered my investment in my staff the following year.'

'Sun Tzu was successful because he was a great leader who rewarded success. He did not win those battles alone. If he could not motivate his troops his highly skilled plans would likely have failed. Incentivising people to be successful is half the victory.'

Chapter 77 – Weekend

She was up bright and early on Saturday, ready to go visit with her mum as she had much to report about progress. The train journeys gave her some three hours of reading time to study the books prescribed during the week.

A little retail therapy on the way back made for a satisfied smile on her face when she returned for dinner.

Sunday was a leisurely morning followed by more self-defence and then tennis. Life was good.

Week 12

Chapter 78 – Monday 5th November

Carmen arrived shortly after Mel who was still in the kitchen with Sebastian. Greetings exchanged he commanded their attention.

'Tonight, ladies, quick gym and then wrap yourself warm as we are going out to celebrate burning Guy Fawkes. Then you are both invited to dinner at a nice restaurant. Off you go. I need you back here, ready to leave, at 7 o'clock.'

As they started for their respective rooms Carmen was confused, 'Who is this Guy Fawkes, and why do you want to burn him?'

'He tried to blow-up our Palace of Westminster – our Parliament. We have bonfire night, tonight, to burn him on a bonfire with a firework's display as a gesture of celebrating our democracy.'

'Watching what happens in your Parliament don't you wish, sometimes, he had succeeded?'

They both laughed as they reached their rooms to prepare for their gym session.

Chapter 79 – Tuesday

As usual Carmen had already left for work by the time Mel appeared. 'Nice evening, and lovely surprise. Thank you. Never saw you as a bonfire and fireworks sort of guy.'

'Do you realise Aldridge sponsored the fireworks? I'm very supportive of the community work by Charles and Jim, and I help to sponsor the youth enterprise scheme Edna chairs. Their community spirit harks back to the days when industry was very much part of providing for the local community, the most famous of which in the UK is Cadbury. Today welfare economics has taken a backseat to the demands by faceless investors to maximise shareholder returns at the expense of any interest in community. Big corporate sponsor the likes of sporting events, but this is more publicity than community spirit.'

'Why don't I know about the community work? I'm still blind to the workings of my company.'

'Don't beat yourself up. You're not yet a local, and it's hardly part of the day-to-day activities of Aldridge. As we get towards Christmas, we'll attend events that will open your eyes to just how much Aldridge puts back into this community. Corporates need to find a formula where greedy investors see such community spirit as a corporate value driver.'

'What a lovely company I work for. By the way, Carmen expressed a concern her visits interrupt my evening lessons. She's happy to participate. What I think she's really saying is she wants to participate. She's really into Sun Tzu and wants more. If you want to teach this evening, your class has doubled.'

'We could do with making some progress, but this would limit your chit-chat in the sauna.'

'No problem. I'm sure there will be evenings when we can skip school if needed. I get useful info from her from a woman's perspective, so not exactly bunking school.'

'So long as you tell me when chit-chat is more interesting than school, so I don't sit here talking to myself. Away with you. You have work to do.'

That evening Mel and Carmen quickly finished their exercise ritual and were relaxing in the sauna.

'How do you feel about the breakdown of your marriage plans, my dear?'

'Strictly between you and me, I feel free to follow my dreams. I became so entwined with the conventional expectations of a woman I lost sight of any ambition for myself. As soon as Seb so brutally opened my eyes to my blindness, or my rose-tinted spectacles as he calls it, it was like I'd been set free from my self-imposed chains.'

'My darling Sebastian was brutal to you?'

'Only in the sense there was no Kleenex and sympathy, just brutal reality. My mistake; my problem. Get back to your job and don't do it again. I wanted to hit him with something hard; but he was right and had me back in the frame in two days. I have the freedom to follow my dreams, so get on with it.'

'Do you find this school hard?'

'I guess yes and no. I feel embarrassed at my age when he exposes my naivety in life, but good he can quickly move me on; if this makes sense.'

'Sebastian has fought many battles in his life. He is like that great General of his; no time to be wounded, learn quickly, and get back into the game. But you scare Carmen when you say brutal. Sebastian is hard, but I think not brutal.'

'Sorry. We have an expression in English about brutal reality, but it's not physical.'

'This is good for Carmen to know. But you feel happy with you quest, yes?'

She reached for Carmen's hands. 'I love it, and you're the icing on the cake.'

'And who is the cake, my dear?'

She laughed. 'I must teach you these quaint English expressions. Seb is the cake, and you're the bonus of the icing on top. We should go or we'll be late for school.'

'Tonight, I want to discuss the problems associate with change. For any business to stay successful it must adapt to changes in the market, regulation, technology, politics, and economics. By far the greatest challenge I experienced was people. At the lower organisational levels, people work to make money to live their lives. They expect to go to work, perform a

the Way

regular task, and then go home. They meet any change to their regular task with disdain even though they will regularly adjust their private lives to fashion, change in family circumstances, etc.'

'At the management level you encounter the corporate immune system. Change that challenges ego, status or workload can be a real hurdle. Only a minority percentage of people find the unknown exciting.'

Turning to Carmen, 'Does this make sense to you?'

'With one exception, my darling. There are also people who want to stay current in their role to maintain their market value and will only stay with you if you allow them to grow.'

'I agree, and we must also include naturally creative people, as well as ambitious people; but none of these resist change; they positively embrace it. Sometimes they are so enthusiastic that reining them in without damping their spirit is necessary, but a different management problem.'

'This evening I want to concentrate of people who resist change. Having studied much on the psychology of such people the most common reasons are fear of losing their job, fear of having to learn new skills, fear of having to work harder, that is, fear of the unknown is the root. Another anxiety is how much disruption will change involve and for how long. The longer this period of disruption, the more resistance you'll encounter.'

'Sun Tzu suggests you have one group of resources who take care of the day-today, and another group of resources to engage in the conflict of change. If you're installing a new computer system, the development process can be essentially invisible to the day-to-day operations until ready to implement. If you're building a new production line, there is little impact until ready to test it. However, much change in the commercial sector requires the co-operation of all resources throughout. Engaging outside support should be a very last resort. I've experienced this approach; usually disastrous. The people you expect to operate in the change environment are your preferred choice to make it happen.'

'There is another factor which requires consideration. Sun Tzu identifies, as a corporate, you are at your most vulnerable during turbulent change. As such, resistance to change needs to be managed to minimise the period of change.'

'Any ideas how we can meet this challenge? Do you have any specific mechanisms in Germany?'

'If we want to make significant changes, we need to put this to our Worker's Council who will examine what we want, they will make any representations they consider relevant, and then we negotiate agreement to make the changes. Once the Worker's Council has agreed our plan, they inform the workers. In our culture once the plan is agreed, all must comply.'

'Ah, the authoritarian compliance approach. Okay in principle, but not conducive to co-operative enthusiasm. Let me put the argument to you that the lower-level people are the most informed about delivering outputs. If there is anything wrong with your plan, or they could propose a better solution to aspects of delivery, you want to encourage this feedback. If you apply authoritarian compliance, you won't get this feedback.'

'You have Carmen's attention, my darling.'

'Let's refer to my basic corporate structure. First comes a strategy which states the intended goal, the essential role of the executive. Then we have line managers who convert strategy into tactical delivery. Finally, we have what I will collectively refer to as operations who are the people who effect delivery of the tactical solution. If the structure does not function as it should there is a feedback mechanism from operations back to either the executive or line managers who feed it up. If such feedback is relevant, it may influence tactics and even strategy at which point modification is fed back down the line. This should be a fluid process. The primary value of this approach is operations people feel part of, and connected to, the process – they feel relevant.'

the Way

'Disclosure of market sensitive goals is not appropriate. The executive needs to disguise such information whilst preserving the intended delivery mechanism.'

'Are we good so far?'

'I assume you have discussed your corporate structure with Mel before.'

'Yes. It's part of my approach to corporate management.'

'I will accept this approach for this discussion but would like to understand this more later.'

'Okay. Let's move on. If this structure is part of your corporate culture at least half of your operations will accept change is coming whether with enthusiasm or quiet resignation. But how to capture all. We need to deploy our *family* culture and Sun Tzu's sharing the spoils of victory. The power of a *family* culture is it closes ranks during times of turmoil. We don't need authoritarian dictate. The operations people who accept the need for change will deal with dissent either by persuasion, or by encouraging dissenters to leave the *family* just as with Sun Tzu's no conscription. Their primary tool of persuasion is the spoils of victory which can be anything of definable value from securing employment for years to come through a share of future prosperity.'

'Wow, my darling. You tell me about your *family* culture before, but Carmen did not appreciate the value in times of change. Mein Gott, it's so obvious. Don't impose; just lead. Fantastic. Mel you have wonderful teacher.'

Mel was smiling at the animation behind her words. Resembled someone telling her the world isn't flat. 'But surely, leadership is at the heart of this approach.'

'Absolutely. The only way you can develop a *family* culture is through good leadership. The patriarch executive must command the respect and support of their commanders and operations people. But not by authoritarian fear. Likewise, the leader needs to understand how to combat any unnecessary constraints and pressure on the *family*.'

Week 12

'The most important of these is to respect the family life of staff, and refrain from setting goals beyond reasonably comprehension. My rule is no long hours unless absolutely necessary, and then only occasionally. Tired people do not perform well. And never set objectives more than three months into the future, even if the goal will take longer. People's lives do not cope well with objectives far into the future. And finally, keep them nourished, especially if giving extra effort to deliver. Always be there for them and take care of their welfare.'

'My darling, Carmen senses you really care for your staff.'

'Carmen, they make me successful. Of course, I care for them. It's called reciprocity. They deliver for me; I deliver for them. Victory is assured.'

He let this soak in. 'Any questions?'

Mel piped in, 'How many executives have you met who operate in this way?'

'Too few to mention. But my aim is you know how to lead and manage people.'

'But who, in your opinion, are the corporate leaders of the day?'

'The first person who comes to my mind is Jack Welch, the President of GE; the former General Electric Company. He has built GE into a successful global corporate, showing great vision and leadership. But I don't know how he runs his Board, as he would currently be classified as a sovereign in the context of Sun Tzu.'

'You should also remember the *family* was only officially born some seven years ago. I was asked to document my management style a few years back by one of the global accountancy companies, but I didn't get around to it as I was busy writing my book *Coaching Corporate Performance,* and then I left the City. But why would anyone outside the financial community know of such executives; they're not celebrities. I certainly never sought celebrity. On the contrary, I try to avoid it. I was only doing my job.'

the Way

'Surely exceptional executives are recognised for their achievements.'

'This is true, but not in ways you would necessarily know about.'

'Were you recognised?'

'Yes, both here and in the USA.'

'And?'

'Didn't you tell me Mary had found my bibliography? I've finished for this evening unless there are questions.'

'Thank you, my darling. Most interesting. You give Carmen much to think about. Good night. Come Mel, my dear. Enough for this evening.'

Chapter 80 – Wednesday

Carmen was taking breakfast. 'As you know my darling, I leave tomorrow as it is the birthday of my wonderful Bernd. If I return today around 5 o'clock would you have time to teach Carmen more self-defence?'

'Why don't you join the program and get all the benefits?'

'I would love to my darling, but my company might not understand.'

'I'm happy to do this so long as you accept you may get hurt, but at your own risk. I don't want your company suing me for damage to their executive.'

'It will be on my time at my request so fear not.'

'I assume you want to perfect the groper move.'

'Yes, as you teach Mel.'

'Okay. See you at 5.'

Mel arrived for breakfast. 'Morning Seb. Interesting evening. Can you cope with twice the class size?'

'My preference is to focus on your development, but Carmen may introduce some interesting angles for you to consider. And it's only three evenings each month, and less if you both bunk school.'

When Mel arrived home, she found Carmen and Seb engaged in self-defence. She detected Carmen had probably had enough for today, so suggested they advance to the gym so they can have a good chat in the sauna.

They were finally settled in the sauna.

'This self-defence is hard work. And you are right about the pain. No mercy from my darling, Sebastian. And you do this every week?'

'Sure. Sometimes more than once. But you get used to it. Do you have any pain now?'

'Carmen thinks she will never write again.'

Mel, remembering how he eased the pain in her wrist, took Carmen's wrist and applied the same therapy. 'Does that feel any better?'

'Does he teach you this as well?'

'Yes. When you fall and feel pain, you need to know how to quickly recover, both physically and mentally.'

'Interesting. He causes you pain, shows you how to fix the pain, and then inflicts the pain again. Carmen has become very interested in how he teaches you. Hard school.'

With a wry smile, 'Not really. He teaches me how to manage pain, so I stay on my feet. Not good for my troops to see me down in pain. Would never pass the grade at this boot camp.'

'Boot camp! What is boot camp?'

'Like a military academy where they toughen you up ready for combat.'

'And you go to war?'

'Only in the corporate jungle. He knows I will take knocks out there. He also knows from experience it's no good having the knowledge if you can't manage the conflict. As a woman, I need

the Way

to be more resilient than a man if I want respect. He prepares me for anything physically and mentally.'

'He is right. Men look for you to fall. He teaches you well. Maybe you teach Carmen more of this resilience.'

'No problem. If you're feeling better, I think it's time for dinner. We have school tonight. Mustn't be late.'

'Tonight, I want to discuss managing people. How you present yourself to people really matters, especially as their leader. If you assume that being given a title and placed in an executive office is all you need to do, you're out of your depth. Any change of guard creates disquiet until you have established yourself and accepted as their new leader. You have one shot at successfully assuming command, so you must use it wisely.

'My darling, you speak much of *family* structure, but where does this come from and how did you develop it? Carmen thinks this structure is fundamental to your management ideas.'

Using the name *family* to define the structure was not me, it was one of my staff. But okay, let's take the opportunity to discuss managing people using my notion of *family*, how to create it, and how valuable it is when considering erratic processes that must complete within one working day.'

'When I first started in banking different processes were structured in fixed departments separated by hard boundaries. This cult of specialisation harks back to the division of labour devised during the Industrial Revolution and globalised by Western Culture. Such specialisation had become a term for what I considered intellectual and professional apartheid encouraging tribalism, exploitation and bias discouraging collaboration, connectivity, and rational perspective. Those who specialised in the same field gathered in tribes where their view of the world is jealously guarded and promoted. This is especially true in the field of IT in today's world. Each department has little or no knowledge of the specific function it plays in relation to others or, more importantly, the significance of their role in the overall process. And some processes served more than one business unit. The accounts department was a centralised process all business units used and relied upon for accurate data, but this tribe tended to be fastidious in the jealous guarding of its methods. This tribalism had both hard, departmental boundaries sometimes with fortification in the form of secured access, and specialised language incoherent to non-tribal members. This tribalism was not conducive to a dynamic market where change was becoming a constant, and the winners would be those who could quickly respond.'

'Investment banking has a peculiarity different to all typical industrial or commercial processing systems. Every trading transaction conducted by a bank in any given day must be processed that same day – no exceptions. Thus, why markets close around the middle of the afternoon to give banks time to complete this task. Failure is a serious offence.'

'I assumed my first management role of a securities business unit just as computers were being installed to consume as much of the manual back-office processing as was possible. This computerisation was undertaken by an external computer software company charged with defining the functions that could be automated in each business process, writing the software, and then installing the system into the bank.'

'I watched this process with some unease having been introduced to Sun Tzu's *Art of War* and could immediately relate to this new philosophy. Systems analysts would watch the processes being conducted manually over some weeks and then translate their observations into a systems specification document which was then passed to computer programmers to write the corresponding programs. At no time did any analyst ask if any of the processes could be done differently if by computer, nor did they investigate how the interfaces with other processes, especially accounts, could be enhanced using computer processing. The resulting computer system was not encouraging. International securities are complex products requiring much understanding of special parameters attached to each bond issue.'

'After a few months of trying to find workarounds and enhance programs, mostly requiring long working hours, my staff were exhausted. For my business unit I cancelled the contract with the software consultants but retained one systems analyst who I thought understood the problem, if not the solution. There were package solutions we could buy, but that would make us the same as the other users. We wanted to be the best, and thus a bespoke solution was the obvious way forward.'

'I hired four programmers. For the first four months all five IT professionals worked in my settlements process as settlements staff. This relieved the load on my exhausted staff and gave the computer personnel direct involvement in the process. I also introduced staff coaching for my line managers. They had a compartmentalised view in keeping with the general departmental structure. And, of course, they all wanted the status of an office. I knew this was a psychological issue so struck a simple rule – offices for Officers of the bank; that is people whose signature could commit the bank. Fortunately, only the settlements line manager qualified, but he was astute enough to know he needed to be in the thick of his people, so none had offices. The coaching reconciled them to this new world of automation and the need to work together as a team.'

'Whilst I think about it, there was another feature of this departmental arrangement I found ridiculous. Internal memos, thousands of them stored in filing cabinets in duplicate, triplicate, or worse, most of which would never again to be read, but gathering dust and occupying valuable floor space. I saw memos that copied someone within the same space as the author. It was bad enough that related process units were separated by artificial barriers. I banned all internal memos unless they recorded something we needed to record for regulatory or other legal reason. Even interdepartmental memos were banned. Families do not communicate by memo; they talk to each other. Not only does it provide a two-way conversation but, more importantly, it creates integrated comradeship. This is what family is about; the glue of comradeship.'

'My darling, does this also apply at the executive level?'

'Of course. Executives are on the field of play. They need to work together as a team to maximise the corporate goal. They have Board meetings – not memos. And let's not forget that a memo can disclose strategy best kept on a need-to-know basis. When the Minutes of your Board Meetings are circulated, are they sent in the internal mail for all to see, or are they delivered in a sealed envelope, or by an exec PA?'

'Always by hand. We take much care to keep such documents away from prying eyes.'

'I foresee emails taking the place of internal memos. The idea that someone can email someone sitting not 3m away is appalling. Discourages cohesion; and fractures any concept of *family*. The impact would be to create many artificial departments of people disconnected from each other, and from the collective goal. I would ban the use of email within the corporate structure for people who are close enough to communicate face-to-face, let's say within a 2-minute walk.'

Let's get back to my evolution of the *family*.'

'After four months I sat with my line managers, the new systems people, and a few of the more experienced settlements staff. I wanted to know what they had learnt about our business processes and could they now see the requirements of automation. Their response was encouraging, so requested they specifically observe over the following two weeks how automation could enhance the working environment in a way the existing staff would embrace this new technology. This changed everything. Much communication – note dialogue; not memos - amongst the whole floor about what could be achieved. We had what today is called a vibe on the floor. Everyone worked together. Within four months we had a system that people embraced, errors were significantly reduced, valuable management information flows multiplied; but more importantly we had a happy band of people all pulling together, and no overtime. People could go home at normal leaving time to see their families and friends.'

'Other business units, frustrated with their new technology, were quick to observe and follow. All our direct processes were now integrated. "Them and us" had gone. There was only "us" – my army of happy troops. But I knew further integration was needed, especially the accounts function. The market was becoming more sophisticated. We needed to up our game; but dealing with internal politics and territorial ego would not be so easy.'

'Step forward a few years. I was asked to create a new investment bank in London for a major US bank. We would occupy floors in their existing building in the City, absorbing their existing securities trading and money markets functions, expand both, and integrate a UK stockbroker and UK Jobber – traders in UK Government securities – both of which operated in the dark ages of technology and procedures. On paper this was not a happy assignment; in reality, it was a real challenge.'

'Integrating traders is easy. They feed off each other. They readily create alliances which expand their profit-making horizons. But technology had moved forward in leaps and bounds. The technology available to traders put enormous pressures on the fabric of the building – much refurbishment to do whilst the existing trading continued. The anticipated daily volume of business would be enormous, I had to integrate the old cash-based accounting of the two UK firms into the accrual-based system of the American bank, and make the entire bank operate as a homogeneous entity within 2 years. This would cost £millions; £6 million just for technology.'

'Space was at a premium, especially during refurb. all internal walls, where possible, were removed, as was any partitioning to create large open spaces for both trading room and operations area. I had control of everything and saw my opportunity to

Week 12

remove all departmental barriers. I put all the operations processing units in one space, encouraging everyone to work together interactively. I recruited line managers and staff who had worked with me before, so knew how I worked. They quickly encouraged integration, including the whole accounting function.'

'The Chairman and CEO of the bank visited with me some 8 months into the project to see how we were progressing. We went onto the operations floor. He looked around, vocalising 'how do you know who does what around here?' One guy stood and started singing the Sisters Sledge hit *'We are family, all my brothers, sisters, and me.'* People joined in until the whole floor of some 180 people was singing. I'll never forget that day. My integrated *family* was born. Wherever I went thereafter, my operations were always referred to as my *family*, and many would follow me from bank to bank. Once *family*, always *family*.'

'Thereafter I had the full support of the bank Chairman throughout some tough challenges and fights, including toppling the powerful Head of Europe for the bank who had no interest in the project until it was clear it would be very successful, and he wanted to take over by right of seniority. The bank came into being on time, on budget, and lauded a major success story – widely reported. But as always in my career, my *family* made it work. I only provided strategy and leadership.'

'After completing this task, and taking a much-needed time-out, I was asked to join another bank to rebuild their securities division. I only had to whisper on the street I needed help. Members I needed from previous *family* came. No discussion about salary and benefits. They knew I would take care of them. Some even used their annual leave allowance to terminate their existing employment early and join me as quickly as possible. Very humbling.'

He stopped to reflect.

'My darling. What a story. You must tell Carmen how to encourage people to work this way. How much time is wasted in business with internal politics and misunderstandings across departments. You eliminate all of this with your *family*. Amazing.'

'Many thought this management idea fanciful. But then, during the night of 15th October 1987, we had the most awful storm in London. Trees were scattered across streets blocking roads, and public transport systems were severely curtailed, bringing London to a standstill. I was staying in London, but it still took nearly an hour to reach the office. We had a major securities issue to launch that day. If we withdrew this launch, we would have to wait at least 90 days before we could re-launch. The company involved needed these funds. When I arrived in the office, we had less than 25% of our staff. I would need to alert the Bank of England of our decision. The available dealers and traders agreed to unite to distribute the issue to the underwriters, and to cover any market-making requirement, a price stabilisation mechanism fundamental to any successful launch. This unity of purpose amongst the traders was good, but we still had to consider the important requirement of processing all transactions generated before 6pm that day.'

'I gathered all my available operations staff, ranging from settlement, accounts, funding, dealer support, IT systems and compliance; less than 30 people out of a head-count of 143 operations staff. My head of settlements had arrived. The collective view of the operations staff was together they would process the transactions. They all knew how to perform these tasks because they had *family* connectivity. We launched the issue to great acclaim. The corporate client sent cases of champagne to the office, and which were distributed to my staff. No-one questioned the power of the *family* thereafter.'

He paused to reflect. Carmen put her hand on his hand.

'My darling Sebastian. In just a few minutes you bring your mighty General to life. I now see why this philosophy is important and Carmen will surely study more of this great man, and of the inspiring man I have the pleasure to call my friend.

Week 12

Carmen has much to learn from you. For future trips, you do not need to suspend your wonderful lessons. Carmen is your willing student.'

'Carmen, I added one more feature to the *family* structure which may resonate with you but it's not the same as your Worker's Council. Let me explain. If you remember, my view is that operations people are best placed to determine the optimal way to process workflows. I asked one person from every process, including traders and dealers, to meet each month to discuss any issues needing address to improve our ability to perform. Our business was organic; processes continually evolving to meet the ever-changing needs of the markets. The goal was a continuous improvement of everything from structure of processes, IT enhancement, including the working environment. This meeting would produce minutes of what they discussed and an action plan to implement any required changes. The bank was afraid I was introducing trade union structures. But, no. This group of people ensured we optimised our trading and processing capability, thus maximising their bonus pools. The minutes of these meetings were an incredible source of feedback for me. The results spoke for themselves; operations performed at their best; and shared the spoils of their success. Other than strategic direction, I was out of a job. But it meant I could travel without fear of problems.'

'We will discuss this more, my darling. Carmen sees the important difference. This would be a better way for our Worker's Council to operate. I like.'

Mel thought this discussion was not complete. 'But what about International operations? You controlled offices across the world. Does your *family* work internationally?'

'Ah yes, my wonderful mentor, Bernie, taught me how to manage troops in distant lands early in my exec career. As a leader, just as you do not address your local troop by memo, you do not address your distant troops by telephone; you visit with them. They must know who you are.'

the Way

Carmen whispered to Mel, 'Who is this Bernie?'

Mel whispered back, 'I'll tell you in the sauna.'

'My troops, or staff if you prefer, were integrated throughout the world. We ran a competition every month where the two best performers in each office in any month participated in an exchange program between offices for two weeks. In this way all staff had the opportunity to meet with, and get to know, their counterparts in other locations. Making it a competition improved performance overall as people competed for these opportunities, and the *family* philosophy became international.'

'Sounds a bit expensive.'

'International financial markets are fickle. They can suddenly rage anywhere in the world requiring additional support. Or maybe it's as simple as people on leave during market volatility. That I had troops I could parachute in, usually within 24 hours, and who could arrive and immediately function meant such risk was eradicated. Trying to train your troops whilst the battle rages is not the way to win battles. The cost of failure in the financial markets can be huge. Impact analysis and risk analysis are fundamental to success.'

'Think about it. Two weeks, all expenses paid trip to New York, San Francisco, Tokyo, Hongkong, or Singapore. Most could not afford such trips from their own funds. My operations staff saw this as a performance reward. I saw it as valuable backup.'

'Darling, can you tell Carmen how she might use this wonderful idea.'

'Okay. If my memory is correct, you have two production lines here, and you're building a third line.'

'This is correct.'

'Do you ever have times when one line is busier than the other?'

'Of course. We respond to market demand. We do not build stock.'

Week 12

'Do you have times when you cannot meet demand on either line?'

'Yes, this happens.'

'Is it machinery that cannot meet demand, or people?'

'All machinery has built-in redundancy. It is people that limit production. We need to use overtime when demand is high.'

'Can the people from one line transfer to the other and function without training?'

'No. Each line has its own workers, but I now know Carmen needs to change this. Before I leave tomorrow, this will change. We make exchange program.'

'When you change methods of production, how do you notify the workers?'

'You embarrass Carmen. We send a change directive. But how should Carmen manage such change?'

'Do you test such changes on your lines in Germany before issuing directives here?'

'Of course. We must see that it works.'

Looking at Mel, 'Okay, Elisa, what is our fundamental philosophy?'

Carmen looked at Mel confused.

Looking at Carmen in her confused state. 'It's okay, he rams this down my throat to make me remember it. It's a line from the movie *My Fair Lady* where Elisa is screaming at her pathetic suitor, Freddie. Don't tell me, show me.'

'Correction, my pretty student. Remember is not enough. You must feel it, eat it, and sleep it. It must be at the very heart of your corporate philosophy.'

'Mein Gott. Then Carmen must do this. Must translate to German.'

'Sag es mir nicht, Zeig es mir.'

'Ah, Carmen forgets her darling Sebastian knows German. But Carmen thinks *Red nicht, Zeigs mir* more potent. But Carmen will feel, eat, and sleep this from now on.'

the Way

'Do you now understand what you need to do regarding change?'

'I don't think you mean Carmen should explain changes as Carmen cannot demonstrate.'

'You reward two good workers; never just one, by sending them to Germany for two weeks to work the line with the new changes already in place. You find two capable people on your German line who want to improve their English to work with these visitors through the changes. Then all four workers will return to Matlock to implement these changes. Don't tell your workers, show them. Can you imagine giving a new soldier a rifle and a manual how to use it? Such an important resource needs to be shown how to perform.'

'Fantastic. It will be as my master teacher suggests.'

'My dear Carmen, you need to structure your resource base to facilitate the dynamics of your markets. Keep it trained and flexible and you can cope with whatever the market throws at you.'

'This is now clear to Carmen. Before my next visit, I will have a plan.'

'When you have these changes working, you have taken your first two steps towards *family*. Then you need to look at the processes you manage to determine where you can apply the *family* philosophy.'

'Carmen is embarrassed. This is so obvious.'

'Think of the *Art of War* as a great music symphony. A conductor (our General) is invited to assemble a full orchestra to play this piece. The conductor organises the orchestra into instrumental groups and rehearses them in the work until they are note-perfect. These musicians are then brought together to rehearse as an orchestra. They play this great work, technically note perfect, to an audience who politely applaud the recital but do not leave the auditorium lifted by the music.'

'Now let's find a conductor passionate about the work who hand-picks the finest musicians available, moulds them in enthusiasm for the piece, not only makes each instrument note-perfect, but harmonises different instruments to change the dynamic and energy to create audible drama. This is now a homogeneous collective, all enthused and ready to work together to deliver something very special. This time the piece moves the audience, find themselves lifted to rapturous applause, leaving the auditorium knowing they have witnessed greatness. Same notes, but completely different interpretation and delivery. The difference is collective enthusiasm, to extract the most from the structure of the music, and the passion to deliver the very best performance possible. They transcend individuality in favour of a common cause – a *family* at its best.'

'In the first example each instrument group of the orchestra could play their parts note-perfect. But there was no synergy between instrument groups. They each performed their parts in splendid isolation, not understanding they needed to work in harmony to achieve greatness. Think department for each instrument group, and the conductor as the responsible executive.'

'You also often see this lack of performance in soccer. Two elite teams confront each other. On paper, there is nothing between them in talent and skills. Yet one team beats the other convincingly. Often you will hear the match commentator state the losing team lacked collective commitment and passion.'

'Sometimes it's one player in the team not focussed on the game causing breakdown of agreed strategy. If the team manager (the General) is slow to realise this player should quickly be substituted for a team player ready to seize the opportunity, by the time the substitution finally takes place the demoralising impact on the performing players could mean the game is already lost.'

'Thus, why you do not carry anyone within a *family* structure. If they don't perform, quickly replace them.'

'Carmen has much to learn, but she is tired so must sleep. Thank you both for a fantastic evening.'

the Way

Carmen departed to her room.

'I felt you relive your story. You obviously have fond memories.'

'When you think about it, my staff were the closest I had to family during those years. More like grandchildren, really. I had the benefit of handing them back to their own families at the end of each day. But it was a marvellous feeling once it worked. I'm so grateful to those people for making my career a success.'

'I would like to speak to some of your *family*. I'm sure it's they who would express gratitude.'

'Then we have reciprocity – perfect harmony. Now off to bed with you. Leave me with my thoughts.'

She went to her room with a smile on her face. She had hit a nerve with him, but this nerve related to fond memories.

Chapter 81 – Thursday

They were having breakfast. Mel had been pondering the revelations from last evening.

'Seb, how do you reconcile your caring for your staff, and your hard-nosed attitude to resource selection? Surely if you cared for your staff, you would be loathed to have to dispense with them when needs changed.'

'You need more understanding of Sun Tzu. I choose the optimal team of resources to meet the demands of the business. This is a simple process of defining the skill requirements and attaching a resource to it. Then I fill my resource list and mould them into my army. Once this is done, I ensure their wellbeing so they can perform at their best.'

'Should the resource mix change to meet fresh challenges I go through the same process but this time matching existing resources to the new requirement, after which I determine if any of the remaining surplus resources can be quickly trained to the new requirement. Any remaining resources still surplus to requirement are let go. My job is to meet the challenges of the market, not provide a social services function. There is nothing hard-nosed about it. It was my job. I was accountable to my CEO, and ultimately to my sponsors, my sovereign, to deliver for them. Does this answer your question?'

'I get it. The hard-nosed bit is ensuring you have the best possible army, and then you nurture them to perform for you.'

'Remember back to our early weeks; except in times of short-term personal distress, we carry no-one. Just a lean, mean fighting machine ready for conquest.'

'Isn't there employment legislation that can be deployed to stop you disposing of staff?'

'If you're referring to the likes of unfair dismissal, there's nothing unfair about it. If I need a plumber, but you're an electrician either unwilling to retrain, or have no desire to be a plumber, I cannot use you, and you cannot deliver for me. Do I detect you feel this process Draconian because nothing could be further from the truth? There is always a severance package attached, which reflects their past contribution. And please remember that hiring and training new people is expensive, so retaining existing resources, if possible, is always your preferred solution. Does this answer your question?'

'I guess it's the process I find hard.'

'Please remember how I dealt with the people in the outsourcing centre. Had I divested responsibility for the deed to human resources personnel, I could readily understand some ill-feeling on the part of those losing their job. I was praised, as the General, by the very people losing their jobs for speaking with them myself. They knew what I did was inevitable. Why didn't the previous management? Treat people with respect and dignity and you will not experience ill-will or bad press. Now on your way or you'll be late.'

'Bye. See you this evening.'

the Way

'Carmen has already left to be back in Germany for her husband's birthday. We are back to normal. As I know nothing of their computer technology base, or how much Carmen knows about technology, this evening I would like to take this opportunity to talk about managing IT projects. Do you know much about the IT systems at Aldridge?'

'Other than the CAD system and the office applications, nothing.'

'IT can be the second largest operating cost after people. Still, many execs do not understand IT and the role it plays in their organisation, and IT professionals can exploit this attitude to enhance their own careers at the expense of the corporate.'

'I think we should examine what type of IT activities I want to address. There are platform systems such as operating systems, word processors, spreadsheets, CAD, and graphic design. These provide the user with increased productivity, and creativity, which is where the value lies. It does not matter that these are software packages because the value resides in how you use them. Then we have computer-aided machines which, again, rely on the user to create the task the machine will be instructed to perform. All such IT systems require minimal support with the primary decision being whether or not to purchase the continual upgrades produced by the provider.'

'The IT systems I want to discuss are the processing systems specific to your requirements and can determine if you're a market leader, or second best. As I explained to you earlier this week, my first experience of such systems was a learning process of how not to do it.'

'The most important consideration is to ensure that if you want the very best, do it yourself. Valuable intellectual property should be closely guarded. If you had an army, would you use hired help to train your troops in tactics, only for the hired help to then go train your enemy's army?'

Week 12

'Up until I started to create a new investment bank in London computer systems were considered an operating cost replacing operations headcount. What I had learnt was much valuable information for traders resided on these computers, if only it could be delivered to them in a timely and useful manner. I started on a quest to convert computers from being an operating cost to a valuable profit contributor.'

'Why don't we start with my satirical view of IT professionals. Many of the IT professionals I've dealt with whom, by definition, are probably some of the best as they tend to migrate to companies who can afford high salaries, fit my profile. Computer systems are their temple, and they are the high priests who protect their temple from mere mortals who should use, but not challenge, or God forbid, offend their temple through ignorant abuse of allowed keystrokes on keyboards. They speak using convoluted mnemonics, the meaning of which are highly guarded secrets only available to the high priests.'

'The content of their temple is a continuously developing being in both speed and complexity. It's part of their creed to always have the best temple possible, regardless of need. They pander to the ever-present proponents of the latest temple developments, salivating at the thought of ownership regardless of the cost. They are consumed with their mighty temple to the exclusion of all others.'

'The reality is this temple is nothing more than a sophisticated adding machine allowing high priests to express themselves. If they become overpowering all you need to do is unplug them, and this is a good juxtaposition to take when considering computer technology. There is no doubt technology will play an ever-increasing role in business but you, as General, need to understand enough to know what the possibilities are, is it cost effective or is it overkill, what are the risks and how can these risks be managed as part of your planning. If they ever annoy or confound, you unplug them until you're at peace. Without power, these temples are useless. A human resource is far more resilient.'

'Let me try to illustrate my point. A General is involved in jungle warfare where he needs to be fleet of foot. His weapons manager has discovered a new type of super weapon called a tank. He's desperately keen to try one, so approaches the General to tell him about this super weapon with amazing firepower. The General asks for a description and data. The weapon manager tries his best to convince the General this tank is a must have weapon. The General uses his experience of weapons to examine the data in detail and determines that a tank is not suited to jungle warfare as it's very large and cumbersome to manoeuvre. His conclusion is a tank is a great weapon in the right situation, but an expensive resource not suited to the current requirement.'

'You are likely to come across this with technology because your IT people always want to stay current, especially as this will enhance their market value. Computer manufacturers churn product far more quickly than the useful life of the previous model. Therefore, you need to understand computing power, how much you need, and can justify as a resource expense.'

'Another ploy of IT professionals regarding latest technology is it will replace your out-dated current resource. Another military example, not least because they are good for illustration purposes, and where getting it wrong can cost lives. I was at the Proof House in London at some function where they were testing the latest sniper rifle. I chatted with a former sniper who had reservations about this new rifle. He told me that during WWII and subsequently, sniper rifles produced in the UK and the USA had what is called iron sights even though they were fitted with modern telescopic sights. Iron sights entails a forend sight affixed to the end of the barrel, and some form of Vernier sight attached at the breach. When the old Lee Enfield No.4 Mk1(T) .303" sniper rifle was replaced with the new 7.62mm calibre sniper rifle, it still had iron sights even though the primary aiming device was a telescopic sight. The rifle being tested had no iron sights, and no means to fix them. His observation from real experience was this new rifle would be limited to fixed position sniper positions where the sniper can easily get to a fixed position where he will stay until mission accomplished or comes under fire. If a sniper needs to manoeuvre such a rifle through bombed-out building in urban warfare to find a suitable position to capture his target, or in jungle warfare manoeuvre through dense undergrowth, there is always the possibility in cramped conditions he can damage the seals on the scope rendering it useless. This would mean abandoning the mission and put the sniper in jeopardy because he has no aiming capability. The former sniper told me when he received a new rifle, the first task was to zero the iron sights before attaching a scope which, again, he would zero. If the scope failed for any reason, he had a backup capability to complete his mission. Although he acknowledged current military scopes are built to withstand combat conditions, and necessary for longer range shots, he would still feel more comfortable with a backup sight. As it was his life on the line, I respected his view more than the assurances of the rifle designer.'

'When computer systems were first introduced into the trading environment, all trading tickets were written by hand. The IT people suggested we could replace trading tickets with traders entering trades directly into the computer. I didn't like this loss of control, especially as traders are generally worse at typing than they are at writing so retained written trading tickets which were then quickly keyed into the computer system for processing by a trading assistant thus retaining a hard-copy record of each trade. One day we had a total power failure rendering all systems useless, but we were still trading and needed to log every trade with the Clearing System that day. Our paper trading tickets meant we could immediately revert to our manual processing systems. Today such buildings have standby generators in the basement and UPS power supplies to ensure an orderly switch to backup power, but I've known generators stall. So, like any great General, (and our former sniper) always have options if all else fails.'

She reflected on his 'family' discussion, 'this is the same as you moving people around your various operations to ensure you could parachute people in at very short notice. Risk and impact analysis. I get it. Always have a failsafe position.'

'Well done. Let's move on.'

'Although you should not consider computer systems in terms of physical size as they will most surely get smaller and smaller over time, we should consider any fixed installation a lumbering giant – a factor you must consider when assigning valuable processing to such technology. If you have a fire in your office, you can evacuate your human resources, but you cannot save your lumbering giant. The more you depend on your lumbering giant, the more you need to consider disaster recovery.'

'This applies equally to external services such as direct end-to-end communications. When we installed direct telephone lines to other banks for trading purposes, we always used at least two telephone exchanges through completely different routing. If one telephone exchange failed, or a terrorist puts explosives under a routing manhole cover, we could continue trading. As communications will become more significant over time, this needs to be considered. There is much discussion on the use of mobile technology communications as a primary medium in the future. But remember that in the event of a terrorist act, or a national crisis, the emergency services will commandeer all such media. The landline will always be the last to fail, so must be a fallback position regardless of advances in alternate technology.'

'Your IT professional will probably be younger in age and experience. Youth tends to believe in invincibility. You must bring a cooler reality to their arguments. The only measure of invincibility is the ability to survive when the lights go out.'

'And you must always remember should the lights go out, all of your resources including your IT professionals will look to you for leadership. Therefore, just as you must understand your human resources in your planning, you must equally understand any, and all technology resources. As you have studied in the Art of War, it is the quality of your planning that will determine success or failure.'

'This is my holistic view of the use of technology as a significant resource. Now I want to turn to management of IT projects as they can be a nightmare in terms of risk.'

'Currently technology is expensive, but if you can afford it you allow computer companies to have sizeable research budgets whilst maintaining expected profitability. In the future, I do not see processing power as an issue. Rather, I see corporations being cajoled by IT professionals to automate ever more of their valuable data – their intellectual capital. The problem I foresee is so much valuable data is stored on computers, a competitor will adopt spies in the form of computer hackers to steal your valuable data and use it against you. Corporations who ignore this risk will be a target for their competitors. When you think of systems always have in your mind the dangers of storing your crown jewels on them. When an IT person tells you that you have the most sophisticated encryption available remember that a person designed it, and thus another person can design a way to beat it.'

'When evaluating an automation opportunity, try to imagine how valuable the data stored would be to a competitor. You must consider how easy it would be for a spy within your organisation to collate and copy valuable data and, if connected to the internet or any other external communications system, how easy would it be for a hacker to penetrate your shield, and always expect this to be possible, and collate valuable data about your positions and future strategy. There is no doubt in my mind

the Way

that systems will be the principal source of valuable data to your competitors. Be on your guard.'

Chapter 82 – Friday

'I appreciate it's Friday evening and you've had a full week, but I would like to briefly complete my intended theme on Wednesday before being distracted. It shouldn't take long as it only deals with the initial requirement to be accepted as a leader.'

'How you present yourself to people, especially as their leader, really matters. Any change of guard, or build of a new army, creates disquiet and uncertainty until you have established yourself and been accepted as their leader. You generally have one shot at successfully assuming command, so you must use it wisely.'

'For the purposes of this discussion I'm assuming you're the General, not the Sovereign, in that you're assuming an executive role within an organisation rather than the CEO role. I'll deal with ultimate leadership another day.'

'We'll discuss ongoing leadership next week, but how do you assume leadership and secure the agreement of staff to follow you?'

'Much about managing others is determined by how you manage yourself. If you lack discipline, your army will lack discipline. If you are constantly agitated, expect them to mimic you. If you can't make decisions, expect derision. If you hide away in your office all day, don't expect them to think you're busy; more cowardly. If you want to engage with them socially as part of the pack, you have no place as their leader. Occasional presence at some special occasion shows you care, but don't stay for long. You can party with your peers, but not your army.'

Week 12

'Let's look at some of the more typical situations where you assume a leadership role.'

'Promotion is one means of achieving leadership. This is probably the most difficult to quickly change the guard because you are typically moving from a tactical role within the army to a strategic role of leadership of the entire army. It's very important you both quickly fill the tactical role you left behind and stamp your authority over the entire army by demonstration. We'll discuss changing the guard later, but it's really important your first delivery to your army is robust as there will be a mindset, at least in the part of the army, you previously acted as a commander; you're one of them.'

'The next situation is where you're assuming the role of leader of an established army during peaceful times. This could be filling the role of a previous incumbent of a stable operation, or you have replaced someone to effect some change in direction or build upon what already exists. This situation is more relaxed, giving you time to assess the current modus operandi before formally changing the guard.'

'Another situation is where you are building an army from scratch. If you remember back to Sun Tzu, the leader needs to generate enthusiasm to support the cause. And how many of the army, if any, will know other recruits? Much turbulence unless you can stabilise the situation very quickly with good leadership skills.'

'The final situation I will add to this list is when you are in rescue mode having been parachuted in with the intent of hitting the beach running. This is typically a failing situation where expectations are focussed on rescue, recovery, and then stabilisation. At best you will have weeks; at worse, just hours to exert your leadership.'

'One of the earlier banks I worked for had a very specific team who could parachute into emergency situations within hours. They were known as Internal Audit and did perform this function when not needed for rescue situations. They were generally continually scattered throughout the world, such that at least one member could be in situ within hours, with a whole team in place within a day. They had power over everyone, including the local executive. They could either assume control of the specific location, or even close it down. Very skilful bunch.'

'Have you ever had to rescue situations during your career?'

'From memory, three times. One of these had to be resolved in just three hours lest the bank would fail overnight.'

'Wow. Does this happen?'

'Yes, it does. But unless such incidents result in failure of a financial institution, the media, and thus the public, never hear of it. Both Governments and banks ensure we see the banking system as stable and trustworthy. The collapse of the German Herstatt Bank in 1974 was the first major failure during my career. Its failure triggered an overnight settlement default which sent ripples throughout the banking sector causing much change in the way International payment systems work. None of the situations I was involved with have ever been reported.'

'But back to the point of this evening. What is the first, and important step to assuming leadership with the full support of your troops?

She tried to think what he was expecting of her. 'I guess the CEO will notify every one of your appointment.'

'This gives you the corporate mandate to act as leader. But this doesn't give you the support of your troops to follow your lead. Want to try again?'

'I don't know. At Aldridge all you get is a memo.'

'Not impressive. Leaders need to be seen and heard. They need to know how to stir belief and commitment to the goal. They need to connect.'

'The only way to have any prospect of being accepted as a leader is to speak with your troops. Address them; let them know who you are, what you stand for, and where you want to go with their help. I fully accept not everyone has good oratory powers, so no Churchillian speech. But you don't need a prepared speech as this would appear contrived and counterproductive. And it should not be stern and formal. You need to be warm and friendly and speak from your heart. Let them know you're strong, but compassionate; have a vision to which they can subscribe; and your intent is all will prosper. Achieve this and you have a loyal and enthusiastic army ready to follow. Any questions?'

'All very Sun Tzu. Don't know if I'm ready for speeches to my army, but as I don't yet have an army, I guess I have time to learn.'

'The first time is always the most difficult. But if you believe in yourself, you'll feel the warmth, and they will believe in you. That's it for tonight.'

'A glass of wine and a long soak will help me to digest your wisdom. Good night.'

Chapter 83 – Saturday

She was up and breakfasted by 9am, ready to go visit with her mum. He noted the books she was taking with her to occupy her on the train.

'See you around 6:30 as I have needed retail therapy on the way back.'

She arrived home with a large smile on her face, went to fulfil her gym routine and presented herself for dinner at 7:30.

'How was your visit with your mum?'

'She was in good spirits. Sent you her regards. Remarkably peaceful, really. She interrogated me about progress, but a good visit.'

'What about your retail therapy?'

the Way

'Mostly essential items' and following up on ideas from Carmen regarding dress code during menstruation. Don't have time to get out at lunchtime. It's much colder up here than in London. Need more layers.'

Chapter 84 – Remembrance Sunday

They were sitting at breakfast. She'd slept in her own bed to get the extra sleep she would not get with him.

'What's the plan today?'

'Today is Armistices Day – the surrender by Germany in the Great War of 1914-18 on the eleventh hour of the eleventh day of the eleventh month. Charles and Jim, both old soldiers from World War II, and their veteran friends take seriously this solemn celebration to remember the fallen. The community around Matlock turns out in numbers as the veteran's parade through the town from the Church to the War Memorial.'

Sebastian did not need any notion of civil duty to participate. Mel saw it as respect for the role of Aldridge in the local community.

Before they left for the church Mel was curious to know Sebastian's position on this annual day of remembrance. 'Can I ask you why you attend the Remembrance celebration here as I have not detected any connection with religion from you nor are you native to Matlock?'

'I belong to Orders of Chivalry out of respect for the freedoms we enjoy today. Many people laid down their lives to provide us these freedoms. I never take for granted the lifestyle I enjoy. I remember the years directly after the second World War where rationing persisted until 1953. More importantly, I remember families who mourned their lost, and widows grieving the loss of their husbands, not able to find another partner because of the devastating loss of soldiers leaving a substantial imbalance between available males and females. One such person, Mrs Taylor, was our next-door neighbour during this time. Although she was very good with us children, her sadness and loneliness at the loss of her husband, after just a few short weeks of marriage, were all to conspicuous. We owe respect to those people who gave and sacrificed so much. Today I salute these people with gratitude for the opportunities they have afforded me in my life.'

'Wow', she thought, *'this is a side of him I've not seen before. Could I be your respectful companion today? I haven't attended such a Remembrance Day since a child with my father. Your explanation has blown away my attendance as a duty to Aldridge. My dad was a soldier in the second World War. It's time to take a leaf out of your book. I need to pay my respects to my dad and his comrades for what I have. Thank you.'*

'Never taking for granted what you have keeps you grounded. Far too many think they are entitled to their freedoms without any regard as to why they exist. Today we will embrace our freedoms and remember the price paid. So come, my companion, and let us go remember. Afterwards we're invited to join Charles, Edna, Jim and Margaret for lunch.'

the Way

Week 13

Chapter 86 – Monday

'This week we'll look at how your behaviour influences your ability to lead. How you present yourself influences how you are regarded. How you manage yourself influences the attitude and discipline of your people. Your attitude to your staff determines the level of respect you can expect.'

'When you are on the field of play in your office environment, you can either stomp around growling at everyone, or you can adopt a friendly, calm air of authority which puts people at ease. If you're stalking around with a sour face, you will create unease, making people wonder what the problem is. You see much of this, especially from so-called leaders who are out of their depth.'

'If your people see weakness or uncertainty in you, they will be filled with unease. And how you respond to genuine problems defines how you're considered by them. If you don't communicate with them, or appear aloof, you will not have content staff. Spend all of your time hidden away in your office, which is off-limits to all but your line managers, will make you appear imperial and distant.'

'And when will you discover how your staff relate to you – when you most need their co-operation?'

He let this sink in. 'So how do we keep our distinction and authority as a leader whilst appearing as someone who cares and is aware? It's all to do with your behaviour.'

'Let us look at defining characteristics of exceptional leaders, including military leaders.'

'Why do you include military leaders in describing corporate organisations?'

the Way

'If you remember back to our discussions about Sun Tzu, before corporations existed, armies were the providers for the Sovereign. They secured the provision required by the State. Leadership of these armies was the most obvious determinant of success or failure. Note any similarities?'

A resigned smile.

'More importantly, leadership of armies is more important than leadership of corporations. A General is asking their troops to be prepared to lay down their life for the cause. Troops must be committed to both their General and the cause if they want to be successful. Laying down one's life is not a requirement within corporate life. And, should you not like your corporate General, you can readily go work for another corporate without being labelled a deserter.'

'Sun Tzu adequately defined the intrinsic characteristics of leaders, namely wisdom, sincerity, humanity, courage and discipline both in their own conduct and with their troops. I would like to use the wisdom of King Solomon in the Bible as an example of administering justice without fear or favour to anyone. Sometimes wise decisions require great courage, as they might well appear brutal. However, such decisions bring perspective to a situation.'

'In my experience sincerity is not taken as seriously as in my early days. Probably the easiest illustration of this failing is the case where people say they will do something, but just not do it. I have seen sincerity deteriorate as a badge of honour descending through commitments that are forgotten as the perception of speed of life has increased to what is now considered as a means of not offending someone to their face only to offend them through non-delivery later. For me, it is imperative for people to deliver on their commitments to others. If you have no sincerity in your commitments, don't make the commitment.'

'Humanity is another interesting characteristic. Far too many so-called leaders start to feed off their own publicity; think Napoleon and Hitler. They quickly forget, stripped of all rank and perception, we're all humans of equal standing. Do unto others as you would have them do unto you comes to mind. Whereas I don't believe all people are born the same, we are all born equal. Some people are born to lead, and others to follow. Without leaders, followers would be lost, but without followers there would be no need for leaders. Neither of these two states carry supremacy.'

'You very often hear troops respect a General who ensures his troops eat before he eats, and he sleeps when his troops are settled. This is a General who understands humanity. A General can devise strategy, but it's the troops who make the victory.'

'Courage is fundamental to leadership. The lonely nature of leadership means tough decisions require strength of character. Without the courage of your own convictions, you cannot lead.'

'As for discipline, if you cannot comply with discipline yourself, what right do you have to inflict it on others? Lead by example comes to mind.'

'Easier said than done, I hear you think.'

'Reading my mind again. Can you teach someone to lead?'

'I'm not sure about teach, but you can show someone how to lead. Much of it is confidence in yourself, which can be coached. Please note I said confidence, not arrogance. People are quick to confuse the two words as the boundary between confidence into arrogance can be a thin line usually defined by how you express yourself. Whereas a leader needs to quietly exude confidence; arrogance must be avoided. You must believe in yourself if you expect other to believe in you.'

'You must also be ruthless in ensuring you can assemble the very best people available. You must always field your best team – no favouritism or prejudice. On the field of play resources are disciplined units of performance with the aim of victory.'

'I was asked to join a bank where I literally had to change everything. They had engaged in the ridiculous idea of outsourcing operations even though this operation was employed by the bank, but they were situated some 40 miles

the Way

outside London. This, alone, told me not even the existing executive understood the securities business. I recruited one of the longest-standing securities settlements people I knew. Ray was his name, he had been in the business longer than me, and what he didn't know about the business was irrelevant. He would be my line manager for securities settlements and his first task was to visit with the outsourced people, find out how many he wanted to bring to London, and then close that office.'

'We would have to let over 30 people go, and some people we could offer positions in London might not want the commute. But no matter as we felt obliged to offer the existing talent the positions, knowing we could quickly fill vacant positions from the City.'

'The executives were paranoid about adverse publicity and saw the closing of this office as a field day for the press to snipe at the bank. They brought in PR people to manage the press, and the Director of human resources organised his team to go tell the bad news. When I told him I would go tell these people on my own, you could see the fear in his face. But I insisted, and whilst I could not stop him being there, I insisted he should be in the shadows to deal with the fallout after I'd finished.'

'The fateful day came. Ray was there. I gathered everyone around me, explained who I was, why I was with the bank, and how I wanted to restructure the securities division, including merging the entire division into the City. I explained we could not offer jobs to everyone and accepted the possibility people we would like to keep may not wish to commute. I thanked them for their contribution.'

'One person stood. I saw the HR Director stand ready to move in if there was to be trouble. But no. He was obviously the spokesperson for the entire group. He thanked me for having the guts to go there and do the deed myself. He knew my reputation in the securities business and saw my presence as respect for the people who had seen this day coming for a long time. Leadership.'

Week 13

Seb reflected for a moment. She wondered what he was thinking.

'Penny for your thoughts.'

'Sorry. There was a junior in this group, I think 18 years old. He had not been selected to come to London through lack of experience. He came to me. Sir, will you take me with you to London? You and Ray are goliaths in this business, and I want to learn. I'll even take a pay cut until I prove myself.'

'There was something about this kid. He had an energy you could feel. I turned to Ray, who had listened to his plea, and told him he could have the headcount if prepared to take him, but no pay cut, and same relocation package as everyone else. This kid worked his arse off, and he was good. Less than 2-years later Goldman Sachs headhunted him at £350,000 salary plus bonus at 20 years old. He was one of the very best Bund – German Government securities – dealers in the City. He had a natural knack for understanding the quirks of German securities.'

'Wow. Why did you let him go?'

'He needed to spread his wings, and I was thinking of moving on at which time Ray wanted to retire. But he never forgot his *family*. It wasn't the first time I'd nurtured someone who went on to make their mark.'

'This what you're doing with me?'

'I hope you'll make the grade.'

'I can feel what it means to you to see others succeed. Do I detect Bernie lurking in the wings?'

'He helped to make my success possible. I know how such selfless contribution feels.'

Chapter 87 – Tuesday

'This evening we'll deal with interpreters. I appreciate you have little use for them here at Aldridge, unless of course you go to places with extreme dialects such as Newcastle, but should you move on to a more international role you will certainly encounter them.'

She was laughing 'And what about scoucers, or even Scots?'

'Most people, in my experience, use interpreters as a necessary evil, and don't know how to get the best out of them. Always remember they are trying to help you communicate with someone.'

'The secret I learnt from a diplomat was to introduce yourself to them, and then spend some 15 – 20 minutes with them explaining what you intend to say, and let them get used to the way you use, and phrase words. If you need to use any technical expressions, ensure you are satisfied they know what you require them to convey.'

'Then there is tone. If they are professional, they will listen to how you want to convey certain messages, ensuring they not only convey the words but also the tone you intend.'

'If you respect them, they will try to help you. I had two interpreters for a lecture I was giving in Brazil. I don't like working from a script, so I spent about half an hour with them beforehand. They really appreciated this effort on my part. They told me I was the first person to sit with them before a presentation. I was informed by someone fluent in both languages they did an excellent job. The Governor of the Central Bank and a Government official praised me for my message to the audience.'

'I learnt this lesson whilst in China during a round of lectures. I got friendly with the interpreter of the Provincial State Governor the evening before. She had been educated in the UK.'

'During the coffee break of the first lecture the following morning she came to me to inform me not only were my words not being interpreted correctly but also the tone was changed. I asked her if she could interpret for me. We went to her boss, who could speak English. He agreed my message was not being conveyed at all. We agreed to start again using his interpreter who stayed with me for three further days of lectures. Without her, my message would not have been conveyed. Because she was a lovely girl, everyone thought I was chatting her up the evening before, but my preparation that evening paid dividends.'

'If you visit countries that have a specific culture, or observe specific rites and social conventions, you must appraise yourself of these before you travel. Using this knowledge will earn you favour and respect, as people appreciate you have made the effort to honour their culture. When in Rome, do as the Romans do.'

Chapter 88 – Wednesday

'I think this evening we will look at how to travel with the least impact on your well-being. We briefly touched on this when we spoke of sexual gratification. But there is much more to it than sex.'

'There are some general rules, especially for long-haul flights of five hours or more; and apply to all countries.'

'If travelling west, as best you can choose flights that will get you to your destination late afternoon or early evening.'

'If travelling East, as best you can choose flights that will get you to your destination early morning, or late afternoon.'

'Try to avoid flights that arrive midday, or middle of the night.'

'Never travel economy on long haul. You need control of your own environment.'

the Way

'When your flight is ready to take off set your watch to the time at your destination. Eat and sleep accordingly. This prepares your body clock for your destination – avoids jet lag.'

'Travel in comfortable clothes. As you never go straight to an office on arrival you can dress comfortably for the journey.'

'Always go to your hotel first. If you arrive late afternoon, you do not meet anyone. A light dinner and early night. If you arrive in the morning sleep until no later than 1pm, do what you need to do in the afternoon, early dinner, and sleep.'

'Any drugs you may need, take with you. Different countries may have unfamiliar names for the drugs familiar to your body. Take the stress out of the situation by carrying your own supply.'

'If you intend to ingest the local tap water, drink, brushing teeth, etc, then it is wise for you to drink a locally brewed beer as the first thing to pass your lips upon arrival. This is equivalent to an inoculation against the local bacteria.'

'Know the local ways of greeting, and what words and expressions to avoid. Do not offend the locals if you want to be successful.'

'Ensure you have appropriate medical insurance and never subject yourself to anything other than emergency treatment in any country not consider as major Western. In most countries, and especially the USA, they will want a credit card before they ask about your problem. If your problem is serious, ensure your medical insurance cover provides for transfer to a competent jurisdiction that speaks your language.'

'Never wear expensive jewellery, including watches, on streets you don't know. Do not make yourself a target.'

'Got all that?'

Additional rules for non-Western countries

'The first thing that passes your lips on arrival should always be a locally brewed beer, if available, for reasons already stated.'

'Know the ingredients that can be mixed at a bar to emulate medicines such as brandy and port for your stomach – same impact as kaolin and morphine. A good barman will know these recipes.'

'Do not indulge in local food more than once or twice per week, even if you're sure of its origin. Give your stomach time to adjust to new food types.'

'Never drink directly from canned drinks. Use a straw, or a glass.'

'Never allow your baggage to be searched without your supervision.'

'Once through immigration do not hand your passport to anyone, not even the police. The hotel may need to see it, but do not leave it with them for any reason.'

'As a woman travelling in the more serious Islamic countries, be alive to dress code. Show respect and you should not be bothered.'

'Sex.'

'The need for sexual gratification is normal, especially if away for some time. However, you need to stay safe.'

'Always carry condoms, even a woman.'

'Never go search for sex in brothels, or on the street.'

'Major brand hotel bars and restaurants are the best source of a suitable partner.'

'If you are single, you can do as you please. If you are married the rule is you bring nothing home other than a memory. No further contact, no calling card, no pictures, no repeats.'

Chapter 89 – Thursday morning

He was starting to prepare breakfast as he knew she had finished in the pool, preparing herself for work. The telephone rang.

the Way

'Hello'.

'Could I speak with Miss Melanie Southgate please?'

'She's in the shower. Could I ask who is calling?'

'I'm calling from Hammersmith Hospital in London, and I need to speak with her urgently.'

'If this is about her mother, then you can speak with me as her guardian.' He knew how to play this game.

'And you are?'

'Sebastian Ryder.'

'Well Mr Ryder, as it's urgent, could you please convey to her that her mother was admitted as an emergency case in the early hours of this morning. Unfortunately, we could not help her, and she died at 4:36 this morning. We offer our condolences to her.'

'My God, this is tragic news. She'll be heartbroken. I'll bring her to the hospital later today.'

'Could you please go straight to the Registrar's Office. We can guide her through the process from there.'

'I understand and thank you for your call.'

'These calls are always sad for us, no matter how many we make. We'll see you later. Goodbye.'

'Goodbye and thank you.'

'My God,' he thought *'so soon after her breakup with Phillip. She'll be devastated.'*

He dialled Charles at home. 'Charles, it's Sebastian.'

'Good morning. What's wrong? I can hear it in your voice. Is Mel okay?'

'I've just had a call from Hammersmith Hospital in London. Her mother was admitted early this morning and passed away at 4:30.'

'Good God, the poor lady will be devastated. Does she know yet?'

'No, she's still getting ready for work.'

'Clearly she's not coming here today. What are you proposing?'

Week 13

'She's the only remaining next of kin so must go to London to take care of funeral arrangements.'

'Please tell her whatever she needs, I'm here for her. I'll alert the London office they are to give her whatever support she needs.'

'That's very kind of you, but I would prefer it if you did no more than for any other member of staff. The last thing she needs is any evidence of favouritism from the Chairman.'

'Wait a minute, Sebastian. You're a hard taskmaster with her, and the results are incredible. But this is different. You need to, as you say, cut her some slack. She's on her own out there. We need to help her.'

'I know she's on her own. That's why I'll be with her every step of the way until she returns.'

'Apologies, Sebastian. I should have known you'll take care of her. Thank you. Anything you need, please call me.'

'Would you and Jim be prepared to join us at the funeral, so the three people left in her life are there for her?'

'Absolutely. Just let me know when and where. What about Edna and Margaret? Two women might be a comfort to her.'

'If they want to come, I agree it would balance things. I don't know of her friends in London, but I know if the three of us show empathy with her, she'll get over this setback very quickly.'

'Sebastian, as always, you never cease to amaze me with your commitment to her, and my gratitude is immeasurable. I'll arrange we stay overnight in London. Can you arrange a wake for her?'

'Yes. I know exactly where I can get that support. If you can stay in the Kensington area, this would make it easy for you.'

'Good. I'll make the arrangements and see you next week in London. Thank you. Please convey our sincere condolences to her from us, and our prayers will be with her.'

'Thanks. I need to alert others before she comes to breakfast so I must go. I'll call you when we have a timetable in place.'

'Bye, Sebastian, and good luck. Take good care of her.'
He called a London number.
'Hello, Richard Beverley here.'
'Richard, it's Sebastian.'
'Hi Seb. To what do I owe a call this early in the morning?'
'I know this is short notice, but I need you to send someone round to open up my apartment this morning. There has been a death in the family, and I need to get there as soon as possible.'
'I'm so sorry. What do you need?'
'Two beds making up. Just eggs, milk, tea, coffee, juice, and bread for a few days. I'll also call you on Monday as there will be two London properties in need of cleanout and disposal.'
'Consider it done. What time do you expect to arrive in Kensington?'
'Not clear yet, as we should go to Hammersmith Hospital first. But might have to leave my car in Kensington as parking might be a pain.'
'I'll alert the doorman of your arrival.'
'Thanks Richard. You're a gem. Bye.'
He could hear her bouncing down the wooden staircase. *What a horrible thing to happen now. How do I break this news?*
'She bounced in and gave him his morning kiss. 'Lovely day.'
He just looked at her.
'What's wrong? What have I done to deserve such a face?'
'Come here.' He held her. 'I've got terrible news for you. Your mother died earlier this morning. I'm so sorry.'
She gasped as tears filled her eyes. 'How? When?'
'She was taken to Hammersmith Hospital early this morning as an emergency case but passed away a little after 4:30 this morning. I don't know what to say,' as tears welled in his eyes.
She collapsed into his arms in floods of tears. She was inconsolable for some minutes.
She looked up, tears streaming down her cheeks 'I have to go there. I need to be with her. There's no-one else.'

He held her close as tears were now rolling down his cheeks as he thought, *'Why has this happened just now to this wonderful woman? This is not part of my program.'*

'Mel, I want to be there for you, if you'll let me. I want to take you to London and help you through this great loss. Will you let me come with you?'

She could hear the pain in his voice. She hugged him tighter. 'Of course, I want you with me. You're all I have left.'

They shared each other's grief as they stood motionlessly entwined.

Eventually some reality returned to her 'I need to call the office to let them know.'

'It's okay. I've already taken the liberty to call Charles on your behalf. You have as much space and support as you need. His prayers are with you.'

'Thank you.'

'Try to have some breakfast as we have a long drive ahead of us. I'll prepare your eggs. Then we both need to pack a bag for about a week.'

'We can stay at my flat now Phil has moved out.'

'Can I suggest you don't know what to expect there. I have an apartment in Kensington, not far from Hammersmith Hospital. We can stay there.'

'Okay.'

He prepared breakfast for her and sat with her while she forced herself to eat, knowing there would be no need to stop *en route* for food.

Having composed herself a little 'My master, can you guide me with some positivity about this event because I only feel loss and despair?'

He looked at her in admiration. She was trying to apply his teaching to probably the worst situation she would encounter.

'There are two positives I can propose. The first is your mother told me of her illness when you took me to see her. She did not want to alarm you because she was so proud of your resolve to better yourself. She knew you would insist on caring for her instead of following your dream. She asked me if you would reach your dream. I told her you would. After your first Board meeting success, I called her to let her know you had graduated with honours at your first big challenge. She was so proud.'

'If you remember when at her home, you came back from the bathroom to find her in tears. I can now tell you what she said that caused those tears. She said after finding your father, the two of them would find the angel who brought us together and thank them.'

Tears were rolling down his cheeks again, 'Is that positive enough for you? Your mother and father are reunited and give thanks for your achievements.'

She went to him and hugged him closely, 'My hard taskmaster has the softest heart I know. I have not dared to say this to you before, but I love you so much for how you care for me.' And kissed him.

She wiped the tears from his face. 'Come my master, we must go.'

He made good time to London, arriving in Hammersmith a little after noon. Although it would have been quicker to go to the hospital, he was keen to get to his apartment, unload, and make a few calls to smooth the way for the coming days. If she noticed, she did not raise any objections. He was with her. She felt comforted with his presence and was used to him having a perfectly logical reason for whatever he did for her.

When they arrived at his apartment block, he drove downstairs to the basement car park where he had an allotted space. They grabbed their bags and made their way to the 17th floor. Opening the apartment door, he was relieved to know someone had already been to prepare for their visit – the smell of fresh bread. She walked in. For a few seconds she forgot why she was there.

'This is lovely. How often do you use it?'

'It was my home before moving to Matlock. Now only when in London; normally two or three nights each month. I still have business interests here, and I enjoy the theatre and the opera. You have consumed my time these past weeks, so I haven't been here.'

'Can I have a nose around?'

'Sure. I left instructions to have two beds made up, but I'm happy for you to stay with me if this will help you to sleep. The master suite is over there,' pointing along the hallway. 'I have some calls to make before we go to the hospital. If you need a drink, the kitchen is that way. A tea would be nice if you're making.'

She took their bags to the master bedroom. As is normal with this man the room was spacious and beautifully decorated. *'Much better than my apartment'* she thought. She decided to unpack for both of before making tea.

He dialled the first of his calls. 'Hello, could I speak with Gino?' He waited while Gino came to the phone.

'Gino? It's Sebastian.'

'Sebastian my friend, we have missed you these past weeks. Where have you been, and what can I do for you?'

'I'm here with my protégé whose mother died last night. She's an only child, and the only surviving next of kin. She's very upset so I would like to block book my quiet table in the corner for lunch and dinner for the next few days.'

'Mama mia, this is terrible news. Of course, you can have your table. I ask Mama to take special care of her and take her up to the apartment if needed. Does she like Italian food?'

'It's her favourite. Her name is Melanie.'

'Then we will spoil her with whatever she wants. Will you come for lunch today?'

'I think something to eat before we go to the hospital would be good. We'll be there in 20 minutes.'

the Way

'Gino will have everything ready, and I tell Mama to be ready for her. Sad news, my friend, but you are family, so we help you through this.'

'Thanks Gino. This lady is very special to me, so I want the next few days to be as painless as possible for her.'

'Leave it to Gino. See you soon.'

The next call went to the concierge at the nearby 4-star hotel. 'Robert, it's Sebastian. I need some good tickets for two. What have you got?'

'Okay I'll take Les Mis, and the opera. I'll collect later today. How much do I need?'

She had finished her tour and was in the kitchen preparing tea. She noticed the fresh food as he walked in to join her.

'Who are you, my master? You flick your fingers and things happen.'

'Forget tea. Come with me. There's family I want you to meet.'

'I'm not really into meeting people today.'

He just looked at her with that look which says everything about resistance.

They strolled out of the building onto Kensington Mews, and then a few streets until they came to a restaurant called Luigi's. He guided her in. Gino was waiting with his wife, affectionately known as Mama.

'Ciao Sebastian, my friend. Lovely to see you. And this must be the lovely, but sad, Melanie. Mama moved in to put her arm around Mel. 'You are with family here. Sebastian is family, and now so are you. Come with me. Mama has a special quiet table for you.'

As soon as Mel was seated Mama sat next to her. 'What can Mama get you?'

'I don't know what you have. I've not seen your menu.'

'Ah. You are family, so no menu. You tell Mama what you like, and Mama fix it for you. Capisci? We are family restaurant.

Week 13

We make everything just like my mama teach me back in Italy. No fancy stuff, just good family cuisine.'

'Could I have just a little pasta with a cream sauce? Fettuccini is the word I was looking for.'

'No problem, and what about to drink?'

'Just water, please.'

'And what about my Sebastian?'

'I think carbonara, not too much, and a glass of soave please Mama.'

Mama shouts across the restaurant in typical Italian style 'Gino, fettuccini for Melanie, and carbonara for Sebastian.'

'Si, Mama.'

'Roberto, a glass of our best soave, and a bottle of water.'

'Si, Mama.'

'I sit with you a while as I like to see my Sebastian, and I want to welcome you to our family.'

'You've already made me very welcome. You obviously know Sebastian very well.'

'Since he was a very sad boy in the City.' She looked at Seb 'how many years, 20 maybe?'

'I first entered your door in 1968 and never left.'

'What is that, eh, 22 years? Long time, si?'

'Any time you want to eat, you come see Mama. Any time you sad, you come see Mama. On Sunday we not open, but you come see Mama. You eat with our family upstairs. Si?'

Mel was smiling, 'Can I call you Mama.'

'I am Mama to family. Mama only have boys. Now Sebastian bring me a daughter. When you feel better Mama celebrate her new daughter, si?'

'Thank you, Mama. I feel better already.'

He knew Mama would be a tonic for her, as she had been to him during those dark days. Italians are the best where family tragedy is concerned.

the Way

They ate well, and she perked up a little. He reached over to cover her hand 'We're now fuelled. It's time to visit with your mum. Are you ready?'

'Seb, I'm so grateful you're with me.'

'I cannot imagine otherwise. If you need the bathroom before we go, it's over there.' Pointing to the *ladies'* bathroom.

'Good idea' and she was off.

Mama came to the table. 'You have a really good lady. You take care of her or you answer to Mama.'

'Mama, I've never taken care of anyone the way I take care of her, so Mama should be happy with me.'

'She opens your heart. For too long it was closed. I like what I see in my Sebastian. You go to hospital now?'

'Yes'

'You come back around 7:30 and Mama take care of her. I know what it is like for a woman to lose her mama. She will need special care. Mama will dine with you tonight.'

'Can I have the bill?'

'No bill. We family. We take care of our own in times of trouble.'

'Thank you, Mama, but I'm happy to pay.'

'Mama happy you don't. You argue with Mama? Go take her to be with her mama. Let her take as long as she needs. Be there where she cannot see you, but where she can feel you near. Say nothing. You hear Mama?'

'I'm listening to your wise words. I'll try my best to be there for her. It's important to me.'

'Sebastian, I can see how you feel for her. You are good man. She comes. See you this evening, si?'

'Yes Mama, but if we are later is this okay?'

'You come at Italian 7:30 and you cannot be late, eh.'

He smiled as he rose to meet Mel and move towards the door. Gino followed him and patted him on the shoulder, 'Our prayers are with you both, my friend.'

Week 13

The hospital was Victorian in architecture, and formerly a Military Orthopaedic Hospital, located in West Acton, rather than Hammersmith. The Registrar's Office was a typical nondescript room, only defined by the sign over the door. Inside there was a counter, the other side of which two ladies sat at two desks joined so they faced each other.

'Good afternoon. Can we help you?'

He let Mel respond, 'My name is Melanie Southgate, and this is Mr Ryder. My mother passed away here this morning.'

'Ah yes. I remember speaking with Mr Ryder this morning. We hate this bit, but could you show us some identification?'

'Of course,' as she reached into her bag for her driver's licence.

'Thank you. Can I explain the procedure to release your mother to your undertaker, and then, if you wish, we can take you to the chapel where you can be with you mother for a while? We try to allow as much time as you need, but it depends on how many people we need to process. As you are later, we do not have any other deceased patients at this time, so hopefully, you're not likely to be disturbed. I hope you'll understand our limitations.'

'Thank you. I understand.'

They went through the formalities and issued the Death Certificate.

They were shown to the chapel, and a few minutes later her mother was wheeled in, already in a lidless coffin.

He was very happy to note her mum really did look at peace and hoped this would comfort her. He remembered what Mama had said, standing close behind her, a little to her right so if she reached for him, contact would be immediate.

She held her mum's hand, and he knew quiet tears were being shed. He could feel her sorrow and wanted to touch her, but held back.

She started to speak, 'I love you so much, mum. Seb told me what you said to him, so I hope you are looking down on us now to see I will fulfil my dream and make you and dad proud of me. Goodbye mum. Give a kiss to dad for me.' She leaned forward and kissed her mum. Then she turned to Seb, falling into his arms, and wept. He let her release her pain.

She eventually turned to the porter, who had quietly witnessed proceedings, nodding her consent to return her mother to the mortuary.

As they left 'We need to go to the undertakers. It is the same company used for dad, so I know where they are.'

He took her hand as they left the hospital and let her lead the way.

By the time they had finished the arrangements for cremation on the following Tuesday, it was after 5 o'clock. They emerged back into the throng of rush hour jostling with people oblivious to her loss. He hailed a taxi to take them back to the apartment.

He phoned Charles to appraise him of the arrangements. He wanted to speak with her.

'Mel, I'm so sorry to hear of your loss. All of us here want to express our sincere condolences. With your consent I would like to attend the funeral with Edna, Jim, and Margaret.'

'You're all very kind to me. If you can spare the time, I would appreciate you being there. You, Jim, and Seb are now the only family I have. I need your strength to overcome my loss and complete my task.'

'We'll be there. You're an inspiration to us all. We'll help you through this.'

Tears started to flow again, so she passed the phone to Sebastian.

'Okay Charles. She's fragile. I'll call you Sunday to confirm everything.'

'Thank you for being there for her. Talk to you Sunday.'

He had things to do. 'Are you alright to chill for a while as I need to pop out? You're welcome to come with me if you prefer.'

'I would like to be with my thoughts for a while, so please go ahead.'

'Anything you want, help yourself. Whatever I have is yours. Make yourself at home as if at Merton.'

'Thanks.'

He met with Robert at the hotel and was pleased with the embassy tickets for both performances. *'Best seats in the house'* he thought, *'This should provide a little respite for her.'*

When he returned, she was sitting with a blank expression, and tears rolling down her face. He left her there and poured himself a drink before going to the bedroom. He wanted to prepare for a deluxe shower to help her wash away her sorrow. He left her alone for nearly an hour but knew she would need a reset to get her out to Luigi's.

He took her hand, encouraged her to her feet, and led her to the bedroom. He started to undress her. She did not resist. After shedding his clothes, he led her to the shower where the water was already flowing.

'It's time to wash away some of your sorrow,' he whispered in her ear.

He doused her in warm water and then started with her hair, ensuring he gently massaged her scalp and the back of her neck. He was slow and methodical; there was no hurry. Let her wallow in the warm water flowing down her body. He applied all his love and care in caressing and massaging her to convey to her she was not alone.

As he reached her back, she leaned into him, using her arms to snuggle closer. She was responding. He wanted her to come back to him and would do whatever it took.

As he rinsed her off, she looked up at him, 'That was so lovely. I could stay here all day.'

'I will happily drown your sorrow as many times as it takes, but can we break for something to eat? Mama will have my guts for garters if I don't feed you properly. Can I get you dressed so we can go to eat?'

'Will you seriously dress me?' as he put a towel around her wet hair.

the Way

'With all the love and care you've just enjoyed in the shower. However, I would like you to dry your hair as I'm no hairdresser.'

She smiled at him, 'I would like to see how you dress me.'

He selected simple, casual clothes that would sit on her easily – nothing tight. She dried her hair and applied minimal makeup while he dressed himself. He sat her on the bed, kneeling to slip her into her shoes. She said nothing, but smiled at him, feeling the love he was applying to her.

'Is my princess ready to eat?'

'Then you must be my prince. I'm ready to go see Mama.'

They got their coats and made their way to Luigi's.

When they walked in Mama was attending another table. Her keen eye had been watching the door for a while. She made her excuses and noisily made for her, scooping her up in her arms. 'My lovely Melanie, so nice to see you. Let me look at you.'

Mama could see her sorrow, but Sebastian had done a wonderful job keeping her afloat. 'Come my dear, come with Mama and let me share you sorrow' as she steered her to their table now laid for three. He stayed to speak with Gino.

'How was it my dear? Did you see your mama?'

Trying to hold back tears 'Yes, she looked very peaceful.'

'This is because she no longer feels pain. She knows her lovely Melanie is in good hands.'

Her tears started to flow, 'My mum was all I had. I lost my dad last Christmas, and now my mum.'

'But your mama meet Sebastian, si?'

'Yes, they met, and she told him she was ill, but not me, and asked him to take care of me.'

'There you are. She know Sebastian is good man. She did not need to endure pain any longer knowing you are loved and cared for. And now you meet Mama and your new family, and we will share your joys and sorrow with you.'

'But why are you doing this for me?'

Week 13

'We met Sebastian after he lost his wife. He was broken man. It took years for him to deal with what happened. We adopted him as one of our own. I like to think with Mama's love he built his career and was very successful. But he has never forgotten his adopted family. He has brought women here for Mama's approval; but none knew how to fix his pain. Today I see a different Sebastian. He really cares about you. A mama knows these things. You have brought him back to life, and he needs you as much as you need him. This makes Mama so happy for both of you.'

'You knew his wife?'

'No, we met the bereaved and tormented result of her tragic death.'

'How did she die?'

'If Sebastian has not told you, be patient. It is very painful for him. Today is about you and your mama, so what can I get you to ease your sorrow.'

'You're very kind to me. I don't really know what I want. Can you think of something for me?'

'What are mamas for?' Turning towards the bar 'Roberto, tell Giuseppe come see Mama.'

'Si, Mama.'

'Giuseppe is my son, and our chef. We will see what he can make for us.'

Giuseppe, being a good Italian son, was quickly with Mama. 'This is Melanie, your new sister. She lost her mama today, so she needs good food to help with her sorrow. She loves Mama's food, so what can we have, including your mama and Sebastian.'

'Leave it to me, Mama. Give me 20 minutes.'

'Off you go. Make Mama proud.' Turning to Mel, 'He's a good boy.'

'What shall we drink? Roberto two nice Grappa please.'

'She couldn't hold back her tears any longer. Mama spotted this and instantly moved herself next to her and held her in her arms. 'Mama is here, your tears are safe with Mama.'

447

the Way

Sebastian joined the table. He knew not to disturb what he saw. He had been there himself many years ago.

Their grappa arrived. Without showing Mel's face, she instructed Roberto to bring a bottle of their best Barolo and pour a glass for Sebastian.

Once Mel had regained her composure Mama encouraged her to pick up her grappa. 'My lovely Melanie we saluti your wonderful mama who created a beautiful daughter and brought her to join our family today. Your mama was a good mama and we are privileged to have you with us. May your mama rest in peace knowing her daughter is safe with us. Your mama, God rest her soul.'

They clinked glasses and drank. 'Thank you, Mama. You have such warmth and generosity.'

Dinner was spectacular, lifting her spirits to the highest point of the day. She could see where Sebastian had acquired his culinary skills and had never felt such kindness and love from a stranger.

When they finally returned to his apartment, she kicked off her shoes as she collapsed onto the sumptuous couch. He poured himself a cognac and joined her.

'You absolutely confound me with what you do for me. Mama told me how you joined the family, albeit not how you lost your wife. You clearly loved her very much, and now I feel that love. You have been my rock today, as always, but extra special.' She gave him her customary kiss, dwelling on his cheek longer than usual, hoping her gratitude was appropriately expressed.

'I do want to be with you tonight. Curled up in your arms is a great comfort to me.'

Chapter 90 – Friday

When he woke, she was still sleeping. He gently eased himself out of bed as he needed the bathroom and a drink. He made tea for two and returned to the bedroom. As he slid in beside her, her eyes opened. She smiled.

'Hello, sleep well?'

'Lovely, thank you.'

'I have tea for you when you're ready.'

'What, no throwing me in the pool this morning?'

'It's in the basement. Long way down.'

'What time is it?'

'Around 8am.'

'Can this be too early today to get up? I want to stay curled up for a while.'

He handed her tea and put his arm around her. 'We have no time considerations today, so relax.'

'What do you need to achieve today regarding your mum?'

'I have to go to her house and select clothes for her and take them to the undertaker. I also need to arrange for flowers and organise putting her ashes next to dad. And I need an urn.'

'Where do you want to start?'

'I need you to drown my sorrows. I'll prepare breakfast to engage in some routine. Will you come with me to mum's house to get her clothes? I need to stay focussed.'

'You don't need to ask such questions. I'm with you every step of the way. You tell me when you want to start with your shower. Until then we stay here.'

'I need to collect my thoughts for a while in case I've forgotten anything.'

He held her until she finally made a move for the bathroom. Their day would now start.

As they approached her mum's house, he could feel her apprehension. 'Look at this visit as ensuring your mum looks her best to go meet your dad.'

the Way

She reached over to touch his arm in appreciation 'If you successfully teach me to be so positive about misfortune, I'll be eternally grateful.'

They entered the house. She quickly found what she wanted, and they were on their way to the undertaker.

Her mum's body had been collected from the hospital, but they wanted to prepare her before any viewings. She could come back later this afternoon. She selected the urn she wanted.

He was hungry. She was mournful. He felt Mama might satisfy both needs.

As they entered, Mama smothered her with attention wanting to know every detail of her day, reinforcing that her mama would be proud of her daughter. Mel took solace in this interrogation as she needed to know she had done everything she needed; Mama would detect any oversights.

After a long lunch she wanted to return to the undertaker to check mum was ready to meet with dad. Mama went with her, knowing this would be the last time she would see her mum, and she could break down. Mama wanted to be there for her. She had really taken to this woman who had broken through the ice-cold barrier of her Sebastian's heart.

Mama quietly indicated to Sebastian he should stay outside. She would go with Mel to see her mama. He knew she would be safe with Mama, so quietly obeyed.

They returned some forty minutes later, Mel wrapped in Mama's arms, still tearful. Her eyes said everything about what had happened in there.

'We take her home now. You take good care of her. Bring her back to Mama when she is ready. Mama will be waiting.'

After dining, they went home to bed. She curled up in his arms and slept.

Chapter 91 - Saturday

'Seb. What are our plans today?'

'I have some ideas, but they need information from you.'

'What do you want to know?'

'I think today should be about gathering your mum's and your friends you want with you. You need to tell them about Tuesday and see who can attend.'

'By the way, I spoke with Gino whilst there on Thursday evening. The restaurant is at our disposal for a wake in honour of your mum. We can go straight there from the funeral and stay as long as we like.'

'That's really kind of them. You think of everything.'

'I have some things I need to do this morning, but I'm available to you from lunchtime.'

'I don't want to bore you with the people I need to see. I'll make some calls, see who is available, and go see some of mum's friends. I won't know how long I need until then.'

'Okay, I'll let Mama know where I am. You need me, call Mama. We have tickets for the theatre from 7:30 this evening.'

'Are you sure that theatre is good at this time?'

'You'll be in darkness, and a little respite will be good for you to recharge.'

'What are we seeing?'

'Les Misérables.'

'Fitting.'

'Have you seen it?'

'No.'

'You'll love it.'

'Have you seen it before?'

'I went to the premiere, and 5 – 6 times since. You cannot tire of such a masterpiece.'

'Praise indeed. Then I guess I should see it.'

'We need to decide on early dinner, or late supper.'

'Late supper sounds good.'

the Way

'I'll be at Luigi's for lunch around 1pm. If you want to bring anyone, just show up.'

'Thank you.'

'How about a deluxe shower, followed by a nice breakfast?'

'Sounds good to me. Let me go first, and I'll get the shower warm.'

During breakfast he handed her money. 'What's this for?'

'I want you to have the option of black cabs today if you need them. That is the only ticket they understand, so please take it. If you don't use it, you can always give it back. I don't want you out there on your own without all the options available.'

She made her calls and organised her visits. They left the apartment together so he could inform the doorman she has unfettered access to his apartment. He gave her a key.

After completing his shopping, he dined alone, returning to his apartment around 3pm. She wasn't there. He was grateful for some time to chill. Although he had no reservations about his commitment to her, being reminded of his own dark past had brought back chilling memories of finding his wife who had been on the floor dead for two days when he found her. These memories needed to be buried again so he could concentrate on the present.

She returned around 5pm, emotionally exhausted. They needed to be out of the apartment by 6:30 to make the theatre in good time. 'What do you need in the next 90 minutes to get you ready for the evening?'

'I want to tell you what happened today. Then another deluxe shower, and some good company.'

'Thank goodness I have all these needs in abundance.'

She smiled as she sat with him. She told him she had eight of mum's friends, and three of her own.

'So, we are 17 in total without Mama. Not bad.'

As the lights came up at the end of the performance, she had tears in her eyes, but this time it was the spectacle she had witnessed. She turned to Sebastian, 'Thank you. It was fantastic; sad; but fantastic.'

'Come. Mama will be waiting.'

They arrived back at the apartment after midnight, ready to sleep.

Chapter 92 – Sunday

Again, it was late when they woke. It was Sunday, so no hurry.

'I have an idea what might be a good to do after a nice brunch somewhere. But I'll discuss it with you when we are up and showered. Whose turn is it to get the water warm?'

She was gone.

Once dressed they sat together. 'I don't want to appear insensitive, but we have the opportunity to take care of some practical issues whilst here in London. I'll tell you what I have in mind, but do not feel compelled to agree with me. We can always come back when all this is over.'

'Seb, the one thing I really appreciate about you is how much you care for me. Tell me what you're thinking.'

'As there is nothing we can usefully do today I suggest we visit your apartment, and your mum's house. What I propose is you clear out from both properties what you want to keep, sell both giving you a fresh start. You can buy a new place with the proceeds to go with your new life as an executive. Sometimes we need to refresh our lives, and this is your opportunity.'

'Always looking for positives, my master. I would like to see how Phil left my apartment. I'm not so sure about mum's house, but I understand your logic. I would need to facelift my apartment before I could sell it and clear out mum's house. I don't have time.'

the Way

'I have someone who will clear out both properties, facelift as necessary, and then achieve the best price possible. Once you have taken what you want, everything else will be dealt with by my property agent. We can meet him tomorrow, or Wednesday, sign any paperwork, and you can concentrate on your future.'

'You believe I should do this now?'

'Think of it as a deluxe cleansing. It washes away the past and allows you to concentrate on making your mum and dad proud.'

'Is this the apartment you shared with your wife?'

'No. I couldn't bear being there. I still own it but have not been back there since.'

'What do you do with it?'

'I have a portfolio of property in London, all of which are contracted as corporate lets. My property agent looks after them for me.'

'Okay, let's go eat and then we can go look at my apartment. Then I'll decide about mum's house.'

She opened the door of her apartment. The stench was rancid. She found the place in total disarray, the fridge door was open, and food was rotting on the table. She burst out in tears.

He looked around and realised there was no way she could clear this mess. He comforted her 'Can you select what you want to keep. I will get packing boxes from the car. You can pack and take it with us.'

She was angry, 'How could he do this to me? We were together for nearly two years. How well did I know him? He's an animal.'

He returned with flat-pack boxes, and a parcel, and put them on the bed. She looked at the parcel, 'What's this?'

'Open it.'

She found the most beautiful briefcase. 'What's this for?'

'Today it's for you to put all the papers you need. Thereafter it befits a woman executive.'

'It must have cost a fortune.'

'It's no good being good if you don't look good.'

She could smell the beautiful aroma of soft leather above the rancid smell of her apartment. Something snapped in her. She quickly filled her briefcase and two boxes. 'I'm finished here, let's go.'

It took more than an hour to go through her mother's house. She was gentle and caring about how she handled things, selecting only the papers she needed and what she felt were precious to her parents.

The car loaded, she locked the house and handed both sets of keys to him. She wanted to close this chapter in her life.

They stopped on the way back to the apartment to buy some food for dinner. Papers needed sorting for the property agent and lawyer and going out for dinner did not appeal to her. The visit to her own apartment had left a bad taste with her, and then visiting her mum's house for the last time had taken an emotional toll on her. He knew TLC was the primary requirement this evening.

the Way

Week 14

Chapter 93 – Monday

While she busied herself making breakfast, he called Richard to confirm his mandate to take care of the property disposal, providing him with the addresses, and the details of his lawyer who would handle her mum's estate. She must be free to pursue her dream. He instructed that the clear-out and facelift costs would be to his account. They would attend his office on Wednesday morning to execute any necessary paperwork.

Her only requirement was to arrange flowers for the restaurant, not least to say thank you to Mama.

'As you have everything in place for tomorrow, how about some shopping therapy for you today?'

'You're the first man I've met who is okay about shopping with me. Can we go to Brent Cross? Everything I would like to see is there; minimal walking, car park, and undercover.'

They had fun. She was soon in a playful mood selecting clothes for him, some serious, and others just for fun. She chose a dress for the funeral, but then changed her mind in favour of a black trouser suit with a white satin blouse, and black patent shoes. Finding a black hat proved troublesome, as black was not in fashion. After much searching and lunch, they found what she needed. She was happy. He was happy to see her happy. Time to relax.

When they got back to the apartment, she quickly ensured all clothes for tomorrow were ready, and in good shape. Then she crashed on the sofa and was soon asleep. He looked at her. *What a lovely lady she is. Why so much pain for her?*

They were at Luigi's at 7:30 with the intent of an early night. Mama was on guard. Mel looked drained. Mama was mindful she might fold for the simplest of reasons. Seb, who was sitting

the Way

next to her in case of her need for a shoulder, found himself frequently holding her hand for any reason. Was this a comfort to her? He didn't know, but she seemed perfectly happy with this contact.

They got back to the apartment a little after 9:30, and she was in bed, asleep by 10:00. He held her in his arms so much wanting to take her away from this seemingly continual pain.

Chapter 94 – Tuesday – Funeral

The funeral was scheduled for 2pm. Charles had phoned to say they would meet at the Crematorium.

The service was brief; but dignified. Mel had elected to let the priest deal with the eulogy, as he knew her mum.

After her coffin had entered the flames, everyone made their way to Luigi's where Mama was in tears because Mel had thought to send such lovely flowers to her at the restaurant. When Mel arrived, she wrapped her in her arms to say thank you, and then showed her the lovely display.

Gino had organised a delicious buffet. Charles, totally unaware of the relationship Sebastian shared with Mama, quickly realised Mel could not afford such a lunch, and Sebastian had already covered far too much on his account. He quietly insisted this wake was to his account. Sebastian pointed him towards Gino.

As Mama could see Mel was amongst friends, especially those of her mum, she stayed in the background, but ready to pick her up if necessary. One of Mel's friends from the London office was very keen to know how she was getting on in Matlock, and desperate to meet Sebastian. Much talk about this man among the fairer sex in the office.

Week 14

The only people left at 5pm were the Matlock attendees. They agreed to a break, not least to allow the restaurant to prepare for the evening. They agreed to reconvene at 7:30 for dinner.

As they walked back to the apartment Mel was silent. He left her with her thoughts until they entered the apartment. 'You did your mum proud today. Are you satisfied with how things went?'

She held him around the waist with her head on his chest. 'I was thinking about what my mum said to you about finding the angel who brought us together. I would also like to thank that angel. What would I have done without you? I should be on my own, but I have you, and Charles, and Jim, and Mama, and …… I feel very lucky to know you all, but especially you. Thank you for making this day good for me and my mum.' He could feel her starting to cry.

'Mel, it's your personality and magnetism that brought these people around you. I also thank the angel that brought us together. You have given me a sense of purpose having lost my way for so long. I have many things, but like you, I have no-one to share with. We both now have purpose in our lives, surrounded by a lot of supportive energy. We need to complete our task together to make good on our good fortune. To help get you through this has been an honour, so what can I do to prepare you for dinner with those who really care for you?'

'Just hold me while I quietly say goodbye to mum. And then I'll get changed for dinner.

Edna was the star at dinner, using her dry wit to keep everyone amused. Mel understood now why Charles had acknowledged to her the important role she had played in the success of Aldridge. She is a strong woman who could rationalise difficult situations and find the funny side. Very much a positive thinker.

By the time they returned to the apartment she was tired, but a contented tiredness. Her mum had been honoured. Now it was

the Way

time to fulfil the destiny her parents had spent their lives mapping for her. She was determined not to disappoint.

Chapter 95 – Wednesday

She woke with a smile on her face. Her life had dramatically changed over the past few months, and she had suffered some difficult situations, especially losing her mum so soon after losing her dad, but she felt blessed with the new people around her, especially the person still sleeping by her side.

She needed breakfast but was not about to shower alone, so went to the kitchen and made breakfast, bringing it back to the bedroom on a tray.

He stirred 'Breakfast in bed today. I think,' as she put the tray on the bed.

'Someone is chirpy this morning.'

'Yesterday has gone. I did my best for mum, but now it's time to move on and fulfil my dreams.'

They enjoyed breakfast, showered, and readied themselves for their trip to Richard.

Richard was a director of a major property agency. He had a conference room waiting for them as they came through the door.

'Good morning, Sebastian. I have everything ready.'

'Good morning, Richard. This is Melanie Southgate, your new client.'

'Welcome Miss Southgate, or may I call you Melanie?'

'Nice to meet you. Melanie is fine with me.'

They assembled in the conference room. Sebastian fully appraised Richard of the situation, including that his lawyer would act as executor of the estate of her mum. She gave him the documentation relating to both properties. Richard explained the paperwork he required her to sign before she executed all.

'By the way Sebastian whilst you're here could I have your signature on some papers on your account.'

Sebastian quickly realised these papers related the clear-out and facelift of both properties; costs he was accepting on his account as they would be incorporated into his accounts as tax deductible. He duly signed them and handed them back to Richard.

Next stop was his lawyer where, again, she had papers to execute, and handed her mum's Will to him. He examined it and indicated it was straightforward and asked about bank accounts and investment. She searched her new briefcase and handed him everything she had found in her mum's home.

Once outside, he suggested they go to Mama for lunch as she had more shopping to do.

Once seated and lunch order she could no longer silence her curiosity. 'Why do we need to shop today?'

'I forgot to tell you we're at the opera this evening, so you need something to wear. It's first night so proper attire is preferred.'

'What are we going to see, and where?'

'Les Contes d'Hoffmann by Offenbach at Covent Garden. The incredible Placido Domingo plays Hoffmann, Robert Lloyd plays the nasty Lindorf, the serene Agnes Baltsa plays the courtesan, with Claire Powell as Hoffmann's alter ego. Wonderful production; and includes an entire act about the deception of rose-tinted spectacles.'

'You've seen this opera before. Your passion for it beams out of you.'

'I saw it a few years ago, again with Domingo. He's truly magnificent in this part.'

'Can't wait. I've never seen him live. He's one of the Three Tenors, isn't he?'

the Way

'My goodness lady. When we're through with your exec training, we need some work on the great classics.'

'I love my university of life, and such a great teacher, so I'll take any excuse to continue my studies there.'

They both laughed. Mama could see them having fun. *'My Sebastian has a real woman this time. I pray to the good Lord he sees what I see.'*

They went to Knightsbridge for their shopping. She tried a range of evening gowns, one very beautiful, but not suitable for sitting for long periods at the opera. Eventually she found a stunning cocktail dress. She tried it. He liked it, bought it, and then started the ritualistic trawl for shoes to go with it.

When they got back to the apartment, it was close to 5 o'clock. 'My hair! Seb, my hair! I can't go like this.'

A quick call to Robert secured her an immediate session with the stylist in the hotel hair salon.

He watched her during key moments during the opera. He would not need to ask her if she enjoyed the performance, she was spellbound.

Chapter 96 – Thursday

'After our shower and breakfast, we should go to settle your mother's ashes with your father. Then it is time to return to Matlock. We need to pack so we can head north directly from the cemetery.'

When her father died, they had buried him, but left the base stone such that it could be slid to allow urns to be interred in the same plot. When they got to the cemetery, she collected the urn and went to his grave along with an attendant who had the tools to move the slab. Once inserted, the slab was closed, and the attendant returned to his duties.

She said a few silent words to both, turned to Sebastian. 'Let's go home.'

When they arrived home, they only unpacked their travel bags. Peter could unload the boxes tomorrow.

They swam together for nearly an hour, during which time they both raced and played. It was good to be back. There was no doubt by either where she would sleep tonight, even though it was a weekday.

Chapter 97 – Friday

He had her up at 6am, and into the pool. He then showered her before sending her off to her room to get ready for work whilst he prepared breakfast.

She arrived at work as normal. Mary had put flowers on her desk and brought her morning tea. She expressed her condolences, but glad she was back. Jim was keen to get her back to work as the journey to London had not been kind to him and he felt he may be forced to have a few days to recover. She understood and was up for it.

Chapter 98 – Weekend

Saturday was back to routine. He felt the sooner she was back on track, the better.

On Sunday they lay in bed together. What do you want to do today?

'It looks like a nice day. Can we go out for the day? I'd like just one day where I can relax and enjoy some time together. I would like to see the Peak District, especially through your eyes. I hear Buxton is very nice.'

'Excellent idea. We can make our way along the prettier south route of the Peak District up to Buxton, and then come back through the bleaker north route along the famous Snake Pass. This should give you a good flavour of the area. I almost chose Buxton over Matlock as a place to live, but it's some 300m above sea level, and a climate to match. It's a much nicer town, but I need my sunshine in the summer.'

'Why is the northern part so bleak? Can't be much distance between north and south parts.'

'They blame the acid smoke from the chimneys of East Manchester during the Industrial Revolution for destroying all the vegetation. In the winter, the moors are bleak. But come, let's up and away so you can see for yourself.'

He chased her down to the pool, impeded her progress during their swim, and then chased her back to the shower. He wanted her in a playful mood. She needed to laugh and have some fun after the dreary events over the past weeks. They were soon breakfasted and on their way.

Week 15

Chapter 99 – Monday

As soon as she arrived home, he could see she was still on the field of play. 'What's on your mind?'

'Charles and Jim have really locked into your view about the imminent recession. I need to understand how this will affect Aldridge, so I understand their planning.'

'No problem. Why don't you go through your normal routine and we'll make it our topic of study this evening?'

'Great. Thanks.' She was off to prepare for the gym.

'As an economic recession has no clear and specific definition, we will only deal with the impending recession. At business school you can have a field day analysing the economic theories on this subject but what they all agree it's a period of zero or negative economic growth as measured by GDP.'

'You will find many economic theories attempt to explain why and how an economy can stall from its long-term growth trend into a period of temporary recession. These theories can be broadly categorised as based on real economic factors, financial factors, or psychological factors, or a mix of all.'

If we revert to **Keynesian** economics, the father of modern economics, his theory of recessions examines the excessive exuberance of a preceding boom time and the deep pessimism of a recessionary environment as an explanation why recessions can occur and persist. In lay terms, this is an overheated or overvalued economy in need of correction.

'I once used an analogy in a lecture along the lines you celebrate a major boom with an overexuberant party with much consumption of food and drink. When exhaustion brings the party to an end, you need a period of recovery from the hangover and consumption excesses where you no longer consume, and you need to pay for the party.'

Keynes also points out that once a recession begins, the gloomy hangover of investors can become a self-fulfilling prophecy of stalled investment spending because of market pessimism, which then leads to decreased incomes that ultimately decrease consumption spending. This market sentiment is very unpredictable, creating volatility in the markets fuelling further uncertainty.

Some theories explain recessions in terms of the behaviour of financial markets. These usually focus on either the overexpansion of credit and financial risk during the good economic times, or the contraction of money and credit at the onset of recessions. When you study this subject, you will bump into Milton Friedman who introduced the idea of capitalism which blames recessions on insufficient growth in money supply which is an excellent example of this type of theory.

Other theories propose that speculative euphoria of financial markets with the likely formation of financial bubbles based on debt which inevitably burst can cause recessions.

For the purposes of this discussion, I would summarise that a recession occurs when political fiscal policy and/or financial markets diverge from economic reality, thus requiring a period for them to realign.

'Are we good so far?'

'You were losing me before your last statement. How do you know when a recession is imminent?'

There is no single way to predict how and when a recession will occur. Aside from two consecutive quarters of GDP decline, economists assess several metrics to determine whether a recession is imminent or already taking place. According to many economists, there are some generally accepted predictors that when they occur together may point to a possible recession.

There are several indexes critically important to banks, investors, and business decision makers because they can give

Week 15

advance warning of a recession. Combine this with officially published data series from various government agencies that represent key sectors of an economy, such as data describing new construction starts, and growth in demand for capital goods. Changes downwards in these metrics may lead or move simultaneously with the onset of recession, in part because they are used to calculate the components of GDP, which will ultimately be used to define when a recession begins.

Okay, I understand some of this, but what is the difference between a recession, a deep recession, and a depression?'

Depends who you talk to. From a banking perspective, a recession will last no longer than two consecutive quarters and is usually some structural correction such as the hangover earlier. Politically throughout the world it is generally agreed that the National Bureau of Economic Research will not declare a country in recession until two quarters of economic stagnation has occurred after which politicians hope to say it has passed lest their economic credentials are challenged by the electorate. To be fair, unless the politicians have introduced some economic strangulation in taxes or investment which reduced the ability to invest, recessions tend not to be their fault, nor do they have the capability to prevent them.

A deep recession will last at least one year but no more than six consecutive quarters and requires significant structural readjustment to realign the economy.

We desperately try to avoid using the "D" word after the devastating depression in the USA in the 1930s. I think the economic definition is more than two years and unemployment reaching 25% and a decline in GDP in excess of 10% but these parameters change over time. I would say, for the purposes of this discussion, a depression is two years or greater with significant economic consequences.

'Why do you think we will have a deep recession on this occasion?'

the Way

'Mainly for events beyond our control. We have the integration of Eastern Europe into Western Europe and the subsequent collapse of the USSR. Costs will be huge. I drove back from Vienna a few months after Germany started its integration program. I wanted to see the old city of Leipzig, the traditional social centre of Germany before the war. Turning right at Bayreuth over the old border towards Leipzig I was stunned with the speed of renewal of transport infrastructure including bridges. I remember reading the reunification budget proposal thinking it typical of such Government infrastructure projects, grossly understated and likely to spend the amount indicated in the first year. Having driven as far north as Berlin before turning west toward Calais I estimated a figure seven times the budget presented was more reasonable.'

'Why do you think they stated a number so wrong?'

'Normal procedure for Governments. They are using taxpayer funds for these projects. If the German taxpayers knew the real number, there would be major protests on the street, and potential resentment toward their new citizens. Think on the recent proposal for the channel tunnel. As bankers, presented with this prospectus, we knew it was understated by a likely factor of three. They start the project. Came back two years later to ask for another tranche stating it is better to continue rather than waste the original £3billion, and a couple of years later refinance the whole project with another large tranche of funding to complete the project. Standard form for any major Government infrastructure project in the UK.'

'We also have the USA in recession with large unemployment slow to recover and incredible demand for funding to renew crumbling infrastructure. As the largest economy in the World when the USA coughs, the world sneezes.'

'Despite these and several other major economies showing quarterly contraction last year, the British economy continued to grow until just recently. We have just entered the European Exchange Rate Mechanism after Margaret Thatcher was pressed

Week 15

to join by her Europhile ministers. Again, my opinion as a banker, is she set the exchange rate so high that ultimately our participation will break the system. In the meantime, we have an overvalued exchange rate which forces up interest rates to attract foreign investment. This has impacted mortgage rates, which will put many people into negative equity, and even lose their houses. This will push down house prices and significantly increase the price of credit. Banks will either withdraw from construction finance or load additional costs with increased interest rates. This is the component that will affect Aldridge.'

'What can Charles do about it?'

'He has faced recessions before, so he understands the dangers and experienced the impact. A deep recession adds to his problems because of the increased timeline. I expect him to fill his order book for as far out into the future as he can, then scan these orders to identify projects that could potentially be put on hold, seek to renegotiate a lower price, or indeed fail. He will then try to achieve further orders to cover these potential gaps and even go beyond this as you tell me he takes non-refundable deposits to cover design costs which adds to his cash flow.'

'By the way I think you're using the wrong name for such deposits as no deposit is non-refundable in law if no consideration has been delivered. In construction projects it is normal that as an order is agreed Aldridge will have a surveyor evaluate the integrity of the project and define an appropriate solution. The deposit will cover this cost and, as such, be non-refundable should the order be cancelled for any reason. If you're buying a house and decide a survey is appropriate before you agree to buy, the fact that you choose not to buy because of the survey report does not mitigate your need to pay the surveyor. I would suggest you change your language to survey fees.'

'Okay, got that. Now I understand what he was discussing with Jim. Which projects might either defer or cancel over the coming year so he can try to fill these gaps with alternate orders. Smart cookie.'

'In both Charles and Jim, you have two people who know how to survive. The process you observed is risk and impact analysis on your order book. Aldridge has no debt, adequate reserves, and forewarned. Aldridge will survive this recession without business contraction.'

'Have I answered your question?'

'And some. Thanks. Whilst on the subject can you discuss inflation and its likely impacts?'

'Again, this will be a quick overview. Much of your supply and demand study is used to describe the impacts of inflation.'

'A reasonable definition of inflation is a sustained increase in the general price level in an economy. In your world, inflation means an increase in the cost of living as the price of goods and services rise. More pronounced without any corresponding increase in your disposable income. To an economist it's a depletion of the purchase power of the currency which means as time goes by prices continue to rise so you get less for your money.'

'The rate of inflation is a measure of the rate increase in prices of goods and services within the economy and is normally an annualised rate. Good economic stewardship encourages fiscal inflation below 4% as this is a factor in overall growth. Above this will start to generate problems.'

'Inflation can occur when prices rise due to increases in production costs, such as raw materials and wages. A surge in demand for products and services can cause inflation, as consumers are willing to pay more for the product.'

'There are four main types of inflation, categorised by their speed. They are creeping, walking, running, galloping, plus hyperinflation.'

'When the rate of inflation slowly increases over time, we refer to it as creeping inflation. For example, the inflation rate rises from 2% to 3%, to 4% a year. Creeping inflation may not be immediately noticeable, but if the creeping rate of inflation continues, it can become an increasing strain on the economy.'

'When inflation is less than 10%, we refer to it as walking inflation. At this rate inflation is still not a major problem, but when it rises over 4%, Central Banks will be increasingly concerned. Walking inflation may simply be referred to as moderate inflation. Our Central Bank will start to adjust fiscal stimulus around the 4% level to slow the economy and thus inflation.'

'When inflation starts to rise at a significant rate, usually defined as a rate between 10% and 20% a year, we refer to it as running inflation. At this rate, inflation is imposing significant costs on the economy and unabated, can easily start to creep higher. Governments and Central Banks must adjust fiscal policy to stem such increase lest you have a runaway economy and thus the label.'

'An inflation rate of between 20% up to 1000% is referred to as galloping inflation. At this rapid rate of price increases, inflation is a serious problem and will be challenging to bring under control. Some definitions of galloping inflation may be between 20% and 100%. There is no universally agreed definition, but hyperinflation usually implies over 1,000% a year. Whereas established economies prevent such inflation, it can easily rage in developing economies where the fiscal know-how and financial reserves are not available to counter.'

'Hyperinflation is an extreme form of inflation – usually over 1,000% although there is no specific definition. Hyperinflation usually involves prices changing so rapidly, that price hikes become a daily occurrence, and the purchase value of local currency will rapidly decline. We are currently witnessing this in some former USSR countries trying to grapple with their newfound fiscal freedom. And, of course, we are constantly aware of hyperinflation in African and South American countries grappling with incompetent and corrupt Government.

the Way

Hyperinflation heralds the collapse of an economy and its currency, rather than simply a tough fiscal period.'

'There are three main causes of inflation: demand-pull, cost-push, and devaluation.'

'Demand-pull inflation occurs when the overall demand for goods or services increases faster than the production capacity of the economy, i.e. growth is too rapid. If demand exceeds supply, firms will respond by pushing up prices. This inflation is good because economic policymakers feel it is within their power to reduce it.'

'The UK experienced demand-pull inflation during recent years. Fuelled by fast rising house prices, high consumer confidence and tax cuts, the economy has been growing by 5% a year, but this has caused supply bottlenecks and firms have responded by putting up prices. Therefore, we encountered creeping inflation. This coming recession should see a downward pressure on inflation to around a more acceptable 2%.'

'Cost-push inflation results from an increase in the cost of production such as raw materials, wages, taxes and import costs. For example, higher oil prices feeding through into higher costs, or lower exchange rate increasing import prices. This is not healthy inflation.'

'Devaluation is either fiscal realignment of local currency exchange rates with other major currencies, or a loss in confidence by the financial markets in the currency. The impact of this within the economy is increasing cost of imported goods, and a boost to domestic demand.'

'To summarise, modest inflation is a sign the economy is approaching full employment. Whereas inflation may have some costs, at least we get lower unemployment as a result, which means more output and tax revenues.'

'Are we good?'

'Great. Thanks.' A little cheekily, 'Does this mean that when my mortgage payments increased as interest rates increased, I am reducing my demands because my purchase power has reduced?'

He could only smile at her playfulness. 'Go rest that brain of yours. It will need a recharge to become part of the discussion tomorrow with your new knowledge. You must understand the process, so you must participate.'

Chapter 100 – Tuesday

It was after 6pm. Mel was not home. He was now alive to the fact she is late but had not called to say she would be delayed. 6:30, still nothing. Just before 7pm, a police car arrived at the gates. He quickly pressed the entry button.

'Mr Ryder?'

'Yes.'

'Good evening, sir. I believe a Miss Southgate lives here.'

'Yes, she does.'

'She's been involved in a car accident. We believe a truck driver drove her off the road into a gully. Fortunately, a driver travelling the other way saw it happen so immediately alerted us. The lorry driver drove on, but the witness identified the truck was from a local company, so we'll find the driver tomorrow. We've cut her out of her car, and she appears to have no injuries other than a few cuts and bruises, but they have taken her to hospital as a precautionary measure. She gave us your name as next of kin.'

'Thank you, officer. I'll go to the hospital to collect her. Was she unconscious at all?'

'Don't think so. Very dazed and confused, but she could speak to us when we got there.'

'Thank you.'

the Way

He quickly closed the kitchen, got into some clothes, and was on his way.

She was in a bed in casualty when he got there. She looked bedraggled and vacant. He went to her and held her hand. 'I hear you've been playing dodgems on the country lanes. How do you feel?'

Tears started to roll down her cheeks 'I thought he was going to kill me. He forced me off the road.'

A nurse appeared. 'Are you Mr Ryder?'

'Yes. I am.'

'She's badly shaken, and in a little shock, but otherwise no injuries other than cuts and bruises. When she's ready, you can take her home.'

'Thank you, nurse.'

'You hear that. I can take you home. Are you ready?' Her tearful face nodded.

'Do you want me to help you?' Again, she nodded.

He gently got her dressed and helped her to his car.

As soon as he arrived home, he took her coat and sat her in the kitchen with a glass of red wine. He wanted her where he could keep an eye on her, just in case she suffered delayed shock.

As he restarted preparations for dinner, he asked her to relate everything that happened from leaving the factory. He wanted to test her level of concentration. She started to tell him everything blow by blow until he appeared at the hospital. He was happy she was fully compos mentis.

Then he wanted to discover the nature of her injuries. He could see the cut and bruise on her forehead, so asked if she had any other injuries. She had a scratch on her neck where her seatbelt had cut in, and bruising on her ribs and legs, but nothing serious. She made no complaint about her neck as the hospital had already checked for any damage.

As he sat down to eat with her, he wanted to know how she was mentally. 'Now we know the extent of the physical damage, how do you feel?'

Week 15

'I nearly got killed this evening. How do you think I feel?'

'I don't know how you feel. All I know is you didn't get killed and, indeed, the angels took excellent care of you. What flashed through your mind as you realised what was about to happen?'

'It was weird. Everything was in slow motion. It was as though I was watching it happen. Then I was on my side in the gully. The crash had impacted the top of the car because the driver's door was jammed. I heard a knock on my door window. It was a man asking me if I was okay. He told me he would get help and was gone, leaving me suspended there. I just sat there confused.'

'What about now?'

'I'm home but dazed in a detached way. I can't feel any pain, and this confuses me.'

'Did they give you anything in the hospital?'

'Two injections, One in my arm, and the other in my bottom.'

'The one in your arm would be for pain, and the one in your bottom would be tetanus. Standard procedure.'

'I should phone Charles to tell him what happened, and I won't be there tomorrow.'

'Why wouldn't you go to work tomorrow? Your injuries are superficial, your mind is working. I'll provide whatever TLC you require tonight, cleanse you in the morning, and then back into play.'

She was angry 'Someone nearly killed me this evening. What don't you get about that? How long did you take off when your wife died?'

He slapped his hand on the table and then pointed at her 'Not as long as you took for your mum, and no-one died tonight, not even close.'

'Just because I didn't die doesn't mean it didn't scare the hell out of me, and I need time to recover. How long did you take to recover?'

'Two days, alone. I knew if I stayed in the apartment playing out what could have been, or should have been, I would descend into the abyss. And my wife did die. I knew I had to get up, grit my teeth and continue just like the Nat King Cole song where he sings "smile, even though you're breaking".'

She saw his head drop and tears well up in his eyes which then rolled down his cheeks 'I spent my days in the office pretending life would go on as normal, and my nights in Luigi's so I would not be alone. This is when Mama came into play. But I knew I had to go on, no matter how painful.'

He looked up at her 'If you can't deal with such a small setback why are you here? Jim gets up every morning and goes to the factory to help you, despite the fact the factory is killing him. He will die faster because he wants you to succeed, and you tell me a few cuts and bruises count for more. Wake up, girl, and don't tell me about pain.'

By now she could see he was back into his despair, tears freely flowing down his face. This was no theatre; she had really hurt him. She jumped up, went to him, and held him tight to comfort him. She was now crying as she understood what she had said. 'I'm sorry, so sorry. I should not have said those things.'

She turned him so she could sit on his lap so she could cup his face. 'Please come back to me. You're my rock and I need you. I'm just a stupid, inconsiderate woman who needs to wake up and learn from my great master. I'll take your wonderful TLC and will take myself to work tomorrow even if I have to walk.'

Later, curled up in bed together, but before he killed the lights, she looked up at him and held his cheek with her free hand 'Seb, I was so wrong tonight. I'm so sorry for what I said. Please forgive me. I will learn your ways and be thankful you are there for me. I love you so much.'

He kissed her forehead as he killed the lights.

Chapter 101 – Wednesday

He woke her at 6am. Took her for a swim on the basis the water would both sooth and heal her cuts and bruises as well as wake her up. He then gave her a long cleansing shower she now enjoyed so much. She got ready whilst he organised breakfast. She noticed he was dressed.

'You're dressed, are you going somewhere?'

'I'm on chauffer duty today when you're ready.'

'She got up from the table and kissed him with a big smile on her face.'

As Sebastian drove through the factory gates, he noticed he was being followed by Charles. Sebastian stopped outside of the main entrance to the office block while Charles parked in his allotted space next to the entrance.

'Good morning Sebastian, what brings you here?'

'Mel had a car accident last night so I'm on chauffer duty.'

Alarmed, he turned to her 'Are you okay my dear?'

'Just a few cuts and bruises, but my car's a write-off.'

'What happened?'

'A truck driver drove me off the road into a gully.'

'Are you sure you're okay? Why are you here?'

'I'm fine, Charles. Seb picked me up, dusted me off, and I'm ready to go.'

'Okay my dear. But only if you're sure about this. This guy is hard, but I'm more understanding.'

'Thank you, but I'm ready for work.'

'Sebastian, while you're here could I have a word. Park up next to me and come up.'

Whilst Sebastian parked up, Charles had organised coffee for them.

'Sebastian, are you sure she's okay to be here today? She looks somewhat shaken.'

'So would you if they had to cut you out of your car. But the angels were there for her, not so much as a broken finger.

Allowing her to dwell on it will only amplify what could have been. The only relevance is she is fully capable of living another day, and this is what she's doing.'

'Have you ever felt real pain because that lady has suffered much these past few months?'

'More than you could ever imagine Charles, now what did you want to discuss?'

Charles realised he had hit a raw nerve and wanted to quickly move on. 'I want to talk about Mel's progress and would like your input. From my perspective she has come on in leaps and bounds in the past three months, so I'm thinking of rewarding her achievement. Jim is over the moon about how quickly she has slotted into that job. He's so relaxed he doesn't fret anymore about the time away he needs for his hospital check-ups. But will rewarding her now interfere with your efforts?'

'Not at all. A reward at this point in her journey would be good for her motivation. You could start with a car as hers is a right off. Do you have a car scheme?'

'Of course. We have a small army of salesforce on the road throughout the country taking care of our small business, retail, and special domestic projects. If she knows what she wants, I could probably have a car for her in the next few days. That's a fortuitous idea, thanks.'

'I don't know how your salary structure works but if you think her current salary does not reward her contribution, then please feel free to fix it.'

'Thanks. I see you as a formidable contributor to her success so did not want to do anything that would hinder your efforts.'

'Thank you for the consideration. It's much appreciated. We are a team with the same goal, so we must play as such. Is that it?'

Seb was still somewhat miffed at being challenged regarding his care for her, so wanted out of there.

'Yes, and thanks for your input.'

Week 15

Later that morning Charles asked Mary to see if Mel's free and bring some tea.

'What happened last night?'

'I was driving along the lane towards the Chesterfield Road when a lorry came up behind me and started to overtake me. The driver obviously saw someone coming the other way and realised he couldn't complete the pass in time. He drove me off the road to avoid the oncoming car. Thankfully, the car driver saw me in the gully, so stopped to help me. I was trapped in my car until the police cut me out. I was taken to hospital for a check-up, and Seb came to collect me.'

'And he expects you to function today after all of that. What is he thinking?'

'You and I are mere mortals who think this way. He's very much of the ilk if you're not broken, keep moving.'

'He acted very strangely when I asked him if he understood pain. I think I hit a raw nerve.'

She sat up concerned 'What did he say?'

He sensed her concern 'I asked him if he had ever felt real pain. He muttered something like more than I could ever imagine.'

Thinking back to last night 'Oh my God, Charles. If only you knew how much pain he's suffered. Even I don't know the full story yet, as he will not talk about it. It's something to do with the tragic death of his wife. I only know because of what Mama told me. You remember the lady at the restaurant in London. She picked him up all those years ago and brought him back from his despair. It took her two years. Sometimes I can see this pain in his eyes. It haunts him.'

'Jesus, what have I done? I must apologise to him.'

'No Charles, not another word. He would not be happy I've mentioned anything to you. Just let him closeout what you said and move on. He knows you don't know, so will not blame you for what you said. Please leave it. I did not have to come today. He did not force me here. He used his knowledge of real pain to pick me up, dust me off, and put me back on the track. And he's right because now I'm here, I'm fine.'

'I'm so sorry Mel. You have been through so much on this journey of yours. I sometimes think he's too hard on you. But I guess I should trust his judgement because you're clearly happy, and the results are incredible.'

'I really appreciate your concern for me but think about it, Charles. How quickly did he get me back on my feet after my breakup with Phil? And how much care did I get when my mum died? Who else would do this for me? And last night he was applying the same care to check I was okay physically and mentally before trying to pick me up and dust me off. What did I do – mouthed off at him. I said some horrible things to him, one of which really hurt him – unforgiveable.'

'But you were in a state of shock. How did he react?'

'Under the teachings of Sun Tzu my fate would be beheading. He told me to leave if I can't hack it. That snapped me out of my righteous self-pity – not shock. He was doing what he's so good at, but I ignored him. He's my university of life, and I have you to thank for sending me there. I love what he's doing for me, and I'm not ready to leave anytime soon. I must make amends first thing this evening. I need his forgiveness.'

'For what it's worth, his words this morning did not hint at you leaving the program.'

'That's a relief, but he needs to know from me I regret what I said, will never do it again, and seek his forgiveness. He needs to know I understand my folly so we can close this chapter and get back to our routine.'

'Although I'm not about to ask him about his motives, I'm at a loss to understand why he's prepared to put so much effort into your development. What's in it for him? Have you ever asked him this question?'

'Yes, I have. His somewhat vague response is he owes it to someone who put it out for him as a junior exec. I don't know for sure, but he has spoken of an aging exec who really looked out for him – almost fatherly. This exec took a major verbal bashing protecting Seb from his CEO during which he suffered a heart attack from which he died. This man, Bernie was his name, had already told Seb it was his duty to mentor as he had been mentored.'

'Wow. What did he do about it?'

'His initial reaction was anger and revenge. But another exec who looked out for him reminded him he should honour Bernie by behaving as would be expected of him. He did eventual topple the CEO – in style. But this painful event stays with him. There is so much pain in his past.'

She sat pensively, looking at her hands clasped in her lap. Without looking up 'My mum saw something special in Seb. She told him, not me, she only had a short time to live. Probably to prepare him to catch me. And Mama thinks this journey is good therapy for him.'

She paused, 'He also knew from the beginning I would break-up with Phil. He was only surprised how long it took for me to realise this. Boy, did he give me a lesson about rose-tinted spectacles after that night. When he decides to press a point, it becomes permanently embossed in your mind.'

She looked up 'Charles, why don't we leave it that unless I come to you and tell you there's a problem, you just accept I'm fully at peace with what's happening no matter how hard it looks. Is this okay with you?'

'Perfectly. I've made a fool of myself. I'll not interfere again unless you come to me.'

He sat back angry with himself 'There's so much we don't know about that man. But I'm so grateful for what he's doing for both of us. I need to get to know him better.'

She let him reflect for a moment. 'Was there anything you wanted to speak with me about?'

'Oh, yes. It's review time for you, young lady. Very opportune because part of your review includes entitlement to a company car. Have you any idea what you would like? As you can see in the car park, an SUV is the appropriate car for these parts but, within reason, you can have what you want.'

'Wow, thanks. Is it possible to have one like Jim's – a Honda I think?'

'Any particular colour?'

'Don't know what's available.'

'As you have a pressing need for a car, let me call our supplier now to see what he has available.'

He dialled his leased car supplier and spoke with him 'if you like silver or dark blue you can have it on Monday.'

'Dark blue, please.'

He finished the call. 'Good, that's done. Leave your driving licence with Mary to arrange insurance. I've also decided to increase your salary by £5,000 starting the first of November, which I think is next Tuesday.'

'Thank you. What a nice surprise! I didn't expect anything before the end of my six months.'

'My dear, I didn't expect half of what we have already. God only knows how good you'll be at the end of six months. Probably fire me. Now, on your way, I have work to do.'

'Thank you, Charles.'

'Oh, and thanks for the heads up on Sebastian. I'll choose my words more carefully in future. And good luck this evening.'

When he collected her at 5:30 he got out of the driver's seat into the passenger seat. She looked at him quizzically. 'You drive. No-one will bother you in this tank.'

She got in, familiarised herself with the controls, started the engine, and off she went.

'Is this so you can avoid chauffer duty?'

'No. But I do want you to restore any lack of confidence in your driving ability. Easier with someone by your side.'

'*He thinks of everything*', she thought.

As they strolled from the garage to the house, she stopped him, turned him towards her, and hugged him. 'Thank you for everything. You were right, as always, and I was horrible. Have you forgiven me?'

'You screamed at me last night.'

'I know. Wallowing in righteous self-pity. Sometimes you need to do something to know you shouldn't do it. It won't happen again, and I'm desperately sorry I brought your pain into the argument. That was unforgivable. I will make amends for my unacceptable behaviour.'

'Then you are forgiven, but please never bring my wife into an argument again.'

'I won't. I promise you I won't,' she kissed him on both cheeks.

She went off dutifully to the gym, and quickly into the pool as she did find the water soothing. At dinner she told him of her review, new car, and pay rise. She was happy and ready for work. He remembered the police had called. They found the driver and charged him with dangerous driving on the strength of the other driver's Witness Statement. They needed a statement from her, including any injuries. The company would take full responsibility for a settlement with her. They decided to go to the police station that evening to get this out of the way. She gave Sebastian full authority to negotiate a settlement with the company.

She went to his bed again. This is where she wanted to be; warm and safe.

Chapter 102 – Thursday

She realised the downside of sleeping with him was being hauled out of bed at 6am in the morning. She now appreciated a swim in the morning, but an hour later would be appreciated even more. The upside was the cleansing shower of which she would never tire. It started the day with such a wonderful feeling.

He went with her to the factory but let her drive. He wanted her confidence fully restored before driving alone again.

Likewise, he collected her in the evening, but again he let her drive.

When seated at dinner 'You have an offer on your flat. What sum would you accept?'

'Probably around £160,000, maybe as much as £170,000 in the current market. What's the offer?'

'So you'd probably accept £185,000 for a quick sale?'

'Wow, you bet. Who's the buyer?'

'No doubt one of Richard's clients' as it is a cash purchase. He obviously can see more value, probably in the rental market, and no doubt he'll manage the rental. He makes good money on both sides.'

'If it's worth more, why wouldn't I ask for a better offer?'

'Sun Tzu. You have a win-win scenario. You don't know how to achieve the additional value. That's his skill. But you exceed your expectations on price – that's also his skill. He more than satisfies your expectations, and he can further increase his own. That's successful business, and why I like Richard who makes around £200,000 per year from me but increases my value by more than five times that amount. We're both happy, as you should be.'

'What about my mother's house?'

'You mother's property needs some work to achieve full value, so a little more time needed. Don't worry. Richard is no slouch. He'll convert that property to money as fast as possible, but at the right price. Shall I ask him to send up the papers on your flat? The deal can be settled by the end of next week.'

'Sure. And please thank Richard for me.'

Week 15

Dinner over he detected she still wasn't quite ready to start school. 'Any other issues you would like to discuss before we get back to our schedule?'

'Could we just go to the living room and chat tonight about whatever comes to mind? I need to feel human again. The past two days have been a little autopilot. Is this okay?'

'Sure. I can see you're a little the day after the day before. Before we do, could I ask for some feedback on the order book decisions on Tuesday.'

'Sorry. Forgot about that. Thanks to you, I now fully understand how they categorise orders for risk of project failure or delay. Charles is applying what he calls an overlay of the order book by 20% to 30%. Although he is very aware of the recession risks, he wants to maintain the integrity ethos of Aldridge. At this level of overlay he can ensure if every order does go ahead, he can use overtime and weekend working to ensure delivery of every order on its scheduled date. Aldridge is known for its surety of delivery, and he wants to maintain this reputation even if it costs in the short-term.'

'The more I understand Aldridge the more I respect Charles. He is a true business survivor. Although you won't learn much about corporate culture at Aldridge, you will certainly understand much about business. You go make yourself comfortable while I clear dinner. What would you like to drink?'

'As clearing up is a normal human activity, let me help you.'

Chapter 103 – Friday

Mel was now back in her stride, feeling happy with life. The cuts and bruises were fading with the memories of that chilling event. The sale of her apartment meant, after repaying her mortgage, she would have nearly £80,000 available as a deposit

the Way

on a new apartment. She was even happier she would not need to find the funds to buy another car, as she did not expect much back from her insurers for her written-off car. More importantly, she was at peace with Sebastian. Life was good, and it was Friday. She pondered what they would do during the weekend although top of her priorities was atonement for her behaviour, albeit she could not think of a suitable form.

These questions danced around in her head during interludes between her daily tasks. Jim was not there, so the occasional song was not out of order.

Charles checked in with her after lunch to see if she was alright; but didn't need to ask. He caught her singing her way through a job spec with a big smile on her face. They chatted for a few minutes about Jim and how she was coping without him. He left for the day, realising any concerns he may have had were unfounded. His young apprentice was in control of the situation.

When she got home, he had a special dinner for her, and then took her to their local pub where many of the tennis club meet on a Friday evening. He thought a little social intercourse would likely freshen her for the tasks ahead.

Chapter 104 – Saturday

After helping with the shopping, she went shopping herself. She wanted to buy something for Seb for helping her through this past week. She had been nasty to him, albeit he was showing her how to quickly recover from her accident. But what do you buy someone who can buy whatever he wants?

She engaged in much window shopping, trying to seek ideas. *'Okay girl, this is not working. Need a strategy. Think team. Think General. Think army.'*

Week 15

She saw it. A T-shirt with a Bruce Springsteen concert logo on it and who was universally known as 'The Boss'. *'That's it. I'll get us a matching team shirt and shorts with The Boss on his and Student on mine. Perhaps Sage would be better for him. We can use them as house clothes. Now to find a shop that prints soccer shirts.'*

Upon arriving home, she couldn't wait to show their team wear. 'Our new house kit. Do you like it? I thought we needed a symbolic team Ryder. Would be good when we're working on something together.'

Chapter 105 – Sunday

They were walking around the grounds to get air before lunch and then their afternoon activities.

'Seb, when is your birthday?'

'26th January.'

'And how old will you be on the 26th January?'

'Fifty-eight.'

'Would you mind if I organised a party for your birthday, maybe a dinner party?'

'Here, or somewhere else?'

'Not sure yet. I'll need to give it some thought now I know I'll still be here.'

'Please remember I value my privacy, so be selective.'

'For someone so accomplished you are very young to be retired. You have so much to offer. Would it be too intrusive to ask why you retired and moved here?'

'You're the first person to ask me so directly so I don't have a pat answer. In the conventional sense of retirement, I don't consider myself retired. I have active investment and trading portfolios, I write articles and books, and I keep myself informed. As for being employed, probably the best description would be a sabbatical of undetermined duration, although I have no desire to be employed, nor the need. I've given so much of myself over the years, but not reaped a meaningful life. I need time to analyse what I want from my life before it's too late to pursue it. What's the point in just making more money when I have no life to invest in?'

She was stunned by his openness. He was not looking at her, just gazing into space as he formulated his thoughts. This was a new version of him. He was sharing an intimate analysis of his loneliness. She felt disturbed, but privileged, he would share such thoughts with her, thoughts she knew were not expressed elsewhere.

'Surely you had a life when you were a banker, lots of social events beyond the reach of urchins like me. You must know many influential and interesting people.'

'That was Sebastian Ryder, executive banker. I'm talking about Sebastian Ryder, person. After Kate died, I didn't maintain much of a relationship with my family or her family, and now my parents have passed away. My brother lives in Australia – haven't spoken to him since the funeral of my father, and that was after some twenty years. Like you, I have no family around me. I've not found anyone to replace Kate, not that I tried. So, I'm taking time out to figure out what I want from the remainder of my life before engrossing myself into anything that might interfere with this process.'

'Doesn't that make me a distraction as I certainly consume much of your time?'

With a smile on his face 'It's true. You do take far more of my time than I initially anticipated. But you also allow me to nurture you, exposing me to the more human elements of interaction. With you, I feel somehow useful. I share your successes, and your sorrow. I find myself caring about another human being – something I haven't done in many years. It's an interesting experience sharing your journey. It gives me a sense of purpose and, on the whole, you're a joy to be with. The only concern I have is your age. You are at a crossroads where you need to

Week 15

make serious choices between career and family. I think I got that balance wrong so I don't want to influence you in a direction you may later regret.'

'Perhaps I can put your mind at rest on that issue. This journey of mine has released much frustration in my career and certainly halted a calamitous mistake regarding Phil. And it's but a short six months that will expand my horizons far beyond any expectations, presenting opportunities and choice. I'm not too old to achieve any lifestyle balance I choose, so please don't let this concern you. I'm very happy with my choices these past months, and to share these months with you has been a truly wonderful privilege.'

He was now looking at her. She decided to be silent, to allow the impact of her words to sink in.

'But you've taken so many knocks these past months – your marriage plans, your mother, even your accident. Do you ever feel fate is testing your resolve?'

'Possibly. But if I look at the positives, I'm well out of my marriage plans, my mum is back with my dad, and I get my first brand new car tomorrow. More importantly, you've made me more resilient – useful when you don't have a family support network around you. I don't expect Jim to survive the six months. He tries hard to hide the seriousness of his illness from me, but I see the pain in his eyes. I've grown very fond of him, so it will really hit me if he dies on me. I'll certainly need a big shoulder that day.'

'I'll be there for you. But I'm concerned the potential result of these continuing knocks will make you so resilient and self-contained you lose your human touch.'

'Do you mean like fortress Ryder?' She leaned towards him 'Seb, when I first came here you were very much a self-contained fortress. The relationship was very proper. You took this challenge very seriously, but you kept yourself remote. You can be a real hermit. Then something changed. After the faux pas by myself and Charles last week, I started to think about our journey to determine when the armour started to crack, and Sebastian's big heart started to reveal itself. At first, I thought it was around my mum's passing. But it was before then. It was the night I broke off with Phil. When you came to the car, you didn't frog-march me in, give me your rose-tinted specs lecture, and send me to my room telling me to man up. You carried me in, tenderly bathed my face, took me to your bed and held me in your arms all night. That must have been one uncomfortable night for you. Then the shower, what a lovely shower. I'll never forget the first time. You didn't just bathe me; you emulated the water caressing away my sorrow. Such care. Then when my mum died you were the perfect definition of a true friend, even to the point when you were unsure what to do you introduced Mama in to help. Mama told me she noticed a big change in you. She saw the wonderful, big-hearted human being who now takes care of me. There is no possibility you will create a fortress Mel because you won't let it happen. Sure, I'll become resilient on the field of play as I need to be, but once off the field I'll revert to me.'

He looked at her with stern eyes 'Analysing our relationship, are we? I only respond to the circumstances as I see them, and I do what I think is best for you to achieve your goal. I've had some lucky breaks to help me such as Carmen and Mama, but I must maintain the mentor and student discipline if we are to succeed.'

'I completely understand and accept your position. I was merely trying to placate your concerns and express why. I think we're both on a journey, and I only hope you profit as much as I will. You're a good man and deserve the life you seek.'

Week 16

Chapter 106 – Monday

She was in high spirits this morning. It was a cold, dank morning, but she was looking forward to receiving her new car. It would be her first brand new car and liked the idea of being the first person to drive it albeit she realised it wouldn't get to the factory on its own.

'Only need my chauffer this morning James. You may have the afternoon off.'

'Thank you, my lady, most kind.'

He liked her in her playful mood. He also knew he could forget schooling tonight. She will reasonably be studying her car User Manual. Even if she did not do this naturally, she would be actively encouraged to do so. And, in any event, Carmen was due to arrive this evening.

They both arrived within a few minutes of each other. Mel was grinning like a Cheshire cat as she admired her new car. Carmen was given a full inspection before both entered the kitchen chatting. They said their greetings to Seb and dispersed to their rooms to get ready for their gym, swim, and sauna session where they caught up on events since they last saw each other. He was somewhat bemused by their behaviour, but he was happy they enjoyed each other's company. Mel needed female friends who were career orientated, and Carmen was a good start.

At 7:30 they both returned to the kitchen, still chatting, ready for dinner. 'My dear ladies, could I interrupt you both for a moment to ask if either of you would like an aperitif before dinner.'

'Not for me, my darling. Just some of your lovely wine will be sufficient.'

the Way

'Same for me, please,' as they sat and resumed their conversation.

Once he sat down for their starters 'You ladies haven't stopped talking since you arrived.'

'My darling, much has happened these past weeks. The sad loss of Mel's mother, and I must meet Mama. Then we have her car accident, the theatre, and the opera. Carmen is surprised we make dinner on time! And most of all my Mel is in good spirit, which means my darling Sebastian is taking good care of her.' She lifted her glass of wine 'Salut dear Sebastian. You are a good man.'

Mel lifted her glass 'here, here.'

'And for you my darling, what happened to cause the loss of your Prime Minister, Margaret Thatcher. Must be a terrible blow for you. We must discuss, but not this evening as we celebrate my darling Mel.'

They chatted some more, including Mel's salary increase and her new company car. He had a thought about remuneration. He knew Carmen had her children whilst she was working so her input into this discussion could prove useful.

'Ladies, this would be an opportune moment to discuss the subject of executive remuneration as I think Carmen can add much regarding how a woman maintains her standing in her career whilst having children. Are you agreeable to such a discussion?'

'My darling, you lead the discussion and Carmen will help where she can.'

'Executives do not get paid by the hour, or for a 9 – 5 working-week. They get paid for devising and implementing ideas and solutions, which add to the value of their company. Theirs is a strategic function.'

'There are two components to executive pay: street value, and compensation for valuable contribution, usually in the form of a bonus or share options. Street value is how much you're worth in the market and defines salary package. It's fundamentally important an executive understands their current worth, and the best source of this information is head-hunters.'

'Valuable contribution occurs when you devise a strategy, product, or solution that adds real and significant value to your company. The rule of thumb is that it is reasonable to expect around 10% of such value after deducting operational costs, including depreciation of any capital component. Another contributor to bonus is performance. If, by your efforts, serious value is realised, you would reasonably expect to be rewarded. Any questions?'

The ladies looked at each other, shook their heads as acceptance.

'What happens when a female executive wants to bear children? Most countries now have legislation that compels companies to support female staff with statutory minimum levels of maternity leave, thus protecting their employment rights. For non-executive staff this is generally not a problem as no company should have dependency on any one member of staff so temporary cover can be organised. Quite rightly, a mother is encouraged to nurture her new-born child through its first months. This is not so easy with a female executive who has direct responsibility for a given corporate function. I have seen this play out in different ways from expecting the woman to suspend her career, be substituted, or encouraged to minimise time away from the office which means foregoing statutory rights, and more importantly, essential bonding with her child. Carmen, as you had both your children whilst an executive, how did it work for you?'

'Ah. Carmen sees the point you try to make. Having children creates a problem with men executives, even though they father such children. They take the view an exec has no time for such things. I think you say show must go on. My career as an executive was established before I decided it was time to have my children. As soon as Carmen knows she is pregnant, she recruits an assistant; I think you call it deputy. And Carmen is smart enough to recruit a female assistant who is likely to want children in a few years, so little chance she can replace Carmen. Also, she is more understanding about childbirth.'

They all laughed at this shrewd thinking.

'My assistant is trained by me to deal with my day-to-day issues, but not my strategic role. Carmen works until she must stop for birth. She takes three months at home, but on the telephone for critical issues. Then she works from home but attends the office for critical tasks until she feels able to hand her child responsibilities to a child nurse but still only attends the office when necessary. My lovely husband also takes responsibility to help with our son. After six months it is invisible Carmen has a young child.'

'What about your second child?'

'Carmen had demonstrated continuity of her duties to the company, so no problem. Interestingly, our chief executive had a bad car accident putting him in hospital for four months and then convalescence for three months. He did work from his bed just as with Carmen, with no problem to the company. As you say, my darling, we executives get paid for performance, not attendance. If a man can function from his bed, so can woman.'

Sebastian turned to Mel. 'Any questions?'

'Smart move with an assistant. Ticks all the boxes for continuity. I have much to learn from you.'

'My dear Mel, as my darling Sebastian will tell you, for every situation you must consider the potential consequences and take steps to mitigate the risks. This is especially true for woman.'

Chapter 107 – Tuesday

Carmen had already left when Mel arrived for breakfast.

Week 16

'There's a concert in the Royal Albert Hall on Saturday I would like to attend. Would you like to come with me?'

'My master. If you would like me to come with you anywhere just tell me where, when and dress code and I'll be there. What's the concert?'

'Georg Solti conducting the London Symphony Orchestra and choir.'

'Is this special?'

'Yes, it is. A rare privilege to have him conduct in London these days.'

'What music will we hear?'

'Stravinsky's Fire Bird, and Beethoven's 9th Symphony.'

'Don't know the Stravinsky, but isn't the Beethoven the "Ode to Joy"?'

'It's part of it, yes.'

'Sounds great. When do we go?'

'If you could leave the office around 3pm on Friday, we could get an early train, and dinner with Mama.'

'Got a better idea. I desperately need to meet some of my architect clients to sell them on our support program. I'll phone around to see who's available. We could leave first thing Friday morning. If I needed to see anyone on Monday, would this be a problem for you?'

'No. I have things I want to do in London, so no problem.'

'Great. I want to drive down in my new car. Need the business miles to keep the benefits tax down.'

'Good morning, Charles. Seb wants to go to a concert at the Royal Albert Hall on Saturday so I'm thinking of going down Friday morning and coming back Monday evening so I can meet with my architect clients to sell them down on our support program. Is this okay with you?'

'Sounds like a good idea. What's the concert?'

'George Solti and the LSO. Stravinsky, and Beethoven's 9th.'

'Solti's in town?' He hit the intercom to Mary. 'See if you can get me tickets for the Solti concert in London on Saturday. I'll pay twice face value.'

She was taken aback 'You like Solti that much?'

'Mel, when conductors like Bernstein or Solti are in town, nothing else is important.'

Mary called back, 'All sold out weeks ago.'

His face dropped. She could see the disappointment.

'Give Seb a call. He has a man who gets him the best tickets at short notice. I think they are embassy reserved seats. He got us the best seats for Les Misérables and the opera when we were there for my mum's funeral.'

He was straight on the phone. 'Good morning, Sebastian. Mel has told me about the Solti concert on Saturday. Do you know where I might get tickets?' He listened 'price is not a problem. Two tickets if you can get them.'

'He'll call back in a minute. Would it be helpful if I came with you to any of these meetings?'

'A commission has just been awarded to Andre Simmons to design two adjacent properties in the City. This would be a great opportunity to really sell our technical support services, and to inform him of the polymer material. Your presence could be valuable, so they know this has support at the very top of Aldridge.'

'Set it up.' His phone rang. 'Sebastian, you're a genius. Thanks so much.'

'Fantastic. He has two seats next to you. Edna will be over the moon. Go set up your meetings and let me know so I can plan our weekend.'

She strolled back via Mary's office. 'What is it with these men? Is Solti really worth all that money?'

'Are you going my dear?'

'Yes, and Seb got tickets for Charles.'

In a knowing tone, 'Then you come tell me what you think when you get back.'

Week 16

After dinner Carmen was visibly agitated. 'Carmen has a problem at the factory. Can I seek help from my dearest friends?'

'Of course, you can. What's the issue?'

'We are refurbishing one of our buildings to produce our new product range. We have twelve maintenance workers covering plumbing and electrical. They are behind schedule and uncooperative. They refuse overtime and weekend working unless we concede to outrageous pay demands. They hold Carmen to ransom, and Carmen does not tolerate such behaviour. In Germany I can appeal to the Worker's Council at our factory to regulate these people. But here I do not know how your trade unions work. Carmen would like to know how to deal with this situation.'

Sebastian was first to speak 'Are these workers employed by the company, or are they contractors?'

'They are employed by us as we have three production lines here to maintain.'

'Is the technology involved special to your company, I mean do you need to protect this technology from your competitors?'

'No.'

He turned to Mel, 'How does Aldridge manage routine maintenance and upgrades?'

'We only have four maintenance people who take care of the routine problems. For major works we outsource to a local company who provide whatever resources are required; usually outside of normal working hours.'

'Is this outsource company reliable?'

'They have been with Aldridge for years so really know the factory, and how we work. I've not heard any complaints about them.'

'Is there any specific logic to why you have four maintenance people?'

'Yes. First, they work in pairs for safety reasons. And when the factory is very busy working long hours on shift, each pair covers different shifts.'

the Way

'So Mel, how would you approach this issue using your knowledge of Sun Tzu?'

'The obvious first step would be to behead them all.' They all laughed. 'Today's equivalent would be to fire all of them and seek an outside contractor to complete this work. But you may inflame the trade union who would likely call for a strike causing disruption to the entire production. It sounds to me like poor planning from the start, so it's time to re-evaluate your plan to complete this line.'

Sebastian turns to Carmen, 'Do you accept Mel's evaluation of your situation?'

'Yes, my darling, and I would really enjoy beheading them as well as our project planner for creating this problem, but what does Carmen need to do to finish this refurbishment on time?'

'Next step, Mel'.

'These maintenance workers need to understand the error of their ways. They think they have the whip hand, so we need to change their position, but avoid conflict. Putting them on notice but allowing them to continue with this project could cause more problems. I would suggest the project is temporarily halted until you can find a contractor prepared to complete it turnkey. This lets the union know the demands of these maintenance workers will not be met. Dispense with the existing maintenance workers, either back to the other production lines, or let someone else in the company, not connected with this project, fire them as surplus to requirement.'

'Not bad. But how do you educate the ongoing general maintenance people about this new production line if they are not involved with the installation?'

'I guess you need to recruit them now and let them work with the contractors.'

'How are we doing, Carmen? Does Mel's proposal sound like a solution to you?'

'I can see the logic my darling but how long will this take? I have deadlines I must meet.'

Week 16

'Back to you, Mel.'

'Okay. I can telephone Carmen tomorrow with the name of our contractor firm, and our senior contact there. Carmen needs to stamp her authority on the suspension of the project, including the maintenance workers and the project manager. Dumping the project manager weakens the hand of the trade union in any protest. I would avoid engaging with the trade union; just reassign the maintenance worker to wherever the project manager found them. Let someone else deal with them. Then it is down to how fast Carmen can conclude a deal that works for her.'

'So, my dear, you suggest I stop my project tomorrow morning, dispense with my project manager who I do not like so this will be easy. You say I can avoid problems with these trade unions if I reassign the maintenance people back to other parts of the factory. This is good. Then I ask your contractor to complete this installation. I think I have to extend my trip until this is done.'

Mel chipped in 'The best deal with the contractor is installation and ongoing major refurbishment or installation of further lines.'

'Thank you, my dear. Continuity is important.'

Sebastian felt an additional parameter would be useful. 'Could I add one small detail to this solution which could prove positive. It would be reasonable to suspect within these twelve maintenance workers there are only two or three ringleaders, and the remainder are merely towing the line. When they realise their demands are not acceptable, and reassignment will probably mean lay-off you may find four of these people very pliant upon reflection. You could bring these four back on the understanding that should they comply with your wishes, they will be the permanent maintenance crew for your new line. Putting them under the direction and control of the installation contractor during installation will also allow them to see how much harder life as a contractor is with long, demanding hours, including weekends and nights, than as an employed maintenance worker. They will learn their lesson well and give you no further trouble.'

Carmen put her hand on Mel's arm, 'This is the hard man speaking. He deals his pain, so you do not forget. Learn well my dear, as Carmen will surely enjoy this part.'

Chapter 108 – Wednesday

Upon arrival at the office, Mel appraised Charles of Carmen's problem. He agreed to call the contractor himself to put a good word in for Aarden. Mel informed Carmen with contact details.

The conversation last evening had left her thinking how little she knew about the maintenance structure in the workshops. It was time to sit with Tom and fully understand this valuable and necessary function, chastising herself for her lack of diligence. *'Assumption is the mother of failure'*, she thought to herself. *'This will be part of my job description so a need to know. Sorry, my master. I will learn.'*

Over dinner Carmen was animated whilst telling how she enjoyed disposing of her project manager and maintenance workers. She had met with the contractor in the afternoon. She was happy the existing Project technical drawings are good enough to bid. She should have an outline bid tomorrow. The Managing Director of the UK operation was at peace with her approach. So far all was going well.

Week 16

Chapter 109 – Thursday

Carmen arrived back at Merten that evening with a large bouquet of flowers. Mel and Sebastian were already in the kitchen talking as her mum's house was under offer at £360,000 and needed action.

Carmen handed the flowers to Mel, 'Thank you my dear. You saved my project.'

'There're beautiful, thank you. But it wasn't me. Seb led me to a solution to which he then applied his superior skills.'

'Ah, my dear. It was not my darling Sebastian who asked Charles Aldridge to personally ask the owner of the contractor to prioritise my project and to treat us as they would Aldridge. This means Carmen can return home tomorrow with an outline proposal, including full project management. My project should recommence in 7 – 10 days and complete on-time. They will project manage until Carmen can find a new manager. Carmen owes Mel, and Carmen will not forget this. Let us away to the gym, and we talk more in the sauna.'

Sitting in the sauna Mel wanted to discuss an article about the gender gap in the workplace and women trying to reach the Boardroom. Carmen explained there are probably differences between the UK and Germany, thus probably better to discuss this with Sebastian after dinner.

Dinner was essentially finished. Mel decided she wanted to set the agenda for tonight before Seb could impose his. 'I read an article today about gender issues in business, the gender pay gap, and why women find it difficult to get into the Boardroom. I mentioned this to Carmen in the sauna. She suggests this is a topic of discussion in which you should be involved. As both of you have such experience, could I get your views on this issue.'

Carmen looked directly at Sebastian, waiting for him to respond. 'I'm not sure I want to go there. Every time I have this conversation with women I've been shot down as a sexist, which

the Way

is not true, but the reaction clearly demonstrates one of the issues. And I'm outnumbered at this table.'

'And what might that be, my darling?'

'That women can take a general objective discussion and make it personal.'

'My darling, you must explain what you mean by such a statement as I certainly do not take comments personally unless they are intended to be personal.'

'Carmen, you now have the experience to know how to take care of yourself on the field of play, but are you seriously telling me that when you first started to climb the executive ladder you did not take objective critique personally?'

'I see your point, but I have experienced men do the same.'

'And how long did they survive on the ladder?'

'Point taken my darling.' She turned to Mel, 'My dear, we can only have this discussion if we are on the field of play. Is this acceptable to you?'

'At this boot camp I get knocked down every time I stray into personal mode when in play. No problem.'

'Ah, this boot camp. I love this expression "boot camp". For this discussion, my darling, we are in boot camp so no emotional or personal content. Please proceed as you have most experience at this table, and you are a man.'

Mel chuckled to herself as she witnessed her master uncomfortable with a subject being pressed upon him by a woman. *'Can't wait to see where this is going.'*

'Okay, ladies, let's start with the gender issue as relates to women engaging as executives in the Boardroom. I'm not about to discuss gender issues relating to other female workers or pay gaps.'

'The terms of reference I hold dear are:

1. The only people who engage in the Boardroom of a mature company should be there on merit, and merit alone. No cronyism. Note the gender-neutral tone of this statement.

Week 16

2. No company should have any legislation imposed upon it which forces women onto their Board. This alienates the very idea that a Board should consist of the very best resources available.'

'We will contain this discussion to women who have the capability to make it to the top, all things being equal.'

'Are we good so far?'

They both nodded in agreement.

'Now to some observations about potential women executives.'

'Women tend to be more agreeable than men – not a helpful consideration in combat. Men will unite towards a common cause without the need for friendship whereas women prefer to unite in friendship. Think back to *My Fair Lady* where Higgins and Pickering are making such comparison citing *Would you mind if I forgot your birthday?* On the field of play, nothing is personal. Focus on the goal.'

'So-called power women back at their desk 3-weeks after giving birth may look good but have forgotten that business is a game. Having children is probably the most important role of their lives and carries far more responsibility. As women are the only gender capable of having children, and this role is important, planning for such an absence is eminently more acceptable than the potential chaos of return to the office during early motherhood. But don't expect men to understand how to plan such an absence. Women must be pro-active in presenting a reasonable plan that is eminently workable.'

'Attachment to a young family can be a distraction. If the game goes into overtime, women want to leave the field of play. Even if they stay, they may not fully focus. This issue is identified by Sun Tzu when selecting people to go to foreign lands who have significant family commitments at home.'

Carmen interceded. 'Bernd would have undertaken my pregnancies if it were possible.'

the Way

He decided to ignore this comment lest he lose his thought process.

'The accepted rules of behaviour in a Boardroom are laid down by men, but not because they were men. They are codes of conduct that maintain a dignified environment in an otherwise combative game. Think of a Court of Law. The professionals involved must, at all times, maintain respect and dignity for all involved, no matter how disagreeable.'

'Do you both understand what this means?'

Mel was first to respond. 'I remember this conversation on the train to London that day we went to buy business clothes. Think clan, not man.'

'Exactly. The Boardroom comprises a clan adhering to a common code of conduct. A female barrister emulates the clan dress code and complies totally with the code of conduct within a Court because it's there to ensure a civilised process, not to indulge men. Scottish clans have the perfect clan culture – both men and women where a kilt from the same tartan.'

'Therefore, a woman cannot assume when she joins a Board, the code of conduct can be changed to suit her needs. Such a process is organic. The clan concept must prevail, and she must learn to be a fully agreeable clan member. No special dispensation; no special provisions.'

'Let me give you an example that may sound silly to you, but I witnessed it happening. I sat on a Board where there was also a female executive. Up until then, she was completely accepted as a capable member. At a Board meeting she remembered it was the birthday of another executive, so wished him happy birthday. You could feel the hostile reaction around the table. In that one act she had reduced her status from being an executive who happened to be a woman, to a female playing executive. Traditionally no-one at a Board meeting would introduce any personal element into the discussion. Outside in the corridor, person to person is okay, but not in a Boardroom. It may sound petty, but nothing is personal on the field of play.'

My darling, are you saying we should not make personal comments in the Boardroom? What about if I like the new suit of a fellow director? Is it so wrong to make comment?'

'Let me answer by telling you about a situation I encountered whilst giving a lecture about my management style at a business school to an audience comprising probably 40% female students. Somehow, during the question time, the subject of female staff came into the discussion. A female student asked for my view of women in the workplace, and how many women as a percentage of my staff I employed, and in what roles. I could remember I had 3 female traders in my dealing room of 140 traders. I could remember this because it was very unusual to have female traders. Dealing rooms are not pleasant places for women. They are not referred to as a bear pit for nothing.'

'When I thought about the operations staff, I knew I had several female staff but embarrassed I had no idea about numbers or percentage. I could state there was no pay gap as everyone was paid on merit, and they all received an equal share of their bonus pool. The student was not impressed.'

'Afterwards I thought about it and concluded that why should I know? Operations was my *family* of resources collectively delivering for me. When I walked into the office in the morning, I was not overtly conscious of the gender differential. I remember shortly after creating this operation there were grumbles amongst some male staff about their limited dress code compared to the females. After due consideration, I compiled a dress code for both males and females to better balance the floor.'

Mel piped in, 'Bet that went down well. A man laying down a dress code for women. Probably deemed sexist.'

'You said you would not make this personal. This is the problem with these discussions. When have I differentiated between male and female? To me they are resources held in the same regard until they make it gender personal.'

the Way

Carmen, putting her hand on Mel's arm, realising he was right, 'My darling, what was the reaction to your dress code?'

'I expected problems, but they generally accepted it. I was confronted by one of the younger females stating my dress code did not allow her to express herself.'

'How did you respond?'

'I suggested the best way to express herself in the office was through the quality of her work. We were not in the business of the mating game. If she needed to change to go somewhere after work, we had a changing room and shower at her disposal.'

'My goodness. You had such facilities available to staff?'

'We had a changing room, shower, and equipped kitchen. On the occasions people such as IT needed to work through the night, or at weekends, they needed these facilities. At the weekend, the City is mostly closed so no cafes, restaurants, or even sandwich bars available. Staff needed to eat and be able to refresh if working long hours. Remember, nurture your troops. When they put themselves out for you, you must ensure their welfare.'

'Wow. You really did look after your people.'

'The first bank I achieved executive status was very much built on reciprocity. The then President of the bank, and my greatest mentor, introduced me to Sun Tzu and very much followed the art of war philosophy. With the cost to fit out my first exec office, you could buy a house. And I had a work of art on my office wall worth more than the office building. The bank had a substantial art collection. Once a year we could go to the basement archive and chose a picture for the following year. Security was tight, but it impressed clients.'

Mel, realising her folly, wanted back in the game. 'You love that word – reciprocity. You use it so often.'

'I first heard this word working on syndicated loans. If a bank asked us to join with them to offer a syndicated loan, we would reciprocate by preferentially inviting them to join with our offerings. This list of preferential banks was called the

Week 16

Reciprocity List. It so encapsulates everything Sun Tzu stood for. You help me, I'll help you. Don't attack me, I won't attack you. You deliver for me; I'll deliver for you. The president of the bank used to refer to us as intrapreneurs and ensured we were well nurtured. Both Roux brothers, the master chefs, controlled our kitchens, one for the exec and guest dining rooms, and the other for the staff dining room. Loyalty to the bank was ensured. But you only survived if you reciprocated by delivering.'

Anyway, ladies, we stray from our subject. Carmen, you have been a Board member for some 8 years; you rose through the ranks, and you had 2 children along the way. Has anything I've said resonated with your experience?'

'My darling, most interesting. You have so beautifully illustrated observations I have not before fully appreciated. I certainly remember the first time I went to a Board meeting. I was very proud to be the first woman on this Board. I arrived dressed very much as a woman and jubilant at my promotion. Carmen quickly learn. You are right. Board meetings are very formal and dignified, and I love your clan idea. Carmen is a member of a Board, not a woman amongst men. I like.'

She turned to Mel, 'This is good. We speak more about this in the sauna because Carmen can now see other things you need to know.'

Turning back to Sebastian, 'You should not think your point about recognising birthdays as silly. Remembering someone's birthday is not a moment of joy if the other person does not remember yours. It is more a moment of endured embarrassment for both. So I now understand that nothing in the Board room should be personal. And I love your comparison with women in the higher Courts. The similarities are obvious, and women are already accepted as equals in that role, even as Judges. Brilliant.'

'Would you also agree that the subject of remuneration is a not an issue? Execs achieve their market value regardless of gender. And they should share equally in the spoils of success.'

'Yes, my darling, this is correct.'

'Would you also agree that transposing gender with ethnicity is also equally valid?'

She thought for a moment, 'Yes, you are right. Just think clan and all such issues do not exist.'

'Good. Have I reasonably responded to your question?'

Mel was quick to respond. 'Surely all corporate Boards do not function as you suggest.'

'There are always exceptions with the common denominator being poor leadership, or dictatorial control. Avoid such companies. I was self-representing a case to a County Court which clearly offended the presiding judge. He thought it improper and beneath his high office that I should choose to represent myself. I requested a specific process in law be accepted. He told me it was his Court, and he would decide on what process should be adopted, and which would favour the opposing barrister.'

'What did you do?'

'I quietly and respectfully reminded him the Court belonged to the people, and he is appointed by the people to honour the law of the land with process that provides a fair and considered hearing. Even in the Courts you will find exceptions and thus why we have appeal courts.'

'Love to have been a fly on the wall that day.'

'My darling, in Germany we are obliged to employ what you might call disadvantaged and disabled people. Does this exist in the UK and where do they fit in your army?'

'Perhaps I should state two points of reference regarding my six months with Mel. In all my teachings I am only referring to frontline staff, your army who accumulate the revenues for the business. I use the word accumulate to include every process needed to convert a sale into income in the bank. When I first entered banking, there was a culture of front office and back office to define this army – us and them in all regards of treatment, remuneration and standing. In the securities business this was absurd but used to ensure the front office shared far more of the spoils than the back office. It took me some time to break this culture, but as with all re-education into the *family* process, it took a demonstration to show the front office they were irrelevant without the back office.'

'Is this another example of don't tell me, show me philosophy? Please tell Carmen as this can be valuable.'

'Traders and salespeople think the trade is job done, profit made. This is not remotely correct. In my case, I assemble the traders and salespeople with one of their trade tickets in my hand. I then ask anyone to step forward who can complete the settlement process through to funds or assets into our corporate account. Securities settlements is a complex process, and most traders and salespeople have no idea of this process. Therefore, I proffer the trade ticket in my hand is but a piece of paper of no value until someone with the necessary skills can convert it into value. The securities business has anomalies requiring great skill to navigate. A highly skilled settlement function – the back office – usually makes the difference between profit and loss. This is why both traders and settlements need to be in close proximity and integrated as a single business function unit. Thus, why settlements have a performance-related bonus pool as with the traders.'

'An extreme example of this would be a buy and a sell of a security with a paper profit. But the trader is either unaware or ignores potential illiquidity in this security, which will make these two trades difficult to settle on their settlement dates. As margins on such trades are relatively small, the cost of funding to carry these trades through to natural settlement can easily be more than the profit generated. A skilful settlements person will immediately know of these difficulties and has an armoury of tactics to minimise the costs to settle. In this case should the trader book the profit in their bonus pool, or should the natural loss be recorded in the trader's bonus pool and the retention of profit in the settlements pool? For me it was both obvious the profit retention belonged in the settlements bonus pool and this mechanism provides discipline to the traders as they would have been advised every morning of every securities issue they are likely to trade with liquidity issues. They trade these issues at their risk.'

'My darling, I don't understand.'

'Carmen, you manufacture and sell air conditioning units. What happens if your salesperson sells 50 units on condition of 1-week delivery, but you only have 20 units available? You tell me you do not accumulate stock. Therefore, to comply with the delivery obligation you must deploy overtime working at additional cost. What about if this additional cost eradicates your profit on this sale? Do you pay the sales commission if the salesperson took the order, knowing it would stress your ability to deliver?'

'Ah, I understand.'

'But can we get back to your original question? If someone is disabled but can function equally on the frontline, they are welcome into the *family*. Just as I do not discriminate gender, race, ethnicity, colour, I do not discriminate in any other way. My only consideration is performance. But there are two branches of economics that also need consideration in non-frontline positions. Just as armies need support such as supplies, feeding, medical treatment, and repairs, corporates need support staff from human resources, security, facilities management, catering, cleaners, etc. These are roles in which disadvantaged people not able to perform frontline roles can be deployed, and corporates have a moral and social responsibility to engage with such people where possible. At business school this came under the heading of social economics. Likewise, corporates should consider a moral undertaking to engage in the local community and environment. At business school this was labelled welfare economics and I distinctly remember a case study where the revitalisation of the UK canal system, which had fallen into disrepair after they were no longer used for transporting raw materials and goods, was achieved by enthusiastic volunteers funded by local corporates. The canal system is now a thriving leisure activity where people can hire a traditional narrowboat and travel these extensive waterways through some stunning countryside. Aldridge plays a major community role here in Matlock. The fireworks night we attended was funded by Aldridge, and I also help to fund a youth enterprise scheme championed by Aldridge and chaired by Edna. I applaud Charles for his commitment to the welfare of this community.'

'I understand better. In Germany we also engage in both your social and welfare economics. Tomorrow I check what we do here. If we need to change, I will speak with you as we want to build a good relationship with this community. It is good we discuss this. Thank you.'

'Ladies, it's late. Have we finished?'

'Most interesting, my darling. Thank you so much. Carmen loves this boot camp.'

'Let me leave you with one all encapsulating thought in answer to your original question.'

'When a woman stops looking at a Boardroom as a male domain, respects the clan culture with associated codes of conduct, and does not expect to change any process with her presence, she will succeed.'

Chapter 110 – Friday

Edna delivered Charles to Merton at 8:30am; she would follow later by train. They were soon on their way with Mel at the wheel.

As soon as she was parked under the apartment block, she left for her meeting. Sebastian and Charles took the luggage up to

the Way

the apartment. They had coffee before going to the hotel for Charles to check in, and to collect their tickets.

Sebastian and Charles were settled at his favourite table at Luigi's.

'You must use this place a lot.'

'About twenty-two years' man and boy. Mama and Gino are family.'

'I sensed at the wake for Mel's mother you had a strong connection here, and the lady you call Mama didn't take her eyes of Mel throughout.'

'Mama adopted her the first time I brought her here and stood ready to pick her up if she folded. Mama has a big heart.'

'As we have some quiet time together can I ask you about your banking days, and why you left it? You're too young to be retired. What are you – early sixties?'

'I'm 57 years old. Investment bankers can retire on full bank pension from the age of 55. Very stressful job.'

'I'm sorry for my error. You're still a youngster. Can you give me a potted history of your banking career as your bibliography glows, but no detail? What type of banker were you, remembering my knowledge is limited to my relationship with my local corporate Barclays Bank?'

'I've never had anything to do with retail banking. The culture is such that retail bankers use a small "b" whereas what are now called investment bankers use a capital "B", I guess to reflect the required skills. When I first joined the banking community, we were called Merchant Bankers. "Big Bang" in 1986 change the face of banking where banks who had never engaged in such activities suddenly wanted in on the act even though their Boards had no idea what they were doing. The result was far too many banks chasing too little business, and a degradation of the whole system.'

'What did this Big Bang change?'

'It deregulated the movement of capital around the world. Most bankers thought new business would explode, forgetting

Week 16

the supply of capital did not increase, just its mobility. All capital at that time was already invested. All that changed was capital could be invested globally more freely, providing more choice for investors.'

'Sounds like a brave new world. Why did you leave?'

'Prior to Big Bang, banking was based on integrity, honour, and prudential risk management. Since then it has degenerated into greed and open risk as bankers chase profit over risk. The concept of asset-backed finance is being replaced by reduced quality good faith sureties. Add to this capital gearing is increasing from 10:1 up to as much as 40:1 for several risky activities, we have a toxic mix likely to explode in the coming years. We will see banks collapse under the weight of poor-quality debt, and some will fold completely. The Central Banks and regulators appear unable or unwilling to curtail these activities. I don't want to be part of it. I've made my money so I'm happy to sit it out.'

'What was your speciality?'

'I've done everything from syndicated loans for major corporates and countries in the early days, then Eurosecurities origination and design, structured project finance, with my final role being risk management of the bank's Balance Sheet. This is where I could see the whole picture. After my concerns were ignored, I decided I was not happy to continue so left after my 55th birthday. That's it. I still sit on several strategic forums and write papers and books.'

'But why was such an important player ignored?'

'If the USA liberate their banks to allow for the pursuit of shareholder value, then everyone else must follow lest the USA banks have a competitive advantage. While the profits role in, bank Boards are not going to reign in their people. Everyone must reign in together or wait for the music to stop.'

'I thought London is the financial centre of the World so surely it can influence how banks operate.'

the Way

'As far as raising capital and maintaining liquidity in global trade, London is most certainly the most important banking centre in the World. And this is unlikely to change, despite the continual attempts by New York and Frankfurt to secure this business.'

'Why do you say this? I read in the papers that New York considers itself the largest financial centre.'

Sebastian laughed. 'New York is the largest market in US Dollars as one would expect. In terms of global banking, London is larger than New York, Singapore, Hongkong and Tokyo put together.'

'But why does London hold this position?'

'Nothing to do with banking; and this is what the USA and Germany fail to understand. The English legal system is recognised as the most dependable and independent in the World. If a global offering is written under English Law, any investor will trust the English Courts to be fair and equitable should the need arise. All global transactions were created and developed in London and thus the legal system was developed here, so lawyers and Courts are familiar with the applicable laws. And adjudication is swift. Neither the USA nor Germany, or anyone else can remotely match this level of comfort.'

'Fascinating. Thanks.' He paused for thought.

'Don't you have any desire to become active again?'

'Not really. I have a property portfolio, mainly here in London, and other investments. If something of interest presented itself, my door is not closed. But no more work for the sake of a salary. In any event, I have a very interesting project nurturing a future corporate executive. This keeps me fully occupied for now.'

'And what an incredible job you've done. By the way, I apologise for my unwitting interference last week.'

'Charles, if you decided to step back a little, she's ready if you give her a few months of oversight. She has the toolbox, and the grit to take good care of your business.'

Week 16

'You really believe she can do it.'

'I know she can. She only needs to understand your touch with your suppliers and retail providers.'

'Please don't tell Edna she's ready. Jim's situation has stirred her to get me to step down from the day-to-day and enjoy life a little. I'm ready to consider change, but I don't want to be pushed, especially by Edna.'

'Fear not. Our conversations are between us.'

'Can I ask you why you do so much for Mel? You really put yourself out for her.'

'Years ago, I asked one of my incredible mentors why he spent so much of his valuable time keeping me on the straight and narrow, and out of trouble. He told me when you identify an opportunity to put some of your good fortune to good use helping the next generation, you should rise to the occasion. He taught me that mentoring was a duty if you find a worthy student.'

'He obviously had a great influence on you.'

'He was far more valuable to me than a university education.'

'Wow. Thanks. I should be getting along to my meeting with Mel. Thanks for lunch. I've asked Gino to keep the bill open for dinner tonight, so have anything you wish. We'll see you here later this evening. I'll call you when Edna has safely arrived.'

Sebastian went off to do some shopping in Bond Street, hiding his purchases when he returned to the apartment. He unpacked for both and settled awaiting her arrival.

He heard the door open. 'Seb, it's me. I'm home.'

She came bouncing in and hugged him.

'Good meeting?'

'Fantastic. They love our idea of technical support, and the new material. I think we should be the font of knowledge for new materials so they rely on us to tell them what's available. Maybe we should have seminars to launch new materials – increase our competitive advantage. Anyway, Charles is delighted he came. We now have to submit a proposal to them.'

'For what it's worth, from a mere banker, I think your Business Development Plan makes good sense, so I'm not surprised with how it's being received.'

She sat next to him and put her arm through his, 'And what's this mere banker nonsense my sage. It's as much your idea as mine. You helped me to put it together.'

'I helped you to articulate your ideas into business language, that's all.'

'Whatever you say. Do we have time for a lovely cleansing shower before dinner? It's only now I realise how grimy London streets are.'

'Go run the water.'

When they arrived at Luigi's it was buzzing with Friday night diners. Mama saw her walk through the door and reached for her.

'Let me look at you, my dear. How lovely and happy you look. Is my Sebastian taking good care of you?'

'Yes Mama. He's great.'

Mama released one hand from Mel to hold Seb's hand, 'You're a good boy. My Melanie is happy. We celebrate.'

'Come, your friends are here. Mama has a nice table for you.'

'A few minutes later Gino appeared at the table with six glasses of Prosecco. Mama re-joined them as each took a glass. Mama spoke 'To my beautiful Melanie, my new daughter. May the good Lord shine his light on you and bring you joy and happiness. And if you are sad, you come see Mama. You are now family. Dear Melanie.' They all toasted her.

Mel got up to hug Mama 'Thank you so much Mama. You don't know how much this means to me.'

'Mama always wanted daughter, so means much to Mama.'

This event beguiled Charles and Edna, but they were happy for her. She needed family now both her mother and father had passed away. Charles was also high from the meeting this afternoon. She had seen the shift in the market before he had, and now she was positioning Aldridge to have a competitive advantage in this new world. She had fully justified his faith in her, and the gamble he took.

Chapter 111 – Saturday

Mel could hear the firebirds sweeping around the auditorium. It was so real to her she was visibly looking for them. And again, the bumble bees humming past her head mesmerised her. During the interval she was literarily buzzing herself. 'That was incredible. How did he do that? I was trying to see the firebirds and the bees flying around.'

Charles and Sebastian smiled at each other, 'Can you now see why Solti is so special? He can make the music float on air.'

'Can't wait for the Beethoven. Probably blast the roof off.'

She floated out of the Albert Hall, and throughout the walk back to Luigi's. Mama could sense her joy and wrapped her arms around her as they hugged and kissed each other.

'Seb took me to the most amazing concert. Incredible music.'

'You float on air, my dear. Do you think you can sit down?'

'Don't know Mama. I can still hear those firebirds and bumble bees flying around my head.'

Mama looked at Sebastian 'It's okay Mama, part of the music this evening.'

'Si, give Mama your coats. You have same booth as last night.'

Although they were only having supper, there was no hurry. Spirits were high. Charles couldn't thank Sebastian enough for securing tickets, and what seats they had in block "K" in the stalls. Couldn't get better. They agreed for any major concert Sebastian would automatically secure tickets for Charles.

Mel was buried in her own thoughts. 'I've got it. I think I've got it.'

the Way

Edna, quickly realising she was referencing *'My Fair Lady'*, 'Gentlemen, or should I say Higgins and Pickering, you should be saying "she's got it. By Jove, I think she's got it" at this juncture.' Turning to Mel, 'and what do you think you've got, my dear?'

'Sebastian tried to explain the difference between a General and a great General faced with the same task. He used two orchestras and conductors playing the same piece, one badly, and the other lifting the roof of the auditorium. Tonight, I experienced the great Sun Tzu and his gallant army of musicians play the *Art of War* to victorious success. Truly amazing how Solti transcends the music, lifting the notes off the page into the hearts and souls of the audience.'

Edna was now confused. 'Who might be this Sun Tzu?'

Charles intervened, 'It's alright my dear. Sun Tzu is a great Chinese General from the era of Confucius. He wrote a series of essays which Mel is studying in-depth with remarkable results. Even I have learnt from these teachings. I have a copy at home if you're interested.' To Mel, 'Interesting analogy.'

As the restaurant emptied Mama came to sit with Mel. 'Tell Mama about these birds and bees flying around your head. Mama no capricci.'

They all laughed as Mel found a new lease of energy using her arms in animation as she explained to Mama.

It was after 1am when they got back to the apartment. She was exhausted. As they crawled into bed and she curled up with him she put her hands around his neck 'This was a truly wonderful evening. Thank you' and kissed him.

Chapter 112 – Sunday

'Anything you want to do today?'

Week 16

I'd like to go visit mum and dad if you don't mind. Then whatever you wish. Perhaps a nice lunch somewhere.

After visiting with her mum and dad, Sebastian drove back to the apartment garage. 'Do you like Dim Sum?'

'Sounds good to me.'

The temperature was crisp, but the sun was shining, making for a good day to walk in London without the noise of the frenzied traffic during the working week. They casually walked from the apartment block, through Kensington Gardens to the Royal China restaurant in Queensway, famous for its authentic cuisine, arriving a little before 12:30 to join the queue. He explained you could not make bookings for Sunday lunch, so first come, first served.

What she experienced was a chaotic, noisy mass of people but serving fabulous Dim Sum in Bamboo pots, arriving at the table until you are full. They then walked along the south side of Bayswater Road where it was traditional on a Sunday for artists to hang their pictures along the park railings hoping to make a sale, or indeed be recognised for their talent.

Once at Marble Arch they walked along Park Lane taking a left along Mount Street to Berkeley Square where he showed her the apartment block on the corner of Hill Street where he first resided in London. Then across the square, up Hay Hill to Dover Street, the centre for art galleries in London.

Seb glanced into a gallery window, stopped in his tracks, took a step backwards and became immersed in the picture in the window. It was an abstract picture called 'Nocturne' with a deep saturation of colour but in some dark place. 'What a great picture. Might come back tomorrow to see what they want for it.'

She quickly mentally noted the name of the gallery and the name of the picture. She had been desperately pondering what to buy him for Christmas. What do you buy for someone who can have whatever he likes and, more importantly, has given so much to her development? She would deflect him from coming back tomorrow and inquire herself once back in Matlock. It was

the Way

in the window so would not be classified as some expensive masterpiece, so she might negotiate a price she can afford now she has the proceeds from her property sales.

They continued their walk along to Piccadilly where they took a left towards Piccadilly Circus and the famous statue of Eros, the god of passion and fertility, commonly referred to as Cupid. She put her arm through his as they gazed at Eros draped in the backdrop of the vast street screens wailing out their various advertising messages. She felt a pang of warmth flow through her body. She was happy where she was – with him by her side.

Week 17

Chapter 113 – Monday

When they awoke and peered out of the window everything was white. It had snowed heavily through the night and continued into the dawn. Sebastian watched the news as she prepared breakfast. 'We need to get out of London by early afternoon if we want to get back to Matlock today. This snow is widespread and will freeze tonight.'

'Great,' she thought. *'No time for him to visit the gallery.'*

Her first meeting on Monday morning was with the lawyer settling her mum's estate. He had finished his work, the Probate Court had approved his filings, and he was ready to distribute the proceeds of the estate. Tears filled her eyes as she read through the paperwork. The conflicting grief of losing both of her parents who loved and nurtured her throughout her life in just a few months and her desire to have them see her achieve her dreams was all she could think about. She suddenly felt very alone. The lawyer knowingly passed a box of tissues as she quietly wept.

It took her some minutes to compose herself before thanking him for his help. He gently pointed her towards the ladies' cloakroom should she need it on her way out.

As she left the building, she felt the need to refocus. *'Okay my wonderful mum and dad. Let me show you I can deliver for you.'* She walked at a firm pace towards Allsops for her meeting.

The meeting with Allsops was very interesting, so found herself quickly back on the field of play. After the meeting she sat in their reception area recalling as much as she could about the meeting before collecting their corporate brochures and putting everything into her prized briefcase before making her

the Way

way to Luigi's where she would meet with Sebastian for lunch before heading back to Matlock.

The tube ride back to Kensington High Street gave her time to reflect on her earlier meeting with the probate lawyer. As she entered the restaurant Mama quickly saw that her lovely Mel was subdued. Mama took her by the arm and led her to a quiet part of the restaurant. 'What is it? Tell Mama why you sad today.'

'This morning I went to the lawyer who dealt with my mum's estate. It left me feeling alone.'

'Your mama did not leave you alone. She left you with a whole new family who love and care for you. Come, we say a prayer for your mama, and then we remember what your mama wanted for you. We never forget our mama. We go on and make them proud.'

'Thank you, Mama. You're so kind to me.'

'When you need Mama, she always here for you. Let us say prayer, and then we go forward.'

When she joined Sebastian at their favoured table, she was feeling much better. 'Are you okay?'

'Fine, thank you. Just needed a word with Mama.'

He knew differently, but could see Mama had dealt with the issue. *'Probably the visit to the lawyer this morning'* he thought.

He left her with her thoughts as they drove home. He would take good care of her this evening to get her ready to enter the field of play tomorrow.

Chapter 114 – Tuesday

Mel breezed into the office despite the icy wind and rain beating down outside. Jim had feedback about the concert from Charles, so amused as she wafted into the office. Mary brought her tea.

Week 17

'Well, my dear. Was it worth all that money?'

'Absolutely fantastic. What a night. Will never forget it.'

'So, you would do it again then?'

'At the drop of a hat.'

'Good. That's why you work hard so you're able to afford such wonderful treats.'

Charles popped in mid-morning. How did yesterday go?

'Great. I think we need to go do a double act at Allsops as they are negotiating some significant commissions.'

'Set it up, lady. I want to start to implement your plan at the beginning of next year. The more real support we have the better. But not this week. I need to visit our people in Manchester before the winter blocks our way. Anytime next week is fine. If I'm not here co-ordinate with Mary.'

As she turned to leave his office, he checked her 'Do you now have the skills to expand your proposal into a full Business Implementation Plan as I would like to understand how you see a full roll-out including the costs and the timeline?'

'Sure. That's what Seb wanted me to do instead of the development proposal to give me the experience of fully presenting my ideas.'

'Why didn't you do it?'

'Didn't want to usurp anyone.'

'My dear Mel, I now understand the quality of your education with Sebastian, and your commitment to learn. You don't need to concern yourself sharing such valuable knowledge with me. I'm not too old to learn from such an accomplished teacher. How long will it take?'

'Seb has some significant sessions he wants to complete before Christmas. I would have to fit it into my daily workload. Say end of next week?'

'Great. Go to it. If you need any financial input, just ask.'

When she arrived home, she was still in good spirit. She went straight to her gym routine before appearing for dinner.

the Way

'Are you ready to start work again after you long weekend break?'

'Refreshed and ready, my master. But before we start, Charles has asked me to expand my proposal into a full Business Implementation Plan. If I gather the data during this week can you help me over the weekend to present it properly?'

No problem. It's an exercise of great importance to your development, and your ideas merit such effort. I'll prepare a list of the data you need.'

'Thanks. What is the subject this evening?'

'This week we're going to deal with the important function of negotiation. We'll deploy the skills of Sun Tzu plus all your game and theatre skills, topped with the importance of silence. We'll also deal with the various protocols needed irrespective of whether you're a lone negotiator or leading a team.'

'But before we start what do you understand as the point of a negotiation as opposed to an agreement, for example, a sales agreement?'

'Your question suggests there must be a difference, so I'm guessing that complexity is one likely difference.'

'Okay, let's look at a sales agreement. One party agrees to provide goods or services and the other party pays an agreed amount as consideration. Unless there is a warranty provided, the transaction is complete, and the agreement falls away. Any warranty will define the extent of any such undertaking, and the remedies available. If anything goes wrong with the transaction and the parties cannot agree remedy, then it is referred to the Court for adjudication.'

'A quality negotiated agreement has the fundamental intent to avoid any recourse to the Court, even if the agreement is no longer viable, unless there is irreconcilable breakdown between the parties. Although some commercial negotiations could be considered adversarial, most are intended as a strategic relationship that benefits both parties. Some are called Strategic Alliances, which define a much deeper integration of business interests to the mutual benefit of both parties. The approach to adversarial and strategic is completely different. In the adversarial situation one party has suffered injury or violation and is seeking remedy – one aggressor and one defender. The approach to strategic negotiation is in a spirit of co-operation in some venture to the mutual benefit of both parties.'

'The essence of a formally negotiated agreement that defines a strategically desirable process for both parties is that it's a complete encapsulation of all the possibilities, including unknowns, that can occur during the relationship. The objective is to maintain continuity of benefit knowing how to deal with inevitabilities such as human error, avoiding any acrimonious and expensive Court battles, especially when dealing across legal territories. Therefore, it will not only define the intended working relationship, it will also include the protocols to be adopted should a review be required to accommodate changes in markets, politics or other influence, dispute resolution, non-performance remedy, arbitration, and an ordered divorce process should change to the business environment render the original intent no longer viable or beneficial. As you can see the intent is to keep the relationship away from the legal system, and you'll see later that I have very firm ideas about the involvement of lawyers in the process. Lawyers are generally not savvy in the uncertainties of the commercial world, and you should never trust a lawyer to completely and properly translate the intent of the relationship into legal speak. This is why a good negotiator will ensure there is a clear summary of the intent between the parties in standard English at the beginning of the agreement, known as Recitals, as in the event of disagreement of legal interpretation, a Judge or Arbitrator will seek to understand the original intent between the parties.'

'Thorough preparation is of paramount importance. You must thoroughly know your subject matter, as much about your opposition's position and possibilities as you can reliably establish, and the background of the people with whom you are

the Way

negotiating. If you prepare well and your required outcomes are reasonable, then you can secretly write down the result before you enter the negotiation, and work towards your expected outcome. If you encounter surprises during the negotiation, and you should know this position, or it's new to the debate, then you must adjourn and regroup. Never leave anything to chance.'

'I think my master refers to planning as per the teachings of Sun Tzu.'

She was playing with him, letting him know his teachings were not wasted on her.

'Go to the top of the class.'

'The first part of the process is to decide what you need to achieve from a negotiation to make it worthwhile. Then look at the other party. Is there any existing or past relationship, or any future possibilities? Can they deliver what you need? Are they the most appropriate party to engage with? What's in it for them? What will be the impact on your company if they fail to deliver?'

'Then we need to identify the primary issues that need to be agreed. Establish any common ground, and options for mutual gain looking from both sides of the table.'

'Armed with this data, we need to understand what type of position we want to take. If there is no existing relationship and no options for mutual gain, then this will be a one-shot deal. This will typically be a win-lose scenario where the stronger party will achieve the most lucrative result.'

'Otherwise work towards a mutually beneficial win-win solution. In addition to identifying the optimal outcome for yourself, try to evaluate their needs, options for mutual gain, what's fair, common ground, and what would stimulate their performance. From this you can prepare a win-win opening statement that establishes the benefits to both sides of engaging any possible resulting long-term relationship and the sharing of information to maintain a close working relationship. The better your understanding of your own interests and those of the other

Week 17

party, the better the chance of a smooth and beneficial agreement.'

'An important process, especially if such agreement is a medium to long-term relationship, is to identify possible future events that could adversely affect the ability of either party to perform or achieve benefit. These could be economic, political, or changes in the market. These need to be defined, and a process of remedy or divorce defined and agreed for each. Then there is force majeure; the unknown. Many lawyers struggle with this eventuality. The commercial solution is usually quite simple. There is a catchall clause in the agreement which states that under such circumstance both parties agree to revisit the original statement of intent to determine if the intent can be modified with knowledge of the unforeseeable event to achieve a modified statement of intent that restores the intended or acceptable benefit to both parties. If so, then the statement of intent is modified, the agreement modified appropriately, and the relationship continues. If not, then an incorporated divorce process is activated. The quality of this part of the agreement is a direct function of the knowledge and experience of the negotiator and their research team.

'Then we need to fully analyse the potential concessions we can offer should the need arise or could be demanded by the opposition. There are two types of concessions. There are concessions you have built into your opening position and can be conceded with no real consequence to yourself but demonstrate during negotiations you can be reasonable. Then there are concessions which have material consequences to you. Every aspect of such concessions must be fully understood to determine whether to accept, reject, or dilute to minimise the consequence. At the same time, you need to understand what concessions would have similar consequence to the opposition and which could be deployed in a tit-for-tat to cancel out the request or equalise the consequences.'

the Way

'Armed with all of this analysis the next decision is solo or team. By solo, I mean one negotiator and a lawyer. If you need a team approach, my preference is a Mutt 'n' Jeff structure. This requires a partner very tuned in to the way you conduct a negotiation. Their role is to identify signs from yourself to interrupt the proceedings without distracting the discussion or moving it on. Every negotiation develops its own rhythm. You need a little time to think but do not want to disturb this rhythm, so you have an agreed signal – as simple as rotating your pen 90 degrees – which tells your partner they should step in and hold the conversation where it is. This can be as simple as lightening the mood with a funny observation, seeking a recap, or asking for more clarification. Whatever your partner does, it must be seamless to the discussion. Therefore, your partner must be credible and knows your signal to bow out again, which also must be seamless.'

She smiled at him 'And what is a Mutt 'n' Jeff structure and where would you use it rather than a solo approach?

'The original Mutt 'n' Jeff was a cartoon strip of two mismatched tinhorns created by Bud Fisher in the early 1900s. My modern-day meaning is 'good-cop/bad-cop'. The lead would be the hard-nosed bad-cop, and the partner would be the affable good-cop. Good-cop can also be used to lighten the atmosphere if the situation requires. It's all down to the way you work together. I had a brilliant good-cop in one of my roles. We were considered invincible at any negotiating table.'

'There are no defined rules regarding solo or team. Much depends on the confidence of each corporate to field a solo representative or want to have a support structure to the lead. My own view is you have a team assemble the research material you need and then go solo if the other side agrees to do the same. If they want to field a team, the Mutt 'n' Jeff structure provides a useful counterbalance. What must be avoided is a team greater than four persons, including their lawyer. The more people present, the less likely you will agree a deal. The other requirement I insist upon to validate a negotiation is the leads can agree head terms which are drafted by the lawyers at the table and signed by both leads before anyone leaves the room. If this is not possible, I don't consider the event as a negotiation; merely exploratory. Is this okay?'

She nodded.

'You're ready to go to the table. But now you meet possibly the worst obstacle of any negotiation – the attitude of the other party. Human nature plays a considerable part in negotiation. Ego, clash of personality, personal objectives as opposed to corporate, intellect, and trust can all influence an outcome, and even destroy the nature of the intended relationship. Thus why it's so important to know as much as possible about each member of the opposition negotiators before engaging. If you detect the lead of the opposition has something to prove, rather than shape a good deal, then a decision needs to be made to either change the lead, or not bother with the negotiations. Sometimes you need to enter the negotiations to prove the unsatisfactory behaviour of such people before adjournment to regroup. I've had occasions when the lawyer of the opposition feels the need to justify their presence without any real-world experience of the subject matter resulting in unnecessary confusion.'

She looked up from her notes, 'How did you deal with that?'

'I have some golden rules developed over the years. Firstly, I try to be last into the room. I walk slowly behind the opposition on the way to my seat, analysing each of the opposition in turn. This requires intense concentration as you are looking for as much data on each person as possible as you pass, not least if they are fielding a dummy lead. I have even had people say to me afterwards they felt the intensity of my analysis as I pass by them. Then I introduce my team and any legal representation, making it clear their role is to record the essentials of our agreement or disagreement, but otherwise be mute. Should either party need to seek any legal clarification, then we should adjourn. I then ask the opposition lead to concur with this process.'

She interceded again 'What is a dummy lead?'

'This is game play. The real lead is at the table but has elected to have someone else play at lead unbeknown to the other side, allowing them the freedom to observe the interactions without needing to get involved. I very specifically look for the signs this is the case as I can use this to my advantage if appropriate. For example, if I'm not happy with this play, I can look the dummy in the eye and ask them to confirm they can agree heads of agreement before leaving the room. If they do not have the authority, they cannot lie in the presence of lawyers, so the real lead must step in.'

'Okay lady. You now have the profile of the preparation for a negotiation. Now the real skills come into play. But we'll leave this until tomorrow as I think you have enough to digest this evening.'

Chapter 115 – Wednesday

'Before we discuss the more interesting negotiating stances applicable to strategic agreements, let me take a minute to say a few things about adversarial negotiations. In business these will typically occur if another company has infringed your copyright or patents rights or utilised your proprietary technology without your consent. These types of conflicts will result in a negotiated settlement if there is no benefit to the owner to allow such violation to continue, or a negotiated settlement for past violation and an agreed mechanism where such use can continue. As you might imagine, whereas the former outcome will be totally adversarial, the latter requires a more measured approach, especially when discussing remedy for any future violation. In my experience the former is conducted by lawyers as they can calculate what a Court is likely to award in the event of no settlement and thus know what amount of settlement is appropriate. Also, they will be alive to the fact, in certain jurisdictions, should the Court award less than being sought by the injured party but equal to or less than already offered by the offender then the injured party are unlikely to be awarded costs and could be asked to pay towards the offender's legal costs. Thus why lawyers usually handle such events.'

'In the case of a continuing relationship lawyers can advise on a likely Court awarded settlement but the actual settlement will depend upon many other commercial factors in the future relationship. The offender will want to gain trust from the injured party so could be encouraged to concede on royalty levels if this means that cash flow does not have to support an onerous amount of penalty to trigger the agreement. There is no point in crippling the ability of the offender to produce goods upon which you will receive royalties by stifling their working capital in upfront penalty settlement.'

Then, of course, hostile takeovers tend to be adversarial, but we are not advanced enough to discuss this type of negotiation.'

'This is all I want to say about adversarial negotiation at this time because, in practice, these events are far less common than strategic agreements. You are far more likely to engage in a strategic agreement, or even a strategic alliance, so this is where I want to focus my attention.'

'Are we okay so far?'

'Yes. I'm with you.'

'To continue from yesterday, we now have our research, our stance, and our objectives. We are ready to commence negotiations, except we need to choose our lawyer. This lawyer needs attributes that favour a smooth negotiation, which can last for days. For much of the time their role will be little more than someone who keeps notes at a Board meeting. However, they need to be informed about the subject matter of the negotiation as they will be required to formulate head terms of agreement at the table, and they need to keep precise notes of the proceedings, especially what are termed as parked issues. They also need to comply with your requirements regarding intervention. In my case, seen but not heard, unless as a specific request, is paramount. If they feel the need for an adjournment, then they pass me a note to this effect, and why. If I disagree then I continue without explanation. As I said last night a negotiation gains a flow and a rhythm and the need to maintain this can be far more beneficial than breaking it for some small technicality in law.'

She interceded 'Do I sense you generally have a low opinion of lawyers?'

'Not at all, but they are not the best people to negotiate commercial agreements. Let me give you an example close to your situation. A new major shopping centre is about to be developed and Aldridge would like to bid on all the window fabrication worth £millions. Clearly the developer would like the best price possible but with certainty of delivery to specification and on time. Aldridge have the credentials to delivery, albeit not the cheapest. The banks financing the project are closely monitoring supply contracts as their biggest fear is what we call event risk, a major contributor to overruns and escalating costs.'

'Can you please explain what you mean by event risk.'

'For commercial purposes there are three essential risks to be considered. Asset risk relates to the value of the project and is important to the financing institutions as this is their security. The first asset is the landbank on which the project will be built. At each stage of the project, this value will change as it becomes developed. Contrary to general logic the value can decrease as development progresses as it goes through a phase when the development has a negative value because, should the project fail, the site may have to be cleared as part of a sale, the cost of which reduces the sale proceeds needed to liquidate the debt financing. Then there is the debt service capability of the project once occupied. For this, banks will require enough quality tenants, called anchor tenants, providing typically 2.5 times in rental income as needed to service the debt. The security here is a term lease with no break clauses within the debt service period, supported by the good credit of the tenant. So, as you can see, a bank will consider the variation in asset value during construction and the quality of the rental income once completed when deciding the level of asset security available for lending purposes. They also want to see events that can delay the project are fully understood and covered with suitable insurance.'

'There are a multitude of event risks that can occur during a major construction project. A crane could fall onto the building causing damage which needs to be repaired but may have many consequential costs, not least delaying the project. The project planning must account for all typical eventualities, mitigating as many as possible in the planning scheme, and then finding insurance cover to remedy the cost implications. The insurance companies will look at the past record of the developer and any risks they think relevant to the project under consideration as the basis to set their premium to cover the risks. A poor record will incur higher premiums or even limited cover. The more robust and seamless the event risk cover, the happier the lending bank will be to finance the project.'

She interrupted 'If I've got this right, banks consider asset value risk, and insurers provide event risk cover.'

'Good. Go to the top of the class.'

'There is one further risk referred to as *force majeure* or Acts of God. These are risks such as a lightning strike which causes a fire or flooding from a storm. Very difficult both practically and cost-wise to foresee or accommodate. You can buy insurance for such events but adds to the cost of the project.'

'Charles would go to the negotiating table seeking a supply only role so he can price competitively without assuming event risks outside of his own factory environment. The developer will seek a supply and install role where most of the event risks fall

the Way

to Aldridge. Let's consider this void between stances. A supply only role requires the windows are made to spec and ready for collection on an agreed date. The only risk to Aldridge is the windows are exactly to spec, undamaged, and ready for loading when required. These risks are fully under the control of Aldridge and thus easily quantifiable. The added risks to Aldridge of supply and install should illustrate my point. Firstly, Aldridge assume delivery risk. This means they need suitable and available transport. This transport needs to safely arrive on site at an agreed time on an agreed date. What happens if the transport breaks down on route? What happens if the transport is involved in an accident that causes damage to the windows? What about traffic jams or even poor weather conditions? Non-delivery can have significant ongoing consequential cost implications, especially if these windows are needed to make the structure watertight to enable fit-out to commence. Aldridge must cover these risks and Charles would need to understand the cost implications before quoting. If the windows arrive damaged or are damaged during installation how quickly can Aldridge provide replacements as every day of delay can incur serious costs. In addition, we have risks of inappropriate access to the site; the installation team do not arrive; the specialised crane does not arrive; the developer has not provided suitable access from the transport to the installation location; and I can give you an example of a real failure where the windows did not fit because of a change to size not relayed to the manufacturer. One of the anchor tenants had been acquired by another retailer during the development phase. This new retailer assumed the retail site, but it had a corporate policy regarding the size of display windows so any major displays such as at Christmas could be designed knowing they would fit in all their stores. This was agreed with the developer, but because this was an unusual event, there was no procedure in the development plan to automatically notify the manufacturer. The windows arrived but did not fit. In this case the developer must assume liability but wants to mitigate as much cost as possible by agreeing terms for a speedy replacement as per a damaged window.'

She smiled at a eureka moment 'Now I understand why Charles has an agreement with Pilkington, our glass supplier, that during the week of delivery of major windows, they guarantee they can provide glass replacement at twenty-four hours-notice.'

'Therefore, you see Charles is aware of the real-world problems that can affect his business. This agreement with Pilkington and probably the extrusion suppliers gives him a marketing edge, and customers will pay for this certainty of delivery because they understand the significant contingency costs of non-delivery. All the risks I have identified and more need to be discussed with remedy and liability agreed before Charles can quote for the job. Lawyers neither have the knowledge nor experience to negotiate such terms. Have I answered your question?'

'Can we now get back on track with the subject of the evening?'

'The next issue for our proposed negotiation is location and environment. The longer the negotiation, the more important this consideration. A light and airy room no bigger than is necessary for the number of people involved with two antechambers close by for adjournments is the ideal. Distance between each party should be two standard desks width minimum, but no separation between desks. You must avoid a 'them-and-us' environment. We are all in this together is a better environment. A Boardroom table is ideal, but not one that can seat many more people than are present. The room should have a good supply of refreshment to avoid the need for unnecessary breaks, and no telephones. Chairs should be comfortable enough for long sessions, but not too comfortable – don't want anyone falling asleep.'

'Target two hours per session as attention span tails off for most people beyond this. Be prepared for longer sessions. I have

the Way

known a single session lasting some five hours, and it was very productive because the flow and rhythm were driving it. No fixed time for meal breaks, but make sure food is available when needed. These sessions tend to be patient marathons rather than sprints.'

'One school of thought suggests that, for complex negotiations, there should be a Chair of proceedings to regulate progress. I'm not of this school of thought because they get bored if they're not involved – the last thing you need. Whoever is hosting the negotiation could have their CEO or Chairman briefly endorse the expectation of the negotiations just to create impetus at the start of proceedings, but then leave.'

'I have seen many negotiations where points of agreement have to be scrutinised by people not at the table before they can be endorsed. I will not engage in a negotiation for which I do not have the authority to conclude a deal, nor one where the lead on the other side cannot do the same. If you are not entrusted to secure a good deal why are you there? Sun Tzu accepts a mandate from his sovereign, but then listening to his sovereign once engaged is at his discretion – and he's right.'

'Sounds to me like one of your rules regarding accountability.'

'It most certainly is. If you're accountable for the outcome, then you must be empowered to deliver it.'

He paused for a moment. 'When you attend important meetings, do you take notes at the meeting?'

'I try to if I can. Why?'

'And how do you record your notes?'

'In my notebook.'

'Using a regular black of blue ink pen?'

'Yes. Where is this going?'

'You may have noted I've never suggested you record notes at a meeting, but immediately afterwards. And if you need to note triggers to remember the detail during the meeting, you should be aware of other people may be recording your notes.

Any skilled executive can read black or blue ink on white paper, even upside down. You may have noticed in American movies they tend to use writing pads with yellow pages. Why do you think this is as paper is generally white?'

'No idea.'

'The most difficult combination of colours to be overlooked is red ink on yellow paper. Therefore, at a negotiating table, should you need some means of recording notes, then this is your preferred choice.'

'But surely you need to record notes as you progress. How do you know where you have been during a long session?'

'I have my lawyer taking notes of the whole proceedings. They sit next to me, so I can quickly flip through their notes if necessary. If they are left-handed, they sit on my right, and on my left if they are right-handed – easier for me to read quickly. Mostly I keep it in my head. I always have my game plan in my head. I do have a yellow pad and red pen by my side, but if I need to jot something down or do a calculation, it is never neat enough for anyone else to read, and the pad leaves with me at the end of a session. In any event, how can you concentrate on proceedings if you're writing notes? Sometimes it's the glance between opposition members, or the little throwaway line providing clues as to where they stand. As lead you don't have time to take notes.'

'Wow. Such precision, and you haven't started to negotiate yet!'

'Would you walk onto a stage to deliver your lines before the set is ready?'

She gave a resigned look.

'I've known negotiators and lawyers who can record their notes in shorthand. Some in their own variation or alternative to regular Pittman shorthand.'

'Isn't shorthand lowly for such people? It's mostly a PA capability.'

the Way

'On the contrary shorthand, in its various forms, was developed by high level people and first recorded in use in the 4th century BC by the Greeks. I think the thoughts of Socrates were recorded in shorthand. Great names such as Julius Caesar, Leonardo Da Vinci, and Galileo all used a form of shorthand. In the case of Da Vinci, he wrote his notes backwards so you would need a mirror to read them. Galileo used mathematical notation as his shorthand to protect what he wrote from the gaze of the Church. Samuel Pepys recorded his famous diaries in shorthand. Oh, no, having a codec only you and your trusted allies can read is as valuable a tool today as it has been over centuries. Mine is a scribble that, hopefully, only I can read.'

'The stage is set. We are ready to start. Whoever is the host will welcome everyone, and introductions made. Each lead will make their opening address, which should be a short and clear statement of why they are here and what they hope to achieve. All very polite and upbeat. And most importantly, throughout the negotiations the language used must focus on communication. Do not use words or vocabulary which could not be used in an agreement. If mnemonics are used, then it must be clear from the outset what they mean with reference to the negotiations. If technical words or expressions are used, then these need to be fully defined.'

'The first item on the agenda is to agree a comprehensive statement of intent which once agreed becomes the agenda. It's helpful if each lead brings their proposed statement of intent with them so easy to determine where there is agreement, and where they differ. It is useful to adjourn after this process so both sides have a little time to reflect and ensure it is complete, not least because this statement will drive the negotiations. A printed copy of this should then be distributed to all at the table as a point of reference. This has a psychological benefit in that should the negotiations start to drift off the agenda, you can use the statement of intent to bring the discussion back without offending anyone.'

Week 17

'Can you give me an example of a clause within this statement as you have already said this statement of intent becomes the recitals in the agreement if I remember correctly?'

'You are correct albeit the wording may be refined where words used have a specific understanding in law. But I can give you a typical example of a divorce clause due to changing circumstances.'

"In the event that market and/or political and/or judicial circumstances beyond the reasonable control of either party deemed to render this agreement materially unworkable in any respect including diminishing profitability below commercial acceptable levels then the Parties shall agree to an ordered dissolution of this agreement minimising any injury to either party. Equitable consequences in mutual respect of each Party shall form the ethos of any such dissolution."

'So here we have the bones upon which we will then add the flesh during negotiations to define circumstance under which a divorce is appropriate, the essential performance criteria of each party during the dissolution process, and any settlement considerations. This is likely to translate (by lawyers) into many pages of text. If you accept that the more text the more chance for error, misunderstanding and interpretation issues then the recital provides a Judge with a clear statement of intent against which to adjudicate. Having attended many Court and arbitration cases in my time, I have seen for myself that a Judge invariably tries to ascertain the commercial intent by the parties in resolving what I call legal confusion. Therefore, the statement of intent needs to be commercially precise, and used as a recitals clause to the agreement.'

'Does this make sense?'

'Do I need to understand legal speak as part of my job? Your recital smacks of legal speak to me. Those words would not be what I call standard English.'

'I have used text that accommodates standard legal definition such as "reasonable" "material" "injury" "equitable". Your

the Way

lawyer would use these words as part of the refinement of your standard English version, but a competent negotiator will know of such words and expressions and their meaning in law.' He paused to see if she raised any other issues. 'Are we okay to move on?' She nodded.

'Conventional textbooks suggest the next step is itemised opening positions. Again, my experience suggests this can be at least a damper on the process, if not a total distraction if vastly at odds with the opposition opening position. I clearly state the objectives but keep the route vague. I want to listen to what the opposition seek. This has three advantages to my way of thinking. Firstly, my mind is not constrained with my own route map. Secondly, their minds are not dampened if our positions are far apart. Thirdly, they may present a route that works fine for me and thus much easier to gain acceptance of any variations that may be needed. It's far easier to get agreement to solutions that your opposition think they tabled albeit carefully re-engineered to your advantage.'

'The next step is to agree as much as you can, parking deadlock situations as soon as they occur. Style of language is important. Both sides must always show dignified respect. Absolutes are not useful, nor is sarcasm, personal attacks, scoring points, or irritators such as "with respect" or "frankly". Your role is to seduce the other party to your way of thinking; slowly but surely wooing them to your tune. Do not hog the floor and listen carefully to what they say. You never learn anything while you're speaking; only when you listen. If they have an idea that sits with your thinking in part, then praise the idea before starting to groom it to the form you prefer.'

'The more you can agree, the easier to convert deadlock into agreement.'

'How are we doing?'

'Theatre, planning, waging war, dispositions, manoeuvre. And did I detect a little coaching? Did I miss anything?'

Week 17

He laughed, 'You're getting too good for me. But does this all make sense to you?'

'And some. I would love to watch you in action. And I love how you vary your play from the textbook approach. You probably destabilise your opposition, and then secure your outcome before they can adjust. Brilliant.'

'Sometimes this can work, but not so easy against a seasoned negotiator. Another important part of the process is to never allow the negotiation to become entrenched, irritating, or frustrating. If you can't park the issue causing this distress, then adjourn the negotiation to allow people to calmly reflect on the issue and only return when there is the possibility of a resolution. This might include informal, off-the-record discussion between the lead negotiators and even reference back to the corporations if appropriate.'

'One last thought about the venue. If it's noisy because of external factors, or negotiations are interrupted by third parties for any reason, change the venue. Do not tolerate irritants, be they environmental or people. Another rule for protracted negotiations is to agree to meet only four days in each week. Tired people tend to get irritable – does not lend itself to robust agreements.'

'I think we've covered enough for today. Any questions?'

'You mean there's more! Negotiation sounds like a profession to me.'

'Most negotiators do undertake specific training as I did. The stakes are usually very high involving many $millions so agreements need to be as bulletproof as possible within the realms of an imperfect business environment. Better, and cheaper, if you get it right at the beginning. Acrimonious and expensive if it ends in tears in Court. For your understanding of the process, I think one more session will be enough. You should also view much of this philosophy as useful in any meetings, especially with other companies. The construction industry is notorious for its hard-headed negotiations where all parties squeeze every last concession out of a deal. You need to be prepared and very savvy in such discussions.'

Chapter 116 – Thursday

'Okay. Let's see if we can finish our sessions on negotiation. Tonight, I want to briefly discuss identifying gaps, how to narrow the gap before considering any concessions that will close the gap, some thought on how to use concessions, gambits that can be deployed and how to counter, dealing with deadlocks, closing tactics, and finally securing executed head terms. Deal done, or maybe not.'

'Not all negotiations deliver an agreement. This is not failure. What appears possible at a macro-level can evaporate once the detail is examined. Any aspect of a proposed negotiation that may prove materially troublesome should be revealed during the initial research. Sometimes it may prove worthwhile for the lead negotiators to informally meet on these issues before starting formal negotiations to establish whether or not they can be overcome.'

'Once you have your statement of intent, each lead negotiator should explain their interests in securing an agreement including how they see it working and explaining any particular ways in which their respective corporates operate and wish to preserve, for example, it's part of their culture. It's also worth remembering that you can write whatever you like in an agreement, but people need to execute what has been agreed. If the agreement does not take account of how the people operate who are expected to comply then there is at least a chance of difficulties if not failure. It's imperative that consideration be given to the types of people expected to fulfil the agreed relationship.'

Week 17

'From this exchange note any serious gaps. The discussion then should explore ways to narrow these gaps. Exchange ideas. Explore 'what ifs'. Change the shape of expectations to find options for further discussion. Then each option should be discussed on merit to find a fair way to bridge the gaps. Try to avoid serious debate or attempt to score points. The odd flinch or gasp are an effective non-combative theatrical way to push back your opponent's expectations. Be true to your aims but be realistic in expectation. This is where concessions, cheap to you but valuable to them, can be bargaining chips to bridge gaps but only give in small slices and on an equitable basis. Remember you are still not in formal negotiations, so all options and concessions are conditional. Stay clear of deadlines for this phase as it is important to understand each gap from both perspectives thus learning about each other ensuring that options considered are practical in execution.'

'For each gap note which have subsequently closed, and which are narrow enough to start the formal process of agreement. It's not important to negotiate the statement of intent in order. Indeed, it's tactically more astute to deal with the least problematic first. The more you can agree, the easier to overcome any gaps. What is important at the conclusion of each statement of intent clause is to convert what is agreed into head terms, usually constructed by both lawyers and leads, executed and held in escrow by both lawyers.'

'What does it mean to hold in escrow?'

'It means that head terms are agreed for a particular statement of intent clause but are conditional on all such clauses having agreed head terms. Avoid revisiting agreed head terms unless both leads agree that subsequent discussion requires an amendment; but beware of slip ins that change the intent.'

'If you can't agree a point, remember to park it on an agreed basis. At the end of each statement of intent clause determine if it's more productive to move on rather than push for a solution.

the Way

If you move on, then record head terms as may be possible but leave open and move on to another clause.'

'Two powerful elements of theatre can win major tactical advantage. The first is putting a key demand into the arena at half your normal vocal volume. You will observe that people tend to listen more carefully if they have to press to hear what you are saying. The second is the power of silence. You put your suggestion or requirement into the arena and then be quiet – for as long as it takes for your opponent to respond. Under no circumstance do you interrupt the silence or appear agitated. Just relax and wait. This is strength.'

She looked up from her notebook 'Do you mean who blinks first loses?'

'Essentially you are right, but this tests the argument and resolve of your opponent. Can they counter, or will they concede?'

'Gambits, or game plays, are generally used by inexperienced negotiators as an emotional power play and more rarely by experienced negotiators trying to refocus a less experienced opponent. They tend to be personal, to exploit any insecurities and to challenge capability. The intent is to extract more value by means of concessions. You need to professionally call their bluff without getting personal yourself. Never concede to gambits lest your opponent sees this as a mechanism to get even more. I'll give you some examples of commonly used gambits and how to counter.'

'We have the Beauty Contest where your opponent implies your terms are not as attractive as another corporate, expecting you to concede more. Your counter would be something to the effect your company is better placed to make this relationship a success, but if you think differently why are we engaging in this negotiation?'

'A more unsavoury gambit is a *fait accompli* where your opponent is demanding a concession, or the deal fails. Your response needs to quietly suggest the negotiation should cease until such demand is reversed. Then feign collecting your papers, make your excuses, and leave the table. If you actually reach the door before your opponent relents, then keep walking.'

'A similar gambit is the Shotgun where your opponent suggests there is no point in continuing unless you concede on a point. Your option here is to park it to see how the remainder of the negotiation evolves, and then return to this point. If this response does not work, then walk away.'

'Gambits involving financial data including budgets are intended to confuse you into conceding points with false data. Ensure all such data is supported in writing and then adjourn to thoroughly check and question such data before proceeding. Show you will always seek support for any financial data and then check it tends to thwart any further attempts.'

'Threats, personal attack, and status challenge are signs your opponent feels they are losing the argument. You must make a quick decision to determine whether you can use this emotional insecurity to win the day or leave until you receive an apology. Another variation of this gambit is they challenge your authority to concede the point, lest a higher authority should be brought to the table. Your response is simply that you are fully mandated to agree or disagree anything related to this negotiation.'

'The contra of this is a gambit where your opponent claims no authority to agree to a point. Your response is simply that all parties agreed at the start of the process they are fully mandated. If this is not the case, then your company should field a negotiator with full authority. If just a gambit they will concede. If not, all current head terms are voided unless and until agreed with a new negotiator.'

'Then we have the Salami gambit where your opponent requires a specific aspect cast in stone before the negotiations are completed – a must have concession. Your response is to reinforce the process of escrow, and such escrow will only be removed once the total package is agreed.'

the Way

'Then we have silence. As I have told you before silence is a very powerful tool. Should your opponent use silence as a force call for an adjournment to allow both parties to consider their position. When you return to the table, take the initiative to summarise where you were before the adjournment and invite any further thoughts. Force your opponent to restart discussion.'

'Another gambit is deadlines. Your opponent states it's imperative negotiations are concluded in a specific timeframe. Ask why, and what happens if this is not possible. We have already dealt with artificial deadlines in your daily corporate life. No difference here. If the demand is unrealistic or artificial, ignore it or walk away. Sometimes a deadline to review progress can keep negotiations moving at a desirable pace, thus can be very useful if your opponent tends to talk points to death or stubbornly makes unrealistic demands. Such review deadline should be used to measure progress to determine if enough progress has been made to warrant further discussion. If the lack of progress is due to your opponent being unrealistic in demands, then this lack of progress can be used as a ploy by yourself to state that any continuance will be subject to a further review deadline at which point a decision will be made to abort if progress is still too slow. Your opponent is now under pressure to be more conciliatory and of course gives you the advantage.'

'As you approach the end of a negotiation, the gambits can be subtle or even cynical. The assumption is you're tired, or you let down your guard as you see a deal concluding in your favour. The first of these gambits is generally termed escalations. These will include new demands not previously considered, late nibbles at already agreed terms, and slip-ins where they attempt to add to an existing agreed term. These test your emotional resolve. At no point do you allow any emotional content into your psyche. You can use theatre to feign frustration, surprise, or whatever response will convey a feeling of dismay at their behaviour. If the new demands are outside of your agreed statement of intent, then suggest these demands are outside of the scope of this negotiation and will require a new agenda. For late nibbles feign surprise and upset stating that you think what has been agreed is equitable and any further modification would require the relevant section to be totally renegotiated. Slip-ins can usually be dealt with by withdrawing all associated concessions and add your own counter-demands. Turn the table against them to determine how serious they are.'

'Then we have the final offer gambit. If this is a take it or leave it demand, then thank them for their time and leave the table. If the statement on either side is essentially, we cannot concede further, then discuss what both sides lose by not concluding an agreement as an attempt to break the psychological deadlock and reshape the conversation. Revisit why you have arrived at this gap to see if there is another way to bridge it. Try to ignore the finality of this demand and placate any anxiety on the other side of the table by praising their efforts to date. If this demand is a tactical gambit, you will get your agreement.'

'Finally, let's deal with deadlocks. We have already discussed that deadlocks during the early negotiating stage should be parked until later. But now you need to address these. Start by summarising the progress you've made, the areas of agreement, and the value to both parties. Then accurately recap the origin of the deadlock using the lawyer notes, if necessary, invite any suggestions and then be quiet. If necessary, propose a different route that on paper seems plausible and then debate this route. When it is seen this will not work, or is inferior to the original route, you have opened the gate to resolving the deadlock. You can also invent new options for mutual gain which essentially act as a fuzzy distraction which then will be discounted whilst softening the deadlock. Sidewinding the deadlock will deflate any undue significance to the problem and ease the way to a rational solution.'

the Way

'If you're still at the table, you have a deal. Ensure all head terms are agreed, celebrate success, and sign the head terms thereby releasing the escrow. It is now down to the lawyers to weave these terms into a legally binding agreement.'

'Has anyone ever tried any dirty tricks on you or even tried to withdraw after leaving the table?'

'I'm not sure what you mean by dirty tricks, but I remember one negotiation had much at stake for both parties and involved many $millions in value to both. The negotiation was in Cambridge, Massachusetts, a very pretty part of the USA. At the end of the first day, we were invited out to dinner at the best seafood restaurant in Boston. When we got there, none of their negotiating team were there. Myself and my partner chuckled at such an obvious ploy to ply us with food and drink and keeping us out late whilst their team were refreshing themselves for the next day. As we were both very resilient in those days, we took full advantage of this ploy having slipped the waiter $50 to ensure our champagne glasses were frequently filled with non-alcoholic 7-UP. But we enjoyed the very best lobster and crab for three nights. After four days we wore them down and achieved the intended deal, but we were tired. It was Thursday evening when we got back to Boston airport. We saw a helicopter ready to leave for Nantucket Island. We jettisoned our flight to New York and took the helicopter, found a fabulous colonial hotel, and had a great long weekend on this wonderful former whaling island completely without cars. When the Chairman saw the result of our negotiation, he happily signed off on our weekend trip including clothes we needed to purchase although the accountants were very aggrieved we had spent close to $10,000 – nothing compared with the value of this agreement to the bank.'

'Should you ever find yourself at a negotiating table with Russians you will see at least one bottle of vodka on the table. This bottle must be empty, and glasses upturned before you start negotiating. You need a friendly waiter suitable primed with money to ensure for every glass you drink of vodka you have a similar glass of water with fresh lemon juice to neutralise the alcohol. Different countries have their traditions, so you must be aware before you go there and be prepared to be resourceful.'

She sat back with a knowing smile on her face, deep in her own thoughts.

'A penny for your thoughts.'

'I get it. I really get it. Whatever the modern heading, be it rules, corporate philosophy, negotiation skills, time management or whatever; they are all subsets of thirteen short essays written 2,500 years ago. What an incredible man he must have been. Reminiscent of Newton's third law in that the Art of War cannot be re-created or dismissed; it merely changes its form. And to have such a wise sage as my master to put his wisdom into context for me is truly wonderful. You are by far the best teacher I've ever had, including my dad. I would love for you to have met him. Not in your league in experience or what you teach me, but very progressive in his thinking.'

'Always remember he laid the foundations for your attitude to learning. He did a fine job, and I would like to have met him.'

'He would have enjoyed sitting through the *Art of War* sessions for sure. I now fully understand and appreciate your inscription in my book, and why you refer to the *Art of War* as a corporate bible. I would think it also has much to offer in general life. Can't believe I've studied so much philosophy in my life, but not the most relevant, until now. I've reread your translations many times, applying them to my work, and what goes on around me. Incredible.'

'My master, I salute Sun Tzu for his wise counsel, and my wonderful master for sharing this wisdom with me. I will endeavour to be worthy of such good fortune.'

'You are most welcome, my delightful student. It has been a pleasure guiding you through his teachings. I suggest you are equipped with the knowledge, but you now need experience. You should encourage Charles to take you with him for any negotiation, to observe the process in action.'

'I'll certainly speak to him about it.'
'Shall we call it a night as we have covered all I wish to at this stage in your development?'

Chapter 117 – Friday

'I have functions to attend next week. On Monday evening I have our tennis club Christmas dinner. Tuesday evening there is a Christmas fundraiser for the youth enterprise initiative I support along with Charles and Edna. On Thursday evening I have a Christmas dinner with friends. You are welcome to join me at all, or any of these.'

'An evening out with my master! Whatever next. I'm grateful for the invitation and would be honoured to go with you to all of them. Can you give me notice of any dress code requirements just in case I need to shop tomorrow?'

'Didn't realise you needed an excuse to shop. However, nothing formal. All casual for me.'

She feigned a frown at him.

'I have no plans for any new lessons before New Year. You've worked hard. I suggest timeout to consolidate your knowledge, and to recharge your batteries. If you want to go away over Christmas or go back to London, it's perfectly okay.'

'I no longer have an apartment in London. Where would I stay?'

'You have a key to my apartment in London; you're welcome to use it.'

'That's very kind of you, but would you mind if we spent Christmas together? We have no-one else in our lives. Might be fun to hang out together out of school. We are invited to spend Christmas Day lunch with Charles and Edna along with Jim and Margaret. It's probably the last Christmas for Jim, so I would like to accept their invitation.'

Week 17

'You're welcome to stay, and I support your sentiment regarding Jim so please accept for both of us.'

'Thanks. I can't imagine Christmas anywhere else but here. It may even snow. What a place to have fun in the snow. Must get some boots.'

Chapter 118 – Saturday

They were sitting at breakfast together. 'Seb, I'd like to study some of the mechanics of business over the Christmas break. Can you direct me to the appropriate reading material? I'm thinking around two hours per day as well as recapping the lessons to date.'

'Very industrious, but don't you need a break?'

'Sure, but not three weeks. And I need to finish my Business Implementation Plan next week, for which I need your help. I'm in the groove and I want to stay there. The material I want to cover is what you term business school. I think I need to understand a Balance Sheet. You say that a Balance Sheet paints a picture of a company. I want to be able to read that picture and understand the component parts. I also want to understand more about value drivers and how to manage them. Do you have the reading material, or can you point me to suitable books?'

'Certainly, I have much of what you need, but a trip to the bookshop whilst we're shopping would prove useful as some of my material is probably stage 2 of your reading. Need the basics first. Let's get cleared up and go see what we can find.'

Chapter 119 – Sunday

Breakfast cleared, they were ready to work through the Business Implementation Plan for which she had assembled all the data requested.

'Let's understand the difference between this plan and the documents that preceded it. We are now at the stage of integrating your proposal into the day-to-day operation of the business. What do you think we need to consider to achieve integration?'

'The principal area of impact is sales in London. They will need to understand how to interact directly with architects. Our sales staff need to be more proactive in providing input to architects to facilitate fabrication solutions that are feasible and within the proposed budget. Certainly, more involvement of our design staff much earlier in the process, and integration into the design team where possible. My idea is we engage the fabrication design capability of Aldridge as early as possible in the building technical design.'

'How do you propose to implement these changes identifying any disruption to the mainstream business of Aldridge.'

'I don't really see any major disruption to the mainstream business as this affects the London office business.'

'Think lady. You are diverting design resources who could well be seconded and even transferred to architects. This will most certainly have an impact on mainstream business. A void that must be considered.'

Think Sun Tzu. Treat this new business opportunity as a new adventure requiring a General to plan a campaign, identify all resources required with all due regard for any disruption to the normal workings of the State. Then what resources are available, and how will you fill any gaps. And I'm talking all resources in whatever form. Do you have resources that can be retrained or configured to fill gaps? If not, where to you seek alliances.'

Week 17

'Sorry, Seb. We've already discussed this process at length. I get it. I'm looking at this from the wrong perspective, but I now understand. Sun Tzu planning. Have you detected any resources I haven't considered?'

'Two obvious ones. On paper, your concession to architects that they may poach your design staff for an appropriate transfer fee does not account for the disruption to your overall design capability. You may have the funds to hire and train new designers, but where is this pool of suitable replacement candidates? I would suggest you consider forming active alliances with appropriate universities to give you access to the cream of new talent. This will have a cost. The other is the printed material you will need to encourage architects to take you seriously. Your brochures today are not suitable for your intended audience. You need a brochure which speaks of your leading-edge approach to new materials and detail any innovative design projects completed by Aldridge. You must align with your new potential clients. There are others you need to consider, but you are now primed. Let's see if you can now plan a campaign to the quality of Sun Tzu.'

He let this rebuke sink in. 'We can skip your martial arts session today, but I will play tennis, and you are welcome to join me, but not essential.'

'I'm so sorry, Seb. I've let you down. I'll work on this until lunchtime. I want to continue our martial arts and I will play tennis with you. As we've finished school for this year, I have time to get this right, and it will be to the required standard of my master.'

the Way

Week 18

Chapter 120 – Monday

Jim was absent. Charles and Mel were sitting in his office discussing her outline implementation plan including the need to identify a pool of design resources to fill expected transfers to architect practices, and the need for new brochures as she had no idea how much this will cost.

'My dear, I agree we must be more pro-active in attracting talent from universities, and I know the universities to approach. Perhaps we should add summer internships for undergraduates before they start their final year. We may not be the sexiest first choice, but it will soon get around we actively engage with some of the best architects around. Good idea. Another source is established designers in large city practices in their 50s and already wanting to move to the countryside for a slower and more tranquil way of life but need to continue working until retirement. This is a lovely part of the country to consider for retirement. We need to cultivate appropriate recruitment agencies to look out for these people. Bet Sebastian hasn't thought of that one.'

'Bet he has. Exactly what he did, albeit he didn't need employment.'

'I agree we need a new corporate brochure to go with our new approach. But this is expensive, so we must take great care to ensure we project the appropriate image. I think we should consider all Aldridge clients. I will think of projects where our input made the difference. We had a project last year for a church conversion. Our innovative designers developed a novel solution which really made that project exceptional. We will need professional help. Give me a few days to think this through. Budget £50,000 for this but will apply to the whole of Aldridge.'

the Way

'I must concede Sebastian's exacting standards open my eyes to so much I take for granted. I can't wait to see the final version of your plan. Do you think you will finish this week? But I would sooner have the exacting version than a rushed form.'

'Fear not. He will not allow anything other than an exacting standards version. The rebuke I received yesterday for not considering some obvious impacts made this clear.'

He chuckled. 'You were working yesterday? When do you have downtime?'

'No more school this year although I want to study and consolidate over the holiday. But I want to finish this plan so we can all think on it before the New Year.'

'Very industrious, my dear, and much appreciated. But you need a break. Could be tough next year. Charge your batteries.'

'This week is social week. We have the tennis club Christmas dinner tonight, the Youth Enterprise dinner tomorrow, and dinner with some of Seb's friends on Wednesday. Probably more taxing on my system than school.'

'I'm pleased you're coming tomorrow. Edna will be delighted to see you. I'll make sure we're all seated together.'

'Could you let Margaret have the details of your architect clients you would like to receive the Aldridge Christmas hamper? Let them know Aldridge is interested in them.'

'By the way, I spoke with Michael Chimes yesterday. We will let Maurice Fulmer go. I want to get Michael into a different mindset for next year.'

'Thanks for telling me.'

'Okay, lady, much to do before closedown.'

Chapter 121 – Tuesday

Jim was enthused to read her draft plan. They spent much of the morning refining the process and associated costs. He could better identify major corporate projects that would appeal to

Week 18

architects. He added yet another consideration – whilst designers were on secondment, how did Matlock stay current in the process. It was rare just one designer work on major corporate projects, not least because of the risk of material error in calculations, especially if the fabrication is part of the superstructure. There are two specialised structural engineers embedded in the Matlock design office who actively engage in all projects.

Another consideration but her plan is now well advanced, almost ready to publish but, yet again, not to Michael Chimes.

She decided on a dress for the Youth Enterprise dinner. Knowing Sebastian's ambivalent view of dress code for events, she had phoned Edna for guidance. They would be on the high table for dinner, thus visible. Charles would oversee the annual awards with the CEO of Rolls Royce, Derby, the guest speaker, presenting the awards. She encouraged Sebastian to be somewhat more compliant than he would prefer.

After dinner Edna sat with Mel for a catchup chat. 'My dear Mel, where are we in the Pygmalion process? Have we passed the rain in Spain event or indeed the first day at the races? I thought to have a chat with Higgins, but I wanted to understand your thoughts. Charles, or should I say Pickering, is certainly impressed with progress.'

Mel was amused at Edna's preoccupation with using *My Fair Lady* as a progress marker. 'We are well passed the rain in Spain. I guess that would have been the confrontation with Michael Chimes.'

'My goodness, yes. Charles was so happy with your performance, albeit you scared the hell out of him with your revelations about the impending recession. Higgins earned much respect that day.'

Amused by her use of Higgins and Pickering, 'I think we could use the Solti concert as the first day at the races. What a night.'

the Way

'Thank you for reminding me. Must thank Higgins for such fabulous tickets. My goodness, what a night. And what a lovely lady you call Mama. You have a good friend in her.' Thinking for a moment, 'I think we only have the Grande Ball left. When do you expect to graduate?'

'I'm not looking forward to graduation. I'm happy with the job, but I dread the events determining this day.'

'You mean Jim.' Patting her hand, 'It will hit Charles hard, but we'll get through it together. Speaking of Jim, in the absence of our respective children on Christmas Day, we've invited Jim and Margaret to lunch. Will you and Higgins be joining us? You're very welcome.'

'Yes. I've already told Charles we'll be there.'

'Excellent news. Much on his mind at present. Say 1 o'clock. We'll eat around 2 o'clock once everyone is settled. Strictly no presents, please. Ah, here's Higgins. Must thank him for his continued support of our Youth Enterprise Scheme, and for the Solti tickets.'

Chapter 122 – Wednesday

It was mid-afternoon. Mel was on her rounds through the workshop. She sensed something was amiss as she was getting sniggering looks from some younger workers. She felt a hand from behind touch her, just below her waist. She instinctively dropped her file, turned, grabbed the offending hand, wrist-locked and turned. She felt her blouse tear as something caught her. He was on the floor, face down, wrist locked in less than two seconds. He struggled. She increased the pressure. He made his pain audible. She moved her position, so there was no way he could floor her. She noticed a sprig of mistletoe on the floor.

By this time there were whistles and applause. When he stopped trying to escape, she threw his hand away from her. She

Week 18

stood over him as he turned over, his face still grimacing from both his fall to the concrete floor, and the pain in his wrist.

She noticed her blouse was torn, revealing much of one side of her bra.

'Get up.'

He got up very sheepishly as a crowd of workers gathered.

'Now pick up my file.'

He picked it up and handed it to her. 'Sorry Miss. Just having some fun, Miss.'

'Not funny. Molesting and groping women is not funny.'

'Back to your work while I decide your future.'

'Please Miss, I didn't mean any harm.'

She walked off back to her office, not attempting to cover her bra. There was much clapping and whistles.

When she walked into the office Jim immediately noticed her blouse. 'What happened down there? Who did that to you?'

She reached into her drawer and pulled out another blouse. 'Just a stupid prank. Don't worry about it.'

'Are you hurt?'

No, but the prankster is not feeling so good.'

She went off to the ladies to change her blouse and binned the torn one when she returned to her desk.

Jim was quickly on to Tom to find out what happened and was told to report immediately. Tom appeared through the office door looking very anxious. 'So sorry, Miss. Are you okay?'

'I'm fine, Tom. How's the prankster?'

'Very embarrassed, Miss. He was put up to it, and stupid enough to try. If it's any consolation you earned a lot of respect down there. No-one will ever try anything with you again. They tell me you were amazing – just threw him to the floor and locked him down. Where did you learn Kung Fu?'

'I have a good master to teach me.'

He turned to Jim. 'His misses just had a baby. If he loses his job, what'll they do?'

the Way

Jim turned to her, 'What do you want to do about it, Mel? You can make a formal complaint. He will be fired, possibly charged with assault. Alternatively, we can give him a warning and have him pay a fine.'

'Jim, it was just a stupid prank. No doubt he'll not live it down on the floor for some time, so let him suffer down there, and learn his lesson. Tom, so long as they all realise that any attempt to touch me for any reason will result in the same, if not more pain, then no harm done.'

'Don't worry Miss, they've seen you in action. You'll have no more problems. And thank you, Miss. I'm not happy with what he did, and he needs to grow up now he has a nipper to consider, but he needs the job. Not much work around here at the moment.'

'Okay Tom, let's all get back to work.'

Mary came rushing in, frantic with worry 'Are you all right? Did he hurt you?'

'No Mary, I'm fine. It's him who needs the first aid.' Jim smiled.

'But I must make a report, and I must inform Charles. This is serious.'

Jim stepped in, 'Mary, you don't have to do anything. The situation is under control, and I'll tell Charles when he returns later. Only Mel can instigate a report, and she has chosen not to for very good reasons.'

She looked at Jim, who was looking very stern. This both calmed her and reminded her of her place. She left the office.

He saw her drive through the gates and park. She skipped to the door, and through to the kitchen, threw herself at him and gave him multiple kisses on both cheeks.

'Slow down, lady. What happened today?'

'I was molested this afternoon.'

'You were what?'

'Molested. And my master's teaching kicked straight in and I floored the guy. He tore half my blouse off in front of the guys

Week 18

on the shop floor, but I dealt with it. You would have been proud of me. I'm still buzzing. It felt great to have this guy pinned to the floor, crying out to let him go in front of all those guys. It took all my self-control to contain myself from a victory dance around the shop floor.'

She kissed him some more.

'Come, sit down and tell me all.'

'I don't want to sit down, I'm buzzing.' She held him around the waist 'my master is forgiven for all the pain teaching me these skills. I love my master so much.'

'Would you like Prosecco to celebrate, or something stronger?'

'Now you're talking. I'll go get a bottle.'

Glasses charged, and still standing, he saluted her.

'How do you feel?'

'I feel totally liberated. I'm no longer a woman in a man's world, I'm a force to be reckoned with. Just like Carmen. It feels great. I salute you, my master. Today marks a new chapter for me, and it's all down to you.'

'Are you going to the gym tonight?'

'Yes, but I need you to help me with something when I get there.'

'Okay, pick me up on your way there.'

She was so high on adrenalin she needed a release. She was back downstairs in a few minutes and led him to the gym.

She sat on the massage table. 'Seb, when a woman is as high as I am the only real solution is rampant sex. But I know it crosses your red line. Will you give me a sexy massage resulting in an orgasm, an extension of the hand in the dark. I so need it.'

'You did well today so I guess a treat is in order.'

She was out of her gym kit and face down on the table before he could say another word. He knew this would not take long. No slow burn on this occasion. She was already primed. All she needed was someone to pull the trigger. He rolled her on her back after just a few minutes, and the whole thing was over in less than ten minutes. He covered her with a towel to let her calm at her own pace.

He had dealt with high-flier women supercharged with adrenalin before when something major had occurred. Even the super-cool Kimberley showed her animal side when they finally got to a hotel near Tunis airport to clean up and chill out before catching an evening flight back to London. As soon as the hotel door was closed her pent-up adrenalin, kept under control for some twelve hours, came bursting out in the form of supercharged sex. They never spoke about it afterwards, and they never got close again. It was just her need to explode.

While she was finishing in the gym and getting herself ready to go out to dinner, Charles phoned to say that Jim had told him of the assault and asked if she was okay. Sebastian told him she was supercharged and burning it off in the gym. Charles would talk to her in the morning after she has slept on it.

She came bounding into the kitchen just before 7:30 full of herself, but much calmer. She gave him a kiss on each cheek. 'Thank you. I needed that.'

'Pour us more Prosecco and tell me about your day before we leave.'

Chapter 123 – Thursday

She had only been at her desk for a few minutes when there was a knock on the door. It was the prankster carrying a bunch of flowers.

'scuse me Miss, can I ave a word?' He looked at Jim, 'Morning, sir.'

Jim sat up waiting to see what was to happen.

'Come in. What's your name?'

'Miles, Miss. Miles Davidson.'

'I want to apologise for yesterday Miss. I'm really sorry, and it won't never happen again.' He gave her the flowers.

Week 18

'Here's thirty quid for a new blouse, Miss.'

'That's okay Miles, the flowers will do nicely, thank you.'

'No, Miss. My missus has told me I ave to make good to you, specially as you didn't sack me. We had a babby three weeks ago, so I need a job. Take it Miss, else my missus won't be happy.'

'Was it a boy or girl?'

'A lovely little girl, Miss. Melts yer eart.'

'Well, you tell your wife I really appreciate what you've done.'

She reached out her hand to shake his hand 'No hard feelings, but do not grope women, even in fun. You hear me?'

'Yes Miss. I's learnt my lesson, Miss.'

'Okay Miles, back to work with you.'

'Yes Miss. Thank you, Miss.' He was gone.

Charles walked through the door, 'Was he the prankster from yesterday?'

'Yes, he came to apologise, brought me flowers, and money for a new blouse. Very sweet.'

'I hear you made quite an impression on the shop floor yesterday. Superwoman appears to be your new nickname. Do I need to ask where you learnt those skills?'

She looked at him and smiled.

'That's one hell of a school. He prepares you for everything. I like how you handled the whole situation yesterday. I don't condone what happened, but you've earned your right to lead that workshop. Congratulations.'

'Thank you, Charles. Much appreciated.'

During lunch time she went to Matlock to buy baby clothes with the £30 and more; and had them gift-wrapped.

Charles poked his head around the door. 'Your parcel from London has arrived. It's in the boardroom. Can I see it before we have it repacked for you?'

'Of course, you can.'

They strolled to the boardroom followed by Jim.

the Way

'Fantastic my dear. Absolutely lovely. He should be pleased with your choice. I'll get the package shop to carefully repack it and then pack it again to obscure the shape of it. Let me have your car keys so they can put it into your car.'

Chapter 124 – Friday

It was the last day before the Christmas shutdown. She asked Tom to visit with her. 'Miles Davidson, what's his wife's name?'

'Sarah, Miss.'

She wrote the name on the envelope stuck to the package. 'Before Miles leaves today, can you give him this for his wife', handing him the parcel.

'Yes, Miss, and thank you. Much appreciated, I'm sure.'

'And Tom, best wishes to you and your family this Christmas.'

'Thank you, Miss. I hope you have a good Christmas. You deserve it. And to you and Margaret' as he looked at Jim. He was gone.

'Young lady, I'm so proud of you this week, and thinking of their young baby after what Miles did to you brings tears to my eyes. You're a fine woman, and a worthy colleague.'

'Thank you, Jim. You forget I have three wonderful mentors who have given me so much. £30 is a lot to Miles, especially at Christmas. I couldn't let that young family suffer after all the good fortune lavished on me this year.'

Chapter 125 – Weekend

Mel certainly had a spring in her step as she prepared to leave for her last-minute Christmas shopping. She felt good about where she is in life. It had been a painful year but handing her Business Implementation Plan to Charles and Jim, having been approved by Sebastian, left her with a sense of achievement, and she had money in the bank, far more than she had ever owned before. No shopping today with fear of maxing her credit limit.

the Way

Week 19

Chapter 126 – Monday – Xmas Eve

Sebastian was somewhat bewildered. Having finished their food shopping his home was undergoing a makeover with Christmas decorations, something he had never undertaken before. Armed with two bags of decorations and the tree she had bought yesterday she was busy putting a shiny, sparkling glow in the hallway, kitchen and living room. *'She's having fun, so why not'*, he thought.

It was 9pm. Dinner cleared. Time to call Carmen. They went to the conference phone in his study and dialled.

'Fröhliche Weihnachten Carmen.'

'Sebastian, my darling Happy Christmas to you. Is Mel with you?'

'I'm here. Happy Christmas. Did you have a good evening?'

'Lovely, thank you, my dear, and so nice to hear from you both. Enjoy your time together with our love and best wishes. We will meet again soon.'

Chapter 127 - Christmas Day

She opened her eyes. It is Christmas Day. Even though the window shutters were closed, the room appeared lighter. She punched the button to open the shutters. Her heart filled with joy as she saw the snowflakes falling past the window. Without even looking to see if he was awake, she tapped him 'Seb, it's snowing. We have a white Christmas.'

She bounced out of bed towards the window. 'How lovely, a proper Christmas Day.'

the Way

He lay looking at her. He sometimes wondered if she really was 32 years old, or just going on a teenager. But he could not imagine her not being there. She brought her own light to his world. 'What a lovely daughter she would make.'

She turned towards him, 'Come on. Special treats for you today. I'll get the shower started,' as she disappeared into the bathroom.

He tried to appear bemused, but he was happy he wasn't alone for Christmas. She invited him into the shower, 'Today we bathe each other.'

He bathed her first, watching her enjoy this unabashed indulgent luxury. When he had finished, she took a while to relish every ounce of pleasure.

It was time for her to return the loving care afforded to her over the past weeks. She found bathing with him really did drown her sorrows. It was such a simple, but compassionate form of giving.

As she was not drowning his sorrows she decided to break from the normal silence. 'What made you think of this method of cleansing me of my sorrows? I don't think you'll find it in any executive training manual.'

'Quite by accident. When Katie, my wife, was grieving the loss of her father she would spend time sitting under the shower. One day I decided to join her. I started to wash away her grief. She responded really well. She came back to me for a while.'

She sensed she was losing him to his dark memories. She needed to wash away his sadness. 'Today is not the day for sorrow. Time for me to care for my master.'

She started again, putting him directly under the shower head to drown him, just as he did with her. Then she applied shampoo and started to gently massage his scalp. She slowly moved down his body. When she reached his genitals, she loaded her hands with bath gel and gently caressed them. Her touch caused him to start to develop an erection. Slowly, but surely, he became fully erect. He tried to move away from her.

'Seb, it's okay. Don't be embarrassed. If only you knew how many times you have my juices flowing, even today. The only difference is your reaction is visible, but I'm so happy to have your attention. I must be doing a good job on you. Let me finish bathing you as I have other surprises for you.'

He was back with her, allowing her to do as she pleased. 'And what surprises do you have in mind?'

'Today is Christmas Day. The staff deserves a well-earned break. I'll be looking after us today, and tomorrow. I'll finish bathing and dressing you and then prepare breakfast. I realise we are with Charles and Edna for lunch, but I'll take care of you throughout the holiday. I owe you so much. It's time for you to have some care and attention.'

'Thank you. Nice surprise. How do you intend to dress me?'

'Today I intend to wear a nice dress and, as my escort, I would like to dress you in smart casual clothes. I would like us to look good together.'

'You better go get your dress so I can see what will work.'

'I've already selected your clothes and put them together with my dress in your wardrobe.'

'Sneaky. When did this happen?'

'Last night while you were preparing dinner.'

'Let's see what you have in mind.'

She opened the wardrobe to reveal her dress next to slacks, shirt, and jacket for him. 'Does my master approve of my choice?'

'I don't know if I want the jacket, but let's see how we look.'

They dressed each other. She looked great, and it was good to see him dressed.

'You look lovely, my dear. I think it's only the third time I've seen you in a dress.'

'I know. The last time was at the opera. Not much call for it in boot camp. Wait a minute. I wore a dress to the Youth Enterprise dinner. Didn't you notice?' chiding him.

the Way

She prepared breakfast: poached eggs on buttermilk muffins (homemade) with smoked salmon, toast and honey, and fresh juice.

'I'm sorry I caused you pain this morning.'

'It wasn't your fault. You didn't know. What you also don't know is my trepidation about using it with you. I knew I needed to pick you up, and dust you off before you could dwell on the fault game, but you could so easily have seen it so differently. It was so close to a red line situation. You'll never know the relief when you told me how great you felt, even though you were unsure about the intimacy.'

'It was surprisingly intimate, but I didn't feel embarrassed. We were already swimming together naked. Happy Christmas Carmen,' as she raised her glass.

'Swimming together overcomes the compromise situation, but there is no physical contact. The cleansing process is very intimately physical – different situation.'

'Seb, I knew you well enough to know I can trust how you care for me. It did take my breath away at first, but it worked fantastically well, and why it's now almost routine when I'm not working. Look how it helped me when my mum died.'

'I sometimes think it's now too routine. It's supposed to be a pick you up and dust you off remedy. It now blurs the lines between us. Look at this morning. Are you my lover, or my student? Mentors do not have sexual relationships with their students – doesn't work.'

'Today is different. It's Christmas. We're both alone in this world. Would you have preferred us to each wake up alone in our own beds on such a day? We're close enough to share special days together. Would you have me wake up today realising I'm alone and then start my day sobbing as I think about the loss of my mum and dad this year? Not you, you understand being alone, and you care.'

She realised this conversation was close to a something she wanted to ask but needed a step closer. 'What about your hand

Week 19

in the dark routine? Where did that come from?' hoping not with Katie.

'That was one of our young executive's club members. Very often she would be asleep when I arrived. She loved to be woken that way as foreplay. I realised, just as with the female members of the club, you had natural sexual urges, but did not need the distraction of another third-party relationship. My choice was to let you go find it elsewhere with potential distracting consequences or keep it in-house. But it still had to be on the right side of the red line. You agreed to my rules, and it seems to work fine for you.'

Now was her chance 'Because your hand cares for me so much, it's delicious. But why have you never tried to make love to me? You must know the door is wide open. I've never felt closer to anyone.'

'Besides the indisputable fact I'm old enough to be your father, there is a bond of trust between mentor and student which should not be compromised by sexual activity. I look at you as I would a daughter. This keeps the intimacy in check.'

'Didn't you have sex with the women in your executive club?'

'Yes, but we were all students with our own mentors. We all knew the rules of sex without commitment, so no distraction.'

'If I openly invited you to have sex with me, how would you respond?'

'Please don't do it. And certainly not while you're my student. We're already at the red line boundary. You asked me to mentor you; you know the rules.'

She felt deflated. This door was now shut.

He saw her disappointment. 'What else do you have in store for us this holiday before we go open our presents?'

'Now we have snow, I would like to go play outside tomorrow, even build a snowman. Do you have a sled?'

'No, I don't. But I'm sure I have something that will suffice.'

'I would like us to go to London for a few days around New Year. I've spoken with Mama and she has something special for

the Way

us on New Year's Eve. I would also like to visit my mum and dad.'

'I also sense a shopping trip quietly hiding in there somewhere.'

She laughed, 'my master is reading my mind. Must buy a hat that shields my thoughts.'

'Anything else?'

'I have some surprises, but if you cannot read them, I want them to stay as such.'

'You've certainly been busy, even with Mama.'

'You didn't really think I would not wish Mama Happy Christmas after what she did for me? We had a good chat, and the request to join them for New Year was more a Carmenesque invitation. She loves you dearly, so let's spend New Year with family.'

'Come, my lovely master, let's go see what Santa brought for us.'

Santa had certainly favoured her. She found a beautiful evening dress (which she had tried during her shopping trip for the dress for the opera, not realising he had quietly purchased it whilst she was changing, and had it shipped), a Cartier watch, and a beautiful, but discreet set of Tiffany earrings. She gasped as she opened each present. 'Seb, they're all so beautiful. What have I done to deserve such fabulous gifts? These are gifts you buy for a lover or wife, not your student.'

'They are my appreciation for someone who has endured a hard taskmaster, suffered personal setbacks in the process, and triumphed over adversity. You richly deserve to be rewarded.'

She held him tight around the neck, 'I have the best master on the planet. How could I fail? Thank you so much.'

As he eased her back so he could see her face, he noticed the tears in her eyes. 'Do not cry, lovely lady. I need you to look your best for lunch.'

She smiled at him under her tears. *'This man does love me. How do I break through his sadness and bring him to my heart?'*

He opened his present. It had been carefully concealed so as not to hint at what was beneath the wrapping. His eyes shone when he finally saw the content. 'Mel, it's fantastic, but how can you afford such a picture? I know how much you must have paid.'

'I had a what-do-you-buy-a-man-with-everything conversation with Charles and told him about how you saw this picture in a gallery and really liked it. He and Jim helped me to buy it as a thank you for all you have done for me. But they don't want you to know they helped, so not a word, please.'

He stood it on a side table against the wall and took a few steps backwards to get a better view. He turned to her, now with tears in his eyes, 'I think this is the most wonderful present I've ever received. What a lady you are.' He reached for her 'Thank you from the bottom of my heart.'

Tears were rolling down his cheek. 'Now, master, no tears. We need to look our best today and, according to my beautiful new watch, we need to get a move on. We're supposed to be there for one o'clock.'

Chapter 128 – Boxing Day & rest of week

After breakfast, which she prepared, she challenged him to find something to use as a sled as she so much wanted to use the open areas of his land to play in the snow, and there was a suitable slope leading down to the adjoining golf course.

They played, but she decided not to abuse her good fortune by trying to get closer romantically. Their discussion on Christmas Day made it clear to her the mentor/student relationship is a rigid structure in his mind, so she must be patient in her quest to move closer to him.

the Way

Other than Christmas Day and Boxing Day she decided to stay with routine, including at least 2 hours each day studying, using him to interface with her study as and when required. This kept her grounded in her pursuit of the benefits of her university of life.

He was impressed with her commitment, thus happy to participate as needed. He stayed with his vision of her as a daughter to nurture when not in mentor mode. It made for a joyful time for both, as he usually spent Christmas in London visiting with friends, but otherwise alone. To have a full-time companion was a new and attractive change to his life.

They decided to leave for London on Friday as she felt the freedom to hit the sales without the usual inhibition of how to pay the credit card bill afterwards. She also found time to speak with Mama about her feelings seeking the advice of someone who really knew him. Mama urged patience.

She heeded Mama's words, 'You cannot lead Sebastian. You only encourage him to look in the direction you wish him to consider. Be patient. Wait until your quest is over. He must then consider life without you. Then you see change. Heed Mama well.'

She thought back to her first week – seeding. *'Hmm, how to seed him.'*

Week 20

Chapter 129 – Monday – New Year's Eve

It is traditional at Luigi's on New Year's Eve to not open at lunchtime to make time for evening preparations for which they only accept bookings from regular patrons. It is a fixed price affair, including champagne, and a fixed multi-selection menu of traditional Italian fare. All tables are clustered so that as many people sat together as possible. Mama saw this as Italian family style celebration of a New Year with fresh opportunities and new friends. They always sell this format out before Christmas to people who felt the warmth exuded by this Italian family restaurant.

Mel had purchased a beautiful cocktail dress specially for the evening and booked a full beauty makeover at a nearby salon. After chrysalis mode in boot camp for four months, she felt the need to open her wings and show her full majesty. Mama hardly recognised her when she walked through the door. When she realised it was her new daughter, she was aghast at the transformation.

'Gino, Mama wants picture with my beautiful daughter.'

A photographer was deployed for people who wanted to recall this special evening. She was quickly deployed in several shots with Mama and Mel, Mama, Mel, Sebastian, and Luigi, and Sebastian and Mel.

They were seated at a table cluster where Mama knew her lovely daughter would have fun whilst Sebastian would have interesting people to engage with. Although Mel was concerned Seb might not enjoy this evening, she was surprised to see him open to these people and fully participate in the event – a side of him not experienced before. The striking of the New Year brought much jubilation and a special kiss between them, and for the first time she saw tears in Mama's eyes as they hugged. It was after 1am before they left the restaurant in good and playful spirit. It would have been a perfect evening for her to express her physical love for this man, but knew this would spoil everything. A hand in the night would have to suffice.

Chapter 130 – New Year's Day

As the restaurant is closed on New Year's Day Mama wanted to go with Mel to visit the grave of her mum and dad. Mama has taken her new daughter to her heart, knowing how important Mel stays connected with her parents but hoping she is also happy with her new Mama. Her hopes are that Mel will find a way into her Sebastian's heart so she will become permanent family. They spent some time bonding together as Mama had no hurry to get back, and when they did decide to return Mel was taken to the apartment above the restaurant to have lunch with the family. For Mama, it was important for her new daughter to know she has a place in the family in her own right and did not need to be with Sebastian to visit with Mama.

Chapter 131 – Remainder of Week

Sebastian needed a couple of days to take care of business neglected these past months. Although she enjoyed shopping with him her financial freedom, and knowledge that London is the place to shop, she was happy to take advantage of the freedom to shop, go to show Mama at lunchtime her purchases, drop them at the apartment, and back out for another round. She was having fun knowing she would be back to boot camp and likely really challenged in the coming months. Each evening he surprised her with a theatre trip.

Week 20

On Friday, now totally shopped-out, they returned to Matlock to prepare themselves to return to their quest. She needed to get back into her routine before returning to the office on Monday.

the Way

Week 21

Chapter 132 – Monday

When Mel arrived at her desk, she could not help but be surprised with the facelift to both the offices and workshops. The Christmas shutdown every year was used to revitalise the workshops for another year of production. All machines had undergone thorough maintenance, one machine had undergone a significant upgrade, and a new machine installed. The workshops had been thoroughly cleaned. Everything looked pristine and ready for business. The office block had undergone some technical upgrades and a lick of paint. There was a freshness to the whole place. What did intrigue her was the addition of what looked like a computer network socket above her desk. *'Must find out what this can do for me.'*

Jim arrived looking better than of late. They were quickly at work preparing the worksheets for all the orders closed by Charles before Christmas. His push to close orders had produced enough work to keep everyone busy.

Late morning, they met with Charles to plan the development of business for the coming year.

Charles was keen to progress her Business Implementation Plan. It fitted well with introducing his new fabrication materials. 'Mel, in your extraordinary teachings, what would be the logical next step for your business proposal which would include production facilities for our new fabrication techniques?'

'According to my teachings I would prepare a Corporate Business Plan to both integrate the new opportunities into the existing business and to provide an impact statement on the business going forward.'

'If we assumed your Implementation Plan is approved, would you feel comfortable to produce a full Corporate Business Plan for Aldridge?'

the Way

'I think it would be a valuable part of my progress into understanding this business. I would require much input, but I'm sure Seb would be keen for me to learn and understand this process. I would add the caveat that, as with my Business Development Proposal and Implementation Plan, he will expect me to work to his exacting standards of delivery.'

Charles chuckled. 'It's okay Mel. The risk section of your proposal really got me thinking about the best way to proceed so no resistance from me. You'll need significant input from Jason, so I'll inform him of your exacting standards. He might even enjoy the process. As a bean-counter he sometimes shows disdain at my short-cut approaches to investment. I can work it out in my head, but he prefers to see it on paper. I will obviously fully support your efforts as will Jim. How long do you think you'll need?'

'Can I discuss this with Seb and let you know when I have a good idea what I must produce to his standards. I assume I'll undertake much of this effort in the evenings under his guidance, so I don't ignore my production duties. Do you have a problem with his input regarding the financials?'

'Now I have seen the impact of his involvement, not at all. His input could be most valuable. But don't burn yourself out. I appreciate your dedication to your program, but I would like you to survive the process. We'll need you in a few months to fully undertake production. It's an important job, so you need to be ready and fit to take over.'

'Don't worry, Charles. He won't let me burn out. He's invested too much to allow failure.'

'We are most fortunate to have such a resource. He has my gratitude and respect for what he's done for you and, indeed, this business. His heads-up on the recession will pay dividends this year. Let me know what he thinks in terms of timing. I have some decisions to make.'

When she returned to her desk, she picked up the phone. 'Seb, the Implementation Plan is accepted, and I'm now required

Week 21

to move directly to a Corporate Business Plan for Aldridge incorporating my proposals and new materials facilities. The Ryder Rolls Royce version is a given. Any idea how long it will take?'

'Is this a dedicated task, or part of your other duties?'

'Part of my other duties.'

'Given all the financial data is available then budget two weeks if we start the process this evening. I can gauge more accurately when I see the quality of the data available. I'll give you a list of data requirements. You do realise Carmen arrives this evening. This task will curtail your chit-chats in the sauna.'

'Didn't think of that. Let's work it out this evening. Thanks, Seb.'

Jim had been listening to her side of the conversation. 'Problem?'

'Nothing we can't work out. Carmen arrives this evening. I find my chats with her very illuminating. Her female perspective of business practice has proven valuable to me. If I start the Business Plan process this evening, I will have to curtail my chats with her.'

'How long does he think it will take to produce a Business Plan?'

'He's budgeted two weeks subject to the quality of available data.'

'End of the month will be fine if this helps you to maintain you chats with Carmen.'

'Thanks, Jim. Let's see what we work out this evening.'

Carmen and Mel arrived almost simultaneously. They walked in together, already chatting.

'Hi, ladies. I can see my presence is redundant already.'

They both laughed. 'Hi, Seb.'

'Hello, my darling.'

'Where were we?'

'Okay ladies. Change of plan this evening. Mel has to restart her studies so dinner at 7:30.'

the Way

'My darling, is this teaching something Carmen can participate? Carmen read everything about you mighty Chinese General in the holidays. Very interesting and very helpful. Carmen wants more of the teachings of our modern day General if possible.'

Mel smiled at her reference to Sebastian. He ignored it.

'We study the structure of a Corporate Business Plan. When we understand all the component parts, we develop a real Business Plan for Aldridge. If you're interested, I can't see a problem until we start to use real data from Aldridge. I'm sure you understand the confidentiality involved. Today and tomorrow will be fine for you to participate. Then we see how far we get.'

'This is good. Come Mel, let's to the gym. We must be on time for dinner.'

Having quickly finished in the gym and the pool, they were spending their last fifteen minutes in the sauna.

'Mel, my darling, tell me everything since my last visit. Aldridge was closed over Christmas, yes?'

'Yes. Shut down for production, but this time is used for maintenance and refurbishment to ready ourselves for the coming year.'

'So, nothing to report about progress at Aldridge for you?'

Feeling a little playful, 'I was molested in the workshop just before Christmas.'

'What! Did he hurt you. What happened?'

'It was a prank. One of the younger guys was set up to try to get a mistletoe kiss from me. Do you remember when you tried to grope me, and I first threw you? This guy got full adrenalin from me and landed on concrete. You should have heard him yell. I wanted to do a victory dance around the workshop.'

'Mein Got. This school is fantastic. We do more of this fighting. Carmen needs these skills. Carmen remembers how she felt after the belly-slap on that nasty manager. Come, we must go to school together. We have much to learn from our masterful teacher.'

Dinner over, it was time to work. 'Ladies, I'm in the fortunate position of having a paper I wrote for SME's which addresses the reasons for, and structure of, a Business Plan. I would like you both to read it before we define what you need for Aldridge. Let me know when you're ready to discuss.'

YOUR BUSINESS PLAN

You can rarely dress up a poor idea or bad business proposition and persuade anyone to back it, but it is perfectly possible to present a good idea or a viable business proposal so badly it never gets off the financial starting blocks. Which is why it is worth putting a great deal of thought and care into that all-important document - your Business Plan.

Do not, though, make the mistake of turning the whole task over to outside experts. Financing a business is really all about supporting the people who run it, so financiers are trying to assess you, the management, and they want to discover both what you think and how good you are at communicating your thoughts. By all means take advice from experts in those areas where you need guidance - but prepare the actual plan yourselves.

Business plans do not have to be prepared to a set formula, but it will ensure you provide all the necessary information if you marshal your facts and figures under different categories. I give the order of a typical Business Plan below, together with advice on what information a financier expects to find.

Presentation counts for much today and it is worth taking advice on how to present your ideas so the reader feels as though you are sympathetic to the amount of such material that they read on a daily basis. Poorly presented information, no matter how good, will at least weaken your bargaining position if indeed your proposal is considered at all. Your Business Plan should paint a picture of your idea so the picture and the style in which it is presented, as with an artist, will determine if the viewer regards it as a work worthy of consideration or just another picture.

Executive Summary

This is increasingly more important because of the vast amount of information financiers need to consider. It is so important to capture the attention of your reader very early in the document. The Executive Summary will usually be the only opportunity to achieve this attention, therefore due consideration to this cannot be over-emphasised.

This summary should be no longer than one page and should present a very succinct account of who you are, what you want to do, why you want to do it, and how much this will yield versus the cost to achieve it over what time frame – Return on Investment.

For those familiar with journalism this is the classic Who, What, Why, When, How, and How Much which must attract your reader to encourage further exploration into your Business Plan.

Business Summary

This is the section in which you list basic information about who you are - business name and address, status of business (Public Limited Company/Limited Company/ Partnership/ Sole Trader), date formed, reason formed, capital structure, professional advisors (names and addresses). Also, a brief history of the business stating how it is now, where it is going, and what you consider to be the most important factors in getting there.

Key Personnel

Here you should give the names, ages, and qualifications of your management team. Also, the position they hold within the company, the length of time they have been there and current remuneration.

Financiers complain that businesses frequently provide insufficient information on the people who are running (or going to run) the business. They also like separate CV's on each director and key personnel to be appended to the plan (details of relevant prior experience, health, family commitments, and include sporting activities and hobbies).

If you have non-executive directors or specialist external advisers (not accountants or lawyers) then they should be included with the reasons for their involvement, and any remuneration consideration.

If you have identified the need for new resources to execute your Business Plan, a profile of such resources should be included and the likelihood of finding such resources in the location in which they are required.

If the project or business is new, the financier will be looking particularly for experience in the business sector chosen. More important still, they will want to see a high degree of commitment to the enterprise both in terms of the cash the directors are prepared to put up and the time they're proposing to devote to the business.

Your chances of getting the money are greatly improved if you show a balanced team of directors with complementary skills and strengths.

Premises

Their size and how much of this is used for what purpose; whether they are freehold or leasehold; their value; outstanding mortgage (if applicable), or, if there is an option to renew any rental or lease commitments. Include rent and business rates plus frequency and date of future reviews. Say also whether you consider the premises suitable for your existing and future use. If not, what alternative is being proposed.

Plant and Machinery, Equipment and Vehicles

Give a brief description of the items which fall under these headings together with their age; estimated replacement date; suitability; how financed (e.g. HP / loan outstanding) and current valuation.

If you anticipate more expense in this area which is not described in the "Financial Summary" section of the plan, detail it here.

Product / Services

Many plans for new products/services fall at the first hurdle because the business idea is just plain barmy (like selling ice to Eskimos!). So, if you are presenting an idea for something new, put yourself in the financier's shoes and ask yourself whether your idea is credible – would you invest your own money rather than prefer other available investments.

List and describe the products or services you offer. If they are technical try to explain their functions in lay terms. Give their approximate value in terms of sales, and if appropriate, their share of *total output.*

If there are any special processes involved that are protected or protectable then explain why and by what means. Any copyright, patents, etc. registered, issued or pending should be mentioned and any new technology development should be outlined with a more detailed scenario (without any confidential information) as an appendix. Are there any technology development grants and awards available? If you have pursued these, then mention the outcome. Alternatively give, by means of your presentation, the opportunity to access the possibility of pursuing such funding on your behalf. Such opportunities greatly enhance the funding possibilities.

Environmental Issues

The interest in our environment has become an issue we cannot ignore. Therefore, the following three areas need to be addressed remembering the tone should be upbeat, not an imposition.

If your product is environmentally friendly or is more friendly than that of your competitors then state why this is, and the cost implication versus the business returns.

If your business is waste disposal or you have unfriendly waste to dispose of then a technical description of the disposal techniques should be included with the cost implications.

If you are purchasing a plant which has a toxic waste disposal problem or other environmentally unfriendly by-products, state how you intend to address this issue and at what cost over what time frame.

Remember that there are many organisations willing to provide soft loans and grants for the protection of the environment. If your case is well presented the financier could well attract such financial assistance thus alleviating the overall investment and/or debt burden on your business.

Sales and Marketing

The information required here is the market size and potential; sales performance; the competition; marketing and sales methods.

An insufficient knowledge of the size and structure of the marketplace mars many a business plan. Whether you're launching a new product/service or trying to expand an existing one, you must be

Week 21

able to profile your buyers, how much they will pay, the price elasticity, and how you intend to get your product to the end-user market.

Financiers expect you to tell them the total size of the market, its trends over the last few years and forecasts for the future. If you do not know this, there is a great deal of already published marketing information. If your local commercial reference library cannot help, try your local Chamber of Commerce. Financiers will expect you to quote your source of information.

If you are in a small market and can give an idea of your present and projected market share, so much the better.

Name your major competitors and their share or status within the market. Financiers like you to define what you consider to be your advantage over them (price, quality, service, location or whatever - but make sure you can justify this).

If you are optimistic about increasing your sales and/or share of the market, explain why. And if you have any sizeable orders in the pipeline, give details.

If you have conducted market research of your own which identified potential prospects, describe the baseline and your findings.

Financiers want to see an aggressive approach to marketing and selling (they will not be impressed with firms whose only method of generating sales is answering the telephone), so describe how you plan to promote your product/service and how much money you are allocating to this. State too the names of your major suppliers, how satisfied you are with them and whether there are any alternatives. If appropriate, briefly describe your methods of production.

Give details of your projected sales over three years, and any elasticity in these figures. If relevant, break them down by product category, and by major customers (financiers are keeping an eye open for potentially risky situations - like, for instance, businesses which rely almost totally on one customer and would thus come unstuck if that customer went to the wall or went elsewhere).

If your product or service idea is a new, you should give information on sales channels, i.e. exactly how your product will reach the customer. How do you know the suggested channel will take it? If you are looking for agents, what do they sell at present? And if it is competitive with your product, will they handle both or give up the old one in your favour? If so why?

Many investors have got their fingers burned when a super new product could not win space on the supermarket shelves, and many an infant company has found that agents and dealers are loathed to give up an established line to risk one that is innovatory.

Trading Performance

In your Business Plan provide a summary of your last three years results (sales, cost of sales, gross profit, overheads, profit before tax) and summarise up to three years of audited profit and loss accounts (if you have them). Explain any unusual features about the accounts - sharp increases/decreases in turnover or profit, for instance.

Copies of the actual audited account are inappropriate in your Business Plan as they tend to be cumbersome. Financiers will expect to see them at some point, but a summary showing the actual results of previous years and projections of future years on one page is easier to digest.

Financial Summary

Again, summarise in your Business Plan how you stand at present (fixed assets, stock, debtors, creditors, net working capital, capital employed and how it is financed - shareholders, loans, overdrafts etc.), and attach up to three years' audited accounts. Explain any apparent anomalies in the figures.

Future Prospects

Financiers need to know what you think are realistic aspirations for the business in the light of your assessment of the market and other related factors. Which means they expect you to prepare cash flow forecasts and balance sheet projections for at least three years ahead.

This is probably the hardest part of the business plan exercises, and an area where you really may be able to benefit from outside help (financiers do appreciate, though, that after the first year or so it's very much a matter of crystal ball projections).

Although annual projections are adequate for the later years, projections for years one and two should be prepared on a quarterly (or even monthly for one year depending on the product cycle time) basis and attached to the plan.

Financial Requirements

Finally, state the amount of finance required with details of why you want it, when it will be needed, how long you need it, and how you propose to fund it. It goes without saying that this section must be worded very carefully, and it must tie in with the cash flow projections that you have prepared.

If you seek a loan, state what term of loan you require and how you propose to repay it - monthly, quarterly, etc. If you are seeking a substantial amount of working capital, are you prepared to part with some equity of your business? Both the size of the share stake taken and the price you pay are negotiable.

State also in this section what assets are available as security (e.g. mortgage on property, key-man and life policies, stocks and shares, guarantees from third parties).

Remember that to have any chance of success your Business Plan needs to excite a potential financier. The reason for which you need the money should be credible and should be explained in a way that is easy to understand with a well-argued and well-worked case. Vagueness is a besetting sin where Business Plans are concerned; financiers hate vague subjectivity. They want to see all the relevant facts and figures and will test you to ensure that you understand them.

Business Risks

This section describes the impact on the business of adverse direct and indirect events. One important aspect of this section is it demonstrates to financiers that you are aware of the primary risks that can impact business performance.

Direct risks can be disruption to your supply chain, or your distribution. The loss of a key resource is another risk, as is defective quality control invoking warranty claims and subsequent product avoidance.

Business disruption risk needs to be included stating what you have planned to mitigate risks such as your premises not being available to you as a result of natural disaster or fire. What insurance cover do you *have, or propose for such event risks?*

If there is any instability in countries that you use for supply, what is your fallback position?

If you export your product what would be the impact of currency rate swings. This also applies if you import components.

Is your product seasonal, or subject to climatic conditions? How would this impact cashflow and profitability?

Indirect impacts could be anything from adverse Government legislation, economic recession, or changes in corporate or employee tax that are currently being rumoured.

There are risks beyond your reasonable control, such as war. Such risks are deemed beyond the scope of your Business Plan.

In Summary

Give some thought to the presentation. It should be neatly presented (easy to read) and well laid out. However, presentation should enhance, but not get in the way of content. Glossy productions with pictures must be relevant or leave them out. And expensive bindings do little to win a financier's heart. Likewise, never present a photocopy version to anyone you would like to read it.

The outline Business Plan indicated inevitably applies best to established companies with hard products. Service companies and start-up businesses will not have anything to enter under certain headings. This means they need to give more emphasis to such things as management skills, identification of the market niche- and approaches to marketing their specific business ideas - and be very convincing about them.

If preparing a Business Plan sounds like a terrible chore, bear in mind that the information financiers require should differ little, if at all, from the information you need to understand and manage your business. Business planning is essentially an exercise carried out for the benefit of the business itself - you cannot identify future potential and possible pitfalls - without planning ahead. And if you do not give some real thought to the future of your business, it might not have any future at all.

He left them in the kitchen. An hour later he returned to find them chatting about what they had read. 'Any comments before we proceed?'

'My darling, you use the word "financiers" throughout. Does this same structure apply to all sources of finance such as banks, investors, and Government funding?'

'Yes, it does, and includes existing shareholders. I would also suggest it equally applies if the company has retained income not already allocated. Such funds are shareholder funds, but not distributed as dividend. They are probably on deposit at some nominal interest rate. A shareholder could take the view they could achieve a much better return if these funds were distributed, albeit there may be tax implications. A shareholder wants to know their money can be deployed by the company at an equal or better return on equity than they could alternatively achieve at the same level of risk. A Business Plan provides this information. I would add that funds not deployed, in whatever form, are one of the principal value drivers in a business.'

'Thank you, my darling. I understand. We maintain reserves we can use if needed.'

'Reserves are very different. Reserves are generally maintained to cover for some potentially catastrophic event where alternate funds may be difficult to secure at short notice, and not securing funding quickly could jeopardise the company. Reserves could be viewed as an insurance fund where commercial insurance cannot be secured or is prohibitively expensive. For example, banks retain reserve funds to maintain capital adequacy in the event of loan defaults. Reserves are intended to mitigate event risk and thus not available for business development.'

'Very interesting, my darling. Carmen will remember this.'

Mel decided to engage. 'As I understand it, the Business Plan is the same structure regardless of whether you want an overdraft or a capital injection, or maybe no funds at all.'

the Way

'Correct. Funding is about ensuring you have the money to engage in business. The label of such funding merely identifies the basis of the availability. Tomorrow I'll give you a diagram to show you how a company deploys funding, and how it calculates its Long-term Equity, its Working Capital Requirement, Short to Medium-term debt, etc.'

'Perhaps I should add that the discipline required to structure a good Business Plan ensures you understand your business and are adequately funded to engage. Overtrading can be as terminal as undertrading. If you haven't structured your corporate funding so you can maintain cashflow liquidity to service your obligations as they fall due regardless of whether you are trading far better than expected, or not achieving your projected trading level, you are insolvent.'

'Surely funding would be available if you were trading much better than expected?'

'Not necessarily. Much depends on the circumstances. It's not generally understood that financiers lend to people, not companies or projects. The company or project is the catalyst that creates the need for funding, but it takes smart people to convert a project or company objective into valuable reward. Many times, people present credible business ideas for funding only to find they are rejected, primarily because the people who want funding are not considered the right people to materialise the value. Overtrading could be deemed a reckless lack of knowledge of the marketplace and thus too risky to support, i.e. wrong people. Therefore detailed information on key players in the business are included.'

'Wow. I never knew that trading far better than expected could be terminal. A bit counterintuitive for the layman.'

'Remember our evening on supply and demand?'

'Must read my notes again.'

'Okay. Let me summarise. A current Business Plan is fundamental to understanding your business objectives, markets, opportunities, and your ability to engage regardless of

Week 21

the funding requirements. You can only optimise your funding needs when you have diligently assembled the data necessary to compile a Business Plan. Any questions?'

Very interesting, my darling. Carmen is happy to be included in these teachings. Thank you both. Carmen will consider this subject again before tomorrow evening. Good night.'

'Now you have the profile, how do you feel about this task?'

'Daunting; but will enjoy seeing Aldridge through your eyes. Hope the data is available.'

'Why don't you take a copy of this paper to Jason and see how he reacts to providing the data required.'

'I'll do that. The sooner he's in the loop, the faster we can build the plan. See you in the morning. Good night.'

Chapter 133 – Tuesday

When she arrived at her desk, there was no evidence of Jim being there. *'Probably another hospital day. Poor man.'*

She decided to engage with Jason as quickly as possible so extracted a copy of the Business Plan paper and headed for his office which was on a wing of the main building tucked away behind the design team. It was a large room partitioned at the far end, using a half-glazed partition to provide a nominal office with a door in the centre. There were four admin staff ranging from 20s to 50s in age, two on each side creating a corridor towards the office.

She said "Good morning" to the admin staff as she approached the office where the door was open. She entered to find every surface cluttered in papers and files, with Jason sitting at a desk facing the partition. Probably late 20s, casually dressed but presentable. He clearly compensated for long hours at a desk with gym and/or sport activity.

the Way

'Good morning, Jason. Do you have a minute?'

'Sure. Charles told me you would come calling. What can I do for you?'

'Can I leave you a paper to read and come back later to discuss? I have been asked to produce a full Business Plan for Aldridge. This paper was written by my mentor, who is a senior banker. I need to comply with this structure. I need your help, especially with the financial data.'

'No problem. This place needs this discipline. Too much seat-of-pants. Charles is very capable, but his way does not help me to help him. What about you come back at 11:30? I should be clear by then.'

'Great. See you at 11:30. Thanks.'

She strolled back to her office amused by his comments, remembering the response of Charles to the first draft of her Development Proposal – more than enough for him, until he was introduced to the section on risk. *'Can't wait to see how he reacts to a comprehensive Business Plan.'* Big smile.

She was snapped out of her thoughts when she saw Tom heading towards her office. 'Hi Tom. I'm right behind you.'

'Hello, Miss. We've got a problem with a fabrication. Can we look at the original requirement to see what we need to deliver?'

'Sure. Which job is it?'

It took some forty-five minutes to resolve the problem, but all would be well. Very satisfying that she did not need to defer to Jim.

She revisited with Jason. He held the paper in his hand. 'This is great. I want to be part of this. Never done a real one. Did something similar at college, but nothing as comprehensive as this. When do we start?'

She laughed, 'I thought we started a couple of hours ago. How much of the data is available?'

'Quite a lot, actually. Possibly not in the form you want, but I can fix that. How do we work this? I have questions for you.'

Week 21

'Much of the work will be in the evenings under supervision of my mentor. Would you be free to join us on Thursday evening? If you arrive before 7:30 you can have dinner with us and then heads down. You can both ask questions and fully understand what's required.'

'Sounds good. I've heard good things about this Ryder guy from Charles. Would love to tap into his knowledge.'

'His name is Sebastian. It's possible I will have more specific requirements tomorrow. I'll let you have them and see how much you can assemble by Thursday evening. Does this work for you?'

'Sounds good. Charles mentioned something about you incorporating ideas you have regarding corporate clients in London. Do you have anything on paper I could look at to assess the financial implications?'

'I wrote a Business Development Proposal and an Implementation Plan to the same standards as I require for the Business Plan. But could you ask Charles for copies? He's very sensitive about some of the data in those reports. I'm not in a position to give you a copy.'

'It's okay. I understand. Very secretive is Charles. I'll speak with him.'

'Thanks.'

'I'll start to assemble data I know for sure you'll require and then you tell me what more you need.'

'Great. Let's talk tomorrow.'

When Carmen and Mel arrived home, they were quickly changed and off to the gym and the sauna.

After dinner, it was time to continue their studies.

'Okay, ladies, any thought from yesterday before we move on?'

'I spoke with Jason today. He read your paper. He's up for it. Will start to prepare what he knows is needed. Wants to know

the Way

what else you need. I invited him for a working dinner Thursday evening where he will present what he has; and agree a final form of our plan. Thought it better to integrate him into the team. He wants to meet you in any event. Charles has given him copies of my Plans, so he'll work up some numbers for the proposed changes.'

'You've been busy. I have a list of data we need. I'll give it to you at breakfast tomorrow.'

'I said last night I would give you a diagram of the financing structure of a company.' He handed them a diagram.

Cash	Short-term Debt
Seasonal WCR	
Permanent WCR	Long-term Debt
Fixed Assets	Equity

As you can see, there are two columns. The left-hand column is cash and use of funds, and the right-hand side is the source of funds. As each component of the source of funds has its own characteristics in terms of the duration of availability and cost, balancing these characteristics against the use of funds is a fundamental task of any competent Finance Director. At its simplest using short-term debt to fund fixed assets is a nonsense unless such fixed assets can generate all the funds required to repay this debt before repayment date.

I don't want to explore the optimum matching sources of funds with the use of funds as this is business school narrative. But this diagram shows a balanced approach to sourcing the funds you need to enable you to conduct business. When formulating your Business Plan your financial requirement should recognise the use of funds which then defines the type of funding requirement.

Chapter 134 – Wednesday

As soon as Mel arrived in the office, she took the list prepared by Seb to Jason. 'Morning Jason. Here is the list of financial data I need.'

He scanned it. 'Very comprehensive, but no problems. May not have all of it by tomorrow evening as I'll need to consult with our auditors on some regulatory details.'

She noticed he had a network socket with a cable to his computer. 'Do you know what I can do with my network socket?'

'Sure. I'm the computer techy around here. Apparently, you mentioned to Charles you had no direct computer linkage with the design team. I had this floor networked over the Christmas break.' He pointed to a computer in the corner of his office. 'That computer over there is called a server and controls access to both the in-house network and email although broadband speeds around here are not great so don't expect too much in the way of access. We need to change your desk PC to get you configured.'

'Why do you need to change my PC?'

'Firstly, it's Windows-based, and out of date. Secondly, I could only connect you to the internet, not the design team. They all use Apple machines. Their preferred CAD software. How come you have a company car but not a laptop? Need to put this right. Do you have a problem learning how to use an Apple computer as you will need it to hook into the design team?'

'If I need it to function properly, then I'll learn.'

'Good. I'll order you a new laptop today. Should be here Friday. Could have it configured on Monday with everything you probably need. If you need to work on the Business Plan only do text, not spreadsheets. I'll do those and transfer them to your new laptop.'

'Will this change slow me down?'

'If you're competent with MS Word, you'll soon pickup Apple Pages. Ditto on spreadsheets. Once you can navigate your way around Apple OS, you'll be fine. The first time a designer needs to screen something for you, they'll show you how to do it. Everything resides on this server and is indexed by Job No. and/or Client so will be available to you.'

'Isn't it risky having all our information on just one machine? What about if it fails?'

'Current work in progress also sits on the designer's laptop. And I backup the server every night and take it home with me just in case the office burns down overnight. When we can get some decent line speeds around here, we'll be able to setup automatic offsite backup and recovery. You should take your laptop home with you every evening to preserve your own work.'

'No problem. I can use it to make notes of the work I do with Sebastian.'

'Okay. Let me get you a new laptop and start to put these financials together.'

She went back to her own office, thinking how she would transfer the data from her current PC to a new laptop. *'He's the techy. Let him do it.'*

When she arrived home, she wanted to speak with Sebastian before starting her routine.

'Jason doesn't like my PC. Thinks it's too old and out of date. He will get me a new Apple laptop ready for Monday so I can communicate with him and the design team. They wired our offices for a network over Christmas, so I need to use Apple because the design team use an Apple CAD system. Better on paper tomorrow, I think.'

'No problem.'

'Would you mind if we bunked school tonight? I want to discuss some issues with Carmen as she leaves tomorrow.'

'Will dinner at 8 work?'

'Great. Thanks.'

'I need to prepare the paperwork you need tomorrow so works for me. See you both at 8.'

Chapter 135 – Thursday

Mel was home on time, through her gym routine, and back in the kitchen by 7pm.

'What can you tell me about Jason?'

'Late 20s. Looks fit. Has been with Aldridge about 6-years.'

'That's it? Where did he qualify? Is he married? Does he have children? What are his interests?'

'Haven't got that far.'

'When will you understand you need to know these things, especially with close collaborators? You made this mistake with

the Way

Michael. Such information can significantly impact the way you put argument to him. Why do you think we include comprehensive CV's in a Business Plan?'

She blushed as she realised her error. 'Sorry. Too busy for chit-chat.'

'This is not chit-chat. It's vital information.' The gate alert sounded. 'Go meet and greet. We'll deal with this later.'

Jason parked his car. Mel, dressed more formally than usual, and quickly back onto the field of play after her rebuke, greeted him.

'Wow, Mel. This place is fantastic. How many people B&B here?'

'Only me, and an executive from Aarden Industries who stays here three nights each month. Come and meet Sebastian.'

'Jason, welcome. Good to meet you. Dinner is nearly ready. Can I offer you a drink?'

'Thank you. It's a pleasure to meet you. Just water for me.'

'How long have you been with Aldridge?'

'Charles took me in as soon as I qualified. Some six years ago now. Saved me a commute to Derby every day to the practice that put me through qualification.'

'Sounds like you're a Chartered Accountant.'

'Yes. Hoping to make FCA in the next couple of years.'

'Who do you use as auditors as I haven't seen any big firms around here?'

'One of the nationals with an office in Chesterfield. Not top drawer International, but certainly more than capable for the needs of Aldridge. They also take care of our regulatory compliance.'

'How did you get involved with Aldridge?'

'My old firm in Derby were the auditors until 3-years ago, but they were a one office practice. So much regulation came into play Charles considered he needed a national firm he could rely on to ensure Aldridge is fully aware of its obligations. Charles is not one to spend time reading directives.'

Week 21

'That makes sense. Charles is old-school businessman. Concentrates on business generation. Let pen-pushers deal with regulations.' Noticing his wedding ring. 'Do you have family here?'

'I was born in Matlock. I'm married to Jenny, a lovely lady I met in Derby. We now live locally with our two youngsters, Katherine and Diane.'

'Do you enjoy being a dad? Are they the reason you look so fit? They must keep you on your toes.'

He laughed. 'There're great. And there're lively. Katie starts school next year. Will be interesting to see how she gels with other kids as she's a real live wire. Wants to know everything about anything.'

'Sounds great. Must keep you busy.'

'They certainly do. But I still play soccer for Matlock. The training night allows me to compensate for sitting at a desk all day, although I try to run at lunchtimes.'

'Is Matlock in a league?'

'Yes. It's minor league but we hold our own.'

'Sorry, I've only lived here a couple of years so still consider myself a stranger in this beautiful region. Let's have dinner before we get down to our task.'

Mel sat there feeling silently chastised as she noted how much information Seb had extracted in just a few short minutes.

They chatted through dinner. She noted how quickly he put Jason at ease, realising he may be a little overwhelmed with the setting and his presence. *'How quickly my hermit master can make someone feel as though they belong here. First time I've seen him on the field of play. Impressive. He has quickly won Jason as both an ally and collaborator.'*

Dinner cleared it was time to work. 'Jason, how do you feel about this task?'

Your paper and Mel's proposals are the wake-up call I've needed to get more active in the future direction of Aldridge. I'm designated as Finance Director but play little part other than

the Way

cash flow management. Jim will only be with us a short time now and Charles must be close to retirement age. I don't see any obvious succession, so I guess it's down to Mel and me to step up to ensure continuity. This Business Plan is a good place to start to fully understand Aldridge. So up for it especially as you've set the bar high. It will help us find any weaknesses we need to address.'

'I like the attitude. Let's go through what you have and then identify what more we need.'

Jason produced the data he had accumulated. They went through it in detail, both to ensure Sebastian could verify integrity, and Mel could understand the numbers, their relevance, and where they fitted into the Business Plan.

'What about event risk? This includes insurance, Life Assurance, indemnities and warranties.'

'We have these. I'll study all of them in the next couple of days and summarise them for you. Hopefully, I can give this to Mel on Monday.'

'Can you note if there are any specific exclusions you may consider material.'

'Sure. No problem. Will be interesting to see if we are as covered as well as we should be.'

'Another subject. What expansion capacity is already available without the new material fabrication facility?'

'None. For the past few years Charles fills his order book and stops looking for what we call current business – business due for delivery in the next financial year. Commercial deliveries tend to have a longer lead-time. He has only started to discuss expansion of the plant for this new fabrication material in the past year, but no expansion of mainstream business.'

'Are you aware of any commercial logic for no expansion?'

'I think he's of an age where he has enough on his plate. I don't understand the logic of the London office as it's only marginal business. Aldridge makes good profits, has no debt, and doesn't have to fight for its current market share. The

Week 21

revelations in Mel's plan about an imminent deep recession explain the large number of orders closed in the past few weeks. Whenever I think Charles needs to think about the future of Aldridge, he demonstrates he's right on it, protecting Aldridge against financial stress. Although I would like to be part of the thinking, I can't fault his business judgement.'

'If your production capacity is full how do you cope with contingent work such as breakages of existing installations? Mel tells me Aldridge guarantee replacement in short order.'

'A full capacity order book assumes a 5-day production week. You're right we do guarantee replacement, and it happens. The factory goes into overtime for such contingencies. We already have all the design and fabrication details so only supply of materials and workshop time. He also has a deal with Pardow that they will help each other out if demand is high, such as was the case with the Manchester street riots a few years ago. Aldridge can cope with whatever is thrown at it and thus its reputation.'

'What about the financial costs of a new processing facility?'

'I'll speak with Jim about this as it will be a significant capital cost.' Looking at Mel, 'You should be part of this discussion as you will inherit it.'

'You both need to be an integral part of every aspect of this plan. I do not want to see at the end of this exercise that either of you needs to refer to the other for any question I might have. A Corporate Business Plan is an expression by the Directors of the business they control. All must be fully aware of the direction of the company and their respective obligations to deliver. Take your time to become totally familiar with this business. There is no rush as you have been given until the end of the month to produce. Are we good on this point?'

Both felt the assertion of this statement – the game had changed.

Mel had a thought. 'I thought you told me Aldridge doesn't need any financing.'

'This is true, but why don't you examine scenarios where the surplus cash is not available for this investment. This will give you both a clearer understanding of how to select appropriate financing options and the cost/benefits of each.'

Jason was quick to interject, 'I'm up for that.' Looking at Mel, 'We need to consider all the options available to us. Our bankers are frequently approaching us with financing opportunities. I would like to take the opportunity how to approach these through the eyes of Sebastian. Might need financial support in the future. What if I assume we reserve the funds owed to Charles for the landbank freehold and dividends elected but not taken? This would consume much of the free cash we have available.'

'Good idea. Make this debt a reserve item to be paid on demand, thus not available to the business. I would also like to add succession planning to this Business Plan, as it will influence funding opportunities. As we all know Jim's days are few as an active participant, and Edna, if not Charles, must be considering Charles' retirement. They run Aldridge and keep much of their strategy secret. Why don't we undertake an impact analysis to determine the risks to Aldridge of losing both these giants in quick succession?'

Jason was quickly in tune with this idea. 'Great idea. When Charles sees it in writing with the associated risks, might encourage him to seriously consider this issue.'

Sebastian thought they had exhausted the discussion this evening. 'Okay, we have a skeleton of a plan. Now we need to add flesh both in numbers and verbiage. Could I suggest, rather than each concentrating on their part, you collaborate so you both understand all aspects of this process. I will provide oversight to help where needed. Any idea when we should assemble again to review progress?'

Jason looked at Mel. 'I can have more detail available Monday, but I think you need to get up to speed on your new laptop so we can share information. Let's give ourselves a little latitude, so can I suggest next Wednesday evening. Give me time to consult with our auditors to see if they have any relevant input.'

She thought about it. 'Sounds good as I do want to make sure I can use this new laptop.'

'Good. Wednesday it is. Jason, can I thank you for your time this evening. It's a pleasure to note your enthusiasm for this task, which will greatly help in my quest with Mel. I will review anything Mel shows to me before next Wednesday, so we resolve any issues as we progress.'

'The pleasure's all mine. I've been waiting to put my education and ideas to good use. And to have such qualified oversight is truly a bonus. I'll see you next Wednesday.'

Chapter 136 – Friday

Once daily demands were completed both Jason and Mel spent much of the afternoon with Jim understanding in detail his thoughts regarding the proposed new production facility. Although much of the capital investment was already embedded in Mel's plan, Jason wanted to understand the working capital issues, especially in the first two years. This was not an expansion of known business, so more risk considerations and contingencies will need to be considered.

Once dinner had been served, he noticed a large grin on her face. 'Someone is feeling happy with herself. Is there something you wish to tell me?'

'I have an admirer.'

'Is this a distant admirer, or someone with amorous intentions?'

'We went to lunch together today.'

'How long has this been developing, and who is he?'

the Way

'His name is Simon. He is one of our better technical designers. Jim selected him to go work with Teresa Yardley, the architect who may use the new polymer materials in her latest design. He's back for a few weeks, and has used every opportunity to visit with me, especially when Jim is not around. He finally asked me to lunch today.'

'How did you feel about this new encounter?'

'Flattered to be asked. Dressing down to do this job does nothing for my femininity or sense of self-esteem. That he sees me as an attractive woman is nice.'

'Using the skills you have learnt can you profile him to me, and any pertinent information gleaned during your lunch.'

'He's testing me after my failure with Jason. Well, my master, I don't need to be told twice. He's probably a couple of years younger than me, single, tall, good looking, and has his own apartment in Matlock. He studied technical architecture at uni, has worked for Aldridge for 6 years, but clearly has ambitions to go much further. He loves working in London with Teresa, and I sense he would like to transfer there on a permanent basis. He's very serious, but not nerdy.'

'Why is he still in the market? Young men of your description of him must be in demand in these parts.'

'I think both his seriousness and his ambition have equally made him appear aloof to local women and keeping himself free to move on to pursue a career.'

'So where do you see this going?'

'Don't know, but it will be interesting to have some social interaction with someone nearer my age.'

'Does this mean you will start dating?'

'Possibly. Would you mind? He has invited me to go clubbing next Friday with some of his friends.'

'Not at all. Your life is your own. Would free me up from cleansing showers, hand in the dark, and you sleeping in my bed.'

Week 21

'Oh no. I'm not ready to surrender such treats for anyone. He'll have to wait until you throw me out.'

He was laughing. She looked at him sternly, 'You've just spoiled my fun.'

'Not at all. Just clarifying your options. But seriously, let us take a moment to look at this encounter from a different angle. Does he know of your ultimate possible directorship of Aldridge?'

'No. This is not discussed anywhere except with Charles and Jim, not least because it's not a given. I must prove myself worthy. As far as anyone else is concerned, I'm a production manager apprentice. Not even Michael is aware of the intended goal. Charles refers to me as his apprentice; hopefully as a smokescreen.'

'Therefore, he probably thinks you are not attached to Matlock, and thus would be happy to move back to London with him to achieve his ambitions – please note his ambitions. You've been there before. You have indicated he is still available to give him freedom to move – but to his ends. I'm sure if he knew your goal, he could see you as a useful resource, or a convenient companion until he moves on.'

'Please Seb. I had a nice lunch with an interesting guy my own age. Now I feel like I'm about to be used, abused, and cast out if I put my career before his.'

'I'm sorry. I could have phrased things better. Please believe me, I'm not trying to discourage this relationship. Quite the contrary. But not as you may see it.'

'Okay, my master. Where are we going with this?'

'Think of the young execs club I told you about. Building useful contacts. You could take the view you don't want a relationship with Simon because this will end in tears when either of you progress to your next level, but you would like him as a friend. He's working with Teresa Yardley. He could provide you with useful insight into the practice that would not be otherwise be available to you. Should he go to work there –

unlikely, as this would probably breach the consultancy agreement between Aldridge and Teresa Yardley – but he could use this assignment to get direct access into another practice in London. This would be useful to you if you don't have his chosen practice as a client. You have your social friendship for the time being without any romantic relationship, but potentially a very useful source for the future.'

'You're a real schemer. Our contract with Teresa Yardley facilitates his transfer if that's his choice. But I think you're suggesting I recruit him as a spy. Am I right?'

'You're getting too good for me. But do you see the opportunity?'

'Yes, I do. But I'm also being asked to consider using him, giving no favour other than social intercourse.'

'You provide him with the opportunity to work with Teresa Yardley. And I haven't said you cannot have a relationship with him if you so desire, albeit I would suggest with no commitment. The rules between you would have to be clear from the outset, but this would probably mean disclosure of your aims within Aldridge. I would advise against this. You only have a few weeks to go to complete your transition, so let nature take its course. But I am serious about the treats here if you enter into a relationship with him.'

'My dear Seb. There is no way I want to lose what we have, and so long as you allow me to stay here, I'll do nothing to jeopardise this lovely world I enjoy with you. Simon needs to look elsewhere if he seeks a sexual relationship. But I need to learn how to recruit my own spies so managing such a relationship with Simon will give me a safe way to practice. As ever my master has taught me how to see opportunity. I will heed his wisdom and keep him informed.'

'Will you still go clubbing next Friday?'

'Why not? Could use a little wild fun. The situation with Jim is taking its toll on me. A little respite might be a useful tonic.'

Week 21

Chapter 137 – Weekend

Sunday was such a dreary day outside with lashing rain and cutting temperature Mel decided to work on her Business Plan text before starting their fighting routine and afternoon tennis.

'Seb, can you give me some pointers how to package my text to minimise rewrites?'

'Sure. You bring several aspects of your teaching into play. First and foremost, keep it brief and to the point. Any statement that does not add anything of value should be removed. You use the same process as we did for the previous reports applying the Who, What, Why When, How and How Much structure. One significant difference is the replacement of "I" with "we" as a Business Plan is a collective statement of all key people. Apply a little rhetoric when appropriate but think objective, not subjective. All the political and economic data can be extracted from your previous work as these external factors apply generally to Aldridge and their business sector. How am I doing?'

'Great. Is there more?'

'You have three main areas of business which should be defined separately. There is your mainstream retail, which will continue without change and is the cash flow engine of the company. You have your corporate business which will integrate working with architects, much of which you already have. Then you must overlay both with new material fabrication which needs somewhat more detail as it has yet to be proven and requires significant capital. I would suggest you need input from both Jim and Charles to comprehend how they see Aldridge position itself with these materials, and where they see these materials being applied in the short-term, medium term, and long-term.'

'Thanks. Got all that.'

the Way

Week 22

Chapter 138 – Monday

When Jim finally arrived at the office just before midday Mel could see he was really struggling. *'What to do'* she thought.

'Jim, I have an idea I want to discuss with you as I need your help to make it work.'

'Let me hear your idea.'

'I need to gain confidence I can do this job without you being so close at hand. As things stand, I have the comfort you're sitting just behind me if I hit a problem. It's too easy to turn to you rather than have the pressure of needing to resolve the issue myself. I also want to test just how capable I am at fulfilling this role.'

'Very commendable. What do you propose?'

'I would like to feel the pressure of being on my own. Can I cut it when it matters? Can I look at a project and define the parameters needed to fulfil it? It would help me to test myself if you worked from home. Any major commission, I would formulate a solution, but bring it to you for your approval before passing it to technical design. For work in progress, or smaller commissions, I would like to engineer through to workshop with Tom raising any issues he feels relevant before bothering you with it. Do you think I'm ready for such a challenge?'

'I can see the logic, and I think your proposal does allow you to develop confidence in your skills. I'm happy to try your idea. Why don't we call Tom up to discuss the process with him? If he's happy then I'm happy. I have no doubts about your technical capabilities. You've worked hard. I don't see any gaps in your knowledge that would give me cause for concern. All I would ask is that you find yourself in doubt, you call me. Agreed.'

the Way

'No problem. I will only find out how good I am when it's my responsibility to solve issues.'

Jim called Tom and asked him to join them. They agreed with the process. Jim went to Charles to explain what had been agreed, and then left for home.

Charles visited with Mel. 'I don't know how you pitched your idea to Jim, but I commend you on your astute observation of his condition. This solution could yield us more of his input without any stress on him. Thank you, and good luck. If I can help you in any way, my door is open.'

'Thank you, Charles. I do need to test myself; and prove myself to the design people and the workshop. I saw the opportunity and hope I've called it well.'

'For what it's worth, Jim thinks you'll shine. He's not concerned at all.'

'Jason and I need some of your time to understand your vision for new materials, and how you see this technology applied.'

'Great. How are things working out with Jason?'

'He's really up for it. Came over to meet Seb last Thursday. We're both now putting our pieces together, and Seb will review our efforts Wednesday evening.'

'Will you thank Sebastian for his input from me. Very much appreciated. I'm nervous about what I'll read so be gently with me.'

Laughing, 'Charles Aldridge, may I present your life's work in words and numbers. A celebration of a worthy businessman.'

He smiled at her, 'Warts and all.'

'We haven't found any warts yet. But I think James is looking. Seb was very exacting about the risk section.'

'Ah, the dreaded risk section. Should I read it first, or leave it until after the best bits?'

'I think it will show you are one slick operator in this business. But if Sun Tzu finds any deficiencies, we must face them together as a team.'

Week 22

'How about 3 o'clock today? This will give us a couple of hours to fully explore the possibilities I've thought about.'

'Great. I'll inform Jason.'

As she walked across the drive to the house Sebastian noticed a serious look on her face. *'Something has happened. Is she nervous, anxious, or just subdued? Need to find out,'* he thought.

'Good evening. Your face tells me we have something to discuss about today.'

She gave him her customary kiss and walked away. 'Need some quiet time in the gym first. Talk to you over dinner.' As it was a cold, bitter day, she flicked the switch for the sauna before going to change. *No time for a soak before dinner.*

She sat in the sauna contemplating what she had done. This was no longer a game. Much rested upon her shoulders. *'This is your real test'* she thought *'are you ready?* As had happened several times over the past few months, revelations had surfaced quite by accident as this job was so second nature to Jim detail so obvious to him was completely unknown to her. *'Okay, lady. You've called the way forward. Time to fill big boots. I hope Seb thinks I've done the right thing. He's my mentor. Should I have consulted him first? Time to find out.'*

They finished dinner. 'I made a decision today without consulting you, but I don't know if it was weak, compassionate, or the best decision for the business. Can I go through my thought processes before you comment?'

'Go for it. As much detail as you can give me.'

'When Jim arrived around lunchtime, he was clearly not well – much worse than of late. And I think this dreary weather, especially the cold, is not helping. I think I adopted my female compassion. I wanted him out of the office, back to the warmth of his home. I volunteered to take over from him with the idea he would be at the end of a phone should I need him. I sold it to him I needed to be tested with a watching brief by him, if required. My instinct tells me he'll never sit at his desk again.

the Way

But am I ready for the challenge? Have I made an impetuous mistake? Sitting in that lonely office this afternoon, knowing he was gone, unlikely to return, was daunting. Charles has offered his support, but that would indicate failure on my part. I need guidance, my master.'

'Phew. What a relief. When I saw your face when you arrived home, I thought you had made some momentous and irrational decision you were now regretting. And before you think me frivolous, I do understand what you're telling me, and your apparent insecurity.' He looked straight into her eyes. 'You've made your first major decision as an executive, and you are to be applauded for your courage and initiative.'

'But I've taken over from him. I've dethroned a titan. Can I fill such boots?'

'Okay. Let's start from the top. You saw Jim as a wounded player. On the field of play, what would you do if another player is injured?'

'Stop the game to allow for that player to be taken for treatment and probably bring on a substitute.'

'And what if there was no suitable substitute?'

'I guess you play on without.'

'Maybe a little restructuring of the field of play?'

'Guess so.'

'To put your primary concern to rest I don't think compassion overruled pragmatic decision making, worthy of an executive. Pure compassion in the sense you suspect would have asked Jim to go home until he felt better – but leaving him with his sense of duty to the business – unnecessary and unhelpful stress. Whether consciously or subconsciously you looked at the dilemma of an important resource and rationalised an optimal solution. Had you invited him to continue, he would likely deteriorate more quickly, and you would be pre-occupied with his health. Neither of you would be performing. I have no doubt Jim would not have left the field of play if he had reservations you could perform; this job has been his life. And you were astute enough to suggest he still provides oversight when sought whether to protect his pride or your insecurity – doesn't matter. It's the impact quality of the decision that counts. Worthy Sun Tzu thinking.'

'I can see your usual positive thinking, but my decision could impact the lives of the people we employ if I get it wrong.'

'Welcome to the executive world. But is this not the aim of this journey of yours?'

'But I haven't finished my six months.'

'You'll never finish your six months until you retire from the field of play. You never stop learning the skills needed to perform at an executive level. This initial six months is just your first step to see if you belong on the ladder. I think today's decision proves your right to be on the ladder. Jim believes it, Charles believes it, and I have no doubts you can make it. Start to believe in yourself – you've earned the right.'

'And what about if I fail to meet expectations?'

'You won't fail. You'll occasionally make imperfect human mistakes; recognise, correct, and move on. Just get on with the job and watch your confidence grow every day. Your first executive position of responsibility is always daunting; but take comfort from the fact you would not be offered such a responsible position if others do not believe in you.'

'Thanks. I'll try to live up to expectation.'

'Good fortune is still on your side. Tackle as large a variety of projects as you can. Remember, you have already factored into your schedule that Jim is unlikely to survive your six months. The more experience you can obtain whilst Jim is on the end of a telephone the less impact his passing. Are we good?'

'Thanks. I'll do my best.'

'I know your best will be good enough so what do you have for me from Jason?'

'It's in the bag with my new laptop. I'll go get it.'

Chapter 139 – Tuesday

When she arrived at the office, the reality struck her that the squeaky chair at Jim's desk would be silent from now on. The inevitability Jim was unlikely ever to sit at his desk again filled her with sorrow and trepidation. She had volunteered to be tested as a compassionate gesture, but now she must fulfil his role. A daunting task to fill his boots, but he had prepared her technically; it was now up to her to demonstrate she was ready to deliver. *'Come on, girl. Time to show what you can do. And you need to speak with Jason, so let's get started.'*

By lunchtime she was pleasantly surprised the in-tray was empty, Tom was happy, and she did not need any other support for any of the jobs. *'Okay girl. Let's go see what Jason has for me. He needs to connect me to his computer server and show me how to use it. Let's see if he can come to me.'*

She phoned Jason. 'Any chance you can come visit and show me how to connect my laptop?'

'Sure. Just off for my run. Say 2 o'clock in your office?'

'Great. Thanks.'

Charles poked his head around the door. 'How are you doing? Any problems?'

Holding up her hand, fingers crossed, 'So far, so good. Even have some time for the Business Plan this afternoon if Jason can get my new laptop connected.'

'Great. I'm away now for the rest of the day. Anything you need, Mary knows how to contact me.'

Chapter 140 – Wednesday

By mid-morning it was evident to her that the design office and Tom had been appraised she was in charge of production,

Week 22

no longer the apprentice. No-one asked anymore if Jim is around, or when he would next be in the office. This simple fact was a real boost to her confidence. *'Thank you, Charles.'*

She spent the morning on production issues and learning how to use her new laptop. Whilst Jason was away on his lunchtime run, she called architect clients to keep them relevant. The afternoon was spent with Jason finalising the draft of their Business Plan to present to Sebastian this evening. She enjoyed this collaboration, learning much about the financial structure and performance of the business. By 5pm they were ready to present their proposals to Sebastian.

After dinner they each presented different parts of the Plan, listening to comments from Sebastian and making notes of any required amendments and additions. Sebastian was very exacting in his analysis of their work, but both were pleased with what they had achieved. They were both content they had assembled the pieces to paint a full picture of where Aldridge is, and where their plan intended to take the business for the coming 3-years.

Chapter 141 – Thursday

Her confidence was building by the day. She no longer looked at Jim's empty chair with any trepidation. She had plenty to occupy her, including gaining necessary knowledge about her new computer. One of the design team spent time with her explaining how to download any job design and spec sheet she needed to see. She even fielded a call from Michael Chimes with no anxiety.

By 4pm they were ready to present their draft Plan to Charles with a copy for Charles to leave with Jim. Charles was out so tomorrow morning would have to do but she decided to deliver a copy to Jim at his home to see how he was. He was looking somewhat frail, which had a disturbing effect on her.

That evening she recapped her week with Sebastian, more to reflect on anything she could have done better, or even forgot to do. His approval gave her much needed comfort she was performing as expected.

Chapter 142 – Friday

'What's your plan this evening?'

'I'll come home as usual and do my routine. Then I can dress in girlie clothes for a change. Simon will collect me at 7:30.'

'Is he driving tonight?'

'Only as far as the railway station. What are you planning for your night off?'

'This proved a dilemma. Can't remember the last time I had a night off. But dinner at the pub with friends will have to do. Not enough notice to do more. What time do you think you'll be home?'

'No idea, but don't wait up. I'll let myself in.'

'Get out of here, and if I don't see you this evening, have fun.'

'Thanks. Can't wait to see what the night life is like. So long since I went out clubbing.'

Charles was in, but only briefly. He took his copy of their Business Plan with him, leaving instructions that no-one else should see a copy. He was aware of the copy to Jim.

Chapter 143 – Saturday

She appeared for breakfast around 9am, looking a little jaded.

'Good night out?'

'Out of practice for late nights. Good night life in Derby centre. Clubs are very loud. And a lot more drunks on the street, including females, than you see in London. Interesting experience. Is it me, or am I too old for clubbing? Couldn't do that very often.'

'How did things work out with Simon?'

'It was very clear he expected me to stay with him last night. After we got back to Matlock around 2 o'clock, he tried every trick in the book to get me back to his apartment. I sensed if we didn't work together, he would have been even more forceful.'

'How did you deal with it?'

'Made it very clear I do not jump into bed on a first date. Got into a cab and came home.'

'What do you expect on Monday?'

'An apology would be a good start.'

the Way

Week 23

Chapter 144 – Monday

As she approached her desk the pile of paperwork in her in-tray took her aback. Charles had been pushing to capture as many orders as possible. She soon found herself very busy. The day passed quickly.

Sebastian sensed the time was fast approaching for the imminent change of the guard meaning Mel will need to overcome any apprehension she has about her role as a director. Whereas Aldridge is not structured as a conventional corporate she did not need any anxiety about boardroom protocols knowing her likely reaction to the death of Jim. It is time to prepare her.

'I think we should spend this evening dispelling any doubts you are ready to assume your role as a Board Director. Your progress over the past six months has proven your ability to perform. Therefore, as you will imminently assume your rightful position as Production Director, perhaps it would be useful to explain the workings of the Boardroom albeit in the knowledge Aldridge possibly do not concern themselves with the protocols and code of conduct normally associated with corporate Boardrooms. However, you need to know what to expect.'

'Has Charles approved your view?'

'I have no doubts about your readiness. The only concern I have is how you manage changing the guard. Jim's demise will affect several people. You must be ready to hold these people together as a leader. It will test your ability, but you've taken knocks of your own throughout this process so I'm hopeful that, on the field of play, you will show your grit.'

'But you were there for me on every occasion.'

the Way

'You quickly recovered. Most would not. You know how important it is to quickly move on. And I will most certainly be there for you when needed.'

'I'll need it but will endeavour to perform as you expect of me.'

'I can ask no more. Shall we progress?'

'We have already discussed the misconception that Boardrooms are alien environments for females. They are a daunting experience for anyone the first time they're invited to participate, even if someone has taken the trouble to brief them beforehand. However, like anything else, once you understand how they work, the less daunting they become.'

'A Boardroom can be used for other meetings, including informal meetings of the executive. What I want to cover is the formal Board meetings that follow accepted codes of conduct and protocols, and for which minutes are recorded and filed in the Minute Book as a record of the subject matter and any Resolutions reached.'

'The only people present are the Board Members and the executive secretary who will have prepared the agenda and will record the salient points discussed and any Motions passed into Resolution, being decisions that will be actioned and complied with.'

'No observers are present. Should the Board decide during a meeting they need advice from an expert, for example, they must adjourn the meeting, invite the guest to sit with them to discuss the matter needing such advice, and dismiss this guest prior to reconvening their meeting.'

'The ambience is very much dignified and respectful no matter the differences of opinion. This is why such protocols and code of conduct exist to ensure a civilised debate without personal attack. This is not alpha male, more human courtesy and respect.'

'Such meetings were once caricatured to me as a gathering of testosterone-driven elite gladiators, having left their weapons at the door, being coerced by their master to focus their energies defeating the competition rather than tearing each other apart. Whereas I have never witnessed such hostility, I have witnessed heated debates requiring reminder of expected conduct. Such debate should never become personal. At the end of the day all members are on the same side playing together to beat competition, not each other.'

'Each participant will have received an Agenda and any supporting documentation for deliberation prior to the meeting. Once everyone has arrived the Chair, usually the Chairman or CEO, will formally open the meeting, and a record of attendees taken. The Chair is then responsible to follow the agenda, allowing debate with anyone who has an interest. A Motion may be tabled to define the way forward for any Agenda item. The members will vote with each vote noted, and a Resolution determined. At the end of the meeting, the Chair will formally close the meeting. That's it.'

'I should add that if you oppose a motion, but the motion is carried, outside of that meeting you comply with the resolution. You most certainly do not copy disloyal Government Cabinet politicians who opposed a motion, lose the vote, and then leave the meeting to brief against the motion, especially to the press. A Board must always appear united. Any discernible discontent will be interpreted by competitors as a weakness to be exploited.'

'If you think back to the meeting with Michael Chimes. You laid down a motion that the company should refocus marketing to architects. As soon as Michael realised he was outvoted, he accepted the position. From what you have told me subsequently, he did go back to London and pursued architect contacts even though he opposed your motion. This is how it should be.'

'But what about his motive? Does he have an agenda?'

'Nothing that can harm you, so don't concern yourself. As regards Aldridge, I think Charles has any loyalty and confidentiality issues covered. We can look at the future of Michael once you're established in your new role.'

'I still have some big boots to fill.'

'Let's look at your personal behaviour in the Boardroom when you fill those boots. You will feel elated and nervous as you approach the Boardroom. Bury these feelings until you're off the field of play. You did not elevate to this seat by winning the lottery. The CEO considers you worthy of contribution at this strategic level. You are an equal member of a team directing a company to success. Remember clan in your dress code; you are not on a date so no overt feminine. You are not there to make a stand for the feminist movement. Acknowledge any welcome and quietly take your seat. Once the meeting is opened, no doubt the Chair will welcome you. Politely acknowledge. Then watch and listen to proceedings to understand the other players, protocol, and tone. If you're asked to comment, think before you speak. Balanced, not controversial. Your time will come to actively contribute once you're established. Any questions?'

'The most important day in your corporate life and you say bury your emotions. How do you do that?'

'First, it's not the most important day in your corporate life. That day is when, as the General, you achieve your first corporate victory. Until then, you are a team member expected to play your part. At this level you are not a junior member or apprentice. You've earned your place at the table so just another day at the office. Remember the coat hook at the entrance to the office. Use it. You controlled yourself at the meeting with Michael Chimes, which was essentially an informal Board meeting. What I'm trying to instil into you is that you belong at the table as a clan member expected to fulfil your role. No *me* and *them*; just *us*. They are your colleagues.'

'Okay. Between you and Carmen, I think I'm no longer daunted by the Boardroom. My real concern is changing the guard, initially in my own head, and then taking responsibility for production led by such a giant of a man for so long. Why should those people adopt me as their new leader?'

'They will adopt you because you can demonstrate your know-how, and you have the endorsement of Jim. He would not have left his post if he is unsure about your ability. Why don't we make this our subject for discussion tomorrow evening? You are ready. You just need the belief to go make it happen.'

Chapter 145 - Tuesday

'Tonight, let's talk about changing the guard. I know we have already discussed this subject in general, but I want to prepare you specifically for your imminent elevation to Production Director. I want us to analyse the situation you face and determine the best way to achieve successful change. Aldridge is very much a male domain. You will need to understand how to overcome any resistance to a female boss.'

'I already cope with the workshops. Since Jim has worked from home, I've had no problems.'

'But you're not the boss, Jim is still seen as their leader. Today you're considered his assistant. Their mindset will most certainly be that they can revert to Jim if need be. We need to change this.'

'What do you propose?'

'Would you change how your process orders, or any other aspect of the production process?'

'Nothing material. As machines come to the end of their useful life, I want to replace them with computer-controlled versions. I observe too many workarounds because a designer does not understand the limitations of the machines with some of the extrusions we use. Computer-controlled versions take instruction directly from the CAD system, which will negate the need for much documentation, and more importantly can simulate the cutting process which will flag any possible cutting

the Way

problems. Other than this, the whole process is very efficient. I would take your advice to walk the floor at least twice per day. Jim can't do this because the workshop environment is not good for his respiratory problem. That's it.'

'Good. Not good to reinvent the wheel too early under your stewardship. We have two scenarios to consider. The first is the regrettable scenario where Jim does not survive before you assume the mantle. This scenario for you will be the hardest emotionally, but easiest as a guard change. The most difficult will be if you assume the mantle because Jim must retire. Jim built this factory and has overseen production for some 40 years. Many of the workshop staff have been with Aldridge for years. Their mindset could be to accept you, but with one eye on Jim should you fail. This is not the type of commitment that will allow you to assume full control for some time.'

Her head dropped. 'As much as it pains me to say it, I don't think Jim will survive unless the medics can quickly find some miracle cure. The day I sent him home, I saw the pain and despair in his eyes. I felt the coldness staring at death. It was horrible. I've been trying to prepare myself for his passing for weeks because I know how I will feel and what you will expect of me.'

He put his hand on hers. 'We'll get through it, and you will make Jim proud of you, which in turn will allow you to change the guard with minimal disruption. Perhaps we should concentrate on this possibility. We can always return to the alternative should Jim surprise us all.'

'Seb, do you mind if we defer this subject? You've just brought Jim's probable passing into focus. I would like not to think about it just yet. Thankfully, I have much to keep me occupied at the office.'

'Understood.'

Chapter 146 – Wednesday

When she arrived at the office, she was intercepted by Mary who was clearly in distress 'Charles wants to see you right away.'

'What's the matter?'

'Jim was taken to hospital last night. It's not good. Go straight in.'

'Mel, good morning. Close the door would you and take a seat.'

'Jim was taken ill last night and is currently in a specialist unit in Derby. The prognosis is not good, and I don't think they will let him work again. I know you've not yet completed your six-month handover, but I need you to officially assume his responsibilities. Do you feel ready? You have certainly impressed both of us with your commitment and skill. If necessary, I can help you as I haven't forgotten how to do this job. Jim and I built this company together, and I had my sleeves rolled up as much as him in the beginning.'

'If you're there when I'm unsure about anything then I'm ready. He has been a very good and patient teacher.'

'Thank you. That's a weight off my mind. It probably is a little odd to you my first thoughts are to continuity of business when my best friend is fighting for his life. But I have nearly 150 people depend upon our ability to function, and I'm obliged to ensure we survive.'

'Please don't apologise for your actions. I've been well schooled in this scenario from the first week here. I know and respect what you need to do for the company, and you can count on my full support. It certainly reinforces what Seb has been drumming into me.'

'Sebastian has done a fine job with you. Your increase in stature these past months is truly remarkable. He certainly knows his stuff, and more importantly, how to teach you.'

the Way

'Now I know you can take control, I can help Jim and Margaret through this. Edna is with Margaret at the hospital. I'm going to join them later this afternoon.'

'Would it be possible to come with you?'

'Let me see how he is, and I'll let you know.'

'Until we know the true state of his health, you will assume full authority of Production Director with my full support. I'll put a note out this morning to this effect.'

'Thank you. Please give my best wishes to Jim and Margaret. I'll await your view regarding coming with you.'

When she got back to her office, her instinct was to shed tears. But she knew her master would tell her she should utilise her emotions more usefully by ensuring the show goes on, and she must now change from understudy to lead role. The factory has over 100 people with respective spouses and children dependent on the company surviving. The misfortune of one person cannot override the responsibility to the others.

She still could not sit at his desk but emptied his in-tray to see what needed to be processed. She was soon busy.

Charles popped his head around her office door. 'It's okay Mel, he would like to see you. Can you be ready to leave a little after 4 o'clock?'

'Sure. Thank you.'

She picked up the phone and dialled. 'Seb, Jim's in hospital in Derby. I'm going with Charles to see him. Can we be flexible with dinner this evening?'

'No problem. Do you know how serious it is?'

'Mary says very serious, and Charles thinks his working days are over.'

'My thoughts are with you Mel. I know how attached you've become to him. Please give him my best wishes.'

'I will.'

'And Mel, if you need anything, and I mean anything, give me a call. I'll be here.'

'Thanks, Seb. Talk to you later.'

Week 23

The drive to the hospital was solemn. She sensed Charles was really concerned, more than this morning. She decided not to probe.

They went straight to Jim's private room. Margaret and Edna were sitting on the right side of his bed. He was sitting, but she was shocked by the change in him. His face was grey, drawn, and he had aged 20 years in a couple of weeks. Tubes and monitors crowded the space around him.

He gave her a faint smile as he saw her. In almost a whisper, he beckoned her to sit with him.

She sat on the left side of him. He held her hand. 'I've let you down, my dear Mel. I promised you six months, but I cannot go on. But you have learnt quickly so I can rest knowing you have what it takes to carry on. You can do this, so make me proud of my pretty apprentice. You must graduate early, but you can do it. You have my full confidence.'

Tears rolled down her cheeks. She knew he was saying goodbye to her. 'You are a wonderful man and a great teacher. I'll try to make you proud. I'll only sit in your chair when I can fill your boots. Until then it will stay empty pending your return.'

He smiled as he shed a tear for her.

She sat outside in the waiting area for a while, thinking about the pain and sacrifice she had endured these past months. She was attempting to differentiate the boundaries between player and human being. Having now fully understood much of what she had been taught, she still found it so hard. When she worked in London, she had no idea what it was like at the top. Her issue now was whether she could live with her new lifestyle with its painful rules and responsibilities. Hard choices were sometimes difficult for her. *'Thank goodness for Seb.'*

Charles came to find her. He put his hand on her shoulder. The tears in his eyes told all. Jim had died.

'To hell with my master' she thought as she burst into tears.

the Way

Charles comforted her. 'He handed you the baton, my dear, in full confidence. Find strength and courage in his words.'

Once she composed herself Charles told her Edna would take her home as he wanted to stay with Margaret.

'Don't worry about me. I'll make my own way home. You and Edna are needed here. Seb will collect me. I'll call him now.'

On her way home she related her visit with Jim, punctuated by periods of tears, after which she was consumed in her grief.

He had prepared a cold table with fresh bread, with an option of fresh pasta if she preferred. Food was the last thing on her mind.

'How do you feel about tomorrow?'

'What do you mean?'

'Jim has handed you the baton. Do you feel confident enough to take it and run with it, or would you prefer to drop it and escape?'

She stared him in the eye. He could see rage. 'I'll go to the office tomorrow, enter the field of play and perform my part in the game as instructed technically by Jim, and managerially by you. Tonight, I'm not on the field of play, I'm a normal human-being grieving the loss of a dear friend.'

She increased intensity 'Perhaps in your high-flying world people just don't count. Tonight, my heart is with Margaret, Edna, and Charles. They have been together for over 40 years. Charles and Jim built Aldridge. Charles went out on a limb for me. In the office, tomorrow he may put on a brave face, but inside he'll be gutted. So, my heartless master, my thoughts are what I can do to ease their pain. It may be weak-minded in your world, but for me it is human compassion; caring about others.'

She stormed out of the kitchen into the living room and opened her heart.

He was livid with himself. *How could I be so insensitive?* 'Why don't I trust her to cope? She has passed ever test thrown at her. The decision on her way forward is hers to make, not mine.'

He went to her. 'I'm sorry, so sorry. I'm totally out of order. Please forgive me. I have no excuses for my inconsiderate behaviour. It's absolutely no excuse, but I have got used to us working scenarios in the evenings to prepare you for such events. What can I do to make amends? I feel wretched.'

She looked at him. He was practically in tears himself. 'There is something I would like from you. I need you close to me tonight, and to wash away my sorrow tomorrow morning. I also want to know that you are on the end of your phone all day tomorrow. I need to go to the office tomorrow prepared to jump without a parachute to help Charles through this. I'll need all of your teachings to hold myself together.'

He saw no opportunity to rephrase his question, so resigned himself to the carnage he had created for himself. 'It's the least I can do. I'll help you through this, have no fear, and with compassion.'

'I know you will, but occasionally can I please be a normal, emotional human-being who cares about the people who care for me?'

Later, just before he put her to sleep, she looked at him in the darkness 'You screwed up tonight. Don't do it again. I need to believe in you.'

Chapter 147 – Thursday

He had her out of bed at 6am, quick swim, a cleansing shower but shorter than usual, and asked her to be as quick as she can dressing as he needed to talk with her.

She appeared at breakfast a little after 7am.

'I know I got it wrong last night but in my clumsy, unforgivable way I was trying to ask you if the task presented to you today is what you want to do. Is this role where you want to be? I fully understand your sense of loyalty, but it's also the day in your life to decide what you want to do. I need to know from you that you are reaching for your dream; not being imposed upon. Just because you now have the skills does not mean you must comply. You have the knowledge to know if this pathway is right for you and I would like to know your thoughts.'

'I remember this conversation when we started this journey. You made it clear to me I must follow my own path and not be obliged to follow a path set by others. Today I feel obliged to Charles and Jim, and especially you, to help my dearest friends through this crisis. Do I feel confident? No. Do I see this as an opportunity to reach for my dream? Yes. I love this business. Every time I walk through the City and see an Aldridge fabrication in a new building, I feel proud to be part of it. I have been blessed with the people around me who have given me the opportunity to play a real part in this business, and to help shape its future. I go today to prove myself capable of playing my part. Does this answer your question?'

'Yes. Therefore, I feel the need to prepare you for today, as you are likely to be really tested. Do you remember back to your first days here when we discussed pillow talk, I told you about one of my mentors, Bernie. He died of a heart attack after taking a punishing verbal battering defending me.'

'Yes, now you mention it.'

'I found out about the death of Bernie whilst in the office. I was totally gutted, not least because he had his heart attack defending a reckless young exec who pushed his luck once too often. I felt responsible. I was angry with the CEO; a bag of raw emotion looking for vengeance. Another wise director who knew how close I was to Bernie; Jim reminds me of Bernie, popped his head around my door and told me I owed it to Bernie and to my staff to honour his legacy in the office, and grieve for him outside. "Behave as he would have you behave" were his parting words to me.'

'Today I pass on this good advice to you. I understand why you feel so strongly for Charles; they were like brothers. And I understand your affections for Jim. Charles will need strong support from you in the coming days. If you really want to help him, you need to be strong for him. And he needs to be convinced you can hold it together before he'll relax enough to grieve for his dear friend. You must be prepared to hold the fort, not only for Jim but also for Charles if need be. It will be very tough, and I'll be on the end of a phone for you all day, but this is by far the best way you can help Charles through this. You have taken some cruel knocks during your journey. Call upon the strength you gained from them and use it to help Charles. I'll give you a pass this evening to allow you to shed your grief here in the safety of my arms.'

She looked at him, tears welling in her eyes. Her wise sage was right. She went to him, hugged him, and gave him two slow kisses to show she understood.

As she pulled away from him, he wanted to get her focussed. 'It's still early to go to the office. I know it's cold outside, but the sky is blue and the air fresh. Why don't you go for a stroll or sit on the sundeck and get your thoughts together whilst filling your lungs with good, fresh air? Will set you up well for the day ahead.'

'I thought I'd go earlier to the office to get myself prepared.'

'Please don't do this. Breaking with routine at this time can be construed negatively by people already on edge. Routine maintains calm.'

'I can see what you're saying. My wise sage, where would I be without you?'

She drove through the factory gates with trepidation, and much sorrow. She knew she'll miss Jim's smile as he greeted her each morning. It gave her the confidence she needed. Today his chair would be empty again, this time for good. No squeaks as he leans backward to greet her. She was determined not to occupy this chair until she was accepted as his rightful heir.

But what about poor Charles? She saw his car parked as usual. What could she do for him?

the Way

When she walked into Mary's office, she was openly sobbing. *'This is your first test'* she thought *'I must hold it together'*.

She put her arms around Mary. She looked up 'He was such a good man, why is life so unkind?'

'We can get through this together. How's Charles?'

'Broken. I've never seen him so down.'

'Mary, can I get you anything? Tea, coffee, anything?'

'Thank you so much dear, but can you help Charles? He needs friends around him.'

'I'll go to him. If I can help him, I will. His pain must be unbearable.'

She knocked on his door and entered. He sat motionless, staring out of the window. She closed the door behind her, walked over to him, and put her hand on his shoulder. He looked up at her. His eyes were moist with tears, but otherwise his expression was blank.

'Hello Charles. Why are you here? Jim gave me his confidence, which gave me strength beyond my imagination. I can do this. I can hold the fort while you grieve your loss. Please trust me. Seb is in the wings if necessary. Please go and help Margaret through this.'

The tears in his eyes started to roll down his cheeks. 'Jim said you're ready, and he handed you his baton to demonstrate his belief in you. If you're telling me you want to prove yourself, then I'm willing to let you try. I'll tell Mary to let you handle everything. Thank you, my dear. I need a day, maybe two, to make all the arrangements for Jim. We'll close the factory on the day of his funeral so that anyone who wants to can pay their respects. I'll let you know when the arrangements have been made.'

'My first executive decision is you should not come back here before Monday. Go, please go, and help your friend. I'll make you proud of me.'

'Thank you, my dear, thank you.'

He gathered his things, told Mary Mel was in charge, and left.

Week 23

Mary looked at her. 'I don't know what you said to him, but I thank you from the bottom of my heart. You need anything, you ask. I know this place inside out, and everyone here. I'll ensure whatever you need done, will be done.'

'Thank you, Mary.'

She went to her office and sat at her desk. There was an eerie silence. She had held herself together, giving Charles the freedom to go do whatever needed for his friend. She felt his pain; but felt able to play the game.

A knock on the door. It was Tom, the shop floor manager. 'Miss, can I have a word?'

'Come in, Tom. What can I do for you?'

'Miss, on behalf of the shop floor and myself, can we offer our condolences? Jim was a good man, and a great engineer. We'll miss him.'

'And, Miss, we know Jim had great faith in you as his replacement. If Jim says you're good, then you're good enough for us. You have our full support.'

'Thank you, Tom. I really appreciate your support. You addressed Jim by his name. My name is Mel, and I hope we can honour the memory of Jim by working together to the benefit of all.'

'Miss, uhhm Mel, we ain't never worked with a woman before. How does it work for you?'

'Simple Tom, just forget I'm a woman. I'll always dress down so as not to be a distraction, just like today, so I'm just your colleague. Does this work for you? I don't want any special attention.'

He looked perplexed.

'I have a deal for you, Tom. I won't sit in Jim's chair until you tell me I can fill his boots. How does this sound to you?'

'Good enough Miss, I mean Mel. I'll get used to it.'

'As my first act as Project Director can I ask you to tell the shop floor the factory will be closed on full pay, for Jim's funeral. Anyone who wishes to attend his funeral will be welcome. We

the Way

want to celebrate the life of one of the founders of this company who, for over 40 years, gave his life and soul to its success. He was widely loved, so let us all be thankful we knew him.'

'Thank you. Most of the floor wants to pay their respects so this will be good news to them.'

'Are there any issues we need to address in the next two days?'

'No, Miss. You already know the work in progress, No problems there.'

'Okay then let us keep this factory working and make Jim proud.'

'We're with you there. And Miss, you won't have any problems on the workshop floor. After the nasty incident before, there's a lot of respect down there. I better get back. Thank you, Mel.'

The telephone rang. It was Mary 'I have Michael Chimes on the line. I've informed him of your position. He wants to speak with you.'

'*Rammed it down his throat, more like.*' She thought. Mary didn't like him. 'Put him through.'

'Michael, good morning.'

'Good morning, Mel. Sad news. Jim was a good man. Can you tell me about the funeral arrangements? There are people here who want to pay their respects.'

'I'll let you know as soon as I know. We're closing on the day of his funeral to allow people to attend. If you have staff who want to attend, we can arrange transport. Let Mary know the numbers.'

'Thanks Mel, I'll let the people know and get back.'

'By the way Mel, congratulations on your appointment. I didn't think you could make it. I was wrong and look forward to working with you.'

'Thank you, Michael. I'll try to make the transition as painless as possible.'

Week 23

'I have every faith in you. You've grown beyond belief. You're a worthy successor. Next time you're in London, come by the office. Interested in your thoughts about the way forward.'

'Okay. I'll let you know. Bye.'

'Bye, Mel.'

She put the phone back on its cradle. *'Okay, my master, was his apology genuine, or was it covering his bases knowing I have the full support of Charles? A discussion for this evening.'*

The day went by pretty much as usual. Mary fielded the calls of condolence. Every time she started to drift into thoughts of Jim, she tried to imagine how her master must have felt that day, not only losing a dear mentor, but feeling responsible for his death. *"Smile, even though your breaking"* came back to her mind. Tough at the top, but it kept her from switching out of the game.

It was late afternoon when Charles called her. 'How are you holding up Mel?'

'I'm making Jim proud. More important, how are you?'

'We have the funeral arranged for 11am next Friday, with a wake at a nearby hotel. I'll let Mary have all the details. Can you inform everyone?'

'No problem. I'll do it tomorrow when Mary gives me the details.'

'Mary tells me you're doing fine, thank you, so I'll heed your instructions not to return before Monday. But any problems, please let me know.'

'Please don't worry. I'll keep this ship afloat for you until you're ready to return.'

'Thanks Mel, you're a star.'

When she got home, she went straight to the kitchen. 'Seb, I want to discuss something with you while I'm still in play as I need to shed some tears later.'

'Tell me what's on your mind.'

the Way

She told him what had happened with Charles, and the subsequent call with Michael, both words and tone. 'What do you think? Covering himself, or quiet resignation.'

'Certainly, not the latter. He's not the type to change his spots. My best guess is he knows he's lost the plot in the marketplace, so is hanging in there for as long as he can. You will see this often as people get physically and mentally tired of playing the game at the highest level possible for them, but they like the trappings of the role. The only benefit to you is you have a tame supporter of your re-structure plan. But will he deliver the results? Another tough choice for you in the weeks to come. Does this answer your question?'

'Perfectly. Thanks.'

She was gone to change.

She sat at the table with a glass of wine, waiting for dinner. The phone rang. 'It's Carmen for you.'

'Hi Carmen. How are you?'

'More important, my dear Mel, how are you? Our Matlock office informed me of the death of Jim. You must be devastated, my dear. Carmen is so sad to hear such news.'

'I'm okay, but it's not easy for me. I now have taken responsibility for the company to give the CEO time to grieve his dear friend, so I have two jobs. But my heart is so sad.'

'My dear, as a woman I know how you feel. This will be your biggest test, but Carmen knows you can do this. Carmen is here for you anytime, day or night. You have my office number and my home number. I arrive home at 5:30 your time. I know my darling Sebastian will take care of you, but if you need to speak to a woman, then you call me. Darling Sebastian is not a woman, so he does not understand all things. I have told Joan in the Matlock office, and my secretary here in Stuttgart if you call me, then it is a priority. They must find me.'

She was now in tears, and Carmen could hear it 'Thank you, Carmen. Very kind of you, and much appreciated. I think I can hold together during the day but need the space to grieve in the evening.'

'That is good. We get through this together. We women executives need to stand together. Can I speak with Sebastian?'

'Sure. Thanks for thinking of me.'

'My dear Mel, we are sisters. We take care of each other.'

She handed the phone to Seb 'Hi Carmen.'

'My darling Sebastian. I know you will take care of Mel but listen to Carmen as you do not know women that well. When she is alone with you let her shed her tears. This is not weakness, just woman showing compassion. Do not say anything, just be there. You hear Carmen?'

'Yes, I hear, and it will be done.'

'Thank you, my darling. You have done a fine job with Mel. She is nearly there. This is big test for her, so give her space to grieve her loss away from the office so she is fresh to take the challenge.'

'I understand. And thank you for caring so much.'

'Mel is a good lady. She had a hard journey. We must help her reach her goal. She can call me anytime. Take care of her, my darling.' She threw her usual kiss down the phone as she terminated the call.

He put the telephone back into its cradle 'Now there's a surprise. She is obviously keeping tabs on events here. You have a good friend in Carmen.'

'She was lovely to me,' still not holding back her tears.

Over dinner, she was recalling the events of the day, and the needs of tomorrow.

'I have to inform all the staff tomorrow about the funeral arrangements, but how do you write such a notice?'

'Do you really think Sun Tzu would approve of such a notice?'

This question brought her back into focus. 'No, he wouldn't. So, what should I do?'

the Way

'You assemble everyone and tell them yourself. This not only adds a human touch but also puts you into their minds as the new pack leader, very important human nature. At this time, they only really know their leader has died, so they feel rudderless.'

She looked at him somewhat surprised. 'What's with the human touch? Is this my master I hear?'

'These people are not your competitors. They are the people who make you successful. They're your troops. They need to know you share compassion with them over Jim, and you're now their new leader. You want them to follow you wherever you go so show them you're real, strong, and ready to lead. I had a simple philosophy with all my staff. You take care of me, and I'll take care of you. It's called reciprocity, and it works like patriarchal family.'

'Is there any special way I should speak to them?'

'Think Aristotle, and use "we" far more than "I". **We** are gathered to remember **our** friend Jim. **We** grieve his loss, but **we** honour his legacy. Get the idea?'

'I've got it.'

'Only when you declare yourself the new leader, do you use "I". Jim has handed **me** his baton, so **I** accept the challenge to fill his boots. A little humility will go a long way. **I** will honour **his** legacy, and you, his faithful colleagues, and friends. You have planted yourself as the new leader. They're focussed again. Job done.'

'Is there anything you don't have an answer for?'

'I've been around in the corporate jungle for a long time, and have experienced both the very best, and the sordid worst of human nature. Aldridge is a minnow in the pool of corporations, so more a family affair than a jungle.'

'By the way, I have one more thought about your conversation with Michael. You do not go to the office in London to meet with him. Think about it. The last time you were there, you were subordinate to Michael; and was so for some years.

Week 23

The staff there do not know of your current standing in relation to Michael. You go there to meet with him, you'll create the perception he's still senior, and he'll do nothing to change this view. The staff there know nothing of your report and its implications. Just as you've changed the guard here, you must do the same in London when the time is right. Until then you call him to meetings here, if required.'

'What about if Charles is with me?'

'Even worse. Think about your battlefield before you make any moves. You are at least a commander. People do not summon you; you summon them.'

'I will have to go to London at some point in the coming weeks to reassure my architect clients all is well, business as usual. What do I say to Michael?'

'Nothing until you're ready. Things need to settle here first. Your focus is to make your entire customer base comfortable. Jim has been around a long time and was held in high regard. Customers need to see you're a worthy successor. Remember your retail customer base is your bread-and-butter income stream. With the imminent recession, you need to maintain calm as your competitors may try to destabilise Aldridge in favour of themselves. Because of Jim's standing in the marketplace, they will see Aldridge as injured. They will probe to see if they can move against Aldridge. This is your priority, especially until Charles returns to the fray. Can you see what I'm saying?'

'I'm sorry, Seb. Events over the past few days have taken my eye off the ball. You're right. My responsibility is to look at the big picture and thwart any potential discord that can harm Aldridge. This is a tough game, but I'll endeavour to make you proud of me.'

'You've had a tough ride these past six months. I'm already proud of your achievements and your commitment to the game. I can fully understand where you are; so much, so fast, would break many people. But we will prevail, and you will get stronger every day. Why don't we clear away dinner and go get comfortable? You need some respite before you face another day.'

Settled on the sofa, he held her as she unleashed her pent-up sorrow before taking her to his bed to start their now ritual of preparing her for another day in the game.

Chapter 148 – Friday

As soon as she arrived at the office, she checked in on Mary to see if she was okay. She knew Mary needed to keep busy so asked her to ask Tom to come see her and prepare a notice about the funeral arrangements to be handed out after she had addressed everyone. Mary would ensure all the admin and design staff will be there.

'Tom, good morning. I want to address everyone at 12 o'clock today in the canteen. Can you ensure all the shop floor people are present? I'll have the funeral arrangements with me.'

'No problem, miss. I'll get right on it.'

She started to scribble herself some notes about what she wanted to say. Her mind was a mess. She summoned her knowledge of rhetoric, but it was content she needed. She already had her brief on style. She started to lose it. She grabbed the phone and dialled. 'Seb, what do I say to these people. They are part of the fabric around here. I'm just an interloper.'

He sensed her dilemma. 'Mel, breath, long and deep. Come back to me.'

He could hear her breathing. 'Are you with me?'

'Sorry, a little panic attack.'

'You know the style so let's look at content. Do you remember what I said this morning?'

'Yes.'

'Then to complete the picture, keep it informative, and from your heart. No notes. You'll find the words once you start. Do not look at anyone specifically, look at everyone as though maintaining eye contact with all of them, but will be a blur to you. Let them think you're speaking directly to each person individually. Open your heart and you'll feel the warmth come back to you. There will be much respect in the room for you because you're speaking to them rather than issuing a faceless piece of paper. Feed on it.'

'Thanks. I wish you were standing with me.'

'Imagine I'm standing just behind you, out of your sight line. Feel my presence and use the strength.'

'Are you okay now?'

'Yes, back on the field of play.'

'You'll be okay. Feel the positive energy around you. Talk to you later.'

'Bye Seb, and thanks.'

It was 12 o'clock. She walked from her office. Mary walked with her carrying copies of the notice she had prepared about the funeral arrangements. She sensed Mel's apprehension, so touched her arm to let her know she was there for her. When they reached the works canteen, it was full but fell silent as they entered. Mary guided her to a plinth she had organised so she could see everyone.

She breathed deep and calmed herself, remembering how to look at the assembled people. *'He's right. It just becomes a blur. Okay, my master. Let's do this.'*

'Thank you all for coming. For those who don't know me, my name is Melanie Southgate. In the absence of Charles, who is rightfully organising a fitting send-off for his old friend, it falls to me to say a few words about our departed colleague and dear friend, Jim, who passed away Wednesday evening. Many of you have long memories of him, but I would like to share mine with you. Jim knew he was sick. Six months ago, he plucked me out of my comfy office in London and brought me to this lovely community to groom me to be his successor. I lost my dad last year, and my mum more recently, so Jim also took me under his fatherly wing. The office will not be the same without his lovely smile in the morning. I was at his bedside on Wednesday. He knew it was time to pass his baton. And I'm truly honoured he thinks me worthy to fill such big boots.'

She paused for a moment.

'I thought we should gather to share our grief at his passing and honour his legacy built up over forty years. He's part of the foundations of this company, and I hope we will all find it in our hearts to continue as he would wish of us. I have accepted the challenge to fill his boots, and I hope you will accept me as a friend and colleague as Jim was to all of you.'

'The funeral will be next Friday. The plant will be closed. Mary has the details for you to take away. All are welcome to attend the funeral and wake. We're all friends together, and we want to celebrate the passing of one of our great friends, and to pay tribute to him, together. Thank you.'

They all clapped. Seb was right. She could feel the warmth.

Tom stepped forward and turned half to her and half to the assembled. 'On behalf of the lads in the workshops we thank you, Miss, for speaking to us today so kindly about our dear friend Jim. We knows Jim had high regard for you, and we want to say we welcome you as his successor, and will help you keep his legacy alive.'

Shouts of 'yeah' filled the room.

'Thank you, Tom.' She looked up to the workshop crowd, 'Thank you.'

She was struggling to hold the welling in her eyes, but she took comfort from the warmth she felt. She got down from the plinth using the guiding hand of Tom. 'That was very kind of you, Tom. Thank you.'

'Miss, you've proved yourself worthy. Just wanted you to know.'

Several people whom she may have seen from time to time, but without interaction, came to introduce themselves, and thank her for her kind words.

Week 23

Mary could see she was losing some of her composure at the overwhelming response, so gathered her up, made their excuses, and lead her back to Charles's office.

She brought tea for them. 'Well, you certainly made an impression today. I can't recall anyone doing that before. Normally it's just a written notice. How do you feel?'

'Both good and sad. Seb was right. The warmth I felt was really comforting. And Tom's little speech nearly had me in tears. So generous.'

'Did I miss anything I should have said?'

'You opened your heart to them, and they loved it. You said everything they needed to hear. Anyone who didn't know you before sure as hell knows you now. I had a problem with the tears as well. It so lovely to have a woman here with such authority. Charles should feel proud of himself for bringing you here, and comfortable to let you run the place while he takes care of Jim and Margaret. How must that lady feel? She loses Jim to his work all these years, and now she doesn't have him in retirement. So sad.'

Mary spent the afternoon sending out funeral notices to the regional centres, and to anyone she thought interested.

Mel, happy to be alone again, and it being Friday afternoon, picked up the phone.

'Hi Seb. It all went well. I felt the warmth. Thank you. See you later.'

She had a thought. She was quickly to Mary. 'Where's the nearest place I can get a decent condolences card?'

'At the Post Office in the village. Why?'

'I want to send some flowers and a card from the shop floor to Margaret to show her they share her pain.'

'Let me go get you a card, I'll organise some lovely flowers, and take the card to them on my way home. They will be delivered tomorrow morning. Mel, only a woman would think of that. Good idea. Back in half an hour.'

'Let me give you some money.'

the Way

'Don't worry, dear. I have enough in petty cash, and we have an account with the florist.'

'But I want to pay for them.'

'It's enough you had such a beautiful thought.' She was gone.

She was sitting quietly contemplating if there was anything else she needed to do when there was a knock on the door. Simon entered. 'Hi Mel. That was some speech down there. Must have taken a lot of guts. Congratulations. I now can see why you didn't want a relationship as you obviously knew you were soon to be my boss. Had you told me, I would have understood.'

She didn't need this. It verged on sarcasm. 'Simon, nothing was a given. I still need to prove myself worthy to fill such boots. But I intend to give it my best shot. You have your ambitions, so we would clash at some point. Why start something that clearly will not survive so soon after my disastrous engagement. I did value your friendship, but today you have shown selfishness that causes me to reconsider. I would like to maintain our friendship, but you do not come to me with selfish sarcasm, especially not today.'

He raised his hands in submission 'Mel, I'm so sorry. You're right. I felt our friendship had been betrayed, but I'm wrong. That mentor of yours has transformed you into a formidable woman, and I have shown myself as unworthy. I would dearly like to count you as a friend and hope you can forgive my insensitivity.'

'James, you have much to learn about the rules of this game. If you prove your friendship with your support, I'll help you to understand the rules. Now please go away as today has presented enough challenges.'

'I'm so sorry. I'll leave you in peace. You can rely on my full support, and I would be honoured to maintain a more considered friendship on my part.'

As he closed the door, her anger quickly subsided. Then a brief chuckle 'I've recruited my first loyal spy.'

Week 23

When Mary returned, she gave the card to Mel who took it down to Tom. 'Tom, I want to send some flowers to Margaret on behalf of the shop floor. Could you write some words in this card to Margaret on behalf of the shop floor?'

I'm not good with words. This is something my missus would think of. Can you help me, Miss?'

'Okay. Ready? Dear Margaret, Today, a dark cloud covers the workshop. We have lost a dear friend. On behalf of everyone on the shop floor, our hearts are with you, and you are in our thoughts. We will all be with you on Friday. Sincere condolences, Tom. Got all that?'

'Don't know if I spelt condolences proper, but otherwise got it all. Thanks, Mel.'

She went back to her office to add her own words before putting the card in the envelope, sealing it, and giving it to Mary. She felt much better.

He saw her park her car. As she got out, he could see she was drained. He went to the door to meet her. She fell into his arms with tears in her eyes.

'Come lady. You did good today. I'm so proud of you.'

She needed to relieve some of her sorrow. He held her close until she was ready to surface again.

He sat her at the table where a glass of wine was already waiting for her. 'What a sad day. I did my best, my master, but now I'm off the field I feel wretched.'

'Then lots of TLC for you tonight. You've earnt it.'

'Seb, am I really cut out for this exec role? I've experienced so much pain but will never get used to it.'

'And I hope you never will. It's your heart that makes you special. I only want to help you deal with pain when you need to be an active player. Otherwise, I like the compassionate lady I see.'

The telephone rang. 'Hello Sebastian. How is she?'

'A little emotionally drained, but otherwise okay.'

'She did great today. Can I speak with her?'

'It's Charles for you' as he handed her the phone. He noticed her quickly compose herself.

'Hello Charles. How are you?'

'All the better from hearing how wonderful you were today. I have spoken with Mary and Tom. Neither can speak highly enough of your performance. And your speech at lunchtime – truly inspirational. You have my gratitude.'

'Thank you. I just followed my instinct.'

'Can I ask a favour of you?'

'Sure, what is it?'

'Would you mind holding the fort until after the funeral? I would like to only come in and out as I need to. Jim's death has hit me harder than I thought. I need some time to reconcile myself to losing him. Do you feel up to this task? But only accept if you feel comfortable. It's a big ask, but on today's performance I feel I can trust you.'

'As I said to you yesterday, you take whatever time you need. I'll hold the fort for you. The worst is over at the factory, so it can only get easier.'

'Thank you so much, Mel. Your courage today shows an inner strength that makes you a worthy executive of Aldridge. Have a good weekend, and God bless you.'

She handed the phone back to Seb, who realised Charles had hung up, so cradled the handset.

She immediately dropped out of composure, but no more tears.

'What did he want?'

'He wants me to hold the fort until after the funeral. I'll need your help this weekend to get me back on track for next week. I have two jobs to do.'

'You'll get whatever you need, have no fear.'

Chapter 149 – Saturday

He opened his eyes around 6am as usual. She was still fast asleep. He was not about to disturb her peacefulness. He needed to change her mindset this morning, but how?

As she opened her eyes some two hours later, he had a plan.

'Good morning. Sleep well?'

'Hmmm.'

She could hear the wind and rain beating against the window 'We don't need to get up yet, do we?'

'No.' He raised himself onto his elbow so he was looking over her. He put his index finger on her forehead, 'I need to flip your mindset before we do anything.' He then tapped her gently on the tip of her nose 'Then I need to put a big smile on this pretty face.' Reaching down to her ribs to gently tickle her, she giggled 'and you need to have some fun.'

'How do you propose to do all of that on such a dreary day?'

'Would you let me try to find some positives out of all this sadness?'

'You're the master of positives, let's hear what you have. I need something to lift me.'

'Just let what I say sink in. Don't fight it.'

'If we recap this week, I can identify several real positives. Let's think about it. There are over one hundred people at the factory who go back with Jim many years, but who does he want to see at his bedside – you. And why does he want to see you? He wants you to know from him that he gives you his baton, knowing you're ready to run with it. He doesn't need to bear his pain any longer. He's entrusting both workshops of revenue generation to you, including the welfare of the workers. So, what do you think he expects you to do with it?'

He touched her lips. 'Don't answer yet. Wait until I've finished.'

the Way

'Yesterday you opened your heart to the people who now depend on you. You reached out to them, and they responded with warmth, and acknowledged you as their new leader. You successfully changed the guard. They now look to you to lead them. If you're down, they'll be down. If you have the courage to lead, they will follow. Remember you've already said your goodbyes to Jim. They must wait until next Friday. Do you consider this a burden, or a privilege?'

'Then there's Charles, the person who plucked you out of obscurity and plotted a glowing future for you. Jim's death has hit him much harder than he expected. He's lost a brother and questions if he's responsible for his death as it's clear the factory environment of past years played a significant role in Jim's health. You're the only person he can trust to give him the respite he needs to come to terms with this loss. Do you consider this a burden, or an opportunity to prove to yourself you can deliver for both Charles and Jim?'

'And finally, if your father were standing here now, what would he be thinking, and what would he say to you?'

She reached up putting both arms around his neck pulling herself up close as she burst into tears. He left her to sob as these are tears she needs to shed as part of her refresh.

As her head slid back past his cheek, she kissed him. 'There is another factor with Charles Mary mentioned yesterday about Margaret. She lost Jim to the company all these years, and now she has lost him before she could enjoy his retirement. I feel for her, so God knows how badly Charles feels.'

She looked him in the eye, 'Where would I be without you? I've just quietly asked my dad what to do. Put me back on the track. I have work to do.'

'Not today, lady. You need some fun. Let's start by putting a smile on your pretty face.'

'That's easy. A lovely shower will do that.'

'Not enough today. I want your smile to last all day. We need to introduce another element.'

'And what might that be?'

'If you need the bathroom, on your way so we can get this show on the road.'

She looked at him to say something but thought better of it as she bounced into the bathroom.

He took her hand and led her downstairs towards the pool, but then turned up towards the sundeck. Before she knew what was happening, he had the door open, and they were standing on the deck in the pouring rain. 'You're crazy. It's freezing out here' as she snuggled into him.

He was animated 'This is defiance. This weather is commanding us to stay indoors. It considers itself more powerful than us mere mortals. I say feel the rain against your skin. It's wildly refreshing. Open your arms and feel invigorated.'

She laughed as she opened her arms to let the rain beat against her naked body.

After a few minutes he took her hand again and ran with her down past the gym and changing room straight into the pool. After some splashing, she challenged him to a race. She was off the mark very quickly. He chased after her. She felt a wild determination and pushed herself to the limit. Laps went by. She could feel him behind her. *'Today he will not pass me.'* It was her time to win. She touched the wall first. She beat him.

He stood in the water looking deflated.

'What's the matter with you?'

'You beat me. I'm gutted. I'll never live this down.'

'Are you serious? I really beat you?'

'Why would I look like this? I'm a sore loser.'

She went to him, jumped up clasping him around his waist with her legs, one hand around his neck, the other waving victoriously in the air as she cheered 'I beat you, yeah.'

She had really beaten him, and he did feel embarrassed, but she was enjoying herself. That's all that mattered today.

the Way

When they returned to the bedroom for their shower, he turned on the radio selecting a station with upbeat music, turning up the volume so they could hear it in the shower.

As they entered the shower she was already dancing. 'Today we have a dancing shower.'

They bathed each other to the music, twirling to reverse the situation. She danced and laughed her way through the whole process. 'This is fun. We should do this more often' as he was trying to pin her foot on his bent leg long enough to wash her foot.

They dressed in preparation to go shopping before going down to breakfast.

'Where're we going shopping today?'

'Somewhere we can get arrested anonymously.'

'Now what are you talking about.'

'All I'll say is look out for low-flying objects around the fresh produce area.'

She got up and went to check his forehead. 'Do you have a thermometer; I need to check to see if you have a fever.'

'I'm okay. Don't you like playful?'

'I've never seen you like this before. I'm concerned.'

'Very remiss of me. Should have added playful fun into our program weeks ago.'

'So, you want to play. Okay my master let's go play. Do you prefer tomatoes or eggs?'

As they drove out of the lane onto the Derby Road, he turned left towards Chesterfield, rather than right to Matlock.

'Now where're we going?'

'I told you. Somewhere where we can play without being recognised. Find some fun music to drown out this rain.' He didn't want to go anywhere today where they might bump into people from the factory. He wanted to keep her totally away from anything to do with work.

Their visit to the supermarket was manic. Seb stood at the fresh fruit section throwing produce back at her. Even when she told him she wasn't looking he was still throwing things back at her. Their trolley was a mess. If anything did fall to the floor, she picked it up and put it in their trolley.

'How many oranges do we need as he was rapidly firing them at her?' She was desperately trying to catch everything whilst laughing at him. Then she saw a member of staff heading straight for them.

'Sebastian, behave yourself, or else you're in for a big smack.' The staff member reached them. Mel was still laughing, 'It's okay. I think he had too much sugar on his cornflakes this morning.' Looking at him 'Come on Sebastian, we have enough for today,' and led him off.

When they arrived at the bakery, he picked up a cream cake in a plastic container, opened it and started to eat it. She was astonished. 'You haven't paid for that!' He threw the empty container in the trolley and pushed the cream cake towards her mouth, inviting her to take a bite. Of course he missed, covering her nose in cream. She looked cross-eyed at the cream on her nose – something he had not seen her perform before. 'Give me that cake, your aim is awful.'

As soon as she had it in her hand, she stuffed it in his mouth, although it wasn't open at the point of impact. The remainder of the cake splattered across his face. She creased up with laughter until she saw the staff member walking towards them again. 'Time to get out of here.'

Even at the checkout he was mesmerising the checkout lady, but a little fun was a welcome respite from the drudgery of checkout duty.

As they walked to the car, she wanted to know who this crazy man was.

He needed to visit a deli in the main shopping area so parked up and they walked. The rain had stopped, but the wind was still howling. They noticed a despondent man with a stall trying to sell barbequed bratwurst in a strong German bread. They bought one each and wander along the street trying to eat it.

the Way

He needed a beer to wash it down, so they popped into a pub for a drink. She really appreciated what he was doing. She was seeing a new side of him, a playful master looking for a little fun. Despite his outrageous behaviour in the supermarket, and the atrocious weather, she was enjoying her day with him.

They finally returned home late afternoon and unpacked their groceries. They had far more than they needed, much of it recovered from the floor in the supermarket.

'How about we make pizza together for this evening?'

'Okay, sounds appropriate after everything else today.'

He suggested they change into house clothes as it could get messy. She changed into a black top and shorts, and him his usual T-shirt and shorts.

They used the kitchen table to prepare the base. He had a flower dusting tin spreading a base on the table as she was mixing the base dough. He went straight across her front with the duster sprinkling flower across her breasts. 'Oops, must be snowing somewhere.'

She knew it was deliberate. She wiped her dough covered fingers across his chest and face. He lay her over the table and sprinkled flower all over her.

She lay there thinking '*If you want to put a real smile on my face, rampant sex will do it*' but was not going to spoil the day by saying it. Then it hit her. '*It's Seb's birthday.*' With Jim's death, she had forgotten.

He saw the change in her face. 'What's the matter?'

Tears filled her eyes, 'I'm so sorry. It's your birthday. I should be spoiling you. Carmen would not forget such an important day – family first. I feel terrible.'

'But wasn't Jim part of your mentor family? You feel his loss as family. Priorities my dear.'

She sat up and put her arms around his neck, 'No positive thinking excuses today, please. You're the nearest I have to family, and I've failed you after everything you've done for me.'

Week 23

She looked him in the eyes 'Happy birthday my lovely, lovely Sebastian' kissed him on the lips, and hugged him tightly.

'I promised you dinner so out of here. Go clean yourself up and get into some clothes. I'm going to prepare us a nice dinner. When you're dressed, please prepare the dining room and put on some of your lovely music. We'll dine and dance the night away.'

He looked at her tears, 'You don't have to do this. This situation is not your fault. And it's not too late to go out somewhere.'

'Seb, I want to do this, so be on your way and let me get on with it. Go.'

After their bizarre shopping trip, she had plenty of choice, so set about thinking about a menu. He had a bookcase of cookery books, so she quickly scanned them for ideas, and was soon busy.

She had a thought. Reaching for the phone she dialled Carmen's home number. Carmen answered. Almost whispering 'Carmen, sorry to disturb you but I've been remiss today and I would appreciate your help.'

'My dear Mel, what do you need from Carmen?'

'It's Seb's birthday, and I forgot all about it until a few moments ago. Could you call him in a few minutes?'

'No problem, my dear. And thank you for telling me. It is also remiss of Carmen not to know this. It will be my pleasure.'

'Thanks Carmen. I must get on with dinner but see you soon.'

'Thank you for the call.'

A few minutes later she heard the telephone ring. '*Thanks Carmen.*'

Once everything was cooking nicely, she slipped away to get dressed. As she passed the living room 'A nice bottle of champagne, and a medium burgundy would be good this evening.'

She was soon in a dress, but only nominal makeup in the time available. She then quietly slipped along the landing into his

the Way

study where she found some A4 card and coloured pens to make a birthday card for him. She had a good hand for sketching so soon had a relevant, albeit cheeky card in tune with their playful day. Then back to the kitchen to finish her offering.

As soon as he killed the lights, she rolled onto her back in submission mode. He held both of her hands above her head as though restraining her and took his time to maximise her pleasure. Her orgasm was explosive. She took some minutes to recover, rolled into his arms, kissed him, and gently drifted into a deep, satisfying sleep.

Chapter 150 – Sunday

She woke with a smile on her face. The storm had passed, and she could see sunshine through the shutters. He was watching her. She curled up in his arms. No rush today.

After breakfast, having cleared up from dinner last night, they were sitting in the lounge. 'Can we spend some time looking at your schedule next week, and where a little preparation would help.'

'What do you have in mind?'

'You're wearing two hats with different responsibilities. Can I suggest you keep these responsibilities separate? This will help you to keep focussed. When you go to the office tomorrow, your first task will be your production role to check all is well. When you are satisfied there are no issues requiring urgent address, go to the office of Charles and sit in his chair. Try to view the world from his perspective. Take a few minutes to feel his world before attempting to deal with his in-tray. His in-tray needs his mindset. Does this make sense to you?'

Week 24

Chapter 151 – Monday

The atmosphere was thick with gloom as she entered the office. Mary was struggling with her feelings of loss.

She dropped her bag on her desk and hung her coat. '*Okay Seb. Let's do this. Let's see if the mighty Seb can lift the gloom from this place.*'

She passed Mary to tell her she would be on the shop floor if needed.

As she walked through the shop floor entrance, she could sense a more subdued atmosphere than usual. As she passed people on the way to Tom's office, she wished them good morning. Tom's face was full of surprise to see her walking towards him and enter his office.

'Good morning, Miss. Is there a problem?'

'No Tom. From now on, I'll visit with you when I arrive each morning. I like to see what projects are in progress, and we can look at any issues that need to be addressed. I may also pop down in the afternoon with any new projects I would like your input. I know this is new to you, but Jim was not allowed onto the floor for health reasons. I will visit the shop floor at least once each day when I'm here.'

'No problem, Miss. In fact, I would like to show you one project causing us a problem.'

He led the way to a production line where an archway window design was being assembled. She could see the problem. With the workers present, she suggested a solution using her engineering skills. They all agreed her idea would work. They thanked her with obvious surprise on their faces. She would pass by the design office to notify them of the variation to the process manifesto.

Once back at her own desk she decided it was time to change her hat and deal with whatever she could in Charles' in-tray. Passing by Mary to inform her where she was going, she entered the office and closed the door behind her. A moment of hesitation as she felt the eerie sense of emptiness. She had never before entered this room without Charles present. Recalling what Sebastian had told her, she went to his desk and slowly sank into his executive chair. She looked around the office trying to extract any information which would allow her to think as Charles would think.

Her mind drifted to how badly Charles had taken Jim's death. *'Poor man. How do we cope with such loss,'* remembering the death of both her mum and dad in one year? *'And what must Seb have felt when he heard of Bernie's death. He's passionate about his mentors. How gutting to lose one in such a tragic manner. If only he knew of the passion and love I have for him both as a student and a woman. I will be gutted to leave him. Only three weeks left. My God. What will I do?'*

The telephone interrupted her thoughts indicating a call from Mary.

'Teresa Yardley would like to speak with you. Do you want to take the call?'

'Yes, please Mary. Can you put her through?'

'Good morning, Teresa. Lovely to hear from you. How can I help you?'

'Simon has informed me about Jim. I never did meet him, but he sounded a lovely and certainly a capable man. I'm so sorry for your loss. How are you coping?'

'It's a great loss but expected sooner or later. We knew of Jim's health problems some months back. This is the reason I moved to Matlock to ensure a smooth transition.'

'Of course. Simon tells me you are now the Production Director. Congratulations. A breath of fresh air to have another formidable woman in this industry. I look forward to building a close relationship with you.'

Week 24

'Thank you. I look forward to working closely with you. There is much to gain from a close co-operation.'

'That I'm sure of. This may not be the best time to raise an issue with you, but we're close to the end of our contracted period regarding Simon's secondment to us. Rather than a renewal I'm considering activating the clause to permanently secure his services. I haven't broached this with him because I want your views on this proposal. We accept the financial terms for such a transfer.'

'We won't obstruct such a move. Our transfer clause is part of a more comprehensive service and co-operation plan with significant architects such as yourself. I developed this new approach from speaking with people like you. We will also be informing you of new material developments and the technical support to incorporate them into your building designs. We want a close relationship with people like you so together we provide optimal solutions both in your design and our costs of fabrication.'

'Wonderful news. I look forward to discussing your novel approach. When next in London we must have lunch and really get to know each other. I think your ideas exactly what we need. Do you have any idea when you will next be in London?'

'I would like a couple of weeks to stabilise things here. Our order books are full. In this period of sadness, we must keep production on schedule. Jim was much loved here, part of the fabric at Aldridge and within the community. It will take a little time to move on. Why don't you speak with Simon about your proposal and let me know if he's receptive? We can always extend the current agreement a few weeks by simple letter exchange if required. I should have a better idea of my travel plans next week. We can plan from there.'

'I completely understand your priorities. And thank you, Mel. Can I assume Simon will still have access to your design resources once with us for continuity purposes?'

'All part of our new service approach.'

'Fantastic news. I really look forward to working with you. Another woman. Breath of fresh air in this industry. I'll speak with Simon later today and let you know if he's interested.'

'Great. Why don't we speak next week? This week will be consumed with Jim's funeral.'

'Of course. My condolences to Jim's family. If I can be of any support, don't hesitate to call.'

'Thanks Teresa. You're very kind. And thanks for the call. You've brightened my day.'

'Let us brighten our futures together. Bye, Mel, and best wishes to you.'

She sank back in her own thoughts again. *Amazing how similar soccer is to business. I've just agreed to our first player transfer.* She chuckled to herself, *'I wonder if Phil understands the correlation between corporate play and soccer.'*

She was interrupted by a voice in her head *'you may be sitting in the chair but when are you going to show me you belong there?'* It was her dad's voice. 'Okay girl. Plenty of time to grieve after the game is over. Sorry, dad. I'm on it. I will make you proud of me.'

As she read the papers in the in-tray Mary walked in carrying teas for two. 'Hello my dear. Thought you might like tea. I can also help you with that pile. There are only two issues that need addressing. The remainder will accept that Jim's passing will occupy us this week. More importantly, how are you coping?'

'Other than the occasional lapse, I'm okay. Seb is masterful at knowing when to keep me focussed, and when I need a little respite.'

'I've never witnessed such influence in my life. Your transformation is staggering. Sebastian must be some incredible teacher.'

She laughed. 'He's no teacher. He's my university of life. Probably write a book about it when I have time.'

'I want the first copy. Only way anyone will believe me.' They both laughed – a needed tonic.

They attacked the pile together quickly dealing with anything needing attention. Tray cleared; it was time to get back to her day job. She left the office with Mary, who went back to her desk.

'*The show must go on*', she thought to herself as she entered her own office.

She arrived home shattered, but in better spirit than she expected. The call from Teresa Yardley had endorsed her new approach. If Teresa indicates support for her ideas, so will others.

Sebastian was ready to catch her, but she didn't fall. 'Hi, Seb. See you at dinner', as she went to her room. A few minutes later he heard her go to the gym. She reappeared in the kitchen a little after 7:15 seeing the already poured glass of wine awaiting her. She went to him, put her arms around his waist and snuggled into him. 'You were great today. Wearing two hats, one at a time, made my task much easier. And sitting in Charles' chair feeling the moment felt good. I can cope. Thanks.'

He put his arms around her. 'Any issues to report?'

'No. Teresa Yardley phoned to congratulate me on my new position, and to support my new initiative with architects. She wants to keep Simon, which he will jump at, and I'm okay with it.'

'Ready for dinner?'

'Will you hold me some more after dinner? Then a long soak. My dad gave me a pep talk today. I want to quietly chat with him some more.'

'Whatever you need, lady. Let's eat.'

Chapter 152 – Tuesday

She decided to keep to the routine adopted yesterday. It worked for her, and Mary was happy Mel kept her informed of where she was, and what she was doing. However, one of the telephone calls this morning was from Michael Chimes. Mary wanted to field it, but Mel took the view she had the power to control the situation.

'Good morning, Mel. I understand you are now acting CEO as well. You've come a long way.'

'What can I do for you, Michael? Holding down two jobs limits my time for chit-chat.'

'Sorry Mel. I've found a potential architect client that fits your profile. Can I use Teresa Yardley as a reference as I understand Simon is still there on secondment?'

'I don't think that's a good idea. We need to keep what architects we already have well under the radar for now and includes Simon's involvement. In any event, I would have to get consent from Teresa before I could use her name. I'm seeing her in a couple of weeks, so I'll ask her how she feels about being used as a referee. Once we have secured a significant order, our involvement will be out there. By then I hope we have quietly carved out a significant market share.'

'Would it be possible for me to meet her with you so I can see first-hand how the relationship works?'

'Let me think about that as Teresa would like to do a girlie relationship lunch to celebrate my new position and to bond as women in this industry. Obviously, you will need to get involved with her at some point, but I'll let you know once I've spoken with her. Could you let Mary know the details of your potential client, so we don't fall over each other? I'm not out there fostering new relationships at present, but one of the architects I have was a referral from another practise that likes my ideas. Once Charles is back, I think we should all meet so we can agree on a strategy.'

'Have you heard from Charles? I can't get him on his home phone.'

'I haven't heard from him since last week. His mind is focussed on a fitting send-off for his old friend, so I won't be chasing him before the funeral. If he makes contact, shall I tell him you want to speak with him?'

'It's okay, Mel. You're right. He needs to put this tragedy behind him. It can wait.'

'Anything else?'

'No, that's all I wanted to ask. See you on Friday. All the staff here are coming.'

'Great. See you then. Bye.'

For the first time since Jim's demise, Mary's face was beaming. She heard the whole conversation as Mel had used the speaker phone. 'Very professional my dear. I know he has been trying to call Charles, probably to ask him the same question. Beautifully fielded. And how inconsiderate of him to try to circumvent you when Charles has made it perfectly clear you're in charge. Well done, Mel. Top of class. Made my day.'

'Have you spoken with Charles recently?'

'The last time I spoke with him was on Saturday. He wanted to use a florist I know to decorate the church and the hotel ballroom. I did speak with Edna last night. Charles is still out rallying support for the funeral. He's planning a big send-off for Jim. Even the Mayor will be speaking at the funeral. Just so you know, I can call Charles if there is a difficulty you're not yet equipped to deal with and cannot be deferred. You're doing a splendid job under difficult circumstances, so we have no such issues. And you don't look out of place in that chair. I think we should leave him to take care of the funeral arrangements. Margaret is staying with Edna and Charles and being kept occupied with the arrangements.'

'Thanks for you vote of support. It means a lot to me.'

'Credit where credits due my dear.'

the Way

'How is Charles? He looked so lost last Thursday. I feel for him.'

'Edna is watching him very carefully. He has taken Jim's death badly. But keeping Charles occupied is good therapy. If Friday is a fitting celebration of Jim's life, I think Charles will consider his duty done.'

'I hope you're right. The air on the factory floor is sombre. They feel Jim's loss. We need to pay all due respects on Friday and then move on just as Seb did with me when my mum died.'

'Charles told me how well he took care of you. What a blessing he's been.'

'Is there anything else we need to address as I need to don my day job hat and keep the factory floor working?'

'My dear Mel. What a tough ride you've had these past months. I have nothing but admiration for you. You go do what you have to do. I'll come find you if anything crops up.'

As they left the office, 'Thanks Mary. Together we'll see this tragedy through.'

Thankfully, the workshop was fully occupied and the initiative by Charles to get as much business closed as possible before Christmas meant everything was running smoothly. No new orders to process as winter sets in and the recession begins to bite. All she had to do was to ensure there would be no deliveries to the factory on Friday, and all contractors requiring product Friday or over the weekend collected on Thursday. Many suppliers had expressed their condolences, and some who had dealt with Jim for many years will be present at the funeral.

A lost day of production would ordinarily cause delivery problems the following week. Some clients were obliging under the circumstances, and the shop floor had agreed extra hours on Monday and Tuesday of next week to make good any shortfall. Many workers have seen the news preaching doom and gloom in the construction industry. They are relieved the order books at Aldridge are full, thus no potential layoffs. They were grateful

Charles was such a shrewd businessman and would therefore ensure they are not responsible for late or damaged fabrications.

When she arrived home, she again was drained but far less insecure about her performance. She felt the support on the shop floor and from the design team. Everyone was pulling together to minimise problems knowing she was wearing two hats. This togetherness energised her just as it had when she addressed everyone last Thursday. She went to the gym and had a swim before presenting herself for dinner.

'You look somewhat more content with life this evening than you have these past days. Are you more comfortable with your duties?'

'I feel the support from the people at the factory. I sense they are working together to help me through the days. It's a warm feeling and helps to energise me. I can't explain it any other way.'

'Does it feel like the warmth you felt when you changed the guard last week?'

'Yes, I think that's it.'

'You are their General. You reached out to them last week. They repay you in loyalty to your cause. You have won hearts and minds. What you feel is the dividend. You've done well. You'll most certainly ride this storm, and they will support you.'

'I still need your full support. Wearing two hats is very demanding and draining.'

'Whatever you need will be there. Even hand in the night if you feel the need. I am by your side every step of the way. Have your heard from Charles?'

'No. Mary told me he is taking Jim's death badly. But he's organising the biggest send-off for Jim. I don't need to interrupt him and have thwarted any attempt by Michael Chimes. Charles needs space to reconcile himself to this loss. I feel privileged I can give him this space after everything he's done for me.'

'Why is Michael Chimes in the picture?'

the Way

'He called me today to get access to Teresa Yardley. He has already tried to contact Charles for the same purpose. I refused access at this time, suggesting we sit with Charles once this sadness is over and agree a strategy.'

'Are you satisfied he understood your instruction?'

'If he does anything to upset my architect clients, or divulge my ideas, I shall use the powers vested in me by Charles to publicly hang, draw, and quarter him in true Sun Tzu tradition before I fire him.'

He laughed as she animated this act. 'That's my girl. Make sure he understands the consequences of betrayal.'

'Are there any issues you wish to discuss this evening?'

'None I can think of. I just need to snuggle in your arms for a while to let the tensions of the day flow away and then put me to sleep. I cannot become complacent. Storms can brew quickly from nowhere. I need to be vigilant and ready.'

'Have you detected any external pressures?'

'Not yet. I asked Mary to keep her ears to the ground as she is far more adept at spotting irregularities. But nothing thus far. Mary even smiled for the first time since last Thursday when I put Michael in his place.'

'Okay. Let's get dinner cleared away and go start your therapy.'

Chapter 153 – Wednesday

She was again following her routine, sitting at Charles' desk adjusting her mindset to the task.

Mary rushed in. 'Mel, my dear, I have Charles on the phone for you. I'll give you a few moments to compose yourself before I put him through.' She was away back to her desk.

'*Breathe, girl, breathe.*' The phone buzzed. She picked it up. 'Good morning, Charles. How are you?'

Week 24

'Content my wonderful apprentice is doing such a fine job. How are you holding up?'

'My Sebastian Ryder crutches are doing a great job. All is well.'

'Mel, whilst I appreciate Sebastian is in the wings, the person performing on the stage is you. And, by all accounts, you are a star performer. You have my gratitude. But this is just a quick call to inform you of an oversight on my part I will take care of today. Any cheques over £10,000 need to be countersigned by me. Mary alerted me that Jason needs to make payments, so I'll pop in later today to sign them. I'll probably pop in and straight out again unless you need to speak with me.'

'Thank you for telling me but as I told you last week your priority is a fitting send-off for Jim. I'm okay, and I can feel the support from the people here. We will prevail for you.'

'God bless you Mel. You're a fine lady. By the way, I'm aware of the situation with Michael. I'm not prepared to discuss anything with him until back in the office. You are in charge and have my full authority and confidence.'

'That's very kind of you. If necessary, I shall make him aware of the Sun Tzu penalty for any act of betrayal. But I think he has the message that now is not the time to disclose our strategy.'

He laughed. 'I forgot that mighty warrior sitting on your shoulder. Any good news to report?'

'I had a call from Teresa Yardley. She fully supports our new approach. She wants to keep Simon on the agreed terms and wants to develop a close relationship with Aldridge. We have our first conquest.'

'That's great news. Thanks, Mel. You've cheered my day. If I don't see you later, I'll see you on Friday. I must go. Still much to do for my old friend. Bye Mel.'

'Bye Charles'

Mary had been listening on her extension. She came into the office. 'Thank you, my dear. To hear him laugh again is such a relief. How about some tea whilst we go through the mail?'

the Way

Later that afternoon, she had dealt with everything she could think of. *'What to do. Time to return some of the warmth I feel from the shop floor.'*

She made her way to Tom's office. 'Tom, if it's not inconvenient I'd like to visit each assembly line and meet the people. I want them to know I'm here for them and thank them for their support at this time of sadness.'

'What a great idea, Miss. They would really appreciate that. Come. Let's start at the shop window line.'

They visited all the production lines with Mel seeking names to establish connectivity. She thanked them for their effort and support. One or two of the more seasoned workers asked her about the impact of the recession. She assured them the order books are full for at least a year with new opportunities in the pipeline. Their only fear should be extra hours to meet demand. She could see the calm descend on their faces. *'Another burden lifted'* she thought to herself. This news would spread around the workshop like wildfire.

When she approached the line where Miles Davidson worked, she made a B-Line for him. 'Hello Miles. How's Sarah and Imogen?'

'The missus is fine, and Imi's a bundle of joy. Breaks yer 'eart every day.'

'Well give Sarah my best wishes and hope to meet them on Friday.'

'I'll tell her, Miss. Thanks.'

She walked back to her office, pleased with herself. She felt the gloom lift. Her army now knew her as a person rather than just a name and a face. It felt good.

Week 24

Chapter 154 – Thursday

When she reached Tom's office, he closed the door behind her to shut out the noise from the workshop.

'Anything wrong, Tom?'

'Quite the opposite, Miss. I want to thank you for what you did yesterday. This workshop is a different place today. I told my missus what you did. She said you have the grit of a man with the compassion of a woman. Says you'll make a great leader. Just wanted to tell you that. My missus can't wait to meet you.'

'Thank you, Tom. I'm very grateful for your kind words.'

'No problem, Miss. My missus thought you would be okay when I told her about the card and flowers to Margaret last week. And she knows about how you dealt with Miles. This workshop is right behind you, Miss. You can count on us to deliver.'

'Thanks Tom. Can't ask for more. Once we say our farewells to Jim tomorrow, we start to build on his legacy and make Aldridge the fabricator of choice across this great nation.'

'Here, here to that Miss.'

'Are there any issues I need to consider today?'

'No Miss. We have a lot more deliver trucks need loading today than usual, but we'll manage. Thank goodness we have plenty of space around the factory. Nearly half-a-million in product is being collected today.'

'Great news. I'd better leave you to it. Need to go put on my other hat and see what I need to do to cover for Charles. Maybe I'll see you later or, if not, I'll see you tomorrow.'

'We knows you have a lot on your plate. So don't worry about us. Everything at this end will be good.'

Chapter 155 – Friday

She woke with an unusual gloom for her. She was thinking of Jim, and how it was not the same in the office without his smiling face and soft, jovial nature. He was looking at her but leaving her with her thoughts. He knew this would be a challenging day for her so soon after the passing of her mother. *'But no rush. The funeral service is at 11am. Plenty of time.'*

After their shower, she opened the wardrobe to reveal what she had chosen for them to wear. He had given her carte blanche to search through all his wardrobes to find something suitable for him just to keep her occupied. She had selected the suit she wore at her mother's funeral, not expecting to wear it again quite so soon. For him, she had to recover a dark suit from his archive wardrobe. Today she wanted them to fully honour her dear friend and mentor.

The church was packed. Margaret and family occupied the front row, with Charles, Edna, Sebastian, Mel, Mary and her husband directly behind with Charles in the aisle seat ready to step out to present his eulogy. Flowers were in abundance throughout the church, lifting the gloom of this sad January morning. On the other side of the aisle were former members of the Royal Engineers Regiment dressed in their uniforms to honour their fallen comrade. It was a fitting turnout for one so loved in his community.

Jim arrived, being carried down the aisle by six bearers, and placed in front of the altar. The preacher started the traditional funeral service to commemorate the life of the man lying before them. The mayor of the local Council, a lifetime friend of Jim, gave a fitting eulogy on behalf of the community. Charles gave his eulogy for his best friend, and which lasted over ten minutes recalling their time together during the war, and then forming the company which was now a pillar of the community. It was clearly hard for him as he was visibly recalling times together with his lifelong friend, occasionally pausing to gather himself before he could continue. Everyone could not help but feel his sadness at the loss of his old friend.

The cemetery was attached to the church, allowing everyone to be present as he was lowered to his final resting place.

Charles had hired the ballroom at a nearby hotel where again no expense had been spared for his dear friend. There was food in abundance whilst family, friends, and colleague paid tribute to and shared memories. Charles, Edna, Margaret, Mary, Mel and Sebastian stood together in a group speaking with anyone wishing to pay their respects.

'A young woman carrying a baby approached Mel. 'Excuse me Miss, are you Miss Southgate?'

'Yes, I am.'

'My name is Sarah Davidson, the wife of Miles, and this is our baby daughter, Imogen. I want to thank you for the lovely clothes you sent us for Christmas. It was a lovely surprise after what my husband did to you.'

Mel could see the baby was wearing clothes she had bought. 'It was my pleasure. Think nothing of it. Imogen looks lovely in them.'

'They tell me you're now the new boss at Aldridge.' She noticed a group of women of various ages had gathered around them. 'Me and the other wives here,' pointing to the other women 'want to welcome you to our community. It's a real surprise to see a sister at the top of Aldridge and we want to stand by you. What you did with Miles taught him a lesson he won't forget, and we respect you didn't sack him. If any of our menfolk give you any trouble you let us know. Around here the wives know how to deal with husbands who misbehave. They call you Superwoman, but we stand ready to help you in any way we can.' There was a chorus of 'Yeah'.

'Thank you, ladies. You bring a cheer to my heart on such a sad day. In a few weeks from now, when a little warmer, I would like to invite you all to the factory for a celebration of a new era at Aldridge and hope you will all come so I can get to know you. You can bring your husbands if you wish.'

They all laughed at her put down. 'We'll be there Miss, have no fear.'

Charles and Sebastian observed this exchange with a smile on their faces. She had already won the full support of the wives. A brave new world indeed.

Edna observed the reaction of Charles and Sebastian. 'I suppose you two are going to smugly sing "we did it, by Jove we did it" referring back to *My Fair Lady*. Well, I concede you have been successful but, more importantly today, Jim will rest in peace knowing Mel will honour his legacy. Sebastian, you've done a fine job with that woman, and we're most grateful. It will be very nice to have my husband back for a while knowing the company is in very capable hands.' She took Charles away to mingle as Mel returned to Sebastian.

Mel noticed Margaret was getting a little tearful. She held both of her hands, 'Margaret, is there anything I can do for you?'

'My dear Mel. Jim was so proud of you. The first time you took on Michael, he wouldn't stop talking about it. And then the incident on the shop floor. That's when he knew you would make it. He started to relax, knowing his legacy was in safe hands. I really believe he held on last week so he could hand over to you himself. You were like a daughter to him, and he thought the world of you. God bless you, my dear.'

By now they were both tearful as they hugged each other.

Many people wanted to meet her, some genuine and others curious to meet this new female star in a male-dominated industry. Tom introduced his wife and daughter, who will graduate from university in the summer. She wanted to know if there was likely to be any prospect of a job. Mel assured her more women would be brought into Aldridge and she would keep Tom informed. There were longstanding suppliers to Aldridge who wanted to meet Jim's successor mostly to make the connection.

Michael Chimes watched all this attention with gloom. How would he fit into the new world according to Mel? Could he make amends for the past; or was it time to move on? Being a consummate salesman, he was gracious towards her and keen to meet the man who had transformed her, as were many of the London office.

Simon approached Mel. 'Thank you for allowing me to go work for Teresa. She told me you'd given your blessing to my move. I hope we can still be friends. You are truly a formidable lady, and I would be honoured to count you as a friend.'

'Did Teresa tell you about the new working relationship with Aldridge? I think you'll be spending time in Matlock as the relationship develops, so we'll have good contact. I wish you well in your new appointment and likewise hope we'll remain friends.'

They were curled up in bed together; the day having taken its toll on her.

'Are you okay?'

'Please put me to sleep. It's been such a sad day.'

He stroked her back. She drifted into a peaceful slumber.

Chapter 156 – Saturday

Edna was not happy with the state of mind of Charles. She encouraged him out to the golf course with his old friend, and primary business competitor, James Pardow. As the owners of their respective companies, they had found over the years that sometimes, working together to thwart an interloper in their business, worked to their advantage. They were content to compete with each other but stood together against rivals.

the Way

Both were now reaching retirement age, but their children were not interested in continuing the family business – not sexy enough. They were pondering what to do.

By the fourth hole James could see his friend was not in good spirit and was already two shots down. James and his wife had attended Jim's funeral, so knew how heartfelt the eulogy by Charles.

'Charles, are you sure you want to play this round, or shall we retreat to the nineteenth hole and share some sorrow?'

'I'm sorry James. I just feel so lost. I don't know if I have the heart to carry on. Jim and I built our business from nothing. We shared the good times, the bad times, and the times in hell, but we stood together, soldiered on, and made things happen. I've lost my comrade and I don't know what to do.'

'But what about this woman you have, superwoman they call her, who is taking over from Jim? Is she not up to it?'

'You mean Mel. She's great. And the guy who is mentoring her has done a fantastic job. Jim was very happy to pass her his baton, and I've passed her mine for the time being. Despite everything, and being thrown in at the deep end, she's doing a great job. But Jim and I were more than the business.'

'Come. Let's to the clubhouse and chat this through because Jim's death has me thinking about my future now my kids have rejected any notion of keeping my business going.'

They were seated in the clubhouse bar with their drinks.

'Charles, what do you want to do with your business? We're both getting on, so how do you see retirement working?'

'I really don't know. What I do know is I would like to take out some capital to give to Margaret. Why I never gave shares to Jim, I'll never know. The business is as much his as it is mine. He wouldn't gamble his money when we bought the airfield, so I took all the shares. I owe him, and I want to make it good with Margaret.'

'I would like to take some capital out of my business, but short of selling the company, I don't know how I can do it.'

Week 24

'James, you've given me an idea. I know a big-time banker who may be able to help us. If you're interested to know what our real options are can you prepare a package of financials, ongoing business, key persons, etc and let me give both mine and yours to him to see what he can suggest. If anyone can really help us, he can. I'll give him carte blanche to find an optimal solution where both of us can extract capital and retain an interest. How does this sound?'

'Who's this banker?'

'His name is Sebastian Ryder. Retired senior executive of one of the biggest banks in the world, his bibliography is extraordinary, and he lives here at Merton Hall.'

'Is he the one who redeveloped that place recently?'

'Yes, and it's fabulous. He spent millions on it.'

'Okay. How quickly do you need the package?'

'How fast can you get it to me?'

'Now we're not playing I can probably deliver it to you tomorrow afternoon. My package will be sealed though, even for my old friend, and the contents to remain confidential.'

'No problem with that. I fully understand, and you can put a note with it regarding confidentiality if you like.'

'Right. We better go busy ourselves.'

Sebastian gently got her up and ready for breakfast. She was not concentrating at all. He was unsure whether to shop in Matlock or keep her away from anyone who might recognise her. He finally opted to shop in Matlock, knowing that if someone did approach her, she would likely pull herself together. The wives had made her welcome yesterday, and this buoyed her for the remainder of the day.

As they walked through the supermarket doors, he suggested she decide what they would have for dinner, both today and tomorrow, and then go select what she needs.

'But I don't know what I fancy.'

the Way

'Well then, go look around until something captures your eye and start from there. I'll be right behind you.'

She was drawn to the fish counter. Not one of Sebastian's first choices. 'Can we have fish pie tonight? I haven't had a good fish pie for ages. Do you know how to prepare it?'

'Do you know how you like it?'

'Of course.'

'Then you know the ingredients.'

'From memory, white fish, smoked fish, salmon, and some shellfish. Potatoes, cream, parsley, mushrooms, milk, white wine. I think that's all. No, we need some hard cheese as well.'

He could hear her engage. He started to assemble what he needed for the week. As soon as she had what she needed, she descended into gloom again.

He wanted to take her out for lunch to celebrate her success, but she did not want to ready herself. They sat in the kitchen enjoying a cold snack knowing they would have a very filling fish pie later.

'Talk to me, lady. You had a tough week, but you not only survived, you came through with flying colours. The idea to visit the workshop and introduce yourself to the workers was brilliant thinking considering the circumstances.'

'Seb, please don't humour me. How many times have you drummed it into me I need to walk the floor twice each day and talk to the people? What you could ask is why it took me so long to do it because I felt the value instantly, and the resulting feedback was uplifting.'

'Lady, you listen to me. Stop this self-inflicted torture now. Ten days ago, you were thrown into the deep end under the most distressing of circumstances. You learnt how to swim the hard way. You successfully changed the guard, and your army could see you were worthy of saving, so they gave you the space to learn. You did it. Do you seriously think Charles would leave his business in your hands if he did not have confidence in you? If he had any doubts, he would at least have sent Edna in to

Week 24

cover for him, and you know she could. So stop beating up on yourself. Sure, you can analyse why you didn't do this or that, but Aldridge survived and everyone we've met acknowledges what a great job you did. Learn from this past week in a positive way, but no negatives. Now go get yourself ready because you're coming out with me.'

'Where are we going?'

'At this short notice I guess a little retail therapy in Derby on my account is the most likely way of putting a smile on your face.'

'You're going to take me shopping? Give me 10 minutes.'

As she was getting ready, a thought came to her head. *'I still owe him a birthday present. Must put this right today. I hate it when he's right, and he pulled out all the stops last week. Ungrateful bitch. Time to put a smile on his face.'*

Chapter 157 - Sunday

When she awoke, she was in a much better place. Her sorrow had diminished, and she was ready to move on. But when she peered through the shutters, rain was beating against the windows. She jumped back into bed. 'No point in getting up. It's not nice out there.'

'Any ideas what you would like to do today?'

'Can we go to the cinema? Haven't watched a good movie in ages.'

'After breakfast find what you would like to see. We can go have some lunch and then cinema. Sound like a plan?'

'Thanks. Could do with a change after the gloom of the past weeks.'

the Way

Week 25

Chapter 158 – Monday

When Mel arrived at the office, she noted the vacant parking space allocated to Charles. She dropped her things on her desk and went to see Mary.

'Is Charles away today? His car is not outside.'

'He phoned in to say he had some things to take care of today. He was here yesterday with Jason. But he wants you to keep an eye on business for a few more days. He obviously missed you this morning before you left.'

She thought nothing of this declaration he was at the office yesterday. *'Probably some more payments to take care of. If I see Jason maybe he can tell me more.'*

Sebastian was sitting in his study watching the markets when the phone rang. 'Sebastian, it's Charles here. Is Mel still there?'

'No. She left about 10 minutes ago, why?'

'Is it possible for us to meet today over lunch? There is something I need to discuss with you in confidence.'

'Why don't you come here around 12:30. I can prepare lunch. Then you can speak freely.'

'I don't want to put you to any trouble preparing lunch. I can arrange for a quiet room at the club.'

'It's no trouble at all. See you here at 12:30.'

'Thanks, Sebastian.'

Mel stuck to her routine. When she went to see Tom, it felt like the sun was beaming into the workshop even though it was raining outside. *'Has someone changed the lighting in here?'*

the Way

Tom was in a good mood. 'Lovely send-off on Friday. Charles did Jim proud. My shop floor people really felt the day and appreciated the wake. No expense spared for Jim. They're all ready for a good year ahead. My missus was pleased to meet you, and thanks for the encouragement for my daughter, Meg. She appreciated your words of encouragement.'

'No problem. Let's see if we can expand the business and make room for some young talent. We could do with some more women around here.'

'I'm up for that, Miss.'

'Any issues we need to discuss?'

'Not at the moment Miss. Everything was dispatched on Thursday, and we haven't heard of any damage or breakages. The maintenance guys were here yesterday checking our machines. Clean bill of health all round.'

'Good. Charles is not back, so if you need me and I'm not in my office, I'll be in his office.'

'Still wearing two caps, Miss. Will try not to bother you.'

'Thanks, Tom. See you later.'

Charles arrived at the gates of Merton at 12:30 sharp. Sebastian let him in.

'Welcome Charles. Please come in.' He was carrying a briefcase.

'Let's sit in the kitchen.'

'What can I get you to drink? I have a good sherry chilled.'

'That will be fine, thank you.'

Sebastian served lunch. Charles was looking down in the mouth. 'Sebastian, I want to talk to you in your professional capacity. I would like to run some ideas past you in total confidence. Not even Edna knows of my thoughts.'

He stopped as though needing confirmation. 'Whatever we discuss will remain between us. What do you have in mind?'

'Since Jim's death I've completely lost my appetite for business. We were partners for so long I feel lost without him, not in business, as Mel is doing a great job, but as brothers. My heart's not in it anymore. I'll be sixty-five in a few weeks. I want out not least to ensure I can give Margaret the funds she needs I feel are due to Jim. I know the owner of our nearest rival, and he needs to think of retiring himself, but has no-one to take over from him. He has a good Finance Director, but no-one suitable to take the helm. Would you look at both companies to see if you can advise on the best way forward? Even a merger would be seriously considered.'

'I'm so sorry, but I understand your position. Mel also feels Jim's loss after just a short relationship. Do you have the detailed financials of both companies, current business prospects, the composition of the Boards, and any other key people?'

'Yes, I have them here', reaching for his briefcase. 'But you already know Aldridge in depth. I've studied Mel's draft Business Plan. I've never seen my company laid so bare before me. Quite revealing.'

'You've built an excellent business worthy of continuation, but your weakness is succession. Let me study this data. Can you come back tomorrow or Wednesday to discuss what I think?'

'Sure. And we expect to pay professional fees for your work. It's time we paid you for something.'

'Charles, before I start this, are you prepared for a brutal assessment of these businesses as I'm not good at soft touch? Obviously, I know how strong Aldridge is from the Business Plan, but any analysis I do will not accommodate any emotional loyalties, only business.'

'Why do you think I came to you? I can't trust anyone else to give me a considered professional opinion, especially just now.'

'Okay, leave it with me. I'll call you in the morning if I'm ready. Otherwise it will be Wednesday.'

'Thanks Sebastian, and thanks for lunch. I've left Mel in charge so I'm free whenever. Use my home phone to call.'

the Way

He took the papers to his study and started to analyse the condition of each company. He was soon lost in the job he had so loved for so many years.

Carmen arrived, dropped her bags, and scooped Mel off her feet. 'How are you, my dear? Let me look at you.'

'Hi Carmen, I'm okay, thanks. Lovely to see you again.'

'You look pretty good. We go do our usual workout and chat?'

'Okay, give me ten minutes to get myself organised. See you in the gym.'

Carmen returned to her baggage and drew out a package and handed it to Seb. 'Happy Birthday, my darling.'

He opened it to find two bottles of Hennessey XO cognac. 'Wow Carmen. What a lovely present. Is there any significance to two bottles?'

'Yes, my darling. One is for your birthday, and the second a special thank you for taking good care of Mel and Carmen. You are an extraordinary man and Carmen knows how valuable you are as a wonderful friend.'

She hugged him and kissed him. 'I must change, my darling, and join Mel. See you for dinner. Please allow us a little extra time if needed.'

Having completed their gym routine and swim, they settled in the sauna.

'My dear Mel, you must tell Carmen everything. The death of Jim must have been a terrible shock. My PA told me the church was full for his funeral. He was well respected here. But how are you coping?'

Mel related events surrounding the death of Jim, and how badly Charles was taking the loss of his dearest friend.

'Has my darling Sebastian understood your situation and cared for you?'

'Other than the night Jim died, he has been my rock.'

'What happened?'

'It doesn't matter, Carmen. He has been there for me whenever needed.'

'Does he know how much you love him?'

This jolted Mel 'What do you mean?'

'Carmen is not blind. I have known for these past three months you have fallen in love with him. Does he know this? Has he responded?'

Mel felt uncomfortable discussing this topic with her. 'I have mentioned to him I love him, but not in a formal way. He sticks strictly to his mentor/student discipline and will not discuss any other relationship.'

'You must be close to your six months. What will happen then?'

Mel hung her head, 'I don't know. I can't bear the thought of leaving here, or him.'

'Then you listen to Carmen. You must find the right moment to confront him with the thought of you leaving. Carmen knows this will be as bad for him as for you once you bring it into focus. Give him time to absorb this loss – a few days, maybe. Then tell him how you really feel about him. He deserves to be loved, and you clearly want this. He has changed so much since you came here. Carmen would be delighted to see both of you happy in love for each other.'

'Carmen, he has a big hurdle with our age difference. He looks at me as a daughter; not a lover.'

'You are a woman, not his daughter. And he is a man, not your father. Love is the strongest emotion known to mankind. Love will conquer the age gap if strong between you. You have reached for your goal; and worked hard to achieve it. Now it is time to apply yourself to this important task for both of you. You have the full support of Carmen to achieve this goal.'

'Wow Carmen. Quite a speech. I want this to happen, but I'm not sure I can break through 23-years of remorse.'

'Wait until I have left on Thursday and confront him with your love and desire to stay here with him. See how he responds.

the Way

Carmen will be available to you at any hour if you need me. But I think you can make this happen if you want it enough.'

'Thank you. I'll do it.'

'Good. Let us see what wonderful delight he has prepared for dinner. And no school this evening. We go to chat as women. You look tired of all this business. Time for woman talk.'

'Are you suggesting we bunk school?'

'What is bunk?'

'We decide we will not go to school.'

'Then we bunk school. Let us go have dinner.'

Chapter 159 – Tuesday

Mel felt refreshed from her chat with Carmen. A welcome return to real life. She would go to work with a refreshed spring in her step. She had dealt with the changing of the guard. The funeral was a real tribute to Jim, but it was time to move on.

Mel left for the office with a spring in her step. Sebastian dialled the home telephone number for Charles. 'Good morning, Charles, I have some provisional thoughts I would like you to consider before going deeper. Can you pop over?'

'I'll come now if it's convenient.'

'Okay. See you in ten minutes.'

Charles arrived and was led to his study. 'My goodness, what a setup. I've always wondered what you did with your time. Do you play the markets?'

'Yes, although not actively. My portfolio is more investment than trading. But I like to keep in touch with what's happening out there.'

'I've fed your numbers, and those of your friend, into an optimisation model. Your business on its own is worth over £68 million, and your friend's business comes out around £42

Week 25

million. If I combine them into one business, and remove duplications, the value is around £145 million. At this level you could list the combined company, take out what you both need in cash, add any investment requirements, and live off the dividends for the rest of your life. What do you think?'

'I'm stunned. Why such a big difference?'

'You're the two principal competitors in your market. You impact each other's margins when you compete. Take that element away, combine production, and cut out overlap, your margins and profitability increase. You have the advantage of a full order book throughout the recession, which makes a significant difference, and attractive to Pardow.'

'How do you see the structure of the combined company?'

'They're in Derby, you're here. They lease their factory. You own yours, and you have plenty of spare space. I would suggest closing the Derby plant and relocating here. All production and management will then be in one place. You both have satellite offices in London so they would merge, and Pardow has offices in Manchester and Liverpool where much redevelopment is about to start. You could take the opportunity to implement Mel's restructure package for the satellite offices. This is an easy placement, and I know just the people to arrange it for you.'

'What do you propose as the next step?'

'Can you bring James Pardow here and see if we can get agreement on a merger?'

'I could probably get him here tomorrow.'

'Then let's do it. Assume we'll need around two hours if he's a willing participant and has the authority to transact.'

'Can I call him now?'

'Please do.'

After speaking with James, 'He'll be here at 9am tomorrow morning. Just so I'm prepared, as I expect him to call me this evening, what will this cost?'

'You should look at a total fee structure of around 7% plus legal and audit. Of the 7% around 2% will come to me. I'll take some in shares which I'll designate to Mel. I think she should head the combined company with you and James staying in there as joint Chair until it all settles down. They have an excellent Production Director, and Finance Director. I've groomed Mel for much more than where she is, and I know she can deliver for you. All Directors must pass through a vetting system and will be given share options as part of the listing to incentivise their performance.'

'Fear not, you have no resistance from me regarding Mel. I'll be very proud to hand over to her. She was an inspired choice for nurturing, and I'm forever in the debt of Mary for pushing me onto you. You've done a fantastic job with her, and she tells me she wants to continue living here. I think she will appeal to shareholders. No brainer.'

'Okay. Let's see if we can put the skeleton of a deal together tomorrow. Should be fun. If we can agree a deal are you prepared to handover the CEO role to Mel straight away so I can show her what is expected of her and educate her regarding being the CEO of a listed company.'

'Of course. I'm not in the frame of mind needed for such a concentrated effort.'

'By the way, Sebastian, dig out your plans for the extension you mentioned. I'll have one of our technical designers look at it. I want to give you that extension before the merger. It's the least I can do for everything you've done for me. And no argument about it, I want this to happen between us.'

'That's very kind of you. I have some thoughts on how to provide for you and Margaret. I don't see any pension provisions in your accounts. You'll need advice from your tax advisers, but can I suggest you consider a generous pension arrangement for both yourself and Jim, including your respective wives and backdate this to the beginning of this financial year or earlier if possible. You could also award Jim a bonus for this year which could be shares or share options which will probably significantly benefit Margaret when listed either as a disposal or as dividend income. I don't know your tax arrangements so you must seek advice, but I can work with such provisions within a listing. You will obviously also recoup the Director loans you have associated with the landbank.'

'It's very kind of you to make me aware of this. I will most certainly pursue this in the coming days. Thanks again. See you tomorrow.'

Mel was sitting with Mary in Charles' office, having completed the demands of her Production Director role. She found she could learn much about suppliers and customers from her, which helped to identify with the signature on letters requiring a response. For much of the mail Mary would fulfil the normal role she played for Charles by composing a response for Charles to review and make any appropriate amendments. This made Mel's task much easier, and she learned so much about the individuals concerned and how Charles privately viewed them. It also gave her the opportunity to examine the supply agreements with major suppliers to understand the special relationship Charles enjoyed with the likes of Pilkington who provide all the glass.

Mel wanted to use these chats to better understand Charles. 'Have you heard from Charles today? He didn't call to tell me he wanted me to continue to hold the fort.'

'He did, my dear, but you had already left. I'm quite concerned about him. I thought the funeral would provide closure, but his mood has not changed. Poor man. I don't know what will happen now. Surely this company cannot cope with both missing.'

'Please Mary, don't you start to worry. Surely you and I can keep Aldridge afloat for some time to allow Charles to mourn his loss. The order books are full, the dark clouds over the workshop have lifted. We're in good shape. The worst is over. We, the women here, will prevail. And I have Sebastian in my back pocket if needed', tapping her bottom.

the Way

Mary smiled, 'sorry my dear, of course we can. My goodness, how far you've come in the past months. What a star. Let's show these men what we can do.'

There was a knock on the door. Jason walked in without waiting. 'Thought I might find you here. I need your signature on this bank authorised signature card. You and I are now joint signatures on the £10,000+ cheques.' He put the card in front of her.

'Mary tells me you were here on Sunday with Charles. Anything I should know?'

'It was a little strange. He called me Saturday evening to ask me to meet him here on Sunday morning. Didn't say why. On Sunday morning he wanted to see our Business Plan and all the supporting documentation, and our current financials.'

'Why didn't he invite me?'

'Don't know, but it wouldn't have mattered. He couldn't concentrate. Took all the documents home with him.'

Mary joined in. 'How did he seem to you?'

'He's having a hard time reconciling himself to the loss of Jim. I can only assume he wanted those documents to see if he can focus on the way forward.'

Mel, feeling a little hurt, 'Surely we need to help him understand our Business Plan. I don't think he's seen such a document before.'

'Mel, this is his business. He built it and knows it better than any of us. I don't think he will have any problems understanding our Plan. He needs a way out of his grief. Until then, what you and I need to do is keep this business running. Getting him to agree to the signature process was too easy. He needs space to think.'

Mary spoke again, 'Jason's right. If he needs us, we're here. But until then we carry on this business for him to give him the respite he needs.'

Still feeling niggled she wasn't invited to the Sunday meeting, 'Alright, I get it.' Looking at Jason, 'Can you and I agree we keep each other informed. I agree you and I need to keep Aldridge working, but we need to do it together.'

'Mel, you're the designated boss and I enjoy working with you so no problem. If anything of significance had occurred on Sunday, I would have told you.' Sensing her disquiet, 'Are we good?'

'Sorry Jason. Wearing two hats can be a little stressful.'

'No problem. Mary knows Aldridge like the back of her hand, and I'll do whatever I can to help you. Share the load a little. You have friends you can trust.'

'Thanks. Thanks to both of you. We can do this.'

Later that evening Mel and Carmen were sitting in the sauna.

'You look a little pre-occupied this evening. Tell Carmen what is troubling you.'

'Charles is not dealing well with the loss of Jim. I don't hear from him, but he asks Jason, our FD, to meet him at the office on Sunday to look at our Business Plan without me. Jason tells me he couldn't concentrate so took all the documents home. I'm wearing two hats but feel out of the loop.'

'As you know, my dear, my PA and your Mary are good friends. Mary is very concerned about Charles. She has worked for Charles for more than 20-years. She knows him well. If you trust this Jason, what is your problem? You are performing well in his absence, are you not?'

'By the seat of my pants, with Seb as my backstop, I'm coping. But it's not easy.'

'My dear, there is no textbook to guide you. You have learnt much these past months, and you have grown as a confident woman executive beyond recognition. You are trusted to play the game, so get on with it. Why did you embark on this journey if this was not your goal?'

'It's stressful. I've been thrown in at the deep end whilst still learning to swim.'

the Way

'Ah, I see. So, you see this role as a burden for which you do not think you are ready. Now you listen to Carmen because your thoughts are negative, and this cannot be. Charles built Aldridge from nothing to a very successful company, yes?'

'Yes.'

'And now, in his hour of need, he trusts you to take care of his business. Mel, this is an honour you should grasp. He would not do this unless he has confidence in you. Feel this honour and go put your hard work to good use. Not many people in your position have this opportunity, and you have people around you who will give you support when needed. Away with this negativity and burden. Carmen needs to see you rise to this challenge with joy at the opportunity. Are we now clear?'

'Wow, some speech. Carmen at her best.'

'Mel, most people in your position wait years for the opportunity to really prove themselves. Carmen has waited 8-years for such a role. You should see this opportunity as a privilege. Come, we have dinner, bunk school again, and speak more. Carmen needs to see you in a different mindset before I leave.'

Chapter 160 – Wednesday

Charles and James Pardow arrived at Merton, and introductions made. Sebastian went through some necessary due diligence with both before outlining his merger plan. They both signed Non-disclosure Agreements to start proceedings. Both Charles and James were in their sixties so realising value from their lifetime's work was naphtha to their ears. They would become wealthy, still have oversight of their business, but know there would be continuity to the next generation whilst having time out on the golf course. James was a little unsure about a woman CEO but was prepared to be guided by Charles and meet her. Sebastian knew this would not be a problem.

Head terms agreed, Sebastian was given the authority to approach his preferred broker to put this deal away. It would take between ninety and one hundred and twenty days to conclude a listing of the merged companies. Seb opened a bottle of champagne to seal the deal. Both would pass the relevant Board Resolutions by the end of the week to commence the merger.

She was sitting at Charles' desk, resetting herself for the task of clearing his in-tray. Mary had not yet joined her. Her thoughts were processing her talk with Carmen when they were interrupted by a familiar voice. It was her father. *'How does it feel to be where you belong?'*

She smiled at the thought of him looking over her. *'Good, dad. I'm getting the hang of it. I will make you proud of me.'*

Mary entered carrying refreshments. 'You look happier today, my dear. Good to see you smile.'

'Had a heavy pep-talk last night. Straightened out my self-pity.'

'Sebastian must be a hard taskmaster, although no one can complain at the results.'

'This wasn't Seb, it was Carmen. Boy, can she lay it on.'

'My friend at Aarden tells me Carmen is a tough lady, but she speaks highly of you, and she adores Sebastian.'

'She's great. Really stood by me these past weeks. Her pep-talk last night really put me in my place. But I couldn't argue with her, so let's to the game.'

Chapter 161 – Thursday

Charles called Sebastian to explain no-one in the company was capable to draft such important resolutions. Could he draft everything needed for both companies and Charles would collect them at lunchtime? Seb found this amusing. He would have to find competent people to insert into this merger to ensure compliance with corporate responsibility of a listed company. He also considered exploring the idea of securing an existing but dormant AIM company to reverse Aldridge and Pardow into it, as this would save much time and paperwork.

Chapter 162 – Friday

Upon arriving home, she went straight to the kitchen to find him. 'Charles is back. I've just signed a Board Resolution to merge Aldridge with Pardow, our principal competitor. I couldn't help but notice this merger would be in the form of a market listing under a financial adviser by the name of one Mr Sebastian Ryder. How long as this been going on, and why didn't you tell me?'

'Only these past few days. But I couldn't discuss this transaction with you. There are rules. It's only with the written consent of Charles I can discuss this with you over this weekend.'

'Well, let me finish the part where Charles confidentially informs me I've been nominated as the CEO of the merged company. I'm interested to know what role Mr Ryder had in this nomination.'

He smiled at her, 'Do you have a problem with this nomination? Aren't you ready for a real challenge? Your nomination has already been agreed, and as of Monday you will be elected the CEO of Aldridge and will be of the merged company upon incorporation. You will be my primary contact to arrange both the merger and the listing. You have much work and learning to do over the coming weeks. In fact, you have much work to do this weekend. You are meeting with James

Week 25

Pardow and his Financial Director on Monday to agree the merger timeline. You will lead that meeting so will need to be ready. The Financial Adviser to the merger will also be there to ensure all the essential components of a merger are understood so you will have some support, but I would like you to conduct this meeting without too much intervention from him.'

She wrapped her arms around his neck and kissed him on both cheeks, 'It's enough you think me ready for this role. I'll do whatever my master requires of me. Wow, what a difference six months makes when in the hands of Mr Sebastian Ryder, superstar extraordinaire. Can we open a bottle of bubbly to celebrate?'

'Go get a bottle from the cellar.'

Dinner over, he was relaxing in the lounge watching TV. She floated in and sat on his knees facing him with her knees towards the back of the couch. He clicked off the TV. 'You have something to say?'

'Yes, we need to talk. We are just two weeks from the end of my six months. I think we both know it will be unbearable to part, but how to go forward. I feel like this is my home, and I can't bear the idea of leaving you.' She let this sink in.

'I've achieved my goal as an executive, and now CEO, albeit acknowledging I still have much to learn. The one aspect of my life where I don't need any input is how I feel. I know where I want to be; here with you. Outside of this beautiful home we have no-one, or at least no direct family. You already know I love you dearly. I want to marry you. I want to be your wife. I want to share my life with you for as long as we live. Will you marry me?'

'What a speech. Can I state my views of where we go from here as I also have some thoughts? I agree for us to part is neither desirable, nor where I want to be. You can live here with me for as long as you wish. I cannot imagine this home without you. My problem is what relationship we'll share. I don't think marriage is good for you as you are half my age. I'm approaching the winter of my life whereas you are in your summer. You have many years ahead of you. Then there is the issue of children. Do you want children? If so, you'll need to consider this in the next few years, latest. I certainly do not want children; I'm far too old. Then there is your career to think about. You could be caring for me, or even lose me, at the very peak of your career when you need a husband at your side. Behind every prominent person there is usually a silent, but important spouse. I couldn't bear to think of you surrendering your career to care for me, or for you to be alone when you most need someone by your side. And please don't tell me we should live for today and let tomorrow take care of itself. I've been there, and I feel the pain to this day. I agree we should stay together, but we must find a more suitable way. When Mr Right comes along, you need to be able to grasp the opportunity.'

'Dearest Seb, I don't need children. For one thing, I don't have the family support structure to help me. I would have to surrender my career. By the time you are old enough to need care which, by the way, I cannot see with your health regime, I'll already be at my peak. Do you seriously believe with what we have, I would care about my job? You're not listening to me. I love you, and that's more important than anything else. It's not as though I need to work. So been there, seen it, done it comes to mind. Now live life, with you.'

'My darling, if anyone looked through the window now and saw us like this what would they think? Their first thought would be we are lovers or, if not, there is some kinky father daughter thing happening. I remember the first time I did this to my dad. I was twelve or thirteen at the time, with something very important to discuss with him. But I was also at the age when it registered that most of the times I had talks with him he was only paying scant attention, not maliciously, but because he knew I would air what I had to say and move on. I can't remember the nature of my need for this serious conversation, but I wanted his full attention. He was sitting in his favourite armchair, so I climbed on his knees like I am now, hands on hips, announcing I had a serious matter to discuss. I looked him straight in the eyes, which glowed with the most loving smile. After I'd finished what I had to say, he reached out to me to come close and rest my head on his shoulders as he wrapped his wonderful arms around me. My world was at peace. After that, right up to when he died if I needed his counsel I would either stand hugging him or sit like this with him. It became our time together, even as a grown woman. When you hold me close, I feel the same peace.' She sat reflecting on those days with her father.

'I have heard some women have the need of a father figure in the man they marry. My father brought me up in his image. I always went back to him when I needed advice, even when with Phil. And look how bad I am at choosing men in my own age group. Can you imagine, if I had not started this process with you, in a few weeks from now I would be walking down the aisle with him, into oblivion. Whew, am I well out of that!'

'However, there is one enormous difference between my dad and you. At the start of our time together you appeared to instinctively know what worked for me in a father and daughter way. But then something changed between us – probably after Phil and I broke up. When the fog cleared after my mother passed away, I started to recall comments made by Mama. She saw it before I did. I had fallen in love with you, not as my father figure, but as my lover. She knew you had changed as well. She commented you had taken women there, but none had warmed your heart. But your steely heart was now warming. Since then I've taken every opportunity to sleep and shower with you, hoping you would realise the same.'

'What else did Mama say?'

'During the time of the funeral she told me to be patient with you. Again, at New Year she knew you love me as much as I love you, but I still needed to wait until you're ready to open up and share your pain with me. Smart cookie is Mama. I thought I'd broken through on Christmas Day when our shower became a two-way event. Having aroused your erection, I then unwittingly stumbled into your dark territory. But I love in hope.'

'Hmm, interesting. I've had one thought over the past few months. I don't know if it's possible, but if you like it, we can go find out.'

'Tell me. I'm listening.'

'Throughout these past months I've looked at you as the daughter I never had. I've really enjoyed watching you grow, nurturing you, taking care of you. And you're the right age. The only thing I don't know is whether it's possible to adopt an adult. I know it's possible in other countries for both reuniting families after adoption at birth, and for inheritance purposes, but I'm not familiar with the law here. If nothing else, I would like you to enjoy what I have as my legal heir for as long as you live.'

'So, you would be prepared to adopt me as a compromise solution to stay with you?'

'Yes. And when Mr Right comes along you are free to pursue him.'

'I already know my Mr Right, but if this is what you want, then let's go pursue it. Does it mean I adopt your surname as well?'

'You can do that by Deed Poll in any event.'

'It's not my first choice, but if it means we stay together as family, I'm willing to take it. And thank you for letting me stay with you. My life would be so empty without you.'

'Letting you go would be devastating for me.'

She thought for a moment, 'If you think back to the first Sunday I was here, Edna made a joke about this situation smacking of Pygmalion. Paradoxically, she was right. You have changed me into someone else. When I went to see my friends when mum died, I no longer had much in common with them. I haven't had the urge to visit with them since. Nor do I miss

London, which is a real shock. My new life is here, with you. I should feel like Eliza, not fitting anywhere, but I feel very content here.'

'Can I sleep with you tonight? I sense much work to do this weekend, so need my sleep.'

'You never need to ask again. Do you need the hand in the night?'

'No, I just need to feel close to you, and sleep. Maybe in the morning, although our cleansing shower is highly competitive.'

'Why not both?'

She kissed him on the cheek, 'You spoil me.' To herself *'Please love me.'*

Chapter 163 – Saturday

She enjoyed both of her treats before they enjoyed breakfast and then did their weekly shop. After lunch, it was time to start her preparation for Monday.

'On Monday you need to walk onto the field of play and give the performance of your life. Think of John Gielgud in full flight – carefully crafted words, the eloquence in delivery, and always remembering the drama in the space between each word.'

'If you're trying to scare the hell out of me, you've succeeded.'

'Mel, you can do this. Today we'll look at the craft, and tomorrow we'll look at the technical substance. No-one at the table will have much, if any, knowledge of the technicalities of a merger pre-listing – that's why I'm here. Therefore, all you need to do is to guide the meeting through a logical course, and then effect a changeover of control, but honouring both Charles and James. You are not taking over to retire off these two titans, you are humbly continuing to build on their success. Your acceptance will depend on how you conduct yourself, and by Monday you will be magnificent.'

the Way

'Yes, my master', in quiet resignation.

Chapter 164 – Sunday

After breakfast they started to work on the substance of the meeting. Seb constructed an agenda noting all the protocol requirements. Then they added a full brief for her to practice after which it was reduced a trigger words to ensure she omitted nothing of importance.

This was quickly a light-hearted affair as she grasped the logic of the process and realised Mary would be by her side, as secretary to the meeting, navigating a written agenda. Although it would be correct protocol to have the Pardow people leave the room whilst an Aldridge Board meeting appointed her as CEO, they agreed such a protocol could be waived as neither company had full Board representation. This was more a shareholders meeting.

By early afternoon she had grasped the process and the content, so they went to play tennis before a leisurely evening together.

Week 26

Chapter 165 – Monday

He had her out of bed at 6am as usual when she slept with him, and into the pool. Then her shower, and off to her room to get ready. She walked into the kitchen looking every bit an executive. She gasped 'Seb, you look fantastic. My God, a suit and tie. Be back in a minute. Must get my camera.'

A few minutes later she was back armed and ready with her camera. 'Come away from the stove into the light. A little more. Great. Say cheese.' She got her picture.

'If you want a record of the day, let me take one of you.'

She handed him the camera and posed. 'No, my dear, you are not posing on the beach. A little more dignified please, but not too stuffed shirt.'

He caught her off guard, laughing at him. 'That will do nicely.'

'Oh no, that's not fair. Take another. I wasn't ready.'

'I caught you in character. It will look very good. Now have your breakfast. Big day ahead.'

Now she was back to earth. 'I've got butterflies already.'

Repeat after me 'I will be great today. I will make my master proud of my progress these past six months.'

'Now believe it. I'll be there to offer guidance if needed, but it's your Chair. Show me you belong there.'

Everyone relevant was assembled at Aldridge by 9:30. Sebastian asked if he could have fifteen minutes with Stephen Hendry, Finance Director at Pardow, to agree the valuation models to be applied during the merger regarding the distribution of shares in the new company.

James Pardow wanted to spend some time with Mel to get to know her. Charles wanted to speak with Jason Tyler, Financial

Director of Aldridge, and then informed Mary this meeting could extend through lunch so cater accordingly.

Finally, they all assembled in the Boardroom. Mary would record the meeting noting the attendees were Charles Aldridge, James Pardow, Melanie Southgate, Stephen Hendry, Sebastian Ryder, and Jason Tyler.

Mel opened the proceedings. 'I would like to welcome everyone to this meeting. I think most now know each other, and a special welcome to Mr Sebastian Ryder, the financial adviser for this proposed merger of our companies. I've been asked to Chair this meeting with the consent of Charles and James. Charles has elected to stand down as CEO of Aldridge but retain his position as Chairman. Therefore, the first item on the agenda is a motion to confirm myself as CEO of Aldridge. Are there any objections to this appointment amongst the Aldridge members?'

Mary recorded no objections. Motion carried.

She continued with a rush of adrenalin 'May I now formally open this meeting to include representatives from Pardow to discuss the merger of Aldridge and Pardow into a new vehicle proposed as Aldridge Pardow plc, with subsequent intent to enter into a public listing of this new company. My understanding is the Head Terms have already been agreed between Charles and James and recorded by Mr Ryder. For the purposes of record can Charles, James, and Mr Ryder please confirm this to be the case.'

Mary recorded that they all confirmed.

'Could I please ask Mr Ryder to outline the terms agreed, and the further methodology proposed to conclude this merger.'

Sebastian outlined the intent of the merger proposal, the financial methodology he proposed to utilise for valuation purposes, and the legal structure of the new entity. Stephen Hendry confirmed he was comfortable with the valuation models, and they would be applied as at today's date. The listing would follow as soon as possible after the merger to realise the investment for the expanded plant and release funds to both owners.

All they needed was an irrevocable confirmation by Charles and James to the merger, and which would then be considered as effective today to allow the exchange of confidential information needed to both integrate the companies, and for Sebastian to construct the appropriate offering document for listing purposes. Sebastian had a suitable document with him, distributing copies to all present and then explained the commitment clauses. He requested they take a few minutes to study this document as, once signed, would be legally binding on both parties with onerous consequences for default.

Charles finally turned to James, 'Are you ready to sign?'

James stood and extended his hand to Charles, who stood in response and shook his hand. 'The competitive game is now confined to the golf course for us. It's time to let the next generation further our business as friends.'

They both signed their respective copies. Stephen, Mel, and Sebastian signed as witnesses.

Charles turned to Mary 'Let it be recorded that Aldridge and Pardow are united, and James and I can be found on the golf course, if needed.' They all laughed.

Mel gently called the meeting back to order. 'Gentlemen, there is much to do over the coming days. I would like to propose the following to maximise the value of this opportunity. First, I would like to structure an interim Board to oversee current operations, and to manage the merger. Mr Ryder will guide us through this process to ensure we are compliant with listing requirements. Can we agree on the composition of this Board today?'

'I have a motion before me appointing me as the CEO of the merged company. Any objections?'

Mary recorded motion carried.

'I would also like to propose Stephen Hendry be appointed as Finance Director of Aldridge Pardow plc with responsibility for liability management and reporting purposes. It is also proposed that Jason Tyler will be appointed CFO of Aldridge Pardow plc with responsibility for asset and cash flow management, reporting to Stephen Hendry. Any objections to this proposal.'

Again, recorded as motion carried.

In addition to those present they agreed that Simon Fowler, the Production Director at Pardow, would be the Production Director of the merged company; a role he would assume as quickly as possible to release Mel to fulfil her role as CEO. They also agreed that both Charles and James be Executive Joint-Chair. The stumbling block was Business Development Director. Mel knew she had to quickly get over this hurdle or risk the first conflict in the merger. 'Gentlemen. I've written a Business Development Plan, based on some two years of research, which radically changes our approach to the market to accommodate the new commercial construction requirements in our major cities. This will change both the philosophy and structure of our regional offices, albeit continue our existing core SME, retail, and domestic sales structure. Could I propose that, as the successful, and most experienced parties at this table, Charles and James spend time together studying my proposals, and then come back to me with an agreed view of how we structure this role.'

Sebastian was beaming with pride, thinking *'Well caught, and deflected. Clever lady.'*

'We also need to confirm Mr Ryder as the financial adviser to both the merger and the listing.' She smiled as they all confirmed his appointment.

'My next proposal concerns potential conflicts in current bids. Putting on my Production Director hat for a moment, I would like to meet with Simon as soon as possible to go through the current bids where we are competing. We should agree between us which adds the most value to the merger and withdraw our competing bids. Then we must look at bids we are proposing and agree a single bid on behalf of the merger.'

James agreed that Simon would be at the Matlock office at 9am tomorrow.

'We should also issue a joint statement to all of our major clients notifying them of the merger. I suggest that Charles and James draft this today so Mr Ryder can check it for regulatory purposes and add some necessary verbiage, including outstanding obligations to both companies. I would like Stephen and Jason to notify our major suppliers of this change in status, to reassure them of our intention to continue to honour our obligations. We will issue a press release on Wednesday afternoon for press on Thursday. All clients and suppliers need to be notified before then.

'I asked Mary to organise a photographer to come here at 2pm to take the requisite photographs for public statements so please don't leave until he's finished. I want to keep control of the pictures used by the media during this merger and listing.'

'Unless anyone has any other business requiring immediate consideration, I would suggest we declare this meeting over and meet weekly to consolidate all the activity during the merger. I would like to create an inclusive atmosphere amongst all employees in this merger, so I suggest we alternate offices for these meetings.'

All agreed.

'Gentlemen, before I close this meeting, I would like to say a few words.' She paused to ensure she had everyone's attention. 'I am truly honoured to have your confidence in leading this merger. I will commit to this task in full respect of the life's work of the two titans sitting at this table who built these businesses with their blood, sweat, tears, vision, and good business judgement. I will ensure this merged entity conducts itself mindful of its name and honours the good names and reputations of its founders. Thank you for your belief. This meeting is closed.'

They all clapped her. Mary was in tears. Sebastian considered his job done. She could hold her own amongst men.

James Pardow stood. 'Melanie, when Charles first suggested that a woman head this merger, I was sceptical. Your conduct today requires me to apologise to my old friend for not trusting his good judgement, and to apologise to you for not considering the possibility. I'm impressed and fully support your lead.'

Her ears filled with a resounding 'here, here.'

Meeting over, Sebastian huddled with Stephen and Jason in the Boardroom to go through the accounting requirements, while Charles, James and Mel adjourned to his office. Mary collected herself after such a momentous occasion and arranged lunch for everyone. Charles extracted a bottle of champagne from his office bar fridge and they toasted the occasion.

Charles asked her when she wanted him to vacate his office.

'I don't want you to vacate it at all. I'm okay where I am for the time being. I need you and James to defer daily trips to the golf course to help me to completely understand your business philosophy, and undertake a project for me, and for which you will need your office. I can use this office when you're not here, if need be, or the conference room when I need of some privacy. I would like to stay with Simon for a few weeks to bed him into our production process.'

'But you still don't use Jim's desk. Why not?'

'I had a deal with Tom that I wouldn't sit at his desk until he told me I could fill Jim's boots. Hopefully, he has forgotten this deal, or else I'm in trouble.' They laughed. 'But it's now Simon's desk, so I'll stay where I am.'

Charles looked at her quizzically 'And what is this project you want us to undertake?'

She braced herself for her first executive strategy – to the most experienced people she knew. She prayed they would support her idea. 'One of the last meetings I had with Jim was to discuss architectural drawings Dennis Potter gave to us demonstrating how his new fabrication material could be used to develop prefabricated affordable housing. As you are aware there are German companies that can prefabricate a wooden house which is then simply put together on-site within a few days. But wood is far more expensive and less versatile than Potter's material.' She paused for breath.

'Just as was the case when you started in business all those years ago, this country has a desperate need for affordable housing as quickly as possible – many thousands. Potter has a drawing for a two-bedroomed house that can be fabricated in a week, and then assembled onto a suitable slab ready for occupation in a week. The prefabrication and assembly costs are less than £20,000 against some £60,000 for a conventional build. My idea is you two are the best people to explore joint-venture deals with municipalities where they provide the land and infrastructure, we provide the slabs and houses, and the whole development financed through Housing Associations that hold the subsequent mortgages. If you can agree a way to develop this idea, you will need to design a new building on this site to accommodate fabrication on a production scale. And it gives us the opportunity to demonstrate the construction efficacy of these materials to our architect clients.'

Charles looked at James in amazement. 'What a brilliant, recession-proof idea. James, I think we are about to return to our roots.'

James held his glass high as he looked up to the heavens. 'Jim, if you're looking on, you trained one impressive lady. God rest your soul, my friend. We miss you.'

They raised their glasses 'Cheers, Jim.'

Charles and James quickly started to discuss how they should approach this opportunity. Mel stood back and watched these two titans develop a new lease for life. Charles has a new partner, and the gloom of losing Jim washed from his brow. She was both relieved they were receptive to the idea, and happy Charles was back to his old self – albeit Edna might not be so enthused.

She was also happy for a little respite to consider the events of such a momentous morning. She drifted into her own thoughts, thinking about how proud her mum and dad would be to know she held her own. And of course, the role played by Seb was never far from her thoughts. *'Can't leave him. He's an integral part of my life. My rock..................'*

She heard her name as she snapped out of her thoughts.

'Mel, we have a plan. We'll put something on paper so you're in the loop on what we propose. It won't be to your corporate standards, but we want your approval before we make a move.'

'Thank you, Charles. I have some input I'd like to share with you as well. But while I have both of you here, there is one other issue which is possibly more pressing.' She had their attention. 'I've been alerted to the possible fallout regarding the changing of the guard, so would like your views on the possibilities from both companies.'

Charles turned to James, 'Do you hear how Sebastian prepares her for everything.' Turning to Mel, 'You've already dealt with the most obvious issue when you cleverly passed the baton to myself and James regarding corporate business generation; for which I applaud you. We're not big corporate. James and I control our respective ships. When we look at your Business Plan, we'll determine where we have overlap and deal with it on your behalf on this occasion, albeit with your full knowledge. There is one obvious overlap – the head of the design unit. We don't want to lose either, so we need to think this through unless the head of the Pardow design team doesn't want to move here, in which case we don't have a problem. While I think about it, the one aspect of your proposal I don't think will work is technical design satellites in any city. Secondment is okay as it's temporary, but no permanent separation. The exchange of knowledge and ideas in our design team is precious. They need to be together. And we'll include as many of Pardow's people as want to move here. This will give us a healthy pool for secondment and allow us to lose a few to architects without damage to our capability.'

Week 26

For the first time this morning Mel felt challenged. Her Business Development Plan moved corporate design to the local city office, but she could see why Charles wanted to keep the intellectual capability at the head office. She also knew that relationship building with architects would be fundamental to building trust. What to do?

'Okay, Charles. I'll accept your view with the proviso that, when appropriate, we send a senior member of the design team with the account manager to relevant meetings so the architects can connect with a real person rather than a design office. Building trust with architects will require personal relationships. We need architects to be comfortable with our design team. This will also remove the onus of accurate feedback from our account manager, and allow our designer to ask pertinent questions, or even offer relevant input to the architects. Our success will depend on the quality of our relationships, especially when contending with main contractors for the fabrication work. The closer we are to the architects, the stronger our position.'

'Agreed. You've shown leadership in fostering these clients. I fully support your instinct for how we consolidate this effort.' Turning to James, 'Do you have any thoughts on this issue?'

'My friend, this new approach of yours has only come to my attention over these past few days. I think the initiative brilliant. I'm listening to how these architects can be useful in securing major corporate contracts. Let's study your development Plan to see if this approach applies to other cities. Edinburgh must be a target city so let's see if we can define a working template for London which can be duplicated in other cities.'

'Good. Then we are agreed about the way forward.' Turning back to Mel, 'On the subject of Main Contractors, during recessions stronger companies tend to swallow weaker ones, and consolidation of larger companies is not uncommon; reduces competition and reduces costs as these companies have to learn to live with smaller margins. Ensuring that you are not backing the wrong horse in such activities is very important. In your new role connectivity will be more occasional, but you must ensure that your account managers keep their distance until the new business contact is identified.'

'First week of my University of Life; don't get into battles before you understand the war.'

'Sebastian has taught you well. I can't believe the progress you've made in just six months.' Turning to James, 'Mel spent some weeks studying the philosophy of some ancient Chinese General, the Art of War. Amazing how it still applies today.'

He continued to expound his knowledge of Sun Tzu. Mel was pleased to watch this rapport. The dark clouds of Jim's death had subsided. Charles had a new partner. He was back to his old self.

Mary popped her head around the door and whispered, 'Lunch has arrived. Where do you want it?'

'As soon as the Boardroom is free, we'll go in there. Thanks, Mary.'

She motioned to Mel, 'Could I have a quick word.'

Mel followed her back to her office.

'Mel, my dear, I'm the proudest woman on the planet. You were fantastic in there. I couldn't wait any longer to congratulate you. Whatever you need, you just ask.'

'Thanks Mary, but you know who should get the praise.'

'No, my dear. If you'd have seen his face. No self-satisfaction; just pride and joy for you. You did it in there, no-one else.'

'Mary, as Charles has stepped down, are you considering the same, or can I rely on your support for at least a few years? You know this company and I would really value your input.'

'My dear Mel. For this past six months you have brought a breath of fresh air to this place. Your appointment as CEO has given me a new lease of life. I'm so proud of what you've achieved. I want to be part of your success for as long as you want me here.'

They hugged each other, 'Thank you. That's a real comfort to me.'

Week 26

They heard the Boardroom door open. 'Can I help you with the food?'

'Absolutely not my dear. You're the CEO. Get back to your role and get these men into line.'

Sebastian was already preparing a special dinner when she arrived home. She hugged him, kissed him, and hugged him some more.

He held her, 'You did real good today, lady. I hope you mum and dad watched that performance.'

Tears came to her eyes, 'My dad would have been so proud.'

He let her weep a little before easing her back to dry her eyes with his thumbs. 'Why don't you get changed while I finish a special treat for you.'

'Does my master not require my gym session today?'

'Today, you graduated with honours. It's now your decision. If you would prefer to come back here and chill, no problem, you deserve it.'

'I'll have a swim to loosen up. No exercise today.'

When she returned to the kitchen, the telephone rang. 'Mel, it's for you.'

'Hello.'

'Mel, this is Edna. Charles has related to me what happened today. I'm so overwhelmed with joy for you. Congratulations, my dear. And tell Professor Higgins he has my gratitude. At last I have my husband back, although he informs me you put him back to work, and I might have some competition with the golf course. I'm organising a dinner to celebrate your success, so hold the next two Saturdays until I've got everyone organised. You can bring Higgins, but it's your night.'

She smiled at this last comment. She liked Edna. 'Thank you, Edna, I'll tell him.'

'That was Edna. She wants to express her gratitude to Professor Higgins. That must be you, my wonderful teacher.

the Way

She's organising a dinner for me. I can take Higgins if I want.' She giggled.

'After dinner, will you sit with me and hold me in your arms while I digest what happened today?'

'Not a problem. Ready to eat?'

Dinner cleared away, they went through to the living room with their respective after-dinner drinks and settled on the couch; him sitting normally, and she laid on the couch resting in his arms.

He broke the silence. 'Can I ask you a few questions about your performance today, or would you prefer to lose yourself in your own thoughts for a while longer?'

'Please ask. It might help me replay some fuzzy parts.'

'When the issue of Business Development Director was raised, what went through your mind?'

'Well, you know I'm no fan of Michael Chimes, and you didn't brief me on their equivalent. So Sun Tzu to the rescue. The supreme art of war is to subdue the enemy without conflict. My report does not support separate regional directors. And it would be better if the appointment is not my decision alone. I thought who better than the titans to resolve this, using my report as the rationale. I know Charles will not favour Michael, and it's for James to convince his old friend of the merits or otherwise of his man, or they ask me to find another. In any event, no-one can point any finger of bias in my direction. Did I do good?'

'That supreme piece of seat-of-your-pants thinking was the highlight of the meeting. First class honours graduation.'

'Where did the photographer idea come from? That wasn't in our brief.'

'A little vanity, my master. After my journey to get here, I could not rely on some paparazzi guy to take a picture that would be splashed everywhere. I think I deserve better than that. And I did want to capture Charles and James in the moment of this merger – especially after such a period of sadness.'

Week 26

'I applaud the thinking, and I'll overlook the vanity on this occasion as we need a good image of you for the investors. Let's hope the photographer captured what I saw today.'

'And what was that, my master?'

'Someone comfortable and confident in her own skin. You radiated professional, and in control.'

'It felt good.'

'How do you intend to inform the employees?'

'The notices will go out tomorrow for both my appointment, and the merger.'

'Not good. Do as you did when Jim died. Get everyone assembled, and you and Charles go tell them. Dress down a little from today. Think what Charles is likely to wear and think clan. Then go to Derby and do the same with James. This will create the image you need to become instantly accepted by all. Let the people in Derby know you're real. Then post the notices.'

'I agree. Will organise first thing tomorrow. Thanks.'

'How do you feel in your new role? Were there any issues or events that clarification might help you be more comfortable?'

'Once I felt the support of Charles and James, I relaxed using my nervous energy to keep me focused. I was the youngest and most inexperienced at the table, but ready to play my part. You still have much to teach me, but I know your knowledge is far superior, and I'll quickly learn. Mary has agreed to stay to help me, which is a great relief. My battlefield is laid, and my troops are primed. Victory will be mine.'

He was laughing. 'So Sun Tzu will be leading the charge.'

'What's so funny? You indoctrinated me with Sun Tzu and now his philosophy guides my every action. It's now second nature when on the field of play. It's like he's sitting on my shoulder watching; and whispering in my ear when I need it. Isn't that what you intended?'

'You are one bright student. I'm in awe at the progress you've made these past months, despite the tragic events. Give me another six months you will not only be battle ready, you'll be battle hardened – ready to face any challenge.'

'Your humble student is most grateful to her master that he is prepared to extend classes by a further six months, but Seb, I could use a break to recharge. I'm emotionally drained.'

'I've already thought of that; but give me a few days to map out when best for you to get away for a couple of weeks. I agree you need it and it will be factored into my plans.'

'Thanks. Do you think we can have an early night as the coming days will be demanding? I'd like to have a soak first and then please put me to sleep.'

'Go use my bathroom and I'll join you after your soak.'

Chapter 166 – Tuesday

Charles finalised a circular officially stepping down as CEO albeit retaining his role as Chairman. He announced that Mel would assume the role of CEO with immediate effect but would retain the role of Production director until Simon could be installed.

In a second circular he announced that Aldridge would merge with their main rival, Pardow. The name of the combined companies would be Aldridge Pardow plc. This name was a marketing ploy suggested by Sebastian to align them psychologically with architect practices. There was a tendency in the market to significantly shorted names, mostly to only initials, but he thought they would stand out from the crowd and retain a proud heritage by keeping the principal names. It continued by stating that over a period of one year they would consolidate the fabrication business on the Matlock site. This would result in a much larger fabrication facility capability to meet the demands of growing cities in the UK. Two new fabrication units would be built at Matlock, which would significantly increase employment.

She found Charles in his office. He was much perkier than of late. She told him she wanted to make an announcement in person to the staff at 12:00. He agreed they should do it together and formally introduce Simon Fowler to them at the same time.

She asked him not to release the circulars until after 3pm. He concurred and arranged with James that she would be at the Derby plant for a 3pm announcement with him.

As soon as she arrived at her desk Tom appeared with a bunch of flowers arranged in a pot the shape of a boot placing it on Jim's desk. I'm sorry, Miss. I thought what I said in the canteen was my approval for you to take Jim's desk. I should have seen this some time back, but I forgot.'

'*Charles*' she thought. 'Thank you, Tom. There're lovely, and I love the boot. Later this morning, I want you to come up and meet the person who will be sitting at Jim's desk from now on. His name is Simon Fowler, and he's currently the Production Director of Pardow. Can you show him around the shop floor for me?'

'But what about you, Miss? This is your job.'

'As of yesterday, I'm the Chief Executive. Charles has stepped down. But I'll stay here for a while to ensure we have a smooth transfer to Simon.'

'Congratulations, Miss. Can I tell the lads?'

'Certainly. You will get two circulars later today that will announce big changes here, but no-one should be worried. In fact, everyone should be very happy that Aldridge is expanding.'

'Tom, can you assemble everyone in the canteen by 12:00. Charles and I will come down to tell everyone, as there's much more than the circulars will say.'

'No problem, Miss. I'll make sure everybody's there.'

He turned to leave but looked back. 'Thank you, Miss. Just let me know when you want me to come up.' He never did get the hang of calling her Mel.

the Way

She met with Simon Fowler, initially to feel him out so she could plan his succession to the role at Aldridge. She agreed with Sebastian's assessment he was good at what he did, and worthy to fill Jim's boots. They agreed how to restructure their bids, and she introduced him to Tom, who showed him around the factory.

Both announcements were well received, and yet again she was thankful for the shrewd input from Sebastian. Where would she be without him?

There was an air of change, and the people were quick to embrace Mel as the new boss. She had made her mark on Aldridge and proved a worthy successor to Jim. They could see she was a formidable boss and, therefore, she would take care of business.

Just before dinner the telephone rang. 'It's Carmen for you' as he handed her the phone.

'Hi, Carmen. To what do I owe the pleasure?'

'Congratulation my dear. I hear you are now chief executive at Aldridge. My heart is so happy for you. You have worked hard, and now rewarded. Welcome to the executive club.'

'Your spies are very alert. Did they tell you we are merging with our closest rival and I will head the combined company? Seb is arranging for the combined company to be listed as a public company.'

'Wow, my dear. I hope my darling Sebastian is prepared to continue with his task. This is a whole new world to a private company.'

'I've notified him of the extension to his contract.' They both laughed. 'Will you continue to visit with us?'

'Most certainly, my dear. My new plant is not yet ready, and it will take time to bed down. And I would not miss seeing my beautiful butterfly open her wings and show her true and glorious colours. And we still have much to learn together from the lovely Sebastian. Have you made progress with him?'

'The jury is out, but I hope when you next visit we have progress.'

'Mel, you can do this. Love is a powerful aphrodisiac. Be strong. Carmen is by your side.'

Chapter 167 – Wednesday

Sebastian asked to meet with Charles at the house.

'What's on your mind, Sebastian?'

'I want to agree a few things with you before we put them into the public arena. The first is that Mel has been subjected to an emotional rollercoaster ride for the past six months, and now she's being asked to take the helm of a public company. During the due diligence phase, I would like to get her out of here for a couple of weeks to give her a break, recharge her batteries, and give me time to prep her as the face of a public company. I would like you and James to cover for her and, as the founding fathers of these companies, structure a practical, and costed integration plan with minimal disruption to production. You two are best placed to make the integration work.'

'Done. We've already started to formulate the integration, so no problem. Just let me know when you've planned your trip.'

'My second request relates to Mel living here. I did not intend to renew our agreement at the end of next week, as I'm happy for her to live here, but there are some regulatory issues which require me to be at arm's length as your financial adviser. Therefore, could I ask you to continue with the arrangement until the listing is complete, at which point, officially, it will become the responsibility of Mel.'

'Sebastian, whatever you need for Mel is a done deal. We need to put a relocation package together for her in any event as she cannot run this company from London. You package what you think will pass scrutiny. You can assume both myself and

James will agree to it. Oh, my God, I haven't raised her package to Director level yet, or registered her as a Director. Must do this today and back-date her package to the beginning of the year.'

'Where're you taking her?'

'Officially I would prefer not to say so no-one interrupts her break. Unofficially I have a villa in the Caribbean. I'll keep contact with the listing guys, but she needs a real break. I can also leave my number with you personally if you wish.'

'Great. You take as long as you need. I agree she needs a good holiday. She had no holiday at all last year other than Christmas, and she banked a week for her now defunct marriage. She's more than entitled. Only you know how long she can be away from the listing process, so take what you can. A couple of extra weeks to get the listing done is no big deal. She's earnt a break. I'm awarding her a £25,000 bonus for last year, so she can enjoy herself a little.'

'That'll keep her busy shopping for a while.' They both laughed.

'Oh, and by the way I haven't discussed the break with her so please keep it to yourself until she says something to you.'

When Mel returned home, she was full of joy even though she was visibly emotionally drained. She greeted Seb with her customary hug, kiss, and big smile. 'I'm now officially registered as the CEO of Aldridge. I can't believe it. In just six months I've come from overlooked obscurity to CEO. What a rollercoaster ride. And you are the architect of my success. My beloved master, I owe it all to you.'

'Dearest Mel. I but showed you the way, occasionally dusted you off, and kept you on the track. You did the rest. You owe me nothing. It was a great pleasure to mentor you through the process, and the result gives me great hope for your future progress. Come, let us drink to your achievements.'

He opened a bottle and poured two glasses. He toasted her with pride in his eyes, which did not go unnoticed.

Week 26

She was pondering with a smile on her face. He watched her, lost in her own thoughts, for a while.

'Can I ask you what you're thinking?'

'I'm thinking about your definition of dusting me off. I'll never tire of your primary method. Cleansing is such a beautiful process; sensual pampering is probably a better name.'

'I have a surprise for you.'

'Are you going to tell me, or tease me?'

'You need a break, and you're due a holiday. I've agreed with Charles that he and James will hold the fort while you recharge your batteries. You have much to do in the coming months, but you're tired. You deserve a break.'

'Great. Where are we going?'

'Who said anything about "we"? I have much work engineering the listing of your company.'

'My master. I know enough to know you intend to supervise my recharge. Where would I go alone? So where are we going?'

'You're becoming too sharp for me. I suggest we go to my villa in the Caribbean. It's on the beach, reasonably secluded, the sun shines 360 days a year, and the turquois water is warm and crystal clear. How does this sound to you?'

'Like paradise. When do we leave?'

'I need to set a few things in motion before we go, so I think two weeks from now.'

She hugged him, 'can't wait.'

Over dinner he needed to raise an issue he forgot to raise with Charles. 'There is something that needs to be done and which must be covert. I'll tell you what it is, but if you feel any reservations, I'll deal directly with Charles as this must happen during the integration.'

'Are we about to descend into your corporate cesspit?'

'The cesspit relates to people. This is about clearing out the past in a way it should not haunt you in the future. Both the need and the opportunity are conveniently encapsulated within the merger.'

Okay, so long as it's not illegal, I want to be part of it. I can't hide behind you any longer. As I see my new position, I need to be aware of everything that can affect me. But why covert?'

'Jim's death and, more important, the cause of his death exposes Aldridge to potential claims that could seriously damage the company. As I've identified this risk, we need to be pro-active in removing it from sight based on *out of sight, out of mind.*'

'What are you talking about?'

'The old cement fabrication hangar. Jim died of respiratory problems. This could easily be associated with concrete fabrication, just as with asbestos in the 1960s. A good lawyer advising Margaret could give rise to a substantial claim. Fortunately, Charles is ensuring Margaret receives substantial funds from the listing, so this possibility is abated. But if any other former employees also died of respiratory problems that could be linked to that facility, then, once a public company, you are a target for a good lawyer, or worse still, a class action. This could destroy the company.'

'If I'm understanding you, what you're proposing is we get rid of the cement fabrication facility in the hope no-one will be provoked into making any such claims. Surely if people did suffer because of that facility then they are morally entitled to compensation.'

'Do you seriously believe Charles and Jim built a factory, in which they both worked in the early years, knowing it would likely kill them? The problem we face is hindsight. Unfortunately, the lure of compensation will far outweigh any historic argument about the lack of knowledge of the long-term effects of cement dust. Lawyers will push for judgement based on the knowledge and health and safety requirements today. I consider this to be unfair and unjust. As such, I want to try to remove this exposure to the company. If the hangar is removed

Week 26

under the guise of integrating and modernising Aldridge Pardow, people will think nothing of it. The base is a concrete slab, so contamination issues will be minimal, thus no need for contamination engineers suited in protection suits wearing breathing apparatus. The problem will quietly disappear. A monochrome picture at the back of the corporate scrapbook depicting a relic of the past.'

'So how do you propose to put this to Charles?'

'I would like you to informally invite him over for drinks, or even dinner. No records in diaries. I'll explain to him my thinking. I'll suggest he tells no-one, not even James, as he could look for a revaluation of Aldridge. He quietly integrates this into the integration plan. No-one will be the wiser. For your part, neither this discussion, nor any other discussion on this subject ever took place. If you are put on the stand in a Court, you must be adamant no such discussion took place. If anyone got wind of what we are doing Aldridge could be complicit in a cover-up. Do you think you can handle this issue?'

'While you were speaking, I saw so much Sun Tzu being applied. I don't lie very well, but I guess I need to learn.'

'Please don't look at it as a lie. You are applying deception on the field of play just as the opposing lawyers would apply current health and safety to their argument. It's part of the game. I'm not asking you to lie in your normal life.'

'This exec role really is a tough game. I see the logic, and I do agree that judging yesterday by today's standards is not reasonable unless there was a deliberate intent to deceive. I'm sure Jim did not plan such a premature and nasty end to his life. He was such a kind and considerate man, loved by this community. He would not knowingly hurt anyone. I must accept this is a necessary requirement to protect the company. I'll play my part.'

'Good. In real terms, the essence is dealing with issues as soon as they are deemed to be a potential problem. If the company decided not to act, then it would be culpable. The sooner Charles has this removal embedded within the integration plan, the better. You will have to build a new concrete fabrication facility, but it will be argued everything needs upgrading, even the building, which is now some sixty years old, and built as an aircraft hangar, not a factory.'

'Any other shocks for me to consider? This one has certainly brought me back to earth with a bang.'

'I will, as part of my due diligence, seek out weaknesses that need to be addressed. This is a very necessary part of my work. You're asking investors to use their money to support your future activities; not pay for past issues. I need to explain to them any such weaknesses, including historic, and how they will be addressed. Clearly, I could not include the potential problems with the existing fabrication hangar. Any other such issues will also be quietly dealt with prior to listing. I'll also brief you how to address risks with potential shareholders and the press.'

'What is my brief regarding the hangar removal?'

'Very straightforward, actually. Your overall message will be the current recession provides an ideal time for the two most respected names in construction fabrication to merge and integrate into a company ready for the coming challenges in fabrication, especially with the introduction of new materials. Although your combined order book will readily see you through the recession, you do have a period of lower activity making it possible to completely modernise your facilities without disrupting production. You need more appropriate modern buildings to accommodate these new technologies.'

'So, I don't get involved in any discussion particularly aimed at the hangar?'

'Absolutely not. It's merely part of the modernisation plan.'

'Don't worry. We'll deal with your face to the world whilst on holiday. By the time we get back you'll be word perfect, and able to handle the shiftiest of reporters.'

'I thought we were going on holiday. Now I here it's a working holiday. Another damper.'

'I promise you a good holiday. But we have some twenty hours of flying we can usefully use. Does this lift your spirits a little? You need a holiday, so start to plan on any needed shopping before we go.'

'Those magic words. I'll prepare a list. On Saturday, shopping, here we come.' She was smiling again.

Chapter 168 – Valentine's Day

She arrived at the office full of the joys of spring. She was met with many messages of congratulations both to her, and on the merger. Her desk was adorned with beautiful bouquets of flowers. All her architect clients had now contacted her to congratulate her on her new appointment.

Charles was decidedly perkier. She informed him Sebastian needed a discreet meeting, off record. He would arrange to meet with him at lunchtime.

Around the factory there was a noticeable air of change. The cloud over Jim's death had lifted. Sunshine poured out of people as she moved about the factory.

Many people in the outside world she did not know wanted to meet her. Mary was a master at regulating diaries and would ensure any such meetings were prioritised and properly prepared.

She was still full of the joys of spring when she arrived home.

Seb informed her that the plan regarding the hangar had been agreed. All concrete fabrication would be transferred to Derby as quickly as possible, and the existing site cleared of all buildings over the coming months, including the offices. James would not be told of the underlying reason, but he had accepted it made sense to clear the outdated components of the Matlock site ready for the merged company plans which would demonstrate to architects the state-of-the-art ethos of the company.

After dinner she adopted the 'we need to talk' position.

'I have studied the law regarding adoption, or to be more honest Mary pointed me towards a lawyer specialising in family law, probate, inheritance, etc. The result is there is no provision for adult adoption in current legislation other than direct family. The only mechanism is under Feudal Law which prescribes that an adult can be adopted for inheritance purposes.'

'It's a long process, with lots of hoops, and a Court hearing. Any evidence of sexual activity will invalidate the Application. I can't imagine you'll want your life putting under a microscope.'

She paused while this information sunk in.

'As much as this could have been a solution for us, it clearly requires much work, and reveals parts of your past that should stay buried.' Again, she paused.

'I appeal to you, on this Valentine's Day, to bind our love in marriage. I give myself to you. I know you still bear the burden of the death of your first wife. Mama explained how badly you took it, that you feel you did not care enough for her to prevent what happened, and I've never ventured to ask. Now I ask you to explain why an event 23 years ago haunts you so much you cannot fully enjoy what we have together. Please tell me so I can understand my rejection.'

He took a deep breath, 'My wife died of a broken heart. I wasn't there for her. I was far too busy selfishly furthering my career.'

She saw the tears well up in his eyes, then rolling down his cheeks. She reached over and kissed the tears away. She could see the pain and sorrow in his eyes.

'I'm so sorry. Can you tell me why she was so broken hearted?'

'She was very attached to her father who doted on her and was the light in her life. When he died, quite suddenly, she was lost. She couldn't get over it. I couldn't understand her grief because, until then, we were so happy together.' The tears were now streaming down his face. She was feeling his pain and started to understand what Mama had told her.

'She could not bear the emptiness without her father, so took her own life to be reunited with him. She was lying in our apartment for two days before I came home and found her. I still have nightmares about what I saw.'

He was now sobbing. She wrapped her arms around him, as he had done for her so many times these past months.

'Please let me share this pain with you. You've shared so much of my pain. It's time for me to help you. Please, please, please, I beg you, let me in.'

He let it all out. She held him tightly.

After some minutes, he gathered himself. 'The only person who knows the truth besides you is Mama who dragged it out of me at a low point in my depression. It took me two years to stop crying, and I still feel the pain. No-one else should know this story.'

'Your life is safe with me, my darling, have no fear.' She held his face in her hands, 'Thank you for opening your heart to me. I feel so privileged.'

'So you see, I'm not a worthy husband, I'm far too selfish. I don't deserve a second chance.'

'You're the most wonderful, caring man I've ever met, as Carmen and Mama are my witnesses.'

'When you're applying your loving hand in the dark, you tell me to fantasise and just go where I want to. I open my body to welcome you in, spending the whole time willing you across your steely red line to become my lover. You give me so much love. I so want to do the same for you. Let go of your pain and let us share our love for each other. I want this more than anything in this world.'

She moved from his lap and stripped naked. Her heart was pounding. She was playing the game of her life. Kneeling on the floor before him, 'Look at me. I'm not your daughter. I'm a woman asking a man to love her as she loves him. I kneel before you and beg you to take me as your wife and let me rid you of your pain. I promise to love and cherish you for better or worse, to honour you, keep you in sickness and in health, and forsake all others for so long as we both shall live.'

'He looked at her, grappling with his emotions. He reached out and picked her up. 'You beg to no man, especially not me. I'm unworthy of your love.'

'How unworthy am I? But I love you, my darling, and this is all that matters. We are but man and wife today, and neither of us wants this to end. I want us to be united together, in love.'

He calmed. 'You sincerely want to marry me? How can I refuse? You bring so much light to my life. Mrs Ryder it shall be. I never thought I would say such words again.' Then an afterthought 'But not until this merger is complete. Not a word, or else I must disqualify myself as adviser.'

She returned to his lap and hugged him tight. 'Then we keep our love between our sheets until then.'

He held her and started to stroke her body. They kissed as lovers for the first time. She felt good having his arms around her naked body as he had done so many times in the past. But this was different. His touch was electrified with passion and urgency. His shackles had gone. His dark cloud had lifted. He had crossed his red line from father figure to lover. She could feel his erection as he held her close. Their lover's kiss had changed their relationship.

She held him tight and whispered in his ear, 'You've delivered for Bernie. You've delivered for me. I'm living my dream. Now we unite in love.'

Week 26

www.ingramcontent.com/pod-product-compliance
Lightning Source LLC
Chambersburg PA
CBHW071112080526
44587CB00013B/1315